CHILDREN
OF UNCERTAIN
FORTUNE

Children
of Uncertain
Fortune

Mixed-Race Jamaicans in Britain

and the Atlantic Family,

1733–1833

DANIEL LIVESAY

Published by the

OMOHUNDRO INSTITUTE OF

EARLY AMERICAN HISTORY AND CULTURE,

Williamsburg, Virginia,

and the

UNIVERSITY OF NORTH CAROLINA PRESS,

Chapel Hill

*The Omohundro Institute of Early American History and Culture
is sponsored by the College of William and Mary. On November 15, 1996,
the Institute adopted the present name in honor of a bequest
from Malvern H. Omohundro, Jr.*

Cover images: Top: *Lady Elizabeth Murray and Dido Belle.* Unknown artist,
formerly attributed to Johann Zoffany. Circa 1780. Courtesy of Earls of Mansfield,
Scone Palace, Perth, Scotland. Bottom: *The Morse and Cator Family.* By Johann Zoffany.
1784. Image courtesy of the Aberdeen Art Gallery and Museums Collections.

Library of Congress Cataloging-in-Publication Data
Names: Livesay, Daniel, author.
Title: Children of uncertain fortune : mixed-race Jamaicans in
Britain and the Atlantic family, 1733–1833 / Daniel Livesay.
Description: Williamsburg, Virginia : Omohundro Institute of Early American
History and Culture ; Chapel Hill : University of North Carolina Press, [2018] |
Includes bibliographical references and index.
Identifiers: LCCN 2017030142| ISBN 9781469634432 (cloth : alk. paper) |
ISBN 9781469634449 (ebook)
Subjects: LCSH: Great Britain—Race relations—History. | Jamaica—Race relations—
History. | Racially mixed people—Jamaica—Social conditions—History—18th century. |
Racially mixed people—Jamaica—Social conditions—History—19th century. | Racially
mixed people—Great Britain—Social conditions—History—18th century. | Racially mixed
people—Great Britain—Social conditions—History—19th century. | Racially mixed people—
Civil rights—Jamaica—History—18th century. | Racially mixed people—Civil rights—Great
Britain—History—18th century. | Racially mixed people—Civil rights—Jamaica—History—
19th century. | Racially mixed people—Civil rights—Great Britain—History—19th century.
Classification: LCC DA125.A1 L57 2018 | DDC 305.23089/0596009041—dc23
LC record available at https://lccn.loc.gov/2017030142

The University of North Carolina Press has been a member of the
Green Press Initiative since 2003.

For Mary

ACKNOWLEDGMENTS

The list of acknowledgments is inevitably long for a first book. I have been the lucky recipient of an incredible amount of assistance, support, and encouragement since beginning this project. Generous funding from a number of different organizations enabled me to undertake research and writing. The History Department at the University of Michigan supported me throughout the whole of graduate school. A Pre-Doctoral Fellowship and Rackham Humanities Fellowship, along with summer funding from the International Institute and the Center for European Studies at the university helped significantly. The Institute of Historical Research at the University of London and the North American Conference on British Studies both provided funds allowing me to spend significant time in archives throughout the United Kingdom. A Fulbright Fellowship to Jamaica was instrumental to work through the fantastic repositories on the island. Short-term grants from the Huntington Library, the American Philosophical Society Library, McMaster University, and the American Society for Eighteenth-Century Studies broadened the scope and increased the depth of the project. A National Endowment for the Humanities Postdoctoral Fellowship at the Omohundro Institute in Williamsburg, Virginia, not only allowed me to finish important sections of research but also helped me to reconceptualize and rewrite the book in ways I never could have done by myself.

The archivists who diligently dragged out countless boxes, pamphlets, and books were key in undertaking this research and vital in discovering crucial corners in the sources that were completely blind to me. My deepest thanks go to Barbara DeWolfe at the William L. Clements Library who first hired me to sort through the Tailyour Papers that formed the foundation of this project. Robert and Sally Tailyour's assistance with the correspondence, along with their hospitality in hosting me in their Somerset home, allowed me to understand their family's wider history. Librarians at the Jamaica Archives, the Island Record Office, and the National Library of Jamaica were patient, kind, and helpful as I stumbled my way through their vast holdings. The archivists at the National Archives of Scotland also opened the channels of communication to consult private papers throughout the U.K. Those records form a key part of this study. The Montgomery and Compton-Maclean families were especially generous to let me read their private letters, and Sir William Macpherson was exceedingly hospitable, opening his house and library to me in

Blairgowrie. I greatly enjoyed our daily lunches while on break from reading his family papers. Finally, I owe a great deal of gratitude to the nearly anonymous workers at the British Library and the National Archives of England who dutifully called up so much material.

Before the project was even a thought in my head, though, I was unbelievably fortunate to come under the guidance of Fred Anderson. Although I was entirely ignorant at the time of how unusual it was for an undergraduate to receive so much mentorship and personal attention, I have since strived to emulate Fred as a teacher, scholar, and human being. My fortune continued in graduate school under the direction of David Hancock, who was equally generous with his time and supervision. David taught me never to be comfortable with my own assumptions or too quick to think that I had solved a particular problem. If this book has been successful in uncovering a group of silenced voices, it is owing to David's help, guidance, and willingness to apply pressure when needed. Julius Scott and Michael MacDonald were also exceptional advisers on my dissertation and gave careful and thoughtful comments at every stage. Scotti Parrish, Dena Goodman, Martha Jones, Tom Green, Sonya Rose, Damon Salesa, Sue Juster, and Kali Israel gave great instruction and feedback in my initial inquiries as well.

A number of scholars have been exceedingly generous with their advice on this project. David Lambert, Zoe Laidlaw, Peter Marshall, and Deborah Cohen all contributed critical mentorship and feedback on early work. The faculty and graduate students at the University of the West Indies, Mona, helped me to sort through archival surveys in Jamaica. The late Glen Richards kindly invited me to present twice to the university. His advice, along with that of Sir Roy Augier, Swithin Wilmot, Kathleen Monteith, Dave Gosse, and Jonathan Dalby pointed me in the right directions for a successful stint on the island. Perhaps most importantly in Jamaica, James Robertson helped me to navigate the archives and was a terrific fellow passenger on rides out to Spanish Town. A book prospectus seminar at the Omohundro Institute gave me more help than I deserved once the dissertation was finished. Sarah Pearsall offered invaluable criticism about how to rethink the book. She has been an ideal mentor since, and I owe her tremendously for her guidance and help. Barry Gaspar, Karin Wulf, and Phil Morgan each helped me to refine those ideas even more and to apply them more specifically to the Caribbean. Likewise, Paul Mapp, Greg O'Malley, Molly Warsh, Jonathan Eacott, Kris Lane, Amanda Herbert, Olwyn Blouet, and Chris Grasso gave critical feedback that enriched my thinking about the book. Finally, a number of scholars of Atlantic and Caribbean history have provided incredibly important comments on my work over the years. Alison Games, Peter Mancall, Kathleen Wilson, Gad Heuman, Christer Petley, Carla Pestana, Brett Rushforth, Michelle McDonald, Rob Taber, Carole Shammas, Bernard Moitt, Roderick McDonald, and Nicholas Popper have each helped to shape my ideas in fruitful ways.

This would have been a much different, and far less effective, book without my time at the Omohundro Institute and the unmatched skill of its editors. I have to thank Ron Hoffman and Sally Mason for making me feel so welcome and for giving me the opportunity of a lifetime. Beverly and Doug Smith, along with Kim Foley and Kelly Crawford, saw to all manner of problems, big and small, with the utmost kindness and patience. I could not have been luckier to have had my two years at the Institute overlap with the inestimable Molly Warsh, who was not only an intellectual powerhouse for me to learn from but also one of the kindest friends one could hope for. My other fellow fellows were something of a murderer's row of young academics. Jonathan Eacott, Greg O'Malley, Alexandre Dubé, and Elena Schneider were each brilliant, funny, and warm, and gave me daily reminders of virtuoso scholarship at work. As an early editor, Fredrika Teute challenged me to think big and write a great manuscript, and her advice was crucial in making the book what it is. Likewise, the suggestions from the manuscript's two reviewers, Sarah Pearsall and John Garrigus, dramatically improved the direction of its argument and scope. Sarah's recommendations were key for thinking through the dimensions of family history, while John's comments helped to sharpen the analysis on the Caribbean. Nadine Zimmerli was a superb editor of the book. Not only did she help me to navigate a long list of fantastic proposals from the reviewers, but she gave expert feedback that clarified the argument and simplified its structure. I owe a tremendous amount to the Institute's apprentices who checked every footnote dutifully and with tremendous patience. An enormous amount of thanks is due to Kaylan Stevenson who suffered through torturous prose to deliver a much more readable and, I hope, enjoyable, book. Her edits were smart, thorough, and invaluable. Finally, I would like to thank Kelly Crawford and Rebecca Wrenn for constructing terrific tables and family trees.

Colleagues in graduate school and beyond have been essential repositories of knowledge and friendship over the years. At Michigan, a solid crew of Atlanticists regularly inspired me. Many thanks to Jennifer Palmer, Katie Cangany, Jeff Kaja, Suzi Linsley, Will Mackintosh, Graham Nessler, Christine Walker, Sara First, and Amanda Moniz. My flatmates in London, Allison Abra and Angela Dowdell, both provided daily encouragement and camaraderie. Alex Lovit and Liz Hudson have been amazing friends and great travel buddies since the beginning of graduate school. At Drury University, I was fortunate to have an exceptional group of Humanities scholars to work with. Hue-Ping Chin, Peter Meidlinger, Chris Panza, Katie Gilbert, Erin Kenny, Greg Renoff, Rich Schur, Shelley Wolbrink, Craig Titus, Jonathan Groves, Ted Vaggalis, and Justin Leinaweaver were model teacher/scholars. Special thanks go out to Ray Patton, Kerry Allen, and Avery Patton for forming a two-family pseudo-commune with us in southern Missouri. At Claremont McKenna College, I've received tremendous support from everyone in the History Department. My fellow Americanists Tamara Venit-Shelton, Lily Geismer, Sarah Sarzynski, and Diana Selig have all welcomed me with open arms. Gary Hamburg and Lisa Cody have been dutiful mentors as well. The Sunday Morning Farmers' Market Crew has also made Southern California even sunnier than usual.

I have been blessed with two (and a half) terrific families who have kept up my spirits all these years. Brian Mathewson has been a friend, therapist, and fellow adventurer for most of my life. He has been on the receiving end of as many discussions about this book as anyone else and has always been a rock of support. My parents-in-law, Kevin and Kathleen McGuinness, seemed as interested in the results of this project as I was, and they continually encouraged me on. I only wish that Kathleen could have seen the book's completion. Angie Ransom and David Livesay are the best type of elder siblings: always ready to keep my ego in check, but always there to lend a hand as well. My late father Joe Livesay and my mother Sonja Livesay both gave me the freedom to pursue my passion for history, even though they had no idea what I would do with it. Their love never faltered, and I always feel it around me. Finally, no one suffered through the tribulations, and rejoiced in the triumphs, of this project more than my wife Mary. Her patience and love remained steady through long periods apart, cross-country moves away from friends and family, and weekends spent competing with this book. I could never properly express my gratitude, but I thank her dearly for being such a wonderful companion.

CONTENTS

❦

	Acknowledgments	vii
	List of Illustrations	xiii
	Abbreviations	xv
	Note on Terminology	xvii
	Introduction	1
1	Inheritance, Family, and Mixed-Race Jamaicans, 1700–1761	20
2	Early Abolitionism and Mixed-Race Migration into Britain, 1762–1778	90
3	Lineage and Litigation, 1783–1788	143
4	Abolition, Revolution, and Migration, 1788–1793	193
5	Tales of Two Families, 1793–1800	249
6	Imperial Pressures, 1800–1812	301
7	New Struggles and Old Ideas, 1813–1833	347
	Conclusion	398
	Appendix 1. *Percentage of White Men's Wills, Proven in Jamaica, with Acknowledged Mixed-Race Children That Include Bequests for Such Offspring in Britain, Either Presently Resident, or Soon to Be Sent There, 1773–1815*	403
	Appendix 2. *Genealogical Charts*	405
	Index	407

LIST OF ILLUSTRATIONS

PLATES

1. Kenwood House, Hampstead Heath, London / 114

2. *Lady Elizabeth Murray and Dido Belle,* unknown artist,
formerly attributed to Johann Zoffany, circa 1780 / 114

3. *Knave of Diamonds,* 1786 / 154

4. *The Wise Man of the East Making His Offering,*
by William Dent, 1788 / 155

5. *The Morse and Cator Family,* by Johann Zoffany, 1784 / 159

6. *Johnny New-Come in the Island of Jamaica,*
by Abraham James, 1800 / 164

7. *The Poor Blacks Going to Their Settlement,*
by William Dent, 1787 / 192

8. Byers Green Hall / 230

9. *Flagellation of a Female Samboe Slave,* by William Blake, 1796 / 246

10. Calderon's Torture, [1806] / 337

11. *William Davidson,* by R. Cooper, circa 1820 / 363

12. *Robert Wedderburn,* 1824 / 367

TABLES

1. Population Estimates for Jamaica, 1661–1834 / 24

2. Percentage of White Men's Wills, Proven in Jamaica, with Acknowledged
Mixed-Race Children That Include Bequests for Such Offspring in Britain,
Either Presently Resident, or Soon to Be Sent There, 1773–1775 / 101

3. Percentage of White Men's Wills, Proven in Jamaica, with Acknowledged
Mixed-Race Children That Include Bequests for Such Offspring in Britain,
Either Presently Resident, or Soon to Be Sent There, 1783–1785 / 190

FIGURES

1. Percentage of Student Body at the University of Edinburgh Medical School and King's College, Aberdeen, from the West Indies Combined, 1744–1780 / 98

2. Total Number of Slaves Shipped into Jamaica (Imports — Exports) in Five-Year Averages, 1705–1774 / 133

3. Percentage of Free Mixed-Race Children Listed as Legitimate in Baptismal Records, Kingston, Jamaica, 1809–1820 / 385

4. Percentage of Free, Mixed-Race Children Listed as Having a White Father in Baptismal Records, Kingston, Jamaica, 1750–1820 / 386

ABBREVIATIONS

APAC	Asia, Pacific, and Africa Collections
BL	British Library, London
BM	The British Museum, London
GL	Guildhall Library, London
GROS	General Register Office for Scotland, Edinburgh (now part of the National Records of Scotland, Edinburgh)
HCSP	Sheila Lambert, ed., *House of Commons Sessional Papers of the Eighteenth Century,* 147 vols. (Wilmington, Del., 1975–1976)
HL	Huntington Library, Art Collections, and Botanical Gardens, San Marino, Calif.
ICS	Institute of Commonwealth Studies Library, London
IRO	Island Record Office, Central Village, Jamaica
JA	Jamaica Archives, Spanish Town
JAJ	*Journals of the Assembly of Jamaica,* 14 vols. (Jamaica, 1811–1829)
JBT	Great Britain, Board of Trade, *Journals of the Commissioners for Trade and Plantations . . . ,* 14 vols. (London, 1920–1938)
LOS	Libres Old Series
LPL	Lambeth Palace Library, London
MBP	Macpherson of Blairgowrie Private Papers, National Register of Archives for Scotland, Blairgowrie, Scotland
MCP	Maclean-Clephane of Torloisk and Carslogie Private Papers, Newby Hall, Ripon, England
NAE	National Archives, Kew
NAS	National Archives of Scotland, Edinburgh (now part of the National Records of Scotland, Edinburgh)
NLJ	National Library of Jamaica, Kingston
NLS	National Library of Scotland, Edinburgh
NRAS	National Register of Archives for Scotland, Edinburgh
OPR	Old Parish Registers, National Records of Scotland, Edinburgh
WCL	William L. Clements Library, The University of Michigan, Ann Arbor, Mich.
WMQ	*William and Mary Quarterly*

NOTE ON TERMINOLOGY

Throughout this study, a number of terms are used to refer to individuals of joint African and European heritage. These include: "mixed race," "person of mixed ancestry," "individual of mixed heritage," "brown inhabitant," and "individual of color." Those traditionally referred to as "black"—that is, without European ancestry—are not included in those categories. Occasionally, the highly imprecise term "nonwhite" is used to refer to mixed-race and black individuals as a group. All of these terms are, of course, fraught with problems, especially considering the incredible genetic diversity among and between African populations as well as those in Europe. Race is simply not a meaningful category at the biological level. Nevertheless, it did serve as a meaningful category to eighteenth- and nineteenth-century observers, and many political and familial changes arose owing to its social valence.

CHILDREN
OF UNCERTAIN
FORTUNE

INTRODUCTION

Robert Morse kept fine lodgings in London. As the eighteenth century turned into the nineteenth, he rented part of a home, which he might have briefly shared with Admiral Horatio Nelson, only blocks from the mansion later to become Buckingham Palace. Morse stocked the dwelling with elegant furniture, exotic goods, and exquisite art. Walking up the first flights of stairs, visitors were greeted by a remarkable painting of a dancer in motion. The piece sat near a chimney mantel, on which Morse kept a golden watch that he dutifully wound every night before bed. Dominating the large parlor was a harpsichord, one of many musical instruments he played in the house. Morse had also purchased a piano and several cellos, which included models built by the famous Stradivari luthiers. Morse was well known for "his fine taste, particularly as a musical amateur." His home also included numerous books, an impressive collection of British engravings, contemporary artwork, and the requisite supply of Madeira and claret. The calico handkerchiefs draping his couches lent evidence of a previous residency in Bengal. A housemaid and manservant kept the home, and Morse's affairs, in order. It was a proper residence befitting the lifestyle of a wealthy and influential barrister in England's capital. It was also a far cry from his birth in Jamaica to a woman of color and a white merchant.[1]

At the same moment, on the opposite end of Britain, the three Hay brothers played alongside their schoolmates. Fergus, John, and Alexander Hay lived in the small seaside town of Dornoch, nestled in the Scottish Highlands. They were not natives of the village, however. Like Morse, they had been born in

1. *The Morning Chronicle* (London), Mar. 29, Apr. 18, June 10, 19, 1816; Baptism of Robert Morse, June 15, 1752, Kingston baptisms, copy register, I, fol. 102, IRO; *JAJ*, May 28, 1747, IV, 66. Morse's house was located at 147 New Bond Street; see P[atrick] Boyle, *With Near Five Thousand Alterations; Boyle's New Fashionable Court and Country Guide; and Town Visiting Directory, for 1798 . . .* (London, 1798), 151. For Nelson's residence at 147 New Bond Street, see "Memorial Tablets," *Journal of the Society of Arts*, XXIV (London, 1876), 613. Additional details of Morse's home come from an Old Bailey trial in which one of Morse's servants stole the watch from his mantelpiece; see *The Proceedings of the Old Bailey Online: London's Central Criminal Court, 1674 to 1913*, "Thomas Gladwell, Thomas Yates, Theft," Sept. 20, 1797, reference number: t17970920-44, www.oldbaileyonline.org. For more on the ubiquity of Madeira in eighteenth-century Atlantic households, see David Hancock, *Oceans of Wine: Madeira and the Emergence of American Trade and Taste* (New Haven, Conn., 2009).

Jamaica. They were also mixed race, the offspring of a Scotsman and, according to a classmate, "a negro woman, as their hair, and the tawny colour of their skin, very plainly intimated." Their father brought them to Scotland to escape colonial prejudices against those with African ancestry. Although they were still young, they likely wished to attain the same level of success as Morse. Later recollections indicate that they got off to a good start. Fergus, who was about twenty years old in 1801, stood out at school as he trained to enter the commercial class. He held such poise and confidence that even the headmaster was known to defer to him. Each of the brothers, in turn, became good friends with their peers. In his later memoirs, the Reverend Donald Sage noted that he and his brother spent their Saturdays and holidays with the Hays and that Fergus in particular "was very handsome . . . had all the manners of a gentleman, and had first-rate abilities."[2]

It might seem out of place for two Jamaican families, the offspring of interracial couples, to be living at both poles of the British Isles at the start of the nineteenth century. Britons tend to think of an Afro-Caribbean presence at home as a phenomenon beginning in the mid-twentieth century and one localized around major urban centers. The topic of interracial unions only began to be addressed in the wake of the Windrush Generation migrating from the West Indies after the Second World War. Yet, the stories of Robert Morse in London and the Hay brothers in Dornoch were not at all unique. Their families were part of a regular migration of mixed-race Jamaicans who arrived in Britain during the long eighteenth century. They were the products of a particular type of family arrangement in the tropics. Interracial sex in the Caribbean was predominantly one of white male violence meant to subjugate and control enslaved women. But, in some cases, white men held long-term, though by no means fully consensual, relationships with free and enslaved women of color. Although most fathers — likely 80 percent — offered no support to the illegitimate offspring that resulted from these unions, a not insignificant number chose to take care of their children. Facing intense discrimination, restricted job opportunities, and virtually no educational options in the colonies, Jamaicans of color took advantage of patriarchal assistance to flee to Britain. Once there, they encountered myriad responses. Although some white relatives accepted them into their homes, others sued to cut them off from family fortunes. Equally, even though a number of fictional and po-

2. Donald Sage, *Memorabilia Domestica; or, Parish Life in the North of Scotland* (Edinburgh, 1889), 149–160; June Evans, "African / Caribbeans in Scotland: A Socio-Geographical Study" (Ph.D. diss., University of Edinburgh, 1995), 83–106.

litical tracts celebrated their arrival, others condemned their presence and lobbied to ban them from landing on British soil. Regardless of these variable experiences, mixed-race migrants continued to come over. Robert Morse and the Hay brothers might have turned heads in the stylish streets of London and the ramshackle roads of Dornoch, but they would not have been a wholly unfamiliar sight.[3]

This book documents the migration of mixed-race Jamaicans to and from Britain during the long eighteenth century. These free people of color were not simply spotted in the metropole, they were also incredibly important to the political and social developments of the British Empire. In the Caribbean, they held an awkward position between an enslaved class defined primarily by African ancestry and a ruling class open almost exclusively to those of supposedly pure Christian European heritage. Yet, owing to the small population of whites on the islands, mixed-race free men and women brought up in Britain were vital to colonial developments. In the eighteenth century, Jamaican officials solicited their loyalty and offered them access to white society in order to maintain control and tamp down on social disaffection. In the nineteenth century, British-educated Jamaicans of color were instrumental in the eventual overturning of racial apartheid and the transfer of colonial governance to those with African ancestry. Their presence was also crucial to definitions of the colonial family. Debates over how best to settle the Caribbean with a significant white population naturally occurred with them in mind because they appeared so culturally and economically similar to European colonists and, therefore, appropriate members of white colonial families. When elites of color left the island, they continued to make waves in their new homes. As illegitimate, African-descended children, these migrants presented challenges to ideas of kinship and belonging. White relatives tasked to care for them were frequently the wealthiest and some of the most politically well-connected people in Britain, and they were likewise integral contributors to the evolving debates on British family membership. In both colonial and metropolitan spaces, then, Jamaicans of color played a significant role in reshaping attitudes toward race and family in the British Atlantic.

Conceptions of race in the long eighteenth century were intimately tied

3. Barry Higman and Richard Dunn both estimate that roughly 80 percent of enslaved children born of white fathers in Jamaica in the eighteenth and nineteenth centuries were kept in slavery; see Higman, *Slave Population and Economy in Jamaica, 1807–1834* (Kingston, Jamaica, 1995), 141; and Richard S. Dunn, *A Tale of Two Plantations: Slave Life and Labor in Jamaica and Virginia* (Cambridge, Mass., 2014), 169.

to notions of family membership, and mixed-race migrants stood at the most contentious intersection of these issues. Their presence helped to push popular opinion in the British-Atlantic world toward more narrow definitions of race and kinship. The path of that transformation was not a smooth one, and it did not progress in a linear direction. There were four main stages to this development. First, beginning in 1733, before the massive enslaved uprisings of Tacky's Revolt in Jamaica, British and West Indian officials alike experimented with the idea of empowering mixed-race elites so that they might form the seedbed for a Caribbean white population struggling to grow. Tacky's Revolt terrified Jamaican rulers in 1760, and they narrowed the potential pool of white progenitors to primarily British-trained migrants of color since they were thought to be the closest, and most loyal, mixed-race islanders. Second, beginning in the 1760s, the early stages of the British movement to abolish the slave trade—and eventually slavery itself—helped transfer these colonial concerns around demography onto Britain as well, especially as English reformers started obsessing over domestic family formation. The potential arrival of emancipated slaves accelerated concerns about the future face of the British people, though mixed-race migrants were not initially targeted as a result of their high class standing. Third, by the 1780s, writers and polemicists began vilifying migrants of color for two reasons: mixed-race elites inheriting massive fortunes came to symbolize the breakdown of stability in British family finances, and officials worried that their education and potential radicalization in the metropole might eventually lead to a Caribbean rebellion, especially after the events of the Haitian Revolution began unfolding in 1791. Finally, the growing disdain toward these rich, illegitimate, African-descended travelers led to their social and familial exclusion in Britain in the early decades of the nineteenth century. Yet, after the prohibition of British colonial slavery in 1833, well-educated migrants of color came to be seen as the proper replacement—not foundation—for a failed white settler society in the Caribbean. Throughout this process, mixed-race migrants both inspired, and were influenced by, increasingly restrictive ideas of race and family belonging. The somewhat fluid ideas of racial status and kinship in 1733 gradually gave way a century later to a simpler differentiation between white and black, relative and stranger.

The number of mixed-race West Indians who traveled to Great Britain in this period was likely in the thousands, and this book tracks more than 360 identified individuals. Examining their lives, even though they constitute a somewhat small pool of migrants, matters because family relations were so critical to the structures and ideologies of Britain's Atlantic empire. Merchant

networks, political patronage, settlement schemes, and conceptions of difference all depended on the ways that families worked, or at least on the ways
that they were expected to work. Close analyses show how individual households were the engines powering the Empire. Yet, scholars have not, by and
large, addressed the question of racial ideology in the British Atlantic as a
family issue. The two have to be considered in tandem because conceptions
of difference were, at their most rudimentary level, built on distinguishing
who belonged within a family and who did not. That point is not meant in
an abstract fashion, based on a loose interpretation of the concept of family.
Rather, questions of kinship were serious considerations at the cornerstone
of the plantation complex driving racial ideologies forward. The transmission of enslaved property to heirs, legislation penalizing interracial sex to reduce manumissions, governmental initiatives to regulate enslaved families in
order to form a self-reproducing workforce: all of these depended on close
negotiation and monitoring of family units. Likewise, the violation of those
mandates spurred on the most nuanced considerations of what racial difference supposedly meant, especially because the idea of a family has always felt
(mistakenly) unchanged. Mixed-race children were an ever-present reminder,
across all imperial spaces, of those regimes' failures to regulate families completely. Focusing on how extended relatives came to conceive of the place of
mixed-race individuals in the family provides the subtlest look at how Atlantic
racial ideologies evolved. As Simon Smith suggests, "Much untapped information about slavery lies buried within family histories."[4]

The story of these mixed-race migrants opens new doors into understandings of early modern racial and family ideology. Although a targeted investigation has not yet been made of the group, a large scholarship exists on
mixed-race people in the Caribbean, and historians of Britain have explored
the presence of nonwhite residents as well.[5] Since the 1970s, scholars have

4. S[imon] D. Smith, *Slavery, Family, and Gentry Capitalism in the British Atlantic:
The World of the Lascelles, 1648–1834* (New York, 2006), 347. For close studies of individual
households and empire, see, especially, Emma Rothschild, *The Inner Life of Empires: An
Eighteenth-Century History* (Princeton, 2011); Elizabeth Buettner, *Empire Families: Britons
and Late Imperial India* (New York, 2004); and Sarah M. S. Pearsall, *Atlantic Families: Lives
and Letters in the Later Eighteenth Century* (New York, 2008). As Peggy Pascoe contends
for North American prohibitions against interracial marriage, policing race is effectively an
exercise in policing family; see Pascoe, *What Comes Naturally: Miscegenation Law and the
Making of Race in America* (New York, 2009), 2.

5. A partial list of the work done on mixed-race people in the Caribbean includes Sheila
Duncker, "The Free Coloured and Their Fight for Civil Rights in Jamaica, 1800–1830" (Mas-

compiled an impressive number of accounts of the colonial "other" arriving in Britain before the twentieth century. Originally, these investigations were motivated, in part, as a reaction to the rise of political parties that claimed an undiluted British racial past under threat by immigration. Scholars such as James Walvin, Folarin Shyllon, and Peter Fryer demonstrated authoritatively that Africans and African-descended people had maintained a visible and continuous presence in Britain from the sixteenth century to the present. The rise of Atlantic studies in subsequent years has widened and deepened that documentation of Britain's nonwhite past. Not only are the names of many of these residents available, but our understanding of British attitudes toward their presence has grown more complex in turn.[6] East Indian, native

----

ter's thesis, University of London, 1956); David W. Cohen and Jack P. Greene, eds., *Neither Slave Nor Free: The Freedmen of African Descent in the Slave Societies of the New World* (Baltimore, 1972); Jerome S. Handler, *The Unappropriated People: Freedmen in the Slave Society of Barbados* (Baltimore, 1974); Gad J. Heuman, *Between Black and White: Race, Politics, and the Free Coloreds in Jamaica, 1792–1865* (Westport, Conn., 1981); Edward L. Cox, *Free Coloreds in the Slave Societies of St. Kitts and Grenada, 1763–1833* (Knoxville, Tenn., 1984); Ann Twinam, *Public Lives, Private Secrets: Gender, Honor, Sexuality, and Illegitimacy in Colonial Spanish America* (Stanford, Calif., 1999); John D. Garrigus, *Before Haiti: Race and Citizenship in French Saint-Domingue* (New York, 2006); Melanie J. Newton, *The Children of Africa in the Colonies: Free People of Color in Barbados in the Age of Emancipation* (Baton Rouge, La., 2008); and Emily Clark, *The Strange History of the American Quadroon: Free Women of Color in the Revolutionary Atlantic World* (Chapel Hill, N.C., 2013).

6. Kenneth Lindsay Little wrote one of the first accounts of black British history in the early modern period, though it suffered from highly problematic ideas of biological difference; see Little, *Negroes in Britain: A Study of Racial Relations in English Society* (London, 1948). On individuals of African descent in Britain, see James Walvin, *The Black Presence: A Documentary History of the Negro in England, 1555–1860* (London, 1971); Walvin, *Black and White: The Negro and English Society, 1555–1945* (London, 1973); Folarin Shyllon, *Black People in Britain, 1555–1833* (New York, 1977); Peter Fryer, *Staying Power: Black People in Britain since 1504* (Atlantic Highlands, N.J., 1984); Douglas A. Lorimer, "Black Slaves and English Liberty: A Re-examination of Racial Slavery in England," *Immigrants and Minorities,* III (1984), 121–150; David Dabydeen, *Hogarth's Blacks: Images of Blacks in Eighteenth Century English Art* (Athens, Ga., 1987); Dabydeen, ed., *The Black Presence in English Literature* (Manchester, U.K., 1985); Ian Duffield, "Identity, Community, and the Lived Experience of Black Scots from the Late Eighteenth to the Mid-Nineteenth Centuries," *Immigrants and Minorities,* XI (1992), 105–129; Paul Gilroy, *The Black Atlantic: Modernity and Double Consciousness* (Cambridge, Mass., 1993); Gretchen Gerzina, *Black England: Life before Emancipation* (London, 1995); Evans, "African / Caribbeans in Scotland"; Norma Meyers, *Reconstructing the Black Past: Blacks in Britain, c. 1780–1830* (London, 1996); Imtiaz Habib, *Black Lives in the English Archives, 1500–1677: Imprints of the Invisible* (Aldershot, U.K., 2008); Kathleen Chater, *Untold Histories: Black People in England and Wales during the*

American, Asian, and Pacific historians have also revealed the regular arrival of other colonial subjects into the imperial metropole. Moreover, French and Spanish scholars have examined this same pattern in those empires as well. At the same time, much of this scholarship has focused on individuals of full African, Indian, or indigenous heritage, rather than those who had multiple ancestries.[7]

As the number of these studies has accumulated, the history of race and slavery has grown far less fixed and static. Although the overwhelming experience of colonial slavery was one of unending toil in a plantation complex, it was also not unusual for an enslaved individual to cross the Atlantic multiple times in service of a master. Olaudah Equiano, the slave-turned-bestselling memoirist, is perhaps most famous to scholars and the public alike. His autobiography demonstrates not only the cosmopolitan experience of a certain class of enslaved workers but also the (albeit narrow) potential for

<hr />

Period of the British Slave Trade, c. 1660–1807 (New York, 2009); and Jacob Selwood, *Diversity and Social Difference in Early Modern London* (Farnham, U.K., 2010).

7. For examples of mixed-race individuals and migrants to Britain, see C[hristopher] J[ohn] Hawes, *Poor Relations: The Making of a Eurasian Community in British India, 1773–1833* (Richmond, U.K., 1996), 102, 122–123; Eric Hinderaker, "The 'Four Indian Kings' and the Imaginative Construction of the First British Empire," *WMQ*, 3d Ser., LIII (1996), 487–526; William Dalrymple, *White Mughals: Love and Betrayal in Eighteenth-Century India* (London, 2002), 67–69, 471–480; Michael H. Fisher, *Counterflows to Colonialism: Indian Travellers and Settlers in Britain, 1600–1857* (Delhi, India, 2004); Durba Ghosh, *Sex and the Family in Colonial India: The Making of Empire* (Cambridge, 2006), 126–127, 174–179, 248–254; and Ardel Marie Thomas, "Victorian Monstrosities: Sexuality, Race, and the Construction of the Imperial Self, 1811–1924" (Ph.D. diss., Stanford University, 1998); Kate Teltscher, *The High Road to China: George Bogle, the Panchen Lama, and the First British Expedition to Tibet* (New York, 2006), 234–253; Alden T. Vaughan, *Transatlantic Encounters: American Indians in Britain, 1500–1776* (New York, 2006); Kate Fullagar, *The Savage Visit: New World People and Popular Culture in Britain, 1710–1795* (Berkeley, Calif., 2012); and Coll Thrush, "The Iceberg and the Cathedral: Encounter, Entanglement, and Isuma in Inuit London," *Journal of British Studies*, LIII (2014), 59–79. Examples of mixed-race migrants to other parts of Europe include Sue Peabody, *"There Are No Slaves in France": The Political Culture of Race and Slavery in the Ancien Régime* (New York, 1996); Dwain C. Pruitt, *"Nantes Noir: Living Race in the City of Slavers"* (Ph.D. diss., Emory University, 2005); Pierre H. Boulle, "Racial Purity or Legal Clarity? The Status of Black Residents in Eighteenth-Century France," *Journal of the Historical Society*, VI (2006), 19–46; Boulle, *Race et esclavage dans la France de l'Ancien Régime* (Paris, 2007); Jennifer L. Palmer, *Intimate Bonds: Family and Slavery in the French Atlantic* (Philadelphia, Pa., 2016); Camilla Townsend, *Malintzin's Choices: An Indian Woman in the Conquest of Mexico* (Albuquerque, N.Mex., 2006), 188–213; and Jane E. Mangan, *Transatlantic Obligations: Creating the Bonds of Family in Conquest-Era Peru and Spain* (New York, 2016).

social advancement once free. Dido Elizabeth Belle, the mixed-race great-niece of England's highest-seated judge with whom she lived in London, has also received a great deal of attention, including a 2014 film based on her life ("Belle"). These stories have long been known to historians of the British Empire, so much so that Ian Duffield grumbled more than twenty years ago that "constant reference in the historical literature to the same few individuals reduces them, despite their importance, to the status of old chestnuts."[8]

To address this criticism, scholars have worked to turn the spotlight onto new characters. Linda Colley has vividly documented the life of Elizabeth Marsh, a Jamaican woman—potentially of mixed heritage—whose experiences took her across the world in the eighteenth century. Colley sees Marsh's ordeal as an extraordinary one, shared only by a select handful of individuals like Equiano. Such globe-trotting, however, was not reserved for an exceptional few. A consistent number of West Indian migrants undertook the same journeys to Britain—and often to India, Africa, Australia, and other spots as well—year after year, and decade after decade. They reveal yet more biographies that demonstrate the vigor by which some bound laborers thrust themselves and their descendants out of slavery and into the realm of global citizenship.[9]

Elite migrants of color were a unique cohort whose experiences were quite different from those of humbler origins. Scholars studying racial ideology in Britain have mostly focused on poor and servile immigrants with non-European heritage. That research has documented a rising tide of racism in the metropole over time. Early-eighteenth-century conceptions of Africans in Britain depended on multiple perceptions of difference, including religious, cultural, and linguistic characteristics. By the end of that century, Britons came to see blackness as rooted in biology. In other words, the rather porous boundaries surrounding British identity at the beginning of the eighteenth century gave way to more fixed and binary ones by the turn of the nineteenth. As these identities cemented, they turned against individuals with African ancestry. When poor colonists with non-European heritage arrived in Britain, fears about interracial unions solidified the notion that to be British one had to be white. Some scholars even go so far as to assert that England developed

8. Duffield, "Identity, Community, and the Lived Experience of Black Scots," *Immigrants and Minorities*, XI (1992), 105; Olaudah Equiano, *The Interesting Narrative and Other Writings*, ed. Vincent Carretta (New York, 2003). See Carretta's introduction for a discussion of Equiano's potential origins.

9. Linda Colley, *The Ordeal of Elizabeth Marsh: A Woman in World History* (New York, 2007), xxiii. See also Gilroy, *Black Atlantic*.

its national identity in reaction to such perceived racial threats from the imperial peripheries. Of course, British ideas of race did not evolve unswerv-
ingly toward a scientific conception of racial difference, and there was never
a single theory of race. Yet, scholars studying racial ideology in the British
Atlantic generally agree that racial discrimination worsened over the eighteenth century and that it became more difficult to escape one's racial category
as the century ended.[10]

The story of mixed-race travelers fits this basic narrative of more strident
racial prejudice developing over time, but it also provides an adapted explanation. Namely, concerns around family membership pushed households on
both sides of the Atlantic to turn against those with African heritage. This correction comes from shifting the focus away from poor and enslaved blacks and
toward those of mixed heritage with familial connections to Britons. If racial
ideas were consolidating and changing in Britain, it was not, as many scholars
presume, solely the result of the arrival of an undifferentiated mass of African-
descended people. It was owing at least partly to increasing interaction with
individuals of color who were familiar through kinship and network connections. That might seem a minor point considering the relatively small number of migrants who made their way from the Caribbean to Britain. However,
there are two important reasons why such a modest cohort deserves sustained
attention. First, British attitudes toward individuals of joint African and European descent were some of the most complicated of the period, especially
when observers were related to them. Scholars have effectively analyzed the
ideologies Europeans built against enslaved Africans, but those were often incredibly distant and simplistic relations between ethnic groups. Negotiating

10. Roxann Wheeler, *The Complexion of Race: Categories of Difference in Eighteenth-
Century British Culture* (Philadelphia, 2000); Dror Wahrman, *The Making of the Modern
Self: Identity and Culture in Eighteenth-Century England* (New Haven, Conn., 2004), esp.
101–129; Felicity A. Nussbaum, *The Limits of the Human: Fictions of Anomaly, Race, and
Gender in the Long Eighteenth Century* (New York, 2003); Isaac Land, *War, National-
ism, and the British Sailor, 1750–1850* (New York, 2009), 77–104; Kathleen Wilson, *The
Island Race: Englishness, Empire, and Gender in the Eighteenth Century* (London, 2003);
Robert J. C. Young, *Colonial Desire: Hybridity in Theory, Culture, and Race* (New York,
1995); Douglas Lorimer, "Reconstructing Victorian Racial Discourse: Images of Race, the
Language of Race Relations, and the Context of Black Resistance," in Gretchen Gerzina,
ed., *Black Victorians/Black Victoriana* (New Brunswick, N.J., 2003), 187. Catherine Molineux presents a more fractured chronology of racial thinking but agrees that slave rebellions
in the 1720s and 1730s turned many opinions strongly against black subjects and slaves; see
Molineux, *Faces of Perfect Ebony: Encountering Atlantic Slavery in Imperial Britain* (Cambridge, Mass., 2012), 110–145.

family membership with a relative of color produced much more careful—
though not always compassionate—considerations of difference, and those
subtleties of understanding are vital to dissecting the intricacies of Atlantic
racial thought. Second, most of these mixed-race migrants were backed by
enormous Caribbean fortunes and were connected to some of the most important politicians and thinkers of the day. Members of Parliament, colonial
assemblymen, merchant kings, and cultural arbiters were often intimately
aware of these migrants and interacted with them in highly personal ways,
including through family relationships. Unlike the thousands of poor blacks
who arrived in Britain during the long eighteenth century, migrants of color
were not wholly segregated socially and geographically once in the metropole.
Elites of color influenced debates around race, abolition, and family membership in disproportionate ways.

These subtleties of racial interpretations brought about by interactions
with interracial kin were also important to the colonial context as well. With
several notable exceptions, scholars have been relatively uninterested in evolving ideas about race in Jamaica. The island was, after all, a terrible hothouse
of slavery in which profit trumped practically all other considerations. For the
hundreds of thousands of enslaved individuals enduring horrific toil, subtle
alterations in racial thinking had virtually no bearing on the misery of their
lives. For the several thousand free people of color living on the island at any
one time in the long eighteenth century, however, small alterations in racial
ideology had important legal and social consequences. Jamaican officials experimented with laws that granted both full and approximate legal whiteness
to mixed-race people in order to stabilize a demographic imbalance in which
enslaved blacks outnumbered free whites ten to one. In the continuous tweak-
ing of that legislation, those officials drew on family connections to determine
who was best suited for white, or semi-white, status. Once again, mixed-race
migrants were key to these developments. Their British education and kinship to important white colonists made them the most ideal candidates to
be included in white society once they returned to the Caribbean, at least
through the perspective of the island's government. Indeed, the group was
vital for the maintenance of social control. Jamaican officials gave concessions
to them when they felt most threatened by enslaved revolution, while simultaneously clamping down on poorer individuals of color. This was meant to
solidify the island's wealthy plantocracy by softening the outermost extremes
of racial thought, allowing some free people of color to buy into the plantation system, rather than to oppose it as a racially exclusive enterprise. Family
belonging thus contributed directly to the debates about what race meant in

the colony. Without this ability to use familial relationships as a lever to adjust racial oppression, albeit for the most elite residents of color, the machinery of Jamaican slavery would have worn down more quickly.[11]

Tracing these migrants' paths illuminates the specific ways in which colonial and metropolitan attitudes toward race interacted. Most scholars analyzing British racial ideologies acknowledge the vital contribution of colonial events and viewpoints; after all, empires were webs of connection with influence traveling in multiple directions. That axiom, however, is often more of an intellectual mantra than a direct line of inquiry. Metropolitan ideas about family did not alter the colonies in amorphous ways. Nor did colonial attitudes about race only vaguely influence Britain. Legal and discursive changes on both ends of the Empire had precise impacts on constructions of family and race. When Parliament revised England's marriage law in 1753, for instance, it not only set about trying to impose similar revisions for its colonies, but it also attempted (the day after the act's passage) to change the scheme for white Jamaican settlement. Similarly, when the Jamaican assembly capped the inheritance of mixed-race colonists in 1761, it provided a legal mechanism for British subjects to begin suing relatives of color in the metropole for a greater share of family wealth, thereby transforming the role of African ancestry within British households. Even the relatively nebulous debates around race within the movement to abolish the slave trade emerged out of specific policy issues. Abolitionist diatribes against interracial sex had their origin in long-standing governmental attempts to quantify and calculate demographics in both the colony and metropole. British ideologies on race and family, then, truly developed in dialogue with West Indian colonies. Migrants of color were often at the forefront, weathering the storm of these ever-changing winds, while simultaneously altering the direction in which they blew.

11. Scholars who have explored the changing dynamics of race in Jamaica include Heuman, *Between Black and White;* Wilson, *Island Race,* 148–168; Linda L. Sturtz, "Mary Rose: 'White' African Jamaican Woman? Race and Gender in Eighteenth-Century Jamaica," in Judith A. Byfield, LaRay Denzer, and Anthea Morrison, eds., *Gendering the African Diaspora: Women, Culture, and Historical Change in the Caribbean and Nigerian Hinterland* (Bloomington, Ind., 2010), 59–87; and Brooke N. Newman, "Gender, Sexuality, and the Formation of Racial Identities in the Eighteenth-Century Anglo-Caribbean World," *Gender and History,* XXII (2010), 585–602. Despite their strengths, these studies are either primarily explorations of racial identities as they relate to political rights or examinations of a single individual. This book aims to build off this scholarship by demonstrating how a large group of mixed-race people navigated a racial identity that was rooted in political struggle but also entrenched in broader social and familial forces.

These exchanges demonstrate that mixed-race migrants were part of an "Atlantic family." Although broad, the term signifies the particular kin relationships that defined transatlantic family networks with joint African and European ancestries. Many individuals in the British Empire had relatives on either side of the ocean, which complicated family membership and interaction regardless of racial questions. Legitimacy, class standing, educational attainment, geographic location, degrees of consanguinity, and personal preference—among others—were all important factors in guiding family units that spanned the globe. But those with mixed-race relations negotiated their kinship through added levels of scrutiny. Statuses of freedom, colonial legal standing, Afro-Caribbean acculturation, and skin coloration were some of the other considerations that went into the acceptance or rejection of mixed-race kin. Yet, these ancillary issues, rooted in questions of race, were not debated outside the normal parameters of family regulation. Whites could, and did, use racial attacks to exclude relatives of color, but rarely was it the only factor—at least not until more stringent notions of racial difference emerged in the nineteenth century. If, for example, they used a colonial law targeting people of color to disinherit a Jamaican cousin, they did so under the guise that this would benefit legitimate family members who were more deserving of filial piety. Of course, this was simply another way to justify racism. But, throughout the long eighteenth century, mixed-race and white relatives attempted to resolve these issues through traditional channels of kinship management.[12]

The Atlantic family, then, functioned as a true family in both Jamaica and Britain. These households were, not ersatz substitutes, but largely normalized versions of so-called traditional family units. Granted, relationships between white men and women of color in the Caribbean were terribly unequal, even in cases that might best resemble a companionate union. Yet, this should not keep scholars from analyzing interracial households within a family framework. After all, white intermarriage among freemen at the time retained strong divisions of power as well, albeit ones more vigorously separated by gender. Inequality did not negate white kinship in those cases, and it should not invalidate the familial dimension of these interracial groups either. Cross-racial relationships abounded in a Jamaican society with a tremendous gender disparity among its white population. They were thus highly normalized, even if published accounts bemoaned the practice. Fathers who took care of offspring born from these unions treated them as children: they paid for their

12. Pearsall, *Atlantic Families*.

upbringing, sent them to school, gave them large hereditary bequests, and in some cases wrote lovingly about them. The children, in turn, looked to their fathers as patriarchs: they drew on them for support, listed their names when appealing for governmental assistance, and took strong positions within their fathers' extended families. Legally, these migrants of color stood outside the traditional bounds of domestic kinship. Functionally, they acted as normal members of Atlantic families that could be complicated in myriad ways beyond race. Despite a much older view that mixed-ancestry relationships fractured Caribbean society and led to its downfall, illegitimate offspring of color were in actuality crucial to familial and social cohesion in the West Indies. Moreover, the illegitimate status held by the overwhelming majority of mixed-race migrants was also not sufficient to nullify family membership across the ocean. Britons were not unfamiliar with illegitimacy, and they frequently accepted children born out of wedlock into kin networks. Nontraditional relatives were, in fact, highly traditional in British society, and it was by no means strange to incorporate individuals with divergent experiences and ancestry into one's family fold.[13]

Nevertheless, none of these family negotiations stayed static over time. Household relationships transformed dramatically from the eighteenth to the nineteenth centuries. The rules surrounding who belongs in a family, and who does not, are always changing, and this was especially true during this period. More particularly, though, the merchant and slaveowning classes that held the highest proportion of mixed-race relatives faced some of the strongest pres-

13. Lowell Ragatz viewed white cohabitation with women of color as emblematic of the social backwardness of West Indian society and a contribution to its decline; see Ragatz, *The Fall of the Planter Class in the British Caribbean, 1763–1833: A Study in Social and Economic History* (New York, 1928), 5, 33. Latin American scholars, by contrast, have long recognized how the creation of a wide spectrum of racial categories could, in fact, "divide and rule" colonial society; see Fernando Ortiz y Fernandez, "Cuba, Martí, and the Race Problem," *Phylon*, III (1942), 271–272. For studies of illegitimacy and its normalcy in Britain, see Alan Macfarlane, "Illegitimacy and Illegitimates in English History," in Peter Laslett, Karla Oosterveen, and Richard M. Smith, eds., *Bastardy and Its Comparative History: Studies in the History of Illegitimacy and Nonconformism in Britain, France, Germany, Sweden, North America, Jamaica, and Japan* (London, 1980), 75–76; Roy Porter, "Mixed Feelings: The Enlightenment and Sexuality in Eighteenth-Century Britain," in Paul-Gabriel Boucé, ed., *Sexuality in Eighteenth-Century Britain* (Manchester, U.K., 1982), 4–13; Andrew Blaikie, "A Kind of Loving: Illegitimacy, Grandparents, and the Rural Economy of North East Scotland, 1750–1900," *Scottish Economic and Social History*, XIV (1994), 41–57; and Stana Nenadic, *Lairds and Luxury: The Highland Gentry in Eighteenth-Century Scotland* (Edinburgh, 2007), 108, 123.

sures to change their kinship patterns. The rise of commercial capitalism in the eighteenth century enriched many of the British men who traveled out to Jamaica and fathered children of color there. But those increased riches also escalated the difficulty with which many merchants and planters could achieve their ultimate goal of buying into British landed society. Only through novel approaches toward marriage and inheritance redistribution could they maintain their commercial networks, let alone join the aristocracy. This meant that direct ties of consanguinity were less important over time than access to credit and independent financial resources. Individuals of color, who were mostly illegitimate, sometimes born enslaved, and often limited economically to their fathers' associates, simply could not compete for full family recognition. As pathways to favored kinship narrowed for many Britons at the turn of the nineteenth century, they virtually ended for Jamaican migrants of color.[14]

⁂

Locating mixed-race migrants and assessing how families interacted with them requires delving into a number of different archives. Two sets of sources are crucial in identifying Jamaicans of color who traveled to Britain. The first is the island's probate records. A sample of more than 2,200 wills proven between 1773 and 1815 contain 122 with bequests for either a mixed-race child soon to be sent to Britain or for those already there. Appendix 1 shows what

---

14. G. E. Mingay, *English Landed Society in the Eighteenth Century* (London, 1963), 12–36; F. M. L. Thompson, *English Landed Society in the Nineteenth Century* (London, 1963), 21–23; John Habakkuk, "The Rise and Fall of English Landed Families, 1600–1800," Royal Historical Society, *Transactions*, 5th Ser., XXIX (1979), 203–205; W. D. Rubinstein, "New Men of Wealth and the Purchase of Land in Nineteenth-Century Britain," *Past and Present*, no. 92 (August 1981), 139–141; J. V. Beckett, "The Pattern of Landownership in England and Wales, 1660–1880," *Economic History Review*, 2d Ser., XXXVII (1984), 11–18; H. J. Habakkuk, "Marriage Settlements in the Eighteenth Century," Royal Historical Society, *Transactions*, 4th Ser., XXXII (1950), 28; Habakkuk, *Marriage, Debt, and the Estates System: English Landownership, 1650–1950* (New York, 1994), 227–231; Christopher Clay, "Marriage, Inheritance, and the Rise of Large Estates in England, 1660–1815," *Economic History Review*, 2d Ser., XXI (1968), 515; Lloyd Bonfield, "Marriage Settlements and the 'Rise of the Great Estates': The Demographic Aspect," *Economic History Review*, 2d Ser., XXXII (1979), 486; Eileen Spring, *Law, Land, and Family: Aristocratic Inheritance in England, 1300 to 1800* (Chapel Hill, N.C., 1993), 183–186; Ruth Perry, *Novel Relations: The Transformation of Kinship in English Literature and Culture, 1748–1818* (New York, 2004), 51–73; David Warren Sabean and Simon Teuscher, "Kinship in Europe: A New Approach to Long-Term Development," in Sabean, Teuscher, and Jon Mathieu, eds., *Kinship in Europe: Approaches to Long-Term Developments (1300–1900)* (New York, 2007), 3–23.

percentage of testators supported children of color abroad, and each of the chapters goes into detail on their individual experiences. Broadly speaking, the survey of wills demonstrates that sending a mixed-race child to Britain was a regular and sustained practice from the late-eighteenth to the early-nineteenth centuries. The second cache of sources comes from the records of Jamaica's lower legislative house, the assembly. From 1733 to 1826—with a twenty-one-year gap at the start of the nineteenth century—the assembly passed private privilege bills for roughly seven hundred elite colonists of color. Initially, these privilege petitions gave full white status to those who received them, but, by the middle of the eighteenth century, they became little more than nominal tokens of distinction. Nevertheless, each privilege bill contains a brief biography of its petitioner, including a note on whether they had spent time abroad. Of those who petitioned, ninety mentioned an education or residence in Britain. These private bills have been virtually unexplored by scholars, and the information within them helps contribute to the family stories presented here.[15]

Understanding the interpersonal dynamics between migrants of color and their families requires consulting an entirely different set of materials. Personal correspondence is not abundant, but several family papers contain surviving letters that address relatives of color at certain snapshots of their lives. These are rarely emotional in tone, but they do provide close reflections on how whites related to kin of color. More substantially, inheritance lawsuits uncover the legal mechanisms by which families arranged their hierarchies. One major suit between Robert Morse's family illustrates just how tricky family maintenance could be when enormous fortunes were at stake. A number of other cases detail just how regular these legal challenges were for migrants of color.

The popular press also gives some wider indication of how both British and West Indian people felt about these migrants. A number of sources stand out. First, the Jamaica assembly records lay out in detail the many legal changes and considerations that colonial rulers undertook for mixed-race

15. The survey of wills was conducted through the volumes of Wills, 1773-1815, LOS, 41-42, 49-51, 57-58, 60-61, 70-75, 87-91, IRO. The only studies that engage with private privilege bills in a substantive way are Samuel J. Hurwitz and Edith F. Hurwitz, "A Token of Freedom: Private Bill Legislation for Free Negroes in Eighteenth-Century Jamaica," *WMQ*, 3d Ser., XXIV (1967), 423-431; and Brooke N. Newman, "Contesting 'Black' Liberty and Subjecthood in the Anglophone Caribbean, 1730s-1780s," *Slavery and Abolition*, XXXII (2011), 169-170.

people. This book offers one of the most complete surveys of those records to trace how island officials monitored and courted migrants of color. Second, many pamphlets and broadsides were published in the long eighteenth century that debated the morality of the African slave trade—and of slavery generally—while simultaneously reflecting on mixed-race migration to Britain. Specifically, pro- and antislavery activists considered how realistic it would be to create naturally reproducing populations in the West Indies that could stabilize white control, while also eliminating the need for imported Africans. This goal turned observers against interracial sex and the mixed-race children born from them, especially those who migrated to Britain and complicated metropolitan anxieties around ethnicity and identity. Novelists joined in this public debate by penning stories with migrants of color. Most of these tales warned of problems around family inheritance and interracial coupling in Britain. Taken together, the popular press came to vilify mixed-race migrants at roughly the same pace that families began to sour in their attitudes toward them.

These various sources reveal both the personal, and the distant, attitudes that whites in Britain and Jamaica had toward migrants of color. Primarily, they uncover the day-to-day relationships between mixed-race and white individuals across the British Atlantic. These were the functional ideologies of race employed by heterogeneous communities and households, rather than philosophical and scientific debates hashed out among the intelligentsia. Scholars of Atlantic racial thought have often put heavy emphasis on those latter opinions. The eighteenth century did see a plethora of theories put forward to explain ethnic difference: stadial theories on the progress of civilization from hunter-gatherer to settler societies, notions that climate influenced both mind and body, debates over single origin (monogenesis) and multiple origins (polygenesis) of the Earth's population, and attempts to connect skin color to biology. Yet, there was never a clear consensus on these theories. More importantly, they almost never trickled into the daily conversations of merchants, planters, or mixed-race households. Therefore, instead of engaging with natural philosophies around race in this period, the focus here is on the personal and political discourses that operated on an entirely different social register that scholars have not yet explored in significant detail.[16]

16. For eighteenth-century theories explaining ethnic differences, see, among others, Young, *Colonial Desire;* Wheeler, *Complexion of Race;* Nussbaum, *Limits of the Human;* and Tillman W. Nechtman, *Nabobs: Empire and Identity in Eighteenth-Century Britain* (New York, 2010), 64–65.

Both private and public sources provide glimpses into white attitudes toward mixed-race relatives, but they unfortunately fail to reveal much of what those migrants themselves felt. Despite that many West Indians of color received a good education in Britain, most did not leave a significant written legacy. Direct correspondence is agonizingly difficult to find, although one of the main families in this study—the Tailyours—did write a handful of letters back to their father once in Britain. Errant bits and pieces provide additional small clues but fail to sketch out full portraits of their subjects. Inheritance lawsuits between relatives, documented extensively in the third chapter, contain some of the most substantive opinions from mixed-race individuals, but they are channeled through the procedural language of legal custom. The most complete record from a mixed-race migrant's own hand comes in a series of published pamphlets by Robert Wedderburn, a Jamaican of color who turned to radical religion after struggling in Britain. Sadly, most information documenting the lives of West Indian migrants comes from white kin, rather than from the perspectives of mixed-race individuals themselves. This is a lingering problem for all scholarship of the African diaspora in the eighteenth century, even, as it turns out, for those individuals with highly elite backgrounds. Although the experience of mixed-race migrants is filtered through white actors, by taking these stories together, collective voices do start to emerge. The following chapters primarily document white attitudes in the British Atlantic, but, in the process, they also resurrect the stories of individuals thought long lost to history.

Focused as it is on the migration of elites of color to Britain, this book naturally concentrates almost entirely on individuals born in the colony of Jamaica. North American colonists rarely treated mixed-race children as kin, owing to much larger and more stable white family units there. In almost no case did mainland colonists send a child of color to Britain for an education. Instead, the West Indies, with greater white gender imbalances, produced many more households of color. Within the English-speaking Caribbean, Jamaica was the epicenter of such interracial family units. As the largest island in the British West Indies, and by the third decade of eighteenth century its most profitable and populated, Jamaica provides the best starting point for this examination. Not only were the majority of migrants to Britain from Jamaica, but the island traditionally stood in for the whole Caribbean in British popular thought throughout the eighteenth and nineteenth centuries. Jamaica also had the largest population of color in the British West Indies. Partly this was a result of the island's overall size, but it also originated from Jamaica's large gender imbalance among white residents. With fewer percentages of white women than its leeward neighbors like Barbados, Jamaica had high rates of interracial unions and thus large numbers of offspring born from them. Moreover, as one of the wealthiest colonies in Britain's eighteenth-century empire, those children were often supported by substantial fortunes derived from slavery and sugar.[17]

Jamaica also merits special attention for its legislative history. Taken from Spain in 1655, the island's laws were some of the most complex on the issue of race in the whole Anglo-Atlantic. Although it is hard to discern how directly the more tolerant Iberian legal models influenced Jamaica, by 1733, the island began experimenting with somewhat flexible racial codes that resembled Spanish and Portuguese laws. Not only did the Jamaican assembly accord legal whiteness to those more than three generations removed from Africans that year, it also began voting on the privilege petitions from elites of color to circumvent certain race-based legislation. Jamaica, therefore, had some of the most complicated and evolving attitudes toward race in the Caribbean, and it also dominated the region's relations with Britain.

Each of the following chapters weaves individual stories with larger political and cultural changes in Jamaica, Britain, and the Atlantic basin. Many of the legislative developments in the Caribbean are set alongside anecdotes from the colonists of color affected by them. Similarly, changing family dynamics in Britain come out of brief snapshots of multiple migrants who temporarily entered the archival record, be it through personal correspondence, a father's will, or a courtroom deposition. Tracking the entire life cycle of individual migrants of color is exceptionally challenging, but three families left detailed records that come close. The Morses, Tailyours, and Rosses were all intimately connected to some of the most powerful and influential people in the British Empire. They are therefore some of the easiest migrants to follow. Each of the chapters begin with stories from their lives as they moved from Jamaica to Britain, and—in some cases—to other parts of the world. Genealogies for each family are included in Appendix 2 to help keep those family relations clear.

The long eighteenth century was a turbulent time in the Atlantic world. Slavery rose and (in some cases) fell, numerous colonial regimes collapsed, and domestic relationships continually transformed. Jamaicans of color who traveled to Britain saw much of this upheaval firsthand. Likewise, they helped contribute significantly to these changes as well. Their lives mattered

17. Handler, *Unappropriated People*, 68–69; Karl Watson, *The Civilised Island, Barbados: A Social History, 1750–1816* (Saint George, Barbados, 1979), 99.

not simply because they appeared exceptional to the seemingly hard-and-fast rules of slavery and racial oppression. Rather, they mattered because they embodied the complications and muddled nature of empire. Europe's imperial regimes were not composed and overseen by isolated individuals, free to drift unhampered across the globe. Empires were rooted by families, deeply connected to one another, and bound by strong ties of kinship that often easily bypassed cultural and social prohibitions. When mixed-race colonists came to the imperial center, they showed Britons the true face of colonialism, not simply its professed ideal. The struggle to look on and accept that image was perhaps the most intimate space of imperial negotiation in the whole of the Empire.

CHAPTER 1

✻✽✻

INHERITANCE, FAMILY, AND
MIXED-RACE JAMAICANS,
1700–1761

As the embers of John Morse's burned Jamaican estate cooled, his business partners struggled to make sense of the devastation. Morse had fled to England as bands of rebels approached his plantation in the autumn of 1760. Even though the first wave of uprisings had crested, hundreds of enslaved insurgents still poured through the colony in what was later named Tacky's Revolt. The rebellion was one of the Caribbean's largest slave insurrections up to that point, taking the lives of as many as five hundred unfree people and dozens of white colonists. It concluded with more than one hundred thousand pounds of property left in ruins, including Morse's plantation. Working through associates still in Jamaica, Morse appealed to the colony's lower legislative house, the assembly, for help. Morse had previously been a member of that body and knew that his former colleagues would do what they could to get his plantation running again. After all, the island's fortunes were bound up with his own and dependent on the productivity of his sugar estates. Morse's six children, who undertook the same journey to England, also relied on those sugar farms to sustain elite, transatlantic lifestyles. Unlike their father, however, they were descendants of slaves, just like the ones who built and maintained the family plantation as well as those who had destroyed it.[1]

1. [Edward Long], *The History of Jamaica; or, General Survey of the Antient and Modern State of That Island . . .* , 3 vols. (London, 1774), I, 462; *London Evening Post,* Feb. 7, 1761–Feb. 10, 1761; *The London Chronicle for the Year 1761 . . .* (1761), IX, 138; *JAJ,* Nov. 14–27, 1760, V, 211, 221; "List of Landholders in Jamaica about 1750," Edward Long Manuscripts, Add. MS 12436, BL; Maria Alessandra Bollettino, "Slavery, War, and Britain's Atlantic Empire: Black Soldiers, Sailors, and Rebels in the Seven Years' War" (Ph.D. diss., University of Texas Austin, 2009), 20–21; Michael Craton, *Testing the Chains: Resistance to Slavery in the British West Indies* (Ithaca, N.Y., 1982), 138; Trevor Burnard, *Mastery, Tyranny, and Desire: Thomas Thistlewood and His Slaves in the Anglo-Jamaican World* (Chapel Hill, N.C., 2004), 10, 170–173; Richard B. Sheridan, *Sugar and Slavery: An Economic History of the British West Indies, 1623–1775* (Kingston, Jamaica, 1994), 300; Burnard, "Passengers Only: The Extent and Significance of Absenteeism in Eighteenth Century Jamaica," *Atlantic Studies,* I (2004),

Because Morse vacated his seat in the assembly when he left Jamaica, he had no say when it reconvened in the fall of 1761 to decide how best to avoid another insurrection. On October 23, the assembly agreed on two core goals: to craft stronger laws against the enslaved and to create a bill combating "the frequent practice of devising large properties to mulattoes and negroes." The latter resolution might have appeared strange to outsiders. Limiting the amount of money that a white father could bequeath to a child of color was seemingly not a direct response to an armed uprising. To Jamaican legislators, though, the flourishing of mixed-race households symbolized an erosion of the divide between enslaved blacks and free whites. Without such a firm distinction, the assembly claimed, bound workers would continue to feel inspired to rise up. For the large number of men who had such families, though, this plan to restrict their bequests aroused a great deal of alarm. Morse, for instance, planned on giving his children in England the majority of his nearly £150,000 fortune.[2]

What must have passed through the assembly members' minds the very next day after crafting this resolution, however, when they received two petitions from mixed-race Jamaicans asking for exemptions from some of the island's harshest laws against individuals of color? John and Dorothy Elletson, who self-identified as "quadroons," and Dugald Clarke, who described himself as a "free mulatto," each appealed for advanced rights based on their substantial wealth and cultural refinement. Like Morse's children, they had also spent part of their upbringing in Britain. If anyone represented the type of excessive privilege condemned by the assembly only one day earlier, it was these two sets of petitioners. Yet, the assembly easily agreed to both requests and gave final approval to the petitions just two days after completing a law that capped the amount of money illegitimate nonwhites could inherit at two thousand pounds. How did the assembly come to these two seemingly contradictory conclusions? For the first half of the eighteenth century, Jamaican legislators openly experimented with policies toward those of partial African ancestry. Racial categories were far from simple, and they were not applied uniformly. Instead, class, upbringing, and family position each became criti-

---

181–185. Unless otherwise noted, all monetary amounts listed are in Jamaican pounds current (roughly two-thirds the value of English pounds sterling throughout the period).

2. *JAJ*, Oct. 23, 1761, V, 273; Richard Sheridan notes that Morse's estate was valued at more than ninety-eight thousand pounds sterling (including debts owed to him) at his death; see Sheridan, *Sugar and Slavery*, 300. Most of that fortune went to his illegitimate children of color; see Will of John Morse, Apr. 18, 1781, PROB 11/1077, NAE.

cal factors in the standing of mixed-race people. And no one had a higher standing than those individuals of color who traveled to Britain.[3]

Initial Debates over Settlement and Race

At the root of Jamaica's deliberations on race were concerns about settlement. From its earliest moments as an English colony, Jamaica struggled with its population. England's navy took the island from Spain in 1655 after a rather bumbling military campaign. Previous successes at cultivating sugar in Barbados made Jamaica an attractive acquisition. But the intense tropical climate, rampant problems with mosquito-borne illnesses, and continual threat of Spanish reconquest dampened its appeal to some British migrants. Nevertheless, the island's boosters loudly advertised its potential. Despite Jamaica's immediate reputation as an unhealthy and wicked outpost, one English transplant insisted in 1661 that the new colony was arguably no "lesse habitable then any other most auspicious settlement." Such claims proved wildly optimistic and speculative, but they represented a legitimate and enduring desire to populate the island with an established core of European colonists.[4]

Initially, the plan seemed to work. British migrants from across the economic spectrum arrived in the hopes of capitalizing on the emerging sugar fortunes of the seventeenth century. Yet, unlike the smaller islands of the eastern Caribbean, Jamaica came under English control *after* sugar had taken over West Indian agriculture. Large plantations had quickly choked off more modest farms, making it difficult for middling white families to thrive.[5] More-

---

3. *JAJ*, Oct. 24, 1761, V, 274, Dec. 19, 1761, 322. Although the printed *JAJ* lists the Elletsons as "mulattoes," their petition notes them as "quadroons" and indicates that their mother was a "mulatto" and their father was white; see Commissioners of Legal Inquiry in the West Indies, Dec. 19, 1761, CO 318/76, NAE. In Jamaican racial taxonomy, a "mulatto" was the child of one white and one black parent. A "quadroon" was the child of one white and one mulatto parent.

4. E[dmund] H[ickeringill], *Jamaica Viewed . . .*, 2d ed. (London, 1661), 2. For more on the English conquest of Spanish Jamaica, see Richard S. Dunn, *Sugar and Slaves: The Rise of the Planter Class in the English West Indies, 1624–1713* (Chapel Hill, N.C., 2000), 149–153; Carla Gardina Pestana, *The English Atlantic in an Age of Revolution, 1640–1661* (Cambridge, Mass., 2004), 177–181; Pestana, *The English Conquest of Jamaica: Oliver Cromwell's Bid for Empire* (Cambridge, Mass., 2017); James Robertson, *Gone Is the Ancient Glory: Spanish Town, Jamaica, 1534–2000* (Kingston, Jamaica, 2005), 15–34; J. R. McNeill, *Mosquito Empires: Ecology and War in the Greater Caribbean, 1620–1914* (New York, 2010), 97–105; and Abigail L. Swingen, *Competing Visions of Empire: Labor, Slavery, and the Origins of the British Atlantic Empire* (New Haven, Conn., 2015), 32–55.

5. Before the "sugar revolution" of the 1640s and 1650s, small-scale family farms suc-

over, the island's climate and reputation for piracy and vice were thought to make it improper for European women. White men outnumbered their female counterparts two to one in 1674, stunting the natural growth of Jamaica's white households.[6] Owing, in part, to this gender imbalance, white men sought out sexual partners among the increasing numbers of Africans arriving each

------

ceeded in Barbados and the Leeward Islands; see Alison F. Games, "Opportunity and Mobility in Early Barbados," in Robert L. Paquette and Stanley L. Engerman, eds., *The Lesser Antilles in the Age of European Expansion* (Gainesville, Fla., 1996), 165–181. Russell R. Menard notes that smaller farms predated large plantations in Barbados but that the emergence of monumental estates occurred before sugar's economic domination; see Menard, *Sweet Negotiations: Sugar, Slavery, and Plantation Agriculture in Early Barbados* (Charlottesville, Va., 2006). John C. Appleby finds the forces of settlement and piracy battling each other in the early years of West Indian colonization; see Appleby, "English Settlement in the Lesser Antilles during War and Peace, 1603–1660," in Paquette and Engerman, eds., *Lesser Antilles,* 86–104. Karen Ordahl Kupperman explores the role of Puritans in the Caribbean Sea as part of the same settlement project of the Great Migration; see Kupperman, *Providence Island, 1630–1641: The Other Puritan Colony* (New York, 1995). See also Natalie A. Zacek, *Settler Society in the English Leeward Islands, 1670–1776* (New York, 2010).

6. Felicity A. Nussbaum, *Torrid Zones: Maternity, Sexuality, and Empire in Eighteenth-Century English Narratives* (Baltimore, 1995), 8–10; Susan Scott Parrish, *American Curiosity: Cultures of Natural History in the Colonial British Atlantic World* (Chapel Hill, N.C., 2006), 77–102; Sarah E. Yeh, " 'A Sink of All Filthiness': Gender, Family, and Identity in the British Atlantic, 1688–1763," *The Historian,* LXVIII (2006), 66–88. These ideas about the tropical climate affecting men and women differently extended long into the eighteenth century. See, in particular, [James Houstoun], *Dr. Houstoun's Memoirs of His Own Life-Time* (London, 1747), 354. For the statistics on white gender demography in the seventeenth century, see table 16 in Dunn, *Sugar and Slaves,* 155; and Lucille Mathurin Mair, *A Historical Study of Women in Jamaica, 1655–1814,* ed. Hilary McD. Beckles and Verene A. Shepherd (Kingston, Jamaica, 2006), 25. Jamaica was thought to be a bachelor paradise, unfit for families and a temporary stop solely on which to make extraordinary sums of money. This narrative continues to be promoted in much of the scholarship about the island; see Orlando Patterson, *The Sociology of Slavery: An Analysis of the Origins, Development, and Structure of Negro Slave Society in Jamaica* (Cranbury, N.J., 1969); Kamau Brathwaite, *The Development of Creole Society in Jamaica, 1720–1820* (Oxford, 1971), 88, 149; Carl Bridenbaugh and Roberta Bridenbaugh, *No Peace Beyond the Line: The English in the Caribbean, 1624–1690* (New York, 1972); Dunn, *Sugar and Slaves;* Alan L. Karras, *Sojourners in the Sun: Scottish Migrants in Jamaica and the Chesapeake, 1740–1800* (Ithaca, N.Y., 1992), 6; Catherine Hall, *Civilising Subjects: Colony and Metropole in the English Imagination, 1830–1867* (Chicago, 2002), 72, 112; Trevor Burnard, "Not a Place for Whites? Demographic Failure and Settlement in Comparative Context: Jamaica, 1655–1780," in Kathleen E. A. Monteith and Glen Richards, eds., *Jamaica in Slavery and Freedom: History, Heritage, and Culture* (Kingston, Jamaica, 2002), 73–88; and James Belich, *Replenishing the Earth: The Settler Revolution and the Rise of the Anglo-World, 1783–1939* (New York, 2009), 29–35.

TABLE 1. *Population Estimates for Jamaica, 1661–1834*

Year	Number of Whites	Number of Free People of Mixed Race	Number of Free Blacks	Number of Enslaved Persons
1661	2,956	—	—	514
1693	7,768	—	—	9,504
1730	7,648	865	—	74,525
1764	15,000	3,000	1,000	146,464
1774	15,300	4,093	—	192,787
1789	18,000	7,500	2,500	250,000
1807	30,000	—	—	350,000
1825	—	28,800	10,000	335,000
1834	16,600	31,000	11,000	310,000

Sources: Governor William Lyttleton's Account of Jamaica, 1764, Add MS. 12409, fol. 7, BL; *JAJ*, VI, Dec. 18, 1773, 486; "Report of the Lords of the Committee of Council . . . Submitting to His Majesty's Consideration the Evidence . . . Concerning the Present State of the Trade to Africa," Apr. 25, 1798, no. 4132, pt. II, in *HCSP*, LXX, 272–274; Gad J. Heuman, *Between Black and White: Race, Politics, and the Free Coloreds in Jamaica, 1792–1865* (Westport, Conn., 1981), 7; B.W. Higman, *Slave Population and Economy in Jamaica, 1807–1834* (Kingston, Jamaica, 1995), 61–62; Richard S. Dunn, *Sugar and Slaves: The Rise of the Planter Class in the English West Indies, 1624–1713* (Chapel Hill, N.C., 2000), 155. Heuman estimates that the total population of nonwhite freemen in 1764 was 4,000, and, in 1789, it was 10,000. His later tallies indicate that roughly three-quarters of that population was of mixed-race, so those earlier figures have been divided under that same ratio. The result seems to fit with estimates from the period. Edward Long claimed that the island's mixed-race population was 3,408 at the midpoint of the eighteenth century; see [Long], *History of Jamaica; or, General Survey of the Antient and Modern State of That Island . . .* , 3 vols. (London, 1774), II, 337.

month. A large population of color developed steadily in turn, while Jamaica's white population struggled.

Slowly, a somewhat diverse colonial society emerged. Rich, white men—mostly planters and slave merchants—stood atop the island hierarchy, accompanied in some cases by white wives. A much larger number of middling and poor whites were next on the societal ladder, working as modest planters, attorneys, overseers, artisans, clerks, and general laborers. Most of them had failed, or would soon fail, to become sugar barons, but, nevertheless, the majority held slaves of their own. Sitting at the bottom of the social scale, but dwarfing both groups, was Jamaica's enslaved population, which grew to ten times the size of the colony's free inhabitants by the eighteenth century. It was composed of island-born (creole), African-born (saltwater), and mixed-race individuals, all struggling under violent servitude. In between the white and enslaved communities were nonwhite freemen. This included free blacks, whose plights were often not much better than the enslaved, and free people of color, who had some family connection to a European forbear. The latter group endured a wide range of experiences. Some held little more than their manumission. Barry Higman and Richard Dunn both calculate that roughly one-fifth of mixed-race offspring fathered by white men were freed, and most of those received little else. Others eked out a living as artisans, or advanced themselves slowly through small-scale planting or pen-keeping. A much smaller proportion, though, took a rather peculiar place in Jamaican society. Treated roughly the same as legitimate children by white fathers, they inherited sizeable sums of money and lived rather comfortable lives. In some cases, they even traveled to Britain for an education or apprenticeship. Throughout the long period of slavery in Jamaica, this elite cohort of color would prove an endless complication to colonial definitions of race, class, and family.[7]

As island officials struggled to understand how to manage such complexity, they continued to campaign aggressively for new white residents. Stocking enough white settlers to provide a demographic bulwark against a far more numerous enslaved population proved one of the most essential tasks to colonial security. Early on, the assembly pushed incentives to bring over laborers and wealthy proprietors, but it did not initially encourage families. A 1664 provision explicitly banned servants younger than fourteen, and a 1667 act "for the greater encouragement and speedier settling or peopling of this his majesty's island" sought primarily men. White migrants responded to these calls in the seventeenth century, and most colonial elites spent more

---

7. Trevor Burnard's survey of estate inventories shows that 80 percent of all whites on the island owned at least one slave; see Burnard, *Mastery, Tyranny, and Desire*, 76. For manumission estates of mixed-race children, see B. W. Higman, *Slave Population and Economy in Jamaica, 1807–1834* (Kingston, Jamaica, 1995), 141; and Richard S. Dunn, *A Tale of Two Plantations: Slave Life and Labor in Jamaica and Virginia* (Cambridge, Mass., 2014), 169. Higman's calculation comes from a number of plantations in the early nineteenth century, while Dunn's comes from one estate from 1762 to 1833. For more on the disincentives for manumission, see Colleen A. Vasconcellos, *Slavery, Childhood, and Abolition in Jamaica, 1788–1838* (Athens, Ga., 2015), 52–58. For the most authoritative survey of free Jamaicans of color, see Gad J. Heuman, *Between Black and White: Race, Politics, and the Free Coloreds in Jamaica, 1792–1865* (Westport, Conn., 1981). See also Verene A. Shepherd, *Livestock, Sugar, and Slavery: Contested Terrain in Colonial Jamaica* (Miami, Fla., 2009), esp. 100–118.

time on the island than off it; but such early efforts were not sufficient to form a self-reproducing free community, owing in large part to the lack of families. Jamaica was failing to attain a stable settler core. A 1702 report on the colony's population laid bare this reality: Jamaica contained only thirteen hundred servants, compared to nearly forty-two thousand slaves. In response, the assembly created a fund to entice more white laborers. Colonists believed that if the island were to survive, then a strong white population would need to emerge to contain and control the growing enslaved class that fueled the economy. These efforts simultaneously put a social premium on whiteness and a stigma on those holding kinship with the enslaved.[8]

In the hopes of strong-arming colonists to bring over European migrants, the assembly wrote up a deficiency bill, the year following its population report. Patterned after a 1701 law from the island of Nevis, Jamaica's deficiency bill required a set number of white residents on each plantation, based on a dehumanizing calculation of the estates' total enslaved laborers and heads of cattle. Those who failed to comply—and most did—faced fines commensurate with the cost of a white servant's passage to the island. Ostensibly, the fees collected from violators were to be used to conscript white labor, but funds rarely went to that purpose. Instead, the assembly used the money to finance other projects, which often included paying for British soldiers to undertake the necessary defense lacking for want of white inhabitants. Yet, despite that

8. *JAJ*, Jan. 20, 1664, I, 2, Sept. 19, 1677, 21, Aug. 19, 1702, 255, Mar. 1, 1703, 266. This very early interest in settler numbers was also part of the government's desire to impose a basic tax structure; see Patricia Cline Cohen, *A Calculating People: The Spread of Numeracy in Early America* (Chicago, 1982), 67–69. This demographic obsession was true across the Caribbean. Saint Domingue, roughly one hundred miles to the east of Jamaica and quite similar in its social and geographic characteristics, undertook the same debate in the mid-to-late seventeenth century. Those considerations eventually led to the creation of the Code Noir; see Malick W. Ghachem, *The Old Regime and the Haitian Revolution* (New York, 2012), 55–57. For more on the struggle of building a stable settler core in the Caribbean, see Henry A. Gemery, "Emigration from the British Isles to the New World, 1630–1700: Inferences from Colonial Populations," *Research in Economic History,* V (1980), 179–231; Jack P. Greene, *Pursuits of Happiness: The Social Development of Early Modern British Colonies and the Formation of American Culture* (Chapel Hill, N.C., 1988), 154–165; Trevor Burnard, "European Migration to Jamaica, 1655–1780," *WMQ,* 3d Ser., LIII (1996), 771–772, 782–783; and Burnard, "Passengers Only," *Atlantic Studies,* I (2004), 178–195. Burnard argues elsewhere that Jamaica was a "failed settler society," but he underplays the value that colonial officials put onto growing Jamaica's white population; see Burnard, "A Failed Settler Society: Marriage and Demographic Failure in Early Jamaica," *Journal of Social History,* XXVIII (1994), 63–82.

the deficiency bills did little to boost Jamaica's white population, they nevertheless built a foundation for stronger legislative discussions around island demography. The original act became an annual bill that the assembly continually modified over the ensuing decades, particularly because it brought in so much revenue. This meant that its yearly debate in the assembly kept issues of population foremost in lawmakers' minds. But it also produced a demographic perspective skewed toward racial apartheid. Only those of full European ancestry could count, or "save deficiency," toward the requirement. Free people of color could initially save deficiency on their own plantations or businesses, but their less affluent mixed-race workers could not, making it difficult for the majority of Jamaica's population of color to find employment. The deficiency bills were some of the island's first race-based laws applied to freemen, and they would set the pattern for future legislation: poor individuals of color were controlled aggressively, while mixed-race elites could often expect a pass.[9]

This increased zeal to augment white numbers came largely out of a parallel concern over the size of the island's enslaved populace. Officials held deep fears about security after the 1702 report claimed that enslaved workers out-

9. An Act for the Encouraging the Importation of White Servants . . . , Dec. 21, 1701, in *Acts of Assembly, Passed in the Island of Nevis, from 1664, to 1739, Inclusive* (London, 1740), 37; *JAJ*, Mar. 1, 1703, I, 266. The 1703 Jamaica act called for one white man to cover a plantation's first ten slaves, two for the next ten, and one more for each additional twenty bound workers. Equally, the law demanded a white resident for the first sixty head of cattle and one per every hundred after that. South Carolina copied this deficiency legislation in 1712; see *The Statutes at Large of South Carolina*, ed. David J. McCord, VII (Columbia, S.C., 1840), 363. Deficiency violations are difficult to track, but parish records from Saint Thomas in the Vale from 1789 to 1802 indicate that roughly two-thirds of its estates were in violation of the deficiency laws; see Vestry Minutes, Saint Thomas in the Vale, 2/1/1, fols. 15–436, JA. England's Board of Trade labeled the acts as little more than money bills in 1718; see *JAJ*, Aug. 16, 1718, II, 262. William Burke noted in 1757 that plantation owners "find it more easy to pay the penalty . . . than to comply with the law"; see [Burke], *An Account of the European Settlements in America . . .*, 2 vols. (London, 1757), II, 113–114. Many scholars agree. Frank Wesley Pitman believes the deficiency acts transformed into revenue makers in 1736; see Pitman, *The Development of the British West Indies, 1700–1763* (New Haven, Conn., 1917), 50–54. Neville Hall believes this transition occurred around 1763, while Lowell Ragatz places it around 1770; see Hall, "Some Aspects of the 'Deficiency' Question in Jamaica in the Eighteenth Century," *Caribbean Studies*, XV, no. 1 (April 1975), 11; and Ragatz, *The Fall of the Planter Class in the British Caribbean, 1763–1833* (New York, 1928), 9. Ultimately, the money collected from deficiency legislation was always important to the assembly. Until it settled on a permanent tax remittance in 1728, the assembly fought incessantly with Westminster over the amount of its duty payments, and deficiency fees helped ease colonial finances.

numbered white servants nearly thirty to one. Such a numerical imbalance was a social powder keg in its own right, but the colony also faced continual threats from foreign invasion as well as from runaway slaves called Maroons living in the island's rugged interior. Before the English conquest, Maroons had originally left Spanish masters, intermixed with aboriginal Jamaicans, and established strong communities that took in new refugees. Planters' attempts to recover those who ran off frequently precipitated clashes, and Maroon numbers grew steadily as more slaves fled. This place of sanctuary obviously compromised Jamaica's slave system, but the Maroon threat frequently compounded when they joined up with small-scale slave revolts. In effect, Jamaica's colonial government waged a continuous, though sometimes dormant, war with the Maroons for the first eighty years of English rule. Opening the assembly's summer session in 1705, Governor Thomas Handasyd railed against the "great disturbances and cruelties which the rebellious negroes (Maroons) daily commit." He insisted that they must be eliminated, "or else I am afraid we may repent when it is too late." Reducing the flood of Africans into the island was not a solution for the budding sugar economy, even if it might dry up Maroon recruits. Altering that commercial current's course by bolstering white numbers was much more realistic.[10]

Handasyd also took a somewhat novel approach to the settlement question by encouraging the weaving together of a tighter social fabric, rather than simply bringing in new migrants. He implored the assembly to fund new roads that might spur the economy as well as help in anti-Maroon campaigns. Perhaps more distinctively, he lobbied for stronger religious institutions and "good schools and nurseries of learning for the education of youth." This latter category had gone woefully undeveloped on the island. The assembly had passed a resolution to establish a free school in the parish of Saint Andrew a decade earlier, but those plans never materialized. The governor's interest in fostering Jamaica's youth now put greater emphasis on a colonization scheme of sustainability and self-reproduction through family development. Decades would elapse before the assembly undertook a legitimate school-building program, but, within a year of Handasyd's appeal, the legislature attempted to

10. *JAJ*, July 11, 1705, I, 365; Barbara Klamon Kopytoff, "The Early Political Development of Jamaica Maroon Societies," *WMQ*, 3d Ser., XXXV (1978), 287–307; Carey Robinson, *The Fighting Maroons of Jamaica* (London, 1969); Orlando Patterson, "Slavery and Slave Revolts: A Sociohistorical Analysis of the First Maroon War, 1665–1740," in Richard Price, ed., *Maroon Societies: Rebel Slave Communities in the Americas*, 3d ed. (Baltimore, 1996), 246–247; Kathleen Wilson, "The Performance of Freedom: Maroons and the Colonial Order in Eighteenth-Century Jamaica and the Atlantic Sound," *WMQ*, 3d Ser., LXVI (2009), 45–62.

increase deficiency fines against absentees and resolved to hire more British ministers. Slowly, such initiatives gained steam. By 1714, the assembly began considering the inclusion of "women, boys, and girls" in deficiency legislation. Although the original law did not allow women and children to save deficiency, they were now part of the debate and would be included fully by 1730. As it was becoming clear in many outposts of European imperialism, monitoring reproduction and family formation could prove a successful strategy for settlement. The colonists themselves might have been far ahead of the legislature in that regard. William Shettlewood excitedly reported in 1706 that he planned to leave Jamaica for England "in order to fetch my wife and bring her here and settle my selfe in these parts." Recreating family life in Jamaica was no longer a fool's errand; it was official policy.[11]

As before, such encouragement of white settlement did not produce significant results. Each of the island's governors in succession bemoaned the stagnation of white numbers and pleaded with the assembly to craft better laws to entice migrants. The assembly responded tepidly with tax breaks and adjustments to the deficiency acts. By 1715, London's Board of Trade had had enough. Tasked with overseeing colonial commerce and legislation, the Board stepped in to determine what needed to be done for "the speedy settling and planting [of] that island . . . for [it] was in a very weak condition." It considered relaxing servants' requirements and doling out land grants for those who

11. *JAJ*, July 11, 1705, I, 365, Jan. 21, 1706, 415, Feb. 18, 1714, II, 133–139; William Shettlewood to Jonathan and Thomas Eyres, Dec. 22, 1706, MS 1850, NLJ. The assembly's session ended before the amendment to add "women, boys, and girls" was passed. By 1730, deficiency laws included those groups. Initiatives to bring over children continued for the next several decades. A 1743 proposal to increase the number of white inhabitants in Jamaica, for instance, suggested that four hundred boys and two hundred girls, between ages eleven and fifteen, should be brought to the island from Britain yearly; see "Proposals for Increasing the Number of White Inhabitants and for Promoting the Further Settlement of the Island of Jamaica," Add. MS 22676, fols. 141–142, BL. Lucille Mathurin Mair contends that the deficiency laws demonstrate an utter disregard for the place of women in Jamaican society; see Mair, *Historical Study of Women in Jamaica*, ed. Beckles and Shepherd, 36–37. However, the eventual incorporation of women into the bills, along with the legislation's focus on demographics, complicates the deficiency laws' initial exclusion of female colonists. On the importance of family strategies in colonization, see Sarah M. S. Pearsall, "Gender," in David Armitage and Michael J. Braddick, eds., *The British Atlantic World, 1500–1800* (New York, 2002), 139–133; and Ann Laura Stoler, *Carnal Knowledge and Imperial Power: Race and the Intimate in Colonial Rule* (Berkeley, Calif., 2009), 47–48. As Jenny Shaw notes, enumerating populations in the British West Indies was also a way of maintaining "the illusion of imperial control"; see Shaw, *Everyday Life in the Early English Caribbean: Irish, Africans, and the Construction of Difference* (Athens, Ga., 2013), 45–47.

arrived. The Board also attacked deficiency fines for not adequately addressing anemic white immigration. Jamaica's upper legislative chamber, the council, agreed. Chosen by the island's governor, who was appointed by British
officials, council members were often at odds with the assembly over colonial
policy. They reported to the Board of Trade that additional laws would prove
superfluous, remarking instead that "what seems most defective in these laws
is, that there is no provision for the encouragement of women." Alternative
measures were needed to spur the development of colonial families.[12]

Looking west from London, Jamaica's settlement problem had a relatively
straightforward solution. As the Board of Trade argued, if the enslaved outnumbered the free and if coerced labor provoked domestic instability, then
the island simply needed more free residents. From the Board's perspective in
England, those free colonists could be of any color. It debated the possibility
"that if all Mulattoes and Indians were declared free, it would be another help
towards the peopling of the island." After all, most mulattoes born into slavery
were the children of European men and had blood ties to white society. It
made some political sense to empower the group, rather than allow them to
toil in slavery. But the Board of Trade might have also been open to such a
solution because cultural constructions of race were not well developed in
Britain during this period. British observers did not yet perceive skin color as
the chief characteristic of social and ethnic status. Instead, metropolitan ideologies of race in the early decades of the eighteenth century included a battery of factors, such as class, religious affiliation, language, education, dress,
gender, and perceptions of cultural civility. Mixed-race Jamaicans, from this
viewpoint, could become valuable settlers if freed and allowed to acculturate to white society. Although British officials did not necessarily anticipate
them achieving the same status as whites on the island, they did believe that
they could be allied with ruling elites against the possibility of enslaved insurrection.[13]

---

12. *JBT*, Mar. 23, 1715, III, 1–15. The Board's attack on the deficiency acts ended in a petition to the king in 1718 to have them revoked for being money bills, rather than proper encouragements for white growth; see *JAJ*, Aug. 16, 1718, II, 262. This came after much debate
with the council; see ibid., Oct. 23, 1716, 224.

13. *JBT*, Mar. 23, 1715, III, 1–15. Jennifer M. Spear demonstrates policing sexuality and
interracial relationships was crucial to demographic planning in French Louisiana as well;
see Spear, "Colonial Intimacies: Legislating Sex in French Louisiana," *WMQ*, 3d Ser., LX
(2003), 78–80, 97–98. On British perceptions of racial difference in the eighteenth century,
see Roxann Wheeler, *The Complexion of Race: Categories of Difference in Eighteenth-Century
British Culture* (Philadelphia, 2000); Felicity A. Nussbaum, *The Limits of the Human: Fic-*

Attitudes toward individuals of color were somewhat flexible in Jamaica at this time as well, but the Board of Trade's suggestion did not excite colonial officials. Mixed-race individuals held complicated social positions in the island's early decades. Africans and Europeans interacted sexually from the start of colonial rule, in mostly nonconsensual ways, and, for the first half century after English conquest, these connections aroused little concern. In 1698, Edward Ward railed against the "Tawny Fac'd *Moletto* Strumpet" with whom a fellow Jamaican-bound passenger's husband cohabited, but most early reports from the island did not draw attention to interracial relationships—certainly not in the ways that would later become a hallmark of West Indian accounts. With kinship ties to whites, free individuals of color occupied a wholly separate category from the enslaved. In 1705, the assembly even debated allowing all mixed-race freemen to save partial deficiency, so long as they served in the militia. Yet, the rapid growth of slavery convinced many officials of the need to erect stronger distinctions between blacks and whites. Perhaps pressured by poor whites competing for jobs, the assembly began passing bills limiting employment for freemen of color. By 1715, they could no longer work in a public office or be employed as navigators, carriage drivers, or plantation supervisors. These were certainly harsh measures, but they were largely directed at keeping people of color out of the island's middling ranks where they might jockey with poor whites. The assembly stopped well short of stripping away all mixed-race rights, though, and it noticeably avoided legal attacks against the wealthiest people of color. Clearly, Jamaican officials distinguished between individuals with some African descent and those with none. But the exclusionary boundary between the two grew increasingly blurry at the higher rungs of the social ladder.[14]

---

tions of Anomaly, Race, and Gender in the Long Eighteenth Century (Cambridge, 2003); Dror Wahrman, *The Making of the Modern Self: Identity and Culture in Eighteenth-Century England* (New Haven, Conn., 2004), 83–115; and Catherine Molineux, *Faces of Perfect Ebony: Encountering Atlantic Slavery in Imperial Britain* (Cambridge, Mass., 2012). Susan Dwyer Amussen also perceives connections between skin color and race occurring in the opening decades of English colonization in the West Indies (both in the colony and metropole), although along different categorical levels than in the eighteenth century; see Amussen, *Caribbean Exchanges: Slavery and the Transformation of English Society, 1640–1700* (Chapel Hill, N.C., 2007), 11–20, 228–229.

14. [Edward Ward], *A Trip to Jamaica: With a True Character of the People and Island...*, 3d ed. (London, 1698), 10; *JAJ*, Sept. 29, 1705, I, 379; Jamaica House of Assembly, Laws and Statutes, etc., 10 Ann. iv. 35 (1711); Heuman, *Between Black and White*, 5. As Ann Laura Stoler contends, interracial relationships were as much an expression of colonial order as they were a violation of it; see Stoler, *Race and the Education of Desire: Foucault's History of*

In the opening decades of the eighteenth century, then, physical distinctions mattered in Jamaica, but not in a uniform and totalizing way. Disagreements emerged as a result of the economic divisions within white society in addition to economic variability among mixed-race people. This effectively produced two separate mixed-race communities. Deficiency bills reduced the incentive to hire middling and poor people of color, and the assembly passed legislation banning them outright from the types of employment they were best poised to take. These restrictions stunted the economic mobility of the vast majority of mixed-race people and signaled that whiteness was a social trump card. Wealthy individuals of color, though, did not yet suffer significantly under the law. All free Jamaican men could vote, but only if they owned an estate with a yearly ten-pound return. That disenfranchised almost all mixed-race people, but elites of color easily qualified to participate in elections. In addition, mixed-race freemen's property stayed protected in the same ways as whites, and they could marry whomever they wished. Of course, extralegal harassment undoubtedly could have made these rights moot. Moreover, many whites—including some in the assembly—were not pleased that the legislature appeared to protect wealthy individuals of color. In 1708, for instance, an assemblyman moved to prevent any "Jew, mulatto, negro, or Indian" from voting. But elites of color continued to have allies in the government—undoubtedly some of whom were relatives—who helped quash the motion. Colonial officials were walking a delicate line between subduing the mass of the island's mixed-race population and allowing a small cohort enough access to property and rights to keep them invested in the continued success of the sugar regime. It would take even stronger pressures around security to push legislators to address this tricky balance more directly.[15]

Insurrection and Legal Changes

Mounting hostilities between colonists and the Maroons ultimately forced officials to make stronger policy decisions toward settlement and mixed-race individuals. Jamaica's enslaved population ballooned in the early decades of the eighteenth century, making the Maroons an even larger threat to white

Sexuality and the Colonial Order of Things (Durham, N.C., 1995), 46. See also Robert J. C. Young, *Colonial Desire: Hybridity in Theory, Culture, and Race* (New York, 1995). Doris Garraway finds a similar narrative absence on interracial relationships in the earliest years of French colonization in the West Indies. Such discourse, she argues, emerged long after idealized binaries of black and white had been permanently obliterated; see Garraway, *The Libertine Colony: Creolization in the Early French Caribbean* (Durham, N.C., 2005), esp. 26–32.

15. *JAJ*, Feb. 12, 1708, I, 439.

rule than before. By 1726, most agreed that "as the Negroes encrease very considerably, and the White Inhabitants every Year diminish . . . the Island will be in Imminent danger." Maroons in the western interior of Jamaica had also recently united under a strong leader named Cudjoe, whose skill and organization butted up against planters' ambitions. After repeatedly failing to retrieve runaway slaves from Cudjoe's forces, Jamaican officials launched a major offensive against the Maroons at the end of the brief Anglo-Spanish War (1727–1729), when the colony was terrified that foreign invaders might ally with rebellious slaves. It would mark the beginning of a brutal ten-year conflict.[16]

The First Maroon War threw Jamaica into turmoil, while also deepening the complicated and fractured policy island officials had toward colonists of color. In the lead-up to hostilities, the assembly looked on free people of color as partners in war. It offered tax relief from deficiency fines if freemen of color served in the militia, or if they paid to have aboriginal Jamaicans or other individuals of color fight in their place. The assembly also considered requiring all nonwhite freemen to stay "equipped with clothes and arms, after the manner of the white men" but ultimately decided to keep membership compulsory only for those with property. Still, many free people of color, including those of meager means, took up arms in the First Maroon War. Numbers are difficult to estimate for this period, but, by 1778, fourteen hundred men of color belonged to the island militia constituting a quarter of its ranks. It is not surprising why so many would fight. As potential defenders against domestic insurrection, free blacks and people of color could assert claims as loyal colonists, if not as full British subjects. If they had any chance of overturning the previous decades' legal attacks, it might come from demonstrating such patriotism.[17]

16. Anonymous, "Haldimand Papers relating to Jamaica," circa 1726, Add. MS 22676, fol. 68, BL.

17. Jamaica House of Assembly, Laws and Statutes, 1 Geo. II xiii (1728); *JAJ*, Feb. 11–15, 1729, II, 669–678; "A General Return of the Militia of the Island of Jamaica, 31 October 1778," Add MS. 12435, fol. 12, BL. For firsthand accounts of the Maroon War of the 1730s and concerns over the ability of Jamaicans to counter it, see "Miscellaneous Papers and Original Letters relating to the Affairs of Jamaica," 1733–1739, Add. MS 12431, fols. 69–134, BL. Military service promoted the assumption, and spread, of British identity throughout the Empire in the eighteenth century; see Linda Colley, *Britons: Forging the Nation, 1707–1837* (New Haven, Conn., 1994). However, claims to accepted British identity were not equally accessible to all subjects, particularly toward the latter half of the century; see Isaac Land, "Bread and Arsenic: Citizenship from the Bottom Up in Georgian London," *Journal of Social History*, XXXIX (2005), 89–110; Cassandra Pybus, *Epic Journeys of Freedom: Runaway*

As the Maroon War progressed, however, the assembly went back and forth in its treatment of the group. At the root of this vacillation was the continued difficulty in accomplishing two separate, yet related, goals: expanding Jamaica's settler base and controlling an enslaved majority. The first seemed impossible if left only to European migration. The legislature still hoped that white families could prosper—even proposing having "boys and girls, of seven years old and upwards, brought over at the public expence"—but it admitted that Jamaica struggled under "the want of numbers of people and families." Free settlement could potentially be accomplished, instead, by opening up full subjecthood to wealthy individuals who nevertheless held some non-European ancestry. Members of the assembly—especially those with children of color—were playing with the idea that economic privilege, rather than racial purity, could be the more successful principle around which free settlement developed. But that idea worked against the second goal, which seemed dependent on further lowering the status of African heritage.[18]

Focused on winning the Maroon war, the assembly initially chose to push harder on the side of black oppression. Attempting to cut off Maroon supplies, the assembly passed a bill in March 1730 prohibiting the sale of goods outside public markets. Although this affected all ethnicities, most small-scale peddlers operating in these arenas tended to be either mixed race or black. As with previous legislation, this clamped down on less affluent populations of color. But the bill did more. It took the unusual step of imposing blanket regulations on all mixed-race people. The act took away nonwhite freemen's rights to give evidence against whites in court, to purchase indentures for white servants, to sell goods freely, and to carry weapons when not with the militia. It also forbade them from living or working within five miles of Jamaica's three major urban centers: Kingston, Port Royal, and Spanish Town. Taken together, these provisions sent a strong message to residents of color. They could not join the colonial economy fully, but they were expected to defend

---

Slaves of the American Revolution and Their Global Quest for Liberty (Boston, 2006), 3–72; and Philip D. Morgan and Andrew Jackson O'Shaughnessy, "Arming Slaves in the American Revolution," in Christopher Leslie Brown and Philip D. Morgan, eds., Arming Slaves: From Classical Times to the Modern Age (New Haven, Conn., 2006), 180–208.

18. JAJ, Mar. 17, 1730, II, 701–702, Mar. 26, 1730, 706. It had been a recent goal of the assembly to build up the newly settled parish of Portland, especially with families. This mission, it seems, was one supported by whites across the island; see The State of the Island of Jamaica . . . (London, 1726), 30. The assembly still attempted to woo white men along with these families, however. Between 1730 and 1732, it encouraged soldiers to settle on the island with promises of land grants; see JAJ, Jan. 12, 1732, III, 53, Sept. 21, 1768, VI, 106.

the island equally. This was also a signal change from the previous class-based legal attacks on individuals of color. Nonetheless, it was not entirely distinct. The prohibition on living near cities came with an exception for anyone owning a ten-pound freehold. Class standing was thus still a vital piece in Jamaican racial designation, but it was potentially losing its importance.[19]

Sensing that their protections were beginning to falter, elites of color wasted no time making their grievances known about the new bill. From their perspective, the assembly was abandoning the custom of making class position synonymous with political privilege. John Golding, a mixed-race planter from Vere, balked at the act's restrictions against indenting white servants for proprietors of color, as it prevented him from employing white workers to comply with the deficiency laws. He petitioned the assembly to have that particular resolution removed. Francis Williams, a free black man educated in England, went further. He petitioned above the assembly's head, writing the Board of Trade to invalidate the law altogether. Both Golding and Williams were at the top of the island's free brown and black communities. They drew their ire from the assembly's failure to provide greater exemptions to the act, thus distinguishing between wealthy and poor inhabitants of color. Officials in Britain agreed. Appointees within the Board of Trade wrote that the law unfairly attacked "free Negroes who are Men of Substance." Ultimately, the protests worked, and, in November 1731, the assembly repealed the bill.[20]

Freshly rebuked, and desperate for results, the assembly considered altering course by including larger numbers of mixed-race people into its settlement schemes. As before, increasing white households was paramount. The assembly formed a committee in 1731 recommending that "women and children are intended to be included" in any proposal for European migration. This was especially important, the island's governor remarked, considering the Maroon threat: "Nothing can prevent the growth of the evils you labour under, but the speedy peopling of the unsettled part of the country." To ac-

19. Acts of the Assembly of Jamaica, Mar. 28, 1730, CO 139/12, no. 22, NAE.

20. *JAJ*, July 8, 1730, II, 725, Nov. 12, 1730, 751; *JBT*, June 30, 1731, VI, 216; Charles Delafay to Alured Popple, July 17, 1731, CO 137/19/1, fol. 73, NAE, Acts of the Assembly of Jamaica, Mar. 28, 1730, CO 139/12, no. 22, Board of Trade Correspondence, 1730, CO 137/20, fol. 33, Popple to Delafay, July 20, 1731, SP 36/23, fol. 248. Francis Williams was well known in Britain; see *The Importance of Jamaica to Great-Britain* . . . (London, [circa 1740]), 16–17; and [Houstoun], *Dr. Houstoun's Memoirs*, 346. See also Vincent Carretta, "Who Was Francis Williams?" *Early American Literature*, XXXVIII (2003), 213–237; and Brooke N. Newman, "Contesting 'Black' Liberty and Subjecthood in the Anglophone Caribbean, 1730s–1780s," *Slavery and Abolition*, XXXII (2011), 169–170.

complish that goal, an assembly committee drafted an act enticing soldiers to stay on the island. More dramatically, though, it recommended that "all the free negroes, Indians, and mulattoes, as shall go and settle" in the frontier parish of Portland would receive a property allotment, provisions, and a yearly twelve-pound stipend. This seemed to go against the previous legal attempts to stymie small-scale planters of color. But, with so few whites present or available to farm in Portland, these mixed-race pioneers posed less of a threat. A joint committee of the council and assembly was even more eager, proposing an amendment that "one hundred mulatto men and one hundred mulatto women be made free at the public charge . . . [and] that there should be fifty acres of land granted to each family." This was far too generous to a nervous assembly, however. It rejected the provision, worried that freeing slaves, albeit ones of mixed heritage, would counteract efforts against the Maroons. Instead, it passed the original bill. Freemen of color were to be part of these new waves of settlement, but the assembly wanted to ensure that they were sufficiently disconnected from an enslaved past and not in direct competition with middling whites.[21]

Taken together, the assembly's considerations reveal a diverse, if not ad hoc, range of thought toward free people of color in the first third of the eighteenth century. Continual fears about enslaved uprisings and Maroon wars resulted in legislation that punished individuals of color in all but the highest tiers of wealth. But the central challenge of settlement emboldened the assembly to experiment with schemes that might enable some mixed-race freemen to contribute to and strengthen the plantation complex. Jamaicans were so obsessed with these demographic issues that when lobbying Westminster for the law that would eventually become the 1733 Molasses Act, the assembly insisted that North America's trade with French and Dutch merchants threatened to eradicate Jamaica's faltering population through economic starvation. Without a robust free community, the island could not control its enslaved workers or fend off foreign invasion. For many whites, the importance of establishing such a permanent group surpassed any disgust with empowering certain individuals of color. And, although it was not stated explicitly in these early debates, members of the assembly likely felt no reluctance in advancing at least their own children who had partial African heritage. For less affluent whites, though, promoting elites of color erased the single characteristic that kept them in the ascendant class. They wanted nothing to do with a relatively open

21. *JAJ*, May 4–7, 1731, III, 3–5, Jan. 4, 1731/2, 47, Jan. 12–13, 1731/2, 53–55, Apr. 20, 1732, 80.

free settler community. A consensus opinion over the social status of mixed-race people, therefore, had not yet emerged. There were simply too many divisions within the white community to create such cohesion. Moreover, diversities of class, phenotype, and familial factors between individuals of color made an accord nearly impossible.[22]

Owing perhaps to such complicated policies, white Jamaicans favoring racial segregation demanded that the assembly take a clearer position. This debate was touched off in the spring of 1733 when John Golding and one of his relatives voted at their parish election. Golding was the prominent mixed-race planter who opposed the bill against free people of color from three years earlier. His political activism might have made him a large target: shortly after the election, the assembly received a complaint that Golding's vote was unlawful. In fact, there were no laws specifically disenfranchising free men of color at that time. The complainant acknowledged that Golding insisted that he held the right to vote and had exercised it openly before. After all, he owned the requisite ten-pound yearly freehold to be considered a voter. But this protest underscored a growing discomfort among some whites over the relative freedoms tolerated for wealthier individuals of color. Those who complained might have done so to test how passionately the assembly was willing to protect the exclusionary value of whiteness.[23]

The decision hanging over Golding's right to vote was an enormous one. Could elites of color continue to participate in island politics, or would Jamaica become a wholly segregated colony? The assembly could have acted broadly, but, instead, it once more made a qualified ruling. Immediately after reading the complaint, it decided that the Goldings, as "mulattoes," lacked the franchise. On its face, this was a comprehensive decision with tremendous repercussions. Free men of color, even those with substantial fortunes, could no longer vote and thus held no stake in the political process. The verdict was

22. Ibid., Nov. 27, 1731, III, 44. White West Indian identity was diverse, multilayered, and contested throughout the Caribbean; see David Lambert, *White Creole Culture, Politics, and Identity during the Age of Abolition* (New York, 2005). In Jamaica, much of this simplification of white status stems from the little-discussed class differences within white society; see Cecilia A. Green, "Hierarchies of Whiteness in the Geographies of Empire: Thomas Thistlewood and the Barretts of Jamaica," *New West Indian Guide/Nieuwe West-Indische Gids,* LXXX (2006), 5–43. In fact, notions of class could attach to the same hereditary ideas associated with race and reproduction in Jamaica; see Diane J. Austin-Broos, "Race/Class: Jamaica's Discourse of Heritable Identity," *New West Indian Guide/Nieuwe West-Indische Gids,* LXVIII (1994), 213–233.

23. *JAJ,* Mar. 30, 1733, III, 123.

unmistakably devastating to the free black community and to the future of Jamaican race relations. But the assembly stopped just short of complete segregation. Realizing the ambiguity of the term "mulatto" in a place as racially diverse as Jamaica, the assembly next resolved "that it should be ascertained who should be deemed mulattoes, and how far their corruption of blood should extend." After a quick debate, members determined that they should copy the Spanish legal tradition applying the legal category of "mulatto" only to those who were less than four generations removed from an African ancestor. This meant that if one had a great-great-grandparent who was black, yet all other immediate ancestors were white, then that person was, by law, white. Or, to put it another way, anyone with less than one-eighth African ancestry was no longer mulatto. Although hardly generous in its genealogical equation, the act's implications were immense: Jamaica, unlike nearly every other British American colony, would not follow a "one drop rule" of racial designation that made any trace of African ancestry grounds for exclusion from white status. One could now become white in the eyes of the law, despite family ties to the enslaved.[24]

With that action, the assembly resolved half the puzzle surrounding mixed-race freemen's status and the island's demographic future. This new pathway to whiteness was a fresh attempt to address an old problem. Jamaica needed European settlers, but British emigration to the Americas had largely dried up, falling from a peak of seventy-two hundred migrants in the 1650s to only three thousand in the 1690s. Moreover, white Jamaican families were not sufficiently reproductive, and the population remained stagnant in the first four

24. Ibid. For more on Spanish legal traditions and the four-generation removal clause, see Ruth Hill, "Entering and Exiting Blackness: A Color Controversy in Eighteenth-Century Spain," *Journal of Spanish Cultural Studies*, X (2009), 46. Virginia made the same determination in 1705 and modified it in 1785; see Thomas D. Morris, *Southern Slavery and the Law, 1619–1860* (Chapel Hill, N.C., 1996), 22–24; and Joshua D. Rothman, *Notorious in the Neighborhood: Sex and Families across the Color Line in Virginia, 1787–1861* (Chapel Hill, N.C., 2003), 202–212. The Bahamas passed an identical version of the 1733 Jamaica law in 1756; see Michael Craton and Gail Saunders, *Islanders in the Stream: A History of the Bahamian People*, I, *From Aboriginal Times to the End of Slavery* (Athens, Ga., 1992), 151–152. North Carolina's legislators did not impose an absolute legal definition of race, but they did pass a prohibition in 1741 against intermarriage between whites and nonwhites that echoed Jamaican law. In this case, "nonwhite" meant anyone three or fewer generations removed from a black ancestor; see Kirsten Fischer, *Suspect Relations: Sex, Race, and Resistance in Colonial North Carolina* (Ithaca, N.Y., 2002), 86. Such a step toward allowing individuals of color to become settlers runs counter to James Belich's claims for total white racial exclusivity in British settlements; see Belich, *Replenishing the Earth*, 29–30.

decades of the eighteenth century (see Table 1, above). If Britons would not sail for Jamaica, and whites would not replenish themselves on the island, then a possible solution might come from altering the membership requirements to be considered white. Nearing its eightieth year under British rule, three generations of interracial relationships had produced a diverse society with incredibly blurred divisions between black and white. By holding out full political equality to those four generations removed from a black ancestor, the assembly incentivized continued interracial pairings that would produce a large cohort of white creole settlers in the coming years. It also hoped this would ensure greater loyalty to colonial rule among light-skinned individuals of color wishing to see their children come into the world with all the political privileges of being white, rather than bearing the civil impediments of being mulatto. At the same time, the calculation of four generations was carefully determined to have a gradual effect: virtually no one would have qualified for the exemption in 1733, thus preventing any significant changes in political rule for a substantial period of time. Nevertheless, this was an aspirational decision that saw individuals of color as a potential seedbed for a new, robust white population. It also showed that a strong settler society trumped any ideological zealotry about conceptions of blood purity. In a way, this concession further legitimated the traditional interracial relationships dominating the island. Just days after the assembly's decision, an Anglican minister wrote that Jamaica's leaders operated under the belief that "people ought to be Encourag'd, or Rewarded, for begetting Mulattos and that That was the best way to People the Islands." With the stroke of a pen, the assembly transformed this customary opinion into governmental policy.[25]

The other half of the assembly's solution to the puzzle of settlement and

25. William May to Bishop Edmund Gibson, Apr. 11, 1733, Fulham Palace Papers, XVII, fol. 258, LPL; Gemery, "Emigration from the British Isles," *Research in Economic History,* V (1980), 216; Verene A. Shepherd, "Questioning Creole: Domestic Producers in Jamaica's Plantation Economy," in Shepherd and Glen L. Richards, eds., *Questioning Creole: Creolisation Discourses in Caribbean Culture* (Kingston, Jamaica, 2002), 177–178. For the evolution of concepts of "purity of blood" and hereditary ties to such "corruption," see María Elena Martínez, *Genealogical Fictions: Limpieza de Sangre, Religion, and Gender in Colonial Mexico* (Stanford, Calif., 2008), 51–75, 267–270; Guillaume Aubert, " 'The Blood of France': Race and Purity of Blood in the French Atlantic World," *WMQ,* 3d Ser., LXI (2004), 439–478; Aubert, "Kinship, Blood, and the Emergence of the Racial Nation in the French Atlantic World, 1600–1789," in Christopher H. Johnson et al., eds., *Blood and Kinship: Matter for Metaphor from Ancient Rome to the Present* (New York, 2013), 175–195; and Sue Peabody, " 'A Nation Born to Slavery': Missionaries and Racial Discourse in Seventeenth-Century French Antilles," *Journal of Social History,* XXXVIII (2004), 113–126.

mixed-race rights came from the free men and women themselves. Days after the assembly disenfranchised him and all other individuals of color, Golding submitted a petition to the legislature. As he had done in his protest of the 1730 bill against mixed-race people, he bristled at the new law's lack of exemptions for the elite. Wealthy people of color had always avoided most legal strictures, and Golding wanted that pattern to continue. Although admitting that "he had descended from mulatto ancestors," Golding nevertheless wanted a legal concession "to entitle him and his children to such rights, privileges, and immunities, as free and natural-born subjects of the crown of Great-Britain, descended from white ancestors." Perhaps expecting such a protest from the start, and cognizant of Golding's substantial land holdings, the assembly approved his request within a week, giving him full political rights. Once again, laws against free people of color came with immunities for those with money. Unbeknownst to Golding, his petition would set in motion a train of similar appeals from elite Jamaicans of color that would last for the rest of the century. His was not the first petition to ask for exemptions from the laws against black and mixed-race residents, but it formed the template for a new type of plea that would become standard for the island's wealthiest free people of color. For the next seventy years, more than six hundred fifty Jamaicans of color would ask for privileged rights. This system of privilege petitioning corrected for the major problem in the generational removal exemption: class distinction. If they did not have enough biological proximity to be considered legally white according to the new definition, then elites of color could at least obtain some portion of those rights through individual appeal.[26]

The privilege bills also encouraged wealthy individuals of color to stay allied with white society. As it had done in redefining the legal term "mulatto," the assembly structured privilege allocations to ensure that subsequent generations would develop increasing biological affinity with Europeans. It did so by giving specific stipulations over how these newly conferred rights would extend. Not only did the petitioner gain added rights, but his or her offspring would receive the same rights as well, provided that the children's other parent was white. So long as privileged Jamaicans stayed politically and sexually loyal to white society, then, their concessions could become hereditary. Thus, these bills not only rewarded class advantage, but they also facilitated and encouraged the creation of white settlers from the island's free popula-

26. *JAJ*, Apr. 6–25, 1733, III, 129–146. This survey of privilege petitioning comes from the Jamaica assembly records; see Acts of the Assembly of Jamaica, 1733–1803, CO 139/13–51, NAE.

tion of color. In this way, both the privilege acts and the generational-removal exemption explicitly promoted increased sexual interaction between whites and those with African ancestry as a policy of settler augmentation. Women of color were by no means universally in favor of coupling with white men, but these laws attempted to persuade them. This certainly altered the position of mixed-race individuals, who could now be seen as potential parents of white offspring. In addition, it complicated social distinctions generally, as white status no longer held a biologically exclusive definition. Racial conceptions in 1733 Jamaica, therefore, came highly mitigated through financial, generational, and familial considerations.[27]

Nonetheless, such apparent permeability between white and mixed-race status existed only for a select group of Jamaicans. For each door now open to individuals of color, many more were suddenly shut. After all, Golding's privilege petition received final approval on the same day as the law formally stripping those now legally defined as "mulattos" of the right to vote. On balance, the legal changes toward mixed-race people in 1733 disenfranchised far more individuals than they empowered. In that way, they were quite consistent with the previous decades' legislation in which poor and middling Jamaicans of color had rights steadily taken away, while elites received exemptions to those bills. Two different communities of color thus emerged by 1733: one that was thought dangerous to an insecure colonial state struggling against enslaved and Maroon resistance and one that appeared poised to join white society on near-equal terms. Antiblack racism therefore increased in Jamaica's early eighteenth century, but it did not affect all individuals of color equally. In the case of the new definition of "mulatto," nearly white was suddenly near enough. Privilege bills following in the wake of this law reinforced the significance of class distinctions to conceptions of social belonging as well. Such subdivision of the mixed-race community was key to formalizing Jamaica's growing racialized state. But financial privilege was not the only way to create distinctions and exclusions. As the petitions for privilege would show, family ties were nearly as important.[28]

27. Kathleen Wilson, *The Island Race: Englishness, Empire, and Gender in the Eighteenth Century* (London, 2003), 148–151. Articulations of race also depended on shifting gendered assumptions of work and class; see Kathleen Brown, *Good Wives, Nasty Wenches, and Anxious Patriarchs: Gender, Race, and Power in Colonial Virginia* (Chapel Hill, N.C., 1996). Jamaica's privilege petitions also support Kirsten Fischer's argument for North Carolina that interracial dalliances had very different meanings for gentlemen than for those in the lower orders; see Fischer, *Suspect Relations*, 74–78.

28. Jamaica House of Assembly, Laws and Statutes, 6 Geo. II ii (1733). This process of

Privilege Bills and Family Bonds

Privilege petitioning became incredibly popular in the eighteenth century and would help reshape Jamaica's elite community of color. It had such an impact that by 1797 the assembly would describe Jamaica's basic social structure to English officials with the practice in mind: "The inhabitants of this colony consist of four classes; whites, free people of colour having special privileges granted by private acts, free people of colour not possessing such privileges, and slaves." After more than sixty years of privilege petitioning, elites of color had established a new racial caste distinguished, not by phenotype, but by considerations of class, kinship, and upbringing. Likewise, the assembly used the petitioners to augment further its certified settler core by siphoning them from the island's most affluent and connected communities of color. These petitions are also invaluable because they provide some of the first documented biographies of mixed-race islanders in the eighteenth century. Whereas people of color exist largely as an anonymous group in the records before 1733, after that date they emerge as individuals with complex family ties, personal histories, and specific social positions. The petitions themselves not only sketch out these biographies, but they also reveal the continual negotiation between elites of color and authorities over status within the colony's wealthiest ranks.[29]

The extraordinary new phenomenon of privilege petitioning came out of the ordinary, legal act of lobbying the government. Organizations petitioned for tax reductions, individuals petitioned for legal changes, and colonial legislatures petitioned for increased support from the mother country. There was nothing astonishing about colonists, even those of color, asking the government for more rights. Jamaican privilege bills drew from this tradition but took on a standardized and scripted form. Any prominent individual of color who wished to stay on the island submitted a privilege dispensation. Nearly all of them were successful owing to the fact that the bills were inordinately expensive to file in the first place. It cost ninety pounds, or roughly the price of three slaves, which automatically disqualified all but the richest Jamaicans

---

using complex racial markers to "divide and rule" was applied throughout the Caribbean; see Fernando Ortiz y Fernandez, "Cuba, Martí, and the Race Problem," *Phylon*, III (1942), 271–272.

29. *JAJ*, July 28, 1797, IX, 647; Brathwaite, *Development of Creole Society*, 105. Brathwaite takes the quote to indicate the assembly's recognition of firm social divisions within Jamaica, but the assembly noted these separate divisions in public service, not necessarily in private interaction.

from applying.[30] In a way, these bills simply codified the informal statuses that most colonists already recognized. White fathers also submitted petitions on behalf of their offspring in order to affirm that they would not become destitute, nor would they grow independent or estranged from white relations. Unlike the Spanish Americas, where for a short time in the eighteenth century a small number of mixed-race colonists petitioned successfully for complete white status, most of these Jamaican indulgences did not confer full legal whiteness. They did provide immunity from many race-based laws, although the extent of those exemptions was on an individual basis for the first thirty years of the practice. No other British island passed them, making Jamaica's concessions toward its populations of color more akin to an Iberian model of racial toleration than that of Northern Europe.[31]

30. Petitioning came out of medieval precedents of appealing to a vassal, although after the English Civil War the practice had become a regular and public act of protest; see David Zaret, *Origins of Democratic Culture: Printing, Petitions, and the Public Sphere in Early-Modern England* (Princeton, 2000). From 1708 to 1733, the assembly heard five separate petitions from free blacks asking for advanced rights, specifically the right to a trial by jury; see *JAJ*, Jan. 30–Feb. 19, 1708, I, 437–446, Nov. 25, 1715–Nov. 10, 1716, II, 152–233, and Nov. 19, 1724–Jan. 21, 1725, II, 510–516. Scholars tend to lump the pre-1733 petitions with those after that date; see Samuel J. Hurwitz and Edith F. Hurwitz, "A Token of Freedom: Private Bill Legislation for Free Negroes in Eighteenth-Century Jamaica," *WMQ*, 3d Ser., XXIV (1967), 423–431; and Newman, "Contesting 'Black' Liberty and Subjecthood," *Slavery and Abolition*, XXXII (2011), 169–170. But, in fact, the two were quite separate in their forms as well as in the biographies of their petitioners. A former member of the Jamaican assembly asserted that the post-1733 bills were legally distinct from those which came before; see [Richard] Barret, *A Reply to the Speech of Dr. Lushington in the House of Commons, on the 12th June, 1827, on the Condition of the Free-Coloured People of Jamaica* (London, 1828), 24–25. For more on the costs and process of applying for the petitions, see Neville Hall, "Law and Society in Barbados at the Turn of the Nineteenth Century," *Journal of Caribbean History*, V (November 1972), 38; and Mavis Christine Campbell, *The Dynamics of Change in a Slave Society: A Sociopolitical History of the Free Coloreds of Jamaica, 1800–1865* (Rutherford, [N.J.], 1976), 94. Slave prices for the period can be found in table 4 in Trevor Burnard, "Evaluating Gender in Early Jamaica, 1674–1784," *History of the Family*, XII (2007), 89.

31. Roughly forty individuals received full white status through petitions in the Spanish Americas beginning in the 1760s; see Ann Twinam, *Purchasing Whiteness: Pardos, Mulattos, and the Quest for Social Mobility in the Spanish Indies* (Stanford, Calif., 2015), 27–30, 425–428. Petitioning in Saint Kitts among free people of color was more in line with general legal petitioning until 1830, when the island began allowing for a more systematic form of privilege petitioning to proceed; see Edward L. Cox, *Free Coloreds in the Slave Societies of St. Kitts and Grenada, 1763–1833* (Knoxville, Tenn., 1984), 96, 149–150. The most focused examination of the Jamaican privilege bills is still Hurwitz and Hurwitz's brief article, "A Token of Freedom," *WMQ*, 3d Ser., XXIV (1967), 423–431. The Hurwitzes largely dis-

John Golding's 1733 petition established the standard privilege bill that all others would copy. It was relatively simple in form. He asked to receive the same rights as white inhabitants and then offered evidence as to why he deserved it. Golding laid out four major claims about his particular status. First, he had been brought up in the Church of England and had raised his children within the same tradition. Second, he strongly asserted his loyalty to the colonial government. Third, he noted the considerable fortune he had derived through his own industry. Finally, he documented his family's genealogy. Unlike most future petitioners, Golding did not have a white father. John Golding senior was a mixed-race planter like his son. But the younger Golding's mother was, he boasted, a white woman. Although maternal European ancestry was highly unusual for islanders of color, it nevertheless raised Golding's profile and indicated a direct filial connection to white society. Such recognized white kinship was crucial to the social progression of mixed-race colonists, especially as they advanced closer to the settler elite. The majority — 59 percent — of subsequent mixed-race petitioners would likewise highlight im-

------

miss the bills as "token" favors of empowerment and not substantial in their novelty. Carl C. Campbell sees the bills as exceptional and proof of the lasting influence of Spanish traditions in Jamaica, long after the English captured it; see Campbell, *Cedulants and Capitulants: The Politics of the Coloured Opposition in the Slave Society of Trinidad, 1783–1838* (Trinidad, Wis., 1992), 22. On the debate over Iberian versus Northern-European systems of enslavement and their relative humanity see, among many others, Frank Tannenbaum, *Slave and Citizen: The Negro in the Americas* (New York, 1946); Robin Blackburn, *The Making of New World Slavery: From the Baroque to the Modern, 1492–1800* (New York, 1997); Kimberly S. Hanger, *Bounded Lives, Bounded Places: Free Black Society in Colonial New Orleans, 1769–1803* (Durham, N.C., 1997); Jane Landers, *Black Society in Spanish Florida* (Urbana, Ill., 1999); Linda Lewin, *Surprise Heirs*, I, *Illegitimacy, Patrimonial Rights, and Legal Nationalism in Luso-Brazilian Inheritance, 1750–1821* (Stanford, Calif., 2003); J. H. Elliott, *Empires of the Atlantic World: Britain and Spain in America, 1492–1830* (New Haven, Conn., 2006), esp. 106–108; A. J. R. Russell-Wood, "The Portuguese Atlantic, 1415–1808," in Jack P. Greene and Philip D. Morgan, eds., *Atlantic History: A Critical Appraisal* (New York, 2009), 82; Winthrop D. Jordan, "American Chiaroscuro: The Status and Definition of Mulattoes in the British Colonies," *WMQ*, 3d Ser., XIX (1962), 183–200; Marvin Harris, *Patterns of Race in the Americas* (New York, [1974]); Gwendolyn Midlo Hall, *Africans in Colonial Louisiana: The Development of Afro-Creole Culture in the Eighteenth Century* (Baton Rouge, La., 1992); Stephen Small, "Racial Group Boundaries and Identities: People of 'Mixed Race' in Slavery across the Americas," *Slavery and Abolition*, XV, no. 3 (December 1994), 17–37; Joyce E. Chaplin, "Race," in Armitage and Braddick, eds., *British Atlantic World*, 155; David W. Cohen and Jack P. Greene, eds., *Neither Slave Nor Free: The Freedman of African Descent in the Slave Societies of the New World* (Baltimore, 1972); and Jennifer M. Spear, *Race, Sex, and Social Order in Early New Orleans* (Baltimore, 2009), 219–220.

mediate white kin whenever they could to narrow the distance between themselves and the island's rulers. Here, then, was the model for all future appeals: assertion of Christian piety and political loyalty, evidence of economic
advancement, and a genealogical map highlighting white kinship. Soon, a
British education would be added to the list of important characteristics.
These were the attributes that the assembly valued and hoped to promote
within the island's small community of mixed-race elites, who were tapped
into vital networks at the heart of Jamaica's ruling core. After debating the
merits of Golding's petition, the assembly gave him all the same rights as
white inhabitants. Once again, he could vote and hold equal legal protections
as whites in court. His unabashed success would inspire others to file their
own petitions, but they would not necessarily experience the same results.[32]

Five years elapsed between Golding's original bill and Jamaica's second
privilege petition, but the outcome was identical. In 1738, Susanna Augier
obtained "the same rights and privileges with Englishmen" for herself and
her two children. Augier's appeal would represent an important phenomenon of the petitioning process: the applications of mixed-race mothers for
their offspring. Women acted as the primary petitioners in 45 percent of all
appeals from 1733 to 1803. This is not altogether surprising. Privilege petitioning was better suited to women of color than it was to mixed-race men.

32. *JAJ*, Apr. 6, 1733, III, 129; Acts of the Assembly of Jamaica, CO 139/13, Apr. 27, 1733,
NAE. The petitions themselves are not extant. Instead, the text of the petition is recorded
in the assembly's minutes held in the Colonial Office records at NAE. Linda L. Sturtz ar-
gues that later versions of the privilege bill created an "associational whiteness"; see Sturtz,
"Mary Rose: 'White' African Jamaican Woman? Race and Gender in Eighteenth-Century
Jamaica," in Judith A. Byfield, LaRay Denzer, and Anthea Morrison, eds., *Gendering the
African Diaspora: Women, Culture, and Historical Change in the Caribbean and Nigerian
Hinterland* (Bloomington, Ind., 2010), 60–67. María Elena Martínez records the importance of genealogical reporting to *limpieza de sangre* (purity of blood) certifications in early
modern Spain, enough so that a new category of businessmen, the *linajudo*, emerged to produce false genealogies to secure "pure blood" status; see Martínez, *Genealogical Fictions*,
75. Likewise, François Weil finds genealogy to have increased in importance during the
first third of the eighteenth century in British North America, among both black and white
households; see Weil, *Family Trees: A History of Genealogy in America* (Cambridge, Mass.,
2013), 29–41. For more on the strength of white Jamaican society and its firm social bonds,
see Christer Petley, *Slaveholders in Jamaica: Colonial Society and Culture during the Era of
Abolition* (London, 2009). Petley chronicles white society during a later period in the eighteenth century during which its members felt under attack by abolitionist forces, perhaps
making them more insular and intensified than they might have been in earlier decades. Certainly this community maintained its close connections in the metropole; see David Beck
Ryden, *West Indian Slavery and British Abolition, 1783–1807* (New York, 2009), 40–82.

Because privileged status could be inherited by children only if their other parent was white, mixed-race women had a greater chance of passing on their special status. After all, very few white women took mixed-race men as husbands or sexual partners. Many women of color likely rejoiced that privilege petitioning offered a new, if not a solitary, way of achieving legal redress for their relatives. They could also assert themselves as the mothers of the new white settler society that the assembly wished to forge out of its mixed-race community. Regardless, like all petitioners, these women had considerable amounts of money. Although Augier did not explain her source of funds, she, like most others, either received a lump sum or allowance from a white paramour or father, or had built up a separate fortune through trade, pen-keeping, or small-scale planting. Augier did note that her children's father was white. References to white companions or relatives were offered whenever possible to obtain the same kinship protections sought by male applicants. In a free society as small as Jamaica's, such connections held real importance.[33]

Augier's bill reinvigorated the submission of privilege bills, but, within weeks of its passage, a row developed between Jamaica's two legislative houses when the mixed-race son of a prominent assemblyman submitted his own petition. Born to Westmoreland representative William Cunningham and a free black woman named Elizabeth Ward, William Cunningham the younger met all the qualifications to receive privileges. He stood to inherit a large portion of his father's estate, which amounted to more than forty-five thousand pounds, and planned to forge his own business in the colony. Even more impressive, Cunningham the elder had "caused his said Son to be Educated in Great Britain," an endeavor typical for planters to undertake for white children, owing to the island's lack of schools. Like many future petitioners, Cunningham's British education would help define his elite identity. Undoubtedly supportive of one of its members' sons, the assembly passed Cunningham's request without delay. The island's upper house, the council, returned the petition, however, asking for an amendment that would deny Cunningham the privileges of both voting and sitting in either legislative chamber and of becoming a magistrate. In a pique, the assembly agreed only to a prohibition on elected office, claiming that the rest of the amendment overstepped the king's prerogative. This refusal prompted a strong rebuke from the council, perhaps nervous about the younger Cunningham's access to governmental

33. *JAJ*, June 17–30, 1738, III, 440–446. Obtaining written record of a privileged status was also imperative for West Indians of color generally; see John D. Garrigus, *Before Haiti: Race and Citizenship in French Saint-Domingue* (New York, 2006), 83–84.

power. It was in the king's best interest, the council chided, "to refuse such favours to the son of a negro woman, as the laws of Great-Britain oblige him to refuse to all foreigners, though of the most illustrious extraction." Still fervently fighting the Maroons—indeed less than a year before suing for peace with them—the council was likely uncomfortable with potentially allowing "the son of a negro," even one trained in a refined British school, to sit in its chambers. Moreover, the council had been chosen by the governor and had fewer personal connections within the island. That the assembly felt less threatened by such a prospect stemmed from kinship ties between the petitioner and a member within its ranks.[34]

The council also worried that the younger Cunningham would open the door to scores of nonwhites who might eventually infiltrate colonial government. In rebutting this argument, the assembly attempted to assuage any hyperbolic concerns about mixed-race advancement. "The number of persons in the circumstance of Mr. Cunningham," the assembly reassured council members, "are inconsiderable." "Besides," the assemblymen insisted, "they are all natives of, and persons who are to possess an interest in, this island, and consequently their attachment to it [is] not to be doubted." The assembly felt confident that only a small, and incredibly privileged, segment of the island's population of color could gain social access to the settler elite. In addition, it trusted that class affiliation overrode racial cohesion, especially because it had worked for decades on legislation to produce such an effect. Possessing an interest in the island as landed planters erased suspicions that mixed-race Jamaicans had competing loyalties beyond material advancement. If the island was indeed a plantocracy, then pursuing economic gain on the backs of enslaved laborers was the defining characteristic of ruling elite identity. Those who held similar stakes, even with some ancestral divergence, could slowly join the fold. Furthermore, this select group of petitioners shared blood ties to

34. Acts of the Assembly of Jamaica, Apr. 14, 1739, CO 139/15, NAE; *JAJ*, Apr. 14, 1739, III, 442; Board of Trade Correspondence, Nov. 8, 1762, CO 137/33, fol. 50, NAE; *JAJ*, July 7–18, 1738, III, 449–454. On the movement of West Indian whites to Britain, see Andrew Jackson O'Shaughnessy, *An Empire Divided: The American Revolution and the British Caribbean* (Philadelphia, 2000), 19–27. Trevor Burnard argues that few West Indian students left for Britain before 1760; see Burnard, "Passengers Only," *Atlantic Studies,* I (2004), 182. But B[arry] W. Higman notes that at least fifty-three Jamaicans attended Eton between 1753 and 1776; see Higman, *Plantation Jamaica, 1750–1850: Capital and Control in a Colonial Economy* (Kingston, Jamaica, 2005), 23. See also Julie Flavell, *When London Was Capital of America* (New Haven, Conn., 2010), 4–9, 67–84; and Daniel Kilbride, *Being American in Europe, 1750–1860* (Baltimore, 2013), 10–11.

that very plantocracy. Ultimately, both houses agreed that Cunningham could have full civil rights, except those of holding office or working as a magistrate. Consanguineous bonds, albeit between whites and children of color in a racially charged society, nevertheless held strong purchase.[35]

Kinship smoothed the passage of privilege bills in the assembly's chambers, but it also bred resentment among some whites. As mixed-race petitions increased in the 1740s, so, too, did the appeals against them. As before, poor and middling whites bristled at the idea that individuals of color might hold equal status as themselves. Distinct racial markers were key, in their minds, to maintain a white ascendancy in which they still towered over those of African ancestry. This was now seen as more important than before. In 1739, the British and Jamaican military gave up its failing war against the Maroons, granting them relative autonomy in return for a promise to return any future runaway slaves. This surrender angered many, and some of those elected to office in this period brought such concerns about encroaching black power to the legislature. After a woman named Elizabeth Ford submitted a privilege request in 1743, several members of the assembly asked to stop hearing petitions for the rest of the session, but the remainder of the house opposed the motion. Although the names of the protesting members are not listed in the record, they were most likely less affluent than their counterparts and shared the hopes of white Jamaicans yearning for stronger racial segregation. Moreover, many of them might have either not had children of color themselves or did not see any need to support those that they did have.[36]

Assembly members who wished to continue hearing privilege petitions often shared deep and complex connections to elites of color. In some cases, these ties were clearly nepotistic. For instance, one year after John Morse—

35. *JAJ*, July 19, 1738, III, 455–456. Ultimately, the assembly lost out to the council, and Cunningham's privilege petition barred him from serving in either the council or the assembly; see Acts of the Assembly of Jamaica, Apr. 14, 1739, CO 139/15, NAE. The historiography on the importance of family in the British Empire is immense and incorporates numerous facets. Suffice it to say that most scholars agree on the importance of familial ties as links between individuals throughout the eighteenth century. Most pertinent to the discussion of such bonds between colonists and mixed-race offspring are Sarah M. S. Pearsall, *Atlantic Families: Lives and Letters in the Later Eighteenth Century* (New York, 2008), 210–239; Durba Ghosh, *Sex and the Family in Colonial India: The Making of Empire* (New York, 2006), 69–106; and Margot Finn, "Anglo-Indian Lives in the Later Eighteenth and Early Nineteenth Centuries," *Journal for Eighteenth-Century Studies*, XXXIII (2010), 49–50.

36. *JAJ*, Apr. 22, 1743, III, 621.

whose estate would later burn in Tacky's Revolt—joined the assembly, he was
tasked with investigating the privilege petition of Mary Augier. Mary was the
sister of Susanna Augier, who had received privileged rights in 1738, and she
submitted this petition on behalf of herself and her children in 1747. It was
Morse's job to question the family to ensure that their biographical claims
rang true, a step taken with all privilege appeals. Mary's daughter Elizabeth
would eventually give birth to five of Morse's six children of color. If their
relationship had started before this interview, then Morse was by no means
an impartial investigator for the assembly's deliberations. If this was their
first meeting, then he clearly did not keep himself a disinterested observer.
No wonder that many nonelite whites began grumbling about the partiality
of privilege dispensations. It was bad enough, to them, that Jamaicans with
African ancestry could join their ranks. It was even worse that the assemblymen made such exceptions in order to keep their family members in high
positions.[37]

White anger grew so strong that Mary Augier's privilege bill set off a new
and more intense round of disputes. Perhaps sensing a growing rage about
the extent of these bills' concessions, the council insisted that it would not
approve the Augiers' appeal unless the assembly banned them from serving
as jurors, prevented them from becoming vestrymen, and prohibited their
testimony against whites in cases not involving battery. The assembly successfully overturned the latter two amendments but conceded the first. The
Augiers, and all future privileged individuals, could no longer sit on juries.
This settled the issue for the government, but, during the debate, a collection of white residents asked for a copy of Mary Augier's petition. Identifying
themselves only as "freeholders and others, inhabitants of the island," these
were likely middling whites who could vote but had very little political power
on the island. Poor whites, such as general laborers and soldiers, might have
joined forces to complain about these bills' enfranchisements. Together, they
might have felt more empowered to attack Augier, rather than previous petitioners, because she was a woman who held significantly less economic clout
than her male peers. The group read Augier's petition and then submitted its
own appeal, complaining that "if the said [privilege] bills should pass into a
law, sundry mulattoes would be entitled to the same rights and privileges with
his majesty's English subjects, free born, of white parents." Quite simply, they
saw that privilege bills were putting elites of color into the same social rank

37. Ibid., Apr. 8, 1747, IV, 66.

as themselves. The assembly could not disagree with these proclamations; indeed, it hoped that the bills would create such an outcome.[38]

Notwithstanding a strong appeal, white petitioners did not convince the legislature to end the practice of granting private indulgences. The assembly continued to award small concessions to people of color. Less than a year after the uproar over the Augiers' petition, the island's attorney general brought forward a bill to allow free mulattoes and blacks to give evidence against one another in court. Immediately, middling and poor whites demonstrated against it. Standing before the Kingston courthouse on May 9, 1748, local wharfinger Archibald Willock read aloud a satirical petition supposedly in favor of the new law. Written in the voice of an enslaved Jamaican, though penned by physician James Smith, it proclaimed that Jamaica "will never flourish till white people are sufficiently encouraged to come and settle in it," and nothing would accomplish that more than "by subjecting the white masters to the black slaves." Smith signed it as "Cudjoe," the name of the Maroon chief to whom the British military supplicated nine years earlier. Many white Jamaicans saw the empowerment of blacks and people of color in any form as an attack on the proper social divisions that kept whites of all means on top and a brutalizing form of slavery in place. Poor protestors also had children of color but felt far less ability, and thus conviction, to take care of them.[39]

38. Ibid., May 1–22, 1747, IV, 79–99. Preventing freemen of color from testifying against whites was somewhat standard issue in the Caribbean. Barbados banned freemen's testimony in 1721. Interestingly, only two years before the Augiers' petition, the governor of Curaçao prohibited free people of color from testifying against whites as well; see Linda M. Rupert, *Creolization and Contraband: Curaçao in the Early Modern Atlantic World* (Athens, Ga., 2012), 146. That the assembly turned over a private petition to a public group was unusual, although, by the eighteenth century, petitioning in general had lost most of its secretive characteristics; see Zaret, *Origins of Democratic Culture*, 95–97.

39. *JAJ*, Apr. 30–May 20, 1748, IV, 120–125. For a full treatment of the petition and its meaning in midcentury Jamaica, see James Robertson, "A 1748 'Petition of Negro Slaves' and the Local Politics of Slavery in Jamaica," *WMQ*, 3d Ser., LXVII (2010), 319–346. British expectations were low for poor men's care of illegitimate offspring, which might have affected white attitudes in Jamaica. Legal requirements for basic provisions, rather than a sense of emotional abandonment, were often the major concern in Britain, at least until the nineteenth century; see John Black, "Who Were the Putative Fathers of Illegitimate Children in London, 1740–1810?" in Alysa Levene, Thomas Nutt, and Samantha Williams, eds., *Illegitimacy in Britain, 1700–1920* (New York, 2005), 50–65; Joanne Bailey, "'A Very Sensible Man': Imagining Fatherhood in England, c. 1750–1830," *History*, XCV (2010), 270; and Bailey, "'Think Wot a Mother Must Feel': Parenting in English Pauper Letters, c. 1760–1834," *Family and Community History*, XIII (2010), 6–10.

Nonelite whites shuddered even more at the thought of slaves' descendants taking on full English subjecthood through privilege petitioning. Despite the contestations over the bills' allowances, by the midpoint of the eighteenth century, almost ninety Jamaicans of color received privileged rights. Slowly, a small cohort of color had carved out a new legislative niche that brought them closer to white status. Moreover, as the island's mixed-race population increased, and more of them inherited their fathers' fortunes, middling and poor whites began to resent the growing preference of economic over phenotypic attributes in island society. Certain members of the council and assembly agreed, as petitions and laws empowering mixed-race individuals drew far from unanimous support. Nevertheless, the key policymakers driving Jamaica forward saw in the island's wealthy class of color its hope for future settlement. Governor Edward Trelawny insisted in 1746 that "having a due Proportion of Freemen (of one Colour or another, white, black or yellow, since white Men enough cannot, at least immediately be got)" would best secure Jamaica from foreign and domestic threats. Class advantages made mixed-race elites good candidates to join white society, but so, too, did blood relation to colonial officials. As family members of the island's ruling core, these privileged individuals of color could more easily transform into de facto white settlers.[40]

Writing to the bishop of London in 1751, the missionary John Venn confirmed this tricky interplay between racial mixture and social acceptance in midcentury Jamaica. With great interest, he commented on Jamaica's 1733 provision making white those more than three generations removed from an African ancestor. The law's effect on society after nearly twenty years was undeniably apparent to Venn. "You cannot throw so great a Slur upon any Man here," he astutely remarked, "as to say, or suspect, he has Negro Blood in his Veins, at how great a distance soever it be deriv'd." On its surface, Venn's comment demonstrates the degree to which Jamaicans viewed African blood as contaminating. Yet, at its core, Venn's observation reveals more completely the complicated identity of those with African ancestry. Locals might have known about a black family member in one's genealogical past, but, at a certain point, now legally defined, a mixed-race Jamaican was in fact white. Insinuating that one was not white violated a fragile new social compact—albeit

40. [Edward Trelawny], *An Essay concerning Slavery, and the Danger Jamaica Is Expos'd from the Too Great Number of Slaves* . . . (London, [circa 1746]), introduction; Gad Heuman, "From Slavery to Freedom: Blacks in the Nineteenth-Century British West Indies," in Philip D. Morgan and Sean Hawkins, eds., *Black Experience and the Empire*, Oxford History of the British Empire Companion Series (New York, 2004), 143.

perhaps one only between elites—that racially legitimated certain colonists of color. In many ways, Jamaica had already realized the goal William Burke would set out for all American colonies in 1757 to find a medium between "liberty and absolute slavery, in which we might place all mulattoes." Genealogy provided that medium, and, while it could advance mixed-race Jamaicans, it could also hover menacingly in their backgrounds.[41]

Family, Marriage, and Illegitimacy

Jamaicans of color stood to gain much from familial position, but they could not depend on that status remaining unchanged. Definitions of family, as viewed particularly through the lens of marriage, underwent strong debate in the 1750s on both sides of the Atlantic. Concerns over illegitimate births and improper marriage prompted vigorous discussion as well as legal reform. For Jamaicans of color, who were almost universally born out of wedlock, such increased attention to formal unions compromised a still-delicate social standing. If they could not rely on white kinship, illegitimate though it was, then they held fewer guarantees of being allowed entry into the settler class.

Legislative initiatives targeting legitimacy and marriage were Atlantic in nature during the eighteenth century. So-called clandestine marriages, in particular, came under intense scrutiny in both the Caribbean and Britain. Clandestine ceremonies were ones in which Anglican ministers wed couples without strictly performing all the duties required by canon law. Men and women chose this method to avoid obtaining parental consent if it was not forthcoming, or simply to rush through nuptials. Authorities disliked these arrangements, not only because they failed to accord with ecclesiastical procedure, but because they could easily produce a range of future complications. Nevertheless, clandestine marriages were official, though religious punishments could still apply. Lawmakers first attempted to discourage them in 1695 when England required a license and the publication of banns, which were announcements of marriage on three successive Sundays before the ceremony. These provisions, however, had little effect on the frequency of the practice. By the 1730s, West Indian assemblies, along with Parliament, returned their attention to these particular family arrangements. In 1734, Barbados's assembly fined spouses married in secret and the ministers who performed the ceremonies. Two years later, Parliament tried, but failed, to pass an act requiring formal parental consent to the marriages of young couples.

41. John Venn to Bishop Thomas Sherlock, June 15, 1751, Fulham Palace Papers, XVIII, fols. 45–47, LPL; [Burke], *Account of the European Settlements*, II, 126.

Nine months after Westminster's attempt, the Jamaica assembly debated, but eventually turned down, a similar bill for "preventing the marriages of heiresses, against the wills of their parents." Barbados added a parental requirement to its act in 1739, and both Saint Kitts and Montserrat passed clandestine marriage bills within that same year.[42]

Why did these ceremonies garner such attention by authorities on both sides of the Atlantic, especially at this point in time? First, the same concern over settler growth in Jamaica weighed on the minds of whites throughout the Empire. Benjamin Franklin held high hopes in 1751 that North America's population growth would eventually outpace England's, thus providing better terms for the establishment of manufactures outside the metropole. The colonial frontier, he believed, provided the perfect place for marriage owing to its wealth of resources that could stabilize household economies. North America's settler population, therefore, might double every generation. "People increase in Proportion to the Number of Marriages, and that is greater in Proportion to the Ease and Convenience of supporting a Family," he observed. In contrast, he noted that "the Negroes brought into the English Sugar Islands, have greatly diminish'd the Whites there," resulting in

---

42. An Act for Preventing Clandestine Marriages, Oct. 1, 1734, no. 165, in Richard Hall, [Sr.], and Richard Hall, [Jr.], eds., *Acts, Passed in the Island of Barbados; From 1643, to 1762, Inclusive*... (London, 1764), 299; A Bill for the More Effectual Preventing Clandestine Marriages, no. 2065, in *HCSP*, VII, 195–196; *JAJ*, Nov. 10, 1736, III, 391–392; An Additional Act for Preventing Clandestine Marriages, Oct. 2, 1739, no. 178, in Hall [Sr.] and Hall [Jr.], eds., *Acts Passed in the Island of Barbados,* 320; An Act for Preventing Clandestine Marriages in the Island of St. Christopher, 1739, no. 104, in Hall [Sr.] and Hall [Jr.], eds., *The Laws of the Island of Saint Christopher* (Saint Christopher, 1832), 107; An Act for Preventing Clandestine Marriages in the Island of Montserrat, 1739/40, no. 120, in *Acts of Assembly, Passed in the Island of Montserrat; From 1688, to 1740, Inclusive* (London, 1740), 117. Jilted spouses who had married clandestinely, for example, could suddenly appear to overturn subsequent ceremonies performed officially, claiming that they had never been properly divorced. Young couples, and sometimes minors, angered parents by marrying in this fashion as well, shunning a family's more preferred match. England's Barebones Parliament required marriages to occur in front of a justice of the peace in 1653—a law overturned immediately on the Restoration, though interestingly one passed on the island of Montserrat twenty five years later; see An Act about Contracting Marriages . . . , 1678, no. 29, in *Acts of Assembly, Passed in the Island of Montserrat,* 33; and Rebecca Probert, *Marriage Law and Practice in the Long Eighteenth Century: A Reassessment* (New York, 2009), 7–8, 169–184, esp. 170. This legal constriction on clandestine marriages was part of a general assault on improper, or ignored, nuptials. Bermuda's legislature passed a bill in 1723, for instance, that formalized prosecutions of illegitimate births; see Heather Miyano Kopelson, "Sinning Property and the Legal Transformation of Abominable Sex in Early Bermuda," *WMQ*, 3d Ser., LXX (2013), 459–496.

the effect of "darken[ing] its People." Franklin's comments echoed those in England. The Reverend Henry Gally had made a strong attack on clandestine marriages the year before, offering the same points about marriage and population growth. "The married State must be allowed to be the most important in Life," he began his 1750 pamphlet, "and it is the Business of Society . . . to promote the Encrease of its Members." Outside of proper marriage, Gally argued, children could not be sufficiently supported and reared. Many would die young or become burdens on the parish, sending England's economy into disarray. The growth of families in the Empire, therefore, proved a lasting goal beyond Jamaica's shores. Strengthening marriages seemed the best way to inspire such increase.[43]

Second, fears over growing illegitimacy in Britain prompted an interest in marriage at midcentury as well. When couples married secretly, Gally argued, they put their children's legitimacy in question. This posed serious problems in a British society committed to smooth property transmission yet seemingly plagued by large numbers of children born out of wedlock. Although data is often inconsistent, it appears that Britain, along with the rest of the Atlantic basin, did see a real increase in illegitimate children after 1700. For England, this might have been the result of a small subset of the population being made more vulnerable to broken family arrangements, or, more simply, owing to changes in record keeping. Scotland experienced some of the highest levels of illegitimacy in Europe during the eighteenth century, perhaps because of its informal marriage regulations. Regardless, Britons reacted to these apparent changes. Not only did Parliament attempt to curb clandestine marriages to prevent future illegitimate offspring, but new institutions arose to care for those who did come into the world. As potential drains on the public treasury, rival heirs to large fortunes, and supposed harbingers of moral decline, illegitimate children emblematized major problems afflicting British society.[44]

43. Benjamin Franklin, "Observations concerning the Increase of Mankind, Peopling of Countries, etc.," in Leonard W. Labaree, ed., *The Papers of Benjamin Franklin*, IV, *July 1, 1750, through June 30, 1753* (New Haven, Conn., 1961), 227–234; Henry Gally, *Some Considerations upon Clandestine Marriages . . .* , 2d ed. (London, 1750), preface. Ezra Stiles would echo these comments several years later, anticipating that the cession of New France would help rapidly expand the population of British North America; see Stiles, *A Discourse on the Christian Union . . .* (Boston, 1761), 120–122. As Lisa Forman Cody notes, England saw population encouragement at this time as a way of outcompeting France; see Cody, *Birthing the Nation: Sex, Science, and the Conception of Eighteenth-Century Britons* (New York, 2005), 18–20.

44. Gally, *Some Considerations*, 17. Themes of illegitimacy dominated English literature

Finally, concerns over marriage escalated as changing economic patterns recalibrated family composition. Although European society at large had long viewed premarital sex and concubinage as immoral and dangerous, illegitimacy took on more insidious connotations in this period. These changes had deep roots in the drastic alterations occurring in the economy. As European empires expanded abroad, the relationship between land and wealth transformed at home. The growth of global commerce, and England's nearly unending warfare during the eighteenth century, unsettled fortunes for all but the wealthiest of Britain's landed elite. As the price of land rose, merchant families struggled to purchase their way into that select group. Many found entry

---

throughout the eighteenth century; see Lisa Zunshine, *Bastards and Foundlings: Illegitimacy in Eighteenth-Century England* (Columbus, Oh., 2005); and Ruth Perry, *Novel Relations: The Transformation of Kinship in English Literature and Culture, 1748–1818* (New York, 2004), 77–106, 337–371, esp. 372–373. Although it was a dominant theme, literary interest in illegitimacy was not exclusive to the eighteenth century; see Michael Neill, *Putting History to the Question: Power, Politics, and Society in English Renaissance Drama* (New York, 2000), 127–147. For scholarship on eighteenth-century illegitimacy in the Atlantic basin, see Ann Twinam, *Public Lives, Private Secrets: Gender, Honor, Sexuality, and Illegitimacy in Colonial Spanish America* (Stanford, Calif., 1999), 7; Peter Laslett, *Family Life and Illicit Love in Earlier Generations: Essays in Historical Sociology* (New York, 1977), 107; Laslett, Karla Oosterveen, and Richard Smith, eds., *Bastardy and Its Comparative History: Studies in the History of Illegitimacy and Marital Nonconformism in Britain, France, Germany, Sweden, North America, Jamaica, and Japan* (Cambridge, Mass., 1980); G. N. Gandy, "Illegitimacy in a Handloom Weaving Community: Fertility Patterns in Culcheth, Lancs., 1781–1860" (D. Phil diss., University of Oxford, 1978); Richard Adair, *Courtship, Illegitimacy, and Marriage in Early Modern England* (New York, 1996); and Belinda Meteyard, "Illegitimacy and Marriage in Eighteenth-Century England," *Journal of Interdisciplinary History*, X (1980), 479–489. Many illegitimate children, however, were born to parents living together unmarried, rather than ones met by casual encounter; see Nicholas Rogers, "Carnal Knowledge: Illegitimacy in Eighteenth-Century Westminster," *Journal of Social History*, XXIII (1989), 355–375; and Black, "Who Were the Putative Fathers," in Levene, Nutt, and Williams, eds., *Illegitimacy in Britain*, 50–65. On Scottish illegitimacy, in particular, see Rosalind Mitchison and Leah Leneman, *Sexuality and Social Control: Scotland, 1660–1780* (New York, 1989); and Andrew Blaikie, *Illegitimacy, Sex, and Society: Northeast Scotland, 1750–1900* (New York, 1993). Blaikie claims, however, that the supposed epidemic of illegitimacy in Scotland has been overestimated; see Blaikie, "A Kind of Loving: Illegitimacy, Grandparents, and the Rural Economy of North East Scotland, 1750–1900," *Scottish Economic and Social History*, XIV (1994), 41–42. Most notably, Thomas Coram created the Foundling Hospital in 1739 to look after both orphans and illegitimate children in London; see Ruth K. McLure, *Coram's Children: The London Foundling Hospital in the Eighteenth Century* (New Haven, Conn., 1981); and Gillian Pugh, *London's Forgotten Children: Thomas Coram and the Foundling Hospital* (Stroud, Gloucestershire, U.K., 2007).

by marrying off children into less affluent peerage and gentry households. Britain's largest landowners reacted by consolidating their wealth through the marriage settlements of daughters.[45] Both strategies reveal just how important regulated nuptials were. Colonization had thus produced a more volatile, albeit more dynamic, economic system that might easily ruin unprotected riches and unmonitored weddings. Households on both sides of the Atlantic reorganized themselves in turn to build more secure credit networks that

---

45. Scholars have charted a turn against illegitimacy within families and the culture at large; see Jack Goody, *The Development of the Family and Marriage in Europe* (New York, 1983), 75-76, 216-219; A. D. Harvey, *Sex in Georgian England: Attitudes and Prejudices from the 1720s to the 1820s* (New York, 1994), 3, 89-93. There is debate over the degree to which bastardy was accepted in social practice. Roy Porter argues that few individuals failed to recognize illegitimate children and that following one's sexual impulses were part of Enlightenment philosophy; see Porter, "Mixed Feelings: The Enlightenment and Sexuality in Eighteenth-Century Britain," in Paul-Gabriel Boucé, ed., *Sexuality in Eighteenth-Century Britain* (Totowa, N.J., 1982), 4-11. Stana Nenadic finds that Scottish lairds also easily recognized and cared for illegitimate children, often within their own household; see Nenadic, *Lairds and Luxury: The Highland Gentry in Eighteenth-Century Scotland* (Edinburgh, 2007), 32-38, 108-149. On the other hand, bachelorhood and illegitimacy could undercut one's manhood; see Pearsall, "Gender," in Armitage and Braddick, eds., *British Atlantic World*, 113-132; and Amanda Vickery, *Behind Closed Doors: At Home in Georgian England* (New Haven, Conn., 2009), 77-82. Although land was still central to the economy, its overall share in Britain's total economic output decreased significantly in the eighteenth century; see G. E. Mingay, *English Landed Society in the Eighteenth Century* (London, 1963), 12-13. John Habakkuk argues that the British government's borrowing to finance military expenditures from 1688 to 1815 raised interest rates so high that middling and indebted landed estates either could not obtain mortgages, or could not repay them, forcing liquidation. This was part of an overall trend in which the wealth gap between large and small landowners increased over the course of the eighteenth century; see Habakkuk, "The Rise and Fall of English Landed Families, 1600-1800," Royal Historical Society, *Transactions*, 5th Ser., XXIX (1979), 203-205. See also W. D. Rubinstein, "New Men of Wealth and the Purchase of Land in Nineteenth-Century Britain," *Past and Present*, no. 92 (August 1981), 139-141; and Mingay, *English Landed Society,* 36. On merchants marrying into the upper classes, see Nicholas Rogers, "Money, Land, and Lineage: The Big Bourgeoisie of Hanoverian London," *Social History,* IV (1979), 444-446. The marriage settlements of heiresses were most important in the first half of the eighteenth century. In part, this was owing to the demographic problem of insufficient male heirs within the peerage; see Habakkuk, "Marriage Settlements in the Eighteenth Century," Royal Historical Society, *Transactions*, 4th Ser., XXXII (1950), 28; Christopher Clay, "Marriage, Inheritance, and the Rise of Large Estates in England, 1660-1815," *Economic History Review,* 2d Ser., XXI (1968), 515; and Lloyd Bonfield, "Marriage Settlements and the 'Rise of the Great Estates': The Demographic Aspect," *Economic History Review,* 2d Ser., XXXII (1979), 486.

could survive such fluctuations. Families did not necessarily become nucleated, but kinship did transition toward more endogamous connections that allowed for safer property transmission. For the merchant and middling classes, in particular, this shift helped to consolidate emerging wealth in the face of rising capitalist pressures.[46] One commentator in 1756, for example, insisted that marriages between those of near kinship would promote national security and the Protestant cause. But illegitimate children, who held no legal rights to inheritance outside of a will, could not assist in this effort at wealth accretion. Instead, they were rival heirs who often held no other financial resources be-

46. The scholarly debate on nuclear versus extended families is long and ongoing. For those arguing for increased nucleation, see, among many others, Lawrence Stone, *The Family, Sex, and Marriage in England, 1500–1800* (New York, 1977); Ilana Krausman Ben-Amos, "Reciprocal Bonding: Parents and Their Offspring in Early Modern England," *Journal of Family History*, XXV (2000), 291–312; and Joanne Bailey, "Reassessing Parenting in Eighteenth-Century England," in Helen Berry and Elizabeth Foyster, eds., *The Family in Early Modern England* (New York, 2007), 209–232. Those arguing against progressively growing nucleation include Philip J. Greven, Jr., *Four Generations: Population, Land, and Family in Colonial Andover, Massachusetts* (Ithaca, N.Y., 1970); Daniel C. Quinlan and Jean A. Shackelford, "Economy and English Families, 1500–1850," *Journal of Interdisciplinary History*, XXIV (1994), 431–463; Richard Grassby, *Kinship and Capitalism: Marriage, Family, and Business in the English-Speaking World, 1580–1740* (New York, 2001); and David Warren Sabean, Simon Teuscher, and Jon Mathieu, eds., *Kinship in Europe: Approaches to Long-Term Developments (1300–1900)* (New York, 2007). Keith Wrightson and David Levine see different forms of nucleation between the upper and lower orders of early modern society; see Wrightson and Levine, *Poverty and Piety in an English Village: Terling, 1525–1700* (New York, 1995). On the importance of kinship reorganization as a tool of class advancement, see Eve Tavor Bannet, "The Marriage Act of 1753: 'A Most Cruel Law for the Fair Sex,'" *Eighteenth-Century Studies*, XXX (1997), 235; Alastair Owens, "Property, Gender, and the Life Course: Inheritance and Family Welfare Provision in Early Nineteenth-Century England," *Social History*, XXVI (2001), 307–313; K. D. M. Snell, "English Rural Societies and Geographical Marital Endogamy, 1700–1837," *Economic History Review*, LV (2002), 262–298; Perry, *Novel Relations*, 38–76, 372–373; Holly Brewer, *By Birth or Consent: Children, Law, and the Anglo-American Revolution in Authority* (Chapel Hill, N.C., 2005), 288–316; and David Warren Sabean and Simon Teuscher, "Kinship in Europe: A New Approach to Long Term Development," in Sabean, Teuscher, and Mathieu, eds., *Kinship in Europe*, 1–32. This consolidation of wealth occurred, to an extent, within the peerage as well; see David Thomas, "The Social Origins of Marriage Partners of the British Peerage in the Eighteenth and Nineteenth Centuries," *Population Studies*, XXVI (1972), 99–111; and Mingay, *English Landed Society*, 32. Bannet and Brewer's claims about Hardwicke's Marriage Act emerging out of desires to consolidate wealth in families are firmly disputed by Probert, who argues for a limited interpretation of the law, although she does not attempt to assign causal explanations for its appearance; see Probert, *Marriage Law and Practice*, 340.

yond a parental connection. As competing claimants to family assets, therefore, illegitimate individuals came under increasing attack.[47]

Within this atmosphere, Parliament created a landmark law against clandestine unions, as part of a broad policy to reform marriage and settlement throughout the Empire. Lord Chancellor, Philip Yorke, earl of Hardwicke, crafted a bill that would eventually take his name. Passed in 1753, Hardwicke's Marriage Act reiterated core principles of the previous Marriage Duty Act of 1695. Publication of banns and obtaining a license were still required for official marriages, although the 1753 regulation demanded only one, and not both, of them. But Hardwicke's Act did allow for the annulment of marriages when parents opposed the match. Taken as a whole, it differed little from previous legislation. Its effective purpose might simply have been to end "Fleet marriages": those conducted without banns or a license in Fleet prison — constituting perhaps as much as half of London's marriage ceremonies. Yet, beyond the specific legal changes it instituted, no matter how limited, the act signaled a more focused concentration on marriage and settlement in England, and later the Empire. Those born outside wedlock took on greater ignominy in the eyes of the law, if not the culture in general. Family networks were still some of the most vital forms of association, but decreasing acceptance of illegitimacy strained certain kinship ties.[48]

47. John Fry, *The Case of Marriages between Near Kindred Particularly Considered* (London, 1756), ix. Such financial accumulation occurred in the colonies as well; see Lee J. Alston and Morton Owen Schapiro, "Inheritance Laws across Colonies: Causes and Consequences," *Journal of Economic History*, XLIV (1984), 277–287; Michael Craton, "Property and Propriety: Land Tenure and Slave Property in the Creation of a British West Indian Plantocracy, 1612–1740," in John Brewer and Susan Staves, eds., *Early Modern Conceptions of Property* (New York, 1995), 512–516; and Kimberly S. Hanger, "Landlords, Shopkeepers, Farmers, and Slave-Owners: Free Black Female Property-Holders in Colonial New Orleans," in David Barry Gaspar and Darlene Clark Hine, eds., *Beyond Bondage: Free Women of Color in the Americas* (Urbana, Ill., 2004), 219–236.

48. Laws and Statutes of Great Britain, 26 Geo. II, c. 32 (1753). For the reorganization of imperial ideas of marriage, see Kirsten Sword's forthcoming work *Wives Not Slaves* (Chicago). Despite these added rights for parents, Hardwicke's Marriage Act failed to close a loophole in which banns could be read in distant parishes to avoid parental knowledge; see *A Letter to the Public: Containing the Substance of What Hath Been Offered in the Late Debates upon the Subject of the Act of Parliament, for the Better Preventing of Clandestine Marriages* (London, 1753), 3–6; and Probert, *Marriage Law and Practice*, 221–236, 340. Probert offers one of the most conservative interpretations of the bill. For those who see it as more revolutionary in scope, see Bannet, "The Marriage Act of 1753," *Eighteenth-Century Studies*, XXX (1997), 234–241; Brewer, *By Birth or Consent*, 288–316; and Douglas Hay and Nicholas Rogers, *Eighteenth-Century English Society: Shuttles and Swords* (Oxford, 1997), 37–53.

Hardwicke's Marriage Act should be seen within an Atlantic-wide dis-cussion about the strategy for increased settlement and formalized families. The day after Parliament passed the act, it voted down a bill for "the better peopling of the Island of Jamaica with white inhabitants." This bill called for a general survey of the island: names of residents, fertility of the soil, quality and amount of buildings, and numbers of enslaved workers listed for each parish. Such a review would determine which properties remained uncultivated and thus open for new land grants. The proposed law emerged out of concerns by an English member of Parliament troubled by a Board of Trade report on the colony's deficient white settler community. Yet, the bill also echoed decades of debate in Jamaica. It demonstrated an empire-wide engagement with the topic of white Jamaican development. Such concern grew up alongside mir-ror interests in population growth at the imperial center. Ultimately, though, the law did not pass. One pamphleteer insisted that Jamaican absentee, and future lord mayor of London, William Beckford exerted tremendous effort to kill the proposition in order to keep competing planters off the island.[49]

Hardwicke himself was also not divorced from issues of slavery, or even migrants of color in Britain. In 1729, he issued a famous legal opinion with Charles Talbot insisting that slavery was legal in England and that baptism did not confer freedom on the enslaved. For more than a generation, Hardwicke and Talbot's opinion influenced freedom trials in England. Additionally, just three years before the Marriage Act, Hardwicke heard the case of William-son v. Codrington, in which a Barbadian planter brought over to England his "two Mulatto boys, whom [he] had by a *negro* woman." In his will, William Codrington devised a large share of his estate to these sons, prompting a law-suit over its execution. Hardwicke conceded that Codrington's wife "must have some resentment against this kind of conduct in her husband" but ad-mitted that "when he had these children, in whatever way, or of whatever colour, it was a natural duty incumbent on him to provide for them." Did Hardwicke's sense of family inform his opinion on giving bequests to ille-gitimate children of color in England? Might he have remembered this de-cision when crafting his Marriage Act three years later? Although he did not comment on these cases' influence, Hardwicke's experience with the legal

49. A Bill for the Better Peopling of the Island of Jamaica with White Inhabitants; for En-couraging the Cultivation of Lands at Present Uncultivated in That Island; and for Making a Proper Distribution of Such Lands, no. 2244, in *HCSP*, IX, 573–590; *A Short Account of the Interest and Conduct of the Jamaica Planters; In an Address to the Merchants, Traders, and Liverymen of the City of London* (London, 1754), 1–3, 13–15.

question of slavery along with the provisions given to mixed-race children traveling to Britain, demonstrated that issues of settlement, family, and inter-racial households were connected topics that spanned the Atlantic in the mid-eighteenth century.[50]

Many Britons were intimately familiar with Jamaican household arrange-ments owing to their regular commercial connections with the island. Ab-sentees, merchants, and family members in Britain routinely oversaw the manumission and care of mixed-race offspring. Sarah Smith in England, for example, learned of overseer John Davis's liaison with Phibbah, an enslaved woman on her Jamaican estate with whom Davis had two children. The reve-lation came because Davis wished to free his family. As long as petitioners either paid or provided substitutes for enslaved relations and companions, plantation owners put up little fuss. Of course, kinship connections often re-vealed these relationships as well. Sorting through his brother George Bar-clay's Jamaican probate, James Barclay made an appeal for part of the inheri-tance on behalf of his mixed-race niece and nephews. James passed a note onto the estate's executor in Britain: "You know my Brother has three Chil-dren here: Sukie and two Lads. I think 'tis hard they should have been forgot in his Will and something should be done for them." Barclay's connection to his mixed-race kin was strong enough that he lobbied for them after they re-ceived nothing from their father. Legislators might have started targeting such relationships because they were so well known in Britain.[51]

The material effects of Hardwicke's Marriage Act on mixed-race Jamai-cans were somewhat uneven. Questions lingered about the law's applicability outside England. Many colonies refused to adopt the measure, claiming it conflicted with local custom. Nevertheless, the law signified a less tolerant wind toward the group's status, and it could still produce complications. Al-

50. Williamson v. Codrington, July 21, 1750, in Francis Vesey, ed., *Reports of Cases Ar-gued and Determined in the High Court of Chancery, in the Time of Lord Chancellor Hard-wicke . . .* , I (Philadelphia, 1831), 511–516; Travis Glasson, "'Baptism Doth Not Bestow Free-dom': Missionary Anglicanism, Slavery, and the Yorke-Talbot Opinion, 1701–30," *WMQ*, 3d Ser., LXVII (2010), 287. Codrington's sons noted having been educated in England in a sup-plemental report; see *A Supplement to the Reports in Chancery of Francis Vesey, Senior . . .* , ed. Robert Belt (Philadelphia, 1825), 226. Codrington gave bequests to several mixed-race children across the Caribbean, some not tied to the lawsuit; see Will of William Codrington, Nov. 27, 1741, PROB 11/713, NAE.

51. Thomas Mosley to Sarah Smith, Jan. 17, 1755, MS 230, fol. 71, NLJ; James Barclay to John Thompson, May 23, 1757, MS 1160/5/9, Gordons of Buthlaw and Cairness Estate and Family Papers, Special Collections Library, University of Aberdeen, Scotland.

though it made no provisions against illegitimate offspring, Hardwicke's Act did make it more difficult for them to marry. In particular, the bill required both parents' consent in cases involving minors. This was less of an obstacle for those staying in Jamaica. Freemen of color who traveled to the metropole, however, might have struggled under the new regulations. Without the consent of a black or mixed-race mother who traditionally never made the voyage across the Atlantic, Jamaicans of color could not marry in Britain before their majority. Jamaica's governor Charles Knowles perhaps hinted at this problem in a letter to Hardwicke, five months after the Marriage Act passed, worrying about the "many minors and orphans in this Island" sailing to England with large fortunes. Without easy access to marriage, they might not be able to establish legitimate family ties in Britain.[52]

If the law produced only spotty changes for the offspring of informal unions, it had almost no effect on the parents' carrying on such relationships. Tighter restrictions on marriage in Jamaica had little application to the small number of weddings that did occur. Indeed, marriage was often seen as a social impediment. A group of Kingston merchants, for instance, drew up articles of agreement in 1752 to allow for the dissolution of their partnership should one of them eventually marry. They did not wish to create new beneficiaries of the business in the likely event that one of them would soon perish in the harsh Jamaican climate. Many other European migrants brought with them a capacious notion of what romantic attachments could be. A host of alternative arrangements involving sex and cohabitation existed in Britain, both before and after 1753, which many couples identified as an equivalent to marriage. Scottish law even recognized simple cohabitation, declarations by consent outside the church, and marriage promised before sex as official unions. Considering the large numbers of Scots in the Caribbean, such porous notions of romantic attachment likely carried over to Jamaica to diminish the enthusiasm of marrying formally. At the same time, these broader conceptions of marriage and kin organization made interracial households not families of a sort, but functionally legitimate ones.[53]

52. Charles Knowles to Philip Yorke, earl of Hardwicke, Oct. 14, 1753, Add. MS 35916, fol. 33, BL; B. H. McPherson, *The Reception of English Law Abroad* (Brisbane, Australia, 2007), 384. Most famously, Hardwicke tried, and failed, to impose his act on Scotland; see Brian Dempsey, "The Marriage (Scotland) Bill 1755," *Stair Society Miscellany*, VI, no. 54 (2009), 75–119. Guardians could substitute as parents to give consent, but that could often complicate matters unduly.

53. "Articles of Agreement between Francis Bright, Kingston, Robert Whatley, Kingston, Jeremiah Meyler, Kingston, and Charles Hall, Kingston," July 1, 1752, in Kenneth Morgan,

Moreover, white men on the island continued to engage sexually with women of color, undeterred by changing attitudes toward matrimony and family. Most of these encounters were part of the violence of slavery; they were crucial to the method of control in that system. Thomas Thistlewood, who arrived on the island in 1750, preyed on enslaved women throughout his life, with little consideration of their own wishes. His attacks reminded women and men, both on his plantation and off of it, of the enormous power he wielded. Yet, some interracial relationships, including at least one of Thistlewood's, operated as quasinormative marriages. Enslaved and free women of color could leverage a romantic attachment to obtain favors. In many cases, these could be minor tokens, in others they could lead to emancipation for themselves and their children. These unions retained the unequal power balance inherent in such a racially exploitative society, but they nevertheless occa-

---

ed., *The Bright-Meyler Papers: A Bristol-West India Connection, 1732–1837* (New York, 2007), 255–256. Even in England, statutory changes produced uneven results in marriage practices, as individuals were slow to alter living patterns. Thomas Turner, for instance, noted the prosecution of two Sussex clergymen in 1758 for violating the strict requirements of Hardwicke's Act. He also recorded the overseas nuptials in 1764 of a woman now considered underage for an English ceremony; see *The Diary of Thomas Turner, 1754–1765,* ed. David Vaisey (Oxford, 1984), Jan. 11, 1758, 130, Nov. 14, 1764, 308. As Probert argues, promises of marriage—often the most common "functional alternative"—did not constitute legal marriage but could be used to force one partner to solemnize the union in church. After Hardwicke's Act, that right of compulsion disappeared, but the contractual component of those promises continued as an option for those not yet ready to marry; see Probert, *Marriage Law and Practice,* 10, 21–36, 221. See also Patricia Crawford, *Parents of Poor Children in England, 1580–1800* (New York, 2010), 91–96. For more on Scottish marriage law and the failed attempt to impose Hardwicke's Act on Scotland, see Eric W. Clive, *The Law of Husband and Wife in Scotland,* 4th ed. (Edinburgh, 1997), esp. 1–48; Norah Smith, "Sexual Mores and Attitudes in Enlightenment Scotland," in Boucé, ed., *Sexuality in Eighteenth-Century Britain,* 47–73; Leah Leneman, *Promises, Promises: Marriage Litigation in Scotland 1698–1830* (Edinburgh, 2003); Leneman, "The Scottish Case That Led to Hardwicke's Marriage Act," *Law and History Review,* XVII (1999), 161–169; and Dempsey, "The Marriage (Scotland) Bill 1755," *Stair Society Miscellany,* VI, no. 54 (2009), 75–119. On the large number of Scots in the Caribbean, see Richard B. Sheridan, "The Role of the Scots in the Economy and Society of the West Indies," *Annals of the New York Academy of Sciences,* CCXCII (1977), 94–106; Karras, *Sojourners in the Sun;* and Douglas J. Hamilton, *Scotland, the Caribbean, and the Atlantic World, 1750–1820* (New York, 2005). Emma Rothschild records an irregular marriage in Scotland that produced a strong and peripatetic family throughout the British Empire. Yet, she contends that the interracial households that these Scottish descendants brought up in the colonies differed essentially from legitimate families in the metropole; see Rothschild, *The Inner Life of Empires: An Eighteenth-Century History* (Princeton, 2011), 15, 199.

sionally offered greater agency to female partners and a modicum of mutual family obligation. If the mothers of mixed-race individuals could bring white partners more closely in line with recognized forms of kinship, then they had a greater chance of advancing their children in Jamaican society.[54]

Personal correspondence shows that some of these efforts were successful, with many mixed-race individuals living as acknowledged and supported family members of white colonists. Although his sexual accounts stand out, Thistlewood's journal also chronicles frequent socialization between racial groups. He hosted a gaming night in 1753, inviting a number of local planters and overseers including "Mr. Kudd a Mulatto, and Kudd's Son." This was not a society wholly segregated along racial lines. Family connections bridged the gap between racial castes in Jamaica, and Thistlewood closely monitored the genealogies of his mixed-race neighbors to understand those ties better. Soon after arriving in Jamaica, he noted of a nearby planter that "Mr. Dorrill has the Whitest Mulatto Son I ever Saw, very fair and has long hair." Much of Thistlewood's knowledge of mixed-race individuals came through such paternal links. He frequently interacted with children of color because of personal relationships with their parents. Visiting Thistlewood's estate in 1756, a Mr. Mordiner "brought his Mulatto Son Tom with him." Tom later stayed with Thistlewood for a week while his father was away. This was not a singular incident. In 1754, Thistlewood recorded that he "let a Mulatto Boy of Mr. Crawfords Sleep here to Night." Nearly all of his interactions with mixed-

54. On Thistlewood, see Douglas Hall, *In Miserable Slavery: Thomas Thistlewood in Jamaica, 1750–86* (Kingston, Jamaica, 1989); Trevor Burnard, "Theater of Terror: Domestic Violence in Thomas Thistlewood's Jamaica, 1750-1786," in Christine Daniels and Michael V. Kennedy, eds., *Over the Threshold: Intimate Violence in Early America* (New York, 1999), 237-253; and Burnard, *Mastery, Tyranny and Desire.* On the experiences of women in these relationships, see Barbara Bush, *Slave Women in Caribbean Society: 1650–1838* (Bloomington, Ind., 1990), 115-116; Verene A. Shepherd, ed., *Women in Caribbean History: The British-Colonised Territories* (Kingston, Jamaica, 1999), 73-76; Hilary McD. Beckles, *Centering Women: Gender Discourses in Caribbean Slave Society* (Princeton, 1999), 178; and Sturtz, "Mary Rose," in Byfield, Denzer, and Morrison, eds., *Gendering the African Diaspora,* 59-87. Marisa J. Fuentes provides the important reminder, however, that women of color's sexuality should not be automatically equated with agency; see Fuentes, "Power and Historical Figuring: Rachael Pringle Polgreen's Troubled Archive," *Gender and History,* XXII (2010), 568, 579-580. Kathleen DuVal also provides a helpful comparison in North America, where the willingness of native American women to sleep with French colonists was by no means universal across space and time—even among enslaved Indians who frequently sought nonsexual paths toward emancipation; see DuVal, "Indian Intermarriage and Métissage in Colonial Louisiana," *WMQ,* 3d Ser., LXV (2008), 267-304.

race people included notes about their parentage. After a "Mulatto child" died in 1758, Thistlewood recorded the name of the infant's father. Within his personal life, then, Thistlewood continued to interact with mixed-race individuals despite encroaching legal pressures on illegitimate children. Lineage factored heavily in mixed-race people's statuses, and Thistlewood related to them in this way throughout the 1750s.[55]

Jamaica's assembly became caught between these public and private forces in the years surrounding Hardwicke's Act. It continued to pass bills encouraging white settlement, and these acts increasingly sought family migration. In 1748, the assembly allowed "children, both male and female, of eight years of age and upwards" to save deficiency. This indicated a greater interest in established families settling in Jamaica, rather than simply adult males. Less than a decade later, the Marriage Act's effects became apparent. Jamaica's 1757 deficiency bill included an allowance that "every man's wife, and each of his children born in wedlock, shall be allowed to save a deficiency." Considering that almost no white men married women of color, despite its legality, the assembly did not direct this clause toward interracial couples. Instead, it mimicked the wider Atlantic interest in promoting proper marriage and cohabitation and in reducing births out of wedlock. White, legitimate families still stood at the pinnacle of Jamaica's most-desired settlers.[56]

In keeping with this restrictive environment, and especially after the protest of poor whites against privilege petitions in 1748, the assembly pulled back on its allowances to freemen of color. Perhaps discouraged from doing so by house members, very few Jamaicans of color submitted privilege appeals in the 1750s. The assembly considered only four privilege bills that decade, and only one of those came after Hardwicke's Act. Stephen Lost's 1756 petition for

55. Diary of Thomas Thistlewood, Thomas Thistlewood Papers, microfilm, reel 1, no. 2 (1750), 283, reel 2, no. 4 (1753), 190, reel 2, no. 5 (1754), 289, reel 3, no. 7 (1756), 88, reel 3, no. 8 (1757), 104-107. This claim of greater social interaction between racial groups runs against the general arguments of Heuman, *Between Black and White,* 6-12; and Christer Petley, "'Legitimacy' and Social Boundaries: Free People of Colour and the Social Order in Jamaican Slave Society," *Social History,* XXX (2005), 481-498. Both Heuman and Petley rightfully see the mass of free people of color living outside the boundaries of white society but explore less fully the connections between mixed-race elites and whites. As a point of comparison, Dominique Rogers charts a highly integrated—though not politically assimilated—free population of color within white society in nearby Saint Domingue; see Rogers, "On the Road to Citizenship: The Complex Route to Integration of the Free People of Color in the Two Capitals of Saint-Domingue," in David Patrick Geggus and Norman Fiering, eds., *The World of the Haitian Revolution* (Bloomington, Ind., 2009), 72-76.

56. *JAJ,* Aug. 12, 1748, IV, 141, Oct. 8, 1757, V, 8.

his offspring of color remained the only such request for an eight-year period between 1752 and 1760. He might have felt more confident in submitting his appeal than other potential petitioners because he had "sent three of his said Children to the Kingdom of Great Britain and will when the other two are of proper age." Educating a mixed-race child in Britain was not unusual at the time, but at this point few privilege petitioners noted such activities. William Cunningham the elder had remarked on his son's English education in 1739, and Elizabeth Pierce noted residing in London with a white husband in a 1746 joint petition with her brother and sister still living on the island. Impressed by the Lost children's accomplishments, the assembly easily approved their appeal. Once again, though, the council dragged its feet. In particular, members of the upper house demanded that the privilege bill bar the recipients from serving as parochial officers or vestry members. Both chambers—presently at war over whether to move the island's courthouses and records from Spanish Town to Kingston—quarreled over the implications of keeping privileged Jamaicans entirely outside positions of government. Eventually, the assembly won; Lost's children could serve in some public function. Even though the assembly had scaled back its private concessions to elites of color and now supported stronger laws toward matrimony, it could not deny certain mixed-race individuals an advanced place in island society. Those educated in Britain, especially, required exemptions, and their experiences abroad informed conceptions of the rarified place of this small cohort of color.[57]

At the end of the 1750s, a generation's time span of allowing mixed-race individuals to become legally white, or at least exempt from most race-based laws, created a new and uncertain racial dynamic in Jamaica. Lineal descent away from African ancestors had fully enfranchised certain individuals, enough so that some visitors noted them as white. Privilege bills corrected for extreme class advancement among those with too much African blood, with

57. Acts of the Assembly of Jamaica, Oct. 13, 1756, CO 139/18, NAE, Apr. 14, 1739, CO 139/15; *JAJ*, May 15, 1746, IV, 54–55, Aug. 25–Oct. 28, 1756, 580–661. Elizabeth Cadogan, a woman of joint European and aboriginal Jamaican descent, also noted that she had a child living in England; see *JAJ*, May 28, 1746, IV, 9. The proposed relocation of the seat of government was, indeed, a major source of tension between the two chambers, which resulted in the governor proroguing the assembly. The records did move temporarily to Kingston but returned within a few years. See *JAJ*, Apr. 22–May 14, 1755, IV, 508–527; *A Letter from a Citizen of Port-Royal in Jamaica, to a Citizen of New-York* . . . (London, 1756); George Metcalf, *Royal Government and Political Conflict in Jamaica, 1729–1783* (London, 1965), 122; and James Robertson, *Gone is the Ancient Glory: Spanish Town, Jamaica, 1534–2000* (Kingston, Jamaica, 2005), 89–93.

almost one hundred Jamaicans of color receiving such dispensations in two and a half decades. Both measures emphasized the importance of genealogy to mixed-race status and the allowance for private exemptions against public laws. Nonetheless, developing concerns in the Empire over illegitimacy and matrimonial increase made the status of these mixed-race elites more vulnerable. By 1760, then, family connections still outweighed legal and cultural restrictions, but the tensions within and between those forces continued to build.[58]

Tacky's Revolt and the Inheritance Cap

Jamaica's long-standing concern with population—both white and enslaved—proved to have been justified on Easter Monday 1760. Nearly one hundred enslaved Coromantees rose up that day from several plantations on the north coast. Numerous outbreaks spread to every corner of Jamaica. Coming toward the end of the Seven Years' War (1756–1763), Tacky's Revolt shocked the colony, forcing its rulers to reconsider domestic security and slave regulation. Within that spirit of change, the assembly revisited its policy toward free people of color and interracial relationships in general. Like it had done in 1733, the assembly crafted a law constraining mixed-race rights, while simultaneously providing paths for wealthy individuals of color to evade those very strictures.

Tacky's Revolt shattered more than two decades of relative calm on the island's plantations. Jamaica's governor had signed a treaty with the Maroons in 1739, ending their war while beginning a new partnership to police runaway slaves. Although some reports surfaced in May 1759 about disturbances among the "wild negroes," these riots did not escalate. The next spring, however, bound laborers on three separate estates joined together into a much larger rebellion. Jamaica's governor Henry Moore delayed calling the assembly, but, by that autumn, the government conscripted a party of free black and mixed-race troops to join white soldiers and Maroons fighting the rebels. Some landowners and prominent whites, including John Morse, fled to safer pastures. Those who stayed witnessed remarkable devastation. "The Negroes in severall parishes have in a state of rebellion rose kill'd and Murdered a

58. An anonymous traveler to Jamaica in 1740 remarked only on three generations of African blood in the island's mixed-race population: "There are also Mulattoes and Mustees; the first are from a Negro and white Man; the other is from the second Generation; and the third are called Castees." Those beyond that descent were white; see *Importance of Jamaica to Great-Britain*, 16. Scholars have yet to study how generational determinations were made and how mixed-race individuals must have exploited this decidedly unscientific endeavor.

Number of People and burned and ruined many opulent plantations," Robert Graham announced in June 1760, "I do not find that we shall be soon able to recover our former tranquility." Before the revolt ended, between three and five hundred bound laborers and more than one hundred whites and free people of color had perished, with at least one hundred thousand pounds of property in ruins. For a moment, the insurrections seemed to unify the island's free population as they battled enslaved rebels. Graham added that "every body without distinction has been oblig'd to take up Arms to destroy the Common Enemy." From the perspective of military service, Tacky's Revolt allowed poor black and brown Jamaicans the opportunity to assert loyalty to the ruling class while also distancing themselves further from an enslaved past.[59]

Immediate reactions to the revolt, however, did not bode well for racial toleration. Numerous theories prevailed about the origins of the upheaval. One rumor attributed the start of the conflict to a personal slight: "The Rebellion in Jamaica of 1760, had its rise from a White Servant or Overseer having taken the Wife of one of this [Coromantee] people to his bed." In this retelling, an interracial sexual encounter sparked the revolutionary fire. The prominent Jamaican historian Edward Long, in his 1774 assessment, shared this suspicion. Having lived on the island during the conflagration, he reported that soon after destroying the first plantations, the insurgents "ravished a Mulatto woman, who had been [an] overseer's kept mistress." Such accounts, beyond any potential veracity, indicate that white Jamaicans might have attributed Tacky's Revolt, at least partly, to interracial unions. This version of events helped ignore the inherent violence of the slave system and the most fundamental and obvious motivations for an insurrection. It also tacitly rebuked

59. *JAJ*, May 3, 1759, V, 119, Oct. 2, 1760, 177; Robert Graham to Nicol Graham, June 16, 1760, Acc. 11335/177, NLS, Edinburgh. Like John Morse, James Pinnock's mother took the family to England in 1760, likely as a result of the uprisings; see Diary of James Pinnock of Jamaica, 1758–1810, Add. MS 33316, BL. The most complete near-contemporary account of the revolt comes from [Long], *History of Jamaica*, II, 447–472. For more details on the rebellion, see C. Roy Reynolds, "Tacky and the Great Slave Rebellion of 1760," *Jamaica Journal*, VI, no. 2 (June 1972), 5–8; Craton, *Testing the Chains*, 125–138; Burnard, *Mastery, Tyranny, and Desire*, 151–173; Vincent Brown, *The Reaper's Garden: Death and Power in the World of Atlantic Slavery* (Cambridge, Mass., 2008), 144–156; Claudius Fergus, " 'Dread of Insurrection': Abolitionism, Security, and Labor in Britain's West Indian Colonies, 1760–1823," *WMQ*, 3d Ser., LXVI (2009), 758–762; Bollettino, "Slavery, War, and Britain's Atlantic Empire," esp. 191–256; Diana Paton, "Witchcraft, Poison, Law, and Atlantic Slavery," *WMQ*, 3d Ser., LXIX (2012), 235–264; and Vincent Brown, "Slave Revolt in Jamaica, 1760–61: A Cartographic Narrative," http://revolt.axismaps.com/project.html.

cross-racial pairings for blurring the vital boundary between black and white, slave and free. Long contended that the upheaval's ringleaders belonged to a planter known for "humanity, and excessive indulgence toward his slaves." Tacky's Revolt suggested that Jamaica's recent experiment with racial accommodation might have failed dramatically.[60]

Once again, though, not all interracial relationships, nor individuals of color, were considered equal. In the middle of Tacky's Revolt, the assembly began debating privilege petitions for the first time in four years. John and Dorothy Elletson, who would later submit a petition the day after the assembly resolved to curtail mixed-race inheritances, lodged an earlier privilege bill in the autumn of 1760. The assembly rejected that appeal on October 6, perhaps because Tacky's campaign had not yet concluded. Yet, one month later, it approved the petition supporting Anna Petronella Woodart, a fifteen-year-old "free Mulatto." Born to one of Kingston's most successful merchants, William Foster, Woodart inherited most of her father's estate, though he had also given a large bequest to London's Foundling Hospital to care for orphaned and illegitimate children. Like the Elletsons, Woodart's father had spent a great deal of money "in procuring the most liberal education for her, in Great-Britain"; in fact, Woodart was still living in England at the time. An assemblyman from Saint Thomas in the East, Gilbert Foord, submitted it in her place. As Woodart's friend, Foord's standing in Jamaica undoubtedly secured her appeal. In addition to serving on the assembly, he acted as the island's attorney general, before advancing to Jamaica's council. Woodart's family and personal connections facilitated the passing of her petition in the face of tremendous anxiety about the island's future. Her status as a young woman in Britain also made her far less of a threat to Jamaican politics, even though she would soon return to the island.[61]

60. John Lindsay, "A Few Conjectural Considerations upon the Creation of the Human Race; Occasioned by the Present British Quixottical Rage of Setting the Slaves from Africa at Liberty" [Spanish Town, Jamaica, 1788], Add. MS 12439, fol. 109, BL; [Long], *History of Jamaica*, II, 449, 472. The Reverend John Lindsay made this claim regarding the revolt's origins in an interracial relationship nearly thirty years after the fact, but it likely originated soon after the event. Because Tacky's Revolt occurred during the Seven Years' War, there were heightened fears about slave insurrections in the Atlantic world generally. Authorities in Bermuda, for instance, uncovered the colony's first slave conspiracy of the eighteenth century within a year of the rebellion; see Clarence Maxwell, "Enslaved Merchants, Enslaved Merchant-Mariners, and the Bermuda Conspiracy of 1761," *Early American Studies*, VII (2009), 140–178; and Michael J. Jarvis, *In the Eye of All Trade: Bermuda, Bermudians, and the Maritime Atlantic World, 1680–1783* (Chapel Hill, N.C., 2010), 382.

61. *JAJ*, Sept. 24–Oct. 6, 1760, V, 168–178, Sept. 26, 1760, 170, Oct. 4, 1760, 178–179;

The assembly continued to allow for private exemptions for mixed-race individuals, even as it began considering measures to curb racial accommodation broadly. On November 21, 1761, it passed an act requiring all "free negroes, mulattoes, and Indians" to register themselves, obtain freedom certificates, and wear a badge on their clothing. Although highly demeaning, this bill was perhaps not the most damaging piece of legislation considered that session. That distinction went, instead, to an act proposed three days later that would cap the inheritance of illegitimate mixed-race and black residents. Tacky's Revolt convinced the assembly that Jamaica's slave regime was in trouble. Even though many had helped put down the revolt, economically mobile free people of color appeared to threaten the racial divide that was so critical to keeping captives enslaved. Limiting the amount of money that the group could inherit would cut short its social advancement and retain white control. But, while crafting the bill, members of the assembly still hoped to promote select individuals of color to stay allied with the ruling class. After the inheritance cap's second reading, the assembly heard the privilege petition of John Clifford, who submitted it "in behalf of Eleanor, Mary, Frances, Martha, John, and Thomas Clifford, free mulattoes," born to him by Phoebe Forord. The Cliffords' appeal sped easily through the legislature, even as the assembly put the finishing touches on the law to constrain mixed-race legacies.[62]

The specifics of the 1761 inheritance cap reveal the Jamaican government's attempt, once more, to institute racial subjugation with class exceptions. Its main provision was simple: illegitimate children of whites and nonwhites could inherit only two thousand pounds — a large sum, but relatively modest

---

Betty Wood and Martin Lynn, eds., *Travel, Trade, and Power in the Atlantic, 1765–1884* (New York, 2002), 31n. Woodart was listed as seventeen, "or thereabouts," in her 1762 marriage agreement; see "Marriage Articles between James Williams and Miss Woodart, etc.," Nov. 3, 1762, in Anna Petronella Woodart, "The Vicissitudes of a Mid-18th Century Female Jamaica Slave: From Slavery to Freedom, to Marriage with a White Englishman and Ownership of a Plantation, 1756-1769," no. 7, University of Minnesota Law Library, Minneapolis, Will of William Foster, Apr. 10, 1756, ibid., no. 1-2. Samuel Vaughan described Foster as one of Jamaica's eight most "eminent merchants"; see Vaughan, *A Refutation of a False Aspersion First Thrown Out upon Samuel Vaughan . . .* (London, 1769), 6n.

62. *JAJ*, Nov. 21, 1761, V, 291, Nov. 24-Dec. 7, 1761, 292-315. In later years, the law was sometimes referred to as the "Drummond Act," though it was not given a formal title at the time; see Joan Vacianna, "Some Primary Sources for the Study of Jamaican History: An Introduction to the Microform Collection of the University of the West Indies Library at Mona," in Monteith and Richards, eds., *Jamaica in Slavery and Freedom*, 9; and Vasconcellos, *Slavery, Childhood, and Abolition*, 56.

compared to the substantial sugar fortunes of many planters. In the law's preamble, the assembly explained its motivations:

> Divers large estates, consisting of lands, slaves, cattle, stock, money and
> securities for money, have from time to time been left by white persons
> to mulattoes, and other the offspring of mulattoes, not being their own
> issue born in lawful wedlock . . . [S]uch bequests tend greatly to destroy
> the distinction requisite, and absolutely necessary, to be kept up in this
> island, between white persons and negroes, their issue and offspring,
> and may in progress of time be the means of decreasing the number of
> white inhabitants in this island.

This explanation set forth some of the strongest language in Jamaican law
toward individuals of color at that point. To some degree, it reversed the
spirit of the previous generation of legal policy. Whereas in 1733 the assembly had allowed some mixed-race Jamaicans to become white through biological means and others to become white through economic and cultural
ones, by 1761 a new cohort of lawmakers envisioned a firmer line "absolutely
necessary . . . between white persons and negroes." This was a much stricter
position to take, but it reflected recent developments. In particular, the legislation targeted illegitimate individuals, now increasingly shunned both in law
and cultural discourse. Additionally, the assembly's defense for the measure
revealed an ever-growing obsession with augmenting Jamaica's white population. Yet, the law, like its predecessors, also provided for some exemptions.
In this original version, the bill did not affect those who had received privilege dispensations. Moreover, it provided mixed-race individuals and white
absentees in Britain additional time to file their wills with the island secretary
in order to avoid the act. This was not done simply in fairness so that those in
Britain would have time to respond. Rather, it was a concession to the island's
most elite residents of color who were educated abroad but would soon come
home to join settler society. In many ways, the inheritance cap was the culmination of decades of legislation: concerns over white settlement and family
legitimacy worked against free people of color, while personal connections
and wealth worked on their behalf.[63]

With its attack on illegitimate, nonprivileged children, the inheritance cap
also revealed a new policy against interracial relationships. The law's provi-

63. Jamaica House of Assembly, Laws and Statutes, etc., 2 Geo. III, viii. 1 (1761); William
Pitt Papers, 1761, PRO 30/8/349/1, fol. 165, NAE. The amount is in Jamaican currency: two
thousand pounds current was equivalent to twelve hundred pounds sterling.

sions were harsh but not wholly debilitating; two thousand pounds was a pit-tance compared to the fortunes accumulated by sugar barons, but it could nonetheless sustain one comfortably in Jamaica for a lifetime. Before 1761, this might have also been a customary bequest for offspring of color. Nathaniel Phillips reported the contents of a Jamaican colleague's will to his relatives in Britain the year before, noting that it included a provision worth roughly two thousand pounds to his mistress of color. In 1758, Malcolm Laing complained about his future mistress's inheritance, which exceeded that amount, opining that "Bessey Fickle's Legacy was too large for one of her colour in this Coun-try." The inheritance cap, therefore, might not have substantially altered tra-ditional inheritance patterns after 1761, although it still represented a major policy shift. Limiting the amount that children of color could inherit was an active attempt to deter middling white men from forming filial bonds with off-spring of color. But, by allowing privileged Jamaicans to avoid this cap, the assembly kept affluent familial linkages central to racial conceptions and be-longing. It also ensured that mixed-race elites would need to stay united with the ruling class, both personally and politically, to maintain their status.[64]

The privilege exemption thus indicates that the original 1761 act targeted the interracial unions of middling whites, rather than those of the uppermost ranks. Jamaica's population of color had grown visibly in the mid-eighteenth century, numbering perhaps less than a thousand in 1730 but more than tri-pling in size by 1764. Most of these were the children of nonaffluent, but not destitute, fathers. The majority of Jamaica's white population was not well off. Three-quarters of whites in the bustling parish of Saint Andrew were likely servants in this period. Poor men who fathered mixed-race children had little to give them, save personal affection. The assembly could easily control these offspring, who were either enslaved or deeply impoverished. It could also handle the mixed-race heirs of Jamaica's sugar and merchant barons, who were dependent on the same slave regime as itself. The assembly could not, however, depend on the strength of its authority over the offspring of middling whites who could bequeath significant, but not remarkable, sums

64. Nathaniel Phillips to Esther Gregg, Jan. 11, 1760, Slebech Collection, MS 11485, fols. 3–4, National Library of Wales, Aberystwyth (the amount was twelve hundred pounds sterling, which was equivalent to two thousand pounds Jamaican current); Malcolm Laing to Frances Perrin, Aug. 28, 1758, Fitzherbert Papers, D239 M/E 16586, Derbyshire Record Office, Matlock, England. For Fickle's legacy, see Will of William Perrin, Sept. 24, 1759, ibid., D239 M/E 16374. Kathleen Wilson believes that the inheritance cap shored up distinc-tions that family connections had allowed to become muddied, but the initial exemption for privileged Jamaicans kept such family lines important; see Wilson, *Island Race*, 148.

of money. That subpopulation of color held the dangerous qualities of being both financially prosperous and politically disenfranchised. If its members could continue to accumulate wealth, then they would surely begin protesting loudly. Limiting their bequests would stymie such financial advancement, while simultaneously discouraging middling whites from treating offspring of color as full family members. The inheritance cap did not impose a blanket assault on people of color, nor on interracial relationships generally. Rather, it dug white Jamaicans' heels further into the ground of accommodation through genealogy and individual exemption while imposing stricter laws against those without such connections.[65]

Nevertheless, the law did not come without its detractors. After the assembly passed it, the inheritance cap next went to the Jamaican council for consideration. Three council members voted against it. In protest, they enumerated a number of major reasons why they did not support the bill. First, it violated the fundamental right of free property transmission, which was a cornerstone of English law. Second, it would hamstring the finances of many prominent individuals of color who might either send their money off the island, if not leave Jamaica themselves. Third, it would eradicate the trust that mixed-race Jamaicans would have toward the colonial government. These first three objections were pragmatic considerations of how the inheritance cap might muck up Jamaica's day-to-day business along with the loyalties of its population of color. Unlike their fellow council members, these protestors felt that more harm than good was done when enforcing full racial segregation at the expense of economic and political efficiency. But the councilmen went further. A fourth objection noted that the inheritance cap might precipitate the making of fraudulent ancestry claims, thereby unsettling white identity even further by injecting suspicion into its assertion. A fifth complaint insisted that the bill would allow relatives to cast dubious allegations of African heritage on rival heirs. Here, they were calling into question the assembly's notion of how whiteness might function in the future. Rather than seeing the bill as making white identity more concrete and circumscribed, these councilmen viewed it as eroding the supposed core strength of that biological category. Finally, the bill's opponents insisted that it would diminish the parental affections of fathers to children who were, in many cases, imperceptibly of mixed ancestry. This effectively mocked the idea of zealous racial policing altogether. Jamaica had already become a richly complex, multicolored society. In these

65. See Table 1, above; Trevor Burnard, "Inheritance and Independence: Women's Status in Early Colonial Jamaica," *WMQ*, 3d Ser., XLVIII (1991), 97.

protestors' minds, it could not successfully reverse course toward full apartheid now.[66]

These council members' objections to an inheritance cap for mixed-race offspring found a sympathetic audience in England. The Board of Trade, presently intent on showing greater administrative muscle over the colonies as the Seven Years' War wound down, baulked at Jamaica's new bill. As its main function consisted of reviewing colonial laws to determine if they conformed to metropolitan standards, the Board struggled to understand the legal merit of constraining legacies, even for people of mixed descent. This formed part of an overall disgust toward Jamaica's legislature over several acts passed in 1761. In particular, the Board flatly refused to approve two laws from that session: one licensing the reexportation of captured goods and another prohibiting the importation of foreign sugars into Jamaica. It also asked for an explanation and defense of the inheritance cap. Few could have anticipated the assembly's answer: it responded that the Board's decisions carried no weight and that it would no longer "suffer them in any respect to direct or influence their proceedings." Governor William Lyttleton heard the news with horror and declared that he was "at a loss to conceive, what can have induced the house to break forth into such expressions." These comments, after all, bordered on treason; as members of the king's Privy Council, the Board of Trade spoke on His Majesty's behalf. Perhaps realizing the gravity of its comments, the assembly amended the response, writing, instead, that it was not used to the style and language of the Board's new members. Indeed, four of the previous eight Lords Commissioners had left after Britain's general election in March 1761. Most notably, George Montagu Dunk, the earl of Halifax, who had served as the Board's president for thirteen years, turned over his position. Together with a significant number of first-term representatives elected to Parliament, along with George III's accession the previous year, Jamaica faced a new English government with differing expectations.[67]

66. Lovell Stanhope, "Reasons in Support of the Bill to Restrain Exorbitant Grants to Negroes etc. and Answers to the Protest of Three of the Members of the Council in Jamaica," circa 1763, CO 137/33, fols. 37–41, NAE.

67. *JAJ*, Oct. 6–9, 1762, V, 351–353. For more on this function of reconciling colonial and metropolitan law in the Empire, see Mary Sarah Bilder, *The Transatlantic Constitution: Colonial Legal Culture and the Empire* (Cambridge, Mass., 2004). For more on changes in the Board of Trade during the 1760s, see Arthur Herbert Basye, *The Lords Commissioners of Trade and Plantations: Commonly Known as the Board of Trade, 1748–1782* (New Haven, Conn., 1925), 105–111; Lawrence Henry Gipson, *The British Empire Before the American Revolution: Provincial Characteristics and Sectional Tendencies in the Era pre-*

After composing itself, the assembly responded in a considerably more measured fashion to the Board's questions on the inheritance cap. It formed a committee in November 1762 to "enquire into what exorbitant grants and devises have been made to negroes and mulattoes" so that it could send hard evidence back to London. Once again, though, the assembly began defending racially oppressive legislation at the same time that it also considered exemptions to such strictures. The very day that it formed the committee to investigate mixed-race bequests, it heard the privilege petition of Robert and Lucy Penny, the reputed children of the island's former attorney general. Perhaps the committee members reflected on the Pennys' appeal when walking next door to the assembly's chambers and into the island secretary's office where they perused the colony's repository of probated wills. There the committee found numerous bequests that appeared to conform to the assembly's original suspicions of "exorbitant grants" to those with African ancestry. Rather than enumerate them all, the committee took a selection of thirteen. This small sample of wills contained well over half a million pounds devolving to individuals of color. Such a sum was extraordinary and potentially indicated an apocalyptic scenario in which the island's fortunes transferred entirely to the descendants of slaves. The assembly prepared a report for the Board of Trade using these wills as evidence of the material threat posed by a growing horde of mixed-race residents.[68]

Yet, within the collection of wills held up by the committee were a num-

ceding the American Crisis, I, *Great Britain and Ireland* (Caldwell, Id., 1936); Charles M. Andrews, *The Colonial Period of American History,* IV, *England's Commercial and Colonial Policy* (New Haven, Conn., 1938), 368–421; Metcalf, *Royal Government,* 156–158; J. C. Sainty et al., comp., *Office-Holders in Modern Britain,* III, *Officials of the Boards of Trade, 1660–1870* (London, 1974); Alison G. Olson, "The Board of Trade and London-American Interest Groups in the Eighteenth Century," *Journal of Imperial and Commonwealth History,* VIII, no. 2 (1980), 44–46; and Eliga H. Gould, *The Persistence of Empire: British Political Culture in the Age of the American Revolution* (Chapel Hill, N.C., 2000), 35–71, 106–136. On the dramatic political transformations in the English government after 1761, see Sir Lewis Namier, *The Structure of Politics at the Accession of George III,* 2d ed. ([New York], 1957); and Namier, *England in the Age of the American Revolution,* 2d ed. (New York, 1961), 56–62, 171–230.

68. *JAJ,* Nov. 6, 1762, V, 372. This committee was formed on September 30, in response to a letter from the island's agent to the government in London, Lovell Stanhope. Anticipating a stronger rebuttal from the Board of Trade, Stanhope indicated that the assembly might need to defend its reasoning behind the inheritance cap. The uproar over the Board of Trade's official letter delayed that committee's work, and, when it was ordered to form once more, the committee had more strict instructions; see *JAJ,* Sept. 30, 1762, V, 345. The total cited includes both real and personal property; see *JAJ,* Nov. 16, 1762, V, 376–377.

ber of familiar names. The majority of testators from the assembly's sample stood out in colonial society. They were not distant interracial families marginalized from the planter elite. Rather, the men who drafted these testaments were members of that very elite, and their children of color lived, to a degree, within that world as well. More than a third of this selection of wills included mixed-race families plugged deeply into the leading social networks of Jamaica and Britain. Nearly half of the wills from this sample, moreover, came from families to whom the assembly had granted privileged rights and who were thus exempt from the law. They were not the ultimate targets for disinheritance, and their inclusion in the sample reveals an element of disingenuousness on the part of the colonial government. Members of the assembly who passed the inheritance cap and attempted to defend it to London, therefore, would have been personally familiar with, and accommodating to, these supposed examples of racial degradation.[69]

The assembly's selection of wills chose to highlight, not Jamaica's rising middle class of color, but instead the island's small and extravagantly wealthy mixed-race cohort. Almost half of the wills reported to the Board of Trade included beneficiaries who had spent at least part of their childhood in Britain. Richard Halhead's estate gave large sums to his three children "by Grace Hazell, a free mulatto woman." Before receiving privileged rights, one of the daughters, Elizabeth, had married Thomas Pierce in London. She still lived there by the time the assembly organized its defense of the inheritance cap. The assembly also noted the bequests of William Cunningham the elder in

69. Even the six families of color within the selection of thirteen who did not have privileged status or who traveled to Britain still came from prominent households. Lucius Levermore was a magistrate from Saint Mary. Peter Caillard was a prominent churchwarden in Kingston and had previously served in the assembly on three different occasions. His mistress, Susanna Augier, was an elite woman of color with houses and property in both Spanish Town and Kingston. Thomas Orgill came from a family who dominated the island legislature in the first half of the eighteenth century. He gave a large bequest to Sarah Shreyer, who received privileged rights in 1745. Thomas Golding was most likely the brother of John Golding, the man whose petition to the legislature started the tradition of privilege appeals altogether. Wills from John Patoun, William Williams, Samuel Seagrove, and William Austin did not include bequests to privileged, or British-educated, offspring, but they nevertheless gave large sums to mixed-race children; see *JAJ*, Oct. 10, 1751, IV, 284, Nov. 16, 1762, V, 376, 377; William Beeston to Josiah Heathcote and Peter Caillard, Oct. 13, 1701, as quoted in Frank Cundall, *Historic Jamaica* (London, 1915), 158; W. A. Feurtado, *Official and Other Personages of Jamaica, from 1655 to 1790* (Kingston, Jamaica, 1896), 17, 73; Acts of the Assembly of Jamaica, July 13, 1745, CO 139/16, NAE, Will of William Williams, Sept. 11, 1751, PROB 11/790.

its report to the Board of Trade as an example of exorbitant grants. This was the same William Cunningham who had been a lion of the legislature and over whose British-educated son the assembly had fought fervently with the council in order to allow him the right to sit in the colonial government. Noting Cunningham as an example of Jamaica's wayward society was insincere protest. The assembly granted privilege rights to individuals whom they hoped could form an elite, loyal class of color, not ones by whom they felt threatened. The assembly also included John Elletsons's will in its sample. His two children, born by the free mulatto Jane Harris, had attended English schools and received privilege dispensations on the same day as the inheritance cap's passing.[70]

Like the Elletsons, Anna Petronella Woodart's bequest joined the pile of evidence on mixed-race wealth, despite having just received privileged rights. Woodart had traveled to England for school when assemblyman Foord submitted her privilege petition in the autumn of 1760. Once in the metropole, she effectively utilized her father's business and personal contacts. James Spragg, a London apothecary acting as executor to her father's estate, helped establish Woodart in the capital. Soon afterward, he introduced her to his associates. The seventeen-year-old Woodart took a strong liking to Spragg's business partner James Williams, and the couple married just days before the assembly drew its sample of wills. They soon returned to Jamaica with children in tow, eventually becoming two of the most prominent pen-keepers in the parish of Saint Catherine. Woodart's progression, including her time spent in Britain, was a model for mixed-race Jamaicans. Likewise, her actions represented the ideal path for individuals of color to take in order to join the ranks of white settler society. She was not an exemplar of the eradication of distinctions "absolutely necessary, to be kept up in this island, between white persons and negroes," proclaimed by the inheritance cap's preamble. Rather, she embodied the successful transition into whiteness for which so many officials strived over a generation's worth of lawmaking.[71]

70. *JAJ*, May 15, 1746, IV, 54–55, Nov. 16, 1762, V, 377; *Public Advertiser* (London), Mar. 19, 1761; Acts of the Assembly of Jamaica, Apr. 14, 1739, CO 139/15, NAE.

71. *Gazetteer and New Daily Advertiser* (London), Feb. 6, 1768; "Marriage Articles between James Williams and Miss Woodart, etc.," Nov. 3, 1762, in "The Vicissitudes," no. 7, "Grant of Rent Charge," Nov. 5, 1762, ibid., no. 8, "Copy Letter of Attorney," Nov. 23, 1763, ibid, no. 10; Sheena Boa, "Free Black and Coloured Women in a White Man's Slave Society, 1760–1834" (M.Phil thesis, University of the West Indies, Mona, 1985), 64–69; Shepherd, *Livestock, Sugar, and Slavery,* 85. Originally, Foord hired Jonathan Rayner to lobby the Board of Trade to confirm Woodart's privilege bill, which included paying the Board's law-

Similarly, the final will in the assembly's sample came from a mixed-race family raised in metropolitan refinement. Gibson Dalzell had served many functions in Jamaica before drafting his will. He had sat as the island's provost marshall, took control over sequestering land on which to build hospitals, and worked as an agent for the South Sea Company. After returning to Britain in 1746, he served as director of the Sun Fire Office insurance company in London, where his father, the highly decorated general Robert Dalzell, had acted as treasurer. Officials on both sides of the Atlantic would have known Gibson. Those in Jamaica certainly recognized his mixed-race companion, Susanna Augier, who had also been the mistress of Peter Caillard, whose will also joined the sample. Moreover, Augier's niece Elizabeth was the companion of John Morse. Webs of interracial connections in the Americas were complex and intertwined. Metropolitan authorities were most likely also familiar with Dalzell and Augier's two children, Robert and Frances, who both settled in Britain, initially living with their father on Clifford Street in London. After attending Westminster School, Robert inherited his grandfather's Berkshire estate and served as an officer in the local militia there. One month after the assembly fingered his legacy as exorbitant, Robert married Jane Dodd, daughter of a member of Parliament. Frances did even better. In 1757, she married George Duff, son of William Duff, the earl of Fife, and had at least two children by him, James and George, before the assembly defended its inheritance cap. Thus, although considered a mulatto in Jamaican law, Frances Dalzell married into Scottish nobility and raised a family effectively disconnected from Caribbean roots. Together, Robert and Frances thrived as wealthy Britons living off the revenues of enslaved labor, not embittered colonists in Jamaica waiting to use their financial power to overturn the colonial system. They posed no threat to colonial society, and the assembly plainly understood that.[72]

---

yer, Matthew Lamb, for a report supporting her petition; see Will of William Foster, Apr. 10, 1756, in "The Vicissitudes," and "Attorney's Fee Bill," September 1762, no. 6.

72. *JAJ,* Apr. 23, 1740, III, 516, Apr. 2, 1747, IV, 64; Will of Gibson Dalzell, July 2, 1756, PROB 11/823, NAE, Will of Robert Dalzell, Oct. 19, 1758, PROB 11/840; *London Evening-Post,* Dec. 18–21, 1762; P. H. Ditchfield and William Page, eds., *A History of the County of Berkshire,* III (1923), 433–437; *London Evening-Post,* Apr., 21–23, 1757; *JAJ,* Nov. 13, 1801, X, 605–606; Burnard, "Passengers Only," *Atlantic Studies,* I (2004), 186; *Oxford Dictionary of National Biography,* online ed., s.v. "Dalzell, Robert (1661/2–1758)," by H. M. Chichester, rev. Jonathan Spain, http://www.oxforddnb.com/view/article/7082; *The Court and City Register; For the Year 1753 . . .* (London, [1753]), 211. Susanna Augier received a privilege bill for herself and her children, including her daughter Mary; see Acts of the Assembly

Was this sample of wills clear evidence, then, of a world turned upside down, at least in the eyes of assembly members? Considering the substantial overlap between the testators and the island elite, it is hard to imagine that the assembly registered any surprise at the bequests it found. Even more, colonial legislators knew these mixed-race households well and interacted with them regularly. They also failed to mention to London officials that many of the beneficiaries they cited now lived in Britain and were consequently unable to challenge Jamaica's racial hierarchy. Moreover, a near majority of the mixed-race children in the sample—those who received privilege rights—would have been exempt from the original 1761 law anyhow. The assembly, therefore, did not support the inheritance cap with an authentic investigation into unseemly estate dispensations. Rather, it ginned up its report to the Board of Trade with individuals many of its members had personally advanced and knew well. Additionally, these were highly successful and experienced migrants of color, raised in both British and Jamaican society. They were the very islanders of color the assembly hoped might augment the colony's feeble settler core. Such an evidentiary justification for the inheritance cap, therefore, reeked of pretense. The assembly hid that these beneficiaries, who numbered in the dozens, were not the ultimate targets of its inheritance restriction; the real target was the mixed-race middle class, made up of as many as one to two thousand members. These selected wills allowed the assembly to defend a draconian law against rising and middling Jamaicans of color by highlighting instead the most refined and wealthy of the island's mixed-race population.[73]

----

of Jamaica, July 19, 1738, Apr. 22, 1741, CO 139/15, NAE. Susanna's sister Mary applied for privilege rights for her daughters, including Elizabeth; see *JAJ*, May 28, 1747, IV, 66. Elizabeth is listed as the mother to John Morse's children in a Chancery suit against his estate; see Morse v. Royal, Apr. 12, 1792, Jamaica Chancery Court Records, 1A/3/154, no. 132, fol. 402, JA. For more on connections between interracial families, see Philip D. Morgan, "Interracial Sex in the Chesapeake and the British Atlantic World, c. 1700–1820" in Jan Ellen Lewis and Peter S. Onuf, eds., *Sally Hemings and Thomas Jefferson: History, Memory, and Civic Culture* (Charlottesville, Va., 1999), 104; and Thomas E. Buckley, S. J., "Unfixing Race: Class, Power, and Identity in an Interracial Family," *Virginia Magazine of History and Biography*, CII (1994), 349–380. Perhaps the most well-known example of the complexities of racial mixture and interconnected families is that of Thomas Jefferson, whose mixed-race lover was also his wife's half-sister; see Annette Gordon-Reed, *The Hemingses of Monticello: An American Family* (New York, 2008); and Rothman, *Notorious in the Neighborhood*, 14–52.

73. This is a very crude estimate of Jamaica's mixed-race middle class. There were roughly three thousand free people of color in 1761. If, as Trevor Burnard notes, about one-quarter of whites were above the servant and working classes in this period, then perhaps seven hundred to one thousand free mixed-race children in the period were born to rising, if not afflu-

The Board of Trade was likely unaware of the assembly's subterfuge, but it nevertheless scrutinized the inheritance cap for legal soundness. Now headed by William Petty, the earl of Shelburne, the Board had its resident lawyer, Matthew Lamb of Lincoln's Inn, read the bill. Lamb admitted his surprise that Jamaica's assembly had passed it without first consulting London. Beyond its racial implications, as a restriction on legacy bequests it violated the sacred rights of property central to English law. He implored the Board to discover what "inconveniencies" the assembly meant to remedy by imposing such unprecedented legislation, "for nothing else can Justify such an Act which takes away the Right of Persons in Giving and Disposing of their own Estates." A number of Jamaican absentees also petitioned the Board to overturn the law owing to this apparent legal violation. Many of them might have been motivated by mixed-race children living with them in Britain, now under financial threat by the colonial legislature. Appealing to the Board's sympathy, perhaps these absentees also knew some of the members' biographies: Soame Jenyns had married an illegitimate heiress, and Edward Craggs-Eliot's mother was also illegitimate.[74]

With Lamb's opinion in hand, the Board agreed to launch an inquiry, as "it appear[s] that this Act might materially affect those gentlemen who have property in this island." It sent letters to Jamaican absentees Rose Fuller and William Beckford to solicit opinions on the inheritance restriction. Beckford had defeated the 1753 parliamentary bill to encourage Jamaican settlers and now served as lord mayor of London. The Board asked him to record the attitudes of his Jamaican friends also. Fuller, one of the wealthiest Jamaicans in England, invited a number of absentees to his London home. Fuller wrote back to the Board of Trade that those in attendance "were unanimous in opinion for the Act," and he noted that Beckford had communicated his own approval for the bill though "he thought it unnecessary." Yet, this did not satisfy

_____

ent, white parents. But, considering that manumitted children naturally came from wealthier families in the first place, that number should be adjusted upward; see Table 1, above; and Burnard, "Inheritance and Independence," *WMQ*, 3d Ser., XLVIII (1991), 97.

74. Matthew Lamb to the Lords Commissioners for Trade and Plantations, Nov. 8, 1762, CO 137/33, fols. 17–18, NAE; *Oxford Dictionary of National Biography*, online ed., s.v. "Jenyns, Soame (1704–1787)," by Ronald Rompkey, http://www.oxforddnb.com/view/article/14766. Craggs-Eliot was also close friends with Philip Stanhope, an illegitimate cousin of Lovell Stanhope; see ibid., s.v. "Eliot, Edward Craggs-, first Baron Eliot (1727–1804)," by E. A. Smith, http://www.oxforddnb.com/view/article/8627. However, Lord Hardwicke's son, John Yorke, also sat on the Board of Trade at this time and might have been inclined toward the inheritance cap's restrictions on illegitimate children.

the Board fully, as many of London's absentee planters had been members of the assembly themselves and stayed loyal to that body. Instead, the Board asked Lovell Stanhope, Jamaica's colonial agent to the English government, to send the specific protests lodged by the three colonial council members who voted against the act and to answer each of those objections. The Board hoped to understand Jamaica's diverse opinions toward mixed-race individuals before ruling on the inheritance cap.[75]

Stanhope responded to the Board in a long letter. He prefaced his remarks, though, with an extensive statement on the general condition of Jamaican society. This introduction struck the normal chords of white settler failure and degradation: blacks severely outnumbered whites; the white population continually decreased; the island did not contain enough European women; "Mulattoes, especially the females," controlled the colonists' "dissolute Minds"; and so forth. Here, even at the behest of Jamaican officials, Stanhope painted a conventional and hyperbolic portrait of debauched white Caribbean society—one familiar to most Britons. Although Jamaicans had been tasked with "prevent[ing] their posterity from being overpowered by Mulattoes," Stanhope declared the mission abandoned. Few could imagine, he theatrically grumbled, "that their Successors would ever degenerate so as to devise their Estates to a spurious Progeny." English officials' recent obsession with clandestine marriages and fecund households surely would have responded powerfully to Stanhope's added claim that the "disinheri[tance] of lawful Heirs," in favor of mulatto offspring, caused "the Destruction of Families." Furthermore, in failing to check the legacies of illegitimate children of color, Jamaica would soon "become a Colony of Negroes and Mulattoes" if the inheritance cap was not upheld. Anticipating, if not inspiring, future comments by Jamaicans such as Long, Stanhope continued:

> All distinction of Colour will at least be leveled, and the Inhabitants of Jamaica, like their Neighbours the American Spaniards, will, too probably, become one day a People without Spirit, Religion, or Morality; for it is undoubtedly to the false policy of the Spanish Laws in America (which destroy all distinction of colour) that those unhappy People are

75. *JBT*, May 6, May 18, 1763, XI, 359–368; Board of Trade to William Beckford, May 7, 1763, CO 138/22, fols. 264–265, NAE, Board of Trade to Lovell Stanhope, May 18, 1763, CO 138/22, fol. 271. Those in attendance at the meeting in Fuller's home included some of the island's most notable residents; see John Morant, Florentius Vassall, and John and Richard Pennant Rose Fuller to John Pownall, May 11, 1763, CO 137/33, fol. 24, NAE; *JBT*, May 18, 1763, XI, 359–368.

now notoriously become the most degenerate and dastardly people upon Earth.

This diatribe encapsulated the worst nightmares of metropolitan officials monitoring American policy. In the wake of the Seven Years' War, any similarities between English and Spanish colonization naturally made British authorities uncomfortable. For Stanhope, portraying British colonial subjects as degenerating racially to the level of Spanish Americans was a safe and effective rhetorical maneuver to defend the strictness of the inheritance cap.[76]

Addressing the dissenting council members' specific complaints, Stanhope responded to their query about whether the bill violated English property rights. British subjects, he contended, did not have license to dispose of estates to the detriment of society at large; granting large bequests to illegitimate children, he contended, eroded the social fabric. Because Jamaicans had been "so degenerate as to give or devise their real or personal property to Savages [and] their Bastard progeny," they needed legal intervention. Otherwise, they would have advanced illegitimate offspring in opposition to the customary restrictions against bastardy in Britain. This reasoning, however, went against English legal protections for testators. The dissenting councilmen had originally pointed to England's 1540 Statute of Wills, which allowed freehold land to be devised to anyone. Furthermore, by 1692, illegitimate children in England held full claim to recorded legacies, although they still possessed no legal recourse when fathers died intestate. Stanhope countered that fundamental differences existed between England and Jamaica, necessitating alternative laws. Ultimately, those distinctions boiled down to the presence of slavery and the "distinction of Colour" that remained unknown in the metropole.[77]

---

76. Stanhope, "Reasons in Support," circa 1763, fols. 34–36. This was also a period of growing tension over nonwhite individuals in the Empire. Linda Colley believes that British and colonial attitudes toward native Americans turned increasingly hostile after the Seven Years' War; see Colley, *Captives: Britain, Empire, and the World, 1600–1850* (New York, 2004), 170–202. See also Peter Silver, *Our Savage Neighbors: How Indian War Transformed Early America* (New York, 2008), esp. 94–124.

77. Stanhope, "Reasons in Support,"circa 1763, fols. 37–38; John Addy, *Death, Money, and the Vultures: Inheritance and Avarice, 1660–1750* (New York, 1992), 8–12. This differed from Luso-Brazilian law, in which ab intestato cases allowed for illegitimate children to make claims on an estate; see Lewin, *Surprise Heirs*, I, 19–41. Stanhope was no stranger to the law, nor to the inner workings of the government's foreign affairs. The year that the assembly passed the inheritance cap, he acted as a law clerk to offices of the secretaries of state, a position he held until 1774 when elected to Parliament for Winchester; see *London Magazine,*

Contrasting colonial and metropolitan law put Stanhope squarely in the middle of emerging debates about the structure and regulation of European empires. Jenyns, a prominent member of the Board in 1762 and friend of Lord Hardwicke, certainly believed that some degree of legal equivalence needed to operate on both sides of the Atlantic, though he supported a strong and leading imperial center. North America's reluctance to abide by the Revenue Acts of the 1760s reflected this tension. For Stanhope, English officials certainly had the right to regulate colonial legislation, but he insisted that they did not properly understand Jamaica's differing racial climate. In his mind, this area of law was best left to the colonists.[78]

The Board's next set of questions, through the council's dissent, focused on the inheritance cap's economic impact on all segments of mixed-race so-

---

XXX (1761), 166; *The State of the Nation, with Respect to Its Public Funded Debt, Revenue, and Disbursement . . . ,* II (London, 1798), 179; Lillian M. Penson, *The Colonial Agents of the British West Indies: A Study in Colonial Administration, Mainly in the Eighteenth Century* (London, 1971), 168–172. Stanhope was also close friends with Lord Halifax, who had recently vacated his long-held seat on the Board of Trade; see *Political Register and Impartial Review* (London), IX (July–December 1771), 232.

78. Eliga H. Gould, "Zones of Law, Zones of Violence: The Legal Geography of the British Atlantic, circa 1772," *WMQ,* 3d Ser., LX (2003), 471–510; Lauren Benton and Lisa Ford, "Magistrates in Empire: Convicts, Slaves, and the Remaking of the Plural Legal Order in the British Empire," in Benton and Richard J. Ross, eds., *Legal Pluralism and Empires, 1500–1850* (New York, 2013), 173–197. In later decades, both pro- and antislavery activists latched onto the debate about legal pluralism in Britain's empire; see Christopher Leslie Brown, *Moral Capital: Foundations of British Abolitionism* (Chapel Hill, N.C., 2006), esp. 209–258. In the French Atlantic, the fallout of the Seven Years' War precipitated a similar attempt at imperial homogenization. Beginning in 1762, French officials started monitoring all "negroes and mulattoes" who arrived in France, as Saint Domingue simultaneously tightened its laws against free people of color; see Sue Peabody, *"There Are No Slaves in France": The Political Culture of Race and Slavery in the Ancien Régime* (New York, 1996), 74–105. Malick W. Ghachem argues that legal debates on slavery were a way for France to impose control over its colonies; see Ghachem, *Old Regime and the Haitian Revolution,* 30, 51–67; and Garrigus, *Before Haiti.* On the Board of Trade's anger at North America's acceptance of the Revenue Acts, see Soame Jenyns, *The Objections to the Taxation of Our American Colonies . . .* (1765), in Charles Nalson Cole, ed., *The Works of Soame Jenyns . . . ,* I (Dublin, 1791), 331–341; *Oxford Dictionary of National Biography,* online ed., s.v. "Jenyns, Soame (1704–1787)," by Rompkey; P. J. Marshall, "Britain and the World in the Eighteenth Century: II, Britons and Americans," Royal Historical Society, *Transactions,* 6th Ser., IX (1999), 1–16. For the Bahamas, in contrast, the Colonial Office essentially dictated the islands' racial policies, although this occurred in the wake of the American Revolution and British attempts to rein in the Empire; see Whittington B. Johnson, *Race Relations in the Bahamas, 1784–1834: The Nonviolent Transformation from a Slave to a Free Society* (Fayetteville, Ark., 2000).

ciety. Stanhope contended that the act only targeted "higher class" mulattoes and not the majority of Jamaica's population of color. It was essential, he argued "to prevent the illegitimate Issue of Slaves attaining a Superiority in Rank, Riches, and, in the Consequence, Power, over free Men and their unmixed Descendants." This was the assembly's rationale behind the act, but Stanhope omitted that the highest class of mixed-race Jamaicans—the richest who held privilege dispensations—would not suffer the law's constraints. Middling freemen, instead, fell most victim to the bill's provisions. Stanhope admitted that of the Jamaicans who took to the streets to protest the inheritance cap, "very few [were] of any considerable fortune" and thus not those of the highest mixed-race status. As a group, rising freemen of color were growing at a quick pace and were slowly accumulating significant amounts of money. Many stood to inherit more than two thousand pounds, which could have helped them establish small plantations from which to build bigger fortunes. The group had also lost a number of its civil rights as the eighteenth century progressed. Financial power and political disenfranchisement were a dangerous pair, and the inheritance cap sought to eliminate the former while also keeping most mixed-race Jamaicans out of the plantocracy.[79]

Stanhope continually used hyperbole and fearmongering in his defense of the act. He grounded his diatribe in previous discussions of legitimacy and the importance of formal family units in the Caribbean. Although he claimed that Jamaicans had abandoned the mission of white settlement, Stanhope nevertheless insisted that the inheritance cap might rejuvenate the failing project:

> It cannot be a Question, whether it would be better that the landed and other real property, should be in the hands of a spurious and illegitimate breed of mulattoes, to the Encouragement of fornication and concubinage, or to encourage the legal propagation of Children by Marriage, and by that means to transmit property and power to a pure and legitimate race.

Stanhope's rebuke of mixed-race individuals was surprisingly strong for the 1760s, although visitors to Jamaica occasionally employed similar vitriol. James Houstoun, for example, railed against a large fortune left more than a decade earlier to mixed-race "Vermin, whilst . . . Brothers and poor Relations were starving for Want." Such condemnation of those with African blood was typically used much later in the eighteenth century. To defend a racialized piece of legislation, though, Stanhope had to employ highly racialized lan-

79. Stanhope, "Reasons in Support," circa 1763, fols. 36–42.

guage, even if his rhetoric was overblown and insincere. His apology for the bill highlighted the Empire's concurrent anxieties over marriage, illegitimacy, settler society, and racial distinction.[80]

In his final set of arguments against the dissenting council members, Stanhope countered a rather sophisticated comprehension of mixed-race experience in the Empire. The councilmen's protest anticipated that the inheritance cap might open up numerous new possibilities for inheritance litigation. Lawsuits surrounding bequests were common in the eighteenth century, including those with mixed-race heirs. Between 1758 and 1761, for instance, Katharine Campbell fought two different sets of relatives over a colonial legacy. Born to a white father and "free mulatto" mother in Jamaica, she inherited more than thirty thousand pounds before resettling in Britain. Both her paternal relations and her Scottish husband's family, however, successfully pried away that bequest. The council assumed that the inheritance cap would facilitate similar cases, particularly because anyone could file suits in Chancery "upon a bare Suggestion that [an] Ancestor or Relation had given real or personal Estates above the Sum limited to such [a] Negro or Mulatto." Implicit in this critique was a concern that functionally white individuals could have legacies stolen away on the revelation of a hidden forebear of color. Such a possibility suggested a dizzying scenario of social chaos in which colonial estates remained perpetually vulnerable to legal attack and in which white settlers could have racial designations challenged at any time. Put simply, the inheritance cap not only threatened Jamaicans of color, the council members believed, but those of supposedly pure European ancestry as well.[81]

This worry over the legacies and statuses of mixed-race people was not only a Jamaican issue. One of the council members' longest objections addressed the migration of mixed-race colonists to Britain and the often ridiculous distinctions between white and nonwhite. They pointed to those only three generations removed from an African, rather than the requisite four required for legal whiteness. These individuals were nevertheless "seven Eights White, and not distinguishable from White Persons." What good was a color

80. Ibid., fols. 39–42; [Houstoun], *Dr. Houstoun's Memoirs,* 293.

81. "Representation for John McLauchlan of Greenhall" Jun. 15, 1761, Maclean-Clephane of Torloisk and Carslogie Private Papers, Bundle 380, NRAS 3283, Newby Hall, Ripon, England, NRAS (My thanks to Mr. Compton Maclean for permission to read his family papers); Stanhope, "Reasons in Support," circa 1763, fols. 38–39. This concern over white legacies coming under question because of a black ancestor became a common theme in antebellum American literature; see Jules Zanger, "The 'Tragic Octoroon' in Pre-Civil War Fiction," *American Quarterly,* XVIII (1966), 63–70.

barrier if one's color could not be visibly determined? More importantly, some of these "indistinguishable" whites retained all the trappings of refined British subjects. Many of them had been "educated in Great Britain, in the most liberal manner." This was not mere speculation, but rather a commonly understood experience:

> It consists with our knowledge that many such Persons have been so educated and brought up, and others are now in Great Britain receiving such Education; and tho' there are some Instances of Laws to oblige Persons to provide for their Children, We never yet heard of any Law to hinder them from doing so, or to restrain their Liberality in making such provision.

How could such refined individuals, raised and educated primarily in Britain, have their rights and inheritance put into question? The Board of Trade, in considering these protests from the council, likely knew many such individuals. It might have also reflected back on the five wills within the assembly's sample of thirteen that included bequests to British-educated Jamaicans of color. Indeed, the Board of Trade's reluctance to pass the inheritance cap likely came from such a firm understanding of Jamaica's racial complexity, especially as it extended to and influenced the metropole. Stanhope was, by no means, helpful in supporting the assembly on these points. His responses to these particular questions were terse: lawsuits would come about regardless of the act, and racial lines had to be drawn somewhere.[82]

Ultimately, Stanhope's defense won out, but not immediately. The Board of Trade remained unconvinced by his argument, but it did not overturn the law. Instead, it demurred granting its assent, and the inheritance cap fell into legal limbo over the next few years. This created confusion for everyone in Jamaica. As late as 1768, after William Patrick Browne submitted a petition to exempt his children of color from the inheritance cap, the assembly admitted that the law was still "depending before his majesty, for his royal confirmation." By the next year, though, it seems to have received the king's blessing. Zachary Bayly hinted that the "Mulatto Bill" had finally been confirmed in a January 1769 letter supporting Browne's petition to the Board of Trade, although he did not explain how the law made it through. Additionally, on a stop in Jamaica sometime around 1769, J. Hector St. John de Crèvecoeur noted that certain island children were now officially "stripped of their Inheritance." British officials, currently struggling to maintain the loyalty of its North American

82. Stanhope, "Reasons in Support," circa 1763, fol. 40.

colonies, likely conceded this piece of legislation to appease its most lucrative imperial outpost.[83]

By the time the inheritance cap finally entered the law books, the statute received some small, but substantial changes. Most important, the act no longer exempted privileged Jamaicans from its provisions. On its surface, this was a significant departure from previous laws against individuals of color. Class exceptions were always part of racial legislation in Jamaica, and, without a concession for holders of privilege bills, the assembly broke with tradition. It is difficult to determine why the change was made. The assembly's records do not list any debates on the matter. There was some turnover in membership during this period, though: between 1762 and 1768, nineteen assemblymen vacated their seats. This was a noteworthy, but not unusual, change in composition, and the new members might have been more eager than their predecessors to clamp down on Jamaica's population of color, perhaps as a result of having witnessed yet another insurrection. In November 1765, an enslaved man named Blackwell, who was thought to have taken part in Tacky's Revolt, led an uprising that killed two men on the Ballard Valley plantation in Saint Mary. The uprising failed, but, within a month, rumors circulated about similar plots throughout the area. These events possibly inspired the legislature to return to the specifics of the inheritance cap in order to make it a stronger attack on individuals of color. Or, the experience of defending the inheritance cap against the Board might have emboldened the assembly to act more universally. In 1766, members were still complaining about their fight with London and the "aspersions and reproach which were undeservedly thrown upon them by the then board of trade." If the Board had, in their estimation, improperly questioned the island's racial policy, then perhaps the assembly needed to take a more radical stance.[84]

Regardless, even though the "Mulatto Bill" no longer accommodated those

83. *JAJ*, Dec. 16, 1768, VI, 152; Zachary Bayly to Josiah Sharp, Jan. 25, 1769, MS 525, NLJ; [J. Hector St. John de] Crèvecoeur, "Sketches of Jamaica and Bermudas and Other Subjects," in Dennis D. Moore, ed., *More Letters from the American Farmer: An Edition of the Essays in English Left Unpublished by Crèvecoeur* (Athens, Ga., 1995), 108. The assembly fired Stanhope within weeks of this exchange for "disobeying the orders of the committee of correspondence," which might have originated from failure to achieve a quick verdict; see *JAJ*, Nov. 24, 1763, V, 425. The council, however, did not want to replace Stanhope as agent; see *JAJ*, Dec. 9, 1763, V, 435. Ragatz dates the passage of the inheritance cap at 1768, perhaps because it did not receive royal approval until then; see Ragatz, *Fall of the Planter Class*, 34.

84. *JAJ*, July 12, 1766, V, 556, Aug. 5, 1766, 591–596, Aug. 12, 1766, 609. For the membership changes, see *JAJ*, Appendix, V, 5–6, Appendix, VI, 5–6.

with privileged rights, the assembly nevertheless still made exceptions. Soon after its passage, mixed-race elites petitioned, and won, exclusions from the inheritance cap. Over the next thirty years, the assembly considered twenty petitions to skirt the cap, passing all but one. Although this was but a token number of individuals, these exemptions demonstrate the durability of personal connections to colonial empowerment, even in the face of increasingly restrictive legislation. More significantly, the inheritance cap energized an expanding population of color eager to apply for privileges. Five times the number of mixed-race individuals received privileged rights in the forty years after the 1761 decree passed as those from the previous three decades. Moreover, while only nine privilege petitioners before 1761 noted that they had spent time in Britain, sixty-five recorded such a journey after that date. Most likely, the increasing restrictions against individuals of color in Jamaica prompted many to leave. Still, members of the assembly, ostensibly worried about the advancement of nonwhites in colonial society, nevertheless continued to allow personal and familial connections to moderate strong attitudes. Although Jamaica's door of accommodation allowing certain individuals of color to pass into white society closed considerably in the middle decades of the eighteenth century, that door did not shut completely. The strict and severe attitudes toward race expressed in the inheritance cap masked much looser and more interesting family dynamics.[85]

Conclusion

Facing a complex, multiethnic society, Jamaican legislators constructed an equally complex set of laws to control its growing free population of color. For the first half of the eighteenth century, this meant the erosion of political rights for the vast majority of the group. But the assembly selected an elite few who might join and augment a failing white settler society. None of these laws did anything to deter interracial unions on the island. For Hercules Ross, who landed in Jamaica from Scotland in 1761, legal strictures took a backseat to companionship. Although he arrived on the island the very year that the inheritance cap passed, he nevertheless had children with a woman of color, Elizabeth Foord. Like many before him, Ross would eventually travel with his mixed-race offspring back to Britain. Countless others took mistresses of

85. This increase in numbers might have been owing to greater numbers of migrants, or to a growing legislative preference for those who noted their experiences in Britain. In addition, Julie Flavell notes that American travel to Britain in general took off after 1763; see Flavell, *When London Was Capital of America*, 4–9, 67–84.

color without considering the legal consequences of their relationships. Even the assembly members' own sexual interests belied their ideological commitment to racial apartheid. Interracial relationships continued, and Jamaica's racial spectrum grew even wider.[86]

Nevertheless, the island's 1761 inheritance cap constituted a major shift in policy toward those with African heritage. It put a significant kink in the flow of wealth from affluent whites to offspring of color, limiting financial freedom to only a handful of elites. In a way, this worked against the previous generation's strategy to incorporate a select, but not insignificant, number of mixed-race colonists fully into white settler society. A midcentury flourish in marriage reform, along with decades of slave rebellion culminating in Tacky's Revolt, convinced colonial legislators of the need to impose greater barriers between black and white. Whereas class and family distinctions had long allowed certain mixed-race Jamaicans to avoid many legal penalties, their social power was beginning to wain in the face of so many other pressures. Only the most elite of the island's wealthy population of color — increasingly those raised partly in Britain — were still accorded social exemptions. Although the island continued to honor its generational removal allowance, in the eyes of the law at least, the vast majority of mixed-race Jamaicans were no longer seen as the hope for a robust, future white population.

This debate did not take place solely on the island, nor did it include only Jamaicans of color confined within its shores. Rather, dynamic questions of family, legitimacy, and race in both Britain and its colonies helped to shape broader Atlantic attitudes. Moreover, when developing their stances toward individuals of color, officials on both sides of the Atlantic used those who traveled to Britain as evidence to support their claims for either restriction or encouragement. The assembly cited five mixed-race families who migrated to Britain, for example, to prove the disorder of Jamaican inheritance dispensations. The Board of Trade, in response, considered British-educated Jamaicans of color as well, although as a counter argument that accommodation worked.

At the individual level, then, governmental bodies on both sides of the Atlantic tolerated elites of color. But the space of toleration in which they

---

86. Elizabeth Foord was potentially the daughter of Anna Petronella Woodart's "next Friend" Gilbert Foord; see Alexander M. Ross, *History of the Clan Ross with Genealogies of the Various Families* (Morgantown, W.Va., 1983), 106; Agnes M. Butterfield, "Hercules Ross of Kingston, Jamaica, and Rossie, Forfar, 1745–1816" (unpublished manuscript, 1982), 94–128. Many thanks to Mr. J. H. St J. McIlwaine for allowing me to read a copy of his aunt's manuscript.

operated was dwindling rapidly. As whites struggled to define the meaning of family in the Empire, the inheritance cap struck a major blow to relatively fluid notions of inheritance and kinship. Furthermore, it helped to structure the debate over the place of African heritage in the Empire when abolitionism took off a generation later. Although abolitionists would embrace Africans within the wider family of man, they would not tolerate them within the family of blood relation. The second half of the eighteenth century, therefore, reverberated with the tones of rhetoric struck in the debate over the inheritance cap. Yet, despite this amplified volume in public discourse, at the level of private interaction such invective was significantly muted. A small group of white Jamaicans continued to form and care for colonial families. Many of those also sent children of color across the ocean, and British relatives accepted them accordingly into their homes.

CHAPTER 2

※❀※

EARLY ABOLITIONISM AND MIXED-RACE
MIGRATION INTO BRITAIN,
1762–1778

At a Kingston debating society in 1774, Hercules Ross stood across the aisle from Thomas Hibbert. Under consideration was "whether the trade to Africa for Slaves was consistent with sound policy, the laws of nature, and morality." This topic came out of the Jamaican assembly's investigation the previous December into the extreme numerical disproportion between enslaved and free and how such imbalance threatened island security. Although he had arrived in Jamaica more than a decade earlier, Ross had thus far failed to distinguish himself and perhaps sheepishly presented his case to the club. A modest tradesman, he dealt in general stores and prize goods, rather than human cargo. Having frequently witnessed captive Africans beaten on Kingston's docks, though, he had come to view the slave trade as an affront to God's will, even if it fueled the island's economy. Hibbert and his supporters disagreed. After making a fortune importing Africans, Hibbert had earned a reputation as the best slave trader of his generation, and he loomed large in Jamaica's meager white community. "God had formed some of the human race, inferior to others," his faction responded, and "negroes appeared to have been intended for slaves." Despite these ideological differences, both men shared similar attitudes toward families of color. Hibbert had sent his two daughters of color, Jane and Margaret, to England four years earlier. Ross had not yet fathered all of his six mixed-race children, but they would join him on his eventual return to Scotland.[1]

1. *JAJ*, Dec. 18, 1773, VI, 486; *Abridgment of the Minutes of the Evidence, Taken Before a Committee of the Whole House, to Whom It Was Referred to Consider of the Slave-Trade, 1791* ([London, 1791]), 145–146; "Minutes of the Evidence Taken Before a Committee of the House of Commons . . . ," Apr. 18, 1791, no. 4281, in *HCSP*, LXXXII, 262–263. The exact date of the debating society's meeting is uncertain. The sole record of this event comes from Ross's testimony to the House of Commons in 1791, in which he noted that the debate had occurred "seventeen years ago" (ibid., 263). See also Vincent Brown, *The Reaper's Garden: Death and Power in the World of Atlantic Slavery* (Cambridge, Mass., 2008), 189. The debate might have occurred at a Masonic meeting, although the connection is not clear. Jamaica had

Jamaican slave merchants had little to fear from Hibbert and Ross's debate. Planter brutality and the disease-ridden environment cut short so many enslaved workers' lives that a steady stream of African captives was necessary to keep sugar estates running. But colonial officials recognized, more than a decade before abolitionism became a popular Atlantic phenomenon, that the slave trade brought with it a number of risks. Namely, the thousands of Africans who arrived each year added further to the island's black majority and escalated the chance for rebellion. Virginians came to the same conclusion in 1772 and attempted to abolish their own slave trade. The seeds of abolition were planted by slaveowners themselves, whose obsession with colonial demography and security produced the terms by which reformers would later attack the Middle Passage. Details of the private Kingston debate came to light when Ross testified about it to Parliament during deliberations over the abolition question.[2]

Concerns over the slave trade were not simply colonial in origin. Britons worried about the effects of slavery on the domestic front as well. Two years before Ross and Hibbert's debate, England's chief jurist determined that enslaved individuals in the metropole could not be forced against their will back to the colonies. Proslavery supporters railed against the decision, insisting that

---

a strong Masonic presence in the eighteenth century—it contained nearly twenty lodges by 1795—although most lodges did not emerge until after 1770; see *The New Jamaica Almanack, and Register . . .* ([Spanish Town], Jamaica, 1795), 129; and F. W. Seal-Coon, *An Historical Account of Jamaican Freemasonry* (Kingston, Jamaica, 1976), 12. My thanks to John Garrigus for his help on Caribbean Masons. For more on the biography of Ross in Jamaica, see Agnes M. Butterfield, "Hercules Ross of Kingston, Jamaica, and Rossie, Forfar, 1745–1816" (unpublished manuscript, 1982), 1–38, 94–128 (My thanks to Mr. J. H. St. J. McIlwaine for allowing me to read his aunt's manuscript); and [Gilbert Francklyn], *Substance of a Speech Intended to Have Been Made on Mr. Wilberforce's Motion for the Abolition of the Slave Trade, on Tuesday, April 3, 1792* (London, 1792), 4–5. Samuel Vaughan described Hibbert as one of Jamaica's eight most "eminent merchants" in 1769; see Vaughan, *A Refutation of a False Aspersion First Thrown Out upon Samuel Vaughan, Esq. . . . .* (London, 1769), 6n. For more on Hibbert, see Frank Cundall, *Historic Jamaica* (London, 1915), 179, 265; and Kenneth Morgan, ed., *The Bright-Meyler Papers: A Bristol-West India Connection, 1732–1837* (New York, 2007), 190n. For more on Hibbert's daughters, especially Jane, see Joseph J. Green, "Jenny Harry, Later Thresher (circa 1756-1784)," *Friends' Quarterly Examiner,* XLII (1913), 559–582; Green, "Jenny Harry, Later Thresher (circa 1756-1784)," *Friends' Quarterly Examiner,* XLIII (1914), 43–62; and Judith Jennings, "A Trio of Talented Women: Abolition, Gender, and Political Participation, 1780-91," *Slavery and Abolition,* XXVI (2005), 55-70.

2. Woody Holton, *Forced Founders: Indians, Debtors, Slaves, and the Making of the American Revolution in Virginia* (Chapel Hill, N.C., 1999), xx, 66; Malick W. Ghachem, *The Old Regime and the Haitian Revolution* (New York, 2012), 309.

slaves would now flock to Britain to seek freedom. In turn, they proclaimed, these new black residents would sleep with poor white Englishwomen, populating the countryside with mixed-race children. Thus, the same demographic fears expressed in Jamaica were now employed in Britain. Yet, they paralleled even more. Although Britons grew anxious over poor individuals of color growing up among them, they originally expressed little animosity over the arrival of mixed-race elites from Jamaica. In the same ways that class and family standing mollified some white colonists in the Caribbean, such markers of status also assuaged many in Britain, especially those who were tasked with caring for relatives of color. In the decade after the inheritance cap, mixed-race migrants found their elite status relatively unchanged in the metropole. But they nonetheless arrived in an environment growing more sensitive to the racial makeup of British society. And, like members of Ross's and Hibbert's households, they came from families contributing directly to the debate over slavery and abolition.

Migration to Britain

In the closing months of 1774, William Cuming, an eight-year-old "mustee," prepared to move to Scotland in accordance with the wishes of his recently deceased father, Duncan. The boy's uncle would take care of him in Inverness until he reached his majority, inheriting the whole of his father's ten-thousand-pound fortune. Duncan might have requested that his son move to Scotland in order to liquefy his Jamaican estate, so that William could avoid the inheritance cap. This was a risky maneuver as British relatives could still easily sue based on the tradition of using colonial law to settle overseas estates. Despite this precaution, William's inheritance nevertheless came under question. Simon Taylor, a rising Jamaican sugar baron, claimed that nearly five hundred pounds of the estate was owed to him in debt. Having received no recompense by the time William arrived at the foot of the Scottish Highlands that next March, he took the young man to court. Financial incentives undoubtedly motivated Taylor's suit, but he might have also resented Duncan Cuming's excessive bequest. Taylor fathered children of color himself but gave only a small allowance to his mixed-race daughter Sally in a 1763 draft of his will. Like many of his Jamaican peers, a general reluctance to equate colonial families with metropolitan ones lessened his sense of duty to relations of color. Although he begged his English employer to take a wife, Taylor insisted that he never thought of matrimony for himself, as he had been "so long in this Hott Country and consequently excessively relaxed." Besides, he commented in 1773, compared to England's "land of Beauties," Jamaica contained none "but Mauritanians and their issue." The Caribbean was still not a place for marriage. But some whites, including Duncan Cuming, had far fewer reservations drawing equivalence between formalized and de facto unions, and they sent children of color to Britain to demonstrate that support.[3]

White settlement and legitimacy remained important goals for Jamaica at midcentury, and officials continued pulling away from policies that incorporated most mixed-race individuals into that fold. Eager to persuade Jamaicans like Taylor to tie the knot, if only as financial encouragement, the assembly allowed "the wives and children of all persons," regardless of age, to save deficiency on estates in 1766. Yet, this tax exemption applied only to those "born of white parents." The provision reflected an ongoing interest in promoting marriage and family growth, although now among a more biologically circumscribed group. Underscoring this limitation, three months later the assembly rejected a similar proposal that any propertied "mulatto be allowed to stand for a deficiency, together with his wife, and children lawfully begotten, in like manner as any other master or owner." As before, this was an attack on middling individuals of color who had acquired small holdings. By once again denying them the ability to save deficiency, the assembly lessened their appeal to potential employers. It also signaled that legislators hoped to promote families of full, rather than partial, European heritage.[4]

3. Will of Duncan Cuming, Sept. 15, 1774, Wills, LOS 42, fol. 21, IRO; Taylor v. Walker, Mar. 1, 1775, Jamaica Chancery Court Records, 1A/3/70, lib. 58, fols. 369-372, JA; Simon Taylor to Sir John Taylor, Jan. 27, 1763, Simon Taylor Papers, ICS 120 II/B/36, ICS; Taylor to Chaloner Arcedeckne, July 25, 1768, in Betty Wood, ed., *Travel, Trade, and Power in the Atlantic, 1765-1884,* Camden Miscellany, XXXV (New York, 2002), 64, Taylor to Arcedeckne, Sept. 17, 1773, 125. In Jamaican racial taxonomy, a "mustee" (or "mestee") was three generations removed from an African ancestor—still subject to the island's laws against "mulattos." On the role of colonial law on the settling of transatlantic property, see Peter Wilson Coldham, *English Estates of American Colonists: American Wills and Administrations in the Perogative Court of Canterbury, 1700-1799* (Baltimore, 1980), v; Peter Walne, *English Wills: Probate Records in England and Wales with a Brief Note on Scottish and Irish Wills* (Richmond, Va., 1964), 19, 49-51. For more on Simon Taylor, see R[ichard] B. Sheridan, "Simon Taylor, Sugar Tycoon of Jamaica, 1740-1813," *Agricultural History,* XLV (1971), 285-296; B. W. Higman, *Plantation Jamaica, 1750-1850: Capital and Control in a Colonial Economy* (Kingston, Jamaica, 2005), 137-165; Brown, *Reaper's Garden,* 95-114; Sarah M. S. Pearsall, *Atlantic Families: Lives and Letters in the Later Eighteenth Century* (New York, 2008), 125-140; and Christer Petley, "'Home' and 'This Country': Britishness and Creole Identity in the Letters of a Transatlantic Slaveholder," *Atlantic Studies,* VI (2009), 43-61; and Daniel Livesay, "Extended Families: Mixed-Race Children and Scottish Experience, 1770-1820," *International Journal of Scottish Literature,* no. 4 (Spring / Summer 2008), 3-4.

4. *JAJ,* Aug. 13-Sept. 12, 1766, V, 636-663, Dec. 12, 1766, VI, 27.

In keeping with tradition, though, the assembly continued to grant privilege dispensations to mixed-race elites, even as it pressed aggressively against Jamaica's rising population of color. Between 1763 and 1778, the assembly approved privilege requests for 148 individuals. No appeals were rejected; the high costs of submission meant all applicants were elite. But lawmakers might have also felt more generous because they simultaneously began diminishing the concessions that privilege bills contained. From the beginning, the individual rights conferred varied between petitioners. All of them could save deficiency—an almost unnecessary luxury as they had enough money not to seek modest labor on plantations. But, beginning in the 1740s, they were barred from serving in office or as magistrates. After Thomas and Elizabeth Majeau submitted an appeal in 1751, the assembly started striking out privileged Jamaicans' rights to serve on juries as well. A decade later, most privilege bills prevented their recipients from testifying against whites in court—except in cases of assault—or voting in elections. Occasional bills did allow petitioners to skirt the inheritance cap, or to have full testamentary rights in court, but the majority retained these same restrictions for the rest of the eighteenth century. By 1762, privilege bills only gave petitioners access to professions otherwise barred by law as well as protections from certain harsh punishments if found guilty of a crime. At this point, Jamaicans sought privileges for two reasons: to obtain relatively stronger economic freedoms and a higher social rank than fellow colonists of color. These economic gains were not inconsequential, and elite status depended on a successful appeal; but privilege bills no longer gave their recipients a position that approximated white status.[5]

Perhaps because of the limited favors now obtained by petitioning, some privileged Jamaicans left for Britain, where such allowance was unneeded. John William Hicks lived in Britain when he received privileges in 1764 and appears not to have returned. He died thirty-six years later just outside Bath, drawing off the proceeds of his inherited Jamaican plantation. Charlotte Stirling won her privilege rights the year before Hicks. Her father, Robert, hoped to educate Charlotte in Britain in order to "qualify her to enjoy the privileges and immunities of a white woman in this island" once she came back. Robert

5. The practice of barring mixed-race persons from holding office began with the debate around William Cunningham's privilege appeal but became a more formal and regular exclusion starting with the petition of Ann Fletcher; see Acts of the Assembly of Jamaica, Apr. 14, 1739, CO 139/15, NAE, May 22, 1742, CO 139/16, fol. 12. On the Majeau's petition, see ibid., Oct. 31, 1751, CO 139/17. On the exclusion of court testimony and voting rights in petitions, see ibid., Nov. 4, 1762, CO 139/22, fol. 3.

died the next year, however, and Charlotte stayed in Britain permanently.[6] Some privileged Jamaicans, though, used the metropole as a launching pad for a successful return. Dugald Clarke, whose petition the assembly read the day after it first considered capping mixed-race inheritances, developed a steam engine to mill sugar while studying in Britain. He petitioned England's Privy Council in 1770 for a general exemption from laws against individuals of color throughout the West Indies. Clarke already held such an allowance for Jamaica, but he hoped to sell his invention to planters in Barbados and Antigua as well. Ultimately, he settled back on the island of his birth, where he received a patent for his machine in 1771. Although Clarke's privileged status would not come close to the rights he held in Britain, he could nevertheless make a tremendous amount of money in Jamaica with his invention.[7]

The diminished reach of privilege legislation induced many to leave, but the greatest factor pushing individuals of color to cross the Atlantic was the island's dearth of schools. Like Clarke, many free people of color wished to expand their fortunes in Jamaica, but they could not receive a sufficient education there. Initiatives for building schools had largely failed in the eighteenth century.[8] Wolmer's, founded in 1729 in Kingston, was Jamaica's most

6. Acts of the Assembly of Jamaica, Dec. 18, 1764, CO 139/22, NAE, Will of John William Hicks, May 15, 1800, PROB 11/1342; *JAJ*, Dec. 8, 1763, V, 431, Nov. 23, 1784, VIII, 26; *Votes of the Honourable House of Assembly of Jamaica; In a Session Begun October 19th, and Ended December 23, 1784; Being the Ninth Session of the Present Assembly* (Spanish Town, Jamaica, 1785), 54. It is possible that Charlotte married in Edinburgh as an older woman. The *Scots Magazine* notes "Miss Charlotte Stirling, daughter of Robert Stirling," married Peter Patrick Sheriff on September 25, 1801; see *Scots Magazine*, LXIII (1801), 660. For more on Robert Stirling, see Bill Inglis, "The Stirlings of Keir in the 18th Century, Restoring the Family Fortunes in the British Empire," *Forth Naturalist and Historian*, XXIV (2001), 93–101.

7. The results of Clarke's appeal to the Privy Council are unclear; see "The Humble Petition of Dugald Clarke," Mar. 14, 1770, PC 1/60/7, NAE; *JAJ*, Dec. 3–21, 1771, VI, 367–392; John Robison, *A System of Mechanical Philosophy* (Edinburgh, 1822), II, 107n; John Farey, *A Treatise on the Steam Engine, Historical, Practical, and Descriptive* (London, 1827), 408; and Elijah Galloway, *History and Progress of the Steam Engine: With a Pratical Investigation of Its Structure and Application* (London, 1829), 849. Veront Satchell's survey of sugarmill technology in the late eighteenth and early nineteenth century finds that nearly a quarter of all patents on sugarmill improvements in Jamaica dealt with innovations based on steam power; see Satchell, "Innovations in Sugar-Cane Mill Technology in Jamaica, 1760–1830," in Verene A. Shepherd, ed., *Working Slavery, Pricing Freedom: Perspectives from the Caribbean, Africa, and the African Diaspora* (Kingston, Jamaica, 2002), 99.

8. Educational endowments were created, but most did not come to fruition; see Saint Andrew's (1695); Drax's in Saint Ann (1721); Wolmer's in Kingston (1735); Vere (1739);

successful institution, but it pulled little weight on the island. The assembly, for instance, took over one of its buildings to hear assize cases without providing any compensation for more than twelve years, despite repeated protests from school officials. Such lack of respect produced an equal noninterest in basic instruction. "Learning is here at the lowest Ebb," a visitor to Jamaica complained in 1740; "To talk of a *Homer,* or a *Virgil,* of a *Tully,* or a *Demosthenes,* is quite unpolite." An Anglican missionary confirmed this sentiment one year later, recounting that the only option for young children was to leave the island, even though they "often Miscarry in their Morals for want of the Watchful Care . . . of a Parent." Jamaica was a place to make money; it was not a site for education.[9]

Manning's in Westmoreland (1737); the free school in Spanish Town (1743); Rusea's in Hanover (1773); and Titchfield's in Portland (1785). These endowments are recorded in the Jamaica House of Assembly, Laws and Statutes, etc.: Saint Andrew: 7 Gul. III. i. 1; Drax's: 38 Geo. III. xxvii. 1; Wolmer's: 9 Geo. II. vi. 1; Vere: 13 Geo. II. x. 1; Manning's: 11 Geo. II. ix. 1; Saint Jago de la Vega: 17 Geo. II. x. 1; Rusea's: 14 Geo. III. cap. X; and Titchfield's: 26 Geo. III. vii. 1. Saint Andrew's school, to be built at Halfway-Tree, never got beyond the planning stage. The free school in Saint Ann's rural hills also never emerged, as Charles Drax's heirs fought the bequest for decades after his death (the numerous lawsuits lodged against the construction of the school can be found in "Cause: Pink v. Pink," 1671–1822, J 90/831, NAE). Vere's school did not begin to arrange its finances until 1768, nearly thirty years after the original endowment. Manning's did not organize until 1780 and Rusea's until 1795, well after their initial grants; see Minute Book of Vere Trust, 4/133/1, private archives, JA; Minute Book of Manning's Trust, 4/137/1, private archives, JA; and Minute Book of Rusea's Free School, 4/138/2, private archives, JA. This school building program was part of a greater initiative in the Caribbean. Christopher Codrington set aside funds for a Barbadian school in 1710, but, by the end of the century, the institution had taught very few students; see George Frere, *A Short History of Barbados, from Its First Discovery and Settlement, to the End of the Year 1767* (London, 1768), 117–118; George Pinckard, *Notes on the West Indies . . . ,* 2d ed., 2 vols. (London, 1816), I, 191–193; and Frank Wesley Pitman, *The Development of the British West Indies, 1700–63* (New Haven, Conn., 1917), 10. Bermuda officials took steps to establish a college in 1727, and the English government set aside land in Saint Kitts for a school the same year; see Warrant from the Attorneys General and Solicitor, July 15, 1727, Add. MS 36126, fol. 241, BL; and Edward L. Cox, *Free Coloreds in the Slave Societies of St. Kitts and Grenada, 1763–1833* (Knoxville, Tenn., 1984), 13. At the same time, free schools to service the poor developed in England as well; see Jeremy Schmidt, "Charity and the Government of the Poor in the English Charity-School Movement, circa 1700–1730," *Journal of British Studies,* XLIX (2010), 774–800.

9. *JAJ,* Nov. 27, 1764, V, 496, Nov. 27, 1776, VI, 661; [Charles Leslie], *A New History of Jamaica, from the Earliest Accounts to the Taking of Porto Bello by Vice-Admiral Vernon . . .* (London, 1740), 35–36; William May to Bishop Edmund Gibson, Apr. 23, 1741, Fulham Palace Papers, XVIII, fol. 9, LPL. The effect of a lack of schools was pronounced across

If they wanted to attend a proper institution, Jamaicans of all stripes had to leave the Caribbean. A small number went to North America, which was quickly becoming populated by newly founded schools and colleges in the eighteenth century.[10] But Britain was still the top choice for Jamaica's wealthiest inhabitants. Perhaps as many as three hundred Jamaicans per year crossed the Atlantic for their education. Anyone wishing to practice law had to attend school in Britain, even if they came back to the colonies. The islands' lack of an episcopacy also forced seminary students to cross the Atlantic. Moreover, a metropolitan upbringing continued to affirm extreme advantage and conferred social refinement. Although many Jamaican youth went to English

---

the Caribbean. Analyzing affidavits from the Leeward Islands at the end of the seventeenth century, Richard S. Dunn determines that nearly half of them were signed with an "X" — a common indication of illiteracy, although it might have only signified an inability to write. Compared to the British population at this time, this might not have been an outrageously low figure. David Cressy's analysis of early modern literacy in England shows that, whereas 78 percent of all Londoners could read and write, less than a third of those outside the capital could do the same. Some have challenged these numbers, but most would agree that literacy in the British Isles greatly surpassed that of the Caribbean by the beginning of the eighteenth century. Regardless of the overall rates, Dunn's findings on West Indian elites are startling; see Dunn, *Sugar and Slaves: The Rise of the Planter Class in the English West Indies, 1624–1713* (Chapel Hill, N.C., 1972), 139, 339–340; Cressy, *Literacy and the Social Order: Reading and Writing in Tudor and Stuart England* (New York, 1980); Keith Thomas, "The Meaning of Literacy in Early Modern England," in Gerd Baumann, ed., *The Written Word: Literacy in Transition* (New York, 1986), 97–131; Margaret Spufford, "First Steps in Literacy: The Reading and Writing Experiences of the Humblest Seventeenth-Century Spiritual Autobiographers," *Social History,* IV (1979), 407–435; Roger S. Schofield, "Dimensions of Illiteracy in England, 1750–1850," in Harvey J. Graff, ed., *Literacy and Social Development in the West: A Reader* (New York, 1981), 201–213; and Michael Sanderson, "Literacy and Social Mobility in the Industrial Revolution in England," *Past and Present,* no. 56 (August 1972), 75–104.

10. The most famous West Indian to attend school in North America was Alexander Hamilton. North American administrators courted West Indians, in particular, with their large fortunes; see John Witherspoon, *Address to the Inhabitants of Jamaica and Other West-India Islands, in Behalf of the College of New-Jersey* (Philadelphia, 1772); and *Candid Remarks on Dr. Witherspoon's Address . . .* (Philadelphia, 1772). A perusal of Harvard graduates shows a number of West Indians who attended the university in the seventeenth and early eighteenth centuries; see Clifford K. Shipton, *New England Life in the Eighteenth Century: Representative Biographies from Sibley's Harvard Graduates* (Cambridge, Mass., 1995); and John Langdon Sibley, *Sibley's Harvard Graduates: Biographical Sketches of Those Who Attended Harvard College with Biographical and Other Notes, by Clifford K. Shipton,* 5 vols. (Cambridge, Mass., 1933). See also Bernard Bailyn, *Education in the Forming of American Society: Needs and Opportunities for Study* (Chapel Hill, N.C., 1960); and Lawrence Cremin, *American Education: The Colonial Experience, 1607–1783,* Book II (New York, 1970).

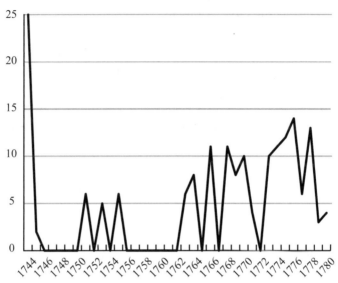

FIGURE 1. Percentage of Student Body at the University of Edinburgh Medical School and
King's College, Aberdeen, from the West Indies Combined, 1744–1780. Drawn by Kelly
Crawford. Table data is based on the matriculation registers in *List of Graduates in Medicine
in the University of Edinburgh from 1705 to 1866* (Edinburgh, 1867); and Peter John Anderson,
ed., *Officers and Graduates of the University and King's College Aberdeen, MVD–MDCCCLX*
(Aberdeen, 1893), 120–175.

On average, the graduating class at King's College, Aberdeen, was roughly six students per
year — though the numbers increased slowly into the nineteenth century. At the University of
Edinburgh, enrollment skyrocketed. Although there was an average of only two graduates per
year in the 1730s, by the 1810s there were an average of eighty graduates each year. Recordings
of student origin are often inconsistent in these registers, so the frequency of West Indian
students might be higher.

schools, a large number undertook their education north of the Tweed. Caribbean students' matriculation in Scottish schools was consistent throughout
the middle of the eighteenth century, despite regular disruptions owing to war
(Figure 1). These young colonists made a noticeable presence. While studying at the University of Edinburgh, Sylas Neville noted in 1772 that Richard
Cumberland's play *The West Indian* had been staged at the request of the
city's many "West Indian and American Students." Elite Jamaicans had their
first taste of absenteeism at a young age when they sought out an education.[11]

11. *The Diary of Sylas Neville, 1767–1788*, ed. Basil Cozens-Hardy (New York, 1950), Jan.
22, 1772, 149. On the movement of young West Indians to Britain for school, see Andrew
Jackson O'Shaughnessy, *An Empire Divided: The American Revolution and the British*

Individuals of color, if they could afford it, had even more reason to travel abroad. Most Jamaican schools were not open to mixed-race students. Wolmer's did not officially allow children of color through its doors during the eighteenth century. When Manning's free school on the western side of the island sought advice about matriculating children of color, Wolmer's confirmed that its trustees did not allow the practice, declaring that "no mixtures whatever were to be in future received." But the social realities of Kingston life demanded leniency when elite students of color applied to the academy. Although Wolmer's charter did not state so explicitly, until 1798 the school admitted some children of color as paid students. Only white children, though, could receive scholarships under Wolmer's original endowment. Considering their fathers' great wealth, however, it would not have been difficult for mixed-race students to afford the annual tuition of sixty pounds. Rumors therefore swirled about the school's admission policy, and, in 1777, the trustees publicly reaffirmed their vow not to allow in any children of color on scholarship. Under such heavy clouds, Jamaicans of color sought other options.[12]

Barred from attending most free schools, students of color frequently relied on private instruction. Many tutors started schools in their homes, but

------

Caribbean (Philadelphia, 2000), 19–26; and B. H. McPherson, *The Reception of English Law Abroad* (Brisbane, Australia, 2007), 477–479. Young West Indians also went to Ireland. Jesse Balrieves, a Quaker boy from Jamaica, attended school in Ballitore, along with "Many West Indians." Mary Leadbetter recorded that Balrieves exclaimed in 1772 on his first sight of snow in Ireland, "O boys! see all the sugar!"; see Leadbetter, *The Leadbetter Papers: A Selection from the Mss. and Correspondence of Mary Leadbetter* (London, 1862), I, 87. Young people throughout the Empire, not just Jamaica, came to British and Irish schools; see "Journal of an Officer Who Travelled Over a Part of the West Indies, and of North America in the Course of 1764 and 1765," King's MS 213, fol. 26, BL; Julie M. Flavell, "The 'School for Modesty and Humility': Colonial American Youth in London and Their Parents, 1755-1775," *Historical Journal*, XLII (1999), 378–379; and Paul Nash, "Innocents Abroad: American Students at British Universities in the Early Nineteenth Century," *History of Education Quarterly*, I, no. 2 (June 1961), 32–44. For personal letters between Scottish migrants in Virginia and the children that they sent back to North Britain, see James McLeod Papers, MS 19297, NLS, and the MacMurdo Family Papers, Acc. 7199, box 3, folder 1, box 4, folders 2–3, NLS. See also the bibliography in Whitfield J. Bell, Jr., "Some American Students of 'That Shining Oracle of Physic,' Dr. William Cullen of Edinburgh, 1755-1766," American Philosophical Society, *Proceedings,* XCIV (1950), 275–281, which is also posted in the Edinburgh University Matriculation Records, GD300/46, NAS.

12. Wolmer's Minute Book, Mar. 25, 1779, MS 97a, fol. 221, NLJ, Nov. 9, 1777, MS 97a, fol. 123-124; Patrick E. Bryan, *The Legacy of a Goldsmith: A History of Wolmer's Schools, 1729-2003* (Kingston, Jamaica, 2004), 20. The tuition costs come from Wolmer's Minute Book, Mar. 25, 1779, MS 97a, fol. 225.

even here they tended to discriminate. In Montego Bay, a Mr. and Mrs. Tetley offered basic lessons but warned in a 1777 advertisement that "none but children of white parents will be received." Even so, a number of tutors took in children of color.[13] Thomas Thistlewood's mixed-race son, John, went to the house of Sarah Bennett in Savannah-la-Mar. Bennett, herself a woman of color, possibly had a reputation for teaching such students. Writing from Scotland, George Kinloch sought a school for his mixed-race nieces and nephew who lived near Bennett. His Jamaican correspondent proposed to "send them to a school near Savanna la Mar . . . to a Woman I have spoke to who Boards several children of the same sort." He suggested this as a cheaper option to having them educated in Britain. Finding a school often required these associational connections. Before leaving for England, Jamaican merchant George Graham emancipated his children, John and Nelly, and wrote to his friend John Somerville about possible tutors. Somerville lived near Savannah-la-Mar and revealed that a mutual friend had sent his mixed-race child to a private instructor nearby — perhaps, once again, Sarah Bennett. Young John eventually went to the same school. Several years later, Somerville reassured Graham of his son's progress, reporting that "John can read and write pretty well" and communicating his intention to "put him with a good Tradesman." Private tutoring filled a gap for Jamaicans of color, but it could not offer the type of instruction demanded by wealthy families. Like their white peers, many mixed-race Jamaicans crossed the Atlantic instead.[14]

How many left for Britain in this period? Estimating exact numbers is difficult owing to the inconsistency of racial notation in the matriculation registers of British schools as well as to the reluctance of some Jamaicans to identify children as mixed race. Privilege bills give some sense of this migration,

13. *Cornwall Chronicle* (Montego Bay, Jamaica), Apr. 12, 1777. Jean Traill lodged a similar ad for a school educating white girls only; see *Cornwall Chronicle,* May 3, 1777. Correspondence from Jamaica in this period regularly contains notes from white fathers to British absentees wishing for their mixed-race children to be emancipated, in some cases so that they could be educated by tutors. Nathaniel Pierce wrote from Kingston to Roger Hope Elletson asking to have his children freed, "to put them out to get Learning which they have not done yet"; see Pierce to Elletson, Aug. 13, 1774, Stowe Papers, STB box 25 (18), HL.

14. Thomas Thistlewood Papers, microfilm, reel 6, no. 19 (1768), fol. 165 (My thanks to Phil Morgan for his help with Sarah Bennett); John Wedderburn to G. O. Kinloch, Dec. 22, 1774, Grange Estate Papers, GD 1/8/35, fol. 115, NAS; John Somerville to George Graham, June 10, 1778–Mar. 14, 1779, Montgomery Family Papers, NRAS 1115/21/6, NRAS, Graham to Somerville, Dec. 13, 1779, Somerville to Graham, Feb. 16, 1784. My deepest thanks to the Montgomery family for allowing me to read through their private papers.

TABLE 2. *Percentage of White Men's Wills, Proven in Jamaica, with Acknowledged Mixed-Race Children That Include Bequests for Such Offspring in Britain, Either Presently Resident, or Soon to Be Sent There, 1773–1775*

Explicit references	9.7
Explicit and implicit references combined	17.2

Source: Wills, LOS 41–42, IRO. For an individual listing of wills, see Appendix 1.

Note: An explicit reference is one in which the child is listed with a racial category (such as "mulatto," "quadroon," "mestee," etc.). An implicit reference is one in which the child is noted as illegitimate ("natural" or "reputed"). In nearly all of the latter categories, the testator also noted having a mistress of color who was likely the child's mother.

as several petitioners noted a British education when applying for advanced rights. Up to 1780, however, relatively few petitioners recorded time spent in the metropole. Of the roughly 250 individuals who applied for privileges between 1733 and 1779, only thirteen explicitly mentioned a British education or residence. Most of those occurred before the inheritance cap's passage. Such modest numbers, though, do not reflect the scale of the movement. After all, those who settled permanently in Britain had virtually no reason to apply for privileges, as the majority of the bills' concessions pertained only to those still living on the island.[15]

Analyzing the inheritance patterns of wealthy white colonists gives a different quantifiable sense of mixed-race migration. Many Jamaicans of color left for Britain without gaining privileges and received substantial legacies from white fathers to facilitate the journey. Of the 364 wills proven in Jamaica between 1773 and 1775, 94, or 25 percent, contained bequests to a mixed-race child. Sixteen of those included provisions for offspring of color who were either in Britain, or soon to be sent there. For this period, then, roughly five households per year made testamentary provisions for individuals of color in Britain. Nine of these wills included beneficiaries labeled explicitly as mixed race, whereas the other 7 were for children almost certainly of color, though only implicitly noted as such. Examples of this latter category were individuals recorded as the "natural" or "reputed" offspring of a white father. The terms "natural" and "reputed" denoted illegitimacy, which almost universally meant children of color in the case of Jamaica. Most of these children were

15. For privilege bills lodged between 1762 and 1802, see Minutes of the Assembly of Jamaica, CO 139/22–51, NAE.

also noted as the sons and daughters of "housekeepers," who were, with little exception, free or enslaved mistresses of color. Among all wills, these legacies for British-bound Jamaicans of color are modest. After all, the majority of mixed-race children not only went unacknowledged in a will but unacknowledged by fathers altogether. But, as Table 2 shows, nearly one of every five white male testators who cared for mixed-race children in Jamaica either sent them to Britain or desired that they should go. This migration, then, was, not an idiosyncratic and episodic phenomenon, but rather routine practice.[16]

Who sent these children abroad? From 1773 to 1775, three testators listed themselves as planters, two as merchants, and one as a physician. Five recorded "Esquire" or "Gentleman" in their wills, which were umbrella terms that generally denoted a planter or merchant. Most of those who sent relatives of color to Britain, then, came from the landed or mercantile class—much the same as those sending white children abroad. Finally, four tradesmen sent offspring to Britain. These were carpenter and shipwright moguls who earned lucrative profits as government contractors and plantation suppliers. Considering the expense incurred in sending children to Britain and remitting enough money for their maintenance, it is no surprise that the island's wealthiest individuals undertook this exercise. These fathers might have given so generously simply because they could. Exorbitant costs might have prevented many others from sending offspring of color across the Atlantic, even if they so desired.[17]

The formalities of testamentary writing make it difficult to discern the personal reasons why fathers wished to remove their children to Britain. Very few wills included any explanation, let alone commentary, regarding intention. Yet, the burden placed on British friends and family left with a mixed-race charge required some testators to defend their actions. Kingston merchant Nathaniel Milward fretted over his associates' opinions on the arrival of three mixed-race children in Britain. When penning his last will and testament in 1775, he hoped for absolution:

16. Wills, LOS 41–42, IRO. To obtain a workable sample of wills over an extended period of time, each of the years 3–5 in the decades from the 1770s to the 1810s were examined (thus 1773-1775, 1783-1785, 1793-1795, 1803-1805, and 1813-1815). Wills from the other decades are analyzed in later chapters.

17. Those listed as "Esquire" and "Gentleman" in the sample were John Nixon, Thomas Blair, Donald Campbell, Duncan Cuming, and Samuel Smith. On the meaning of those titles, see David Hancock, *Citizens of the World: London Merchants and the Integration of the British Atlantic Community, 1735-1785* (New York, 1995), 279-319; and O'Shaughnessy, *Empire Divided*, 19.

For the trouble I have here given my good friend Mr. George Bush by thus taking the liberty to appoint him Guardian and Trustee to these swarthy Illegitimates, I am at a loss what apology to make in their behalf (who are blameless) I must rely on his humanity, in my own, I have to hope his good nature will excuse the follies of youth, and to consider the provision here made as the most eligible attonement to render them usefull to Society.

Sending mixed-race children to Britain, in Milward's mind, was as much an act of redemption as it was a response to the social and legal inequalities that his offspring faced in the colonies. Couched in this way, many in Britain accepted these children into their homes to complete the redemptive process. After all, men like Milward simply followed the advice of Francis Douglas in 1771 toward married fathers in England: "By training up his children to the love and practice of virtue, and giving them a decent education, he draws upon himself the respect due to a good citizen." Nonetheless, Milward's apology for imposing a burden would prove prophetic: Bush continued to supervise the children's finances for the next decade and a half.[18]

Fear could also rise to the surface in these testamentary documents, specifically as it related to sexual pairings. Fathers who asked that mixed-race children travel to Britain frequently did so with the desire that subsequent generations would become legitimate and thus more phenotypically white. They implored guardians to keep vigilant watch over their children's sexual behavior and marriage prospects in the metropole. In 1773, George Hall, a prosperous Jamaican carpenter and millwright, demanded of his "mulatto son Francis" in Britain that "if he will marry a white woman he shall be intitled to one third of my said property . . . but in case he should live in a lewd way with any woman he shall only be intitled to [only a few slaves]." Hall set the same stipulations for his daughter. He might have enjoyed an unsanctioned relationship in the colonies, but, fearful that his children would take similar steps in Britain, Hall regulated their marriage prospects intensely. This prerequisite reflected the importance of matrimony, even, if not especially, for illegitimate Jamaicans of color. Marriage would bestow the legitimacy these migrants lacked, giving them entrée to social respectability in Britain. Moreover, it would reorient the racial heritage of subsequent British descen-

18. Will of Nathaniel Milward, June 15, 1775, LOS 42, fol. 133, IRO; Francis Douglas, *Reflections on Celibacy and Marriage* (London, 1771), 23. David Duncombe noted that the bequests to Milward's children were still being settled fifteen years after his death; see Duncombe to Lowbridge Bright, June 19, 1790, in Morgan, ed., *Bright-Meyler Papers*, 548–551.

dants. Mixed-race men in particular had little or no chance of marrying white spouses in the colonies. Moving to Britain increased the prospect of a biological whitening of the family line.[19]

Who left? Nearly all of the migrants in this period of the sample were free. Only two of the children were still enslaved when their father crafted a last testament, so most of these mixed-race beneficiaries were already living outside the worst abuses of colonial society. But the discriminatory realities of Jamaican life nevertheless shaped who was sent off the island. Both genders crossed the Atlantic, but preference was given to boys. From 1773 to 1775, testators made provisions for fifteen boys and thirteen girls to go to Britain. Fathers sent both genders abroad because all children could benefit from a metropolitan education. When siblings were singled out to remain in Jamaica, they tended to be female: six girls compared to one boy stayed behind while other family members departed for Britain. This originated primarily from the disheartening opinion that women of color had greater opportunities to find continued white patronage in Jamaica through sex than their brothers did through business. Of those who left, most simply headed to school with no other direction from their fathers. But five of the testators did lay out a future employment path. Three wanted their children to enter a trade; one wished to see a son trained as a physician; and Milward asked that his two sons enter the foundry and carpentry professions, while his daughter was to become a midwife. Milward did not specify, though, with whom the children would stay in Britain. He was not alone. Only four testators identified guardians who would supervise their offspring in the metropole: three were to stay with family, while the other was to lodge with a friend. The remaining fathers asked only that their children attend school across the ocean, without any stipulation about who should care for them.[20]

Where did they go? Mixed-race beneficiaries landed throughout Britain and Ireland in the 1770s, although most went to England and Scotland. Northern England, in particular, proved popular to both English and Scottish fathers. Milward sent both of his boys to a boarding school in the tiny hamlet of Kirby-Hill in Yorkshire. Reverend Henry Hale kept a school there for

19. Will of George Hall, Oct. 21, 1773, LOS 41, fols. 169–170, IRO.

20. The claim that women of color could succeed as concubines in the colonies, while their brothers could move to Britain, was voiced by antimigrant factions in the early nineteenth century; see Pinckard, *Notes on the West Indies,* II, 136–137; and James Walker, *Letters on the West Indies* (London, 1818), 170. Milward's plan for the children came after fairly extensive correspondence about British schools with Lowbridge Bright in Bristol; see Bright to Nathaniel Milward, Aug. 3, 1774, in Morgan, ed., *Bright-Meyler Papers,* 462–463.

thirty-five years and likely trained other West Indians. Yorkshire was a magnet for mixed-race children. In 1763, a Jamaican attorney wrote to a British colleague about his son's education: "I have taken the liberty of troubling you with the Case of a Molato Boy . . . when he arrives youl be pleased to send the said Boy down to School at Knayton near Thyrsk in the North part of Yorkshire." The attorney placed his son in this particular institution because there were "several Boys from this Island now at that School." An absentee in London sent his mixed-race son to school in Thirsk as well. The young man settled permanently in the small village, working as a surgeon. Reputation might have guided these fathers' choices, but the geographic proximity of these institutions is striking: Thirsk was less than thirty miles from Hale's school in Kirby-Hill. Yorkshire could have been an attractive option because the area provided a convenient location for children of color from Scottish families who wished to have their children nearby but still at a distance; the same might have held true for fathers from the Home Counties. Similarities between the Scottish and northern-English educational systems also possibly encouraged West Indian Scots to send children of color to Yorkshire schools. Frugality might have persuaded others to eschew an education in the capital's more expensive institutions.[21]

21. Will of Nathaniel Milward, June 15, 1775, LOS 42, fol. 132, IRO; JF to [More?] and Bayly, Apr. 28, 1763, Attorneys Letter Book, MS 14280, fol. 28, GL; Will of John Fletcher, Dec. 5, 1785, Wills, LOS 51, fol. 114, IRO; Will of John Harriot Fletcher, Feb. 3, 1798, PROB 11/1301, NAE. A brief summation of the school at Kirby-Hill can be found in an advertisement it took out the year after Milward crafted his will; see *Daily Advertiser* (London), May 10, 1776. See also Madge Dresser, *Slavery Obscured: The Social History of the Slave Trade in an English Provincial Port* (New York, 2001), 76. Not all fathers with offspring of color in Britain joined them in the metropole. Personal proximity then, was not always the only choice. Milward asked that his sons travel to Bristol after their schooling to be apprenticed to Lowbridge Bright, a former Jamaican merchant and Milward's business partner who was one of the top sugar merchants in Bristol; see Will of Nathaniel Milward, June 15, 775, fol. 132; and *London Evening Post*, July 30, 1774. For more on Bright and Milward's partnership and connections to a larger merchant community in New England and Britain, see Morgan, ed., *Bright-Meyler Papers;* and James W. Roberts, " 'Yankey Dodle Will Do Verry Well Here': New England Traders in the Caribbean, 1713 to circa 1812" (Ph.D. diss., Johns Hopkins University, 2011), 220–222. The quality and style of schools in Yorkshire could have precipitated this trend of sending young mixed-race students to the north of England. R. A. Houston believes that socioeconomic similarities, particularly in terms of agricultural and apprentice labor, between lowland Scotland and Northern England produced similar educational systems; see Houston, *Scottish Literacy and the Scottish Identity: Illiteracy and Society in Scotland and Northern England, 1600–1800* (New York, 1985). The African missionary Philip Quaque noted that Yorkshire was an economical option for schooling African students of

Many fathers simply wished to avoid London altogether, perhaps to prevent children from falling prey to the capital's supposed moral hazards. Jamaican attorney and assemblyman Malcolm Laing asked a former employer's son William Philip Perrin to help find a school in England for Robert, his six-year-old mixed-race child. Such requests were common between transatlantic contacts, but Perrin might have felt some familial obligation as well: Robert's mother, Elizabeth Fickle, had also been mistress to Perrin's late father. Laing asked for Perrin's opinion because he knew virtually nothing about which schools to choose, longing simply "to give [Robert] such an Education . . . that might enable him to go into some business." Although Robert first stayed with his aunt in London, his father did not want him to remain in the capital. Part of his reasoning centered on cost. If Robert was going to return to Jamaica eventually, there was no need to incur heavy debts in the expensive capital. Yet, Laing also desired that Robert be "kept as much out of London as possible, that place, being the ruin of all young people except where they have parents to give continual Attention to them." Throughout his long correspondence, Laing betrayed an obsession with his son's morality. He wished to ensure that Robert never followed "the road of Disipation and what is called high life" while he stayed in England. Unsure as he was about a British education, Laing hoped his mixed-race son would not endure too much temptation. This worry also betrayed Laing's anxiety about a young West Indian of color strolling the streets of the Empire's vibrant capital.[22]

What sorts of experiences did these migrants have? Testamentary documents say virtually nothing about these migrants' lives. Moreover, those left to toil at their books in cold Yorkshire schoolhouses generally did not make lasting impressions on their surroundings, which was perhaps exactly the point of such isolation. Not all fathers, however, directed their children away from the capital, nor did they refrain from continuing correspondence with them. Many of the Jamaican migrants of color who passed into the archival record lived in London. Once there, they carved out spaces in refined society, seemingly distant from West Indian origins.

Jane and Margaret Harry, Thomas Hibbert's daughters with the free mu-

---

color in the metropole; see Quaque to William Morice, Aug. 6, 1782, in Vincent Carretta and Ty M. Reese, eds., *The Life and Letters of Philip Quaque: The First African Anglican Missionary* (Athens, Ga., 2010), 158.

22. Baptism of Robert Laing, 1768, Kingston baptisms, copy register, I, fol. 198, IRO; Malcolm Laing to William Philip Perrin, Jan. 10, 1774, D239 M/E 16777, Derbyshire Record Office, Matlock, England, Laing to Perrin, June 9, 1776, D239 M/E 16834, Laing to Perrin, Nov. 4, 1776, D239 M/E 16827.

latto Charity Harry, arrived in the village of Barnes, just outside London, sometime around 1770. It is possible that the Harry sisters left Jamaica with their father on the same ship with Bryan Edwards, who would later become a member of the assembly and eventually a leader of the Caribbean's key parliamentary lobbying body, the West India Committee. At Barnes, Jane and Margaret stayed with Nathan Sprigg, their father's former slave trading partner. Under his care, both would begin assimilating into polite English society. Margaret soon left for boarding school, while Jane stayed with the Sprigg family. Sprigg had married the former Miss Arabella Benfield, a London socialite, and the couple frequently entertained guests, including such luminaries as Samuel Johnson, at their Surrey manor house. They also took young Jane with them on trips to the spa town of Cheltenham, to mingle further with England's elite.[23]

Despite such comfort, Jane's recollection of these times was one of withdrawal, rather than social participation. "It has often been observed by my friends and by most of my acquaintances that I was of a grave and solid turn of mind," Jane wrote to her father several years after arriving at Barnes. Although she studied ethics and morality during adolescence, her real passion rested in illustration and the arts. "Drawing began to engross much of my time and attention," Harry recalled, so that "I found it more easy to engage myself in this employment than any literary one." Yet, within a few years of arriving in England, Jane suffered a devastating blow: her sister Margaret died in London at only ten years of age. Jane herself was not yet twenty and grieved intensely. She experienced something of a spiritual awakening, shifting away from "the folly of metaphysical reasoning" as well as Anglican doctrine, which she per-

23. In a letter to Vincent Boscoe, Nathaniel Phillips wrote of Thomas Hibbert's plan to travel from Kingston to England in June 1770. Hibbert had been plagued by gout and hoped to consult with a German doctor recommended to him by his former Jamaican partner, Nathan Sprigg, who had since returned to England. If that was the case, then the Harry daughters shared the voyage with Edwards; see Phillips to Briscoe, May 27, 1770, Nathaniel Phillips's Letter Book, Slebech Collection, MS 11485, fol. 165, National Library of Wales, Aberystwyth, and Phillips to Walter Brett, June 4, 1770, fol. 166. Edwards also reported to the Jamaican assembly in 1770 that he was in bad health and heading soon to England to recover; see *JAJ*, Feb. 14, 1770, VI, 240. Joseph Green's work does not note that Margaret attended a London boarding school, but Judith Jennings has found evidence of her education in the capital; see Jennings, "Jane Harry Thresher and Mary Morris Knowles Speak Out for Liberty in Jamaica and England," in Amar Wahab and Cecily Jones, eds., *Free at Last?: Reflections on Freedom and the Abolition of the British Transatlantic Slave Trade* (Newcastle upon Tyne, U.K., 2011), 61–84. For Sprigg's marriage to Benfield, see *London Chronicle*, June 8, 1773.

ceived to have strayed from New Testament teachings. She found comfort in the friendship of a frequent visitor to the Sprigg residence, Mary Knowles. A devout and zealous Quaker, Knowles consoled Jane over the loss of her sister while encouraging her to continue questioning the Church of England. Perhaps sensing a conversion, she became close friends with Jane, whom observers later commented was highly enamored of Knowles. Still in her teens, Jane stepped into the bustling social circle of one of England's most prominent elite women.[24]

Through her connection with Mary Knowles, Jane made the acquaintance of many famous figures. She had already met Samuel Johnson, but the "Good Doctor's" friendship with Knowles put him into even greater contact with Jane. A later account noted that "Dr. J[ohnson] . . . loved and respected Jenny H[arry]." Better suited to her passion for drawing, Harry also met Joshua Reynolds. The country's preeminent painter took a strong interest in Harry's work and lent her some of his own pictures to copy. Her abilities flourished yet more, and, with Reynold's encouragement, she soon submitted an original painting to the Society in London for the Encouragement of Arts and Commerce. The society, which gave cash prizes to young female artists, later awarded Harry a gold medal for her piece in 1778. It was a proud accomplishment, recounted by the *Gentleman's Magazine* as an especially high honor to receive from "that learned body."[25]

Although it is unclear whether anyone in Jane's social circle knew of her full genealogy—no one referred to it publicly—people were at least aware of her background in the West Indies. Poet Anna Seward informed James Bos-

24. Jane Harry to Thomas Hibbert, circa 1778, as quoted in Green, "Jenny Harry," *Friends' Quarterly Examiner*, XLII (1913), 562–566; Anna Seward to James Boswell, n.d., as quoted in W. Beck, W. F. Wells, and H. G. Chalkley, eds., *Biographical Catalogue: Being an Account of the Lives of Friends . . .* (London, 1888), 334. For more on the connections between Jane Harry and Mary Knowles, see Judith Jennings, *Gender, Religion, and Radicalism in the Long Eighteenth Century: The 'Ingenious Quaker' and Her Connections* (Burlington, Vt., 2006), 49–72, 99–120.

25. M. S., *Gentleman's Magazine: And Historical Chronicle*, LXI, pt. II (London, 1791), 700; Helen Pennock South, "Dr. Johnson and the Quakers," *Bulletin of Friends Historical Association*, XLIV (1955), 26–27; "Rewards Bestowed by the Society for Promoting the Polite and Liberal Arts, from the Year 1775 to the Year 1782 Inclusive," *Transactions of the Society, Instituted at London, for the Encouragement of Arts, Manufactures, and Commerce*, II (London, 1789), 132; Green, "Jenny Harry," *Friends' Quarterly Examiner*, XLII (1913), 561; Jennings, "Jane Harry Thresher and Mary Morris Knowles Speak Out for Liberty," Wahab and Jones, eds., *Free at Last?*, 61–84; *Gentleman's Magazine: And Historical Chronicle*, LIV, pt. II (London, 1784), 716.

well that Harry was "the daughter of a rich planter in the West Indies [who] sent her over to England to receive her education in the house of his friend." Jane's cousin Thomas certainly knew of her African ancestry, although he socialized with the proslavery interest in London, rather than with Johnson's retinue. Surely reports of Jane's mixed heritage would have circulated around the capital. But the lack of explicit comments among her friends indicates that Jane's artistic talents and high social connections trumped any racial concerns that might have existed. As Jane reported to her father, this social circle "treated me with great respect, and some of them with much affection; they made me of some consequence among them at their places of publick resort." Her skills as an artist and socialite helped to establish her in England's upper ranks.[26]

John Morse's children also took up residence in London and capitalized on the Empire's opportunities. Morse, the former assemblyman who fled Tacky's Revolt in 1760, had five children with the privileged Jamaican of color Elizabeth Augier: Jack, Robert, Catherine, Ann, and Sarah. Each of the siblings relocated to England by the 1770s. Nineteen-year old Catherine married her father's former clerk Edmund Green in June 1777, and the two soon moved to London. The couple occupied a house on Lincoln's Inn Fields, where Catherine would later give birth to three daughters and four sons. Robert studied law nearby at the Inns of Court and argued cases before England's highest magistrates as a young barrister. Perhaps reflecting on his father's success in Jamaica, Robert yearned for greater economic rewards than his profession offered in England. The month before his sister's wedding, he set off on the *Seahorse,* bound for India. Also on board was a fellow West Indian, one Mr. Arnott, the illegitimate son of navy captain Frederick Maitland and "a native woman of Jamaica" and thus most likely a migrant of color himself.[27]

26. Seward to Boswell, n.d., as quoted in Beck, Wells, and Chalkley, eds., *Biographical Catalogue,* 333; Harry to Hibbert, circa 1778, as quoted in Green, "Jenny Harry," *Friends' Quarterly Examiner,* XLII (1913), 562–563. The potential lack of concern over Harry's heritage in this period, owing to her class privilege, conforms to literary analysis on the connection between skin color and discourses on race. Both Felicity A. Nussbaum and Roxann Wheeler argue that complexion was only part of a battery of markers that constituted "race" in the eighteenth century; see Nussbaum, "Women and Race: 'A Difference of Complexion,'" in Vivien Jones, ed., *Women and Literature in Britain, 1700–1800* (New York, 2000), 69–88; and Wheeler, *The Complexion of Race: Categories of Difference in Eighteenth-Century British Culture* (Philadelphia, 2000).

27. Baptism of Catherine Morse, Dec. 4, 1757, Kingston baptisms, copy register, I, fol. 135, IRO; Will of Edmund Green, Apr. 4, 1802, PROB 11/1422, NAE, Will of John Morse, Apr. 18, 1781, PROB 11/1077; William Hickey, *Memoirs of William Hickey,* ed. Alfred Spencer, 9th

Little is known of Robert's English experiences before leaving London, but his travel to India reveals the type of character he formed while in Britain. In particular, he demonstrated a self-identification with elite British society, wholly divorced from any subordinate, colonial roots. On landing in Bengal in November 1777, Robert and his companions marveled at the natives before them "laugh[ing] heartily, not only at the language so new to our ears, but at the whole scene that presented itself and the many grotesque figures that appeared amongst the spectators." Moreover, each of them found intense amusement with "the ludicrous figures and postures the black people put themselves." Robert fit in well with this cadre of English voyeurs studying the natives. Further distanced from his West Indian and African heritage through an English upbringing, he could assert an equal claim to metropolitan identity against a colonized people. It might not have been a conscious construction on his part, but Robert's participation in the ridicule of Indian natives formalized his own imperial advancement. Ironically, though born in the Empire's periphery, his reengagement with other colonies helped clear away his peripheral past.[28]

Soon after arriving in Bengal, Robert was admitted as an advocate and began making "a great deal of money" in his legal practice.[29] But he grew tired of the law and desperately sought new employment. Eventually, he switched careers and took a job with the East India Company as paymaster for a battalion of Bengalese troops. That position did not last, however, and he rejoined the bar in Calcutta, despite that his inclinations were "naturally averse" to the profession. Robert now "sat whole days in Court, unemployed, a circumstance that mortified him excessively, for . . . he had a large share of pride." Yet, he persisted. By 1783, he won an appointment as sheriff. Eventually, Robert returned to London, where he invested in his brother-in-law's

ed., 4 vols. (New York, 1948), II, 103–107. The location of Catherine and Edmund's wedding is unclear, but the *London Evening Post* records the marriage, noting Green's origins in the Isle of Wight; see *London Evening Post,* June 17, 1777.

28. Hickey, *Memoirs,* ed. Spencer, II, 118–120.

29. Despite Morse's ultimate success as a lawyer, he nevertheless found initial difficulties in Bengal. Immediately on their arrival, Morse and his friend William Hickey discovered that Stephan Caesar Lemaitre, a justice in Bengal's Supreme Court of Judicature for whom both men had introductory letters, had died. Morse had met his letter's author, a Welsh judge, at a dinner in London shortly before embarking for India. After reading through two pages of the recommendation without a single mention of his name, Morse found himself inserted into the letter's final line: "This will, I believe, be delivered to you by a Mr. Morse, who the devil he is or what sort of a man I cannot tell, never having seen him in my life!" Networks were thus not always reliable; see Hickey, *Memoirs,* ed. Spencer, II, 122–130, III, 156.

brewery and acquired a share of property in Covent Garden. Success on the subcontinent distanced Robert Morse from his Caribbean origins, and he arrived back in England as something of an Indian nabob, rather than as a descendant of slaves.[30]

Two of Robert's sisters followed him to India. Perhaps thoughts of marriage motivated the journey. With so many unmarried men making substantial fortunes, India was a prime location for finding a husband. However, few single Englishwomen left for South Asia. Women of color, who might have experienced resistance to marriage in Britain owing to their African heritage, possibly expected to find more receptive partners there. In Calcutta, Sarah and Ann Morse met two thriving Englishmen. William Cator, an associate of Robert Morse, worked as a merchant factor for the East India Company. For Sarah, attaching herself to a rising English family was the best method by which to reinforce her social legitimacy. In the autumn of 1780, Sarah wed Cator in Calcutta. The week before, Ann married Nathaniel Middleton, a junior merchant and later a company servant. Both sisters would eventually return to England with their husbands, bolstered by newfound imperial connections to India as well as added colonial fortunes. In less of a position to articulate their inclusion into British society through professional development, as Robert could, the Morse sisters instead constructed a refined identity through marriage.[31]

30. Hickey, *Memoirs*, ed. Spencer, III, 191. Nathaniel Middleton, Morse's brother-in-law, wrote of his concern about Morse's struggles on reentering the bar after leaving his paymaster position; see Nathaniel Middleton to Elijah Impey, Aug. 12, 1782, Correspondence of Sir Elijah Impey, Add. MS 16263, fols. 273-274, BL. For more on Robert's activities on arriving back in England, see Will of Robert Morse, Feb. 29, 1816, PROB 11/1577, NAE. Morse, along with his sisters and brothers-in-law, invested in the troubled brewery of William Cator, husband of Sarah (née Morse). For more on the financial settlement surrounding the brewery, see Watney Mann Records, 1799, 789/201-33, City of Westminster Archives Center, Westminster, U.K.

31. Hickey, *Memoirs*, ed. Spencer, II, 123, 155; Marriage of William Cator and Sarah Morse, East India Company Returns of Marriages, Nov. 4, 1780, APAC, N/1/2, fol. 145v, BL, Marriage of Nathaniel Middleton and Ann Morse, Oct. 26, 1780. In Samuel Foote's play *The Nabob*, Matthew Mite offers to transport two women "to Madrass or Calcutta, and there procure them suitable husbands"; see Foote, *The Nabob; A Comedy, in Three Acts* (London, 1778), 9. Much like British planters in the West Indies, Middleton had several children with a native woman: Eliza, Charlotte, and George. Oddly, Middleton baptized his daughter Eliza on the same day that he wed Ann; see *Oxford Dictionary of National Biography*, online ed., s.v. "Middleton, Nathaniel (1750-1807)," by T. H. Bowyer, http://www.oxforddnb .com/view/article/69059; Will of Nathaniel Middleton, Aug. 1824, PROB 11/1470, NAE, and Robson and Robson v. Leake and Smith, 1834, PROB 37/909.

The Morses and Jane Harry each found relative acceptance in Britain in the 1770s. As the children of wealthy Jamaicans, they held the financial trappings of resettled colonial elites. Skin color and biological heritage does not appear to have entered into immediate, or at least explicit, consideration of their place in metropolitan society. As two of the many mixed-race families transported from Jamaica to Britain up to the American Revolution, they might have simply fit into an accepted and understood migration. With family and class associations more in keeping with Britain's finest residents than with enslaved Africans, these migrants had little trouble assimilating into a privileged life an ocean away from Jamaica. For those of African heritage without such wealth, British society was far less accommodating.

Somerset, Slavery, and British Demography

Dido Elizabeth Belle was just ten years old when James Somerset fled his master Charles Steuart in October 1771. In certain ways, the two had much in common. Dido's mother had been enslaved—possibly in Africa—and taken to England, where she gave birth to her daughter who was later freed. Somerset was born in Africa, captured and sold to the New World, and also brought to England. The two even resided near one another: Dido in the tony London neighborhood of Bloomsbury Square and Somerset in the city's thriving eastern end. Here, though, is where their stories diverge, for, despite their proximity, the two lived worlds apart. Dido's father was a captain in the Royal Navy, and he asked his uncle William Murray, Baron Mansfield, to raise her alongside her cousins, two other great-nieces whom Mansfield had also adopted. Under Mansfield's watchful care, Dido lived in relative splendor, eventually moving to his estate in Hampstead Heath (see Plate 1).[32] Somer-

32. Numerous historians have examined Dido's life; see Folarin Shyllon, *Black People in Britain, 1555–1833* (New York, 1977), 40–41; Gretchen Gerzina, *Black England: Life Before Emancipation* (London, 1995), 90–132; Asher Hoyles and Martin Hoyles, *Remember Me: Achievements of Mixed Race People Past and Present* (London, 1999), 65–66; Simon Schama, *Rough Crossings: Britain, the Slaves, and the American Revolution* (New York, 2006), 40–41; *Oxford Dictionary of National Biography,* online ed., s.v. "Belle, Dido Elizabeth (1761?–1804)," by Reyahn King, http://www.oxforddnb.com/view/article/73352; and Gene Adams, "Dido Elizabeth Belle, a Black Girl at Kenwood: An Account of a Protégée of the 1st Lord Mansfield," *Camden History Review,* XII (1984), 10–14. Her life has also been dramatized in the 2013 movie *Belle.* Details of her birth are speculative. Thomas Hutchinson reported, after meeting Dido, that she was the daughter of an enslaved black woman taken from a captured Spanish vessel in the Atlantic; see Thomas Hutchinson, *The Diary and Letters of His Excellency Thomas Hutchinson, Esq.,* ed. Peter Hutchinson, 2 vols. (London, 1883–1886), II, 276. However, these details have never been confirmed and are most likely untrue. She

set, on the other hand, bitterly detested his situation. Still bound to Steuart, he decided to run away, perhaps with the encouragement of new friends in the capital's growing community of free and enslaved blacks. Steuart tracked him down, however, and imprisoned him on board a Jamaican-bound ship docked in the Thames. One week later, several of Somerset's friends appealed to the Court of King's Bench, on which Mansfield sat as chief justice, to issue a writ of habeas corpus on his behalf. Mansfield would ultimately decide in Somerset's favor, proclaiming in June 1772 that no individual, not even those enslaved, could be taken involuntarily out of England. Although the ruling did not grant freedom to captive workers in England, it did give them certain bargaining rights with owners not to be returned to the colonies against their will. It is unclear what, if anything, Mansfield told his mixed-race niece about the case. Dido's thoughts on the matter are also lost to history, although she might have drawn no parallels between herself and Somerset. Britons familiar with the trial portrayed it as a judgment on the future of Britain's racial composition. This was not simply a legal debate over slavery; it was the culmination of years of concerns over family, race, and demography on both sides of the Atlantic.[33]

—————

might have had a brother, John, as such a person is listed in her father's will as a "reputed son" with whom she was to split a one-thousand-pound trust; see Will of Jonathan Lindsay, June 13, 1788, PROB 11/1167, NAE; and Shyllon, *Black People in Britain*, 41. King claims that the John and Elizabeth listed in Lindsay's will were two other illegitimate children and that Elizabeth had no brother-german. Her life story is similar to one recounted in the previous century. William Heath, acting as an agent for the Guinea Company in Gamboa, married a native black woman, Speranca (later renamed Hope Booker), in 1693. After she became pregnant, Heath sent her to England, where she gave birth to their daughter Elizabeth in November 1694. William died before he could return to England himself; see "A President relating to a Whitemans Marryage with a Black Woman at Gamboa in Guinea," Book of Cases, II, 1695–1738, fols. 103–104, Religious Society of Friends Library, London.

33. For the details of the Somerset case, see [Francis] Hargrave, *An Argument in the Case of James Sommersett a Negro* (London, 1772), 3–6. Legal analyses of the Somerset case tend to debate the amount of freedom given to slaves in England. For those who view Mansfield's decision as emancipationist, or at least liberally empowering, see William R. Cotter, "The Somerset Case and the Abolition of Slavery in England," *History*, LXXIX (1994), 31–56; and Kathleen Chater, *Untold Histories: Black People in England and Wales during the Period of the British Slave Trade, c. 1660–1807* (New York, 2009), 77–101. For those who perceive Mansfield's decision as strictly an issue of habeas corpus rights, see James Oldham, "New Light on Mansfield and Slavery," *Journal of British Studies*, XXVII (1988), 45–68; Paul D. Halliday, *Habeas Corpus: From England to Empire* (Cambridge, Mass., 2010), 174–176; and Dana Rabin, "'In a Country of Liberty?': Slavery, Villeinage, and the Making of Whiteness in the Somerset Case (1772)," *History Workshop Journal*, LXXII (October 2011), 5–29. For

PLATE 1. Kenwood House, Hampstead Heath, London. Photograph by the author

PLATE 2. *Lady Elizabeth Murray and Dido Belle.*
Unknown artist, formerly attributed to Johann Zoffany. Circa 1780.
Courtesy of Earls of Mansfield, Scone Palace, Perth, Scotland

Somerset was not the first escaped slave in Britain brought before a court; he was not even the first escaped slave brought before Lord Mansfield. Owing to the vagaries of Mansfield's ruling, he would not be the last black man to claim freedom in Britain either. Masters sought runaway servants throughout the Stuart and Hanoverian eras, and test cases on slavery abounded in the eighteenth century.[34] Mansfield's decision did galvanize private interests and public opinion in ways previous events never had. The specifics of the case are well known, and the exact legal meaning of the decision is not under investigation here. More important to this study, instead, is the general discourse around the issue of slavery in Britain both before and after the case. Scattered questions on slavery, freedom, demography, and marriage crystallized around

----

those who interpret it as an ambiguous decision, see William M. Wiecek, "*Somerset:* Lord Mansfield and the Legitimacy of Slavery in the Anglo-American World," *University of Chicago Law Review,* XLII (1974–1975), 86–146; Douglas A. Lorimer, "Black Slaves and English Liberty: A Re-examination of Racial Slavery in England," *Immigrants and Minorities,* III (1984), 121–150; and James Walvin, *The Zong: A Massacre, the Law, and the End of Slavery* (New Haven, Conn., 2011), 132–137. A forum in the *Law and History Review* reassesses each of these perspectives; see "Forum: Somerset's Case Revisited," *Law and History Review,* XXIV, no. 3 (Fall 2006), 601–671. For more generalities on the case and its actors, see Shyllon, *Black People in Britain,* 20–41; Gerzina, *Black England,* 90–133; and Christopher Leslie Brown, *Moral Capital: Foundations of British Abolitionism* (Chapel Hill, N.C., 2006), 98–101.

34. In 1771, Mansfield heard the case of *Rex v. Stapylton,* which also revolved around an escaped slave—in this case Thomas Lewis—threatened with deportation to Jamaica. However, Mansfield left Lewis's fate in the hands of a jury, which found him to be free. One year after his decision in the Somerset trial, he would also oversee the negotiations for the freedom of Little Ephraim Robin John and Ancona Robin Robin John, two African slave traders wrongfully enslaved and eventually imprisoned in Bristol; see Randy J. Sparks, *The Two Princes of Calabar: An Eighteenth-Century Atlantic Odyssey* (Cambridge, Mass., 2008), 96–106. For more on slave trials in Britain, see Shyllon, *Black People in Britain,* 20–26; and Travis Glasson, "'Baptism Doth Not Bestow Freedom': Missionary Anglicanism, Slavery, and the Yorke-Talbot Opinion, 1701–30," *WMQ,* 3d Ser., LXII (2010), 279–318. Holly Brewer's forthcoming work *Inheritable Blood: Slavery and Sovereignty in Early America and the British Empire* (Cambridge University Press) also explores the development of English slave law in the seventeenth and early eighteenth centuries. France experienced quite similar legal contests over individual claims to freedom; see Pierre H. Boulle, "In Defense of Slavery: Eighteenth-Century Opposition to Abolition and the Origins of a Racist Ideology in France," in Frederick Krantz, ed., *History from Below: Studies in Popular Protest and Popular Ideology in Honour of George Rudé* (Montreal, 1985), 221–241; Boulle, "Racial Purity or Legal Clarity? The Status of Black Residents in Eighteenth-Century France," *Journal of the Historical Society,* VI (2006), 19–46; and Sue Peabody, *"There Are No Slaves in France": The Political Culture of Race and Slavery in the Ancien Régime* (New York, 1996), 57–137.

the trial. Suddenly, these "somewhat abstract issues matter[ed] in England in a concrete way." Somerset's case was the child of these long-standing concerns, but it also birthed its own set of debates on the future of race and migration in a changing empire. Foremost among these, it helped to erode British notions of a separate metropole and periphery. Jamaican matters of race and society now applied to Britain as well.[35]

In deciding that masters could not take enslaved people forcefully off English soil, Lord Mansfield energized an old debate about the presence of blacks in the metropole. From its beginning, the transshipment of Africans across the Atlantic naturally landed small numbers of black men and women in England, Scotland, and Wales. Their presence garnered relatively little attention until 1729, when colonial missionaries sought a legal opinion to declare that baptism did not confer freedom — thus calming planters' fears about evangelical efforts among the enslaved. Philip Yorke, later Lord Hardwicke, and Charles Talbot wrote an opinion exactly to that effect, adding that enslaved laborers retained their status while in England. Observers at the time certainly noticed more bound servants in the metropole. A 1730 tract on colonial slavery remarked: "So many Negroes are now to be seen in *England* itself." The author worried that many of them, like Somerset forty years later, might head off to "some remote County" with the help of black friends when their masters prepared to leave for the colonies. Once free, the author continued, "This Negroman can be of little use in *England* except to fill up a Number, and to consume the Food of another." Such pre-Malthusian concern with population and resources led London's lord mayor to pass an ordinance in 1731 that "no *Negroes* or other *Blacks* be suffered to be bound Apprentices at any of the Companies of this City." Fears of interracial sex followed, in some cases justifiably. The West Indian magnate and future lord mayor William Beckford, for example, fell into intense despair as a young man in the 1730s when the "mulatto boy" he brought over from Jamaica impregnated his white lover in London. Clearly, by the first third of the eighteenth century, free and enslaved blacks in England aroused considerable concern about the nation's population.[36]

35. On the Somerset decision making abolitionism more institutional in nature, see Brown, *Moral Capital*, 98. The Somerset trial's proceedings can be read in Henry George Tuke, ed., *The Fugitive Slave Circulars* (London, 1876), 23–73.

36. *A Letter to the Right Reverend the Lord Bishop of London* . . . (London, 1730), 34–41; "Ordinance of the Lord Mayor of London," Sept. 16, 1731, Printed Books, Broadsides 6.34, GL; Shyllon, *Black People in Britain,* 84–85. For more on the Hardwicke-Tablot decision, see Glasson, " 'Baptism Doth Not Bestow Freedom,' " *WMQ,* 3d Ser., LXII (2010), 303–305. Another proslavery tract, published six years after the 1730 tract, told the fictional story of

Yorke and Talbot's opinion appears to have calmed much of the broad legal debate on slavery in England for the next forty years, but it did not end it. Black servants continued to file individual claims of freedom, despite English judges' general support for the Yorke-Talbot reasoning.[37] As a British phenomenon, however, legal definitions of slavery in the metropole were not uniform. Scottish jurists did not incorporate the 1729 opinion into their decisions, causing some concern among those who brought black attendants to North Britain. This sounded an alarm among antislavery supporters as well. The Edinburgh lawyer George Wallace, inspired by David Hume and other members of the Scottish Enlightenment to see slavery as economically inefficient, worried that Scotland did not have a solid legal position on slavery. Perhaps hoping to draft an opinion as influential as Yorke and Talbot's, he insisted in 1760 that Scottish law did not tolerate enslavement, so that "every one of those unfortunate men, who shall happen to get into Scotland, is, and is entitled to be declared to be a free man." Wallace's claim was as much a warning to slaveowners not to bring captive laborers north of the Tweed as it was a celebration of Scottish legal freedoms. Demography certainly weighed on his mind as well, particularly when it came to the idea of emancipated slaves. He encouraged American planters to set their workers free, "and, in

_____

an enslaved Jamaican who attended his master's son at a grammar school in Yorkshire, then at Oxford; see *The Speech of Mr John Talbot Campo-bell, a Free Christian-Negro, to His Countrymen in the Mountains of Jamaica; In Two Parts* (London, 1736), 5-6. The incident with Beckford's servant occurred sometime in the mid-1730s and is related in at least two biographical descriptions of Beckford; see [Cyrus Redding], *City Biography, Containing Anecdotes and Memoirs of the Rise, Progress, Situation, and Character, of the Aldermen and Other Conspicuous Personages of the Corporation and City of London* (London, 1799), 78-79; and *Memoirs of William Beckford of Fonthill . . .*, I (London, 1859), 18. For more on the presence of blacks in Britain in the sixteenth and seventeenth centuries, see James Walvin, *The Black Presence: A Documentary History of the Negro in England, 1555–1860* (London, 1971); Walvin, *Black and White: The Negro and English Society, 1555–1945* (London, 1973), 1-27; Shyllon, *Black People in Britain*, 1-25; Peter Fryer, *Staying Power: Black People in Britain since 1504* (Atlantic Highlands, N.J., 1984), 1-67; Gerzina, *Black England;* Imtiaz Habib, *Black Lives in the English Archives, 1500-1677: Imprints of the Invisible* (Burlington, Vt., 2008); Chris Evans, *Slave Wales: The Welsh and Atlantic Slavery, 1660–1850* (Cardiff, 2010); and Chater, *Untold Histories*, 1-25.

37. Lorimer, "Black Slaves and English Liberty," *Immigrants and Minorities*, III (1984), 140. Yorke and Talbot's opinion did not close the debate, even on the question of baptism and slavery. Edmund Hoskins agreed with the 1729 brief twenty years later when an enslaved man belonging to Dudly Crofts refused to return to the West Indies from England. Hoskins's consideration of the issue, though, shows that Yorke and Talbot's opinion was not taken as authoritative; see *A Letter to Philo Africanus, upon Slavery . . .* (London, 1788), 29-32.

a few generations, this vast and fertile continent would be crowded with in-habitants." Wallace meant this as a celebration of the progress of manumis-sion, but promoting emancipation for its effect on fecundity likely did not sit well with Scottish readers worried that freed blacks might intermarry and reproduce liberally with white women at home. Many likely shared Hume's sentiments, proclaimed twelve years earlier, that "there are Negroe slaves dis-persed all over Europe, of which none ever discovered any symptoms of inge-nuity." Even though reformers, like Hume, wished to see slavery modified if not ended, most did not push for any degree of racial equality.[38]

Combining slave reform with demographic analysis came directly out of colonial debates. Jamaican examinations of enslaved populations always co-incided with concerns over white settlement. Should Jamaica's unfree com-munity grow too large, then white control would dissolve. Decades before British humanitarians, Jamaica's governor called for an end to the slave trade on exactly these grounds. Writing anonymously in 1746, Edward Trelawny professed that he would "be content, if no more Slaves be imported." The reasons were clear. "Negroes go on increasing by Importations every Year," he noted, but "the *Whites* rather diminish yearly." The outcome, he believed, was equally obvious; he contended that "the further Importation of Negroes for Sale in the Island should be forbid by a *British* Act of Parliament." Like Wallace, Trelawny maintained that West Indians of African descent would have no problem reproducing themselves without future imports. Although he did not advocate for emancipation, Trelawny believed that reform might en-able such demographic increase. Preventing interracial and extramarital sex, moreover, would also spur reproduction, as slaves "lie with both Colours, and do not know which the Child might prove of," and thus supposedly under-took frequent abortions. For both Trelawny and Wallace, then, a reformed, if not eradicated, system of slavery would keep Africans and their descendants in the colonies and would end the worst horrors of the transatlantic slave com-

38. George Wallace, *A System of the Principles of the Law of Scotland,* I (Edinburgh, 1760), 88–96; David Hume, "Of National Characters," in T. H. Green and T. H. Grose, eds., *Essays Moral, Political, and Literary,* I (New York, 1889), 252n; David Brion Davis, "New Side-lights on Early Antislavery Radicalism," *WMQ,* 3d Ser., XXVIII (1971), 585–594; Brown, *Moral Capital,* 96n. Scotland had a number of enslaved blacks in its borders in the eigh-teenth century; see June Evans, "African / Caribbeans in Scotland: A Socio-Geographical Study" (Ph.D. diss., University of Edinburgh, 1995), 34–75; and Iain Whyte, *Scotland and the Abolition of Black Slavery, 1756–1838* (Edinburgh, 2006), 9–15. Hume's attack was likely inspired by his distaste after learning about Francis Williams, the privileged black Jamaican who went to school in England before returning to the island.

plex through demographic balance. Furthermore, interracial unions on both sides of the ocean might decrease substantially in turn.[39]

These appeals for demographic surveillance blossomed in the 1760s, as imperial migration escalated and more people of color arrived in Britain. Jamaican absentees traveled to the metropole in much greater numbers after the Seven Years' War, alongside North American colonists on grand tours of Europe. Many brought along black servants, a practice that rested uneasily with certain residents of the capital. A 1764 editorial in the *Gentleman's Magazine* fretted over the supposed twenty thousand black residents in London who "cease to consider themselves as slaves in this free country." In 1765, a London physician made a stronger claim, insisting that he knew several instances of black and white intermarriage in both the capital and in York. A high-ranking magistrate, John Fielding, complained three years later about the number of foreign servants generally intermixing in Britain. He targeted those of a darker shade specifically, imploring that "the immense Confusion that has arose in the Families of Merchants and other Gentlemen who have Estates in the West-Indies, from the great Number of Negro Slaves they have brought into this Kingdom, also deserves the most serious Attention." Fielding alleged that enslaved blacks caused dissension in families they served, if they stayed with them at all, and attempted to claim freedom by marrying English brides. Although Fielding did not explore this idea further, such weddings plainly unsettled him.[40]

39. [Edward Trelawny], *An Essay concerning Slavery, and the Danger Jamaica Is Expos'd from the Too Great Number of Slaves . . .* (London, 1746), introduction, A3v, 18–34. It was not uncommon for enslaved women to use abortifacients and contraception to regulate their reproduction, especially when attacked by white men; see Jerome Teelucksingh, "The 'Invisible Child' in British West Indian Slavery," *Slavery and Abolition*, XXVII (2006), 240–241. On Trelawny's authorship, see Trevor Burnard, "Slavery and the Causes of the American Revolution in Plantation British America," in Andrew Shankman, ed., *The World of the Revolutionary American Republic: Land, Labor, and the Conflict for a Continent* (New York, 2014), 58–59.

40. "Short Notes from the Papers," *Gentleman's Magazine: And Historical Chronicle*, XXXIV (London, 1764), 493; James Parsons, *An Account of the White Negro Shewn Before the Royal Society . . .* , in *Philosophical Transactions of the Royal Society*, LV (London, 1765), 47–48; John Fielding, *Extracts from Such of the Penal Law as Particularly Relate to the Peace and Good Order of This Metropolis . . .* , 2d ed. (London, 1768), 143–145; Trevor Burnard, "Passengers Only: The Extent and Significance of Absenteeism in Eighteenth Century Jamaica," *Atlantic Studies*, I (2004), 178–195; Julie Flavell, *When London Was Capital of America* (New Haven, Conn., 2010), 4; Daniel Kilbride, *Being American in Europe, 1750–1860* (Baltimore, 2013), 10–15.

Multiple newspaper editorials concurred about a looming threat to British society. One author lamented in 1765 the "vast importation of Negroes, Mulattoes, and Blacks" with whom "our Whites will be so infamously base as to intermarry." Observers were particularly concerned about the potential for mixed-race partnerships among the poorer classes, declaring that "the English complexion . . . shall in less than half a century, be utterly defaced amongst the common people." The threat to British culture and civility also worried the author, who hoped that black and mixed-race servants would be ordered back to the colonies. An editorial in London's *Public Advertiser* two years later similarly claimed that blacks "swarm in every street" of the capital and that Parliament needed to pass a law taxing all "foreign servants and Negros" landing in England.[41]

Even reform-minded Britons struggled to accept the biological outcome of an increased black presence. Granville Sharp, the lawyer who would later help to shape Somerset's legal strategy, wrote of similar discomfort the year after Fielding's publication. He roundly condemned slavery, especially in Britain, but also disparaged the "national inconvenience" of Caribbean planters increasing the "stock of black Servants in this kingdom, which is already much too numerous." Equally disturbing to the abolitionist was "the mixed people or Mulattoes, produced by the unavoidable intercourse with their white neighbours" in England. Thus, even among those advocating for black residents, the issue of slavery in Britain inevitably led to demographic handwringing. To them, British slaves did not represent a political threat but instead a biological one.[42]

Such concerns were bound up with intertwined anxieties around marriage and family formation. British polemicists continued to worry, like their Caribbean counterparts, about the growth of proper family units. Until Thomas Malthus's declarations about overpopulation at the end of the eighteenth century, Britons routinely complained that the metropole was not crowded enough. In 1767, a Scottish physician insisted that sexual vice had produced too many unsupported illegitimate children who would either die or fall on public support. Promoting marriage was the only way that Britain could stave off population decline and transform Jamaica into a "well-peopled Island." Fellow Scottish writer Francis Douglas echoed these comments in 1771. Hor-

41. *Gazetteer and New Daily Advertiser* (London), Sept. 21, 1765; *Public Advertiser* (London), Sept. 30, 1767.

42. Granville Sharp, *A Representation of the Injustice and Dangerous Tendency of Tolerating Slavery . . .* (London, 1769), 74–75, 109.

rified by the "scandalous and reiterated accounts of conjugal infidelity [reported] in England," he declared that marriage conferred honor, whereas concubinage and bachelorhood imparted disgrace. In consequence of men going unmarried, Douglas insisted that "the state is depopulated, the specie locked up, and many an amiable woman suffered to bloom, to fade, and to die unmarried, who might have been the happy mother of healthy and virtuous children."[43] Parliament also stayed vigilant on this topic. It repeatedly introduced legislation to adjust and improve England's clandestine marriage laws as well as regulate the treatment of illegitimate children thought to be financial drains on local parishes. If Britain did not promote marriage while discouraging bachelorhood, then population growth, economic development, and moral respectability would decline precipitously. Put another way, the same fears of white demography long torturing Jamaicans now energized Britons in a much more focused manner. The king's ministers worried so intently about depopulation that in 1773 they undertook a census recording all emigrants leaving the Isles.[44]

At the same time, observers insisted that not all marriages were equal. In particular, misalliances presented their own complications. Douglas did not simply want an explosion of nuptials, he wanted to ensure that like married like. Unions between individuals of different social ranks, he argued,

43. Thomas Short, *A Comparative History of the Increase and Decrease of Mankind in England, and Several Countries Abroad . . .* (London, 1767), 25–28, 72; Douglas, *Reflections on Celibacy and Marriage*, 36, 60–61; C. A. Bayly, *Imperial Meridian: The British Empire and the World, 1780–1830* (London, 1997), 3. Amanda Vickery demonstrates that bachelorhood in eighteenth-century England was seen as emasculating, particularly because it denied men a type of virility connected to domesticity and heading families; see Vickery, *Behind Closed Doors: At Home in Georgian England* (New Haven, Conn., 2009), 49–82. See also Joanne Bailey, *Parenting in England, 1760–1830: Emotion, Identity, and Generation* (New York, 2012), 22–26.

44. For legislation regulating marriage, see, in particular: A Bill to Repeal an Act, [26 Geo. II, c. 33] . . . and to Encourage and Facilitate Marriages . . . , Feb. 13, 1765, no. 3032, in *HCSP*, XXI, 81–85, A Bill to Amend an Act, [26 Geo. II, c. 33] . . . for the Better Preventing of Clandestine Marriages. . . , May 1, 1772, no. 3131, XXII, 437–439, A Bill for Regulating the Settlements of Bastard Children, May 2, 1772, no. 3132, 441–447, and A Bill for Better Regulating the Settlement and Providing for the Maintenance of Bastard Children, Apr. 28–29, 1773, no. 3172, XXIV, 27–41. Two major works survey the extent of information from these emigration records; see Bernard Bailyn, with Barbara DeWolfe, *Voyagers to the West: A Passage in the Peopling of America on the Eve of the Revolution* (New York, 1986); and Peter Wilson Coldham, *Emigrants from England to the American Colonies, 1773–1776* (Baltimore, 1988).

destroyed trust and bred resentment.[45] An anonymous pamphleteer—most likely Douglas himself—lamented in 1772 that mixed marriages between rich and poor produced undue complications of wealth that tore apart households. Ill-suited matches could lead to disinheritance or financially dysfunctional relationships. These matrimonial admonitions reflected the previous two decades' interest in combating clandestine marriages across the Anglophone world. George III's own disgust over his brothers' infelicitous matches inspired the Royal Marriages Act of 1772, which required monarchial consent to the nuptials of His Majesty's siblings. Whereas Jamaican officials fretted over improper pairings based on distinctions of race, Britons largely worried over similar mismatches of class. But questions of ethnic heritage inevitably infiltrated these discussions. Sarah Scott's 1766 novel *The History of Sir George Ellison* highlighted such concerns. After returning to Britain from Jamaica with several black and white servants in tow, the titular character forbids intermarriage. "For though he promoted their marrying," the narrator observed, "he did not wish an union between those of different complexions, the connection appearing indelicate and almost unnatural." Such unions had aroused little disgust in the Caribbean, but they now suddenly appeared a threat in Britain.[46]

45. Douglas, *Reflections on Celibacy and Marriage,* 39–41. Fears about improper marriages had a long history, stemming from concerns about class and religion. Moses West's 1707 tract *A Treatise concerning Marriage* warned against mixed marriages between Catholics and Protestants—grounded in a religious argument about the biblical prohibitions against Jewish and gentile nuptials—and underwent multiple printings in the eighteenth century; see West, *A Treatise concerning Marriage* . . . (London, 1707). There are various patterns to observe about marital exogamy between social classes. For the peerage, social exogamy in marriage was significant in the eighteenth century; see David Thomas, "The Social Origins of Marriage Partners of the British Peerage in the Eighteenth and Nineteenth Centuries," *Population Studies,* XXVI (1972), 99–111. Among the rural poor, geographic—and thus socioeconomic—endogamy in marriage was strong; see K. D. M. Snell, "English Rural Societies and Geographical Marital Endogamy, 1700-1837," *Economic History Review,* LV (2002), 262–298.

46. *Considerations on the Causes of the Present Stagnation of Matrimony* . . . (London, 1772), 1–24. Holly Brewer believes Francis Douglas to have written this tract as well; see Brewer, *By Birth or Consent: Children, Law, and the Anglo-American Revolution in Authority* (Chapel Hill, N.C., 2005), 317n. For legislation concerning royal marriages, see 12 Geo. III, c. 11 (1772); and C. d'O. Farran, "The Royal Marriages Act, 1772," *Modern Law Review,* XIV (1951), 53–56. The Rockingham Whigs opposed the Royal Marriage Act in 1772 because they worried that the crown might gain too much control over marriages generally; see W. M. Elofson, "The Rockingham Whigs in Transition: The East India Company Issue, 1772-1773," *English Historical Review,* CIV (1989), 956–957. An interesting comparison can

Within this heightened rhetorical environment, James Somerset came before Lord Mansfield. His trial focused predominantly on English laws toward bound subjects, especially medieval regulations on villeins and their applicability to concepts of chattel slavery on which England held no statutes. Yet, lawyers did not avoid the issue of British demography. William Davy, Somerset's lead attorney, echoed Sharp and Wallace's racial comments at a pretrial hearing in February 1772. Davy hoped to win Somerset a writ of habeas corpus, not to protect his fundamental rights, but to forestall future importations of bound workers into Britain. According to Davy, England already dealt with the consequences of that migration. "Now and then we have some Accidents of Children born of an Odd Colour," he acknowledged. If Mansfield confirmed Somerset's rights, then West Indian planters would stop bringing black servants who would then flee and intermix with whites. If Mansfield denied those rights, then slaves would accompany their masters in even greater numbers, heralding a new social frontier. "I don't know what our Progeny might be, I mean of what Colour," Davy warned in such case; "a Freeman of this country might in the course of time be the grandfather of half a Score of Slaves for what we know." Davy clearly fretted over the racial implications of further black arrivals into Britain, but these fears fixated entirely on enslaved immigrants. The notion of whites fathering enslaved children in Britain signaled a rapid breakdown in familial structure as well as a disintegration of an emerging English racial identity.[47]

With such professed anxiety about the arrival of enslaved blacks both before and during Somerset's trial, it is little surprise that observers expressed the same concerns after the case concluded in his favor. Most famously, Jamaican absentee Edward Long foretold of a world turned upside down after Mansfield made his determination. Long had returned to England only three

___

be made to Spain, where in 1776 a Royal Pragmatic on Marriage required parental consent for the marriage of anyone under the age of twenty-five. The law was passed with similar goals as England's 1772 act: namely, to prevent matches between those of unequal social rank. For Scott's novel and the wider implications behind it, see Sarah Scott, *The History of Sir George Ellison*, II (London, 1766), 48; Moira Ferguson, *Subject to Others: British Women Writers and Colonial Slavery, 1670–1834* (New York, 1992), 104; Felicity A. Nussbaum, *The Limits of the Human: Fictions of Anomaly, Race, and Gender in the Long Eighteenth Century* (New York, 2003), 135–150; and Brycchan Carey, *British Abolitionism and the Rhetoric of Sensibility: Writing, Sentiment, and Slavery, 1760–1807* (New York, 2005), 50–57.

47. William Davy, Feb. 7, 1772, as quoted in David Brion Davis, *The Problem of Slavery in the Age of Revolution, 1770–1823* (New York, 1999), 495; Rabin, "'In a Country of Liberty,'" *History Workshop Journal*, LXXII (October 2011), 18–19; and Kathleen Wilson, *The Island Race: Englishness, Empire, and Gender in the Eighteenth Century* (New York, 2003), 11–16.

years earlier, after serving in the assembly and as a vice admiralty judge in Jamaica. He had also been present in London's West India Merchants Committee when the group debated what to do in case Mansfield set Somerset free. Long was astonished when that potential situation became a reality. He proclaimed that, suddenly guaranteed habeas corpus rights, *"three hundred thousand blacks,* now scattered over our different colonies," would mutiny and traverse the Atlantic "where, by only swallowing one single mouthful of British air, they may enter upon the rights of *free-born Britons.*" Trading in gross exaggerations and fearmongering, he further speculated that one of those migrants might potentially win the lottery, enabling him to purchase a rotten borough seat so that he could take a place in the hallowed halls of England's House of Commons. "Complexion," he pronounced ominously, "will be no disqualification." None of Long's rhetorical forebears anticipated that freed blacks would take the reins of English government, but such a thought tapped into previous premonitions about social change in Britain should slaves escape to the metropole. These ideas were not entirely beyond the pale when Long penned his polemic.[48]

As hyperbolic as Long's claims were, he parroted near-identical concerns expressed by those who came before him. Much like Sharp and Davy, Long imagined rampant interracial unions if black men continued to come over. Those who had already arrived, according to Long, fell "into the company of vicious white servants, and abandoned prostitutes." Mixed-race children, naturally, would soon begin populating England's poorer ranks. They would stay there, Long insisted, owing to the negligence of black fathers who "make no scruple to abandon their new wife and mulatto progeny to the care of the parish." In Long's portrayal, interracial relationships resembled the worst

48. Edward Long, *Candid Reflections upon the Judgement Lately Awarded by the Court of King's Bench, in Westminster-Hall . . .* (London, 1772), 50, 59; *Oxford Dictionary of National Biography,* online ed., s.v. "Long, Edward (1734–1813)," by Kenneth Morgan, http://www .oxforddnb.com/view/article/16964?docPos=2. Long acquainted the West India Merchants Committee with Rose Fuller's introduction of a failed bill in the House of Commons on May 25, 1772, "for providing certain Regulations relative to Negroe and other Slaves, who shall hereafter come or be brought into *Great Britain* or *Ireland"*; see *Journals of the House of Commons,* XXXIII ([London], 1804), May 25, 1772, 789; Minutes of the West Indies Merchant Committee, June 2, 1772, Microfilm Minutes of the West Indies Merchants Committee, reel 1, M915, ICS; and Lorimer, "Black Slaves and English Liberty," *Immigrants and Minorities,* III (1984), 143n. For more on vice admiralty judges in the West Indies, see Michael Craton, "The Role of the Caribbean Vice Admiralty Courts in British Imperialism," *Caribbean Studies,* XI, no. 2 (July 1971), 5–20; and Carl Ubbelohde, *The Vice-Admiralty Courts in the American Revolution* (Chapel Hill, N.C., 1960).

types of sexual unions already plaguing England. Children born of servile blacks and destitute whites fell into the same category of illegitimate offspring troubling British observers throughout the eighteenth century. Cross-racial pairings in England, then, fit into an older perception of problematic households and dysfunctional reproduction.[49]

Where Long differed from previous commentators was on the scope of predicted social change. Those observing black immigrants in England before Mansfield's decision envisioned localized problems of interracial cohabitation and individual family upheaval. Long anticipated, though with polemical exaggeration, widespread cross-racial coupling. Trading on fears of black male sexuality, he insisted that white women — especially poor white women — lusted brutishly after African bodies. United together, they would have "a numerous brood." These children of color would then multiply exponentially, so that "in the course of a few generations more, the English blood will become so contaminated with this mixture . . . till the whole nation resembles the *Portuguese* and *Moriscos* in complexion of skin and baseness of mind." Here, Long's remarks diverged once more from previous commentators. Sharp and Davy both saw interracial relationships in England as a problem within the poorer ranks. Long agreed and targeted formerly enslaved black men as the culprits in bringing forth this racially amalgamated future. But, in amplifying his claims to terrify a British audience, he warned that the effects of these relationships would not stay contained within one segment of society. He bellowed that "this alloy may spread so extensively, as even to reach the middle, and then the higher orders of the people." He went so far as to label this process an "ulcer" that would spread "until every family catches infection from it."[50]

Taken as a whole, Long's tract reveals the importance of class, gender, and family considerations to his understanding of England's racial future. The supposed source of this racial transformation was not from a vague black threat but rather from a specific concern over the arrival of poor and enslaved men of color. Themes of violation and animalistic passion consumed Long's sense of black male sexuality. Moreover, he attributed the same forces of immorality to England's working-class women. Interracial matches, then, were simply another expression of improper sexuality and family organization endemic to England. Long worried over the prospect of this phenomenon reaching into the wealthier ranks, but this was a qualified anxiety. African blood might even-

49. Long, *Candid Reflections*, 47–48.
50. Ibid., 48–49.

tually permeate into England's middle and upper orders, but only in Long's most apocalyptic formulation. The more immediate and likely threat was still among England's laboring poor. This situation was nearly identical to the one in Jamaica. Colonial officials worried about the growth of a mixed-race population from more modestly successful whites and enslaved blacks—demonstrated through the passage of the inheritance cap—while fretting little over such children from elite whites, as shown through the approval of privilege bills. Britons agonized in much the same way over interracial matches at home.

As overinflated as Long's comments were, his sense of an impending corruption of English blood influenced social critics and individual opinions alike. Samuel Estwick, who had lived in Barbados and would later serve as the island's London agent, called for a ban on slave importation into England based on similar reasoning. Writing at the same time as his Jamaican peer, he believed that this prohibition would "preserve the race of Britons from stain and contamination." An Antiguan absentee concurred, claiming in the same year that such an edict would "save the natural beauty of Britons from the Morisco tint." Three years later, an Irish author warned the English populace that, "if they pursue the addition they have lately begun to make to it, by mixing with Jews and negroes, their progeny will not much longer have reason to value themselves on their beauty, wit, or virtue." North American visitors drew similar conclusions. On leave from his South Carolina plantations in 1774, Henry Laurens proclaimed that he was "astonished" at the number of black servants in London—one of whom, Robert, was his own. Laurens wished "to See the Kingdom cleaned from every one of [Robert's] Colour," especially as he expected that in six years' time "there will be at least 20,000 Mulatties [sic] in London." This was especially problematic as "half a dozen Boroughs [seats] . . . may be purchased" by them in due time—a direct imitation of Long's hyperbolic claims. Likewise, the popular travel writer Philip Thicknesse railed against the pairing of black men with English women, asserting in 1777 that "in almost every village are to be seen a little race of mulattoes, mischievous as monkeys, and infinitely more dangerous." His simian comparison made obvious connections to the racist notion of Africans as a separate species. But the supposed danger that he pointed to was familial, rather than political.[51]

51. [Samuel Estwick], *Considerations on the Negro Cause* . . . (London, 1772), 44; Samuel Martin, *A Short Treatise on the Slavery of Negroes in the British Colonies* (Antigua, 1775), 12 (this edition notes that the original was printed three years before); [Charles Johnstone], *The Pilgrim* . . . (Dublin, 1775), 127; Henry Laurens to George Appleby, Feb. 28, 1774,

Long, then, was not a lone voice crying out in the wilderness. His forewarning of a social and racial breakdown in England after Mansfield's decision came out of more established commentary about the presence of black attendants in the metropole. For most, this appeared a scourge coursing through Britain's poorer ranks. Should runaway slaves intermix with white servants in the metropole, a disenfranchised and destitute group of African descent would emerge that might compromise Britain's imagined political and biological stability. A heightened interest around race in Britain after the Seven Years' War brought multiple perspectives to this debate. Ukawsaw Gronniosaw's 1772 autobiography of his time spent in slavery, along with his new life as a freeman in Britain, made repeated mention of his white wife and children of color. Gronniosaw noted that many people objected to his marriage, not out of racial concerns, but because his beloved was poor. Although commentators did not mention him by name, Gronniosaw's account surely confirmed the fears of those worried about the future face of Britain's working classes. The timing of his autobiography fed perfectly into this paranoia.[52]

---

in George C. Rogers, Jr., and David R. Chesnutt, eds., *The Papers of Henry Laurens,* IX (Columbia, S.C., 1981), 316–317; Philip Thicknesse, *A Journey through France, and Part of Spain; Including Many Curious and Interesting Observations,* 4th ed., II (London, 1798), 101–112 (the first edition was published in 1777, and Thicknesse compared the arrival of African-descended people in France to his observations of England). Although Long might be seen as holding much more strident racial ideas than his peers, he nevertheless was very influential; see Fryer, *Staying Power,* 161. On Estwick's role in the London-based West Indian community, see Lillian M. Penson, *The Colonial Agents of the British West Indies: A Study in Colonial Administration, Mainly in the Eighteenth Century* (London, 1971), 251. Long and Estwick are the two most referenced commentators after the Mansfield decision; see Jack P. Greene, "Liberty, Slavery, and the Transformation of British Identity in the Eighteenth-Century West Indies," *Slavery and Abolition,* XXI, no. 1 (April 2000), 16–17; and Srividhya Swaminathan, "Developing the West Indian Proslavery Position after the Somerset Decision," *Slavery and Abolition,* XXIV, no. 3 (December 2003), 40–60.

52. Catherine Molineux argues that a racial consciousness emerged in Britain in the 1760s and 1770s, which produced a larger market of black imagery and political debate. These new images increasingly depicted blacks within the urban working class; see Molineux, *Faces of Perfect Ebony: Encountering Atlantic Slavery in Imperial Britain* (Cambridge, Mass., 2012), 14, 201. For more on Gronniosaw, see [Ukawsaw Gronniosaw], *A Narrative of the Most Remarkable Particulars in the Life of James Albert Ukawsaw Gronniosaw, an African Prince, as Related by Himself* (Bath, circa 1772), 39–47. Vincent Carretta notes that Gronniosaw's narrative went through at least ten editions, a translation, and a serialization before 1800, demonstrating that it had popular appeal; see *Oxford Dictionary of National Biography,* online ed., s.v. "Gronniosaw, Ukawsaw [*pseud.* James Albert] (1710x14–1775)," by Carretta, http://www.oxforddnb.com.ccl.idm.oclc.org/view/article/71634.

Even supporters of Mansfield's ruling in the Somerset case employed a discourse around interracial unions. A 1772 report on the judgment in London's *Public Advertiser* decried detractors' claims of a link between skin color and natural slavery. Yet, the author continued on, mentioning that black and white pairings were well established in Britain: "If Negroes are to be Slaves on account of Colour, the next Step will be to enslave every Mulatto in the Kingdom; then all the Portuguese; next the French; then the brown-complexioned English; and so on till there be only one free Man left, which will be the Man of the palest Complexion in the three Kingdoms!" *The Dying Negro,* a poem written by John Bicknell and Thomas Day the year after Mansfield's decision, also used interracial matches to defend its antislavery stance. The authors recounted the true story, similar to Somerset's, of an enslaved black man facing deportation in London. Rather than be separated from his white English wife, with whom he hoped—in the words of the authors—to "blend with mine the colour of thy fate," the man killed himself. The poem used sentimental attachments between black and white lovers to advocate for the rights bestowed by Mansfield's decision. Thus, even for those in opposition to Long and company, interracial unions were a fundamental part of the discourse surrounding an African presence in the metropole.[53]

Such anxieties and debate reflected, to a large degree, the types of demographic concerns dominating discussions in Jamaica. The island's assembly had capped mixed-race inheritances a decade before to stunt further the economic strength of a mixed-race underclass it could barely control, while simultaneously allowing elites to skirt those laws through private petitioning. Poor Britons of color could potentially upset metropolitan society in the same way, particularly as interests in formalized marriage and reproduction had expanded tremendously over the previous quarter century in England through Hardwicke's Marriage Act and the general cultural interest in illegitimacy and clandestine nuptials. Class and race, then, were closely linked on both sides of the Atlantic, with financial advantage overtaking perceived problems of African heritage. Although Long made a passing reference to formerly enslaved individuals winning the lottery, most commentators in 1772 saw the problem

53. *Public Advertiser,* May 18, 1772; John Bicknell and Thomas Day, *The Dying Negro: A Poetical Epistle, Supposed to Be Written by a Black (Who Lately Shot Himself on Board a Vessel in the River Thames;) to His Intended Wife* (London, 1773), 3; Carey, *British Abolitionism and the Rhetoric of Sensibility,* 75–84. George Boulukos argues that the Somerset decision was a catalyst in the rise of sentimental considerations of race; see Boulukos, *The Grateful Slave: The Emergence of Race in Eighteenth-Century British and American Culture* (New York, 2008), 6–8.

of racial mixture in Britain as one entirely afflicting the working poor. As in Jamaica, the prospect of such unions among the elite did not pose a substantial risk.

Proto-Abolition and Mixed-Race Migration

At the same moment that observers argued over Britain's racial future and its legal definition of slavery, one of the first concrete proposals emerged seeking to abolish the institution altogether. In 1772, Maurice Morgann anonymously published *A Plan for the Abolition of Slavery in the West Indies*. His motivation for publishing the tract came directly out of the Somerset case, but his scheme was not inspired by the trial. Instead, he had developed his ideas nearly a decade earlier in response to Britain's acquisition of Florida after the Seven Years' War. Morgann's was one of several examinations of the territory after the Peace of Paris. Hoping to forestall the growth of a slave system in the new territories, he suggested an experiment in free labor as part of an overall moral reform in Britain's expanding empire. Only after the tumult of Mansfield's decision, however, would he feel compelled to circulate his theories.[54]

Morgann's plan was simple enough. If Westminster outlawed slavery in West Florida, the colony would develop much faster than with bound workers. Like George Wallace in 1760, Morgann thus argued that slavery was not only immoral but inefficient. More important, he contended that enslave-

---

54. [Maurice Morgann], *A Plan for the Abolition of Slavery in the West Indies* (London, 1772), i–iii. Morgann published the tract anonymously, but Daniel A. Fineman has discovered that Morgann was, in fact, the author, and Christopher Brown has confirmed it with additional evidence; see Fineman, ed., *Maurice Morgann: Shakespearian Criticism* (New York, 1972), 6–7; and Brown, *Moral Capital,* 214n. Brown also gives a detailed account of the development of Morgann's ideas in 1763 and their publication after Somerset (213–238). For more on Morgann's influences, including his Welsh roots, see Fineman, ed., *Maurice Morgann,* 3–11; and Evans, *Slave Wales,* 77–81. Such settlement schemes abounded for both East and West Florida, often with disappointing results; see Hancock, *Citizens of the World,* 109–110, 152–157. For other examinations investigating the new territory of Florida and abolition of slavery after the Seven Years' War, see, in particular, William Roberts, *An Account of the First Discovery, and Natural History of Florida* (London, 1763); and [William Stork], *An Account of East-Florida . . .* (London, 1766). John and William Bartram would also provide natural histories of Florida from visits conducted in the 1760s and 1770s; see John Bartram, "Diary of a Journey through the Carolinas, Georgia, and Florida . . . ," ed. Francis Harper, American Philosophical Society, *Transactions,* New Ser., XXXIII, part 1 (December 1942); William Bartram and Francis Harper, "Travels in Georgia and Florida, 1773–74; a Report to Dr. John Fothergill," American Philosophical Society, *Transactions,* New Ser., XXXIII no. 2 (November 1943); and Christopher P. Iannini, *Fatal Revolutions: Natural History, West Indian Slavery, and the Routes of American Literature* (Chapel Hill, N.C., 2012), 177–217.

ment also bred rebellion. Although he left it unpublished until 1772, Morgann developed his strategy in 1763, just two years after Tacky's Revolt ended in Jamaica, and he did not wish to see continued uprisings in Britain's vulnerable new territories. Free labor would ease this problem, but Morgan suggested something radical to ensure total pacification. He recommended that male and female children from Africa be brought to Britain and educated until they reached sixteen years of age. At that point, these black students would then settle in Florida to act as leaders of the new colony. A fresh group of African children would arrive annually for fifteen years to create a deep pocket of British-educated, nonwhite colonists. Consistent with other settlement strategies, Morgann directed that each student marry before leaving Britain. Perhaps a testament to the popularity of Long's ideas, Morgann indicated that these migrants might wed blacks already resident in Britain, in order to take them back to the Americas. With married free blacks in West Florida, the territory would easily become populated by settled families. Indeed, Morgann insisted that black fecundity, though only under free conditions, was so great in the tropics that a naturally reproducing society would emerge quickly. Led by British-educated black settlers, these colonies would thrive.[55]

Where did Morgann develop such an audacious plan? To understand his published manifesto from 1772, one must consider his experiences up to 1763. Born in Wales, Morgann entered into governmental service through the connections of Sir John Phillips, although it is unclear if he ever met Caesar, an enslaved Senegalese boy living on Phillips's Welsh estate. Phillips introduced Morgann to William Petty, the earl of Shelburne, who in 1762 appointed him as his private secretary—a post he would hold for many years. The next spring, Shelburne took over as president of the Board of Trade, where he mediated the dispute with Jamaica's assembly over the inheritance cap. Did Morgann think of the assembly's list of wills with bequests to British-educated Jamaicans of color when composing his plans for Florida that same year? Might he have drawn from the Jamaican council's own examples of mixed-race English residents when proposing that Africans come to British schools as well? Morgann had the entirety of his personal correspondence destroyed, so it is difficult to determine how invested he was in that squabble. But he and Shelburne worked closely with John Pownall, the Board's permanent secretary and Lovell Stanhope's primary correspondent in his defense of the inheritance cap. Moreover, from Morgann's public writings he appears to have held a strong belief—even stronger, in fact, than Shelburne—in colonial sub-

55. [Morgann], *A Plan*, 2–20.

servience to the mother country. He would have wholeheartedly agreed with the Board's hesitancy to pass the inheritance act, particularly as it seemed to violate the central tenants of English common law.[56]

From the language behind Morgann's proposal, it seems likely that the inheritance cap dispute did indeed affect his ideas about slavery. When arguing with the assembly—which at the time included Edward Long—the Board of Trade deferred to the Jamaican council's claims that of the large estates "left to Mulattoes[,] . . . no Evils have attended the Possession of Property by them," and that the inheritance law would destroy mixed-race industry. Furthermore, it insisted that Jamaican officials should not punish those "seven Eighths White, and not distinguishable from White Persons." Morgann expressed a more radical conception of freedom and race in his tract by including less affluent individuals of color in his settlement scheme. If enslaved blacks were freed, he insisted, they would become "more industrious, more skilful, and, upon the whole, work cheaper than slaves." Eventually, they would marry whites:

> The produce of such marriages, partaking of both climates and both complexions, will possess the middle space; the present prejudices arising from complexion, will wear away, and colour will be no longer opprobrious: the whites will inhabit the northern colonies; and to the south, the complexion will blacken by a regular gradation. . . . [T]he middle parts will link the two extremes in union and friendship.

It is not difficult to see close parallels between Morgann's *Plan* and the Board's questions on the inheritance cap. Interracial sex, and the children produced by it, did not automatically signify social decline to either. Rather, mixed-race individuals in these portrayals were an important buffer in colonial societies

56. Rory T. Cornish, "Maurice Morgann (c. 1725/26–1802)—A British Undersecretary of State Revisited," *Proceedings of the South Carolina Historical Association* (2004), 1–2; Evans, *Slave Wales*, 55–56, 76. Pownall received and answered most of Stanhope's letters when corresponding about the inheritance cap; see Lovell Stanhope to John Pownall, May 9, 1763, CO 137/33, fols. 20–32, NAE. Historians traditionally see Morgann as a strong defender of metropolitan right over colonial liberty; see R. A. Humphreys, "Lord Shelburne and the Proclamation of 1763," *English Historical Review*, XLIX (1934), 247–252; Humphreys, "Lord Shelburne and British Colonial Policy, 1766–1768," *English Historical Review*, L (1935), 258–269; and Franklin B. Wickwire, *British Subministers and Colonial America, 1763–1783* (Princeton, 1966), 93–97. Cornish believes that Morgann held a much more liberal, and freedom-minded, attitude toward the colonies than previous scholars have suggested; see Cornish, "Maurice Morgann," *Proceedings of the South Carolina Historical Association* (2004), 1–12.

beset by oppression and ethnic stratification. Arguing for a racial spectrum that might tolerate those between white and black was a vital initiative for both Morgann and the Board of Trade. Surely his promotion of British education for African children, who might further bridge the gap between racial groups through an elite upbringing, came out of this same debate as well.[57]

Morgann's British-centered approach to slave reform paralleled concurrent changes emanating outward from Jamaica. Island officials never seriously debated emancipation in the eighteenth century, but some did consider reducing, if not stopping altogether, new African imports. The arrival of saltwater slaves increased the disproportion between black and white and fueled future uprisings as Africans were thought to be more rebellious than creole laborers. Governor Edward Trelawny's anonymous appeal in 1746 claimed that if Jamaica did not stop importing Africans it might otherwise "be overrun, and ruined by its own Slaves." This suggestion by no means gained universal support, particularly among planters who needed a continuous stream of captive laborers. Nevertheless, most saw little problem regulating the slave trade's flow; Jamaica appeared awash in Africans. The colony became the epicenter of Britain's slave trade in the eighteenth century, particularly after the Treaty of Utrecht in 1713 when the South Sea Company began using the island as a storehouse in its transshipment of Africans to the Spanish Empire. Colonists grew to hate the company, as they believed that it flooded the island with slaves and took away the best of those for sale to the Spanish Main. Beginning in 1717, the assembly passed slave export duties in retaliation. Company officials rushed to the Board of Trade in London to complain, and, for the next two decades, the Board and the assembly waged a continuous battle over the latter's right to impose tariffs on Africans whom the company claimed it had only stopped briefly on the island for "refreshment." Import and export duties wavered through the middle of the eighteenth century, but, by 1774, the assembly decided to act boldly.[58]

57. Lovell Stanhope, "Reasons in Support of the Bill to Restrain Exorbitant Grants to Negroes etc.," circa 1763, CO 137/33, fols. 39–41, NAE; [Morgann], *A Plan*, 25–26.

58. [Trelawny], *Essay concerning Slavery*, 18–23. The most straightforward account of this battle is recounted in James Knight's *Some Observations on the Assiento Trade, as It Has Been Exercised by the South-Sea Company* . . . (London, 1728), which argued that the company's asiento contract took away employment in Jamaica and flooded the island with cheap slaves. In response, Richard Rigby drafted *An Answer to a Calumny* . . . (London, 1728), insisting that the company and its asiento contract benefited Jamaica. Much of the back and forth about slave duties can be followed in the *JBT,* Nov. 6, 1717–Jan. 27, 1718, III, 301–233, Feb. 23–Mar. 12, 1725, V, 147–155, Mar. 16–May 24, 1727, 314–335, July 12–27, 1732,

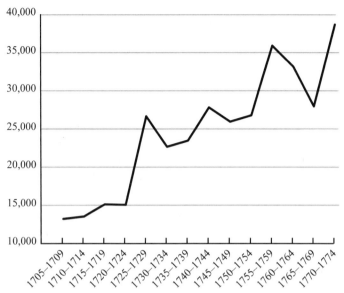

FIGURE 2. Total Number of Slaves Shipped into Jamaica (Imports-Exports) in Five-Year Averages, 1705–1774. Drawn by Kelly Crawford. *JAJ,* Nov. 30, 1775, VI, 598

As North American colonists began making overt declarations against the king, Jamaican officials prepared for war. In December 1773, amid heightened colonial clamor, a committee of the assembly reported that the island needed greater military protection, as much on the grounds of the "rebellions of our slaves, as on the dread of any attack from a foreign enemy." It also noted that between 1693 and 1740, the island's white population had only doubled, while its enslaved populace had increased tenfold. A later report indicated that the number of Africans landed on Jamaican docks in 1773 had been nearly twice as large as the year before. As Figure 2 shows, slave imports grew dramatically during this period. Hoping to combat the seemingly exponential increase of slave arrivals, the assembly quintupled importation duties from ten shillings to two and a half pounds per head in 1774. It might have also relished the op-

---

VI, 304–310, and July 10–Dec. 4, 1734, 399–431. Gregory E. O'Malley details the transshipment of slaves from Africa to Jamaica, before heading to ports across the circum-Caribbean, including these stoppages for "refreshment"; see O'Malley, *Final Passages: The Intercolonial Slave Trade of British America, 1619–1807* (Chapel Hill, N.C., 2014), 40–41. See also Colin Palmer, *Human Cargoes: The British Slave Trade to Spanish America, 1700–1739* (Urbana, Ill., 1981). Jamaica's assembly printed a list of its import and export duties in 1775, in response to the Board of Trade's disgust at a recent import tariff; see *JAJ,* Nov. 30, 1775, VI, 598. These should not be taken as gospel, as many of the duties printed were in dispute with the Board before passing officially.

portunity to upset British merchants after the fallout of the Empire's massive credit crisis from two years before.[59]

Merchants in London, Liverpool, and Bristol attacked the tariffs as a violation of the king's prerogative, and the battle over slave trade regulation reignited. Jamaica's governor Basil Keith explained the increased duty, stating that "a great Number of the Assembly and of the People of Property [are] under the greatest alarm, and apprehension from the vast increase of Negroes, already out of all prudent or safe proportion to the White Inhabitants: who I am sorry to see are decreasing." Members of the assembly did not seek to abolish the trade, but they did wish to control it, especially to secure the island as Britain's Empire marched hesitatingly toward civil war. Jamaica's assembly ultimately declared its loyalty to the crown, rather than to the North American colonies pulling away from Westminster. It chastised Parliament for a supposed plan "enslaving the colonies" but nevertheless conceded that the island could not survive without support from the mother country. Its members' attempt to limit slave imports came out of fears that North American secession would inspire enslaved insurrection—a panic not unfounded. Though it held no sympathy with antislavery arguments such as Morgann's from two years earlier, the assembly's tariff scheme added to the public consideration on the possibility of abolition. Amid this furor, Thomas Hibbert and Hercules Ross debated the morality of the slave trade.[60]

59. *JAJ*, Dec. 18, 1773, VI, 486, Nov. 30, 1775, 598; "Copies of an Act Passed by the Assembly of *Jamaica,* in the Month of February 1774 . . . ," Mar. 14, 1796, no. 4609, in *HCSP*, C, 161-181. These numbers match, almost exactly, those recorded up to 1751 in a Jamaican ledger—most likely owned by Rose Fuller—written around 1752; see "Jamaican Plantation Records from the Dickinson Papers, 1679-1849," microfilm, M 2157, reel 2, DD/DN 513, John D. Rockefeller, Jr., Library, Williamsburg, Va. West Indian merchants were far less damaged by the 1772 crisis than those in North America, but it still greatly strained their credit and debt standing; see Richard B. Sheridan, "The British Credit Crisis of 1772 and the American Colonies," *Journal of Economic History,* XX (1960), 165-166, 172-173.

60. *JAJ*, Feb. 12-13, 1774, VI, 508-510, Dec. 23, 1774, 569-570; Basil Keith to George Legge, earl of Dartmouth, June 12, 1775, CO 137/70, fol. 77, NAE; Robert Livingston Schuyler, *Parliament and the British Empire: Some Constitutional Controversies concerning Imperial Legislative Jurisdiction* (New York, 1929), 135; Andrew Jackson O'Shaughnessy, *An Empire Divided: The American Revolution and the British Caribbean* (Philadelphia, 2000); Richard B, Sheridan, "The Jamaican Slave Insurrection Scare of 1776 and the American Revolution," *Journal of Negro History,* LXI (1976), 290-308; N[eville] A. T. Hall, "Some Aspects of the 'Deficiency' Question in Jamaica in the Eighteenth Century," *Caribbean Studies,* XV, no. 1 (April 1975), 19. Later observers would claim that this was an early form of self-imposed abolitionism. Member of Parliament William Burge insisted in 1831, for instance, that the measures taken by the assembly in 1774 were an attempt to unshackle them-

The same year that officials in Jamaica applied the brakes to slave importation, Long took up his pen again, writing a supportive appeal in England to curb Jamaica's Africa trade. Long published his three-volume magnum opus *The History of Jamaica* in 1774, both to describe his former residence and to prescribe its future development. Throughout the work, Long built a case for greater creolization—not race mixing, but a stronger internal society with more infrastructure that might spur increased reproduction among both blacks and whites. He reflected at length about the barriers to island fertility and believed that certain measures, including reduced slave importation, would accelerate fecundity. Although they came from a stridently vocal supporter of slavery, these ideas later became central pillars of the abolition movement's arguments.[61]

Along with this proto-abolition theme, Long railed against interracial sex. Motivated to make Jamaica a more self-reliant colony, he disparaged cross-racial pairings because they did not contribute to his two primary goals: increased white settlement through reproduction and improved enslaved fecundity that would eliminate the need for future African imports. Interracial unions, instead, produced a middle group that did not fit easily into the island's racial and economic dyad. Long held little sympathy toward enslaved Africans, insisting that they had no moral sensations and were perhaps even a different species from Europeans. This made white sexual interactions with them all the more problematic, especially as they undercut the development

---

selves from slavery; see *Report of the Debate in the House of Commons, on Friday, the 15th of April 1831; on Mr. Fowell Buxton's Motion to Consider and Adopt the Best Means for Effecting the Abolition of Colonial Slavery* (London, 1831), 33.

61. [Edward Long], *History of Jamaica; or, General Survey of the Antient and Modern State of That Island . . .* , 3 vols. (London, 1774), II, 432–447. Later writers picked up Long's promotion of creole—rather than African—slave growth; see William Wilberforce, as quoted in *The Debate on a Motion for the Abolition of the Slave-Trade, in the House of Commons, on Monday the Second of April, 1792 . . .* (London, 1792), 13; and Thomas Gisborne, *Remarks on the Late Decision of the House of Commons respecting the Abolition of the Slave Trade*, 2d ed. (London, 1792), 17–18. Long hoped to reduce white importation in order to inspire greater fecundity as well; see Hall, "Some Aspects of the 'Deficiency' Question," *Caribbean Studies*, XV, no. 1 (April 1975), 12; Claudius Fergus, "'Dread of Insurrection': Abolitionism, Security, and Labor in Britain's West Indian Colonies, 1760–1823," *WMQ*, 3d Ser., LXVI (2009), 759–780. Long's creolization plan was part of a more general initiative across the Caribbean to bolster white West Indians' reputations in Britain; see Trevor Burnard, "West Indian Identity in the Eighteenth Century," in John D. Garrigus and Christopher Morris, eds., *Assumed Identities: The Meanings of Race in the Atlantic World* (College Station, Tex., 2010), 71–87.

of legitimate white families. "Many are the men, of every rank, quality, and degree here," he observed, "who would much rather riot in these goatish embraces, than share the pure and lawful bliss derived from matrimonial mutual love." He reiterated his fears from two years earlier about racial dissipation in England to warn of similar social ruin in Jamaica: "Let any man turn his eyes to the Spanish American dominions, and behold what a vicious, brutal, and degenerate breed of mongrels has been there produced." The taint of Iberian imperialism permeated both publications: English becoming Portuguese in the metropole, and Jamaicans turning Spanish in the periphery.[62]

Despite these calls for increased racial segregation, Long maintained qualified ideas about mixed-race Jamaicans in his *History*. Class, family standing, and inheritance were crucial parts of his attitudes toward individuals of color. His discussion of the problems attendant with interracial sex came out of a defense of none other than the 1761 inheritance cap. Long had served in the assembly when the bill passed, and he maintained that the act was good law despite being "objected [to] by many, and with great warmth." He conceded that the cap was repugnant to English statutes, but only because Jamaica countenanced slavery, which English law also failed to recognize — a lesson made painfully clear to Long in the Somerset case. He contended that capping the inheritance of mixed-race Jamaicans honored the spirit of English traditions against illegitimate children. Drawing from earlier debates about settlement and marriage in both Jamaica and Britain, Long made an appeal for matrimony arguing that "the institution of marriage is regarded as one of the main links of society . . . [and] is doubtless of as much concern in the colony, as it is in the mother country." Because the former contained so many slaves, however, "a man's right of devising his property by will ought justly, therefore, from the constitution of our West India colonies, to be more circumscribed." Interracial children recognized as heirs, then, not only compromised racial distinctions, they also violated a social compact honoring legitimate families. Long disparaged concubinage in England as well and compared mixed-race bequests to legacies given to the offspring of English prostitutes. "It might be much be better for Britain, and Jamaica too," he contended, if white Jamaicans would "abate of their infatuated attachments to black women, and, instead of being 'grac'd with a *yellow offspring not their own*,' perform the duty incumbent on every good cittizen, by raising in honourable wedlock a race of unadulterated beings." Illegitimacy, not simply biology, factored heavily

62. [Long], *History of Jamaica*, II, 327–328, 338–356.

into Long's conception of mixed-race Jamaicans. He decried illegitimacy and concubinage in England among his other writings published that same year.[63]

Long also supported the dispensation of favors, particularly privilege bills, to those with higher class standing. In defending the inheritance cap, he stated that the law essentially targeted middling and poor Jamaicans of color. It protected, in particular, against "foolish, and indiscriminate devises." Yet, Long believed that exceptions could, and should, be made. When a testator had no lawful kin and "his illegitimate child may be, by the polish of a good education, and moral principles, found well deserving to possess it," the assembly should confer de jure legitimacy. This referred, of course, to Jamaica's privilege bills, which after 1761 included at least nineteen separate families that received exemptions from the inheritance cap. Large bequests to elites of color "might not be so likely to produce the same inconveniences" as those to poorer Jamaicans and thus the privilege bills should empower those who deserved them. The favoring of such an allowance was a legacy of the privilege bills' original intention: to provide certain elites of color with immunities that would effectively allow them to join white society. If, through privilege bills as Long claimed, Jamaicans of color "might be made legitimate," then they might also be made white.[64]

Ultimately, Long held complicated and sometimes conflicting attitudes toward mixed-race elites, in part because they seemed so similar to whites. Long's desire to see the growth of a creole population in Jamaica led him to disparage absenteeism in all its forms. He especially lamented the lack of colonial schools. Without proper educational facilities, young Jamaicans, including those of color, left in droves. Long noted that "every father here, who has acquired a little property, [sends] his children, of whatever complexion,

63. Long continued his attack against Mansfield's decision in his *History of Jamaica,* insisting that English and Jamaican law were distinct, though connected; see [Long], *History of Jamaica,* II, 89, 323–327. Legal pluralism was a contentious issue in the Empire, especially in the years surrounding the American Revolution. Colonists and Britons wanted legal uniformity in some cases and legal distinctions in others — often the two were in conflict; see Mary Sarah Bilder, *The Transatlantic Constitution: Colonial Legal Culture and the Empire* (Cambridge, Mass., 2004); Lauren Benton, *Law and Colonial Cultures: Legal Regimes in World History, 1400–1900* (New York, 2002), 31–79, 127–209. Long penned a general comment about social life in England, including calls for improved marriage and decreased concubinage; see [Edward Long], *The Sentimental Exhibition; or, Portraits and Sketches of the Times* (London, 1774), 63–72.

64. [Long], *History of Jamaica,* II, 326–327.

to Britain, for education." Such a practice damaged Jamaican society but also hurt those who left. Long believed that life in England instilled immoral behavior, especially with all of the capital's temptations, each available beyond the reach of parental supervision. West Indians learned nothing in Britain, he claimed, other than a "riveted prejudice against a colony-life," and, once returned, "they regret their exile from the gay delights of London." Time spent away from Jamaica further entrenched absenteeism, remitting innumerable riches to British institutions that might be better spent on the island.[65]

These youthful sojourns were not simply problems among absentee whites. Long disparaged mixed-race education in Britain for almost identical reasons. On the one hand, Long contended that sending a child of color across the Atlantic was, at best, a silly indulgence of parental affection:

> Young *Fuscus,* in whom the father fondly imagines he sees the reflected dawn of paternal genius, and Miss *Fulvia,* who mamma protests has a most delicate ear for music and French, are both of them sent early to England, to cultivate and improve the valuable talents which nature is supposed to have so wantonly bestowed, and the parents, blind with folly, think they have discovered.

Here, Long acknowledged the role that mothers of color had in lobbying for their children's future, but he mocked the seriousness with which their paramours took them. On the other hand, Long asserted that a metropolitan education worked against mixed-race students in much the same way as it did against whites. After attending Eton, or a finishing school in Chelsea, Long insisted that Jamaicans of color would be ruined if they returned home: "Miss faints at the sight of her relations, especially when papa tells her that black *Quasheba* is her own mother," and a mixed-race son could now only "converse with *Quashee* and *Mingo,* instead of his school-fellows, *Sir George,* or *My Lord;* while mademoiselle, instead of modish French, must learn to prattle gibberish with her cousins *Mimba* and *Chloe.*" The delights and refinement that spoiled white colonists did exactly the same to mixed-race migrants, but with added problems. Jamaicans of color who returned to the Caribbean, Long believed, would never be fully accepted into white society—at least not to the degree that they had in Britain. Left only to converse with those

65. O'Shaughnessy, *Empire Divided,* 19–27; [Long], *History of Jamaica,* II, 246–249; Kilbride, *Being American in Europe,* 29. Long disparaged English boarding schools generally in another work; see [Edward Long], *English Humanity No Paradox; or, An Attempt to Prove, That the English Are Not a Nation of Savages* (London, 1778), 36–37.

deprived of an education, they would surely grow to resent their colonial station.[66]

Such similarities between white and brown elites complicated Long's sense of a strong, ruling white community. A general disgust toward Africans tainted his view of those holding any such heritage. He believed that endogamous mixed-race unions produced no offspring because both partners were "of the mule-kind." Yet, he did not hold mixed-race individuals in total contempt. He advocated for "the enfranchisement of every Mulatto child" who would "form the centre of connexion between the two extremes" of black and white in order to stabilize colonial relations. This made elite, light-skinned Jamaicans of color a tricky variable for Long's prescriptive equation. His treatment of the group was simultaneously dismissive and inclusionary. Writing of those who became legally white owing to generational removal from a black ancestor, Long noted, "To call them by a degree inferior to what they really are, would be the highest affront." Such perceived offenses were supposedly worse among those who returned from Britain. "However well this yellow brood may be received in England . . . a well-educated Mulatta must lead a very unpleasant kind of life here," he reasoned. One can see a conflicting impulse on Long's part to exculpate seemingly impure whites from ruling society while also envisioning them as crucial to white growth. Long decried mixed-race migration partly because it removed influential members of the community: "The opulent among them withdraw to England; where their influence, if they ever possessed any, ceases to be of any use." Ultimately, they represented the central problem for settlement in Jamaica. Without marriage, the colony would not grow naturally, and absenteeism, including mixed-race absenteeism, would continue unabated. Long summed up his feelings: "If their fathers had married, the difference would have been this; their white offspring might have remained in the colony, to strengthen and enrich it: the Mulatto offspring desert and impoverish it."[67]

66. [Long], *History of Jamaica*, II, 328–329. Long's sense that British instruction did little for mixed-race girls echoed similar gender stereotypes about education. One author in 1772 opined, "The books [women] read, however well calculated for information and improvement, can have but little influence on them"; see *Considerations on the Causes*, 24. "Fuscus" and "Fulvia" were characterizations of enslaved (or formerly enslaved) individuals' names.

67. [Long], *History of Jamaica*, II, 329–333, 335. Notions of sterility in mixed-race people were common in the eighteenth and nineteenth centuries, particularly as the idea that Africans and Europeans formed different species still held some purchase; see Robert J. C. Young, *Colonial Desire: Hybridity in Theory, Culture, and Race* (New York, 1995), 6–9.

Mixed-race migration to Britain, then, formed a critical part of Long's analysis of colonial society, but it did not figure into his sense of metropolitan racial degradation. Despite numerous comments on British-educated children of color in *The History of Jamaica*, Long did not connect this phenomenon to the same worries of blood dissipation expounded in his tract about the Somerset decision from two years earlier. In fact, he joked that people in England believed that white children turned "swarthy" in the Jamaican climate because of the "many Mulatto, Quateron, and other illegitimate children sent over to England for education." That he included "mulattos" and "quaterons" in the same series as "illegitimate children" speaks to the importance of white kinship to his concept of racial difference. Even for a notorious race-baiter like Long, an elevated class standing and connection to white family moderated the most serious perceived threats to British society.[68]

Conclusion

When Massachusetts's recently deposed governor Thomas Hutchinson visited Lord Mansfield's Hampstead Heath home in 1779, the Somerset trial still lingered in the air. Hutchinson met Dido Elizabeth Belle, Mansfield's mixed-race great-niece, and noticed her socializing in the normal fashion: she took coffee with the other ladies at dinner and walked arm in arm with them through the garden. Hutchinson, himself, was not impressed with her appearance, but, even in his critique, he recognized her energetic attempts to adopt English custom. "She had a very high cap, and her wool was much frizzled in her neck," he observed, "but not enough to answer the large curls now in fashion." Watching her mingle reminded Hutchinson of his host's famous legal decision from seven years earlier, and he recalled in his diary a Jamaican planter who had remarked before the case that Somerset "will be set free, for Lord Mansfield keeps a Black in his house which governs him and the whole family." Rumors could not escape the tightly bound Jamaican network in London, but Hutchinson's recollection reveals an understanding of the normalcy of mixed-race residents in British households. Surely Edward Long and Samuel Estwick knew of Dido as well, and their lack of commentary on her presence speaks to the perceived divide between mixed-race and poor black immigration in the metropole. Yet, as Hutchinson's diary demonstrates, Somerset's case had not adjourned in the court of public opinion.[69]

68. [Long], *History of Jamaica*, II, 274.
69. Hutchinson, *Diary and Letters of His Excellency Thomas Hutchinson*, ed. Hutchinson, II, 276. David Beck Ryden traces in great detail the connections between West Indians

The 1772 trial continued to arouse interest because it had not settled the issue of slavery in Britain. The year before Hutchinson visited Mansfield's home, an identical case came before Scotland's highest legal body, the Court of Session in Edinburgh. Joseph Knight, an enslaved African purchased by John Wedderburn in Jamaica and brought to Scotland in 1769, fled his master after hearing of Mansfield's decision. Soon apprehended, Knight came before a Perthshire court that ruled in 1774 that Scotland did not allow enslavement. The Court of Session upheld the decision in 1778, officially banning slavery north of the Tweed. The case turned on exactly the same principles as Somerset's, but the Scottish judges gave a definitive statement on slavery, whereas Mansfield had simply deflected it. Surprisingly, the trial did not provoke the same degree of outrage as Somerset's had, even though it was a stronger legal decision and Knight had actually married a white woman in Britain. Indeed, he and his wife Ann Thomson had a child together. Only Henry Home, Lord Kames, commented on the marriage and its product. Channeling Long, Kames believed that Knight fled his master because, "never having received any wages, he became uneasy for want of means to maintain his family." Marriage and family concerns still dominated conceptions of enslaved blacks in Britain, although an interracial couple in Scotland perhaps appeared less threatening than one in the imperial capital.[70]

The Somerset case, along with Britain's other freedom trials from the period, brought colonial concerns with race and demography to the metropole. Between 1772 and 1778, slave supporters and opponents alike decried the arrival of black men and women as the beginning of a racial decline that

in London; see Ryden, *West Indian Slavery and British Abolition, 1783–1807* (New York, 2009), 40–82.

70. Henry Home, Lord Kames, *Principles of Equity; The Third Edition; In Two Volumes* (Edinburgh, 1778), II, 134n. For more on the Knight trial's proceedings, see *Decisions of the Court of Session; From January 1778 to December 1781* (Edinburgh, 1791), 5–9; John Mac-Laurin, [Lord Dreghorn], *The Works of the Late John MacLaurin . . . ,* I (Edinburgh, 1798), xxiv–xxv; John Millar, *The Origin of the Distinction of Ranks . . . ,* 3d ed. (London, 1779), 346–361; Shyllon, *Black People in Britain,* 26; Evans, "African / Caribbeans in Scotland," 55–73; Whyte, *Scotland and the Abolition of Black Slavery,* 47; and Emma Rothschild, *The Inner Life of Empires: An Eighteenth-Century History* (Princeton, 2011), 91–93, 203–205. Samuel Johnson also discussed the case, although he did not delve into aspects of Knight's marriage; see James Boswell, *The Life of Samuel Johnson . . . ,* II (London, 1791), 179–180; and *Gentleman's Magazine: And Historical Chronicle,* LXXIII, pt. 1 (London, 1803), 598. On the implications of Knight's mixed-race children, see Brooke N. Newman, "Contesting 'Black' Liberty and Subjecthood in the Anglophone Caribbean, 1730s–1780s," *Slavery and Abolition,* XXXII (2011), 179.

would transform Britain into Jamaica, or, worse still, into Spain or Portugal. This trepidation over Britain's racial future was part of the same demographic and settlement debate that had raged for years in Jamaica and that had energized interest in domestic marriage during the previous two decades. However, this was not a blanket fear of African blood. Rather, it was a directed concern over racial degradation among Britain's laboring poor. Mixed-race Jamaicans barely registered in these alarms over metropolitan character. If anything, elites of color who came to Britain were simply seen as unimportant, perhaps because they arrived in such modest numbers. But they were not hidden. Many came over during the 1770s and lived relatively charmed lives. Moreover, they were related to a number of the principal commentators of these debates. Indeed, Robert Wedderburn, a mixed-race Jamaican agitator who arrived in England the same year that Knight's trial concluded, would later claim descent to Knight's owner. Brown migration, then, coincided with and connected to black migration, although the former had not yet aroused the same types of fears because of the modifying effects of class advantage and family position.[71]

Nevertheless, the bewildering array of nonwhite immigrants, with different ethnic heritages, financial resources, and kinship ties, produced a great deal of confusion to British observers. A 1776 editorial in London's *Public Advertiser* underscored just how puzzled many were about Britain's growing racial complexity. The editorial railed against the recent barring of a black man, John Satia, from trading goods in the capital simply because of his skin color. This seemed a bad omen for English liberty, and the author worried: "If a black Man is excluded, may a Mulattto *[sic]* be admitted? or if a Mulatto be excluded, may the next Generation (purified once more by a white Mixture) be admitted? Who shall draw the Line and say, in what Generation the Descendants of a black Man become sufficiently bleached? and what Persons are fair enough to be made Citizens of London?" In the midst of the American Revolution, officials and observers on both sides of the Atlantic struggled with that very question.[72]

71. Robert Wedderburn, *Truth, Self-Supported; or, A Refutation of Certain Doctrinal Errors, Generally Adopted in the Christian Church* (London, circa 1790), in Iain McCalman, ed., *The Horrors of Slavery and Other Writings by Robert Wedderburn* (Edinburgh, 1991), 65–66. The evidence connecting the two Wedderburns, however, is thin. Iain Whyte believes that the two were not related; see Whyte, *Scotland and the Abolition of Black Slavery*, 47. A recent novelization of the case, however, suggests that they were indeed family; see James Robertson, *Joseph Knight* (New York, 2003).

72. *Public Advertiser*, Jan. 8, 1776.

CHAPTER 3

✾❦✾

LINEAGE AND LITIGATION,
1783–1788

As Britons began reflecting on the legal and moral dimensions of slavery, they simultaneously turned their attention toward abuses throughout the Empire. The American Revolution, having just concluded in 1783, had unsettled the entire imperial project, and officials sought out evidence of other colonial mishandlings in order to forestall future turmoil. India, in particular, came under close scrutiny, and, in 1786, Parliament initiated a formal inquiry into Bengal's erstwhile governor Warren Hastings on charges of mismanagement and bribery, setting off one of the most publicly discussed cases in Georgian Britain. Several months after the start of the investigation, London's popular daily newspaper the *Morning Herald* reported on some of the lavish riches brought over from the East that came to symbolize these accusations. Hastings's wife, the *Herald* noted in July 1786, had shipped home large quantities of gold and silver muslin on the couple's return to Britain the year before. The paper also recorded that Mrs. Kater, a fellow nabobina recently arrived in England from India herself, had such expensive taste that she "wore a new muslin or chintz gown every other day on her passage home." Such anecdotal evidence confirmed the suspicions of Britons growing increasingly convinced that colonial rule in India, like that in the Caribbean, was corrupt and that its agents were awash in immoral luxury.[1]

1. *Morning Herald* (London), July 11, 1786. Marian Hastings might have brought over as much as forty thousand pounds worth of goods to England from India; see Frances Burney, *The Diary and Letters of Madame D'Arblay,* II, *1787–1792,* ed. W. C. Ward (New York, 1892), 93. British attitudes toward nabobs extended to their wives, whom Tillman W. Nechtman calls "nabobinas"; see Nechtman, *Nabobs: Empire and Identity in Eighteenth-Century Britain* (New York, 2010), 187. Hannah Barker claims that the *Morning Herald* became one of London's best-selling newspapers soon after its founding in 1780; see Barker, *Newspapers, Politics, and Public Opinion in Late Eighteenth-Century England* (Oxford, 1998), 64. The *Herald*'s founder and proprietor, Henry Bate, was perhaps London's most prominent newspaper editor; see *Oxford Dictionary of National Biography,* online ed., s.v. "Dudley, Sir Henry Bate, baronet (1745-1824)," by Barker, http://www.oxforddnb.com.proxy.wm.edu /view/article/8152. However, it would not be until the 1830s that the *Herald* would take its place as one of the capital's leading political newspapers; see H. R. Fox Bourne, *English Newspapers: Chapters in the History of Journalism,* 2 vols. (London, 1887), II, 17-19. On the

A correction about Mrs. Kater in the next day's edition, however, might have caused some surprise. Tipped off by one of its readers, the *Herald* stated that the woman's surname was actually spelled "Cator" and that she was "the reputed daughter of a West-Indian merchant, deceased, by a Mulatto woman in Jamaica . . . [who] determined to quit this country, and try her fortune in the East." In fact, Sarah Cator was the daughter of the late John Morse and was now married to the East India Company merchant William Cator. The *Herald* did not identify its informant, but most likely the culprit was Edward Morse, Sarah's English cousin currently in the middle of suing her and her siblings for control over John Morse's Jamaican fortune.[2]

If Edward Morse did reveal this information, he had a clear purpose. In his lawsuit, Edward alleged that his cousins could only receive two thousand pounds apiece from their father's estate, owing to Jamaica's 1761 inheritance cap against mixed-race individuals. The rest, he claimed, belonged to him and his legitimate relatives. Proving that Sarah and her siblings were by law "mulattoes" was essential to win the case. Not only did the suit isolate the Jamaican Morses from British kin, it challenged their ability to assimilate, both through reputation and economic standing, into metropolitan society.

That Edward also potentially chose to take this information to the court of public opinion shows something even more significant about the lawsuit. By distinguishing Sarah Cator as an East Indian grandee with Afro-Caribbean roots, Edward connected her family's story to substantial concerns in the Empire. Britons confronted three major imperial crises in 1786. First, the trauma of the American Revolution continued to linger and called into question the organization and moral imperative of empire. The arrival in Britain of several thousand black loyalists who fought in the conflict helped to inspire in January of that year the formation of the Committee for the Relief of the Black Poor, which hoped to address the influx of African-descended people into the metropole. Second, one month after the Committee for Relief organized, parliamentarian Edmund Burke began his formal investigation of Hastings and the apparent corruption of British officials in India. Finally, the momentum of the British movement to abolish the slave trade had built up tremendous speed, inspiring Thomas Clarkson to publish his first abolitionist tract the month before Sarah Cator arrived from India. Britons in 1786, therefore, were rethinking their empire in terms of both administration and social com-

---

particular fear of East Indian luxury in Britain, see James Raven, *Judging New Wealth: Popular Publishing and Responses to Commerce in England, 1750–1800* (Oxford, 1992), 224–225.

2. *Morning Herald*, July 12, 1786.

position. Sarah Cator and her siblings embodied each of these issues pressing against imperial identity: African heritage in Britain, East Indian opulence, and connections with Caribbean slavery.[3]

Edward Morse's lawsuit against his Jamaican cousins exposes the private dimensions of these much larger public debates in the 1780s. Estate litigation is driven by its own familial idiosyncrasies, but it is also highly influenced by cultural expectations, while simultaneously reflective of pressing social issues. In his attempt to pilfer the inheritance, Morse employed a number of topical racial attacks that not only held strong purchase in the law but also in general British discourse. Judges and juries might have been swayed by Morse's invocation of Indian corruption, not because they saw Hastings's trial solely as a political issue, but because they worried that it might be emblematic of a much larger social problem. Fears of East Indian corruption and luxury spreading to England and racial anxieties about the influx of African-descended people into the metropole were unquestionably hyperbolic, but polemists did not construct them out of whole cloth. Instead, these concerns originated largely from the contested kinship of families like the Morses and others. A close examination of their inheritance suit, as well as the tribulations facing similar families, reveals the tumult about race and identity facing Britain's Empire following the American Revolution.

After the Revolution

Sarah Cator returned from her sojourn in India amid rising tensions over a mounting black presence in Britain. Following the American Revolution, thousands of formerly enslaved individuals, having gained their freedom fighting for the British, arrived in England after being evacuated from North America. They joined a community in precarious straits. Work was difficult

3. Christopher Leslie Brown notes that the perceived excesses of East Indian nabobs and West Indian grandees were conflated in Britain starting after the Seven Years' War but more substantially after the American Revolution; see Brown, *Moral Capital: Foundations of British Abolitionism* (Chapel Hill, N.C., 2006), 156–158, 201–203. On black poverty and the arrival of black loyalists in Britain, see Stephen Braidwood, *Black Poor and White Philanthropists: London's Blacks and the Foundation of the Sierra Leone Settlement, 1786–1791* (Liverpool, U.K., 1994); Simon Schama, *Rough Crossings: Britain, the Slaves, and the American Revolution,* 2d ed. (New York, 2006), 176–192; and Cassandra Pybus, *Epic Journeys of Freedom: Runaway Slaves of the American Revolution and Their Global Quest for Liberty* (Boston, 2006), 103–110. Maya Jasanoff estimates that as many as five thousand black loyalists arrived in England; see Jasanoff, *Liberty's Exiles: American Loyalists in the Revolutionary World* (New York, 2011), 127.

to find for many free blacks and people of color, who numbered as many as ten thousand in London itself. Slaves who left masters in Britain faced even bleaker prospects: a young woman named Jess fled her Scottish mistress in 1782 and actually returned to Jamaica, along with the child she had by a white man, in the hopes of passing as a freewoman on the island, rather than staying enslaved in the metropole. Owners frequently ignored the Somerset decision of 1772 that gave habeas corpus rights to the enslaved in England. Sam Oats, for instance, left his master Henry Fleming but came back into servitude after being convicted of "small theft." A justice of the peace turned Oats over to Fleming, who then sent him to Virginia to be sold in 1786. William Beckford mourned these "poor neglected negroes [who] are constantly seen lamenting in the streets" of London and whom he believed were bound to become "pick-pockets, thieves, or murderers in consequence of emancipation." Over the next several years, reformers would work less to relieve Britain's black inhabitants than to resettle them permanently in Sierra Leone.[4]

The conspicuous increase of black faces on London's streets after the American Revolution revived earlier debates about race in the metropole, inviting fears of invasion that echoed Edward Long's cry in 1772 that the Somerset decision would bring thousands of formerly enslaved people to England's shores. The Committee for Relief, and those following its actions, paid close attention to the numbers of black poor requiring assistance. Less than a month after its founding, the committee reported that it had discovered 250 black individuals needing charity. The committee's chairman wrote to London's West India Committee two weeks later noting that he intended to "procure an Act of Parliament, to prevent any Foreign Blacks being brought to this Country to remain." The *Morning Herald* made its own observations, commenting nervously in 1785 about the "poor Blacks who infest our streets." Even abolitionist claims that emancipation would produce better industry in the Caribbean were countered by the supposed poor example of free blacks in Britain.

4. *Royal Gazette* (Spanish Town, Jamaica), July 6, 1782; Henry Fleming to Charles Yates, Feb. 13, 1786, Papers of Henry Fleming, microfilm, M-1376, John D. Rockefeller, Jr., Library, Williamsburg, Va.; W[illiam] Beckford, Jr., *Remarks upon the Situation of Negroes in Jamaica . . .* (London, 1788), 96. On the Committee's intentions with the Sierra Leone scheme, Isaac Land argues that the Committee for Relief essentially defined London's black community as impoverished; see Land, "Bread and Arsenic: Citizenship from the Bottom Up in Georgian London," *Journal of Social History,* XXXIX (2005), 89–110. On the cultural imperative in Britain to establish the colony of Sierra Leone, see Douglas A. Lorimer, "Black Slaves and English Liberty: A Re-examination of Racial Slavery in England," *Immigrants and Minorities,* III (1984), 140.

Of the "ten or twelve thousand able negro men now in England," absentee sugar planter James Tobin queried, has anyone "ever saw a single one employed in any laborious task?" James Ramsay, an abolitionist and former West Indian resident himself, conceded partially to Tobin's assertion, but maintained that such idleness among the majority of Britain's black population could easily be explained: "Those to be found in England *have [never] worked in the field, or been brought up from childhood to hard labour.*" Both men registered discomfort with the group's presence by claiming that its members were drains on local parishes. Other observers picked up Long's attendant worries over the subsequent relationships formed with working-class white women, prompting one writer to laud the Committee for Relief's goal to send the recent immigrants abroad to "prevent the unnatural connections between black persons and white; the disagreeable consequences of which make their appearance but too frequently in our streets." In the wake of the influx of black loyalists, many in Britain felt threatened by the presence of an impoverished black community in their midst and the potential for a mixed-race population that might tarnish British racial purity.[5]

Sarah Cator's African ancestry was not the only cause for concern in this environment. Although Britons were far more anxious about black immigration in the eighteenth century—principally owing to stronger prejudices toward those of African ancestry as well as toward those who had been previously enslaved—the arrival of East Indians also challenged an emerging British sense of whiteness. Having returned from India, Sarah faced the parallel scrutiny ap-

5. *Morning Herald,* Aug. 13, 1785, Feb. 1, 1786; Benjamin Johnson to the West India Committee, Feb. 17, 1786, reel 3, Planters-Merchants Minutes, West Indies Merchants Committee Minutes Microfilm, ICS; John Pugh, *Remarkable Occurrences in the Life of Jonas Hanway* . . . (London, 1787), 210–211; James Tobin, *Cursory Remarks upon the Reverend Mr. Ramsay's Essay on the Treatment and Conversion of African Slaves in the Sugar Colonies* (London, 1785), 117; James Ramsay, as quoted in J[ohn] S[amuel] Smith, *A Letter from Capt. J. S. Smith to the Revd Mr Hill on the State of the Negroe Slaves* (London, 1786), 34–35 (emphasis in original). Tobin later noted that the Committee for Relief had "freed the streets of the metropolis from a large number of useless and miserable poor creatures, who had been long a burthen to private charity"; see [James Tobin], *A Short Rejoinder to the Reverend Mr. Ramsay's Reply* . . . (London, 1787), 99. Ramsay's original letter can be found in his unpublished manuscript "African Slaves in British Colonies," 1785, Add MS. 27261, fol. 180, BL. The formerly enslaved African Ottobah Cugoano wrote from London in 1787 that "the labour of freemen . . . would be attended with greater blessings"; see Cugoano, *Thoughts and Sentiments on the Evil and Wicked Traffic of the Slavery and Commerce of the Human Species* (London, 1787), 137. See also John Millar, *Observations concerning the Distinction of Ranks in Society,* 2d ed. (London, 1773).

plied to those who might bear Eastern heritage. Two English plays published in the same year as the Somerset decision drew strongly on the idea of racial transformation in the metropole through Eastern influence. William O'Brien's farce *Cross Purposes* revolves around the three Bevil brothers who display differing complexions owing to their respective residences: fair-skinned Frank who remains in England, olive-skinned George returning from India, and dark-skinned Harry coming home from either the West Indies or Africa. George's phenotypic changes parallel his inner corruption, as he quickly wastes a vast fortune on his arrival from the subcontinent. Samuel Foote's *The Nabob* trades more aggressively on thoughts of interracial relations, as the play's East Indian grandee entertains "some thoughts of importing three blacks from Bengal" to establish a London harem. The sexual and social cultures of India were thus thought transportable to the imperial center, and their threat mimicked that posed by Caribbean travelers to Britain.[6]

Movements for imperial reform following the Seven Years' War and the American Revolution helped perpetuate British anxieties over the arrival of both East and West Indians, particular those of mixed race coming for a metropolitan education. Maurice Morgann's 1772 suggestion to train a small number of black Americans in English schools found traction in the developing debate over colonial slave reform. In 1781, the African missionary Philip Quaque—himself educated in England—revived his hopes of educating mixed-race Africans in Britain and even traveled with his two children to their English schools three years later. Likewise, one 1782 abolitionist pamphlet envisioned instructing an enslaved West Indian at an English school. After receiving a refined education, the young man could then "appear at the bar as the advocate for the rights of his brethren, the unhappy children of Africa." Perhaps one day, the author conjectured, he might even "address the Commons of England." The prominent Irish politician Edmund Burke, reflecting on how to ameliorate West Indian slavery, made a similar proposal in 1780. He recommended that one enslaved boy each year should travel from Jamaica to Britain to study under the bishop of London before returning

6. Michael H. Fisher, *Counterflows to Colonialism: Indian Travellers and Settlers in Britain, 1600–1857* (Delhi, India, 2004), 11, 102; [William O'Brien], *Cross Purposes: A Farce of Two Acts* (London, 1772); Nechtman, *Nabobs,* 137; Samuel Foote, *The Nabob; A Comedy, in Three Acts . . .* (London, 1778), 38. The New Theatre in Jamaica staged a performance of O'Brien's play in 1784, perhaps in reaction to the parliamentary debates about East Indian administration; see *Cornwall Chronicle, and Jamaica General Advertiser* (Montego Bay, Jamaica), May 1, 1784, Supplement. Although published in 1778, Foote's play was first performed in 1772.

to the colonies as a free man ready to convert slaves. A comparable scheme from 1784 emerged in India, as the Bengal Military Orphan Society advocated sending mixed-race foundlings to England. These Eurasian students could then return to the subcontinent as cadets in support of the East India Company. Although none of these proposals ultimately took form, they nevertheless fed into a growing unease with the appearance of mixed-race colonists from across the globe.[7]

Despite a developing metropolitan identity that increasingly rejected the colonies after the Seven Years' War and especially after the American Revolution, many white fathers continued to send mixed-race children to British schools. In fact, the percentage of mixed-race travelers per household found in East Indian probate records is roughly the same as that for Jamaica. But the capacity of class and kinship to moderate racial attitudes was beginning to wane. Observers increasingly dismissed or grumbled at the practice for both Indian and Caribbean children. The English army officer Innes Munro even linked the two together in 1789. He believed that at least 10 percent of England's seminaries contained mixed-race colonists but that their education was of little benefit. "Measures might easily be fallen upon, both in the East and West Indies, to give those mulattoes a decent education in the country where they are born," he declared. Keeping them in their native climate would shield them from any kind of prejudicial reproach in Britain. More importantly to Munro, perhaps, it would also prevent "a commerce, that may so sensibly degenerate the race, and give a sallow tinge to the complexion of Britons." Whereas Long worried over the arrival of enslaved blacks altering the English visage in 1772, Munro took Long's concerns one step further, fret-

---

7. [Maurice Morgann], *A Plan for the Abolition of Slavery in the West Indies* (London, 1772); Philip Quaque to William Morice, Oct. 20, 1781, in Vincent Carretta and Ty M. Reese, eds., *The Life and Letters of Philip Quaque: The First African Anglican Missionary* (Athens, Ga., 2010), 153, Carretta and Reese, "Introduction," 16; "A Speech in Favour of the Unhappy Children of Africa: A Vision," *Hibernian Magazine; or, Compendium of Entertaining Knowledge* . . . (Dublin) (July 1782), 341; Nini Rodgers, *Ireland, Slavery, and Anti-Slavery: 1612– 1865* (New York, 2007), 179; Edmund Burke, "Sketch of a Negro Code," in Warren M. Elofson et al., eds., *The Writings and Speeches of Edmund Burke,* 6 vols. (New York, 1990–1996), III, 576–577; C[hristopher] J. Hawes, *Poor Relations: The Making of a Eurasian Community in British India, 1773–1833* (Richmond, U.K., 1996), 56–57. The East India Company vetoed the plan to send orphans to England in 1784 and banned John Turing, a Eurasian man living in London, from joining the company army seven years later. Turing's rejection produced a blanket prohibition against any mixed-race East Indian joining the company's civil or military branches. Turing's case is discussed in more detail in Hawes, *Poor Relations,* 55; and Fisher, *Counterflows to Colonialism,* 201–207.

ting about mixed-race elites' impact on British bloodlines. The high economic standing of these migrants of color, originating in the vices of colonial plunder and oppression, was becoming a liability, rather than a virtue.[8]

The political and ideological fallout of Britain's imperial conflicts had thrown a strong spotlight on the perceived corruption of Britain's empire as a whole. Taxation was a key administrative issue after 1763 in both the western and eastern colonies, but for India the stakes were much direr. Of the many trophies it took after the Seven Years' War, perhaps Britain's most alluring was the right to collect taxes in Bengal for the Mughal emperor. The concession stood to enrich the East India Company dramatically, but its directors mismanaged the affair terribly, exacerbating a deadly famine in 1769 that cost millions of Indian lives and sunk company profits. Bengal's governor, Robert Clive, came up for investigation over the matter, right at the same moment that William Murray, Lord Mansfield, began hearing the Somerset case. In an odd twist of history, the British government appointed John Lindsay, whose

8. Innes Munro, *A Narrative of the Military Operations on the Coromandel Coast . . .* (London, 1789), 50–51; East India Company Directors Court Minutes, Apr. 19, 1791, IOR/B/113, fol. 17, APAC, BL. For more on Eurasian children in Britain, see Hawes, *Poor Relations,* 55–56, 102–123; and Ardel Marie Thomas, "Victorian Monstrosities: Sexuality, Race, and the Construction of the Imperial Self, 1811–1924" (Ph.D. diss., Stanford University, 1998). On the case of Jane Cumming, a half-Scottish, half-Indian transplant, see William Dalrymple, *White Mughals: Love and Betrayal in Eighteenth-Century India* (London, 2002), 67–69, 471–480; Fisher, *Counterflows to Colonialism;* Durba Ghosh, *Sex and the Family in Colonial India: The Making of Empire* (New York, 2006), 126–127, 174–179, 248–254; Kate Teltscher, *The High Road to China: George Bogle, the Panchen Lama, and the First British Expedition to Tibet* (New York, 2006), 234–253; Peter Robb, "Children, Emotion, Identity, and Empire: Views from the Blechyndens' Calcutta Diaries (1790–1822)," *Modern Asian Studies,* XL (2006), 178–185; Margot Finn, "Anglo-Indian Lives in the Later Eighteenth and Early Nineteenth Centuries," *Journal for Eighteenth-Century Studies,* XXXIII (2010), 49–65; and Deborah Cohen, *Family Secrets: Shame and Privacy in Modern Britain* (New York, 2013), 13–46. For wills referencing the education of mixed-race children from India, see Ghosh, *Sex and the Family,* 123–127. Ghosh examines more than six hundred wills in the opening decades of the nineteenth century to find that 10 percent of white male testators asked that a mixed-race child be sent to Britain or noted that he or she was already there. This fits well with the percentages for Jamaica; see Appendix 1, below. On the transformation of British imperial identity after the Seven Years' War and the American Revolution, see Stephen Conway, "From Fellow-Nationals to Foreigners: British Perceptions of the Americans, circa 1739–1783," *WMQ,* 3d Ser., LIX (2002), 77–82, 86–100; Kathleen Wilson, *The Island Race: Englishness, Empire, and Gender in the Eighteenth Century* (New York, 2003), 11–12; and Dror Wahrman, *The Making of the Modern Self: Identity and Culture in Eighteenth-Century England* (New Haven, Conn., 2004), 220–221, 246.

mixed-race daughter Dido Elizabeth Belle lived with Mansfield (his uncle) in London, as its first representative on the subcontinent to combat Clive's corruption. Ultimately, Parliament agreed to bail out the company and to exonerate Clive in 1773. But the taint of that affair would continue to follow East Indian matters, and it cast a permanent shadow over Clive's successor, Warren Hastings.[9]

Parliament's ongoing frustrations with the East India Company and its continuing abuses on the subcontinent came to a head after the American Revolution. Britain's government hoped to institute substantial reform in the Empire after losing thirteen of its colonies, and India was a prime target. Beginning in 1783, Charles James Fox submitted a proposal in the House of Commons to put India under greater governmental control at the expense of the East India Company. In a show of support for Fox's bill, fellow parliamentarian Edmund Burke attacked the company and its agents for their supposed corruption. "He that goes out an insignificant boy, in a few years returns a great Nabob. . . . loaded with odium and with riches," Burke opined. He declared that company servants had plundered India's native nobility and exploited all of its classes, draining them of any natural bounty. He went further in his parliamentary speech, however, condemning returning nabobs for bringing that corruption to Britain as well: "They marry into your families; they enter into your senate . . . they cherish and protect your relations which lie heavy

9. For general documentation of the East India Company at midcentury up to the 1773 Regulating Act against the Company, see P. J. Marshall, *The Impeachment of Warren Hastings* (New York, 1965), introduction; W. M. Elofson, "The Rockingham Whigs in Transition: The East India Company Issue, 1772–1773," *English Historical Review*, CIV (1989), 947–974; H. V. Bowen, *Revenue and Reform: The Indian Problem in British Politics, 1757–1773* (Cambridge, 1991); and Nicholas B. Dirks, *The Scandal of Empire: India and the Creation of Imperial Britain* (Cambridge, Mass., 2006), 10–68. Biographies of Clive abound, which include various depictions of his actions in India. See, for instance, Thomas Babington Macaulay, *Lord Clive* (New York, 1877); Allen Edwardes, *The Rape of India: A Biography of Robert Clive and a Sexual History of the Conquest of Hindustan* (New York, 1966); and Robert Harvey, *Clive: The Life and Death of a British Emperor* (New York, 1998), 285–388. John Lindsay's commission from the East India Company, along with his correspondence while there, can be found in "Appointment of Sir John Lindsay," 1769–1770, Add. MS 18020, BL. The results of both the Seven Years' War and the American Revolution similarly prompted a spirit of reforms in the French empire. Some French officials advocated for a divestment or halt in acquisition of Indian territory. After Britain returned France's primary Indian port of Pondicherry in February 1785, the French state pushed to halt further investment in the subcontinent in favor of supporting the Caribbean slave colony of Saint Domingue; see François-Joseph Ruggiu, "India and the Reshaping of the French Colonial Policy (1759–1789)," *Itinerario*, XXXV, no. 2 (2011), 25–43.

on your patronage; and there is scarcely an house in the kingdom that does not feel some concern and interest [for them]." Though Burke focused on the transmission of corruption and luxury, rather than social diversity, into the metropole, his criticism proved once more reminiscent of Long's rhetoric of invasion and intermarriage expressed a mere decade before over the prospect of the arrival of enslaved blacks into Britain. His oratory was so heated that many diarists privately wondered, justifiably so, if the East India debates could dissolve Parliament. Even Jamaican newspapers worried that Fox's bill might "convulse the State to its very foundation." Ultimately, his proposal did not pass. Instead, the House of Commons singled out Hastings after he resigned from a twelve-year governorship of Bengal in 1785. It charged him formally with inciting revolt, encouraging bribery and corruption, and presiding over innocent deaths in India. The British public could now have its imperial reckoning. In its shadow, the Morse family and others like them would untangle their family legacies, shaped by Britain's transforming Empire.[10]

The Trials of Warren Hastings and the Morse Family

On the very day that Parliament officially brought charges of corruption against Warren Hastings, the former governor fell victim to incredible chance. The House of Commons agreed on June 13, 1786, to try Hastings for having provoked the raja of Benares into an open and deadly revolt during his governorship. That same morning, an Indian diamond—estimated to weigh a massive 110 carats—arrived in England. The nizam of Hyderabad had sent the jewel as a gift to George III, and Hastings happened to be in attendance when the king received it the next day. Although Hastings had no personal connection to the diamond, the timing of its arrival provided rich fodder for

10. Edmund Burke, "Speech on Fox's India Bill," Dec. 1, 1783, in Elofson et al., eds., *Writings and Speeches of Edmund Burke*, V, 403, 443. Sexual imagery, in slightly different ways, also permeated Burke's comments about Hastings and India. Parliamentarians speaking out against Hastings pointed frequently to the supposed sexual exploitation of the Begums of Awadh, when the governor sent troops into their private quarters to collect tribute. Burke spoke of the East India Company's spoliation of India in general in similarly sexual language throughout the trial; see Anna Clark, *Scandal: The Sexual Politics of the British Constitution* (Princeton, 2004), 84–112. On public reactions to the parliamentary proceedings, see, for instance, "The Diary of Nicholas Brown," in John Crawford Hodgson, ed., *Six North County Diaries*, Surtee's Society, *Publications*, CXVIII (London, 1910), December 1783, 253, Mar. 25, 1784, 257; *The Diary of a Country Parson: The Reverend James Woodforde*, ed. John Beresford, 5 vols. (London, 1926–1931), II, Dec. 23, 1783, 111; *Cornwall Chronicle, and Jamaica General Advertiser*, Mar. 20, 1784, Supplement. In fact, Parliament dissolved in March 1784, forcing the prime minister to call a general election.

the press, and it came to symbolize the accusations of bribery against him. Caricaturists quickly seized on the event to represent the apparent corruption of East Indian affairs. A satirist depicted Hastings sitting atop a bulse of diamonds in 1786 (Plate 3). William Dent later portrayed Hastings genuflecting to the king with a similar offering of jewels and gold (Plate 4). The event continued to serve as shorthand for East Indian extortion for years afterward as Hastings's case slogged forward.[11]

The clamor over the nizam's diamond in 1786 brought John Morse's children, recently returned from India, once more to public attention. Just two weeks after the *Morning Herald*'s report on Sarah Cator's bounteous muslin gowns, the paper printed another anonymous letter about her family. Famous for its attacks on political corruption, the *Herald* directed its attention this time to Sarah's sister Ann Middleton. Why, the paper's correspondent asked, should so much fuss be made over the nizam's gift when "it is well known that diamonds are of so little estimation in India." The writer continued, "Mrs. *Middleton* (sister to Mrs. *Cator* lately arrived) on her marriage with N[athaniel] M[iddleton] Esq. sent one as a present to [Giuseppe] Baretti, her Italian master, *of whom she had received six lessons,* that was valued here at 500 guineas!" Like Hastings, Ann Middleton (née Morse) stood accused of throwing about lavish Eastern bounty in Britain. Her decadence suggested impropriety, if not outright immorality. Above all, her generosity exposed an outrageous fortune.[12]

11. *Morning Herald,* June 16, 23, Dec. 12, 1786; *The Debate on the East India Relief Bill, in the House of Commons, on Monday the 26th of June, 1786: in Which Is Included the History of the Diamond Delivered to the Right Hon. Lord Sydney by Major John Scott* (London, 1786), 21–28; John Watkins, *Memoirs of the Public and Private Life of the Right Honorable R. B. Sheridan . . . ,* 2d ed., 2 vols. (London, 1817), I, 336–338. See also Sir Alfred C. Lyall, *Warren Hastings* (New York, 1889), 194–295; and Marcia Pointon, "Intriguing Jeweler: Royal Bodies and Luxurious Consumption," *Textual Practice,* XI, no. 3 (Winter 1997), 503; Ian Balfour, *Famous Diamonds* (London, 2000), 117–125; Dirks, *Scandal of Empire,* 102–105; and Nechtman, *Nabobs,* 162–165. Balfour reports the diamond to have been 101 carats, while the *Morning Herald* noted it as weighing 110 and worth one hundred thirty thousand pounds; see *Morning Herald,* Dec. 12, 1786.

12. *Morning Herald,* July 26, 1786; Barker, *Newspapers, Politics, and Public Opinion,* 85. News of Middleton's gift long outlived the *Herald*'s report. Multiple biographies of Baretti indicated that the diamond had been much needed and that Middleton continued to support Baretti financially for years to come. See *Annual Register; or, A View of the History, Politics, and Literature, for the Year 1789* (London, 1792), 39; and Eleazar Lord, *Lempriere's Universal Biography; Containing a Critical and Historical Account of the Lives, Characters, and Labours of Eminent Persons . . . ,* 2 vols. (New York, 1825), I, 166.

PLATE 3. *Knave of Diamonds.* 1786. BM Satires 6966.
Image courtesy of the Trustees of the British Museum

PLATE 4. *The Wise Man of the East Making His Offering.* By William Dent. 1788.
BM Satires 7274. Image courtesy of the trustees of the British Museum

Beyond the simple revelations of Ann Middleton's extravagant gifts and Sarah Cator's luxurious wardrobe, the *Morning Herald*'s reports in the summer of 1786 contained a complex set of information meant to excoriate John Morse's daughters and uncover rampant colonial vice. First, Middleton's Italian teacher, Giuseppe Baretti, was a notorious and popular figure in London. His friends included the actor David Garrick and writers Samuel Johnson, Hester Thrale, and Fanny Burney. In 1769, Baretti faced a well-publicized murder charge but was acquitted by Lord Mansfield, influenced, perhaps, by the intervention of Garrick, who entertained Mansfield's home (including, potentially, Dido Elizabeth Belle) with a passage from *Othello* during the trial. Baretti also became close friends with John Cator, Sarah's socially prominent brother-in-law who would later introduce the Italian, along with many other famous figures in London, to Ann Middleton. The Jamaican sisters' friendship with Baretti indicated their high social standing and connection to some of the capital's leading lights. By announcing Ann and Sarah's ties to Baretti, the *Morning Herald* demonstrated that the sisters were, not only decadent nabobinas, but elites enmeshed in the exact networks of power now coming under scrutiny with Hastings's trial.[13]

Second, Ann Middleton's marriage—noted in the *Herald*'s report—indicated her strong affiliation with Hastings himself. Nathaniel Middleton, who wed Ann in Calcutta, had served as Warren Hastings's representative in Lucknow. The two were friends who corresponded regularly—the Middletons even named their firstborn Hastings—and, despite eventually losing the governor's confidence, Middleton remained loyal to his old superior.[14] He

13. *Gentleman's Magazine: And Historical Chronicle,* LIX, pt. 1 (London, 1789), 569–571; [Frances Burney], *Diary and Letters of Madame D'Arblay,* [ed. Charlotte Barrett], I (Philadelphia, 1842), 68, 222–256; Lacy Collison-Morley, *Giuseppe Baretti: With an Account of His Literary Friendships and Feuds in Italy and in England in the Days of Dr. Johnson* (London, 1909), 182, 206–208, 301–329. John Cator was well-known in England as a successful timber merchant, sheriff of Kent, and member of Parliament for Ipswich. He socialized with Samuel Johnson, Hester Thrale, and Fanny Burney; see Norman G. Brett-James, *The Life of Peter Collinson* (London, 1926), 222–224; and Pat Manning, *The Cators of Beckenham and Woodbastwick* (Eastbourne, U.K., 2002), 6–23.

14. Marriage of Nathaniel Middleton and Ann Morse, Oct. 26, 1780, East India Company Returns of Marriages, N/1/2, fol. 145v, APAC, BL; *Saint James's Chronicle; or, the British Evening-Post* (London), Aug. 25–Aug. 28, 1781; William Hickey, *Memoirs of William Hickey,* ed. Alfred Spencer, 9th ed., 4 vols. (New York, 1948), III, 155–156; Marshall, *Impeachment of Warren Hastings,* 44–52; *Oxford Dictionary of National Biography,* online ed., s.v. "Middleton, Nathaniel (1750–1807)," by T. H. Bowyer, http://www.oxforddnb.com /view/article/69059. Middleton's correspondence with Hastings can be found in "Original

did so in part because he became swept up in the same allegations as Hastings. Bengal's ruling council had investigated Middleton, along with two other East India Company officials, in the summer of 1783 for what Edmund Burke deemed the "grossest peculations." That inquiry failed to reach a verdict, but it saddled Middleton with the standard taint of East Indian abuse. When building his case against Hastings in the House of Commons, Burke described Middleton as the governor's "confidential Resident" in suppressing the nawab of Awadh in Lucknow. During Hastings's trial, Middleton divulged little information, earning the nickname "Memory Middleton" in the press — a sobriquet that followed him for the rest of his life.[15] Readers who monitored Hastings's plight closely certainly would have known of Nathaniel Middleton when the *Morning Herald* discussed his wife. Ann's present to Baretti, then, appeared to be not simply a coincidental gift to that of the nizam's diamond. Rather, it served as a metonym of East Indian corruption generally and of direct associations with Warren Hastings specifically. Linking Ann to her husband affixed the label of colonial degradation more firmly onto the Jamaican Morses.[16]

Correspondence of William Hastings," Dec. 20, 1778, Add. MS 29142, fols. 214–215, Add. MS 29143, Apr. 2, 1779, fols. 172–173, Add. MS 29146, Nov. 20, 1780, fols. 274–275, and Add. MS 29155, Jun. 9, 1782, fol. 478, BL.

15. Burke, "Speech on Fox's India Bill," Dec. 1, 1783, in Marshall, ed., *Writings and Speeches of Edmund Burke*, V, 405–422; *Memoirs of William Hickey*, ed. Spencer, III, 155–156; *The Diary of Joseph Farington*, XIV, *January 1816–December 1817*, ed. Kathryn Cave (New Haven, Conn., 1984), Oct. 18, 1817, 5090; Marshall, *Impeachment of Warren Hastings*, 44–52. Cartoonists even satirized Middleton's lack of disclosure, noting the "Select Passages" of his "Oriental Tales"; see William Dent, "Bad Memory, an Imperfect Work," 1788, BM Satires 7327, BM. When Middleton added a level to his Hampshire manor years after Hastings's trial concluded, a London newspaper wittily reported that "*Memory Middleton . . . forgot* to build [it] when the Mansion was first erected"; see *True Briton* (London), July 17, 1800. Middleton was an important focal point in Hastings's trial. The House of Commons subpoenaed Middleton's correspondence and read his letters to Hastings as well as to Sir Elijah Impey, Bengal's chief justice, in court. Those letters included personal accounts of Middleton's wife, Ann, as well as their son, Hastings Nathaniel. They also included information about Ann's sister Sarah and her husband, William Cator, whom Middleton helped to advance within the East India Company; see, in particular, Middleton's letters to Impey in *Minutes of the Evidence, Taken Before a Committee of the Whole House of Commons; on the Articles of Charge of High Crimes and Misdemeanors, Presented to the House, against Warren Hastings, Esq; Late Governor General of Bengal; Being the Examinations of Nathaniel Middleton, Esq. and Sir Elijah Impey* (London, 1787), 21–28.

16. Ann's support for Hastings matched her brother's own enthusiasm. While still in Bengal, Robert signed his name to a 1785 petition of "British Inhabitants of Calcutta" who

Finally, by noting that Sarah Cator's mother was a *"Mulatto* woman," the *Morning Herald* exposed Sarah, and later her sister, as a mixed-race Jamaican. The revelation by the anonymous correspondent implicitly charged her with disguising this West Indian past by parading as an East Indian returnee. Certainly, there was an element of truth to such an interpretation of the Morses' self-fashioning. Before coming back to Britain, Ann, Sarah, and their brother Robert commissioned a family portrait that eliminated any visual evidence of a connection to either the East or West Indies (Plate 5). Classical architecture and European instruments, instead, asserted a settled and uncomplicated domestic British identity. Years later, Ann and Nathaniel Middleton's son cagily declared to a correspondent that he was uncertain if his parents had met and married in India or even if he himself was born there. John Morse's children seem to have wished only to integrate into elite British ranks, wanting little interrogation of their origins. The editorial submission to the *Herald,* then, undercut the family's extensive pains to assimilate as rich Britons firmly rooted in the metropole. Likewise, revealed as "mulattoes," the Morse children fell vulnerable to the increasingly negative associations made with individuals of African heritage, particularly after the arrival of so many formerly enslaved North Americans in Britain. They desperately wished to avoid being called what Francis Grose first labeled in his 1785 dictionary of English slang "Dingey Christians": "Any one who has . . . a lick of the tar brush, that is, some negroe blood in them."[17]

---

declared a "general Satisfaction in the whole Tenour" of Hastings's administration; see "To the Honourable Warren Hastings, Esquire, Governor General," Feb. 1, 1785, in *Minutes of the Evidence Taken at the Trial of Warren Hastings Esquire, Late Governor General of Bengal, at the Bar of the House of Lords, in Westminster Hall, upon an Impeachment against Him for High Crimes and Misdemeanors, by the Knights, Citizens, and Burgesses, in Parliament Assembled, in the Name of Themselves, and of All the Commons of Great Britain,* VI ([London], 1788), 2451-2452.

17. Hastings Nathaniel Middleton to William Leake, Nov. 7, 1819, Hastings Nathaniel Middleton Letter Book, 796/1, fol. 213, City of Westminster Archives, Westminster, U.K.; [Francis Grose], *A Classical Dictionary of the Vulgar Tongue* (London, 1785), s.v. "Dingey Christians." It appears that the first published identification of the term "Dingey Christians" comes from the 1785 edition of Grose's dictionary; see Eric Partridge, *A Dictionary of Slang and Unconventional English,* ed. Paul Beale (Abingdon, U.K., 2005), 310; and Jonathon Green, *Cassell's Dictionary of Slang,* 2d ed. (London, 2005), 406. This erasure of visual connection to the colonies was consistent with other nabobs; see Richard Leppert, "Music, Domestic Life, and Cultural Chauvinism: Images of British Subjects at Home in India," in Leppert and Susan McClary, eds., *Music and Society: The Politics of Composition, Performance, and Reception* (New York, 1987), esp. 68–88; Beth Fowkes Tobin, *Picturing Imperial*

PLATE 5. *The Morse and Cator Family.* By Johann Zoffany. 1784. Image courtesy of the Aberdeen Art Gallery and Museums Collections. From left to right: Robert Morse, Ann Middleton, Sarah Cator, and her husband, William Cator

The relatively simple accusations thrown at Sarah Cator and Ann Middleton thus attempted to inflict tremendous damage to their personal reputations. The sisters had, according to the letters published about them, incredible wealth derived, in part, from spoils linked to East Indian corruption. Moreover, their lavish spending and extravagant gifts indicated a deep attach-

<hr />

Power: Colonial Subjects in Eighteenth-Century British Painting (Durham, N.C., 1999), esp. 121–123; and Madge Dresser and Andrew Hann, "Introduction," in Dresser and Hann, eds., *Slavery and the British Country House* (Swindon, U.K., 2013), xiii.

ment to the vice of luxury. Personal and professional associations with War-ren Hastings, Bengal's foremost symbol of dishonesty and fraud, further en-trenched this idea in the minds of the *Herald*'s readers, who were sympathetic to the paper's endorsement of the former governor's prosecution. Indeed, the paper proclaimed strong support for Hasting's prosecutors, Charles James Fox and Edmund Burke. The revelation of the sisters' African ancestry was an effort to assign to them the growing stigma against blacks in Britain. It also validated the claims recently made by their cousin Edward Morse in a lawsuit against the family's enormous Caribbean fortune.[18]

If the anonymous letters published by the *Morning Herald* did come from Edward Morse, he sent them in a state of general despondency about his future. A lawyer trained at Gray's Inn, Edward anticipated a bright legal future when he obtained the seat of chief justice of Senegambia in 1772. He arrived in Africa at the end of that year, but, by the next spring, an inflammation of the eyes forced him to return to England. Edward voyaged back to Senegam-bia in 1776, but he fled to England within a year as French forces stormed the colony. His impermanence in Africa led to disputes with the colony's gover-nor as well as complications involving his salary. Edward struggled to recoup back pay, a housing allowance, and personal expenditures for travel between England and Africa. Most damaging to his finances was the loss of his posi-tion of chief justice once the French recaptured Senegambia. Anticipating a lifelong appointment, or perhaps viewing the seat as a sinecure, Edward ex-pressed utter confusion at how he might support himself now that the posi-tion was gone. He badgered officials throughout London and Westminster for any kind of employment, either at home or abroad. "All Countries are equally indifferent to me," he wrote. With a pregnant wife, four children, and "an aged Mother" depending on his salary, Edward pleaded for help. Having exhausted his credit, he warned Thomas Townshend, Lord Sydney, that he would soon be turned out "into the Street with my little family," only to be-come "in the strictest Sense of the Word, *Beggars*." Under such pressures, Edward targeted his wealthy cousins of color for the lion's share of their late father's estate.[19]

18. Barker, *Newspapers, Politics, and Public Opinion*, 57–60; Jeremy Black, *The English Press in the Eighteenth Century* (Philadelphia, 1987), 183.

19. Edward Morse to William Pitt, Oct. 20, 1784, CO 267/8, NAE, Morse to George III, Jan. 9, 1784, Morse to Thomas Townshend, Lord Sydney, Oct. 29, 1784 (emphasis in origi-nal); Joseph Foster, *The Register of Admissions to Gray's Inn, 1521–1889* . . . (London, 1889), 382. Morse replaced Christopher Milles in the position of chief justice on the latter's death; see *The Annual Register; or, A View of the History, Politics, and Literature, for the Year 1772*

Inheritance challenges were by no means rare in the Atlantic world, and Edward Morse's suit drew on long-standing precedent. Taking a rival heir to court was routine in the British Empire, and the ubiquity of death in Jamaica made the island a hotbed for estate litigation, especially for people of color. Katherine Campbell, for instance, was sued by her aunts after their brother left his massive Jamaican estate to Campbell's father and his "lawful heirs." Born an illegitimate quadroon on the island, Campbell's rights of inheritance to the fortune after her father died were questionable. But the case took an even more complicated turn in 1749 when a Jamaican attorney brought her to Britain, where she married Hugh McLachlan. Now attached to his wife's disputed inheritance, McLachlan traveled to Jamaica to secure the birthright but died within weeks of arriving. His death prompted McLachlan's relatives to file their own suit, alleging that Campbell had "dazzled [him] with the prospect of so rich a Succession," eventually leading to his downfall. Beyond such language, tied to ideas of sexual ensnarement by colonial women of color, this trial—much like the initial one lodged by Campbell's aunts—turned entirely on Campbell's illegitimacy and rights as an heir, not her skin color, which was never explicitly mentioned. This might have been owing partly to timing: the more stringent notions of race developing at midcentury had yet not fully emerged. Racial accusations, therefore, did not saturate either proceeding, but family considerations did. Campbell was most vulnerable because of her birth out of wedlock, but this was a problem that faced most elite Jamaicans of color.[20]

(London, 1773), 160. Morse published an account of the events leading to his financial difficulties in 1787; see Edward Morse, *Case of Edward Morse, Esq.* ([London], 1787). A number of letters between Morse and the secretary of state detail the case even further; see "The Humble Memorial of Edward Morse Esq. Chief Justice of His Majesty's Province of Senegambia in Africa," Jan. 14, 1777, T 1/538, fol. 251, NAE, "The Humble Memorial of Edward Morse Esquire Chief Justice of His Majesty's Province of Senegambia in Africa," Dec. 17, 1777, T 1/542, fol. 219, "Sierra Leone Correspondence," 1778–1784, CO 267/4–8.

20. Representation for John McLauchlan of Greenhall, June 15, 1761, bundle 380, NRAS 3283, MCP, "Information for Daniel Katharine Campbell Defender against John McLachlan of Greenhall Pursuer," 1760. Many thanks to Mr. Compton Maclean for permission to read his family papers. On inheritance suits in this period, see John Addy, *Death, Money, and the Vultures: Inheritance and Avarice, 1660–1750* (New York, 1992), 149; and Lloyd Bonfield, *Devising, Dying, and Dispute: Probate Litigation in Early Modern England* (Burlington, Vt., 2012), 65–78. Vincent Brown documents the struggles between legatees and executors in Jamaica; see Brown, *The Reaper's Garden: Death and Power in the World of Atlantic Slavery* (Cambridge, Mass., 2008), 102–107. Jamaica's Chancery Court heard numerous cases in which executors failed to compensate mixed-race beneficiaries. Bernie D. Jones finds quite

Edward Morse knew that he could wage a similar attack against his own relatives because he had a long personal history with them. He claimed to have been "brought up and Educated" by John Morse, the father of his mixed-race cousins, who sent him to Jamaica as his "Acknowledged Heir." Once in Jamaica, Edward came to learn the intricacies of his uncle John's professional and domestic life. Edward moved into John Morse's home, where he lived alongside his uncle's mistress, Elizabeth Augier, as well as his mixed-race cousins. Augier had come from the island's privileged class of color and had received a small but significant bequest from her affluent father, William Tyndall. Such an advanced financial and legal position ushered Augier into the upper ranks of Kingston's society of color. With Augier's social advantages and their father's wealth and clout, the Jamaican Morses grew up in extreme privilege compared to that of their mixed-race peers, the vast majority of whom toiled in slavery or abject poverty. Edward Morse undoubtedly recognized that when he moved to Jamaica and remembered it years later as his uncle's health started to fail. When John Morse suffered a stroke in 1777 and returned to England permanently, Edward began contemplating his wider family's fortune.[21]

Immediately after John Morse passed away at his London home in 1781,

---

similar results for mixed-race heirs in the United States several decades later; see Jones, *Fathers of Conscience: Mixed-Race Inheritance in the Antebellum South* (Athens, Ga., 2009). For more on cultural beliefs in colonial women of color as temptresses, see Mary Louise Pratt, *Imperial Eyes: Travel Writing and Transculturation* (New York, 1992); Carol Barash, "The Character of Difference: The Creole Woman as Cultural Mediator in Narratives about Jamaica," *Eighteenth-Century Studies,* XXIII (1990), 406–424; and Marlene L. Daut, *Tropics of Haiti: Race and the Literary History of the Haitian Revolution in the Atlantic World, 1789–1865* (Liverpool, U.K., 2015), 198–204.

21. Morse v. Green, Feb. 22, 1785, Chancery Court Records, C 12/604/16, NAE. Both sides in the suit over the family fortune acknowledged that John Morse cared for Edward, even going so far as to pay for the rights to Edward's position of chief justice of Senegambia. Three of Edward Morse's opponents noted the time he spent in his cousins' house; see Morse v. Royal et al., Apr. 12, 1792, Jamaica Chancery Court Records, 1A/3/154, no. 132, fol. 405, JA; and Royal v. Morse, Jan. 21, 1796, Chancery Court Records, C 12/660/5, NAE. Mary Augier, Elizabeth's mother, had also accumulated a modest degree of affluence, possibly owing to her connection with Tyndall. She possessed both land and a house in Kingston worth sixty pounds of rent per year as well as two other substantial homes. Added to this were fourteen slaves and a large number of household goods. Mary's extended family also obtained a degree of financial security. Her sister's relationship with Richard Ashton netted her a near-equal fortune to Mary's, and her nephew came into an inheritance of five hundred pounds from his father's bequests; see Acts of the Assembly of Jamaica, May 28, 1747, CO 140/33, fol. 66, NAE.

Edward began obstructing the execution of his will, which had left the majority of money to his mixed-race children. First, Edward lodged a complaint with the Prerogative Court of Canterbury, in an attempt to prevent it from proving the document. Like many litigants in the eighteenth century, Edward alleged that the recently deceased had been non compos mentis when crafting his last wishes. Deathbed testaments were common in both Britain and the colonies. Recurring illnesses regularly provoked such amendments, so much so that satirists mocked the phenomenon in Jamaica, especially considering the island's unhealthy climate for British transplants (see Plate 6). The frequent distress and delusions often present in that state convinced many judges not to honor their stipulations. If the courts found such accusations of lunacy to be true, they could nullify the document, which would necessitate the use of an older version of a will or the sending of assets into intestate proceedings. Edward insisted that John Morse had written the will after his debilitating stroke, which prevented him from speaking or simple reasoning. This had long been rumored in Jamaica: a plantation attorney reported from Spanish Town in 1778 that John Morse "labours under a degree of insanity . . . [from which] the doctors have little hopes of his recovery." In such a case, the will would be invalid and Morse's property distributed according to intestate custom, meaning that only Morse's legitimate relatives could inherit his sizeable fortune.[22]

Edmund Green, the attorney for Morse's children, disagreed, claiming that the will was drafted long before Morse became sick. More effectively, Green managed to convince Edward to drop his petition to the court by claiming that the deceased's Jamaican holdings were deeply in debt and would be settled only after years of litigation. John Morse's other creditors were, in fact, already complaining. Instead, Green offered to pay Edward a lump sum of fifteen hundred pounds to satisfy his claims on the estate. For cash-

22. Will of John Morse, Apr. 18, 1781, PROB 11/1077, NAE; Edward East to James Brydges, Duke of Chandos, Oct. 23, 1778, Stowe Papers, STB box 26 (46), HL (the next year, however, East reported an update that Morse was now supposedly "perfectly restored to health"; see ibid., June 16, 1779, STB box 26 [48]); Morse v. Green, Feb. 22, 1785, Chancery Court Records, C 12/604/16, NAE. For more on non compos mentis charges in England, see Addy, *Death, Money, and the Vultures*, 113–118; and Michael MacDonald and Terence R. Murphy, *Sleepless Souls: Suicide in Early Modern England* (New York, 1990), 133–142. Several such cases turned up in Jamaica's Court of Ordinary records. See, in particular Rowe v. Mitchell et al., 1811, Jamaica Court of Ordinary, 1B/11/11/2, JA, Ash v. Ratigan, Sept. 3, 1808, 1B/11/11/3, fols. 8–24, and Dispute over the will of John Sleater, Oct. 3, 1789, 1B/11/13/1, fols. 143–154.

John sends for Mr Codicil & bequeaths his Kit.

PLATE 6. *Johnny New-Come in the Island of Jamaica*. By Abraham James. 1800.
Image courtesy of the National Library of Jamaica. Caption Reads:
"John sends for Mr. Codicil and bequeaths his Kit."

strapped Edward, presently writing in vain for monetary assistance from the
British government, the offer brought a modicum of relief, and he reluctantly
accepted it. But Edward's immediate needs severely clouded his judgment.
Edmund Green was not a disinterested individual. Not only was he an executor of John Morse's will, Green was also Morse's son-in-law, married to
his Jamaican daughter of color, Catherine. Moreover, the couple lived with
Morse in his London home in Charterhouse Square during the last months
of the patriarch's life. Edmund and Catherine stood to inherit an equal share

of Morse's Jamaican fortune under the terms of his disputed will, and paying off Edward removed the chief obstacle preventing the attainment of that bequest. Green later denied making these declarations about debt on the estate to Edward, with little surprise: within four years, John Morse's Jamaican plantations were turning over tremendous profits.[23]

Learning of the strength of his late uncle's colonial estate, Edward Morse went back to the courts in 1785. He had received favorable legal encouragements to sue from Henry Maddock and Alan Chambré, two of England's most prominent jurists. Taking an entirely new legal direction, Edward's suit went beyond the traditional confines of domestic inheritance litigation and instead became a race trial in England. He presented a simple legal argument to England's Court of Chancery pointing to a solitary colonial statute. Highlighting Jamaica's 1761 inheritance cap against illegitimate children of color, Edward protested that his mixed-race cousins' legacies exceeded the law's maximum allowance. Though he might have overvalued his uncle's estate at £330,000, John Morse's property certainly numbered in the tens of thousands of pounds. With most of that bequeathed to his mixed-race children, each individual inheritance would have gone well over the £2,000 limit enacted by Jamaica's 1761 edict. To ensure that the court had clear evidence of his cousins' racial ancestry, Edward also sketched out their genealogy. Elizabeth Augier, he noted, was the illegitimate mulatto daughter of Mary Augier, who was herself the illegitimate mulatto daughter of "a negro woman" in Jamaica. Elizabeth's children with John Morse, then, were only three generations removed from a black ancestor, and therefore each within Jamaica's legal definition of "mulatto." He did not reveal their privileged status, most likely because he understood that it might complicate his simple argument. Edward's case nevertheless rested on an intimate knowledge of family history. A strong genealogical comprehension of colonial relatives—including those with non-European heritage—was critical, not only for understanding overseas kin structures, but for managing transatlantic families. If determined to be "mulattoes" according to Jamaican law, the Morse children could not legally inherit more than £2,000. Edward Morse made his case plainly. None of his

23. Ezekiel Dickinson to Caleb Dickinson, May 14, 1785, in "Jamaican Plantation Records from the Dickinson Papers, 1675-1849," microfilm M 2175, reel 4, 282/2, John D. Rockefeller, Jr., Library; Morse v. Green, July 15, 1785, Chancery Court Records, C 12/604/16, NAE, Feb. 22, 1785. John Morse's son and namesake noted that the home was located in Charterhouse Square; see Answer of John Morse, Feb. 6, 1787, C 12/610/30, NAE. The residence also appears in an advertisement for a London school run by Mrs. Campbell, a former West Indian; see *Public Advertiser* (London), June 16, 1770.

cousins were born in wedlock, and, because they were mulattoes, they could not inherit the whole sum of their father's fortune. As next of kin, Edward proclaimed that he and several other British family members stood to inherit the bulk of John Morse's estate, as the provisions for his children had violated colonial law and rendered the stipulations of the will null and void.[24]

From a legal perspective and Edward's selective evidence, arguments to deprive his mixed-race cousins of the majority of their inheritance rested on a sound foundation. Colonial law had ultimate jurisdiction when probating a colonial estate. British courts administering wills of individuals dying overseas had to abide by colonial law and had no jurisdiction over real property. Probated estates were divided into real (land and buildings) and personal (everything else) holdings. Though both were officially administered according to laws of geographic origin, disputes over the former had to comply firmly with colonial legislation, if they were not tried in colonial courts.[25]

24. Morse v. Green, Feb. 22, 1785, Chancery Court Records, C/12/604/16, NAE. In a later deposition to the court for a different, though related, trial, William Mitchell reported that Edward Morse held legal opinions from Maddock and Chambré in 1785; see Morse v. Royal, July 21, 1801, Chancery Court Records, C 13/2394/27, NAE. See also *Oxford Dictionary of National Biography,* online ed., s.v. "Maddock, Henry (d. 1824)," by J. M. Rigg, rev. Jonathan Harris, http://www.oxforddnb.com.proxy.wm.edu/view/article/17756, and s.v. "Chambré, Sir Alan (1739–1823)," by James Oldham, http://www.oxforddnb.com.proxy .wm.edu/view/article/5086. In many ways, Edward's attempt to prove the mixed-race ancestry of his relations resembles, in reverse, the genealogies constructed by families in the Spanish Atlantic to ensure that a mark of African or indigenous ancestry was not present in a family line; see María Elena Martínez, *Genealogical Fictions: Limpieza de Sangre, Religion, and Gender in Colonial Mexico* (Stanford, Calif., 2008), 62–75, 217–225. Edward Morse later proclaimed that his uncle's will had been drafted to "evade and elude the force and Effect of the said Act" of 1761; see Morse v. Royal et al., Mar. 10, 1792, Jamaica Chancery Court Records, 1A/3/154, no. 132, fols. 253–254, JA.

25. Peter Wilson Coldham, *English Estates of American Colonists: American Wills and Administrations in the Perogative Court of Canterbury, 1700–1799* (Baltimore, 1980), v; Peter Walne, *English Wills: Probate Records in England and Wales with a Brief Note on Scottish and Irish Wills* (Richmond, Va., 1964), 19, 49–51. According to David P. Gauthier, John Locke exalted this system of using overseas law in the settling of property in his *Second Treatise of Civil Government* (1689). Locke believed that the administration of wills in conquered lands should follow the custom of the conquered country, otherwise the colonizer claimed ownership of the land, which violated the civil compact; see Gauthier, "The Role of Inheritance in Locke's Political Theory," *Canadian Journal of Economics and Political Science / Revue canadienne d'economique et de science politique,* XXXII (1966), 38–45. Often claiming itself as a conquered territory, Jamaica and its officials supported this theory. British opinion differed, however, when it came to the administration of expatriate Britons' wills overseas in competing empires' territories. Muriel Nazarri notes that Britain demanded the ability to

Declarations from many assemblies, including Jamaica's, that enslaved people were real, and not personal, property reinforced colonial over metropolitan law when it came to inheritance resolution, considering that most West Indian fortunes consisted of land and slaves. Mixed-race people in Britain, therefore, fell subject to tight Caribbean estate regulations. Such restrictions opened a clear path for white family members to litigate. If John Morse's bequests violated Jamaican legal strictures, his will could not be enforced.[26]

By taking this position, Edward Morse uncovered his cousin's African heritage and thus reimposed a Jamaican status on them, even though they now lived in Britain. In his arguments to the Chancery Court, Edward asserted a firm understanding, not only of Jamaican law, but of the island's social history. He cited the colony's 1733 edict allowing Jamaicans more than three generations removed from a black ancestor to become legally white. In the time between that decision and the 1761 inheritance cap, Edward proclaimed that the island's mixed-race population had exploded. Echoing the inheritance law's preamble, he justified the necessity of the act, declaring that this demographic shift had "decrease[d] the Number of white persons whereby Insurrections frequently happened." The Jamaican Morses, according to their cousin, represented these improper and potentially dangerous kin and therefore needed to incur the punishment intended for such wayward families.[27]

What Edward did not make clear, though, was how this law, grounded in specific colonial concerns of demographics and slavery, had any bearing on those now resident in the metropole. Having left the West Indies, the Morse children obviously no longer compromised the distinctions between black and white on the island. Yet, Edward said nothing about the potential impact of mixed-race individuals in Britain, reciting only Jamaica's legal code. His intentions were most likely only pecuniary, not political, and he utilized no other

---

implement British inheritance law over its subjects living in Brazil; see Nazarri, "Widows as Obstacles to Business: British Objections to Brazilian Marriage and Inheritance Laws," *Comparative Studies in Society and History*, XXXVII (1995), 781–802.

26. Several of Britain's North American colonies likewise defined chattel slaves as real property: Virginia from 1705–1792; South Carolina in 1690 — although the Privy Council overturned that decision; Louisiana; and, after the Revolution, Kentucky from 1798–1852, and Arkansas from 1840–1843; see Thomas D. Morris, *Southern Slavery and the Law, 1619–1860* (Chapel Hill, N.C., 1996), 63. Colonial slave laws were also frequently used to attack black and mixed-race people in France, which had no positive law on slavery; see Pierre H. Boulle, "Racial Purity or Legal Clarity? The Status of Black Residents in Eighteenth-Century France," *Journal of the Historical Society*, VI (2006), 19–46.

27. Morse v. Green, Feb. 22, 1785, Chancery Court Records, C/12/604/16, NAE.

racial language beyond the scope of those edicts. Nevertheless, by making this legal argument he asserted that Jamaican social concerns surrounding race also mattered in Britain, as mixed-race grandees brought their inappropriate family units into the metropole. Moreover, his lawsuit demonstrated the incredible legal and financial vulnerability of West Indians of color, even in Britain. Traveling across the Atlantic could separate one from the worst abuses of Caribbean prejudice, but it could not provide a full divorce from the colonial edicts that divided individuals by race.

Despite these legal vulnerabilities, the Morse children were not devoid of protective options. As their representative, Edmund Green employed a number of tactics to stall the case. Initially, he issued demurrers to each of Edward Morse's complaints in order to stall the proceedings—a strategy typical for Chancery Court trials—and to exacerbate Edward's mounting debt. Edward quickly recognized this and protested that these measures were "calculated merely for delay and for the purpose of harassing and oppressing your petitioner and rendering it expensive and difficult . . . to prosecute his just rights." Green next directed the court's attention toward John Morse's disputed will, which Edward invoked in his Chancery allegation. Green insisted that Edward's claims were an attempt to defraud the family. John Morse was not only sane when he crafted his will, Green argued, but he had "refused to speak to or see" Edward in his last years and therefore intended nothing for him anyhow. Green conceded that Morse's children were indeed illegitimate but that their bequests were valid nonetheless. This claim was true: England's Statute of Wills had declared in 1540 that freehold land could be devised to anyone—even those born out of wedlock—and, by 1692, one could freely allocate one's personal property to whomever he or she wished. John Morse had acknowledged his offspring in his will, and they were therefore entitled to inherit from his estate. Green effectively argued that John Morse had recrafted his family, turning away from legitimate kin and toward reputed relations with whom he held more affective bonds. This drew on a general understanding in the Atlantic world that colonial families, even if illegitimate, could still be considered as functional households.[28]

28. Morse v. Royal et al., Mar. 10, 1792, Jamaica Chancery Court Records, 1A/3/154, no. 132, fol. 258, JA; Morse v. Green, July 15, 1785, Chancery Court Records, C 12/604/16, NAE, Green v. Morse, May 13, 1785, Chancery Court Records, C 12/137/37; J. H. Baker, *An Introduction to English Legal History*, 3d ed. (Boston, 1990), 122–130; Henry Horwitz, *Chancery Equity Records and Proceedings, 1600–1800: A Guide to Documents in the Public Record Office* (London, 1995), 9; David Lemmings, *Law and Government in England during the Long Eighteenth Century: From Consent to Command* (New York, 2011), 56–57, 79; Addy,

Edmund Green eventually answered Edward's claims about his in-laws' ancestry as well. One year after the start of the suit, Edmund and his wife Catherine sent a response taking issue with Edward's genealogical report. They alleged that they knew little of Jamaica's inheritance cap and certainly nothing of the "numbers of mulattoes" who might have increased on the island since 1733. In direct attack to Edward's claims, though, they disputed his account of Catherine's heritage. The couple insisted that they did not know if she and her siblings were "above three degrees removed in a lineal descent on the Mothers side from a Negroe Ancestor" and instead demanded that Edward furnish exact proof of such an accusation. Somewhat brazenly, they even asked Edward to verify that Elizabeth Augier was, in fact, his cousins' mother.[29]

Other members of the family further muddied these genealogical waters. In a later statement to the court, eldest son Jack Morse asserted that Elizabeth Augier's heritage was not adequately understood. Augier's mother, he contended, was decreed a "mulatto," but it remained unclear if this label originated from "Negro Ancestors . . . or a person descended from an Indian." If this was true, the Morses' biological roots would not have been tied to slavery, but rather to indigeneity. However, this supposition was—from all available evidence—false. Aboriginal descent was a recognized category in privilege bills, and the Augier family was not listed as such on theirs. Moreover, the term "mulatto" was almost never used to describe an individual of Amerindian heritage in Jamaica. But Jack's suggestion contributed to the Morses' case in two ways. First, it threw another racial variable into the mix, further complicating the already bewildering set of facts surrounding the Morses' ancestry. Second, it gave the court reason to believe that even if the children were found to be descended from nonwhites, they were nevertheless unbound by the inheritance cap; indeed, the 1761 act put no restrictions on the children of white and Amerindian parents.[30]

Death, Money, and the Vultures, 8–12. In practice, the social tradition of giving substantial amounts of money to illegitimate offspring of color in Jamaica through a will mimicked the Luso-Brazilian legal custom of allowing bastard children to inherit, even in cases where the deceased had no will; see Linda Lewin, *Surprise Heirs,* I, *Illegitimacy, Patrimonial Rights, and Legal Nationalism in Luso-Brazilian Inheritance, 1750–1821* (Stanford, Calif., 2003). Christer Petley, however, notes that these large bequests were the exception, and not the rule, in Jamaica; see Petley, "'Legitimacy' and Social Boundaries: Free People of Colour and the Social Order in Jamaican Slave Society," *Social History,* XXX (2005), 481–498.

29. Morse v. Green, May 17, 1786, Chancery Court Records, C 12/604/16, NAE.

30. Royal v. Morse, Jan. 21, 1796, Chancery Court Records, C 12/660/5, NAE; Jamaica

All of this was legal posturing, intended to delay the trial's progression. Yet, it was also brilliant strategy utilizing the essential ambiguity, and inherent ridiculousness, of Jamaican racial categorization. The island's assembly and courts did not always maintain, nor were they effectively capable of maintaining, a consistent record of mixed-race genealogies. These institutions frequently used "mulatto" to refer to anyone of joint African and European heritage, even though that term specifically meant the child of one black and one white parent. Considering that the 1733 act to determine racial status distinctly decreed anyone more than three generations distant from a black ancestor to be white, such vagueness complicated matters severely and unduly. Some individuals with less than three generations' removal passed into legal whiteness owing to such indeterminacy. William Jones, for example, noted after visiting Jamaica in 1778 that many people lived as white on the island, even though they were only two or three generations from a black forbear. By the same token, some Jamaicans beyond three generations had a white status questioned or denied. There is no available evidence describing how the assembly actually conferred whiteness to those receiving it under the 1733 act. It appears, instead, that a black ancestor, no matter how far distant, could always remain a legal liability. For instance, Robert Cooper Lee, a business partner of John Morse, won a privilege exemption to the 1761 inheritance cap for his children even though they were legally considered white. This was technically unnecessary, but he worried about "any Evil or mischief, that may attend such Children, by attempts hereafter to bring them within the Intent and meaning of the said Act" simply because they had an African ancestor somewhere in the family tree. By questioning Edward Morse's genealogical claims, then, Edmund Green hoped to transport this racial ambiguity from the colonies to England's courts.[31]

House of Assembly, Laws and Statutes, etc., 2 Geo. III, viii. 1–11 (1761). There are three privilege bills from indigenous petitioners in the Jamaican records. The first appellant was Elizabeth Cadogan; see Acts of the Assembly of Jamaica, May 28, 1746, CO 140/33, NAE. The second came from the Majeau family: Acts of the Assembly of Jamaica, Oct. 31, 1751, CO 139/17, NAE. The third was from the Jones family: Acts of the Assembly of Jamaica, Dec. 22, 1775, CO 139/31, NAE.

    31. *The Diary of the Revd. William Jones, 1777–1821*, ed. O. F. Christie (New York, 1929), 33; Acts of the Assembly of Jamaica, Nov. 16, 1776, CO 140/56, NAE. Racial determinations in slave societies often took ridiculous forms, especially in court. Ariela J. Gross finds personal reputations, including one's ability to dance, to be key when one's race was called into question in the United States; see Gross, *What Blood Won't Tell: A History of Race on Trial in America* (Cambridge, Mass., 2008).

As a final retort, Green pointed to another legal conundrum in Jamaican law. Seemingly in contradiction to his previous challenges regarding the Morses' lineage, Green eventually admitted that their mother Elizabeth Augier had received a privilege concession in 1747. This, he argued, proved that her offspring were not bound by the inheritance cap. Specifically, he highlighted a key passage within Augier's privilege allocation: so long as a white man fathered them, the decree stated that her children would be "free and naturall born Subjects of the crown of Great Britain . . . [as if] descended of and from white Ancestors." This provision was found in all privilege bills. From the perspective of Jamaica's assembly, the stipulation sought to increase the further whitening of Jamaica's elite residents of color. For Green, it meant that Augier's children did not simply inherit her privileged rights but that they were de jure white owing to their father's European ancestry. The inheritance cap, therefore, should hold no power over individuals, declared by law, to be natural subjects of Great Britain.[32]

By taking this line of argument, Edmund Green effectively unraveled the frayed thread of Jamaican racial legislation. The final version of the 1761 inheritance cap did not allow privileged individuals to avoid its measures, although the assembly did consider separate petitions afterwards that conferred such exemptions. But the legislature did not make clear the status of those petitioners' children who, according to the language of the bills, would become "natural born Subjects" should their other parent be white. Did this mean that the children of privileged Jamaicans were free from the inheritance cap's strictures? Did it mean that the group had total immunity to all of the island's race-based legislation? Later protests by Jamaica's mixed-race population seem to indicate that the assembly did not formally take this stance. Rather, it still considered the children of privileged individuals to be bound by the inheritance cap as well. Nonetheless, Green's protest teased out a major

32. The specific language of the clause regarding Augier's white parentage originally came from John Golding's privilege petition; see Acts of the Assembly of Jamaica, Apr. 27, 1733, CO 139/13, no foliation, NAE. Augier's privilege petition, including the recurring considerations of it, can be found in *JAJ*, Apr. 8–May 19, 1747, IV, 66–96. Edmund Green referenced the clause in his rejoinder to Edward Morse; see Morse v. Green, May 17, 1786, Chancery Court Records, C/12/604/16, NAE. Although the *JAJ* do not include this clause, each privilege petition contained it in the manuscript copies of the Acts of the Assembly. The exact meaning of "subject" was in tremendous flux during this period as well and did not have a singular meaning, especially in the colonies; see Hannah Weiss Muller, "An Empire of Subjects: Unities and Disunities in the British Empire, 1760–1790" (Ph.D. diss., Princeton University, 2010).

flaw of the island's discriminatory legislation and one considered seriously by England's Chancery Court. The Morse children, by virtue of their elite standing, were not clear targets of the inheritance cap that had been crafted two decades earlier by their father's colonial associates. Their legal defense brought forward the complexities and contradictions of Jamaican racial ideology more forcefully into the metropole.[33]

Green's responses and the trial's slow pace drew Edward Morse into desperation. He never admitted to having leaked information about his cousins to the *Morning Herald,* but he did openly present his personal hardships to the public as the inheritance suit began to stall. In 1787, he published a short, functionally titled pamphlet, *The Case of Edward Morse.* The tract aired his grievances over the previous decade and a half. Morse recounted his difficulties after taking the post of chief justice of Senegambia in 1772, his subsequent travels between England and Africa as he grew ill, and the loss of salary incurred after France regained the colony in 1783. He laid the majority of blame for his economic woes on England's colonial secretary, Lord Sydney, for having ignored his requests for another governmental appointment. Worst of all, contended Morse, Sydney had failed to promote him to recently opened judicial positions. A vacancy in the seat of chief justice of the Bahamas was a particular prize for Morse, who begged Sydney for the post. Morse craved the seat owing to the "proximity of these Islands to the Island of Jamaica . . . [where] a Suit at Law I have depending there for the recovery of a large Estate, of Right belonging to me, as Heir at Law of an Uncle deceased." Sydney, however, had not advanced Morse's candidacy.[34]

In publishing this short tract, Edward Morse openly subjected his family's inheritance trial to public scrutiny. Those who either knew Morse, or knew of his lawsuit, would find in his pamphlet a perfect representation of the major crises confronting Britain in 1787. Morse's experiences in Senegambia, a colony that Britain attempted to use in the reform of its African slave trade, overlapped with an emerging popular abolition debate. His inheritance suit in Jamaica connected strongly with concerns over Britain's western territories, as he directly appropriated the language of colonial officials worried about white settlement and mixed-race growth in his legal challenge. Finally, for those close to Morse, his cousins' experiences and affiliations in India tied these issues to the Hastings scandal, which had already captivated the nation.

33. "Commissioners of Legal Enquiry in the West Indies," 1822–1828, CO 318/76, fols. 101–106, NAE.
34. Morse, *Case of Edward Morse,* 9.

Considering the family's elite networks and associations with some of Britain's most powerful individuals, their inheritance trial must have attracted a significant audience. They seemed the epitome of family complication in the Atlantic world that so many reformers were struggling to deal with: mixed-race and illegitimate individuals who were also globally mobile and wealthy. Indeed, the *Morning Herald* maintained its curiosity with the family as the trial progressed. The paper reported once more on Ann Middleton in 1788, discussing not only her matrimonial adventures in India but a pair of diamond boot buckles worth thirty-five thousand pounds sterling that she had allegedly brought back with her to England. Public obsession with the family's colonial wealth did not die easily. Many observers likely followed the lawsuit nervously to see how an English court would settle a private family matter that embodied—if not inspired—the imperial concerns of so many Britons.[35]

It is unclear what either the English or Jamaican Chancery courts made of the Morses' suit. Between 1785 and 1794, both Edward Morse and Edmund Green issued claims and counterclaims that circled around the same issues of Jamaican law and inheritance administration. They both lodged appeals in Jamaica's Chancery Court, alongside similar actions in England. Each additional petition effectively restarted the case anew according to equity procedure. None of the surviving court documents include the chancellors' reflections on the case. Despite strong argumentation about Jamaican law and biological taxonomy, it is also uncertain how much these racial questions informed the opinions of jurists on either side of the Atlantic. Instead, the case continued to slog on, bound up more by court procedure than legal debate.[36]

With mounting frustration owing to the length of the suit, Edward Morse moved to Jamaica in the hopes of pressing the governor for a favorable decision. He eventually died there, firmly committed to the cause of wresting John Morse's fortune from his cousins' hands. In his will, probated in February 1795, Edward recorded: "Whereas I am Intitled to a very large Estate real and personal in this Island as Nephew and heir at Law of John Morse . . . it is my Desire that my Executrix and Executors . . . do continue the said Suit." Two months later, Jamaica's Chancery Court moved to abate the trial in light of

35. *Morning Herald*, June 23, 1788; Philip D. Curtin, *Economic Change in Precolonial Africa: Senegambia in the Era of the Slave Trade* (Madison, Wis., 1975), 153–187; Brown, *Moral Capital*, 276–314; Brown, "The British Government and the Slave Trade: Early Parliamentary Enquiries, 1713–83," in Stephen Farrell, Melanie Unwin, and James Walvin, eds., *The British Slave Trade: Abolition, Parliament, and People* (Edinburgh, 2007), 37–39.

36. Horwitz, *Chancery Equity Records*, 9; Baker, *Introduction to English Legal History*, 129–130.

Edward's demise. Although Edward's relatives did carry the case forward, by 1799, England's chancellor was ready to come to a decision. London newspapers announced in January of that year that Edmund Green had finally won the suit and protected the riches of his mixed-race in-laws.[37]

The trial's conclusion seemed to foretell calmer days ahead for the Jamaican Morses. It also appeared to close the door on a very public discussion of their African ancestry. For Ann Middleton and her household, it began anew the process of becoming fully British. Her husband Nathaniel had been somewhat startled to learn of his wife's background when the lawsuit came to trial. In a deposition, Middleton declared that he was "an entire Stranger" to his in-laws' past, "having resided in India . . . and having never heard or been informed" of such circumstances. Ann's erasure of her Jamaican history appears to have succeeded, at least during her courtship. Now the couple set up a residence at a classically constructed estate at Townhill Park in Hampshire. Behind Townhill's grand exterior, built in the traditional style of England's eighteenth-century manor homes and described as "superb and spacious," the Middletons kept an extensive collection of Indian artifacts, cultivated from years spent abroad. Townhill's walls hid these colonial treasures behind a conventional English façade; they also concealed a distant African ancestry of the residents living within. For Ann and her siblings, this was simply part of a process of assimilation that originated with her mother's privilege petition half a century earlier. For British polemicists at the end of the eighteenth century, the Middletons' home symbolized the very anxieties many had about racial infiltration in the heart of England.[38]

37. Will of Edward Morse, Feb. 28, 1795, Wills, LOS 61, fol. 89, IRO; Morse v. Royal, Apr. 23, 1795, Jamaica Chancery Court Records, 1A/3/166, no. 143, fols. 204-208, JA; *Lloyd's Evening-Post* (London), Jan. 21-23, 1799; *Star* (London), Jan. 23, 1799; *Morning Chronicle,* Jan. 23, 1799; *True Briton,* Jan. 25, 1799; *E. Johnson's British Gazette, and Sunday Monitor* (London), Jan. 27, 1799. Morse died sometime in the late spring or early summer of 1794; see *True Briton,* Aug. 13, 1794.

38. "The Joint and Several Answer of Nathaniel Middleton and Anne Frances Middleton," Feb. 9, 1787, Chancery Court Records, C 12/610/30, NAE; William Page and H. Arthur Doubleday, eds., *A History of the County of Hampshire,* 5 vols. (n.p., 1908-1911), III, 481-489; John Bullar, *A Companion in a Tour Round Southampton . . . ,* 2 ed. (Southampton, U.K., 1809), 215; Nechtman, *Nabobs,* 169. The Middletons' estate was consistent with many English country homes built on imperial profits at the time; see Laurence Brown, "Atlantic Slavery and Classical Culture at Marble Hill and Northington Grange," in Dresser and Hann, eds., *Slavery and the British Country House,* 91-101.

Challenging Family Dynamics in Britain

The Morses were not the only ones to struggle with British relatives during, and immediately after, the American Revolution. Clamoring discussions on race in Britain grew increasingly loud, layering on top of the earlier tirades expressed by Edward Long and others. Paranoid fears over racial mixture and mixed-race people became an increasingly permanent fixture of British social and political discourse. For elite Jamaicans of color, such heightened racial rhetoric threatened their ability to assimilate into metropolitan society. Seen another way, the arrival of Jamaicans of privilege into wealthy metropolitan households, in fact, *inspired* these increased calls to police interracial relations in Britain.

Peggy Ker never won the acceptance of her Scottish relatives. Described as a mulatto in family correspondence, she landed in Scotland from Jamaica sometime between 1775 and 1776. Her father, David Ker, served as a physician in Jamaica, staying on the island as the American Revolution commenced while his daughter sailed for Britain. For her Scottish family, the arrival of a mixed-race girl was not a welcome one. Peggy had, at first, lodged with a great aunt, but the arrangement did not last. Recalling her initial appearance, David's cousin noted: "My Mother took the charge of her for some time but as she discovered vicious habits I would not allow my aged Parents to be troubled with her." Such bad behavior must have exhibited itself late, as Peggy lived with the aunt for at least seven years. Peggy next traveled to Forfar, to lodge with her step-grandmother, Clementina Ker. Yet, for reasons unknown, Clementina "was neither able nor willing to take any further charge." Peggy's Scottish relatives considered their available options with David still in Jamaica. Living in nearby Perth, David's cousin Henry Burt took over the management of Peggy's affairs. Having "no friend [who] would take upon them to care for her," he placed Peggy in a Perth boarding school. Burt paid for a year's instruction, "expecting between then to get notice from [David] what he intends to do with the creature." Peggy's matriculation was less out of the family's desire for her formal education than for someone to take over her day-to-day supervision.[39]

39. Henry Burt to James Ker, Apr. 21, 1783, Lynedoch Papers, MS 3591, fol. 100, NLS, Burt to David Ker, Apr. 9, 1783, fol. 100, Burt to James Ker, Apr. 21, 1783, fol. 100. The family genealogy is a bit unclear. From letters in the Lynedoch Papers at NLS, Clementina Ker is noted as David Ker's mother-in-law. Ker was not the surname of his later wife, however, and it appears through the family correspondence that Clementina Ker was married to his late father, which would mean that she was his stepmother and not his mother-in-law. Timing

Throughout the correspondence on Peggy, Ker's family wrote dismissively of its new charge. Her uncle, James Ker, supported his stepmother's decision not to care for Peggy after her first move. "I think Mrs. Ker is right not to meddle with the Mullato Girl," Ker wrote to his cousin Burt, "and I think you will likewise be right in keeping her at School till you hear from [David]." Despite the blood tie and David Ker's wish to protect his daughter, the family had little patience for the child. For her part, Clementina Ker was hostile. Referring to Peggy as "the Indian," Clementina wondered antagonistically, "what is to be don[e] with that Creten." Peggy, perhaps through no fault of her own, had not made a good impression; British relatives immediately sided with Clementina. Henry Burt insisted that his cousin David provide "some acknowledgement" to his stepmother "for her trouble in fitting out Peggy." Indeed, Clementina frequently alluded to the necessity of some kind of recompense. Driven by mercenary considerations, rather than familial ones, Peggy's relatives did not provide an environment conducive to her acculturation and integration. Her time in Britain, then, would not conform to her father's original expectations. With little assistance from metropolitan kin, Peggy decided to return to Jamaica in 1783. Showing stronger familial support than his relatives, David Ker wrote dejectedly to Burt, "I beg you'll be kind enough to send my poor little Peggy to Glasgow." Suspecting only minimum assistance, Ker hoped that his stepmother would be able, at the very least, to provide some clothes for Peggy on her return voyage. Without family encouragement once in Britain, West Indians of color had very little likelihood of success. Although Peggy's relatives blamed bad habits, rather than ancestry, for the breakdown in their relationship, prejudice against illegitimacy and African heritage likely compounded attitudes as well.[40]

Other families and correspondents recognized similar prejudices escalating in the metropole. Robert Laing's arrival prompted vigorous discussion among his English guardians about the chances of success for a young man of color. William Philip Perrin, the son of Laing's father's employer, took over supervisory duties in London. But Perrin worried about Laing's prospects in the metropole, considering his background. He wrote to two Kingston slave

---

might have weighed most heavily on Clementina's decision not to take on Peggy. Her husband—David Ker's father—had only recently died of pleurisy, and she herself was afflicted.

40. James Ker to Henry Burt, Apr. 19, 1783, Lynedoch Papers, MS 3591, fol. 104, NLS, Clementina Ker to Henry Burt, Sept. 1, 1783, Sept. 8, 1783, fols. 124–126, Henry Burt to David Ker, Sept. 15, 1783, fol. 131, David Ker to Henry Burt, June 22, 1783, fols. 115–116. Peggy's father paid for her transport from Perth to Glasgow and finally to Greenock. From there she sailed back to Lucea, Jamaica, where her father lived with a white wife.

traders in 1783 soliciting advice about the differences between Jamaica and England in terms of professional options for mulatto men. "The circumstance of Colour, which you seem to think will operate against him in England," the two reassured him from Jamaica, "will still be in greater force here." In particular, Perrin wondered if Laing would find greater success practicing law—his preferred subject—in the colonies rather than in England. His Jamaican contacts disabused Perrin of that notion, assuring him that "the circumstance of Colour would operate very forcibly" against Laing as a barrister in the West Indies. So Laing stayed, and two years later he was admitted to Lincoln's Inn to train in law. Racial prejudice did not preclude him from such a professional choice, but the concerns raised by his guardian indicate that British attitudes toward those of African heritage were not always tolerant.[41]

Interpersonal strains also appear to have emerged in this period, even for those who had already taken up residence in England. Jane Harry, who had arrived in the capital sometime around 1770, experienced a tremendous amount of disruption in her life, owing primarily to her Quakerism. But a Jamaican heritage might have also started to influence her reputation by the time of the American Revolution. James Boswell reported that her acquaintance Samuel Johnson invoked the Caribbean when learning that Harry had converted: "I compared him at this time to a warm West-Indian climate, where . . . heat sometimes produces thunder, lightening, and earthquakes in a terrible degree." In drawing on Caribbean imagery, Boswell might have been hinting at the common knowledge of Jane's heritage, although the insinuation was by no means explicit. Nevertheless, she found her metropolitan relationships under stress. Her father's business partner, Nathan Sprigg, cast her out of his home after she joined the Friends. She eventually found a stable residence with the Lloyd family in Birmingham, acting as governess to the household's seventeen children. But she felt isolated and wrote dejectedly to her father about the recent loss of friends as well as her concern that he might abandon her too: "I hope you will not also be irreconcilable, for I have much need of your parental love, and who have I else in this World to look unto?" Despite a

41. John Jacques and Ralph Fisher to William Philip Perrin, Apr. 24, 1783, D239 M/E 16972, Fitzherbert Papers, Derbyshire Record Office, Matlock, England; *The Records of the Honorable Society of Lincoln's Inn*, I, *Admissions from a.d. 1420 to a.d. 1799* (London, 1896), Dec. 7, 1785, 516; Charles Viner, *A General Abridgement of Law and Equity*, 2d ed., I (London, 1791), vii. The two Kingston traders were the prominent slave merchants John Jacques and Ralph Fisher who were also the executors of Laing's father's estate; see *Royal Gazette*, Jan. 19, 1782. For more, see Kenneth Morgan, ed., *The Bright-Meyler Papers: A Bristol-West India Connection, 1732–1837* (New York, 2007), 513n.

dearth of extant correspondence between the two, Jane and her father appear to have maintained a connection.[42]

Such ties did not extend to Jane's broader white family. After the death of her father in 1780, she appealed to his nephew, also named Thomas Hibbert, for a portion of the estate. Writing back to Jane, the younger Hibbert noted that she was to receive a bequest of two thousand pounds from the estate and that her mother, still in Jamaica, was to inherit half that as well as a small house. Perhaps angered that Jane had asked for a larger amount, Hibbert claimed that his uncle had initially allotted only one thousand pounds before Sprigg convinced him to double the bequest. Hibbert chastised her for ingratitude, asking Jane to reflect on her circumstances in the metropole. "How many Daughters of some of the best Families in England, with whose Education and Style of Life and Company you yourself would not compare your own, are little better portioned?" he queried. His experiences in Jamaica turned him against relations of color wanting adequate portions of the family fortune. According to his 1807 will, Hibbert had most likely lived with several women of color himself. Perhaps with a mixed-race family all his own, Hibbert understood Harry's privileged position and bristled under a perception of ungratefulness.[43]

42. James Boswell, *The Life of Samuel Johnson,* II (London, 1791), 232; Jane Harry to Thomas Hibbert, circa 1778, as quoted in Joseph J. Green, "Jenny Harry, Later Thresher (circa 1756-1784)," *Friends' Quarterly Examiner,* XLVII (1913), 576-577. Friends of both Johnson and Harry challenged the viciousness of Boswell's reports, insisting that the doctor had always respected her; see M. S., *Gentleman's Magazine: and Historical Chronicle,* LXI, pt. 2 (London, 1791), 700-701. If Johnson did invoke this imagery to point to her racial background, it was most likely not for pejorative reasons. Despite Johnson's general conservatism, he was outspoken against enslavement in both Britain and the Americas. His loyal friendship to a freed Jamaican slave in England, Francis Barber, attests to his capacity for racial tolerance. For more on Harry and Quakerism, see Judith Jennings, "A Trio of Talented Women: Abolition, Gender, and Political Participation, 1780-91," *Slavery and Abolition,* XXVI (2005), 55-70. Joseph J. Green believes Sprigg to have evicted Harry in 1779, but the *Dictionary of Quaker Biography* places the move at 1778; see Green, "Jenny Harry, Later Thresher (circa 1756-1784)," *Friends' Quarterly Examiner,* XLVIII (1914), 49; and "Dictionary of Quaker Biography," s.v. "Sampson Lloyd III," Friends House Library, London.

43. Thomas Hibbert to Jane Harry, Dec. 15, 1780, as quoted in Green, "Jenny Harry," *Friends' Quarterly Examiner,* XLVIII (1914), 44-45. In the absence of Jane's letters, a reconstruction of her correspondence with her father's nephew derives from the younger Hibbert's response. Rumor spread from Anna Seward, through James Boswell, that Hibbert had originally offered Jane one hundred thousand pounds if she were to stay with the Church of England. This was unfounded, particularly as Jane labored under Jamaica's 1761 inheritance cap; see Seward to Boswell, n.d., as quoted in W. Beck, W. F. Wells, and H. G. Chalkley,

Hibbert further asserted that his cousin did not have a valid place within their British family. He insisted that her father never considered himself a parent of Jane, or her sister Margaret, nor ever called them daughters. Hibbert gainsaid her claims about paternal piety, averring that, "so far was my late Uncle from desiring that you should be 'held up to the World as his Child,' that no Consideration gave him more Uneasiness, than that of your being so publicly known to be so; of which the Change of your Name is of itself a sufficient Proof." He further argued that Jane's father had been "extremely desirous, while it was possible, to conceal the Nature of his Relation" to her. Hibbert's rant was most likely intended to stymie any legal maneuvers on the Jamaican estate. With frequent litigation over colonial fortunes, he might have wished to intimidate his cousin from demanding more money. At the same time, Hibbert's miserliness and vitriol was supported by a general turn in Britain against individuals of color. Moreover, as one of the more outspoken opponents of abolitionism in later years, Hibbert was never sympathetic to the plight of slaves or their descendants. With more and more published tracts in Britain calling for an end to the slave trade and the amelioration of slavery by 1780, he might have been reacting viciously to Jane's African ancestry.[44]

With severed ties to her father's family, Jane Harry replaced bonds of blood with bonds of matrimony. While serving as governess in the Midlands, Harry met Joseph Thresher, a surgeon and fellow Quaker, from nearby Worcester. He quickly grew enamored stating that "her amiable qualifications soon attracted my attention, and by degrees made such an impression on my mind, that I at length found myself very tenderly attach'd to her." Anxious to solemnize their relationship, Thresher began applying for the requisite permissions. Their fellow Friends approved of the match, but both he and Jane wished for parental support. They worked together on a letter asking for the consent of her mother Charity Harry, who was still in Jamaica but nevertheless continued to have an important role in her daughter's life. Jane made several corrections

eds., *Biographical Catalogue: Being an Account of the Lives of Friends* . . . (London, 1888), 334. A later edition of Boswell's *Life of Johnson,* although not pointing to the 1761 edict, dispelled the rumor by noting an original provision of one thousand pounds, supplemented by an equal amount at a later date; see James Boswell, *The Life of Samuel Johnson, LL.D.* . . . , ed. John Wilson Croker, IV (London, 1831), 155n. After returning permanently to Britain, Hibbert removed two codicils from his will that gave one hundred pounds each to Sarah Winter, a "free quadroon of Kingston," and Henrietta Coot Luisa, a "free mulatto"; see Will of Thomas Hibbert, Nov. 18, 1807, PROB 11/1470, NAE.

44. Hibbert to Harry, Dec. 15, 1780, as quoted in Green, "Jenny Harry," *Friends' Quarterly Examiner,* XLVIII (1914), 46.

to the letter that, she admitted, "may perhaps have render'd it less elegant, but I think its form is rather more simple, and may therefore be better understood." Although a member of Jamaica's privileged class of color, Charity was perhaps unfamiliar with Thresher's long and florid style. The couple's desire for Charity's permission demonstrates that the mothers of mixed-race migrants could remain actively involved with their children and even help direct their decisions. Despite that very few joined their offspring in Britain, this distance did not mean that they lost all familial ties, or even parental duties. It is unknown if Charity gave her explicit consent, but Jane and Joseph wed at the Friends' Meeting House in London on November 26, 1782. From there, they moved to Worcester and lived with Joseph's brother Ralph. Once again, Jane asserted an alternative claim to social acceptance, this time built on domesticity and family associations forged in nuptials. Marrying a physician, albeit a nonconformist one, allowed her an even greater claim to respectability and removed her one more degree from the mark of black, Caribbean ancestry.[45]

Although increasingly distanced from her roots in Jamaica, Jane's correspondence with Joseph nevertheless reveals an undercurrent of racial conspicuousness and concern. He likely knew of his wife's ancestral makeup and colonial past, having maintained a correspondence with Charity. Friends around him understood these facts as well and kept Joseph cognizant of their knowledge. He wrote to Jane of an incident in which an associate, Samuel Neale, asked him, *"How does that West Indian Girl do?"* Joseph replied without affront but noted that another friend "observed, that much archness seemed concealed under that question." Such suspicion reflects the sensitive nature of Joseph's alliance with a mixed-race woman. Even if Neale had no knowledge of Jane Harry's ancestry, nor clues of it based on her appearance, his question insinuated a black past. Britons sometimes suspected all Caribbean whites of containing at least some African members in their family trees. Foregrounding geographic origins made implicit claims about biological background, to such a degree that others understood the veiled critique. If Jane did pass as white, then questions of her origin immediately threw her into an uncertain racial taxonomy.[46]

45. Joseph Thresher to Charity Harry, circa 1782, as quoted ibid., 59, 60. Jane's note about her corrections appears in an amendment to the letter printed in Green's article, but it is unclear which sections she altered. For Jane and Joseph's marriage announcement, see *Whitehall Evening-Post* (London), Nov. 28–30, 1782; and *Morning Herald, and Daily Advertiser,* Nov. 29, 1782.

46. Green, "Jenny Harry," *Friends' Quarterly Examiner,* XLVIII (1914), 59, Joseph Thresher to Jane Harry, June 3, 1781, 55; Will of Charity Harry, Nov. 13, 1783, Wills, LOS

Joseph intended his new wife to avoid, if possible, these challenges by cutting ties to the West Indies. Emboldened by the developing abolition movement, Jane Harry had at one time considered returning to Jamaica to free her mother's slaves, in order to spread the Quaker religion among them. Her later obituary noted that, although "she was well qualified" to provide such instruction, "the great commotion of public affairs frustrated her noble design," and she was never able to leave for the island. Jane's husband might also have been instrumental in scuttling the trip. The year before their nuptials, Joseph decried the "snares and temptations" of Jamaican "wickedness" and begged Jane to reconsider her mission. He might have simply not wanted to pay the steep price for their manumission, but he also worried about his wife's return home and how it might endanger her status in Britain. Reestablishing herself deeper in Jamaican society would undercut the advances she had made across the ocean. Considering that this admonition came immediately after discussing Neale's question about *"that West Indian girl,"* Joseph most certainly worried about others' impressions of her forays to the Caribbean.[47]

Ultimately abandoning the return to Jamaica, Jane quickly settled into British domestic life. Not long after moving to Worcester, she became pregnant and gave birth to a son, Edwin, in May 1784. Now a mother, Jane possessed the full collection of domestic trappings to place her in a socially acceptable position, in spite of her heritage. Such social stability would prove only temporary, however. Owing either to complications from Edwin's birth or to severe infection shortly thereafter, she grew gravely ill. She died on August 17, 1784, just three months after Edwin's arrival, and was interred in the Friends' burial plot at their Worcester meetinghouse several days later. Her obituary ran in the *Gentleman's Magazine* the next month, noting, among other things, that Jane wished for her husband to undertake the mission to free her mother's slaves in Jamaica. Family bonds, sanctified through marriage, bound West Indians of color to Britons in a number of ways. As much as Joseph might or might not have wished his wife to renounce her Jamaican origins, those bonds did not dissolve on marriage, nor even on death. Joseph gave a twenty-pound annuity to "my Mother in Law Charity Harry of Kingston" when he followed his wife to the grave two years later. Considering that inheritance allocation increas-

58, fol. 71, IRO. Suspicions of mixed-race ancestry in Caribbean immigrants were alluded to in fictional accounts at the time; see Agnes Musgrave, *The Solemn Injunction*, I (London, 1798), 182–184.

47. *Gentleman's Magazine, and Historical Chronicle,* LIV, pt. 2 (London, 1784), 716; Thresher to Jane Harry, June 3, 1781, as quoted in Green, "Jenny Harry," *Friends' Quarterly Examiner,* XLVIII (1914), 55–56.

ingly favored nuclear, over extended, families, and male, over female, beneficiaries, these bequests were an even greater signal of affection for his mother-
in-law. Charity Harry reciprocated. Although she would outlive Joseph by
seven years, she asked in her original will that he emancipate her enslaved
workers in the case of death. Through her marriage, Jane Harry joined another
Jamaican family of color to a white British household.[48]

Jane Harry's triumphs and struggles in Britain demonstrate the new challenges facing Jamaican migrants of color. Relatives could either clear the
way or throw up obstacles to success in Britain. In her case, affinal ties built
through marriage and female domesticity could successfully replace blood
relations severed through disownment. Peggy Ker and Robert Laing also arrived from Jamaica with the assistance of extended kin and associates. But
they were not granted automatic acceptance, encountering instead family and
friends who were, at best, nervous about their assimilation or, at worst, actively working against them. Ongoing debates about race in Britain, stoked
by fears of an increasing number of nonwhite immigrants, undoubtedly made
their lives harder. British families tasked to oversee relatives of color began
questioning the exact nature of their kinship in light of these broader Atlantic discussions. For those in the metropole, pulling away from mixed-race
relatives was one way of signaling a changing view about who was an appropriate member of the family. But family ties, in the case of Laing and Harry,
ultimately won out.

Jamaica after the Revolution

If Britons were beginning to question the nature of their relationship to
mixed-race kin, they had almost no effect on white men's attitudes toward
the continued creation of such households in Jamaica. The year before Jane
Harry died, Scottish merchant John Tailyour stepped onto a bustling Kings-

48. Green, "Jenny Harry," *Friends' Quarterly Examiner,* XLVIII (1914), 61–62; *Gentleman's Magazine, and Historical Chronicle,* LIV, pt. 2 (London, 1784), 716; Will of Joseph
Thresher, July 18, 1786, PROB 11/1144, NAE; Ruth Perry, "Women in Families: The Great
Disinheritance," in Vivien Jones, ed., *Women and Literature in Britain, 1700–1800* (New
York, 2000), 111–129; Alastair Owens, "Property, Gender, and the Life Course: Inheritance
and Family Welfare Provision in Early Nineteenth-Century England," *Social History,* XXVI
(2001), 299–318. Like many slaveowners, Charity Harry did not wish to erode the base of
her economic prosperity and therefore wanted to wait until death before emancipating her
workers. She also noted that, barring Thresher's ability to free them, John Boyd of Britain was to carry out the task, demonstrating her connections to Britain; see Will of Charity
Harry, Nov. 13, 1793, Wills, LOS 58, fol. 71, IRO.

ton dock, concluding a long journey from New York. He arrived in the spring of 1783 a defeated man, broken by the results of the Revolution in North America. Jamaica was a destination of last resort, after having failed on three separate occasions at trade on the mainland. His cousin Simon Taylor pleaded with him to quit New York for the island in 1781, as it became clear that Great Britain could no longer restrain its rebellious colonies. John was more than eager to accept the invitation from his wildly successful relative: "I have long had thoughts of trying to settle in Jamaica and the Manner in which you write has very much encouraged me to it. Under your protection I think there is little doubt of my doing well." Departing for the Caribbean, he joined a train of loyalists hoping to reestablish their devastated plantations further to the south. They were helped along in the form of massive tax incentives held out by Jamaica's assembly eager to induce the loyalists "to settle here." For his part, Tailyour settled in Simon's home, Prospect Pen, just beyond Kingston's parish boundaries. He would eventually grow accustomed to the island lifestyle.[49]

Jamaica did not initially impress Tailyour, however, and he continued to hold equal amounts of anger and resentment toward the outcome of American independence. Like many others, he believed that peace with the rebellious colonies was "shamefull and disgracefull" and that the "Glory of Britain is not and [in] all probability, never to rise again." Indeed, there was a general crisis in imperial identity throughout the British Empire over the loss of the North American colonies. Not only did the Revolution challenge British notions of imperial administration, it separated Britain from the majority of its overseas white population. Suddenly estranged from more than two million white settlers, the Empire's colonial subjects were now, on average, of a much darker hue.[50] Tailyour reflected less on these specific racial issues and more

49. John Tailyour to Simon Taylor, Jan. 3, 1782, Letter Book I, Tailyour Papers, WCL, Tailyour to Messrs. Campbell and Hagart, Mar. 25, 1783; *JAJ*, Feb. 11, 1783, VII, 544. For more on the migration of loyalists out of North America, and especially to the Caribbean, see Wallace Brown, "The American Loyalists in Jamaica," *Journal of Caribbean History*, XXVI (1992), 121–146; Whittington B. Johnson, *Race Relations in the Bahamas, 1784–1834: The Nonviolent Transformation from a Slave to a Free Society* (Fayetteville, Ark., 2000); James Robertson, *Gone Is the Ancient Glory: Spanish Town, Jamaica, 1534–2000* (Kingston, Jamaica, 2005), 129–134; and Jasanoff, *Liberty's Exiles*, esp. 215–277.

50. John Tailyour to John MacKenzie, Mar. 29, 1783, Letter Book I, Tailyour Papers, WCL, John Tailyour to Joshua Loring, Mar. 30, 1783. The American Revolution helped to bring to light systematic problems in British imperial administration, which simultaneously produced a more authoritarian type of regulation along with a more complex language of moral prestige meant to heal the damaged empire; see Stephen Conway, *The British Isles*

on the reported abuses meted out by patriots against loyalists who stayed in North America. Yet, despite his lamentations, Tailyour regretted his own departure. Had he remained just a few months longer, he insisted to his brother in Scotland, he could have made a fortune in Virginia's tobacco market before the stipulations of the peace had been determined. Instead, he would have to try his hand in Jamaica at a trade he knew virtually nothing about: the commerce in human cargo. Tailyour's ignorance, however, did not presage failure. He arrived in Kingston at the start of the island's final sugar boom. He would build his finances off the battered backs of one of the last waves of imported Africans into Jamaica.[51]

Tailyour also gained terrific advantages through his relation to his cousin Simon. Born on the island though educated in England, Simon rose from a relatively humble position as a plantation attorney to become one of the largest—and estimated the richest—landholders in eighteenth-century Jamaica. He served as a member of the assembly for Kingston and Saint Thomas in the East as well as chief justice of the Court of Common Pleas, lieutenant governor of the militia, and a chief magistrate of the island. Few could rival Simon's power and extensive network on the island, and Tailyour was overjoyed to capitalize on his cousin's reputation and knowledge. As he giddily noted to his brother, "[Simon] is of very great influence here and has a fortune little inferior to any in Jamaica." That influence quickly compelled Tailyour to standardize his surname to accord with Simon's, in order to trade

---

and the War of American Independence (New York, 2000), 315–340; Brown, *Moral Capital,* 209–258, 455–456; and Jasanoff, *Liberty's Exiles,* 177–243. These changes helped to simplify, some scholars argue, British identity; see Wahrman, *Making of the Modern Self,* 220–246; and Conway, "From Fellow-Nationals to Foreigners," *WMQ,* 3d Ser., LIX (2002), 82–100. However, this new, simplified identity turned away from overseas possessions; see Linda Colley, *Britons: Forging the Nation, 1707–1837* (New Haven, Conn., 1992); Eliga H. Gould, *The Persistence of Empire: British Political Culture in the Age of the American Revolution* (Chapel Hill, N.C., 2000), 208–214; Wilson, *Island Race;* Land, "Bread and Arsenic," *Journal of Social History,* XXXIX (2005), 89–110; and Catherine Molineux, *Faces of Perfect Ebony: Encountering Atlantic Slavery in Imperial Britain* (Cambridge, Mass., 2012), 219–246.

51. The *Cornwall Chronicle* reported on the harassment experienced by loyalists in North America soon after Tailyour arrived; see *Cornwall Chronicle,* Sept. 27, 1783, Supplement. See also John Tailyour to J. Shacham, Oct. 28, 1783, Letter Book I, Tailyour Papers, WCL, and John Tailyour to Hercules Tailyour, Mar. 30, 1783. On the rush to import Africans at the end of the eighteenth century, see David Beck Ryden, *West Indian Slavery and British Abolition, 1783–1807* (New York, 2009), esp. 221–253; and Audra A. Diptee, *From Africa to Jamaica: The Making of an Atlantic Slave Society, 1775–1807* (Gainesville, Fla., 2010).

off his cousin's high standing (for clarity of distinction, though, this study will continue to refer to him by his original appellation).[52]

Relying heavily on Simon's connections, John Tailyour seems to have emulated his cousin's domestic habits as well. Never marrying, Simon Taylor was notoriously single, with a reputation for going after women of color. Later in life, Simon was visited by the wife of Jamaica's governor, Lady Maria Nugent, who described Taylor as "an old bachelor, [who generally] detests the society of women." However, she also met one of Taylor's "mulatto girl[s]." Expressing surprise at the young girl's presence, Nugent inquired of her to Taylor's housekeeper, who informed Nugent that the girl was "his own daughter, and that he had a numerous family, some almost on every one of his estates." Simon Taylor kept mistresses of color for the entirety of his adult life, giving some substantial provisions that approached the 1761 inheritance cap on mixed-race bequests.[53]

52. R[ichard] B. Sheridan, "Simon Taylor, Sugar Tycoon of Jamaica, 1740–1813," *Agricultural History*, XLV (1971), 285–296; B. W. Higman, *Plantation Jamaica, 1750–1850: Capital and Control in a Colonial Economy* (Kingston, Jamaica, 2005), esp. 137–165; *The New Jamaica Almanack, and Register . . .* , 2d ed. ([Spanish Town], Jamaica, 1791), 109; W. A. Feurtado, *Official and Other Personages of Jamaica, from 1655 to 1790* (Kingston, Jamaica, 1896), 94; John Tailyour to Hercules Tailyour, Mar. 30, 1783, Letter Book I, Tailyour Papers, WCL. Tailyour changed his name to "Taylor" in 1784; see John Tailyour to George Carnegie, Mar. 20, 1784, ibid.

53. [Lady Maria Nugent], *Lady Nugent's Journal of Her Residence in Jamaica from 1801 to 1805*, ed. Philip Wright (Kingston, Jamaica, 1966), 68. In 1763, three years after returning to Jamaica on completion of his studies in England, Simon Taylor drafted a will that included a substantial provision for his housekeeper, Grace Donne, whom he described as a "free Quadroon Woman" as well as for one of his children of color. Donne lived in Taylor's house on Orange Street, in East Kingston, having moved in soon after Taylor returned to the island. Simon gave her his land and house in Kingston, nine slaves, a horse, and a £150 gift as well as his furniture, bedding, and silverware in return for her "Faithful Services." The bequest was a large sum, and he confessed to his brother John: "You will say I have made a great Provision for the Woman who Lives with me. I own it, but She has been a Faithful Servant To me, and I never had occasion to call twice for any thing, or awake her in any of my Severe Fitts of Illness." Taylor also gave an allowance to his "Natural Quadroon Daughter" Sally Taylor, including ten slaves and an annuity of £20; see Simon Taylor to John Taylor, Jan. 27, 1763, Simon Taylor Letters, ICS 120 II/B/36, ICS. Sally's mother was never identified; most likely she was not the daughter of Grace Donne as both were labeled "quadroons." Thus, even by the young age of twenty-three, Simon Taylor had had multiple relationships with women of color. By the time Lady Nugent visited Simon Taylor at the end of his life, his family had grown, and his female companions had changed. Soon after the death of Grace Donne, Taylor revised his will in 1808. The revisions included a £500 bequest to Donne's niece Grace Harris. Sally Taylor's inheritance remained unchanged. In the years between the

In his extensive relationships with women of color, Simon Taylor provided a model for his cousin John on the sexual politics of Jamaican life. Living in Simon's house and drawing as he did on Simon's connections, Tailyour was fully aware of his cousin's personal activities. He would even monitor Simon's plantations while Simon was off the island. Such supervision gave him full view of his cousin's colonial family, whom he would then manage. During one of these absences in 1785, for example, Tailyour informed Simon that his mixed-race son Jack had acquired a fever. Several years later, in 1789, he wrote Simon a short, ambiguous letter about Simon's mistress of color Grace Donne. Tailyour insinuated that Donne had slept with another man and cagily suggested that he might himself have been the offender. Like most interracial sex on the island, Tailyour's actions might have been outright rape. But it is possible that, in Simon's absence, Donne attempted to build connections to other white men who might assist her and her offspring. This presented tremendous risk if Simon found out. But the precariousness of life in Jamaica, especially for those of white companions, made it necessary for women of color to maintain a broad set of attachments. Regardless, such interactions with Simon's mixed-race mistresses and children gave Tailyour a firm understanding of the island's sexual status quo.[54]

More importantly, John Tailyour began his own relationship with an enslaved woman belonging to Simon. Polly, born Mary Graham, was noted as "mulatto" in the baptismal certificates of her and Tailyour's children. Like most mixed-race individuals, she was not emancipated by a father, nor was she ever expected to leave the island. Like Grace Donne, she utilized instead a sexual connection in the hopes of advancing herself and her future children. That opportunity came not long after Tailyour landed in Kingston. Polly met him on one of Simon's estates and took a place in his home as many island

wills, Taylor had taken up residence with Sarah Blacktree Hunter, a "free Mulatto woman" who replaced Donne as his housekeeper sometime around 1778. Hunter bore him at least one child, named Sarah Taylor. When amending his will, Simon gave Sarah Hunter a £500 gift, in addition to several pieces of furniture. Sarah Taylor initially received £1,000, but he increased the amount by £1500, along with a £30 annuity, in an 1813 codicil. Taylor also allocated a £500 lump sum, a £50 annuity, and a slave to his granddaughter Sarah Hunter Taylor Cathcart, the child of Sarah Taylor; see Will of Simon Taylor, September 1813, PROB 10/7400/7, fols. 2–4, 58–59, NAE. For more on Simon's relationship to these mistresses, see Christer Petley, "'Home' and 'This Country': Britishness and Creole Identity in the Letters of a Transatlantic Slaveholder," *Atlantic Studies*, VI (2009), 43–61; and Petley, "'Legitimacy' and Social Boundaries," *Social History*, XXX (2005), 481–498.

54. John Tailyour to Simon Taylor, Jan. 22, 1785, Simon Taylor Letters, ICS 120/XIV/A/1/17, ICS, Tailyour to Taylor, August 1789, ICS 120 XIV/A/1/44.

women did: by acting as his nurse. Travelers usually became quite ill in the West Indies, owing to a climate with which they had no familiarity and to diseases with which they had no immunity. The month before Tailyour arrived, Jamaica's *Cornwall Chronicle* announced that a fellow loyalist displaced from New York had died shortly after landing there. Tailyour complained constantly of illness during his stay on the island, and Polly nursed him through each bout. She also took care of him after he sustained serious injury by falling from a horse.[55]

Although still enslaved, Polly lived with Tailyour, and soon children came into their family. They had four offspring together between 1786 and 1792. Eldest son James was born on August 28, 1786, and baptized in November of that year. Simon, the next child, arrived on October 11, 1788, but was not baptized until February 24, 1791. He might have died quite young: there are almost no letters about him from any of Tailyour's personal contacts, and it would not have been unusual that Simon's late baptism arose out of a fear of impending death. Polly gave birth to the couple's third son, John, on October 31, 1790, who was baptized on the same day as Simon. The couple's only girl, Catherine, was born on September 22, 1792, and baptized two months later.[56]

The two eldest children, James and Simon, were born enslaved. Because one's status of freedom in Jamaica was matrilineally determined, Tailyour's children were slaves along with their mother. Not long after Simon's birth, Tailyour resolved to emancipate his growing family, following the advice of

55. *Cornwall Chronicle,* Feb. 8, 1783, Supplement; John Tailyour to John and Alex Anderson, Jan. 30, 1791, Letter Book 3, Tailyour Papers, WCL; John Campbell to John Tailyour, Aug. 12, 1791, Tailyour Papers, WCL. Tailyour's fall also made the news, as reported in the *Cornwall Chronicle, and Jamaica General Advertiser,* Jan. 22, 1791. "Mulatto" might not have been an accurate description of Polly's racial background, as baptismal registers sometimes used the term as a blanket reference for any person of mixed race. There are two entries for a Mary Graham in the Kingston parish records that correspond with her age: one Mary Graham was born on January 29, 1748, to Susan Ripley, "a mulatto woman," and William Graham; another was born to "a mulatto woman named Grace" on January 15, 1752, without any notation of paternity; see Kingston baptisms, copy register I, fols. 99, 110, IRO. In all likelihood, this was not Tailyour's mistress, as Mary / Polly was still enslaved when they met. It is also possible that Polly was born in one of the island's other parishes and sold at a later date to Simon Taylor. The most complete analysis of the virulence and destruction of colonial disease can be found in J. R. McNeill, *Mosquito Empires: Ecology and War in the Greater Caribbean, 1620–1914* (New York, 2010).

56. Baptism of James Taylor, Aug. 28, 1786, Kingston baptisms, copy register, I, fol. 371, IRO, Baptism of Simon Taylor, Baptism of John Taylor, Feb. 24, 1791, fol. 425, Baptism of Catherine Taylor, November 1792, fol. 454.

Jamaican men such as Benjamin Vaughan. Before his younger brother's departure for the island in 1777, Vaughan recommended avoiding the example of "those who have mulattoes as their offspring, yet can neither patronize, *educate*, nor enrich them; and must see their own blood and substance grovelling in low insensibility or shame." This was the usual course for the children of interracial unions, who were freed at most 20 percent of the time. But, perhaps owing to a strong sense of familial obligation, Tailyour wished to set his family free. Without legal possession, however, he had to apply to his cousin Simon for their emancipation. This required Tailyour to compensate Simon as well as pay hefty manumission fees for Polly and each child.[57]

In purchasing their freedom, John Tailyour's appeal revealed strong affections. Addressing his cousin in early 1790, Tailyour wrote: "I take up the Pen to request a favour of you, which tho I have often wished to do verbally I have not been able. It is, that you would grant Polly her Freedom and that of her Children." Tailyour's inability to bring up the matter with his cousin face-to-face perhaps demonstrated his trepidation about Simon's response, or at least his reservation to discuss such delicate matters. Nevertheless, Tailyour cared deeply about their fate. "Having now for several years experienced [Polly's] care and attention both while I have been in sickness and health," he confided, "I confess myself much attached to her, and I find myself very much so for her Children; which makes me very desirous of putting them in a more respectable situation." His letter uncovers a level of compassion that bound some interracial couples together. To him, Polly was more than a sexual partner; she was a companion and a nurse as he struggled with failing health. He wanted to offer Polly and the children an opportunity to rise out of slavery and to obtain a more comfortable life. This affection grew out of codependence in a brutal and devastatingly unequal colony, but it existed nonetheless. Tailyour closed his appeal, "I feel my self more anxious to obtain this Favour than I can describe." The plea worked, and, by August of that year, Simon had set in motion the emancipation process. Polly and the children became free, and John and Catherine, born after the transaction, entered the world unburdened by the shackles of enslavement.[58]

57. Benjamin Vaughan to Charles Vaughan, Oct. 24, 1777, Benjamin Vaughan Papers, Ser. II, American Philosophical Society Library, Philadelphia; B. W. Higman, *Slave Population and Economy in Jamaica, 1807–1834* (Kingston, Jamaica, 1995), 141; Richard S. Dunn, *A Tale of Two Plantations: Slave Life and Labor in Jamaica and Virginia* (Cambridge, Mass., 2014), 169.

58. John Tailyour to Simon Taylor, Jan. 3, 1790, Simon Taylor Letters, ICS 120/XIV/A/50, ICS.

John Tailyour and Polly's family was emblematic of continued interracial relationships in Jamaica after the American Revolution. Many white men who chose to leave North America after that conflict recreated such familial organizations in keeping with Caribbean custom. Despite any wider Atlantic concerns about slavery, family, and race that emerged out of the Revolution, then, social practices did not change fundamentally in the West Indies, and whites continued to father mixed-race children. Indeed, satirists persisted in lampooning this behavior: the loyalist hero of the 1787 farce *Adventures of Jonathan Corncob* decried the ongoing "way of washing the blackmoor white" that he found on arriving in Barbados. For John Tailyour, this did not simply mean unfettered sexual abandon, although it certainly could have. Owing to either his own sense of fatherly responsibility, or to Polly's assertiveness and resolve in the face of paternal apathy, Tailyour offered a measure of support to these offspring as well. He was by no means the only one.[59]

Jamaicans like John Tailyour also continued to send young children of color to Britain despite emerging polemics about metropolitan racial infiltration. Tailyour, for instance, moved each of his offspring across the Atlantic, beginning the same year as their emancipation. He perhaps drew inspiration from Hercules Ross, a close colonial friend of Simon Taylor who resettled only a few miles from Tailyour's boyhood home in Scotland. Ross had sent each of his Jamaican children of color to Britain several years before Tailyour. More generally, white Jamaicans continued to provide for mixed-race offspring in Britain through hereditary bequests in the 1780s (see Table 3). Although the percentages decreased from the previous decade (see Table 2), owing perhaps to the disruptions of the American Revolution, a substantial portion of white men in Jamaica gave money to offspring of color in Britain. Nearly 14 percent of white male testators who acknowledged mixed-race children asked that their offspring be sent to Britain, or noted that they were already there.[60]

Jamaica's privilege bills also show a sustained interaction between mixed-race colonists and the metropole. Of the more than 150 individuals who petitioned for privilege exemptions between 1780 and 1787, 24 noted that they had spent time in Britain.[61] This was a greater percentage of demonstrated

---

59. *Adventures of Jonathan Corncob, Loyal American Refugee* (London, 1787), 125.

60. Agnes M. Butterfield, "Hercules Ross of Kingston, Jamaica, and Rossie, Forfar, 1745–1816" (unpublished book manuscript, 1982), 94–102. My thanks to Mr. J. H. St. J. McIlwaine for allowing me to read his aunt's manuscript.

61. Survey comes from Acts of the Assembly of Jamaica, 1779–1787, CO 139/37–43, NAE.

TABLE 3. *Percentage of White Men's Wills, Proven in Jamaica, with Acknowledged Mixed-Race Children That Include Bequests for Such Offspring in Britain, Either Presently Resident, or Soon to Be Sent There, 1783–1785*

Explicit references	4.5
Explicit and implicit references combined	13.5

Sources: Wills, LOS 49–51, IRO. Out of the 379 wills proven in Jamaica between 1783 and 1785, 89 gave at least some portion of money to a mixed-race child. Of those, 12 contained bequests to mixed-race children in Britain or requested to be sent there. For an individual listing of wills, see Appendix 1.

Note: An explicit reference is one in which the child is listed with a racial category (such as "mulatto," "quadroon," "mestee," etc.). An implicit reference is one in which the child is noted as illegitimate ("natural" or "reputed"). In nearly all of the latter categories, the testator also noted having a mistress of color who was likely the child's mother.

migration within the privilege bills than in previous decades. Many of these petitioners had returned to Jamaica, but several would settle permanently in Europe. Robert Hilton Angwin, for instance, monitored his livestock pens on the island but traveled back and forth to Britain, eventually retiring in western England where he died in 1833. His siblings John, Sarah, and Frances each traveled to Britain as well. Frances soon married in England and had two children before moving to East Greenwich. Bryan Mackey, a free quadroon who earned his privileged rights in 1780, also lived the remainder of his life in England. He eventually became rector of the small village of Coates in Gloucestershire. Some were too young for transatlantic travel but would make the journey later. William, Edward, and John Hiatt, for instance, won privileged rights in 1780, but they would not leave for Europe until 1790. The next year, their father submitted another privilege bill for them to avoid the inheritance cap and noted that "they shall all remain [in Europe] during life." Thus, mixed-race migration across the Atlantic persisted, even if observers were looking with fresh eyes on the quality and conduct of Britain's changing Empire.[62]

62. Acts of the Assembly of Jamaica, Dec. 22, 1787, CO 139/43, NAE; Will of John Angwin, May 4, 1790, PROB 11/1191, NAE, Will of Robert Hilton Angwin, Oct. 7, 1833, PROB 11/1822, Will of Frances Hurle, Feb. 10, 1783, PROB 11/1386; *Trewman's Exeter Flying-Post; or, Plymouth and Cornish Advertiser* (Exeter, England), July 16, 1818; Verene A. Shepherd, *Livestock, Sugar, and Slavery: Contested Terrain in Colonial Jamaica* (Kingston, Jamaica, 2009), 85, 102–106; Acts of the Assembly of Jamaica, Apr. 21, 1780, CO 139/37A, NAE; *T. Gentleman's Magazine*, XXIX, New Ser. (London, 1848), 213; Jack Ayers, ed., *Paupers and Pig Killers: The Diary of William Holland a Somerset Parson, 1799–1818* (Gloucester,

Conclusion

In the immediate years after American independence, Britons across all social strata began reassessing their attitudes toward individuals with non-European ancestry, both at home and overseas. Demographic and racial questions that had long been the purview of a limited policy debate in the colonies were now thrust into a much wider Atlantic market of ideas. These realities of imperialism, both to the East and to the West, met at the Empire's center. In 1787, this point of contact seemed to threaten Britain's whole web of exchange. That year William Dent, who would later portray Warren Hastings offering jewels to George III (Plate 4), encapsulated all of these issues in a single satiric print (Plate 7). He depicted Charles James Fox and Frederick North, Lord North, the parliamentarians who had attempted to pass the bill regulating the East India Company four years earlier, as poor blacks leading a train of individuals on their way to Sierra Leone. The problems of East Indian reform, the loss of the North American colonies, and the resettlement of black Britons in Africa cohered into a solitary image of imperial woe. The Empire was in crisis; British identity was almost wholly unmoored.[63]

These ideological evaluations were not only negotiated in the public spheres of abolitionist debate, political imagery, and imperial discourse. Just as importantly, they were contested and settled within private households, caught up with the material realities of racial mixture and extended families spread across the globe. These direct concerns over kinship produced a range of reactions to the issue of race and family belonging. Edward Morse's inheritance contest with his Jamaican cousins embodied these internal disputes. In Edward's estimation, race could be understood as constrictive and concrete, anchored firmly to legal definitions and unalterable biological qualities. In the arguments of his cousins, race could be seen as porous, ill-defined, and dependent on geographical and genealogical context. Likewise, family could be constructed along lines of legitimacy and European endogamy, or it could

---

U.K., 1984), 39, 216–220; Kathleen Chater, *Untold Histories: Black People in England and Wales during the Period of the British Slave Trade, c. 1660–1807* (New York, 2009), 106; *Cornwall Chronicle, and Jamaica General Advertiser*, Apr. 17, 1790, Supplement; and *Votes of the Honourable House of Assembly of Jamaica; In a Session Begun the 25th of October, and Ended the 22d of November, 1791; A Session Begun the 23d of November 1791, and Ended the 10th of March, 1792; and a Session Begun the 13th, and Ended the 15th of March, 1792; Being the Third, Fourth, and Fifth Sessions of the Present Assembly* (Spanish Town, Jamaica, 1792), Dec. 9, 1791, 113.

63. For a close reading of Dent's print, see Molineux, *Faces of Perfect Ebony*, 219–222.

PLATE 7. *The Poor Blacks Going to Their Settlement.* By William Dent. 1787.
BM Satires 7127. Image courtesy of the Trustees of the British Museum

be defended as expansive, affective, and capacious. Peggy Ker, for instance, received virtually no recognition from British kin but benefited nevertheless from parental support. Similarly, Jane Harry found her father's relational connections cut off in England, but she easily formed new kinship networks through marriage instead.

Thus, competing ideas about race and family coexisted in the 1780s, without any firm resolution. Neither definition held greater sway in the Morse's legal case, nor the Ker and Harry families, nor perhaps in British society generally. Instead, public concerns raised about racial infiltration in Britain butted up against the private needs of households to navigate familial membership. These conflicts would persist as long as white men continued to father children of color in Jamaica and send them off to Britain, which they did with little interruption even after the great turmoil of American independence. That conflict had brought a number of imperial and ideological questions to mind, but it had not completely eliminated the acceptance of mixed-race kin in Atlantic families. It would take another revolution in the Americas to shift the argument firmly to one side.

CHAPTER 4

🐾

ABOLITION, REVOLUTION, AND MIGRATION,
1788–1793

One can only guess what passed through James Taylor's mind when he landed in the small Scottish seaport of Montrose in 1791. He was only four years old and surely had few memories of his first three years spent in slavery. He had absolutely no knowledge of his Scottish relatives—most still using the original surname of Tailyour—whom he was about to meet. What was clear was that the young boy had not enjoyed the voyage from Jamaica. Storms had raged in the North Sea, making the journey's final leg treacherous. Other factors on board could have been a problem, as they occasionally were for travelers of color. John Graham, the child of a British migrant and an enslaved black woman named Eve, was assaulted violently by the ship's captain on his voyage from Jamaica to London six years after James's trip. The reasons behind Graham's confrontation are unclear; perhaps racial factors played a role. Multiple issues could have plagued young Taylor's passage as well. Regardless, immediately on meeting his grandmother James admitted that the voyage had been "very long and disagrible" without further explanation. Family hospitality helped ease the transition, and James took an immediate liking to his British cousins. They shared all of their time, studying in school, playing at home, and even receiving smallpox inoculations together. James became a favorite of the British Tailyours. With pride, his aunt Catherine cheerfully remarked, "He is a very fin[e] Boy."[1]

If he was like most small children, James had little cognizance or interest in the political debates of the time, but those around him did. The month before James arrived in Montrose, a man in the village received a letter that would transform his life. Hercules Ross had resettled in his hometown eight years earlier, after living more than two decades in Jamaica. He was part of the large white absentee and émigré community from the West Indies, and, like many

---

1. Thomas Lincoln to Thomas Graham, circa 1814, Montgomery Family Papers, NRAS 1115/21/6, NRAS (Many thanks to the Montgomery family for access to the collection); Jean Tailyour to John Tailyour, Jan. 24, 1791, Tailyour Papers, WCL. James's father John changed his surname to Taylor in Jamaica, although most of the Scottish branch retained the original spelling of Tailyour. For clarity, this study will refer to the elder John as Tailyour, while giving his children their legal name of Taylor.

194   ABOLITION, REVOLUTION, AND MIGRATION

of his peers, Ross brought Jamaican children of color with him to Britain. Life in the Caribbean had enriched his finances, and it had also precipitated the arrival of this important dispatch. The letter came from William Wilberforce, the young parliamentarian mounting an effort to abolish Britain's slave trade. Wilberforce had learned of Ross through a friend and hoped that the aging Scot could provide information on West Indian slavery. Perhaps he had heard of Ross's arguments against the slave trade at the Kingston debating society in 1774; maybe Ross had made more vocal pronouncements since leaving Jamaica. Rising British naval commander Horatio Nelson, a close friend of Ross, might have also made the recommendation.[2] Regardless of his source, Wilberforce hoped to submit Ross's account to a committee of Parliament before Christmas. He apologized profusely for such a brash and rushed demand by an unfamiliar correspondent but insisted that "the importance of the subject . . . may excuse and almost justify a departure from the ordinary ceremonial."[3]

Having received Wilberforce's letter on December 10, Ross felt unsure if he could make the Christmas deadline. First, he would have to decide whether he was even ready to collaborate with the antislavery movement. Wilberforce had tried unsuccessfully since 1788 to pass legislation in the House of Commons prohibiting the slave trade, and political camps quickly formed around pro- and antislavery arguments. Many, if not all, of Ross's Jamaican friends

2. Agnes M. Butterfield, "Hercules Ross of Kingston, Jamaica, and Rossie, Forfar, 1745–1816" (unpublished book manuscript, 1982), 94–102. My thanks to Mr. J. H. St. J. McIlwaine for allowing me to read his aunt's manuscript. For more on the British West Indian community, specifically in London, see David Beck Ryden, *West Indian Slavery and British Abolition, 1783–1807* (New York, 2009), 40–82. Hercules Ross discussed his involvement in the Kingston debating society meeting in his later testimony to the House of Commons; see "Minutes of the Evidence Taken before a Committee of the House of Commons Being a Select Committee, Appointed to Take the Examination of Witnesses respecting the African Slave Trade . . . ," Mar. 17, 1791, no. 4281, in *HCSP,* LXXXII, 263. See also Chapter 2, above. Nelson met Ross in Jamaica during his West Indian tours and eventually served as godfather to his first legitimate son and namesake, Horatio. For correspondence between Ross and Nelson, see Nelson Papers, 1783, Add. MS 34903, fols. 9, 110, and Add. MS 34917, fol. 382, BL. See also Thomas Joseph Pettigrew, *Memoirs of the Life of Vice-Admiral Lord Viscount Nelson, K. B. . . . ,* 2d ed., 2 vols. (London, 1849), II, 233–234; Frank Cundall, *Historic Jamaica* (London, 1915), 72; and Alexander M. Ross, *History of the Clan Ross with Genealogies of the Various Families* (Morgantown, W.Va., 1983), 106.

3. William Wilberforce to Hercules Ross, Dec. 8, 1790, MS 587, NLJ. The rashness of the request came up later in parliamentary debate; see *The Debate on a Motion for the Abolition of the Slave-Trade, in the House of Commons, on Monday and Tuesday, April 18 and 19, 1791 . . .* (London, 1791), 17.

did not wish to see an end to the trade, especially as their estates in the West Indies still depended on fresh imports of bound Africans. Conspiring with Wilberforce would undoubtedly destroy those relationships. Ross waited nearly a week to respond, writing that Wilberforce's letter was "an application so unexpected, [that it] has rather agitated me," and concluding that he had been gone too long from Jamaica to provide much help.[4]

Thinking it over that night, however, Ross decided to keep the doors of communication open. He quickly dashed off another letter to Wilberforce the next day, admitting his fear of being exposed "to resentment, or the loss of many valuable friendships," should he continue the correspondence. In particular, he worried that his "intimate friend" Robert Cooper Lee, who had his own children of color in Britain and who was an associate of the late John Morse as well, would cut ties. He also was concerned, justifiably, about his relationship with Simon Taylor, the cousin of John Tailyour whose mixed-race son James would arrive in Ross's hometown within weeks. Regardless of these social pressures, Ross decided to lend support. Might his children of color, if not those of his neighbors, have influenced his decision to aid the antislavery struggle?[5]

For the two Montrose families supporting mixed-race children, their relatives' genealogies likely served as a direct reminder of the increasingly passionate calls in Britain to end the slave trade. Decades-long debates about colonial demography and settlement in Jamaica now became popular topics of conversation as everyday Britons considered the possibility of a ban in human trafficking. Should blacks and whites reproduce themselves by natural means, the conversation went, Britain's sugar islands would be secure and imported Africans would no longer be needed. This made the status of children like James all the more precarious, as interracial sex was now an especially virulent threat to these twin demographic goals. Public commentators thus eyed the arrival of such children in Britain with increasing cynicism. Nevertheless, families like the Tailyours and Rosses continued to accept them into

4. Hercules Ross to William Wilberforce, Dec. 16, 1790, MS 587, NLJ.

5. Ibid., Dec. 17, 1790; Butterfield, "Hercules Ross," 56. Robert Cooper Lee's children were, according to Jamaican law, white, as they were four generations removed from their black ancestor. Nevertheless, he applied for a privilege petition for them; see "Commissioners of Legal Enquiry in the West Indies," 1822–1826, CO 318/76, fol. 102, NAE. Lee was both a creditor and trustee to John Morse's estate; see Morse v. Green, July 15, 1785, C 12/604/16, Chancery Court Records, NAE. Ross lived just outside Montrose, on Scotland's eastern coast. John Tailyour's son James first arrived in Montrose from Jamaica in January 1791; see Jean Tailyour to John Tailyour, Jan. 24, 1791, Tailyour Papers, WCL.

their homes. Within months of James's landing in Britain, however, an en-slaved revolution in the French colony of Saint Domingue, originally blamed on antislavery activism, would forever alter perceptions of such migrants. The advent of abolitionism made mixed-race migration to Britain a cause of offi-cial interest.

Abolitionism, Demography, and Racial Mixture in the Colonies

It bewilders the mind to consider what the Africans onboard the *Eliza* experi-enced during their weeks at sea before finally landing in Kingston on July 19, 1789. Most had been captured in the Bight of Biafra and sold at New Calabar to Captain Edward Bullock, who had set off for the West African coast from Bristol, England. In total, 283 men, women, and children in chains stepped onto the ship, now headed for the Caribbean. Details of the early days of the voyage are unclear, but, as the *Eliza* approached Barbados, a number of its passengers began to exhibit the trademark pustules indicating smallpox infection. The ship's doctor and his assistant had little luck fighting the ill-ness, nor could they prevent the rapid spread of dysentery that killed many others. When the *Eliza* finally pulled into port in Jamaica, 73 Africans, more than a quarter of those taken on board, had perished. This was a higher mor-tality rate than usual for the Middle Passage, but it was certainly not unprece-dented. Unfortunately for those taken ashore in Kingston, reaching land did not stop the course of illness. Thirty more died within weeks of arriving. Many others were permanently disfigured and blinded by the ravages of disease. They now faced the prospect of yet another sea voyage to a different colony or potentially a short trip to a nearby Jamaican plantation. All were assuredly intended to spend the rest of their lives undertaking backbreaking toil.[6]

Details of the *Eliza*'s fraught journey, and the misery endured by its pas-sengers, come from the pen of James Taylor's father. He wrote of the voyage the year before sending off his young son of color to family in Britain. John Tailyour came to know the ship's history so intimately because he was respon-sible for selling its cargo. The recent efforts he had undertaken to educate and assist his formerly enslaved children appear to have had no effect on how he

6. For information on the *Eliza*'s passage, see *Voyages: The Trans-Atlantic Slave Trade Database*, no. 18041, www.slavevoyages.org. See also *Cornwall Chronicle, and Jamaica Gen-eral Adversiser* (Montego Bay, Jamaica), Aug. 8, 1789, Supplement; and David Richardson, ed., *Bristol, Africa, and the Eighteenth-Century Slave Trade to America*, IV, *The Final Years, 1770–1807* (Bristol, U.K., 1996), 151. For more on the spread of disease on slave ships, see Alexander X. Byrd, *Captives and Voyagers: Black Migrants across the Eighteenth-Century British Atlantic World* (Baton Rouge, La., 2008), 37–41.

carried out his professional activities. His letters about the deaths on board the *Eliza* reveal a slave trader utterly disconnected from the moral realities of his business. The loss of life upset him, not for its human tragedy, but for its impact on his reputation. Visible signs of smallpox on the Africans' bodies could have lowered their appeal and price, he huffed. With a bizarre sense of pride, he congratulated himself on nevertheless selling them at some of the highest rates of his career. Tailyour made no mental connection to a previous ship coming into port in Jamaica seven years earlier, the *Zong*, whose crew had famously murdered more than one hundred Africans on board, helping to accelerate the anti–slave trade movement in Europe. Growing calls in Britain to reform, if not end, the commerce in human cargo had done little to diminish Tailyour's zeal in profiting from African labor. In one of his longest letters on the *Eliza*'s fatal journey, he expressed relief that Parliament had recently failed to pass a bill against the slave trade.[7]

Is it possible that Tailyour reassessed his feelings two months later when the Jamaican assembly asked him to explain what had gone wrong on the *Eliza?* Owing to increasing protests from the abolition movement, London's Board of Trade commanded Jamaica's governor to issue a report on the slave trade, and a committee of the assembly spent most of the year in 1789 collecting evidence to send back. On December 3, the committee presented its findings, which included Tailyour's testimony about his experiences earlier in the fall. Tailyour insisted that smallpox, not cruelty, had caused the heavy loss of life and that the *Eliza*'s doctors had done well to prevent the virus from spreading more aggressively. He even praised himself for having inoculated the healthy Africans who arrived once the ship came into port. As a financial beneficiary of the slave trade, Tailyour clearly did not favor abolition. His testimony to the Jamaican assembly, however, demonstrates his connections and contributions to the discussion surrounding it. The House of Commons in England read Tailyour's report on slave trading as well as that of his British business partners John and Alexander Anderson. Abolitionism, therefore, was not a peripheral issue to the Scottish slave trader. It was an attack on his

7. On the *Eliza*'s passage, see John Tailyour to Thomas Jones, Aug. 9, 1789, Letter Book II, Tailyour Papers, WCL, Sept. 15, 1789, John Tailyour to William Miles, Sept. 15, 1789. Jones was one of the owners of the *Eliza*. Health was generally the most important issue that concerned Jamaican slave traders; see Audra A. Diptee, *From Africa to Jamaica: The Making of an Atlantic Slave Society, 1775–1807* (Gainesville, Fla., 2010), 4–5, 48–49. For more on the *Zong*, see James Walvin, *The Zong: A Massacre, the Law, and the End of Slavery* (New Haven, Conn., 2011). The *Zong* arrived in Jamaica in 1781, but the details of its passage did not come to light until the ship's owners applied for insurance recompense in 1783.

profession, and Tailyour was as active as anyone on either side of the Atlantic in engaging with the terms of its debate. A profitable slave trade was also critical to the financial success of his offspring of color in the metropole.[8]

The assembly's report, to which Tailyour's testimony contributed, underscored the island's long-standing obsessions with demography and family formation as they related to slavery. Writing to Parliament, the assembly crafted twelve reasons why the slave trade should continue. According to the list, slavery was neither immoral nor deadly, and the assembly insisted that ending the slave trade would obliterate Jamaica's economy. On this latter point, the legislature argued for the impossibility of growing either the black or white populations on the island should Parliament prevent new Africans from arriving. Owing to a gender disparity among enslaved Jamaicans, the assembly contended that more captives were needed "before any segmentation can be expected from natural increase by generation." Moreover, island officials had previously held out "great encouragement for the introduction of white families" with little success, and chipping away at the profits of the sugar economy would effectively forestall any potential increase in white numbers. Concerns over the balance between black and white populations, as well as obsessions with white settlement, had preoccupied the assembly's time throughout the eighteenth century. They now dominated the island's official response to abolitionism.[9]

The Jamaican assembly maintained its interest in demography because slave trade reformers latched onto the issue in their own attacks. Initial

8. *JAJ*, Dec. 17, 1788, VIII, 481, Dec. 3, 1789, 526; *Daily Advertiser* (Kingston, Jamaica), Feb. 5, 1790; "Minutes of the Evidence Taken before a Committee of the House of Commons . . . against the Abolition of the Slave Trade," Feb. 20, 1790, no. 4212, pt. II, in *HCSP*, LXXII, 201, "Minutes of the Evidence Taken before a Committee of the House of Commons . . . to Consider the Circumstances of the Slave Trade . . . ," no. 4160, LXVIII, 341–345. Bryan Edwards discussed his inquiry into the *Eliza* in a speech to Jamaica's council and assembly on November 19, 1789; see Edwards, *A Speech Delivered at a Free Conference between the Honourable the Council and Assembly of Jamaica, Held the 19th of November, 1789; on the Subject of Mr. Wilberforce's Propositions in the House of Commons, concerning the Slave Trade* (Kingston, Jamaica, 1790), 26–27, appendix, x–xi; and *Report, Resolutions, and Remonstrance, of the Honourable the Council and Assembly of Jamaica, at a Joint Committee, on the Subject of the Slave-Trade . . .* (London, 1790), 15–16. The assembly included the evidence of another Jamaican with a relative of color who had traveled to Britain: Robert Hibbert, the cousin of Jane Harry Thresher, who died in 1784. Hibbert provided information on the number of Africans his uncle's firm imported between 1764 and 1774; see *JAJ*, Nov. 12, 1788, VIII, 429–430.

9. *JAJ*, Dec. 3, 1789, VIII, 524–528.

humanitarian appeals before the early 1780s had used religious and Enlightenment rationales against the commerce in human bodies. But the tremendous profits flowing out of the West Indies forced a new strategy that generally conceded the economic necessity of slavery but attacked the economic inefficiency of the slave trade. Demography, an emerging field of empirical inquiry, provided the rhetorical tool for just such an argument. "If a planter treats his slaves well, and encourages population," Thomas Clarkson declared in his second abolitionist tract, "they *must* increase." Amelioration would allow the Caribbean's enslaved laborers to reproduce, thereby eliminating the need for any fresh imports of bound Africans. Clarkson's Committee for the Abolition of the Slave Trade held firmly to this belief, or at least espoused it with strong conviction. At one of its first meetings in January 1788, members maintained that they held accounts from a number of West Indian estates that had gone years without purchasing saltwater slaves, owing to more humane practices in the field. In making this claim, abolitionists appropriated a long-standing discourse around colonial demography, turning it against the West Indian planters and merchants who had regularly engaged in such considerations themselves.[10]

By this point in the late 1780s, Jamaican officials continued to insist that natural reproduction among both enslaved blacks and free whites was a high social priority. Fewer imported Africans would reduce costs and lessen rebelliousness; more white settlers would increase domestic security. But decades of failed demographic stability, owing to endemic colonial diseases and increasingly more demanding labor regimes that devastated enslaved fecundity, revealed how little encouragement had actually been given to facilitate reproduction. Planters had done virtually nothing to improve conditions for enslaved workers. Granted, between 1781 and 1788, the assembly had passed a series of slave acts meant to reform the institution. Maiming and killing enslaved persons now resulted in stricter punishments, but for the most part

10. [Thomas Clarkson], *A Summary View of the Slave Trade, and of the Probable Consequences of Its Abolition* (London, 1787), 14; Minutes of the Committee for the Abolition of the Slave Trade, Jan. 15, 1788, Add. MS 21254, fol. 28, BL; Christopher Leslie Brown, *Moral Capital: Foundations of British Abolitionism* (Chapel Hill, N.C., 2006), 239–258, 335–352; B. W. Higman, "Slavery and the Development of Demographic Theory in the Age of the Industrial Revolution," in James Walvin, ed., *Slavery and British Society, 1776–1846* (Baton Rouge, La., 1982), 164–194; Seymour Drescher, *The Mighty Experiment: Free Labor versus Slavery in British Emancipation* (New York, 2002), 35–49. The philosophy of amelioration, as Colleen A. Vasconcellos demonstrates, did not produce results; see Vasconcellos, *Slavery, Childhood, and Abolition in Jamaica, 1788–1838* (Athens, Ga., 2015), 21–37.

these internal changes lacked any kind of legal teeth and did little to allevi-
ate the daily brutality of field work. Likewise, the assembly had all but given
up on forging a strong white settler community by the start of the American Revolution, as evidenced by the development of the island's deficiency
laws. Initiated in 1703, the laws required, under threat of often steep fines,
each estate to house a certain number of white inhabitants proportional to its
nonwhite laborers. Originally intended as a spur to white immigration and
growth, the deficiency acts eventually became more of a direct tax. As early
as 1757, William Burke commented that colonists preferred paying the fines
over importing white servants. Officials were equally happy collecting the
dues. Nearly one-quarter of the Jamaican government's income came from
such fines in 1771, and the revenues continued to rise. The parish council
of Saint Thomas in the Vale, for instance, saw steady increases in its deficiency fee collection, from less than four hundred pounds in 1789 to more
than twelve hundred pounds in 1800. At the end of the 1780s, then, very few
Jamaicans continued to propagate the illusion that the deficiency laws encouraged white growth. A Jamaican newspaper advertisement from the summer
of 1785 laid bare that fiction. A white family of five posted a somewhat brazen
notice that it was seeking "a House, rent free, for saving DEFICIENCIES, upon
any property."[11]

Despite their lack of efforts to promote conditions conducive to slave family
formation, Jamaican officials and planters instead blamed black workers
themselves for demographic decline. Proslavery supporters dismissed abolitionist assertions that slave numbers were growing naturally under humanitarian conditions. Many insisted that bound laborers were incapable of such
increase. Both the extremities of the West Indian climate as well as cultural

11. [William Burke], *An Account of the European Settlements in America*, 2 vols. (London, 1757), II, 113–114; Vestry Minutes, Saint Thomas in the Vale, 1789–1802, 2/1/1, fols.
15–436, JA; *Cornwall Chronicle, and Jamaica General Advertiser*, July 30, 1785. See also
Chapter 1, above. A similar ad appeared in the Nov. 17, 1792, edition of the *Cornwall
Chronicle*. For more on the increasing demands on enslaved labor in Jamaica and beyond
in the eighteenth century, see Justin Roberts, *Slavery and the Enlightenment in the British
Atlantic, 1750–1807* (New York, 2013). For a brief, and remarkably clear, history of the legal
changes around Jamaican slave laws in the 1780s, see *The New Act of Assembly of the Island of
Jamaica . . . Commonly Called, the New Consolidated Act . . .* (London, 1789). Neighboring
Saint Domingue instituted a similar revision of its slave codes in 1788 to reduce torture and
murder; see Malick W. Ghachem, *The Old Regime and the Haitian Revolution* (Cambridge,
Mass., 2012), 167–206. For more on Jamaican officials and the deficiency acts, see N[eville]
A. T. Hall, "Some Aspects of the 'Deficiency' Question in Jamaica in the Eighteenth Cen-
tury," *Caribbean Studies*, XV, no. 1 (April 1975), 11–12.

traits brought over from Africa supposedly inhibited reproduction. Multiple anonymous pamphleteers contended that African polygynous practices came to the New World, stunting natural growth. Assemblyman Bryan Edwards made the same point in a 1789 joint session of Jamaica's two legislative houses. In comments later published, Edwards claimed that enslaved women "hold chastity in so little estimation, that barrenness and frequent abortions, the usual effects of a promiscuous intercourse, are very generally prevalent among them." Philip Gibbes concurred based on the evidence he saw on his Barbadian estates. "The *early* and *promiscuous* commerce between the sexes," he held, was "the great enemy to propagation." Gibbes's observation fit with emerging studies of demography: Thomas Malthus declared in 1798 that "misery and vice" were the chief impediments to population growth as they prevented parents from properly caring for their young. For those supporting slavery, African habits, rather than colonial brutality, were to blame for social instability in the Caribbean.[12]

Abolitionists, too, conceded to the claims that sexual immorality within African culture inhibited black population growth and proposed familial reforms to correct the problem. In an early sermon on amelioration, the abolitionist bishop Beilby Porteus commanded that the enslaved should be converted to Christianity in order to eliminate promiscuity. A society of Glaswegians against the slave trade joined this idea to the population issue in 1791. Planters, they argued, needed to pay more attention to their workers' families. "Marriage, so important for that end, will be encouraged among them," allowing enslaved numbers to increase, they projected, and "all the parental and filial relations will be strengthened." This reform in marriage and kinship practices among captives mirrored Edmund Burke's suggestion in 1780 to settle black laborers into village-like communities that would allow nuclear families to flourish. For the next century, abolitionist and humanitarian reformers alike would continue to emphasize the importance of imposing British systems of

12. *Considerations on the Emancipation of Negroes and on the Abolition of the Slave-Trade, by a West-India Planter* (London, 1788), 14; "Short Reasons against the Abolition of the Slave Trade," (1789), 2, Add. MS 12431, fol. 221, BL; Edwards, *Speech Delivered at a Free Conference*, 34; [Philip Gibbes], *Instructions for the Treatment of Negroes, &c. &c. &c.,* 2d ed. (London, 1797), 125; [Thomas Malthus], *An Essay on the Principle of Population . . .* (London, 1798), 107–108. Gibbes's account was first printed in 1786. Polygyny was practiced in many West African societies; however, the general gender imbalances of enslaved populations in the New World made such relationships nearly impossible—though polyamory was not unheard of. See James H. Sweet, *Recreating Africa: Culture, Kinship, and Religion in the African-Portuguese World, 1441–1770* (Chapel Hill, N.C., 2003), 34–40.

sexuality and family formation onto enslaved (or formerly enslaved) individuals in the colonies. Proslavery supporters did not necessarily disagree. Dominica's assembly passed a law in 1788 requiring owners to allow their slaves to
marry one another. English pamphleteer John Ranby anticipated numerous
obstacles in getting bound workers to marry but felt that wedlock might improve reproduction, even as he rejected the intentions of abolitionism. Likewise, a 1792 apology for slavery held that, if planters wished to increase their
slave stocks organically, then "negroe *young girls* . . . [should be] trained before they arrived to maturity for *marriage*." For advocates on both sides of the
abolition debate, changes in West Indian family structures provided one solution to the Empire's ongoing problems with the slave trade.[13]

This focus on enslaved family life brought greater attention to the issue of
motherhood on the plantation. The treatment of fertile women became a central topic in Westminster's discussions of African enslavement. One witness
testified to the House of Commons that he had seen pregnant slaves working
"till within a few hours of their delivery." Many accounts emerged echoing one
author's claim that, "in some estates, it is usual to dig a hole in the ground, in
which they put the bellies of pregnant women, while they whip them." Abolitionist James Ramsay, having lived for a time in Saint Kitts, lent support
to these statements. He believed that plantation owners had little sympathy
toward enslaved women, especially expectant mothers. As most white men in
the tropics were bachelors, Ramsay believed that both planters and overseers
had no understanding of pregnancy and viewed motherhood as an impediment to productivity. "Nothing raised a manager's resentment sooner," he
observed, "than to be informed that a negress was with child." This concern

13. Beilby Porteus, "The Civilization, Improvement, and Conversion of the Negroe-Slaves
in the British Islands Recommended," 1783, in *Sermons on Several Subjects; by the Right
Reverend Beilby Porteus, D.D., Bishop of Chester* (Dublin, 1784), 263–264; *An Address to the
Inhabitants of Glasgow, Paisley, and the Neighbourhood, concerning the African Slave Trade*
(Glasgow, 1791), 13–14; Edmund Burke, "Sketch of a Negro Code," in Warren M. Elofson
et al., eds., *The Writings and Speeches of Edmund Burke*, 6 vols. (New York, 1990–1996), III,
576–577; An Act for the Encouragement, Protection, and Better Government of Slaves, Dec.
23, 1788, Acts of the Assembly of Dominica, CO 73/9, fol. 82, NAE; [John Ranby], *Doubts
on the Abolition of the Slave Trade . . .* (London, 1790), 67–71; Ranby, *Observations on the Evidence Given before the Committees of the Privy Council and House of Commons in Support of
the Bill for Abolishing the Slave Trade* (London, 1791), 164; Jesse Foot, *A Defence of the Planters in the West-Indies . . .* (London, 1792), 96–100; Catherine Hall, *Civilising Subjects: Metropole and Colony in the English Imagination, 1830–1867* (Chicago, 2002), esp. 112–125, 174–
208; Henrice Altink, "Forbidden Fruit: Pro-Slavery Attitudes towards Enslaved Women's
Sexuality and Interracial Sex," *Journal of Caribbean History*, XXXIX (2005), 201–235.

over the bodies and reproductive capacities of African women had fascinated Europeans from the first days of the slave trade. Motions to end that commerce aroused such interests even further. Parliament even began compiling statistics on specific population changes in West Indian estates and peppered its witnesses with questions on how to improve enslaved fecundity.[14]

Within this discourse of population and reform, interracial families and mixed-race children came under increasing scrutiny. If both abolitionists and proslavery pamphleteers could agree that naturally reproducing enslaved black and free white populations were vital for the West Indies and that movements away from promiscuity and toward marriage could accomplish that goal, then concubinage and mixed-race households were even more problematic than before. Visitors to the Caribbean had long registered distaste for white and black coupling. Openly accepted extramarital sex, to say nothing of interracial intimacy, violated many Britons' sense of propriety. But the added political pressures of abolition galvanized those worries. Evidence given in Parliament by antislavery activists between 1790 and 1791 noted that white overseers effectively used black workers as prostitutes and thus diminished their reproductive capacities. A 1790 account of Caribbean customs similarly railed against the practice of whites keeping black and mixed-race mistresses, who "from their youth up are taught to be whores." "Creole men commonly keep black or mungrel women till a day or two before they enter

14. *An Abstract of the Evidence Delivered before a Select Committee of the House of Commons in the Years 1790, and 1791; on the Part of the Petitioners for the Abolition of the Slave-Trade*, 2d ed. (London, 1792), 52–53; James Ramsay, *Objections to the Abolition of the Slave Trade, with Answers* (London, 1788), 5–6, 50–51. Others made the same accusation about pregnant women being beaten; see Samuel Bradburn, *An Address to the People Called Methodists; concerning the Evil Encouraging the Slave Trade* (Manchester, U.K., 1792), 4; *A Short Address to the People of Scotland, on the Subject of the Slave-Trade* . . . (Edinburgh, 1792), 15. For parliamentary testimony on pregnancy and slavery, see, for instance, "Barbadoes: Report of a Committee of the General Assemby . . . ," Feb. 18, 23, 1788, no. 4187, in *HCSP*, LXVII, 395, "Report of the Lords of the Committee of Council . . . ," Apr. 25, 1789, no. 4132, LXX, pt. 2, 272–279; and "West Indian Islands, Papers relating to Antigua," William Pitt Papers, 1788–1793, PRO 30/8/348/1, fols. 61–249, NAE. Medical views on exertion during pregnancy were divided in this period, but most agreed that women should not work as actively up to the moment of birth; see Judith Schneid Lewis, *In the Family Way: Childbearing in the British Aristocracy, 1760–1860* (New Brunswick, N.J., 1986), 125–126. Jennifer L. Morgan has observed a general trend in Atlantic history of imperial obsession and fascination with the body of the enslaved female and that body's ability to perpetuate the slave economy; see Morgan, *Laboring Women: Reproduction and Gender in New World Slavery* (Philadelphia, 2004).

into the serious bond of marriage," the author complained. "In one family I have seen white, mestee, quadroon and mulatto children, all brothers and sisters, playing together." White men's encouragement of mixed-race households appeared to violate proper family formation and unduly complicated colonial society.[15]

Such public and polemical attacks against interracial unions revealed changing attitudes about families in the Empire. More directly, these topics were now central to governmental planning. Although English visitors to the Caribbean had long turned away at the sight of white and black coupling, those relationships did not originally provoke political jeremiads. Illegitimate children and functional alternatives to marriage had been common, and to some degree accepted, features of families on both sides of the Atlantic in the early eighteenth century. But concerns over population and economic stability made those issues of state interest in the century's second half. In Britain, there was a tightening in marriage law as well as in the continued inheritance suits lodged by family members against illegitimate relatives. In the West Indies, the notion that white and black households had to be segregated and regulated in order to augment natural reproduction gained support. With increasing governmental scrutiny, imperial observers advocated more sharply for reformed familial codes.

Jamaican whites tended to agree publicly with admonitions against interracial sex, even if their actions betrayed such support. Edwards disparaged his fellow Jamaicans' propensity to sidestep matrimony for pleasure. "No White man of decent appearance, unless urged by the temptation of a considerable fortune, will condescend to give his hand in marriage to a Mulatto," he bemoaned. But even wealthy women of color rarely wed white men. Those bachelors who did not marry nevertheless closely considered the financial standing of the mixed-race women they took as long-term companions. These extended relationships, of course, created a number of complications, as seen with John Morse's inheritance dispute in the previous chapter. Interracial unions undercut legitimate family formations and compromised the island's professed demographic ideal of separate reproductive white and black communities. A 1789 letter to the editor of a Jamaican newspaper lamented how white men improperly organized their families. Men of all stripes, "in defiance of shame, keep women of colour as their common prostitutes, in their very houses," the author decried. Worse still, these white men "cherish[ed]

15. *Abstract of the Evidence*, 120–221; J. B. Moreton, *Manners and Customs in the West India Islands* . . . (London, 1790), 106, 129.

their nankeen [yellow] breed as legal offspring." The approximation, or performance, of legitimacy in these illegitimate households was perhaps the most troubling aspect of interracial relations. Bastardy was not uncommon in the Atlantic world, but the wiping away of its cultural blemish was a novel outgrowth of the colonial setting.[16]

The supposed ubiquity of cross-racial relationships meant that commentators believed that the islands' only significant demographic growth would come in the form of mixed-race individuals. "The brown people, or mulattoes, quadroons, and mestees, increase every day," a former resident complained of Jamaica. This demographic shift was seen as especially bad in light of his claim that both the white and enslaved populations were decreasing. The realities of West Indian life, and whites' desires for mistresses of color, meant that a growing bloc of mixed-race people was nevertheless unavoidable. Jamaica's free population of color expanded dramatically over this period, perhaps increasing tenfold from roughly three thousand to thirty thousand between 1767 and 1834. Its enslaved population of color likely boomed at the same rates. But, although the island's white populace did see a brief increase of 90 percent at the end of the eighteenth century, it ultimately returned to pre-1788 levels by the time of emancipation. Jamaican native Benjamin Vaughan witnessed these changes firsthand, proclaiming in 1792 that the "number of the people of color in the colonies must inevitably increase." Vaughan was the rare commentator that did not express this fact alarmingly, but he failed to share the optimism of Jamaican officials from two generations earlier that this class of color could eventually become white settlers. "Intermixture being once made it never can be retrograde," he pronounced; "the people of color never can return to the race of whites or of blacks." Again, notions of family belonging and racial status had shifted significantly from the earlier periods of the eighteenth century, which sought to include certain fractions of the island's people of color into white society. Instead, a new political consensus had emerged. The twin pillars of West Indian stability were still increased white numbers and greater enslaved fecundity. But interracial sex could no longer produce children who could eventually contribute to either of these basic goals.[17]

16. Bryan Edwards, *The History, Civil and Commercial, of the British Colonies in the West Indies*, 2 vols. (Dublin, 1793), II, 22; *Cornwall Chronicle, and Jamaica General Advertiser*, Dec. 12, 1789, Supplement.

17. [Peter Marsden], *An Account of the Island of Jamaica; with Reflections on the Treatment, Occupation, and Provisions of the Slaves . . .* (Newcastle, U.K., 1788), 7; Benjamin Vaughan, "Concerning the Whites and People of Color in the Colonies," circa 1792, Benjamin Vaughan Papers, ser. III, Amscy, American Philosophical Society Library, Phila-

Both pro- and antislavery supporters alike railed against individuals of mixed ancestry as they did not fit easily into the islands' social and economic ambitions. The group's capacity to work became a crucial topic in a debate fixated on questions of labor. West Indian absentee James Tobin countered early emancipation proposals by remarking that people of color generally refused to work in sugar fields, especially those who had become free. Even the noted abolitionist Ramsay conceded this point when responding to his critics. In a 1788 tract, he agreed that mixed-race people not only worked less strenuously but, if freed, would not undertake serious manual labor. This denigration of the capacity of mixed-race persons to work emerged out of a broad conception that Europeans could not exert themselves effectively in the Caribbean climate and that their blood diluted the robust industry of those with African heritage. Many others echoed this claim, including fellow critics of the slave trade. One abolitionist pamphlet from 1787 decried the place of mixed-race people in the Caribbean economy: "*Mulattoes* are . . . the greatest receivers of stolen goods; and the female mulattoes are little else than mistresses. *Negroes,* are, then, the only class that will stand the climate, and, at the same time, labour." Other authors parroted this supposition. In a 1790 defense of Jamaican slavery, William Beckford stated, "The colour of the mulatto, his birth, and education, naturally exclude him from the possible severity of toil." With near universality, pro- and antislavery commentators believed that only those of full African ancestry could endure heavy activity in the West Indies. Any mixture of European blood supposedly compromised that ability, thus undercutting the plantation system. In the eyes of imperial observers, the children of interracial unions inherited not only the taint of patriarchal immorality but also a dissolute biology that eliminated their usefulness to colonial society.[18]

The abolition debate was thus not solely centered on the slave trade but also on the future face of British colonialism in the Caribbean. The desire

---

delphia, Pa.; Gad J. Heuman, *Between Black and White: Race, Politics, and the Free Coloreds in Jamaica, 1792–1865* (Westport, Conn., 1981), 7; Thomas C. Holt, *The Problem of Freedom: Race, Labor, and Politics in Jamaica and Britain, 1832–1938* (Baltimore, 1992), 87. See also Table 1, above.

18. [James Tobin], *Cursory Remarks upon the Reverend Mr. Ramsay's Essay on the Treatment and Conversion of African Slaves in the Sugar Colonies* (London, 1785), 116–119; Ramsay, *Objections*, 31–32; *Thoughts on Civilization and the Gradual Abolition of Slavery in Africa and the West Indies* (London, 1787), 11; [Marsden], *An Account of the Island of Jamaica*, 38; William Beckford, *A Descriptive Account of the Island of Jamaica*, 2 vols. (London, 1790), II, 322. Despite this denigration of mixed-race labor, Ramsay still believed that free people of color could serve as an important social bridge between blacks and whites.

for a secure and stable West Indian economy escalated the need for self-reproducing populations on the islands, bringing a long-standing ambition of the Caribbean plantocracy to the attention of officials on both sides of the Atlantic. Sugar provided enormous profits for those who farmed it, traded it, and facilitated its purchase. Whether to continue to harvest the crop was not up for debate. Rather, who would cultivate it and how long that system could carry forward weighed on the minds of everyone who reflected on slavery. A Jamaican newspaper editorial from the fall of 1787 imagined a letter written thirteen years in the future describing an ascendant isle, filled with well-funded charity schools, wide boulevards, lush public squares, and settlements of an "industrious and laborious race of white people . . . [so that] the inhuman custom of importing slaves, may be rendered unnecessary." Such flights of fancy, grounded in very real demographic challenges, meant that mixed-race individuals were more of a colonial threat than ever before since they were no longer thought to contribute properly to either the free or enslaved communities.[19]

Abolitionism, Demography, and Racial Mixture in Britain

Questions on colonial demography in the abolition debate naturally led to similar considerations of social composition in the metropole. Just as Britons had appropriated colonial concerns over black and white intermixture in the 1760s and 1770s, popular abolitionism continued to press such examinations into the ensuing decades. The hyperbolic rhetoric around interracial unions in Britain espoused by Edward Long after the Somerset decision of 1772 did not die down. Instead, abolitionist debate rejuvenated and sustained such concerns. Once more, the prospect of slave reform signaled in the minds of many metropolitan observers the breakdown between the Empire's periphery and center. If British freedoms and humanitarianism extended to those beyond the line of the Old World, then the demographic distinctions between the metropole and its colonies were equally subject to standardization. This meant that abolitionist critiques of interracial relationships and their offspring abroad led to parallel concerns at home. Discussions of abolitionism, therefore, continued to include considerations of mixed-race West Indians in Britain.[20]

---

19. *Cornwall Chronicle, and Jamaica General Advertiser,* Oct. 6, 1787, Supplement.

20. For the legal and political component to the question of imperial homogeneity, see P. J. Marshall, "Britain and the World in the Eighteenth Century: II, Britons and Americans," Royal Historical Society, *Transactions,* 6th Ser., IX (1999), 1–16; Eliga H. Gould, "Zones of

Observations on migrants of color sat alongside ongoing commentary on servile blacks in the metropole. Racially charged reactions to the Somerset decision had focused exclusively on enslaved or recently freed individuals in Britain. London's substantial black community at the time gave a visible face to these responses, and the continued arrival of nonwhite servants and sailors sustained these worries. When black loyalists landed in Britain after the American Revolution, politicians and reformers alike accelerated their interest in addressing this expanding social group. In many ways, the rhetoric spouted by Long and others in 1772 did not change significantly over the course of the next decade and a half. One 1784 letter attacking abolitionists in London's *St. James's Chronicle; or, British Evening-Post* directly channeled Long, stating: "[Blacks] will intermarry with our white Women, and produce one of the most wicked Races of Men the World is cursed with. . . . England will become thereby such another Race of Men as the Portuguese." Lingering uncertainties about the legal status of enslaved blacks in England after the Somerset decision led to repeated proclamations that Britain was to follow in the racially compromised footsteps of its Iberian neighbors. Little had evolved in arguments against British racial intermixture, perhaps because the rhetorical gestures of both abolitionists and their detractors at the end of the 1780s drew so heavily from those of previous years.[21]

Polemicists found some potential solutions to the perceived problem of mixed-race individuals living in Britain by looking across the Channel. France had passed legislation in 1777 that effectively prohibited anyone with African blood from entering the country and closely regulated those currently there. As abolitionism gained steam, some observers insisted that Britain follow suit. English writer Philip Thicknesse urged collateral legislation after the first bills to end the slave trade were introduced in the House of Commons in 1788. "The prudent policy of the French nation should not be overlooked," he urged, for "they will not suffer a Negro to land in their Kingdom, therefore we

---

Law, Zones of Violence: The Legal Geography of the British Atlantic, circa 1772," *WMQ*, 3d Ser., LX (2003), 471–510; Mary Sarah Bilder, *The Transatlantic Constitution: Colonial Legal Culture and the Empire* (Cambridge, Mass., 2004); and Lauren Benton, *A Search for Sovereignty: Law and Geography in European Empires, 1400–1900* (New York, 2010).

21. *St. James's Chronicle; or, British Evening-Post* (London), Oct. 26–28, 1784; James Dore, *A Sermon on the African Slave Trade, Preached at Maze-Pond, Southwark, Lord's Day Afternoon, Nov. 30, 1788*, 3d ed. (London, 1788), 17; Robert Robinson, *Slavery Inconsistent with the Spirit of Christianity . . .* (Cambridge, 1788), 19–20; G[ilbert] Francklyn, *Observations, Occasioned by the Attempts Made in England to Effect the Abolition of the Slave Trade . . .*, 2d ed. (London, 1789), x–xiv, 11–12.

shall soon be *peopled* with them from *all* quarters." If Parliament did not produce its own ban, then "the English nation would in another century, degenerate into a race of Portuguese." Once again, proslavery supporters insisted
that the reputedly more tolerant Iberians' lapse into racial degeneration would
afflict Britain should it grow too compassionate and abolish human trafficking. Fellow anti-abolitionist Clara Reeve echoed these comments four years
later. She believed that black colonists would "flock hither from all parts, mix
with the natives, and spoil the breed of the common people . . . [to] produce
a vile mongrel race of people, such as no friend to Britain can ever wish to in-
habit it," unless the British copied the French. That same year, another writer
urged a French-style ban against black immigrants to prevent Britain from
becoming a "sink of all the earth, for mongrels, vagrants, and vagabonds."
Perhaps the recent enslaved uprising in France's principal Caribbean colony
of Saint Domingue inspired these fears. Regardless, Britons continued to express worry about the arrival of servile blacks in the same ways that they had
in 1772. Britain's working-class blood was still seen as most vulnerable to
corruption, although these polemics hinted at an eventual overwhelming of
national heritage generally.[22]

Even as commentators begrudged the idea of poor blacks arriving in the
metropole, they held more conflicted notions about elites of dual ancestry.
Just as Long had viewed mixed-race education in Britain as a waste of money,
rather than as a portent of doom, so, too, did William Dickson, a former West
Indian resident, lightly dismiss the practice in a 1789 reflection on slavery
and the slave trade. "Should you think of sending home young men, of your
number, to be regularly educated for the church, in this country," Dickson
wrote in a letter to Barbados's free population of color, "it is to be feared that
a mistaken generosity might induce you to allow them more money than is
absolutely necessary for their support." This was less of a condemnation of
their children's arrival in Britain than an exhortation to monitor finances. One
of Dickson's correspondents, the Barbadian planter Joshua Steele, also held
little concern about people of mixed heritage in Britain. Steele, whose own
mixed-race children would move to England after his death, took a pragmatic

22. Philip Thicknesse, *Memoirs and Anecdotes of Philip Thicknesse . . .* (London, 1788),
282 (emphasis in original); Clara Reeve, *Plans of Education; with Remarks on the Systems of
Other Writers; in a Series of Letters between Mrs. Darnford and Her Friends* (London, 1792),
90–91; John Scattergood, *An Antidote to Popular Frenzy, Particularly to the Present Rage for
the Abolition of the Slave-Trade . . .* (London, 1792). For more on French law, see Sue Peabody, *"There Are No Slaves in France": The Political Culture of Race and Slavery in the Ancien
Régime* (New York, 1996), 106–119.

stance on the "Descendants of Negroes, some of whom may now, perhaps, be seated among the Nobles and Commons in Parliament; (for, without doubt, there has crept a little Negroe Blood among them . . .)." The realities of imperialism and influence of familial and biological connections to white Britons meant that the arrival of West Indians of color in the metropole was still seen somewhat separately from that of poor blacks. Steele's intimation about Parliament, though, hinted that those feelings were nevertheless complicated and unresolved.[23]

Prompted by these discussions about slavery and mixed-race migration, the British government undertook an investigation. In 1788, England's Board of Trade joined Parliament in soliciting information broadly on the transatlantic slave market. Among other topics, the Board sought evidence on the practice of sending black and mixed-race children from African slaving ports to Britain. England's black students were often discussed in abolition debates about African mental faculties, and the Board wished to learn more. These children piqued the government's interest because they might eventually help Westminster to secure a stronger colonial foothold in Africa as well as reform and regulate the slave trade now under such intense scrutiny. Delegates from Liverpool's slave interest fielded the questions. Their chief representative John Mathews drafted his "Observations on the Conduct of Mulatto and Black African Children, Who Had Been Educated in England," which detailed the experiences of six black and eight mulatto children from Africa who had come to Britain as scholars. Most of the mixed-race individuals were the offspring of slave merchants and native women, whereas the black children primarily descended from African royalty.[24]

23. William Dickson, *Letters on Slavery* (London, 1789), 176; Joshua Steele, *Barbados Gazette*, Nov. 21, 1787, in *Letters of Philo-Xylon . . .* (Barbados, 1789), 13. Steele's letters were reprinted in Dickson, *Mitigation of Slavery, in Two Parts* (London, 1814), 82.

24. "Mr. John Mathew's Observations on the Conduct of Mulatto and Black African Children, Who Had Been Educated in England on Their Subsequent Return to Their Native Country Prepared in Pursuance of Minutes Delivered by Their Lordships Order of 19th April 1788 to Mr. Tarleton One of the Delegates from Liverpool," 1788, BT 6/11, NAE; my thanks to Ian Barrett for the reference. John Beatson railed against the slave trade in 1789 by insisting that, if Africans were "to be brought into England, [and] trained up according to our mode of education, . . . they would, in all the various branches of science, be equal to a similar number born of English parents"; see *Compassion the Duty and Dignity of Man; and Cruelty the Disgrace of His Nature . . .* (Hull, U.K., [1789]), 16–17. The next year, J. B. Moreton, though no particular friend to those of African heritage, likewise claimed: "If blacks were tutored from their infancy in England, they would be as virtuous as white[s]" (Moreton, *Manners and Customs*, 160). See also "Report of the Lords of the Committee of Council

In his testimony to the Board, Mathews said little of the black students in England but commented extensively on those of mixed ancestry. Of a Miss Norie, he wrote, "On her return to her Native Country, she continued to dress in the English fashion and appears to be a sensible and intelligent woman." Describing Jeremy Clinton, son of a merchant on Bance (Bunce) Island, Mathews noted, "His attachment to Europeans is strong, as he is, as well as all others who pertake of European Blood, proud of the distinction." After discussing another African trader's son, he concluded, "To sum up his Character in a few words—with a white man he is a white man, with a Black Man a Black Man." Mathews's remarks on these Africans of color show a fascination with identity and cultural practices in light of mixed heritage. He believed that the students' joint African and European ancestry could work to tremendous advantage in regulating the slave trade. As most of these children eventually planned to return home, Mathews argued that an English education would make them better mediators between African and British slave merchants. He also believed that their presence would help in "promoting Civilization," which would reduce chaotic slave raids and more thoroughly formalize the trade.[25]

Mathews's evidence eventually made its way into the Board of Trade's report on transatlantic slavery. In 1789, the Board released a lengthy account of the commerce in human cargo, which included details provided by Mathews on students of color in Britain. Overall, Liverpool's traders believed that the students were "improved by their Education, particularly the Mulattoes, who pride themselves on the Acquisition of European Knowledge and European Blood." Although the report focused specifically on children from Africa, rather than the West Indies, it still concerned itself broadly with the impact of students of color in Britain as they related to the abolition movement. The Board identified mixed-race immigrants as unique subjects who might potentially reform the slave trade. Abolitionism, then, brought the issue of mixed-race colonists in Britain further to light and within the government's purview.

Appointed for the Consideration of All Matters relating to Trade and Foreign Plantations," Apr. 25, 1789, no. 4132, in *HCSP*, LXIX, pt. 1, 82–86.

25. "Mr. John Mathew's Observations," 1788, BT 6/11, NAE. C. B. Wadstrom also made a comment about one of these children, John Cleveland's son, in his tract, *An Essay on Colonization, Particularly Applied to the Western Coast of Africa, with Some Free Thoughts on Cultivation and Commerce . . .* , pt. 2 (London, 1794), 15. For more on the Clevelands and other Anglo-African families that sent their children to Britain, see Randy J. Sparks, *Africans in the Old South: Mapping Exceptional Lives across the Atlantic World* (Cambridge, Mass., 2016), 19–23.

For the Board of Trade, a mixed-race presence in England could help accelerate commercial reform, even if there was a disquieting sense of uncertainty about these migrants' social positions.[26]

Imperial and abolitionist discourse invigorated a metropolitan interest in mixed-race migration. This combined attention contributed to a heightened monitoring—both officially and informally—of mixed-race elites. Concerns over British interracial pairings at the end of the 1780s differed little from those of the previous two decades. However, specific interests in metropolitan elites of color now took on a more political tone, as they had for racially mixed people in the colonies. Reform-minded officials at the Board of Trade eyed migrants of color generally as potential collaborators in a restructured Atlantic slave trade. Laymen continued their curious notice of these individuals as well, especially as such travelers might signal the intellectual and assimilationist potential of those with African heritage in Britain.

Jamaicans of Color Leaving for Britain at the Start of Popular Abolitionism

British interest in migrants of color coincided with a sustained, if not accelerated, pace of mixed-race Jamaicans leaving for the metropole. Quantitative assessments of the phenomenon are challenging, but a survey of Jamaican wills shows more white men sending children of color to Britain in the 1790s than in previous decades. The growing awareness, if not outright surveillance, of these individuals in Britain does not appear to have dissuaded fathers from financing transatlantic trips. Likewise, mixed-race migrants who returned to Jamaica continued to revel in the prestige of a metropolitan education. Privilege petitioning on the island, which granted small legal concessions in court and in employment options, skyrocketed between 1788 and 1791. In that period, 125 people applied for privileges, which was greater than in any other four-year span of time—so many that Bryan Edwards complained in 1793, "Half the time of the House [of Assembly in Jamaica] during the last five years . . . was taken up in passing Mulatto privilege Bills." Moreover, 29 of the petitioners in this period noted that they had attended a British school. As con-

26. *Report of the Lords of the Committee of Council Appointed for the Consideration of All Matters relating to Trade and Foreign Plantations; Submitting to His Majesty's Consideration the Evidence and Information They Have Collected in Consequence of His Majesty's Order in Council, Dated the 11th of February 1788, concerning the Present State of the Trade to Africa, and Particularly the Trade in Slaves; and concerning the Effects and Consequences of This Trade, as Well in Africa and the West Indies, as to the General Commerce of This Kingdom* (London, 1789), [83–86].

cerns about the group in both Britain and Jamaica mounted, elite Jamaicans of color came and went frequently from the island.[27]

Even at the end of the eighteenth century, sending a child to Britain, no matter the color, was essential if Jamaican parents wished to matriculate them at good institutions. Jamaica's numerous founded but unfunded schools provided few educational options. Wolmer's in Kingston did have its doors open and unofficially allowed in scholars of color until 1798, but it was still modest in size. Stephen Fuller, Jamaica's British agent, begged the island's planters and merchants in 1776 to finance Wolmer's fully, "especially at a time when the Expences of an English Education are so enormous." Manning's free school in Westmoreland was effectively the island's only other functional landed institution. But a massive hurricane in 1781 that devastated Barbados swung through Jamaica's western parishes as well, obliterating Manning's humble campus. Private tutoring flourished in this learning vacuum — Montego Bay's *Cornwall Chronicle, and Jamaica General Advertiser* regularly advertised such institutions — but not all homes admitted mixed-race children. Even those that did were not ideal. Davis's Academy was so intent on proving that its white scholars would be prevented from "talking in the negro dialect" that it boasted, "Children of colour have separate seats and classes from the whites." This was an essential goal for young white Jamaicans. One mother living in the capital of Spanish Town hoped that her grandson had "intirely forgot the Negro dialect" after starting lessons with a governess. Such fear came out of general anxiety among whites about the influence of servants in the upbringing of affluent children. British schools would help young white Jamaicans to avoid black acculturation, and, in many ways, parents of mixed-race children held the same aspirations.[28]

Absentee education took on greater political importance during the aboli-

27. Bryan Edwards, "The Legal Capacities Annexed to a Mulatto in Jamaica, That Is the Principal Laws relating to a Mulatto in Jamaica and the Principal Laws, relating to a Mulatto in St. Domingo," May 16, 1793, CO 137/91, fol. 149, NAE. For a survey of 1790s Jamaican wills, see Appendix 1, below.

28. Stephen Fuller to Paul Phipps, Mar. 5, 1776, Wolmer's School Manuscripts, MS 97a, fols. 151–152, NLJ; *Cornwall Chronicle, and Jamaica General Advertiser*, Oct. 27, 1787, Supplement; Anne Gardner Brodbelt to Jane Gardner Brodbelt, Dec. 24, 1792, in Geraldine Mozley, ed., *Letters to Jane from Jamaica, 1788–1796* (London, 1938), 47. A substantial report on the hurricane damage to the school can be found in *JAJ*, July 6, 1781, VII, 371; and Matthew Mulcahy, *Hurricanes and Society in the British Greater Caribbean, 1624–1783* (Baltimore, 2006), 147–182. On trepidations over servants' influence on children, see Joanne Bailey, *Parenting in England, 1760–1830: Emotion, Identity, and Generation* (New York, 2012), 250.

tion era, as some commentators believed that it held the key to slave reform. Britons made much hay out of the notion that whites were fundamentally different in the Caribbean compared to home. In this telling, West Indians were more dissolute, mean-spirited, authoritarian, and lascivious. Slavery and the tropical climate supposedly produced such distinctions, and some insisted that, without a British education, Caribbean planters would be even more tyrannical. A proslavery polemicist countered Thomas Clarkson's proclamations that West Indians were overly severe by stating that they were, in fact, softened by their upbringings in England and therefore not liable to punish their workers excessively. When testifying to the House of Commons in 1792 about the slave trade, a Mr. "Baillie"—most likely prominent Jamaican planter Nathaniel Bayly—concurred. Bayly vouched for the "temper and dispositions of the inhabitants of our West India Islands" by asking, "Are not our children educated in this country, and instructed in those principles of affection and loyalty?" An anonymous abolitionist constructed a similar argument that same year. British schools were good for West Indian children, the author claimed, as they would shame the students into despising slavery. For these proponents, a British education was essential to connect the West Indies closer to the home country. Without that link, slaveholding could only become worse and abolition never realized.[29]

Despite arguments supporting a British education, sending West Indian children home to the metropole for instruction did not meet with universal acclaim. Long had lambasted the practice in 1774, intent on demonstrating that education abroad hindered the development of a strong, white creole society in Jamaica. It was needlessly expensive and destroyed the intimate connection between parents and children. A decade later, writers on both sides of the slave trade debate appeared to have agreed. In criticizing Caribbean social norms, abolitionist James Ramsay remarked that a West Indian student in Britain knew "no other relationship between him and his parent, than that of a banker." Challenging most of Ramsay's tract, proslavery writer James Tobin nevertheless conceded that absentee education hurt Caribbean families and bemoaned its apparent increase in popularity. Parroting Long, Tobin went on to state that West Indian girls in London schools "acquire only the exterior

29. G[ilbert] Francklyn, *An Answer to the Rev. Mr. Clarkson's Essay on the Slavery and Commerce of the Human Species* . . . (London, 1789), 236–237; *The Debate on a Motion for the Abolition of the Slave-Trade, in the House of Commons, on Monday the Second of April, 1792* . . . (London, 1792), 61–62, 81, 87; *Remarks on the New Sugar-Bill, and on the National Compacts respecting the Sugar-Trade and Slave-Trade* (London, 1792), 80.

and frivolous accomplishments . . . so ill adapted to the sphere in which they are most likely to move." Numerous authors echoed that sentiment. In one of a series of fanciful letters published by Jamaica's *Cornwall Chronicle* that were dated years into the future, an author rejoiced in the eventual extinction of customarily sending children to Britain. Island schools in this distant world took the place of those in the metropole, preserving the "natural affection" between parent and child. Money could be saved, and parents could delight that a "darling daughter, instead of the dreadful risques attending the going to England for education, advances gradually, under her mother's eye." That this utopian vision was still so far away reveals the frustration many Jamaican whites felt about the island's stunted development. Inadequate schools, as with demographic decline, signaled the ongoing problems of settlement that had plagued the island since the inception of English colonization. Keeping Jamaican children in the colony was one way of turning a corner on these problems. Regardless, owing to a lack of educational initiative, parents continued to send their children, both white and brown, to Britain.[30]

If many commentators on both sides of the Atlantic had soured on the effect of absentee schooling, mixed-race Jamaicans vigorously defended the importance of that tradition in their own lives. As in previous decades, a British education helped Jamaicans of color to win privileged rights from the island assembly. Between 1788 and 1791, 125 individuals of color appealed for privileges. Of those, 29 noted that they had spent some time in Britain or were planning to attend school there. This percentage of British visitors was double that for privilege appeals in the rest of the eighteenth century. The continued inclusion of this biographical detail signified the value placed on a metropolitan education for Jamaicans of color not only for the students themselves but for the white officials who conferred on them privileged status.[31]

Many British-educated Jamaicans returned to the island to settle as planters and merchants. Each of John Russell's quadroon children and every one of George Leslie's mulatto offspring went to Britain intent on eventually

30. [Edward Long], *The History of Jamaica; or, General Survey of the Antient and Modern State of That Island . . .*, 3 vols. (London, 1774), II, 246–247; James Ramsay, *An Essay on the Treatment and Conversion of African Slaves in the British Sugar Colonies* (London, 1784), 267n; [Tobin], *Cursory Remarks,* 71–72; *Cornwall Chronicle, and Jamaica General Advertiser,* Nov. 15, 1788, Supplement. For similar remarks to Ramsay's and Tobin's, see Moreton, *Manners and Customs,* 112; and Thomas Atwood, *The History of the Island of Dominica . . .* (London, 1791), 214–216.

31. The number of individuals applying for privileges is calculated from the Minutes of the House of Assembly of Jamaica, 1788–1792, CO 139/45–47, NAE.

coming back to Jamaica. The free mulatto woman Susanna Young won privileges for her quadroon children, all of whom but the youngest were already in
England. She made no mention of her eventual intention for them, perhaps
because their white father did not open doors to his British relatives. Others
receiving privileges crisscrossed the Atlantic in the fashion of the Empire's
elite citizens of the world. One of them, Thomas Charles Cadogan, claimed
descent, not from an African ancestor, but from an aboriginal Jamaican and
went back and forth to Britain. Years later, he came into the orbit of London's
Old Bailey court, after being robbed of some goods. Richard Clarke, who
described himself as a quadroon in his 1788 petition, left for England at a
young age and married there. His wife stayed behind when Clarke returned to
Jamaica years later. In submitting privilege appeals during the start of popular
abolitionism, mixed-race Jamaicans still held up British instruction as a virtue
meriting special treatment. The assembly appears to have responded in turn,
conferring privileged rights on all but one of those who mentioned such an
upbringing.[32]

The single exception was for the young girl Bridget McDermot Kein. In
December 1790, Bridget's father Patrick Kein submitted a privilege appeal
for her and her mother Sarah Symes, a free mulatto. In the petition, Patrick
bragged of his intention to "send his reputed Daughter to Great-Britain, to
be brought up in a decent and creditable Manner." Patrick was a prosperous
planter in the parish of Saint Mary and had more than enough money to afford
the expense. He had achieved so much success in his work that he published
an advice manual on running plantations six years after submitting Sarah and
Bridget's privilege appeal. Abolitionism, if not his own family experiences, influenced his tract, as he commanded planters to treat slaves rationally and as
fellow creatures. Patrick Kein was no abolitionist, but he did believe that reform would benefit all in the plantation system. Nothing in his 1790 privilege
appeal indicated a potential problem with either Bridget's or her mother's
background that might compromise the request. The assembly simply refused
to vote on the petition after its initial reading. This was a rare occurrence. The
assembly turned down only a handful of petitions in the eighteenth century,

32. The petitions can be found in Acts of the Assembly of Jamaica, Dec. 6, 1788, CO
140/73, fols. 21, 102, 123, Dec. 16, 1791, CO 140/77, fol. 96, May 28, 1746, CO 140/33, fol. 9,
NAE. For the robbery perpetrated against Cadogan, see *The Proceedings of the Old Bailey
Online: London's Central Criminal Court, 1674 to 1913*, "William Henry Rawlinson, John
Rawlinson, John Rawlinson, Theft," Jan. 14, 1818, reference number: t18180114-121, www
.oldbaileyonline.org.

particularly because the exorbitant fees incurred simply for lodging a privilege appeal made them available only to the most elite individuals of color.[33]

The issue plaguing Kein's petition appears, rather, to have been rooted in long-standing personal animosities and demonstrates the extreme vulnerability that mixed-race migrants faced even when they had a generous father. The story began in 1760, when Sarah Symes was an enslaved woman on the Brimmer-Hall plantation in Saint Mary. That year, Sarah left the plantation to live with Patrick. It is unclear if her father, Robert, had attempted to free her before she left the estate; if he had, he failed to file the necessary paperwork. Over the course of the next nine years, Brimmer-Hall changed hands twice: first to the prominent planter Zachary Bayly in 1762 and finally to his son Nathaniel Bayly, uncle to Bryan Edwards, the famous political commentator, assemblyman, and chief member of Britain's West India Committee lobby. In 1776, Sarah gave birth to Kein's daughter, Bridget. The occasion prompted Patrick to inquire if Sarah's manumission had been effected properly. Because Nathaniel Bayly was off the island, Patrick approached his nephew Bryan Edwards instead. Edwards broke the news that an emancipation had never been officially filed, making Sarah, and thus Bridget, still legally enslaved. At the same time, Sarah's father Robert appears to have written Nathaniel Bayly in the hope of purchasing their freedom. It is not clear how Bayly responded, but, from later newspaper reports, Bryan Edwards either granted the manumission himself or provided some kind of assurance soon after Bridget's birth that she and Sarah were no longer considered property of Brimmer-Hall. Either way, the freedom of both mother and daughter dangled in the balance, with only hazy legal clearance, even as Kein prepared to send his daughter to Britain.[34]

Things came to a head when Nathaniel Bayly ran for public office in 1787. Bayly had only recently returned to Jamaica and canvassed Kein before the election. Enraged by Bayly's apparent reluctance to acknowledge his mistress's and daughter's manumissions, Patrick turned away the candidate. Not surprisingly, this did not please Bayly, and, on the day of the election, he issued Patrick with a creditor's demand to return Sarah and Bridget to

33. *Votes of the Honourable House of Assembly of Jamaica; in a Session Begun October 26th, 1790, and Ended March 5th, 1791; Being the Fifth Session of the Present Assembly* (Spanish Town, Jamaica, 1791), 97; Patrick Kein, *An Essay upon Pen-Keeping and Plantership* (Kingston, Jamaica, 1796), 18–19. See also, Roberts, *Slavery and the Enlightenment*, 216–233.

34. The account of the Keins' trial comes from the *Cornwall Chronicle, and Jamaica General Advertiser,* Sept. 20, 1788, Supplement, and Sept. 27, 1788, Supplement.

Brimmer-Hall. The issue eventually made its way to Jamaica's Supreme Court and caught the public eye. Jamaica's *Cornwall Chronicle* reported on the case, and a large number of inhabitants testified on behalf of Patrick and his "unfortunate child." The newspaper recoiled at the spectacle of "dreadful uncertainty hanging over [Patrick's] mind, whether [Bridget] might not possibly be adjudged the slave of a man, whom he conceived his bitterest enemy." Indeed, Bridget made a strong impression. The paper described her as "a most beautiful girl of about 11 or 12 years of age [who] interested the beholders in a high degree." Perhaps her charms worked. In the fall of 1788, the court decided in favor of the Keins. Sarah and Bridget were now officially free.[35]

The Keins' case reveals the vulnerabilities attendant on any kind of familial connection to slavery, even for those who were future candidates for privileged rights and European travel. Bridget was bound for Britain, but her ancestral past was grounded in chattel labor. Reenslavement was all too common in the Caribbean and could happen to even the indulged child of color. Moreover, the personal animosities between Kein and Nathaniel Bayly demonstrate the occasional breakdown in white-Jamaican solidarity. By standing up for his family, Patrick picked a political fight that undercut his own status, even as a thriving planter. Nathaniel Bayly won his bid for assemblyman of Saint Mary in 1787, and he continued to sit in the house through 1790, when the Keins' privilege petition appeared in its chambers. As a member of one of Jamaica's most influential families, Bayly would have had no problem killing the appeal, even with his own fraught reputation. Indeed, Bayly was most likely responsible for the bill's failure. The privileged networks of white society could thus cut both ways for elite Jamaicans of color. Connections to prominent fathers often led to advanced rights and even an education abroad. But, as shown in the Kein case, whiteness was not the sole linkage in Jamaica's networks of influence. Wealthy Jamaicans of color could sometimes share kinship to the wrong white family.[36]

Kein's plan to send his daughter of color to Britain shows the significance of that act in the last decade of the eighteenth century. Having narrowly escaped

35. Ibid., Sept. 27, 1788.

36. Reenslavement could easily occur, and legal documentation was vital for individuals of color to avoid it. For a comparison, see the case of Paul Carenan in John D. Garrigus, *Before Haiti: Race and Citizenship in French Saint-Domingue* (New York, 2006), 83–84. The year before Kein's privilege bill came before the assembly, Jamaica's Supreme Court found Bayly guilty of trespassing on the estate of Alexander Grant and cutting down twenty acres of sugarcane with free and enslaved workers; see *Cornwall Chronicle, and Jamaica General Advertiser*, Dec. 12, 1789, Supplement.

reenslavement, Bridget's removal to the metropole was surely intended to bestow a status fully divorced from colonial bondage. Other Jamaicans of color with more secure claims to freedom undertook the same migration for similar effect. Some of them might have paid for the passage themselves, rather than relying on a white benefactor. The private benefit of this practice outweighed whatever public scorn was beginning to mount against elites of color in Britain. Nevertheless, those debates were prominent and only grew more so as abolitionist fervor increased. Whites in Jamaica who were all too familiar with the realities of racial mixture might have dismissed some of these arguments as old or exaggerated, but interested Britons maintained their attention. This meant that families welcoming relatives of color into their British homes at the end of the eighteenth century did so within a cultural milieu more attuned to such a phenomenon. When mixed-race kin arrived from Jamaica, they could not escape this new political atmosphere.[37]

Arriving in Britain

On a summer's jaunt through Hampshire in 1784, English composer John Marsh met with family and friends for a quick visit to the Isle of Wight. Marsh noted without further comment that the boat that took them from Gosport to the island was "row'd by 6. blacks." The presence of these nonwhite sailors outside bustling London is hardly astonishing considering the large number of African-descended inhabitants in eighteenth-century Britain. More peculiarly, though perhaps still not unusual, Marsh attended the violin concerto of the mixed-race Guadeloupean Joseph Boulogne in England three years later. Even Marsh's home bore evidence of a black cultural influence. He humorously recorded an instance in which his son compared Marsh's friend to the portrait of a black bassoon player displayed in the family study. Not only did he routinely witness individuals of African descent in servile and performing capacities in England, but he stayed closely informed of emerging discussions about race and slavery in the abolition movement: he sat through antislavery sermons by Beilby Porteus and abolition debates between William Wilberforce and Bryan Edwards in Parliament. Like many other Britons, Marsh en-

37. Evidence of Jamaicans of color leaving the island can be found in passenger manifests printed in Montego Bay's *Cornwall Chronicle*. See, in particular, the notes for Susannah and Sarah Shermer and for Joseph Rodney Ibanks—all of whom were listed as free quadroons sailing from Jamaica; see *Cornwall Chronicle, and Jamaica General Advertiser*, Oct. 23, 1790, Supplement. They could have potentially afforded the trip on their own. Self-financed voyages became more regular at the turn of the nineteenth century, as households of color began accumulating larger troves of wealth.

gaged with metropolitan black residents as well as with the popular uproar over the slave trade.[38]

Within this sphere of activity, Marsh came to learn of a relation of color. In 1786, John received a message that his brother Edward had died in Jamaica. During a long tour on the island with the Royal Navy as captain of the ship *Europa,* Edward fell from a horse and broke his leg. Within weeks, a bacterial infection coursed through his body. Gangrene eventually claimed Edward's limb and ultimately his life in September 1786. News of his passing crossed the Atlantic, reaching the Marsh family several weeks later. Thomas Williams, husband to Edward and John's sister Mary, first read the report, which he then conveyed to the rest of the family. John Marsh was obviously upset to learn of his brother's fate. The uncertainty of life in the Caribbean, let alone of early modern medicine, perhaps reduced Marsh's surprise. But he was not prepared to discover from the same letter that a mixed-race nephew was living in Jamaica. Edward had left behind a son of the same name by a "West India wife."[39]

38. *The John Marsh Journals: The Life and Times of a Gentleman Composer (1752–1828),* ed. Brian Robins (Stuyvesant, N.Y., 1998), Aug. 24, 1784, 326, Apr. 7, 1786, 372, Apr. 1, 1787, 400, 410, Sept. 28, 1788, 439; John Marsh Autobiography, April 1797, XVIII, fols. 95–96, HM 54457, HL. Marsh was not a member of Parliament but attended the debate as a visitor. For Marsh as a prominent musician, see John Brewer, *The Pleasures of the Imagination: English Culture in the Eighteenth Century* (Chicago, 1997), 531–572. On the regular presence of black Britons in the eighteenth century, see, for instance, James Walvin, *The Black Presence: A Documentary History of the Negro in England, 1555–1860* (London, 1971); Walvin, *Black and White: The Negro and English Society, 1555–1945* (London, 1973); Folarin Shyllon, *Black People in Britain, 1555–1833* (New York, 1977); Peter Fryer, *Staying Power: The History of Black People in Britain since 1504* (Atlantic Highlands, N.J., 1984); Gretchen Gerzina, *Black England: Life before Emancipation* (London, 1995); Kathleen Chater, *Untold Histories: Black People in England and Wales during the Period of the British Slave Trade, c. 1660–1807* (New York, 2009); Norma Meyers, "Servant, Sailor, Soldier, Tailor, Beggarman: Black Survival in White Society, 1780–1830," *Immigrants and Minorities,* XII (1993), 47–74; Meyers, *Reconstructing the Black Past: Blacks in Britain, 1780–1830* (London., 1996); Douglas A. Lorimer, "Black Slaves and English Liberty: A Re-examination of Racial Slavery in England," *Immigrants and Minorities,* III (1984), 121–150; and Isaac Land, "Bread and Arsenic: Citizenship from the Bottom Up in Georgian London," *Journal of Social History,* XXXIX (2005), 89–110. For more on the popularity of the abolition movement and the degree to which it saturated British society at every level, see Brown, *Moral Capital;* Seymour Drescher, *Capitalism and Antislavery: British Popular Mobilization in Comparative Perspective* (Oxford, 1986); and James Walvin, "The Propaganda of Anti-Slavery," in Walvin, ed., *Slavery and British Society,* 49–68.

39. John Marsh Autobiography, Nov. 25, 1786, X, fols. 181–182; *John Marsh Journals,*

Edward Thomas Marsh was born in Jamaica on July 2, 1785, and was only a year old when his father died. His mother was either a black or mixed-race woman who likely depended on her companion's largesse. The death of Edward senior might have radically changed her social position on the island. Without a living white lover, her patronage options were much different. As correspondence circulated across the ocean, Edward Thomas and his mother waited behind, suddenly bereft of a white patriarch who might partially shield them from the inequities of colonial society.[40]

John Marsh's initial reaction to the news of his nephew was not explicitly concerned with questions of race. Instead, Marsh responded skeptically to the boy's lineage: "I must confess I at first rather demur'd . . . under the idea of its being a common bastard that co'd not be certainly authenticated to be [Edward's]." Illegitimacy marked Edward Thomas more so than heritage, but the accuracy of his genealogy was most important. Casting doubt on kinship was not wholly unreasonable. Many colonists hid illegitimate children of color from British family members and did not disclose their existence until death freed them from the burden of maintaining the secret. Wills frequently served as official messengers, bearing witness to their authors' colonial indulgences.[41]

Marsh's cynicism about his nephew of color speaks to the insecurity that Britons held toward family fortunes in the periphery. Beyond their fears that white relatives had formed mixed-race households who might dissipate family wealth, Britons such as Marsh also worried that illegitimate relatives of color could be the products of outright scams. Ann Fraser Robertson balked at the supposed will of her brother John, who died in Spanish East Florida. On discovering that she would share her late brother's fortune with his four mixed-race children, one of whom attended school in Liverpool, she filed suit to

---

ed. Robins, Nov. 25, 1786, 391. Edward Marsh died in the early part of September in Spanish Town; see *Cornwall Chronicle, and Jamaica General Advertiser,* Sept. 16, 1786, Supplement; *Morning Chronicle, and London Advertiser,* Nov. 25, 1786; Bern Anderson, *Surveyor of the Sea: The Life and Voyages of Captain George Vancouver* (Seattle, 1960), 23–25. A "West India Wife" was a euphemism for a black or mixed-race companion.

40. John Marsh Autobiography, July 1788, XII, fols. 59–60. For more on the small avenues of redress that came with a relationship to a white man, see Barbara Bush, *Slave Women in Caribbean Society: 1650–1838* (Bloomington, Ind., 1990).

41. *John Marsh Journals,* ed. Robins, Nov. 25, 1786, 391. Probate procedures often revealed mixed-race relatives kept hidden behind thousands of miles of ocean; see Vincent Brown, *The Reaper's Garden: Death and Power in the World of Atlantic Slavery* (Cambridge, Mass., 2008), 107–120.

dismiss John's will as fraudulent. Her plea incorrectly assumed that the estate was "devised to certain persons of Colour who it is pretended are the natural children of the said John Fraser . . . but it is not known whether the said persons of Colour . . . are in existence." Without firsthand knowledge of the colonies, family members such as Robertson had to trust the veracity of strangers charged to resolve their kin's estate. British society at large fretted over illegitimate children and their capacity to unseat family legacies. Popular literature regularly employed the trope of an illegitimate pretender to the bequests of middle- and upper-class households. In Marsh's case, his brother had little to protect. The deceased left behind a modest two hundred pounds that legally devolved to his brothers and sister in England, as he had failed to craft a will. Overcoming their objections to Edward Thomas's illegitimacy, John Marsh and his siblings "all agreed to give up [the sum] for the maintenance and bringing up of the infant." Caring for such a child without any legal recourse to his father's estate required strong allegiances between family members to honor a deceased relative's wishes at the expense of their own finances.[42]

John Marsh did not formally dispute the veracity of his nephew's genealogy, nor did he balk at the news that Edward Thomas was on his way to live with the family in England. The Jamaican naval officer who passed along all of this information apparently provided sufficient evidence to satisfy the English family. "The Mother really lived with my Brother," Marsh declared, "and had certainly cohabited with no other person during that time." This was his only observation about her, perhaps owing to a lack of knowledge or to a refusal to maintain any ties. But he did accept responsibility for her son. "I not only consented but wish'd to cooperate . . . in providing for the Child, especially as it seem'd that my Brother had intended taking him with him to England, had he lived."[43] Once again, Edward Thomas Marsh's inclusion in the family was considered along consanguineous, rather than racial, lines. A commitment to his father's wishes inspired kinship, even when it would demand taking full care of a new child. Considering the important role that guardian-

42. Petition of William Robertson and Ann Fraser Robertson to the Superior Court of East Florida, 1823, John Fraser Estate Collection, folder 27, WCL; John Marsh Autobiography, Nov. 25, 1786, X, fols. 181–182. On the Fraser case generally, see Daniel L. Schafer, "Family Ties That Bind: Anglo-African Slave Traders in Africa and Florida, John Fraser and His Descendants," *Slavery and Abolition*, XX, no. 3 (December 1999), 1–21. For discussions of general British fears about illegitimate children as rival heirs, see Lisa Zunshine, *Bastards and Foundlings: Illegitimacy in Eighteenth-Century England* (Columbus, Ohio, 2005), 121–123.

43. John Marsh Autobiography, Nov. 25, 1786, X, fols. 181–182.

ship, fostering, stepparenting, proto-adoption, and—to a diminishing degree by the eighteenth century—godparentage played in the early modern world, such inclusion of illegitimate relatives was not wholly out of the ordinary. The regularity of bastard children might have also been an influence.[44] John Marsh dealt with the issue again when his son Henry later admitted to having a daughter out of wedlock. Much more a pragmatist than an ideologue, John Marsh accepted the realities of daily life. Familial complexity was, to him, a given, and Edward Thomas was yet another nontraditional relative in need of support.[45]

44. For guardianship, fostering, stepparenting, proto-adoption, and godparentage, see Helen Berry and Elizabeth Foyster, "Childless Men in Early Modern England," in Berry and Foyster, eds., *The Family in Early Modern England* (New York, 2007), 158–183; Richard Grassby, *Kinship and Capitalism: Marriage, Family, and Business in the English-Speaking World, 1580–1740* (New York, 2001), 234; Stephen Collins, "'Reason, Nature, and Order': The Stepfamily in English Renaissance Thought," *Renaissance Studies,* XIII (1999), 312–324; and Will Coster, *Baptism and Spiritual Kinship in Early Modern England* (Burlington, Vt., 2002). For illegitimacy rates, which soared in the eighteenth century (although changes in measurement might have played as much a role as those in behavior to account for this shift), see Ann Twinam, *Public Lives, Private Secrets: Gender, Honor, Sexuality, and Illegitimacy in Colonial Spanish America* (Stanford, Calif., 1999), 7; Peter Laslett, Karla Oosterveen, and Richard M. Smith, eds., *Bastardy and Its Comparative History: Studies in the History of Illegitimacy and Marital Nonconformism in Britain, France, Germany, Sweden, North America, Jamaica, and Japan* (London, 1980); Richard Adair, *Courtship, Illegitimacy, and Marriage in Early Modern England* (New York, 1996); Rosalind Mitchison and Leah Leneman, *Sexuality and Social Control: Scotland, 1660–1780* (New York, 1989); John Black, "Who Were the Putative Fathers of Illegitimate Children in London, 1740–1810?" in Alysa Levene, Thomas Nutt, and Samantha Williams, eds., *Illegitimacy in Britain, 1700–1920* (New York, 2005), 50–65; Nicholas Rogers, "Carnal Knowledge: Illegitimacy in Eighteenth-Century Westminster," *Journal of Social History,* XXIII (1989), 355–375; Peter Laslett, *Family Life and Illicit Love in Earlier Generations: Essays in Historical Sociology* (New York, 1977); Andrew Blaikie, *Illegitimacy, Sex, and Society: Northeast Scotland, 1750–1900* (New York, 1993); Laslett, "A Kind of Loving: Illegitimacy, Grandparents, and the Rural Economy of North-East Scotland, 1750–1900," *Scottish Economic and Social History,* XIV (1994), 41–57; and Belinda Meteyard, "Illegitimacy and Marriage in Eighteenth-Century England," *Journal of Interdisciplinary History,* X (1980), 479–489.

45. Henry had waited twelve years to divulge the secret to his father, reassuring him that the young woman was at a school in northern England. Once more, John Marsh reacted calmly to the news. Ultimately, he was relieved to find that there was no "seduction" involved with the woman and that further interaction had stopped; see John Marsh Autobiography, 1816, XXXI, fols. 25–26. Marsh was also not shy in acknowledging sexuality and its manifestations; see William Weber, "The Fabric of Daily Life and the Autobiography of John Marsh," *Huntington Library Quarterly,* LIX (1996), 158–161.

The final right of acceptance came on the young Jamaican's landing in England in the summer of 1788. He had traveled from the island with another child, possibly also of mixed heritage herself, under the supervision of a naval captain. They arrived at the house of John Marsh's sister Mary and her husband Thomas Williams. If the family secretly held any suspicions about the child's paternity, they dissolved on seeing his face. "I was much struck with his resemblance," John Marsh proclaimed, "to my Brother Edward when he was a Child." Blood ties overcame any objections to the young boy's status or non-European heritage. Marsh's only comment on the children's foreignness came at the expense of their clothes. "Both he and the little Girl then made but an uncouth appearance, being dress'd according to the taste of the Country they came from." Yet, this sartorial and cultural distinction was easily overcome, he remarked, for their attire "was now soon altered by my Sister for a better." Edward Thomas was colonial and perhaps exotic but not unchangeably so.[46]

Within the Marsh family, personal reactions to the arrival of a mixed-race relative were not heavily concerned with the issue of African heritage. Despite the current furor over abolition, illegitimacy and colonial status were still greater impediments to family inclusion than biological ties to enslaved Jamaicans. This is not to claim that notions of race did not inform the Marshes' attitudes toward Edward Thomas. John Marsh's initial reluctance to acknowledge his brother's paternity as well as his surprise at the resemblance between father and son contained implicit anxieties about the place of a mixed-race child in the English family. But those racial cues did not dominate the family's process in coming to terms with Edward Thomas's presence and were certainly not stated outright. The young man was eventually adopted by Thomas and Mary and led a life in England effectively disconnected from a past rooted partly in slavery. John Marsh recorded frequent visits with Edward Thomas over the ensuing years. Together they attended concerts, played music, and fished. Inclusive kinship, not enlightened ideals of racial equality, cleared a path toward metropolitan assimilation unburdened from colonial origins.[47]

James Taylor's family in Scotland prepared for his arrival in much the same

46. John Marsh Autobiography, July 1788, XII, fols. 59–60. John Marsh writes that the captain's surname was "Countess," but Nevil Harvey Williams notes that in later letters the captain's name is referred to as "Hutt"; see ibid., fol. 59; and Williams, "The Williams Family in the 18th and 19th Centuries in the UK" (unpublished manuscript), 45. Many thanks to Nevil Harvey Williams for allowing me access to his manuscript.

47. *John Marsh Journals*, ed. Robins, Oct. 22, 1788, 440–441, Dec. 17, 1790, 483, Aug. 14, 1791, 497, May 29, 1794, 555, Aug. 21, 1801, 738, Sept. 22, 1801, 739.

way. Before the boy came over, his grandmother Jean showed regular interest in his early progress. "Tell me what has becom of your Baby that you mentiont to me" she implored her son John soon after James's birth, for "I would be very happy to have it under my Car[e]." When John failed to provide sufficient information on the boy, she scolded him, demanding, "Why have you not in your last two letters Sead one word of My Young Friend James if he is Still doing well, lett me know in your next." Although John revealed his Jamaican offspring to British relatives, Jean often received news of her grandchildren of color from extended family. She learned of the birth of John's second and third children, for example, through the relatives of her son-in-law. In choosing to make public his private life in the colonies, John Tailyour prepared to connect his Jamaican and Scottish families. He would depend on the latter for his children's success in Britain.[48]

From the start, the Scottish Tailyours wrote of Jamaican relatives from a familial perspective when managing their affairs. Yet, aspects of the children's race seeped into this correspondence in a much more explicit fashion than the Marshes. James's uncle Robert was one of the first to learn of his future arrival and proved instrumental in finding him a school. When writing back to John about a plan of education, Robert assured him: "I approve very much of your sentiments respecting your little family. . . . It is surely incumbent on us to provide for our Offspring whether Black or White." Robert's letter demonstrates two points. First, he understood James to be an acknowledged and supported child of his brother. Although his diminutive reference to John's "little family" indicates Robert's distinction between the Jamaican and Scottish Tailyours, he nevertheless described James as a member of his brother's household. This might have been a difficult concession for Robert to make. Caring for illegitimate children was not altogether unusual, especially for members of Britain's upper classes, but openly acknowledging them was. Second, Robert's mention of James's African ancestry stands in contrast to the Marshes, who made no overt reference to Edward Thomas's heritage. Such recognition would influence his future associations with James.[49]

48. Jean Tailyour to John Tailyour, Aug. 14, 1787, Tailyour Papers, WCL, Feb. 21, 1789, Nov. 20, 1789. British commentators at the end of the eighteenth century generally held that grandparents were important actors in the upbringing of a child; see Bailey, *Parenting in England*, 200–210.

49. Robert Taylor to John Tailyour, Aug. 27, 1791, Tailyour Papers, WCL. Throughout the eighteenth century, children were understood to be deserving of support, regardless of their situation; see Alysa Levene, *The Childhood of the Poor: Welfare in Eighteenth-Century London* (New York, 2012), 8–10. For more on the steps wealthy fathers took for illegitimate

The remainder of Robert's remarks balanced carefully between issues of family position and racial makeup. Much like John Marsh's concern over Edward Thomas's illegitimacy, Robert worried that the mark of bastardy would most hamper James's success. He conceded that Jean "would treat him with the same Kindness and attention as if he had been born in [we]dlock" but anticipated that his illegitimacy would "mortify him the more, as soon as he has Sense to know the disadvantages with which he has been ushered into Life." Bastardy was indeed burdensome, but it was not unusual. Illegitimacy rates in Scotland, particularly in the northeast inhabited by the Tailyours, appear to have increased from the eighteenth to the nineteenth centuries. Moreover, some evidence suggests, albeit for the Highlands, that the Scottish elite regularly treated illegitimate children similarly to younger, legitimate offspring. Half-siblings on both sides of the legitimacy barrier were often raised in the same homes or fostered by the same families. Yet, on the question of bringing up James with Scottish relatives, Robert demurred: "By keeping him at a distance from his own Relations I think there is the greater chance of concealing from him his Inferiority and preventing the Mortification of being slighted by relations who from early habits he might consider himself perfectly upon a footing with." Such "Inferiority" might have been a nod to James's African heritage, but it fits better with Robert's more immediate concerns over illegitimacy. Without legal claim to an inheritance and thousands of miles from a colonial family only recently freed from slavery, James's finances and social standing were tenuous. Class difference frequently trumped racial distinction in the treatment of illegitimate offspring in Britain, but, without any solid right to their fathers' immense fortunes, mixed-race children taken to the metropole were often just as financially indeterminate as they were racially ambiguous. For Robert, James's fiscal disadvantages tied to illegitimacy, more so than coloration, kept him apart from full family recognition. Abolitionist discourse might have aroused some racial indignation in the Tailyours — Robert called Wilberforce "ridiculous" and John labeled his followers "Rogues and Fools" — but it did not overwhelm their approach to James. After all, most eighteenth-century parents wanted nothing more

---

children, see Patricia Crawford, *Parents of Poor Children in England, 1580–1800* (New York, 2010), 86–91. Adult brothers often depended strongly on one another, both for personal and professional help, and uncles were frequently called on to care for nieces and nephews for short periods; see Leonore Davidoff, *Thicker Than Water: Siblings and Their Relations, 1780–1920* (New York, 2012), 175–179.

than to place their children into the ordered and prescribed lines dictated by society.[50]

Robert's suggestion to remove James from Montrose demanded some critical reflection from the family. The Scottish seaport was not an educational epicenter, but it was also not a backwater; young James would not necessarily have floundered there. The American traveler Jabez Maud Fisher described Montrose in 1775 as a "neat well built town," especially compared to its modest surroundings. Among the Angus burghs radiating out from Dundee, Montrose held the highest proportion of genteel residents and was one of the wealthiest towns in the region. Cities and towns throughout Scotland underwent dramatic improvement in the eighteenth century, though not necessarily at the same time, nor at the same pace. Montrose was an exemplar of this movement to update Scotland's civic institutions and apply Enlightenment thinking to urban living. The town redesigned its High Street in 1734 as a means of beautification, and its residents formed the Montrose Club in 1760 to host balls and assemblies for gentry scattered throughout the county. In the spirit of this reform, many town members came out against the slave trade in the 1790s. Ironically, though, much of the money for these changes came from returning sons who had made their fortunes in the West and East Indies. John Tailyour and Hercules Ross were included within that number, and they certainly would have seen themselves as the type of enlightened Scots now dominating Montrose's elite. If Tailyour wished to offer his son

50. Robert Taylor to John Tailyour, Aug. 27, 1791, Tailyour Papers, WCL, Robert Taylor to John Tailyour, Nov. 2, 1791; John Tailyour to John and Alex Anderson, July 12, 1789, John Tailyour Letter Book, II, Tailyour Papers, WCL. For more on illegitimacy in eighteenth-century Scotland, see Blaikie, *Illegitimacy, Sex, and Society;* Laslett, "A Kind of Loving," *Scottish Economic and Social History,* XIV (1994), 51–55; Stana Nenadic, *Lairds and Luxury: The Highland Gentry in Eighteenth-Century Scotland* (Edinburgh, 2007), 45, 123, 149. Scottish kinship was perhaps even stronger abroad, as fictive relations helped cement bonds in the colonies; see Douglas Hamilton, *Scotland, the Caribbean, and the Atlantic World, 1750–1820* (New York, 2005), 22–27. On Eurasian children in Britain, see Margot Finn, "Anglo-Indian Lives in the Later Eighteenth and Early Nineteenth Centuries," *Journal for Eighteenth-Century Studies,* XXXIII (2010), 59–61. Peter Robb finds that Richard Blechynden also commented more on his mixed-race child's illegitimacy, rather than his race, after the young boy was sent to Britain from Bengal; see Robb, "Children, Emotion, Identity, and Empire: Views from the Blechyndens' Calcutta Diaries (1790–1822)," *Modern Asian Studies,* XL (2006), 175–201. For the importance parents placed on adhering to prescribed social roles for children, see Anthony Fletcher, *Growing up in England: The Experience of Childhood, 1600–1914* (New Haven, Conn., 2008), 51.

James a good education and refined upbringing, then he could have chosen much worse locations than his hometown. No doubt his brother's recommendation to find a school outside Scotland influenced Tailyour heavily, and distance between his white and mixed-race families grew to become a vital factor in his decisions for James.[51]

Once Tailyour approved to settle James in England, Robert sought advice on appropriate schools south of the Tweed. London seemed out of the question, as it appeared to offer too many temptations. Robert claimed to have witnessed personally the ruin of many mixed-race migrants in the capital, stating, "Such has been the fate of two thirds of the Young men who I have known of [James's] description." Moreover, the expense of London was simply too much, especially if their ultimate fate might be back in the colonies, rather than in Britain. Just two months after offering his original suggestions to Tailyour, Robert discovered several prospective institutions in northern England. In a postscript to a 1791 letter, Robert noted, "I have heard of a School in Yorkshire which I think will answer for your Young ones." He did not specify if the institution had a reputation for teaching children of color, but he had certainly asked his correspondents for guidance, including a former Jamaican assemblyman and slave trader from Kingston, Jasper Hall, whose own son attended the school. "From what Hall mentioned of it to [Simon] Taylor and myself," Robert relayed, "I have no doubt it Will answer the Purpose you Wish." Robert eventually settled on the institution run by John Bowman

---

51. *An American Quaker in the British Isles: The Travel Journals of Jabez Maud Fisher, 1775–1779*, ed. Kenneth Morgan (New York, 1992), Oct. 1, 1775, 60–61; Gordon Jackson and S. G. E. Lythe, eds., *The Port of Montrose: A History of Its Harbor, Trade, and Shipping* (Wainscott, N.Y., 1993), xix–xxv; Bob Harris, "Towns, Improvement, and Cultural Change in Georgian Scotland: The Evidence of the Angus Burghs, c. 1760–1820," *Urban History*, XXXIII (2006), 195–212; Harris, "Merchants, the Middling Sort, and Cultural Life in Georgian Dundee," in Charles McKean, Harris, and Christopher A. Whatley, eds., *Dundee: Renaissance to Enlightenment* (Dundee, U.K., 2009), 243. For more on the quality and unevenness of Scottish improvement in the eighteenth century, see T. M. Devine, "The Making of a Farming Elite? Lowland Scotland, 1750–1850," in Devine, ed., *Scottish Elites: Proceedings of the Scottish Historical Studies Seminar University of Strathclyde, 1991–1992* (Edinburgh, 1994), 62–76; Richard B. Sher, "Scotland Transformed: The Eighteenth Century," in Jenny Wormald, ed., *Scotland: A History* (New York, 2005), 177–208; and Bob Harris, Charles McKean, and Christopher Whatley, "An Introduction to Georgian Dundee," in McKean, Harris, and Whatley, eds., *Dundee: Renaissance to Enlightenment*, 132–159. On issues more pertinent to Montrose, see Iain Whyte, *Scotland and the Abolition of Black Slavery, 1756–1838* (Edinburgh, 2006), 43, 84; and Harris, "Towns, Improvement, and Cultural Change," *Urban History*, XXXIII (2006), 201–206.

just outside Durham. He also recommended another Yorkshire school, kept by the Reverend James Milner, for when James became a little older. Once again, Yorkshire schools proved an attractive option to Jamaicans resettling mixed-race kin. The county's simultaneous remoteness from, and proximity to, Scotland likely convinced Tailyour of its useful location.[52]

When word came to Jean Tailyour that her grandchild would be educated in England, she grew sad about his future distance from family. Robert broke the news to his mother, who then lamented to John, "Bob told me that you was to Satel James in Ingland as he had wrot you that he thought it much better then in this Country." Jean understood but grew anxious that James, only five years old at the time, would be too young on his own. Unlike Robert, Jean did not wish to push James out into the periphery of their family circle, especially as the young boy had so ingratiated himself with the clan. Her daughter Catherine, who took care of James, agreed with the decision. Still, Jean noted that, on learning of James's departure, Catherine "was Sorry for . . . he is a very Cl[e]ver good tempert Boy." She hoped that John would "let him Stay Some time with [Catherine] as he is So very young and not proper to go to a publick Scool." Under the guidance of his aunt, James could better continue the transition from Jamaica to Britain. "Had I been living in the Country I would Sertenly have kept him with me," Jean offered hypothetically, "but this Town (Montrose) is not So proper." Jean had moved to the town after the death of her husband Robert in 1780. The family had been forced to sell both of its large rural estates in the wake of his passing, and Jean took up residence in nearby Montrose. It is unclear if she believed that James would suffer less discrimination in the countryside or if she simply did not wish to have neighbors commenting on her mixed-race grandson in the more compact environs of a town.[53]

Bowman's school, more than two hundred miles from Tailyour's family,

52. Robert Taylor to John Tailyour, Feb. 1, 1792, Tailyour Papers, WCL, Oct. 5, 1791, Oct. 26, 1791, Jan. 4, 1792. During this period, Durham fell into the county of Yorkshire. An advertisement for Hall's slave sales can be found in the *Jamaica Gazette* (Kingston), Jan. 3, 1765. Milner kept his school at Scorton, near Catterick, charging sixteen pounds per year for each student; see *Diary; or, Woodfall's Register* (London), Apr. 1, 1791. See also, Chapter 2, above.

53. Jean Tailyour to John Tailyour, Sept. 24, 1791, Tailyour Papers, WCL, Mar. 27, 1792. The family estates were Kirktonhill, on which the family house was built, and Balmanno. Colonel David Gairdner purchased Kirktonhill, and Alex Smith purchased Balmanno after Robert Tailyour's death. See Andrew Jervise, *Epitaphs and Inscriptions from Burial Grounds and Old Buildings in the North-East of Scotland* (Edinburgh, 1875), 134.

PLATE 8. Byers Green Hall. Photograph by John Alderson Photography.
Courtesy of Lil Cassie

was not a cosmopolitan alternative to Montrose. The proprietor instructed students at Byers Green Hall, the former homestead of the Trotter family, just outside Durham. Complete with three hearths, the stone building was the largest of its village in the seventeenth century. Within the spirit of eighteenth-century improvement, the Trotter family had expanded and remodeled the home. By the time Bowman's father took it over as a school in the middle of the century, it bore a sophisticated, modern look (see Plate 8). Byers Green itself was a small enclave, and James Taylor would have found few things there to distract him from his studies. In fact, he was a dedicated student. Soon after his arrival, Bowman informed John Tailyour, "I am happy to say that James is very hearty and few there be that can exceed him in learning at his Age." Reputedly bright, James eagerly studied a variety of topics. Mathematics and grammar were the first subjects he tackled, but slowly he added Latin, advanced accounting, and bookkeeping. These courses prepared James for a possible career in overseas trade. Under private instruction, the young Jamaican acquired the rudiments of a refined education—a professional requirement for a potential British merchant and gentleman. James's family monitored his learning from its outset. Robert believed Bowman's teaching would be "sufficient to give him all the Instruction that Will be necessary to enable him to make his way in the World with a little of [Tailyour's] Assistance." Like many young men in Britain, James's absence from family while at boarding school likely proved hard to endure, but a closely supervised education would enable him to thrive when he reached maturity.[54]

The Tailyour family's decisions put James on a path toward relative financial independence. Kinship was vital to achieve such success as West Indians of color had few options beyond their families. An English newspaper announcement in Bath from 1788 reflected this vulnerability, reporting on "Two Jamaica Youths of *Colour,* In Great Distress" after their father failed to send remittances. Similarly, English poet Robert Southey recalled that "the natural son of a wealthy planter by a woman of color" who attended his Bristol school in the 1780s—one of "a good many Creoles at this school"—later killed himself when his father stopped sending money. Most parents were not so negligent. Business associates were often called on to help when fathers stayed in the Caribbean. John Robertson, for instance, used professional contacts in Glasgow to maintain the accounts of his mixed-race children in Scotland between 1786 and 1789. Such assistance was nevertheless still built on family networks. The Tailyours' actions reflected a general desire to care for kin but also demonstrated a simultaneous reluctance to have relations of color too close, both physically and economically, to a legitimate household. Like many other mixed-race Jamaicans, James Taylor's arrival in Britain precipitated a flurry of family activity and preparation. Edward Thomas Marsh's relatives

54. John Bowman to John Tailyour, Apr. 14, 1793, Tailyour Papers, WCL, Dec. 31, 1795, Robert Taylor to John Tailyour, May 2, 1792, Nov. 28, 1792; Adrian Green, "Tudhoe Hall and Byers Green Hall, County Durham: Seventeenth and Early Eighteenth Century Social Change in Houses," *Vernacular Architecture,* XXIX (1998), 33–42. By the time that James arrived, Bowman's school had been in family hands for years. London's *Daily Advertiser* included an advertisement for the school in 1783, which noted that his father had previously run the school for thirty years. It also reported that students were instructed in classics, grammar (without learning Latin), mathematics, and drawing for twelve guineas a year; see *Daily Advertiser,* Mar. 20, 1783. The price had increased to thirteen guineas by 1792; see *Diary; or, Woodfall's Register,* Aug. 4, 1792.

worked just as hard when he landed in England three years earlier. Neither household made strong, nor terribly direct, comments about the children's ancestry despite how discourse surrounding the slave trade, including pronouncements on racial intermixture and mixed-race migration to Britain, was beginning to influence public opinion. Private attitudes had not yet adopted the growing disdain spouted in public toward the arrival of these elites of color, even if Britons with such relatives were closely engaged with those debates, both from the abolitionist side (Hercules Ross and John Marsh) and its opposition (the Tailyours). Family linkages no doubt helped to smooth out these differences.[55]

Saint Domingue and Migrants of Color

Mixed-race migration to Britain was not deliberated solely within the narrow band of abolition discourse, nor was it limited strictly to familial considerations. The Atlantic world appeared alive with change in this period. George III suffered a major bout of mental illness in 1788, prompting a crisis of genealogical succession in the royal household. That same year, Warren Hasting's trial officially commenced in Westminster, throwing still more attention on the moral and administrative character of Britain's Empire. Without question, the French Revolution of the next year would forever alter Britons' conception of political stability and civil society. As the Revolution progressed, and society unspooled, observers across the Channel began reconsidering the effects of moral reform. For Jamaicans of color in Britain, the most important developments to their own lives originated from the Caribbean. In 1790, several individuals of color in France returned to their home colony of Saint Domingue only to lead a small uprising against Dominguan officials that might have helped contribute to the colony's much larger slave rebellion the next summer. The Haitian Revolution forever altered West Indian politics and society. Officials in Jamaica reacted to the insurrection by offering some concessions to free and enslaved individuals with African heritage while simultaneously clamping down on those same populations. For both Jamaican and British observers, the minor uprising led by French-educated West Indians of color in 1790 tempered their acceptance of mixed-race schooling in the metropole generally.

Like Britain, France hosted a regular cohort of mixed-race students from

55. *Bath Chronicle* (Eng.), Nov. 6, 1788; Robert Southey, *The Life and Correspondence of Robert Southey,* ed. Charles Cuthbert Southey (New York, 1851), 42; Anonymous Journal of Glasgow Merchants, 1786–1789, Court of Session Papers, CS 96/1526, fols. 91–165, NAS.

its colonies. Most of these scholars came from the bustling and lucrative Caribbean colony of Saint Domingue.[56] The events of the French Revolution pushed some of these migrants to lobby for colonial reforms that would benefit freemen of color. Julien Raimond was one of the most vocal of these proponents, and he pushed the National Assembly to consider mixed-race enfranchisement in the Caribbean among its other reforms. Fellow Dominguan of color Vincent Ogé joined Raimond in petitioning for these rights in France. Ogé—a potential distant relation to Elizabeth Augier, the mother of John Morse's children of color—had a great deal of experience in the metropole. In 1768, he had left the West Indies for school in Bordeaux, before returning several years later to Saint Domingue. Despite having apprenticed as a goldsmith in France, once back Ogé became active in various colonial trades: coffee, real estate, and coastal commerce. Two of his sisters later departed for the same Bordeaux school, and Ogé traveled once more to France to bring them home. He also wished to collect on outstanding debts as well as appeal for reimbursement after colonial officials built a road through his coffee plantation. During Ogé's trip, Parisians stormed the Bastille. These revolutionary events inspired him, and he met with Raimond and other freemen of color in Paris to begin lobbying for the rights of the Empire's *gens de couleur libre* (free people of color).[57]

Ogé decided to travel back to Saint Domingue in 1790 after observing what he thought was the passage of an edict enfranchising the colony's free population of color. Parisian deputies had drafted an ambiguous colonial election

56. Still, nonwhites from other French colonies also indulged in the practice. In July 1789, Scottish physician Jonathan Troup met "the Mulattoe Accoucheur" in Dominica who had attended Parisian schools to learn anatomy, surgery, and midwifery; see Journal of Jonathan Troup, July 15, 1789, MS 2070, fol. 28, University of Aberdeen Special Collections Library, Aberdeen, Scotland. The most thorough and quantified consideration of nonwhites in eighteenth-century France (both black and Asian as well as mixed-race) comes from Pierre Boulle's *Race et esclavage dans la France de l'Ancien Régime* (Paris, 2007), esp. section III, "Les non-blancs dans la France de la fin du XVIIIe siècle." See also Jennifer L. Palmer, *Intimate Bonds: Family and Slavery in the French Atlantic* (Philadelphia, 2016), 1–18; and Dwain C. Pruitt, "*Nantes Noir:* Living Race in the City of Slavers" (Ph.D. diss., Emory University, 2005).

57. According to John D. Garrigus, Ogé claimed in his interrogation after the failed uprising that his surname originally began with an "Au," making his given name either "Auger" or "Augé"; see Garrigus, " 'Thy Coming Fame, Ogé! Is Sure': New Evidence on Ogé's 1790 Revolt and the Beginnings of the Haitian Revolution," in Garrigus and Christopher Morris, eds., *Assumed Identities: The Meanings of Race in the Atlantic World* (College Station, Tex., 2010), 19–45, esp. 22.

law that appeared, to him, to be an equality bill. Encouraged by the increasing associations, both in Britain and France, between armed service and citizenship, Ogé brought with him a military uniform to play the part of citizen soldier. After he arrived, Ogé met with Jean-Baptiste Chavannes, a free man of color who served in the colonial militia as a noncommissioned officer. In October, they demanded that Saint Domingue's government uphold the Parisian enfranchisement bill. The government refused. In response, some three hundred freemen of color gathered in the mountains outside Cap-Français to form a new militia, ready to fight for equal rights. The government, after two attempts, put down the inchoate rebellion. Ogé and Chavannes fled to the Spanish-controlled area of Hispaniola but were soon captured and returned to Saint Domingue. Authorities interrogated Ogé about the events before exacting ultimate justice. They broke him on the wheel, decapitated him, and placed his head on a pike as a warning to future rebels. But Ogé's mission had not been one of revolution. He did not wish to see an emancipation of the colony's enslaved populace; rather, he pushed only for the same rights of equality that all males in France now enjoyed. When asked in his interrogation if he had ever been insulted based on his color, Ogé responded with a simple "No." Although he had challenged colonial authority, Ogé did not fly a banner of racial equality. Yet, reactions to his failed uprising would turn on that very point.[58]

Six months after Ogé's execution, enslaved laborers in northern Saint Domingue rose up against their masters. The event terrified observers throughout the Atlantic, and many commentators in both the French and British empires looked to Ogé's coup as the catalyst. The connection between the Haitian Revolution and Ogé's uprising, though, is by no means clear. By blaming Ogé, observers diminished the political capacities of enslaved Dominguans and displaced critiques over colonial slavery. Nevertheless, officials worried that news of Ogé's actions would inspire the type of insurrection that the colony would in fact soon endure. Despite a public execution, authorities attempted to tamp down public interest in the affair. Saint Domingue's government tried Ogé in secret and forbade any local newspapers from reporting on it—a prohibition that did not extend to nearby islands, as Jamaica's *Cornwall Chronicle, and Jamaica General Advertiser* wrote regularly on Ogé's

58. Ibid., esp. 24; Garrigus, *Before Haiti*, 240–265; C. L. R. James, *The Black Jacobins: Toussaint L'Ouverture and the San Domingo Revolution*, 2d ed. (New York, 1989), 67–76; Laurent Dubois, *Avengers of the New World: The Story of the Haitian Revolution* (Cambridge, Mass., 2004), 60–89.

rebellion. Such secrecy foreshadowed the linkage many would later make between the two uprisings.[59]

Although it was enslaved Dominguans who revolted in August 1791, reports on the event frequently obsessed over rumors of atrocities carried out by mixed-race freemen. Often these accounts fixated on patricide in interracial households. Deputies from Saint Domingue carried news back to France about young men of color slaughtering their fathers. At a speech to the French National Assembly in November 1791, these envoys testified that a Monsieur Cardineau "had two natural sons of colour [who] . . . had been the objects of his tenderest cares." Filial piety, they claimed, broke down at the start of the revolution. "They accosted him with a pistol at his breast, and demanded his money," they relayed, "but no sooner had they obtained it than they stabbed him to the heart." Likewise, Monsieur Chauvet du Breuil's sixteen-year-old mulatto son supposedly assassinated him, despite being heir to his large fortune. Members of the National Assembly responded in shock. Of all the atrocities listed by colonial deputies, perhaps the most perplexing and tragic to those in France was that the "white father falls a victim to the unnatural rage of his Mulatto son." Such narratives fit into a long-established French discourse on improper, libertine families in the Caribbean that produced disturbed and vengeful children of color. English publishers translated and sold copies of these speeches to an eager British audience that was both fascinated and repelled by the accounts. The Jamaican assemblyman Bryan Edwards, who visited Saint Domingue in the early months of the revolution, repeated these stories in his own history of the ongoing conflict after returning to England in 1792. If ever there was a sign that West Indian whites headed improper and immoral households, it was here, in the crucible of revolution, when sons fought against fathers, rather than with them. To outside observers, all of the overtures made by planters about the bonds of affection between white fathers and children of color appeared to disintegrate immediately when put under stress.[60]

59. Marlene L. Daut, *Tropics of Haiti: Race and the Literary History of the Haitian Revolution in the Atlantic World, 1789–1896* (Liverpool, U.K., 2015), 126–129, 560–566; Garrigus, "'Thy Coming Fame,'" in Garrigus and Morris, eds., *Assumed Identities*, 20; Michel-Rolph Trouillot, *Silencing the Past: Power and the Production of History* (Boston, 1995), 102–103. For reports on Ogé's rebellion, as observed in Jamaica, see in particular the *Cornwall Chronicle, and Jamaica General Advertiser* supplements for Sept. 11, 1790, Nov. 27, 1790, Dec. 11, 1790, and Jan. 1, 1791.

60. Saint Domingue General Assembly, *A Particular Account of the Insurrection of the Negroes of St. Domingo, Begun in August, 1791: Translated from the French*, 4th ed. (n.p.,

When commentators attempted to explain the onset of revolution, these broken relationships gave strong evidence of an unstable society. Generally unwilling to consider the possibility that slavery could form the ultimate root of such discontent or that a slave revolt could eventually succeed, both the French National Assembly and Edwards pointed their fingers instead at injustices done to Saint Domingue's free population of color. Lacking many of the same rights as white inhabitants, the colony's gens de couleur had ample reason to revolt. Not only did the law disenfranchise them, but, according to the National Assembly, "White Colonists excluded them from their social circles, from their assemblies, from their municipal functions." Still optimistic that enslaved Dominguans had been radicalized by free people of color and were soon to be pacified, the National Assembly concluded in 1792 that the uprising "must be attributed to the degradation of the People of Colour . . . and above all, to the injustice of which the Whites have been guilty in refusing to let the Mulattoes partake of the blessings of liberty." Once again, Edwards echoed these comments to an English audience. Saint Domingue officials repressed free individuals of color, Edwards claimed, naturally leading to rebellion. In an attempt to calm nerves in Westminster, he assured readers that mixed-race people in Britain's Caribbean possessions were much better treated. The four-generations-removal clause giving whiteness to certain individuals of color in Jamaica was not to be found in Saint Domingue's law books, and Edwards insisted that it would have pacified the French colony. Jamaica, in this retelling, had presciently allowed a white populace to emerge out of a mixed-race one, thus underscoring the continued interest in demographic debates even during revolution. Exalting Jamaican law further, Edwards believed that the inheritance cap was also vital to colonial security. Without a check on mixed-race finances, a politically disenfranchised, but economically privileged, class of color would grow too large. Elite colonists of color were the culprits in Edward's history of the as-yet-unfinished Haitian Revolution. As Atlantic observers focused on free people of color, rather than enslaved individuals as the agents of rebellion, Ogé's uprising took on much greater importance than the subsequent Haitian Revolution in explaining Caribbean unrest.[61]

———
[1791]), 4–5; French National Assembly, *An Inquiry into the Causes of the Insurrection of the Negroes in the Island of St. Domingo . . .* (London, 1792), 5; Bryan Edwards, *An Historical Survey of the French Colony in the Island of St. Domingo* (London, 1797), 74; Doris Garraway, *The Libertine Colony: Creolization in the Early French Caribbean* (Durham, N.C., 2005); Daut, *Tropics of Haiti,* 345–372.

    61. French National Assembly, *Inquiry into the Causes,* 10, 28; Edwards, *Historical Survey,* 7–10.

With this viewpoint in mind, commentators scrutinized Ogé's biography, particularly his time spent in Europe. France's National Assembly concluded that abolitionism and the French Revolution had radicalized West Indians of color in Paris. Ogé had fallen victim to these ideas and carried them back to the Caribbean. Even Britain's chief abolitionist, Thomas Clarkson, believed that Parisians of color were central to the Haitian Revolution. Attempting to defend the struggling British abolition movement against claims that it had inspired the Caribbean rebellion, he drafted his own history of the affair in 1792. Having dined with Ogé and several other prominent men of color in Paris the year before the coup as well as hosted Ogé when he passed through London on his way back to Saint Domingue, Clarkson maintained that factions between white and mixed-race Dominguans had ultimately inspired the uprising. Although he did not begrudge the reforms demanded by French-educated Dominguans of color, Clarkson did believe that Ogé's actions, along with the continued pressures asserted by mixed-race individuals still living in France, encouraged the social divisions necessary for an enslaved rebellion to begin.[62] William Wilberforce agreed in his speech to the House of Commons that same year. Caribbean observers felt similarly. A Bahamian resident wrote to England that "the Coloured people of St Domingo are many Characters of superior Cast for Intelligence—whose minds have been highly cultivated"—a reference to the effects of a metropolitan education. Edwards believed that "these unfortunate people resident in France . . . were thus inflamed into madness" from such schooling and experience. Additionally, Europe's general political upheavals of the period startled a group of Irish missionaries working in the Caribbean who worried about the return of a mixed-race man named Thomas Gordon from England in 1792. As he shared the surname of the famous agitator in London who inspired the 1780 Gordon riots against Catholic appeasement, the missionaries grew anxious that Thomas might potentially bring a similar insurrection to the tropics. With so many observers blaming mixed-race colonists, particularly those educated in Europe, for pro-

62. French National Assembly, *Inquiry into the Causes,* 13; Thomas Clarkson, *The True State of the Case, respecting the Insurrection at St. Domingo* (Ipswich, 1792), 4–8; Garrigus, " 'Thy Coming Fame,' " in Garrigus and Morris, eds., *Assumed Identities,* 28. See also Gerzina, *Black England,* 189–190. An anonymous author concurred that the divisions between white and mixed-race society enabled the Haitian Revolution to commence; see *Short Address to the People of Scotland,* 30. This idea of strong ruptures between white and mixed-race individuals in Saint Domingue fits with Malick Ghachem's theory that legal contests between colony and metropole over the status of subjects and slavery divided society, thus enabling revolution; see Ghachem, *Old Regime,* 234–248.

voking Saint Domingue's enslaved revolution, the act of sending a child of color abroad came under greater scrutiny.[63]

Fear spread throughout the Atlantic that Saint Domingue's uprising might prompt other Caribbean populations of color to rise up as well, empowered by the general calls for slave reform. Clarkson cast blame on Ogé for the revolution in part to deflect criticism of abolitionists for inspiring freemen and slaves to rebel. Jamaica's assembly immediately pointed its fingers at abolitionists, as did Saint Domingue's legislature. Parliamentarians threw out similar accusations in Westminster. North American writers also used the revolution to counter growing calls for emancipation in the United States. These views were frequently expressed in private as well. A correspondent of Wilberforce wrote mournfully to him in February 1792 that the revolution would poison attitudes toward humanitarianism. John Tailyour and his contacts complained regularly that abolitionism would eventually destroy Jamaica, as it had the French Caribbean. In a letter written just days after he had excitedly reported finding a school for his mixed-race nephew in Yorkshire, Robert Taylor complained to John: "I sincerely hope the troubles which have become so serious in Hispaniola will not reach Jamaica and I think they will be serviceable in Opening the Eyes of People in this Country to Mr. Wilberforce's mad projects and mistaken humanity." To proslavery supporters, abolitionists were, responsible not simply for creating a spirit of change generally but for directly causing these problems. Edwards insisted that France's "*Amis des Noirs* [Friends of Blacks] formed an intimate connection" with "a considerable body of the mulattoes from St. Domingo and the other French islands, [who] were resident in the French capital." These abolitionists, in Edward's estimation, "poured out such invectives against the white planters, as bore away [the migrants'] reason and moderation." Not only that, but the *Amis des Noirs* held supposedly close links with abolitionists in London. Connections did exist between the groups, but Edward's accusation hinted at the possibility that Jamaican migrants of color might become radicalized in Britain in the same way that Dominguans had in France. These opinions continued to linger well after Haitian independence.[64]

63. William Wilberforce, as quoted in *Debate on a Motion* (1792), 11–12; John Wells to George Chalmers, July 19, 1793, Correspondence of George Chalmers, Add. MS 22900, I, fol. 195, BL; Edwards, *Historical Survey*, 40; John Holmes, *Historical Sketches of the Missions of the United Brethren for Propagating the Gospel among the Heathen, from Their Commencement to the Present Time* (Dublin, 1818), 375. The *Cornwall Chronicle, and Jamaica General Advertiser* likewise referred to Ogé as a "very intelligent mulatto"; see *Cornwall Chronicle*, Jan. 1, 1791, Supplement.

64. *JAJ*, Nov. 3, 1791, IX, 5–6; Saint Domingue General Assembly, *Particular Account*

The potential threat of rebellion appeared to materialize in December 1792 when a group of free Jamaicans of color drafted a petition to the assembly demanding greater civil justice. The petitioners noted that they were entitled to the same rights as Britain's natural subjects, as they had been born free in its territories. Laws against the group not only violated this fundamental privilege but actively damaged its members' lives. In particular, the petitioners begrudged their inability to give evidence freely in court, a problem that left them unsafe from "White Persons invading their Properties." They also condemned unequal punishments and deficiency laws that weighed on them more heavily. Likewise, as taxpayers, the petitioners demanded a greater place in civil society — a not so subtle reference to the recent peace with the United States. Finally, the petition highlighted the now-decades-old inheritance cap as a particularly gross injustice. The 1761 act, according to the appeal, was "so immediately repugnant to the *parental feelings of good men,* that it requires no illustration to point out its oppression." Here, then, was the response of Jamaica's mixed-race elites to Ogé's uprising and the subsequent slave rebellion. The island's freemen did not take up arms. Instead, they professed loyalty to the government but insisted that such allegiance could only be main-

---

of the Insurrection, 5–6, 13; Speeches of Mr. Baillie and Charles James Fox, as quoted in *Debate on a Motion* (1792), 51, 133; Noah Webster, *Effects of Slavery, on Morals and Industry* (Hartford, Conn., 1793), 18; Samuel Hoare to William Wilberforce, Feb. 20, 1792, in Robert Isaac Wilberforce and Samuel Wilberforce, eds., *The Correspondence of William Wilberforce,* 2 vols. (London, 1840), I, 89–90; Robert Taylor to John Tailyour, Nov. 2, 1791, Tailyour Papers, WCL (for similar letters within the family, see ibid., Feb. 17, 1792, Simon Taylor to John Tailyour, Nov. 2, 1791, Mar. 2, 1792); Edwards, *Historical Survey,* 17, 85–86. Jacques Pierre Brissot, founder of the *Amis des Noirs* not only contacted England's Committee for the Abolition of the Slave Trade but also published a pamphlet urging the formation of a similar group in France with links to its British counterpart. The committee inducted Brissot as an honorary member in 1787 and encouraged him in the formation of the *Amis des Noirs* but declined lending any pecuniary support; see [Jacques P. Brissot de Warville], *Discours sur la nécessité d'établir à Paris une société pour concourir, avec celle de Londres, à l'abolition de la traite et de l'esclavage des nègres* (Paris, 1788); and Minutes of the Committee for the Abolition of the Slave Trade, Aug. 27, 1787, Add. MS 21254, fol. 13, BL. Thomas Coke also argued that the *Amis des Noirs* had radicalized Saint Domingue's Parisian-educated migrants of color in his 1811 account of the Caribbean; see *A History of the West Indies . . . ,* 3 vols. (London, 1808–1811), III, 410. Joseph Marryat expressed the same opinion five years later; see *More Thoughts, Occasioned by Two Publications Which the Authors Call 'An Exposure of Some of the Numerous Misstatements and Misrepresentations Contained in a Pamphlet, Commonly Known by the Name of Mr. Marryat's Pamphlet, Entitled Thoughts, etc.' and 'A Defence of the Bill for the Registration of Slaves'* (London, 1816), 114–115.

tained with broadly conferred equalities. Not unexpectedly, they also cast their appeal within the language of family obligation.[65]

The petitioners never formally submitted this appeal, but drafts of the document leaked to the colony's assemblymen, who reacted strongly. Immediately, legislators sought out its author. A quadroon man named Dickson wrote the petition but died before presenting it to the government. Officials saw in Dickson a close resemblance to Ogé. Jamaican governor Adam Williamson wrote to the British secretary of state that Dickson had "been sent home and regularly bred to the Bar" in England. Williamson must have believed that such time spent in Britain had radicalized Dickson in the same way that time in France had Ogé. Indeed, Williamson drew equivalence between the two migrants' aims: "On [Dickson's] coming out here he had been at some pains to seduce the people of Colour." Members of the assembly came to the same conclusion. In a report drafted just days after the petition was found out, several members furiously penned a terrified letter to their agent Stephen Fuller in London. Dickson's petition, they wrote, "is expressed in the Language of Fanaticism." Considering "what has happened at Hispaniola," they warned, "we have every reason to believe that these people of colour have it in their power to lead our Slaves into Rebellion." On top of this, the assemblymen worried that news of the petition might "get into the hands of the pretended friends of freedom and Equality in Great Britain," thereby accelerating the supposed feedback loop between abolitionism and Caribbean revolution. This was not altogether a fantasy. In 1794, police arrested Henry Redhead Yorke, a man claimed by investigators to be a West Indian whose "natural Mother . . . is a Mulatto," in northern England for giving seditious speeches that included calling for an end to slavery. His activities seemed to confirm the fear that mixed-race migrants in Britain were bound to cause imperial instability. Planters and overseers echoed these concerns. Writing from Jamaica, Thomas Barritt warned his absentee employer in London about the petition from "the People of Colour about the towns" who "suffer from the Preachers of absurd Doctrines, as also from what has happened at St. Domingo." Having witnessed recent slave uprisings in Martinique—and soon Guadeloupe—as well, white colonists felt sure their fears were justified.[66]

65. "The Humble Address and Petition of the Free People of Colour," December 1792, CO 137/91, fols. 39–41, NAE [emphasis mine]. For more on the petition, see Mavis Campbell, *The Dynamics of Change in a Slave Society: A Sociopolitical History of the Free Coloreds of Jamaica, 1800–1865* (Rutherford, N.J., 1976), 67; and Heuman, *Between Black and White*, 23–24.

66. Adam Williamson to Henry Dundas, Mar. 9, 1793, CO 137/91, fols. 119–120, NAE,

Jamaican officials might have felt eager to suppress and bury Dickson's un-filed petition, but implicated parties in Britain debated its merits. Learning of the petition in London, George Hibbert, whose mixed-race cousin Jane Harry Thresher had died a decade earlier in the English Midlands, wrote to Edward Long about his own apprehensions. With large tracts of property in Jamaica, Hibbert described Dickson's appeal as a "Germ of evil" but never-theless believed that some concessions had to be made, or else the island risked upheaval. "We have the example of St. Domingo, Martinique, and Guadeloupe before us," he cautioned. Fuller went even further in his per-sonal deliberations. Acting as Jamaica's British agent, he wrote down loose thoughts on the island's mixed-race population after learning about the peti-tion. Fuller, who held deep genealogical roots in Jamaica, recorded in his journal that free people of color were vital to island security and therefore should have the same rights accorded to British subjects. Without holding a demographic majority, he scribbled, whites could not sincerely convince freemen of color to submit to legal disenfranchisement. Instead, he believed that an older approach needed to be taken. "It seems to me to be expedient to make some positive, notorious, established distinctions of the People of Colour," he stated, "to reduce them to classes, in proportion to the distance of remove from the Negro Ancestor, and to establish a new code of Laws, by which they should approach by degrees nearer and nearer to all the benefits of White Men and succeed to them by gradation." This tactic essentially rep-licated the ideas set out by the Jamaican assembly sixty years earlier in an at-tempt to augment the island's white population through racial mixture. Legis-latively, the assembly had modified that strategy over the previous generation, but such methods were not completely abandoned in popular debate.[67]

Report on the Petition by People of Color to Stephen Fuller, Dec. 5, 1792, CO 137/91, fol. 38. See also "Most Secret and Confidential, House of Assembly Jamaica," Dec. 5, 1792, Add. MS 12431, fol. 223, BL, John Griffith to Philip Yorke, Lord Hardwicke, June 14, 1794, HO 42/31, fols. 124-125; *Oxford Dictionary of National Biography*, online ed., s.v. "Yorke, Henry Redhead (1772-1813)," by J. G. Alger, rev. Peter Spence, http://www.oxforddnb.com.proxy.wm.edu/view/article/30241; *Times* (London), Oct. 31, 1794, July 28, 1795; and Thomas Bar-ritt to Nathaniel Phillips, June 28, 1792, Slebech Collection, MS 8399, National Library of Wales, Aberystwyth. An insurrection in Martinique predated the general enslaved revolu-tion in Saint Domingue. Guadeloupe's Trois-Rivières uprising occurred shortly afterward in April 1793; see Laurent Dubois, *A Colony of Citizens: Revolution and Slave Emancipation in the French Caribbean, 1787-1804* (Chapel Hill, N.C., 2004), 85-89, 126-131.

67. George Hibbert to Edward Long, Jan. 28, 1793, Add. MS 12431, fol. 230, BL, Feb. 1, 1793, fol. 232; Stephen Fuller, "Notes on Mulattos," 1793, DD\DN/508/62-66, fols. 1-10, Somerset Record Office, Taunton, U.K. Many thanks to Ian Barrett for the reference.

Edwards, himself a member of the assembly, reflected on the role of mixed-race persons in a 1793 tome on Jamaican history. Drawing from his own experiences, along with many of the same records used by Long in his 1774 history, Edwards constructed an ethnographic sketch of the island and its peoples. Heavily influenced by Long, Edwards introduced his section on mixed-race individuals in the same way as his predecessor: he detailed their legal status. Noting their disenfranchisement and inability to give evidence against whites, Edwards closed this section by highlighting the inheritance cap. He wrote hesitatingly about the act. Noting that although privilege bills could give exemptions, Edwards nevertheless conceded that it was a contentious edict. It was possible to modify it, he added in a footnote, but "to repeal it altogether, is a deep and difficult question." The problem he found with these legal impediments was the ridiculous advantage of rights that poor whites held over elites of color. Gesturing toward the practice of mixed-race schooling abroad, Edwards lamented "that the lowest White person, consider[s] himself as greatly superior to the richest and best-educated Free man of Colour." Echoing Fuller, Edwards suggested that gradation should continue to matter in social status. He recommended that anyone just two or more generations removed from a black descendant should be enfranchised. Despite being one of the most popular and influential members of the assembly in his day, Edwards's 1793 proposals did not prompt any immediate legislative action. Nevertheless, his extra-parliamentary opinions show the survival of early-eighteenth-century ideas about demography and graduated rights well into the abolitionist period.[68]

Another Briton with strong connections to Jamaica also believed that the mixed-race condition needed to be considered thoughtfully but did not share Fuller or Edwards's enthusiasm for throwback policies. Benjamin Vaughan was born in Jamaica, but his parents moved the family back to London when he was a young man. He nonetheless continued to monitor events in his birthplace and felt certain that the island's population of color would continue to increase exponentially. The assembly therefore had to provide the group some political relief. African heritage, he contended, was not a useful dividing line in a society so saturated with racial mixture. Liberty would be a better social barrier, properly separating free from enslaved in a pragmatic and logical manner. Yet, Vaughan understood that there was not a singular population of color on the island. "Riches, knowledge, fashion, habit and a variety of other circumstances" differentiated people of mixed heritage, and those distinctions

68. Edwards, *History, Civil and Commercial*, II, 17–21n.

would continue to matter in the future. Moreover, Vaughan suggested, "it will be important for the whites to divide the mulattoes, if it should be found impossible to content the whole of them." It is clear that this was not a call for racial equality. Nor was it a roadmap, like Fuller's plan, to forge a white class from one of color. Vaughan insisted that African heritage could never be erased generationally. This was a preliminary sketch of a Jamaican society that many would come to accept in the early nineteenth century: the replacement of the island's white populace with one of elite mixed ancestry. Yet, in one area Vaughan betrayed a regressive attitude. Elites of color, he hinted, should continue to have some type of upbringing in Britain. Vaughan argued that mixed-race Jamaicans would assimilate by becoming more like whites, which potentially included an education abroad. Experience showed, he contended, that it was not "strange to see people of color becoming citizens of Europe." If the island was to advance, then these British-schooled Jamaicans of color would have to form a new core of island settlement and citizenry. Unlike his fellow commentators, then, Vaughan envisioned a world in which mixed-race migration to Britain could forestall Caribbean revolution, rather than fore-shadow it.[69]

All of this debate, emanating from the aborted 1792 petition, did little to change the status of mixed-race Jamaicans significantly. The assembly did not clamp down harshly on its population of color after the first rounds of insurrection began in neighboring Saint Domingue, but it also did nothing to improve that group's lot. Yet, the reverberations of the Haitian Revolution did ultimately push the assembly to act. In 1796, it finally allowed freemen of color to testify against whites, but only in cases in which they were vic-tims. Ostensibly, the concession came as a reward for mixed-race assistance in hunting down insurgents during a large Maroon rebellion from the previous year. The 1795 uprising of the island's Maroons, however, was not isolated. It was part of a series of larger, circum-Caribbean revolts that year that saw slaves conspire and take up arms in Guyana, Curaçao, Grenada, Venezuela, and Louisiana. Undoubtedly, Jamaica's assembly hoped that by holding out a small legislative token to mixed-race people, the island could ward off fur-ther social upheaval.[70]

69. Vaughan, "Concerning the Whites and People of Color in the Colonies," circa 1792, Vaughan Papers, Ser. III.

70. *JAJ*, Mar. 25, 1796, IX, 471; Sheila Duncker, "The Free Coloured and Their Fight for Civil Rights in Jamaica, 1800–1830" (Master's thesis, University of London, 1956), 22–23; Jane G. Landers, *Atlantic Creoles in the Age of Revolutions* (Cambridge, Mass., 2010), 53;

Ultimately, the timing of the 1792 petition was deeply unfortunate for Jamaicans of color. Island officials and British observers each cast blame on mixed-race individuals for instigating Saint Domingue's revolution. Moreover, the biography of the Jamaican petition's author, Dickson, read much too similarly to that of Ogé's. Having attended an English school and carrying ideas of European reform back to the colony, Dickson appeared the model of political dissent in the abolition-era Caribbean. Commentators across the Atlantic had grown wary of mixed-race West Indians traveling to the metropole for their studies, especially as many authors and theorists wished to simplify the Caribbean's diverse racial and economic characteristics. Migrants of color were not universally reviled, but they were now under closer supervision as both Britain and France reimagined their empires.

Conclusion

Just three months after the first letter arrived from William Wilberforce, Hercules Ross testified to Parliament about his time in Jamaica. Wilberforce had found him a useful contact. Immediately after receiving Ross's promise to help, the parliamentarian begged him to solicit Scottish friends "who have been in the W[est] Indies, to come forward as Witnesses," who he believed were "numerous beyond what one could imagine." Ross certainly would not have to look far for neighbors with Jamaican experience: James Taylor was currently playing with his cousins just miles from Ross's home, and his own children of color might have been running through the house when he drafted letters to Wilberforce. Neither set of these children of color in Britain came up in the correspondence. Ross appears to have hidden these domestic arrangements and kept his involvement with Wilberforce private until addressing Parliament for two days in March 1791. When speaking before the Commons, though, Ross played up his credentials. He had, according to his testimony, visited every parish in Jamaica, toured the island with colonial governors and British admirals, and even lived briefly in Saint Domingue. If anyone could comment about the state of West Indian slavery, surely it was him.[71]

Much of the questioning centered on the plight of Jamaica's enslaved laborers, and Ross provided Parliament with many of the salacious details

Linda Rupert, *Creolization and Contraband: Curaçao in the Early Modern Atlantic World* (Athens, Ga., 2012), 201–211.

71. William Wilberforce to Hercules Ross, Jan. 25, 1791, MS 587, NLJ; "Minutes of the Evidence Taken before a Committee of the House of Commons, Being a Select Committee, Appointed to Take the Examination of Witnesses respecting the African Slave Trade," Mar. 16–17, 1791, no. 4281, in *HCSP*, LXXXII, 253–264.

it sought. In particular, the House asked about punishments given to slaves on the island, to which Ross responded that reprimands were given "with severity, and I fear sometimes without just cause." This brought to his mind an incident he had witnessed years before in Savanna la Mar, on Jamaica's western end. During a stroll through town, Ross heard several loud shrieks in the distance. He followed the sounds to an enclosure in which he saw a young woman suspended from a tree by the wrists, her toes barely able to touch the ground. An overseer held a torch up to her genitals for long moments at a time, as her master watched on "with an unmoved countenance applying this torture." Based on the timing and location of the event, the master might very well have been the notorious Thomas Thistlewood. This act of flogging slaves suspended by the wrists was customary in the West Indies. Ross noted that the practice regularly occurred on Kingston's wharfs, with the added punishment of weights applied to the victims' feet. News of this particular method of torture elicited a great deal of distress among Britons, and it came to symbolize the helplessness of enslaved people alongside the barbarity of Caribbean whites. This horror found visual manifestation in William Blake's *Flagellation of a Female Samboe Slave,* published in John Gabriel Stedman's enormously popular 1796 autobiography (see Plate 9). Ross's testimony to Parliament helped to contribute to popular awareness of these abuses.[72]

Amid such dramatic accounts, Ross touched on the demographic issues at the root of British consternation over abolitionism. "I always considered Negroes best adapted for labour in those climates," Ross answered when questioned about the ideal West Indian workers. Likewise, he responded that an end to the slave trade would "prevent the making of new settlements in the islands." In this way, he agreed with claims of the proslavery interest about the economic damage awaiting the Caribbean should Africans stop arriving. Irrespective of those problems, though, Ross boldly declared that every European nation had a moral duty to "abolish the inhuman traffic." Tellingly, Ross insisted that he had not come to such a conclusion in a state of passion. He proclaimed that it had been his opinion for decades, noting the instance of his 1774 debate in Kingston with Thomas Hibbert—another father who sent his Jamaican children of color to Britain—about the ethical quality of the slave trade. Ross promoted his experience and standing in Jamaica to highlight the point that abolitionism was not a new question recently sprung on Caribbean planters. Rather, West Indian whites had long considered the advantages and

72. "Minutes of the Evidence Taken before a Committee of the House of Commons," Mar. 16-17, 1791, no. 4281, in *HCSP,* LXXXII, 253-255.

PLATE 9. *Flagellation of a Female Samboe Slave.* By William Blake. 1796.
From J[ohn] G[abriel] Stedman, *Narrative, of a Five Years' Expedition, against the Revolted Negroes of Surinam . . .* , 2 vols. (London, 1796), I, plate 35. This image is reproduced by permission of the Huntington Library, San Marino, Calif.

drawbacks of regulating, if not eliminating, the slave trade. If economics were truly the only stumbling blocks to West Indian acceptance of abolition, then Ross intended to show that there had never been a majority opinion on that point.[73]

Humanitarians cheered Ross's account. Publishers of the testimony expressed "unfeigned respect and regard" for him, Wilberforce regularly repeated Ross's information that "merited every degree of praise that could be bestowed upon it," and Thomas Clarkson later exalted the "peculiar benefit which had resulted from his testimony to the cause." Hercules Ross, like James Ramsay before him, used his Caribbean past to undercut the proslavery camp's claims to particular expertise. Moreover, he showed that demographic calculations were still nearly universal in the debate.[74]

It is tempting to see direct connections between Ross's abolitionism and his sending mixed-race children home to Britain. Surely the forces compelling him to educate his children in Britain overlapped, at least to some degree, with those convincing him of the immorality of human trafficking. Yet, absent his personal reflections on the matter, it is unwise to jump to that conclusion. One should not dismiss the idiosyncrasies of such decisions. More importantly, the question of family cannot be omitted in this deliberation. Ross and Hibbert could both care for offspring of color in Britain and nonetheless support different sides in the abolition debate because they could easily separate family obligations from ideological determinations. John Tailyour perhaps best embodies this racial compartmentalization. He wrote of the need to uphold his parental duties to young James, all the while continuing to profit from the import of kidnapped Africans. Simultaneously, he actively dismissed Wilberforce's reform efforts. Could Britons, Tailyour wondered to associates weeks after James landed in Montrose, "be so mad as to abolish the slave trade"? The question was not paradoxical in light of his domestic situation. The heavy distinction between freedom and slavery in Jamaica, along with still relatively open ideas of kinship in the Atlantic, meant that conceptions of

73. Ibid., 256–263.

74. *Debate on a Motion* (1791), 17–18; *Heads of the Speeches, Delivered on the 18th and 19th April, 1791, in a Committee of the House of Commons, on a Motion Made by Mr. Wilberforce, for the Abolition of the Slave-Trade* (Liverpool, U.K., 1791), 13; Thomas Clarkson, *The History of the Rise, Progress, and Accomplishment of the Abolition of the African Slave-Trade by the British Parliament*, 2 vols. (London, 1808), I, 351. Of course, others jeered Ross, and his supposed high standing in Jamaica; see *Morning Chronicle*, Mar. 19, 1792; and [Gilbert Francklyn], *Substance of a Speech Intended to Have Been Made on Mr. Wilberforce's Motion for the Abolition of the Slave Trade, on Tuesday, April 3, 1792* (London, 1792), 4–6.

race were not singular and unmitigated, even for slave traders. Likewise, Tailyour's engagement with abolitionism, both in private correspondence as well as in public testimony, did not compromise outlays to Jamaican offspring, even though the discourse around mixed-race migration had already begun to erode.[75]

Between 1788 and 1793, abolition and revolution saturated Atlantic notions of the West Indies and its people. Long-standing demographic concerns turned into acute questions in abolitionist debate, and families of mixed heritage came under increasing scrutiny. Britons' continued interaction with that discourse invigorated parallel anxieties about interracial relations at home. Vincent Ogé's metropolitan experiences, which British and French observers blamed for Saint Domingue's revolution, accelerated the interest in elite Jamaicans of color in Britain. Individual families worked out those issues in private, and belletrists exercised them in public. But the two were not divided. Just as the principal players in Warren Hastings's impeachment were aware of Edward Morse's mixed-race cousins, so, too, were abolitionists personally connected to migrants of color. Wilberforce was quite familiar with Britons of color—he knew Ross's household intimately and would later befriend John Marsh as well. Tailyour's Jamaican family likely became known to parliamentarians reading his testimony in Westminster, and George Hibbert undoubtedly reflected on his late cousin of color when condemning humanitarians. Mixed-race migrants mattered to Britons because of abolitionism and the revolution in Saint Domingue. Equally, abolitionism and Caribbean rebellion mattered to Britons because they knew mixed-race migrants personally.[76]

75. John Tailyour to John and Alex Anderson, May 31, 1791, Letter Book III, Tailyour Papers, WCL.

76. John Marsh Autobiography, 1816, XXXI, fols. 167–169.

CHAPTER 5

TALES OF TWO FAMILIES,

1793–1800

Beset by financial troubles, Jack Morse went to court in the spring of 1795. The eldest mixed-race son of Jamaican merchant John Morse, Jack had grown weary, like his siblings, of the ongoing inheritance suit lodged by his cousin Edward. Still four years from being resolved, the case was now entering its second decade, and Jack desperately needed money. Rather than countersue his opposing litigants, Jack targeted other members of the family: first, he set his sights on a white cousin who had been helping the Jamaican Morses; second, he turned against his own brother and sisters. Namely, he alleged that these relatives had bilked him out of a proper share of his birthright, leaving him destitute. His actions would set off parallel rounds of litigation that further complicated John Morse's bequests to his children, even after Edward Morse's original challenge was defeated.[1]

At the turn of the nineteenth century, mixed-race migrants remained deeply vulnerable to litigious relatives, especially in cases involving substantial inheritances. The normal affairs of Atlantic commerce and estate settlement regularly brought migrants into the court system. But these lawsuits were not simply instances of white attacks against people of color. Occasionally, white Britons went to trial in cases that ultimately supported mixed-race kin. Additionally, as lineages grew and the size of colonial fortunes expanded, some migrant families of color like the Morses sued one another. Jamaicans of color were becoming more and more independent in Britain, even as new children arrived to live with white relatives. In many ways, intrarelational lawsuits between mixed-race kin evidenced a high degree of metropolitan assimilation; there was nothing so quintessentially British in the long eighteenth century as taking a rival heir to court. More importantly, these probate challenges only seemed to confirm to nervous metropolitan observers that chaotic family organizations stood to disrupt traditional transmissions of property through household lines.[2]

1. Royall v. Morse, May 7, 1795, Jan. 21, 1796, Chancery Court Records, C 12/660/5, NAE. For more on the Morse family inheritance battle, see Chapter 3, above.

2. John Addy, *Death, Money, and the Vultures: Inheritance and Avarice, 1660–1750*

Settling family legacies became even more complex when fathers of mixed-race migrants returned to Britain and formed new, legitimate families. After taking up residence once more in Montrose after living in Jamaica, John Tailyour, for instance, bought back his parents' Scottish estate and married the daughter of his former Glasgow employer. He would go on to have numerous children with his wife, which conferred stronger social respectability than his Caribbean arrangement. Indeed, fathering legal heirs was one of several tasks that faced white men migrating between the Caribbean and the metropole. Buying land, furnishing elaborate homes, and readapting to British life were imperatives for these absentees. Family obligations in the islands, however, never left them, and, in some ways, West Indian households initiated and developed their skills as patriarchs. Extended relatives in Britain generally favored legal successors who could receive and retain property more successfully, but the creation of new, legitimate family lines did not necessarily eradicate the acceptance of mixed-race kin.[3]

Competition among and between Caribbean and British families aroused considerable consternation in the popular press, most notably in the sentimental literature of the time. Novels began incorporating elite migrants of color into their plots in the 1790s, primarily after the political zealotry of abolition started to decline. Repeated attempts to prohibit the slave trade in Parliament had failed, and, by 1793, the mighty wind propelling the movement forward had dwindled to a mere breeze. Yet, reduced passion among polemicists did not signal that Britons had lost their curiosity about Jamaicans of color in their midst. Rather, sentimental literature took the mantle from political debate to reflect closely on what such migration meant to British households. In particular, these novels obsessed over the impact on inheritance practices when children of color contended with white family in the metropole. Moreover, well-provisioned characters of color frequently operated as foils to white protagonists who had been denied a rightful bequest or spouse. For a decade after the start of the Haitian Revolution, then, British authors found a useful cultural trope in the mixed-race migrant, a figure of increasingly popu-

(New York, 1992), 149; Lloyd Bonfield, *Devising, Dying, and Dispute: Probate Litigation in Early Modern England* (Burlington, Vt., 2012), 65–78.

   3. Although not all West Indian men wished to settle permanently back in Britain, many—particularly Scots—held that as a top priority; see Alan L. Karras, *Sojourners in the Sun: Scottish Migrants in Jamaica and the Chesapeake, 1740–1800* (Ithaca, N.Y., 1992); and Bill Inglis, "The Stirlings of Keir in the 18th Century, Restoring the Family Fortunes in the British Empire," *Forth Naturalist and Historian*, XXIV (2001), 94–100.

lar interest as ideas of kinship composition came under scrutiny in light of contested inheritances within Atlantic families.

Continued mixed-race migration, both in reality and in fiction, coupled with fortunes that liberated mixed-race kin from white benefactors while also resulting in complex lawsuits heightened British fears over a breakdown in family order. Illegitimacy and inheritance, which had been long-standing concerns in Britain, took on even greater importance. Whatever uncertainties existed about mixed-race migrants before this period began to coalesce around a general discomfort with the social implications of their presence in Britain. Whereas previous polemics focused on the visible effects of interracial relations in the metropole, British observers at the end of the eighteenth century turned their attention toward the economic confusion that migrants of color induced in the domestic sphere.

Rival Heirs

In contesting their cousin Edward Morse's original Chancery suit, the mixed-race Morses presented a united front. When Edward attempted to use Jamaica's inheritance cap to assume the majority of his cousins' legacies, they fought back aggressively in court. Eventually, Edward moved to Jamaica to help advance his case. He died there in 1794, but his passing did not terminate the lawsuit. Instead, other British relatives took it on for the next five years. Immediately following Edward's death, however, Jack Morse lodged his own complaint against the colonial fortune still locked up in litigation. Though he initially took action against the executors of his father John's estate, he would soon turn against his brother and sisters as well. His efforts would begin the process of unspooling the family's unity as new rounds of litigation kept the colonial fortune in legal limbo. The Morse family inheritance battle was one of many inheritance contests that tied up the affairs and compromised the financial stability of mixed-race migrants.

Jack Morse's decision to sue dated back to the immediate years after his father's death in 1781. By all accounts, Jack was a spendthrift. As a young man, he had found success in the military, rising to the rank of lieutenant in the British army's First Troop of Horse Guards. But he proved unable to live within his means. Just three years after John Morse died, Jack was scrambling for money. Owing to cousin Edward's initial challenges, his father's will had not yet been proven, and Jack's inheritance was still only a line on paper, rather than cash in hand. In 1784, he impulsively sold his birthright—nearly one-fifth of John Morse's substantial Jamaican estate—for a paltry five thou-

sand pounds to a white cousin, John Vanheelin. Disappointed by such reck-
lessness but nevertheless willing to help, his sister Ann transferred her portion
of the inheritance to Jack and their brother Robert. Having just returned from
Bengal with an enormous fortune, Ann and her husband Nathaniel Middleton
felt comfortable forgoing their claims on John Morse's Jamaican estate, which
they believed to be severely burdened with debt anyway. Although she acknowledged that their father had comfortably provided for Jack and Robert,
she nevertheless felt that the brothers needed the money much more than
her immediate household. Within a month, Jack sold this new acquisition to
Vanheelin as well for twenty-five hundred pounds. By 1789, four years after
these sales, John Morse's executors—of whom Vanheelin was a member—
reassesed his colonial possessions, finding them to be much more profitable
than initially suspected. Jack, still "in great want of money," demanded that
Vanheelin take the honorable step of sharing some of this newfound bounty
with him, having sold his legacy at too low a price.[4]

Until his death, Vanheelin argued bitterly with Jack Morse about the next
turn of events. Sensing Vanheelin's unwillingness to comply with his demand,
Jack threatened to sue if his cousin did not pay a recalculated sum. Vanheelin
railed to a friend that such intimidation was an "ungentleman attack." More
damaging was the lack of familial respect in these proceedings. Litigation was
no way to treat a relative tasked with stewarding one's finances. Had Jack
"pursued a different line," Vanheelin lamented, "he would ever have found
me a generous friend." Wary of enduring a protracted lawsuit and eager to
reduce family tensions, Vanheelin submitted to an arbitration proceeding in
1789 overseen by Edmund Green, Jack's brother-in-law and Vanheelin's close
associate. Months passed in arbitration, however, and tempers flared. Van-

4. Royall v. Morse, May 7, 1795, Jan. 21, 1796, Chancery Court Records, C 12/660/5,
NAE, Morse v. Royall, Dec. 21, 1798, Jan. 22, 1802, Chancery Court Records, C 13/2394/27,
Morse v. Middleton, May 11, 1804, "Answer of Nathaniel Middleton and His Wife Anne,"
Chancery Court Records, C 13/2407/39; Francis Vesey, Jr., *Reports of Cases Argued and
Determined in the High Court of Chancery, from the Year 1789 to 1817*, 2d ed., XII (London, 1827), 355–378. For a list of Jack Morse's promotions, see *London Gazette*, Dec. 7–10,
1776, May 23–27, 1780, and Oct. 11–14, 1783. In the original sale between Jack Morse and
John Vanheelin, it appears that a man named George Wootton was also part of the transaction. Vanheelin had only recently returned from Jamaica, having served as a member of
its assembly in 1787 and 1790; see W. A. Feurtado, *Official and Other Personages of Jamaica,
from 1655 to 1790* (Kingston, Jamaica, 1896), 97. He had been a slaveowner who had written
about the proper modes of running a plantation; see Alexander X. Byrd, *Captives and Voyagers: Black Migrants across the Eighteenth-Century British Atlantic World* (Baton Rouge,
La., 2008), 81–84.

heelin's own finances were in bad shape, and he hardly had the money to pacify a petulant relative. As negotiations stalled, Vanheelin wondered if he should "preserve peace or go to war." Ultimately, he decided to comply with Green's terms in 1790 to give Jack an additional seventy-five hundred pounds, doubling the amount he originally received. Within months, though, Vanheelin's assets became insolvent, preventing him from paying the full sum. By the end of the year, tragedy struck once more, and Vanheelin was dead.[5]

Vanheelin's untimely death did little to curb Jack's crusade. Settling in a London residence at 31 Weymouth Street, not far from his brother Robert who rented a house near Buckingham Palace, Jack filed lawsuits against Vanheelin's children and the remaining executors of his father's estate for the rest of the settlement owed him from the 1790 arbitration. The case came before England's chancellor in May 1795, just months after Edward Morse had died. Jamaica's Chancery Court had acted to abate Edward's lawsuit after his death, but the case was still active in England. Jack Morse's challenge, then, came at an extremely inopportune time. His opponents wrote bewilderedly of Jack's mysterious reasoning in suing the estate before it had been secured from Edward's legal attacks. The executors noted in court that they had hoped Jack "would have abstained from so doing until such times as the said Claim as the said Edward Morse shall have been disposed of" before rather dejectedly concluding, "But now so it is." Jack had dragged the family into yet another suit between the white and mixed-race families of John Morse. Perhaps worst of all, he did so in order to recover—in relative terms—the somewhat modest sum of two thousand pounds.[6]

In spite of the dry language of these legal filings, the family's exasperation with Jack oozes off the page. Jack attempted to corral his siblings into supporting his complaint but to no avail. He grumbled that Robert and two of his sisters pretended to agree with him but refused to get involved in the case itself. His sister Catherine Morse Green, whose husband Edmund was a defendant in Jack's original suit, likewise had little remaining patience for her brother. Feeling betrayed, in 1798 Jack included each of his siblings in another Chancery action against the executors of his father's estate. He claimed that their shares of the Jamaican property came at the expense of his unfilled arbi-

5. John Vanheelin to William Mitchell, Sept. 17, 1789, in Morse v. Royal, July 21, 1801, Chancery Court Records, C 13/2394/27, NAE, "Answer of William Mitchell," Oct. 7, 1789, C 13/2394/27.

6. P[atrick] Boyle, *With Near Five Thousand Alterations; Boyle's New Fashionable Court and Country Guide; and Town Visiting Directory, for 1798* (London, [1798]), 151; Royall v. Morse, May 7, 1795, Chancery Court Records, C 12/660/5, NAE.

tration agreement. Family cohesion broke down as finances became strained, and the mixed-race family was now at war with each other.[7]

The origins of the Morse family troubles were rooted in the divergent experiences of the siblings. They did not enjoy equal levels of success in Britain, eliciting Jack's jealousies and need. For most of Jack's siblings, his litigiousness caused more heartbreak than bitterness. Catherine and Ann had both married wealthy men and could weather this new legal squall. Robert had come into his own money outside the inheritance, through travels to India and business ventures in London. But, for his sister Sarah Morse Cator, Jack's lawsuit came at a terrible time. After returning from India, her husband, William Cator, had not properly monitored their finances. He had tried and failed at establishing a brewery just north of the City of London. The venture appears to have sunk his savings, and Jack's lawsuit only aggravated matters. In 1799, the year after Jack filed his complaint against the family, William admitted his desire of "quitting and wholly giving up" the brewing business. He entrusted the remaining stock he held to his brothers-in-law, Robert Morse, Nathaniel Middleton, and Edmund Green, and set sail once more for India in the hope of winning back the lost fortune. On board a merchant ship to Bengal, William became gravely sick. Anticipating the worst, he wrote a will on May 14, 1800. His instinct was correct; William passed away while still at sea. Sarah could have been forgiven if she assigned some blame for her husband's death to Jack's greed. She could also rightfully resent his destruction of their intimate relationship; the two had been close siblings born less than a year apart.[8]

Even after these events, Jack did not let up, and his relatives began to turn on him. He filed a suit directly against his sister Ann and her husband Nathaniel, in the hope of having his original arbitration with Vanheelin honored by someone in the family. For the Middletons, this was the last straw. Having originally donated her portion of the inheritance to Jack, Ann not only refused to give him more money but countered that her gift was now void. She might not have been motivated only by spite. Reports had reached them of yet another increase in value of their father's colonial estate. In a re-

7. Morse v. Royall, Dec. 21, 1798, Chancery Court Records, C 13/2394/27, NAE.

8. "Articles of Agreement," July 10, 1799, 789/201, City of Westminster Archives, Westminster, U.K., "Abstract of Release and Assignment from Mr. Cator," Aug. 7, 1799, 789/202, "Grant of Power of Attorney by William Cator," Apr. 9, 1800, 789/203; Will of William Cator, Aug. 14, 1802, PROB 11/1379, NAE. The eldest children in a family were commonly quite close throughout the eighteenth and nineteenth centuries; see Leonore Davidoff, *Thicker Than Water: Siblings and Their Relations, 1780–1920* (New York, 2012), 120.

sponse to the Chancery court, the Middletons asserted that they turned over Ann's bequest to Jack under "such ignorance of their rights" and without being properly examined about the transaction. They wanted their share back. Catherine's family also pushed against Jack's designs. Her husband died in December 1804, but Jack felt no scruple in filing a new case specifically aimed at their household. The couple's two sons, now both grown, took over responsibility of the suit. Charles Green, like his father, had become a lawyer. He was ready to argue in court in the place of his brother Edmund Francis, who had since moved to Jamaica. The root household of color might have been transplanted from the island, but branches of the family tree nevertheless sprouted back toward the West Indies.[9]

Jack Morse's suits ostracized him from his relatives as each case made the family's inheritance all the more vulnerable. By the time England's chancellor ultimately decided to dismiss each of the various suits in 1806, John Morse's estate had been frozen in court for twenty years. Edward's had been the most vicious attack and was not settled until 1799. Jack's attempts to renegotiate the terms of his inheritance buyout had only prolonged the resolution of all this litigation. In the meantime, British observers watched as the family duked it out. Edward had publicized his lawsuit in a tell-all memoir of his trials and tribulations. Interest continued as Edwards's case progressed, and London's newspapers announced its conclusion. Jack's legal action made less of a public impact, but it brought far more people into its orbit. Not only did he sue another branch of the white family—the Vanheelins—but he went after several generations of the Jamaican Morses, too. Thus, multiple family spheres had to engage with the inheritance contest between mixed-race migrants. If Britons were growing more concerned with how families divided property, then their anxieties originated from both public and private understandings of households such as the Morses.[10]

The Morses were not the only Jamaican migrants of color to lodge inheritance suits against one another in this period. The mixed-race descendants of Gibson Dalzell also entered into their own internal family squabble in 1801, although the case had long historical roots. Gibson had two children, Frances and Robert, with the free mulatto Susanna Augier. Interestingly, Susanna was

9. Morse v. Middleton, May 11, 1804, Chancery Court Records, C 13/2407/39, NAE, Morse v. Green, May 2, 1805, June 13, 1805, Chancery Court Records, C 13/2412/40.

10. Vesey, *Reports of Cases,* XII, 378; Edward Morse, *Case of Edward Morse, Esq.* ([London], 1787); *Lloyd's Evening-Post* [London], Jan. 21–23, 1799; *Star* (London), Jan. 23, 1799; *Morning Chronicle* (London), Jan. 23, 1799; *True Briton* (London), Jan. 25, 1799; *E. Johnson's British Gazette, and Sunday Monitor* (London), Jan. 27, 1799.

the aunt of Elizabeth Augier, the mother of John Morse's children. Frances and Robert moved with Gibson to a house on Clifford Street in London before his death in 1756. They had some early legal challenges with their father's executors, but the chief family contest did not emerge until later on. Having resided in Berkshire for decades, Robert decided to get rid of his share of the Jamaican estate to reinvest in British acquisitions. As his health deteriorated, Robert drafted his will. Confident that he had already provided sufficiently for his eldest son, John Thomas Robert, he left the young man only a token bequest. Robert gave the majority of his fortune instead to his daughter Juliana Ann, now living in London and married to Edward James Mascall. His other daughter, Henrietta Theresa Carolina, living in Surrey with husband John Jackson, had inherited a large amount of money from her maternal uncle, and Robert thus gave her only a small legacy as well. Flush with an alternative family fortune, Henrietta made few complaints. John Thomas Robert, however, grumbled at the perceived hereditary slight. He sued his siblings for a greater part of the estate, dragging their children into the proceedings as well. The case lasted for years up to the 1820s, originating from a bequest nearly a century old. Like the Morses and their respective extended white families, the Dalzells used inheritance litigation to extract as much colonial wealth as possible for metropolitan-based households.[11]

11. Gibson Dalzell's 1756 will was part of the collection of testamentary documents that Jamaica's assembly presented to the Board of Trade in 1762 to justify its inheritance cap; see *JAJ*, Nov. 16, 1762, V, 376; and Will of Gibson Dalzell, July 2, 1756, PROB 11/823, NAE. In 1801, Frances filed a suit in Chancery claiming that her father's executors were not properly overseeing the estate. Now in her late twenties, Frances had married George Duff, and Gibson's creditors had started harassing the couple for unpaid debts on the colonial property. Her brother Robert, only fourteen at the time, nervously wrote to the court that he would be unable to continue his education if such debts were not cleared. Gibson's executors, including Frances and Robert's grandfather, balked at the claim, insisting that the estate had plenty of money. The litigation died off before a month had passed, and Gibson's children appear to have taken full possession of his fortune; see Baptism of Robert Dalzell, Nov. 8, 1742, Kingston Baptisms, copy register, I, fol. 70, IRO; and Duff v. Dalzell, July 7-26, 1757, Chancery Court Records, C 12/2305/33, NAE. Robert's decision to give up his share of the estate required an exemption from the Jamaican assembly, which he obtained in December of that year; see *JAJ*, Nov. 13–Dec. 10, 1801, X, 605-652. For the particulars of Robert's bequests, see Will of Robert Dalzell, Sept. 1, 1821, PROB 11/1648, NAE. For the bequest of Henrietta Theresa Carolina's uncle, see Will of John Dodd, May 11, 1816, PROB 11/1580, ibid. For more on these various cases involving the preceeding generations of the Dalzell clan, see Dalzell v. Jackson, Jan. 22–Oct. 16, 1823, Chancery Court Records, C 13/772/21, ibid.; Dalzell v. Welch, May 14, 1828, in *The English Reports*, LVII, *Vice-Chancellors Court II* . . . (Edinburgh, 1905), 808-811.

Mixed-race Jamaicans fought one another, in part, because their finances were increasing, allowing them to depend less heavily on white benefactors. A generation after the inheritance cap cut off mixed-race offspring from their father's massive fortunes, wealth accumulation started to recover among the group. Endogamous marriages between Jamaicans of color avoided the 1761 inheritance law altogether, and entrepreneurial ventures into pen-keeping and coffee plantations had proven highly successful for some mixed-race people. One need only look at Jamaican wills to find the first glimpse of such independence. Of a sample of more than twenty-two hundred wills proven on the island between 1773 and 1815, the first instance of a mixed-race individual bequeathing money to a person of color in Britain came in 1793. The testator in question was none other than Charity Harry, companion of Thomas Hibbert and mother of Jane Harry Thresher who had passed away a decade earlier in England. After Hibbert died in 1780, Harry cultivated the property left to her and increased its value. She gave money, household goods, and plots of land to various relatives of color, including her nephew Charles Cosans who was currently living in Britain. Cosans might have had funding from a white father as well, but his aunt's bequest surely helped make his time in the metropole more secure. In the next two decades, more testators of color would give bequests to mixed-race children in Britain. This practice showed that a metropolitan education was valued not only among white Jamaican fathers but also among mixed-race parents on the island. That individuals of color could now finance such trips themselves indicates their successful accumulation of property, which undoubtedly caught the eye of white lookers-on.[12]

Even as growing access to financial resources regularly brought migrants of color into the court system, inheritance battles with white extended relatives could still turn principally on issues of family rather than race. Robert Hilton Angwin, a mixed-race Jamaican who traveled back and forth to Britain, had to defend his family's Caribbean estate against William Hurle, who married Angwin's sister Frances in England. Frances's death pushed Hurle to claim her birthright, and he and Angwin spent years in litigation. None of the court documents noted the siblings' racial status or Jamaica's race-based laws. Similarly, the Lyons and Angell families, all mixed-race Jamaicans living in Britain, each became entangled in lawsuits between rival executors to an

12. Harry also did not forget Jane's memory in the original draft of her will; she gave Joseph Thresher, her daughter's widower, seven hundred pounds to free her slaves once she died, in keeping with Jane's original wishes. When Joseph died soon afterward, she took out this provision; see Will of Charity Harry, Nov. 13, 1793, Wills, LOS 58, fols. 71–73, IRO.

administered will that did not make explicit mention of race. Neither family suffered under the suits, but the legal wrangling lasted for a significant period. The trust supporting Alexander Lowes, a young man of color transplanted to Yorkshire, also came under legal threat without any racial commentary. Islander George May had lost five thousand pounds to Lowes's mixed-race uncle, Isaac Ochterloney, in a verdict handed down by Jamaica's Supreme Court over an improper land expulsion. May pleaded to the Court of Error, which heard appeals against the Supreme Court, adjudicated by the House of Lords in Westminster. It was an extraordinarily exclusive court and the legal refuge of the island's most rich: a bond of five hundred pounds was required by both sides just to begin proceedings. That Ochterloney could use the elite court and also fund a nephew of color in Britain demonstrates the great wealth that some individuals of color had accumulated. Ultimately, the Lords rejected the appeal, and the Lowes family kept its massive legal windfall.[13]

Whether driven by questions of race or family, these largely probate- and business-based suits kept migrants of color financially anchored to Jamaica, and they also created opportunities for women of color left on the island to maintain familial connections. Three quadroon women in northern Jamaica, for example, sued to have their father's estate properly divided in 1792. One of the sisters persuaded her white husband to act as lead litigant in order to go to trial. This would clearly enrich him, but the case would also assist one of the sisters' mixed-race half-brothers who had gone to Britain with no other recourse to funds without their intervention. Likewise, mothers still on the island advocated on behalf of offspring abroad. After he left for Britain, Charles Wright depended on his mixed-race mother in Jamaica to arbitrate his father's intestate fortune. She worked to secure authority over the property in order to ensure her son's continued financial well-being, especially as he was a minor. Free women of color in Jamaica, then, continued to exert a large degree of control in their extended families' financial and business dealings. Even though many of them had not been given the option to travel to Britain, they nevertheless retained a great deal of responsibility in monitor-

13. Hurle v. Buford, May 16, 1805, Chancery Court Records, C 13/79/14, NAE, Hurle v. Angwin, Jan. 21, 1806, Chancery Court Records, C 13/55/4, "Further Answer of Robert Hilton Angwin," Feb. 25, 1808, Chancery Court Records, C 13/90/41, Hurle v. Angwin, Aug. 15, 1808, Chancery Court Records, C 13/91/10; Lyon et al. v. Innes, Aug. 8, 1817, Jamaica Court of Ordinary, 1B/11/11/4, fols. 45–46, JA, Webb v. Angell, Mar. 17, 1818, Jamaica Chancery Court Records, 1A/3/331, no. 308, lib. 327, fols. 117–118. See also Angell v. Angell, Jan. 24, 1811, ibid., 1A/3/268, no. 245, fol. 130, and Ochterloney v. May, Aug. 19, 1815, Jamaica Court of Error Records, 1B/11/10/12, fols. 89–95.

ing those who had. These women's efforts to safeguard the interests of their mixed-raced kin brought more Britons into litigation with Jamaican families and, in particular, with Caribbean women of color.[14]

Family disputes between white litigants could also unintentionally benefit mixed-race relatives in the metropole. In 1801, white members of the Tulloh family in Jamaica lodged a bill of complaint against the executors of a brother's estate. The Tullohs claimed that the brother's will had not been complied with, including provisions for his two mulatto boys, James and John McKenzie, who had both gone to Britain. Although the Tullohs did not advocate for the boys directly, the two young men became central to the case when executors alleged that the costs of sending them to Britain — plus two more children of color from their father — kept the executors from properly administering the patriarch's final wishes. That same year, Sarah Young from Bermondsey, England, sued the executor of her brother's estate for taking similar control of a Jamaican property instead of dividing it between his heirs. She held an equal share of the estate with her brother and sisters as well as her mulatto nephew, Isaac Young Jobling, now living in Britain. Her lawsuit, if successful, would have given Jobling full access to his colonial trust. Although neither the Tulloh nor Young families actively crusaded for mixed-race kin, such legal efforts ultimately sought to secure their relatives' fortunes. The outcomes of these cases are nearly impossible to track owing to the state of Jamaica's Chancery Court Records, but their existence demonstrates how routinely white and mixed-race family members came into one another's legal worlds. Even when their intentions were benign, British litigants became intimately familiar with mixed-race relatives in the metropole as well as with the complexities of their wider families' household structures.[15]

Yet, for as much as Jamaicans of color inadvertently benefited from inheritance litigation, they more frequently suffered from it. Most often, bequests came under attack when litigants, like Edward Morse, disputed which version of a will to use. Robert Tefler drafted a will asking that his mixed-race daughter Jeany be sent to Britain with a small trust at his death. Nine years later, he

14. Cunningham et al. v. Williams et al., Feb. 24, 1792, Jamaica Chancery Court Records, 1A/3/154, no. 132, fols. 1–6, JA, Writ of Grace Israel, Apr. 28, 1809, Jamaica Caveats of Administration, 1B/11/16/1; Linda L. Sturtz, "Mary Rose: 'White' African Jamaican Woman? Race and Gender in Eighteenth-Century Jamaica," in Judith A. Byfield, LaRay Denzer, and Anthea Morrison, eds., *Gendering the African Diaspora: Women, Culture, and Historical Change in the Caribbean and Nigerian Hinterland* (Bloomington, Ind., 2010), 66–71.

15. Tulloh v. Marshall, May 30, 1801, Jamaica Chancery Court Records, 1A/3/190, no. 167, fols. 323–324, JA, Young v. Kiddell, May 2, 1801, fols. 167–171.

drew a line through that bequest and replaced it with a smaller provision for a different daughter of color. Later disputes over the will did nothing to compensate Jeany. In another case, John Whittaker's two mestee sons, who both moved to Britain "never to return to Jamaica or any part of the West Indies," according to his will, became entangled in a lawsuit. Whittaker had provided handsomely for both sons, but for only one of their mothers, Mary Graves. In a last-minute revision, Whittaker took Graves out of his will completely, substituting another woman of color in her place. The court decided against Graves, and she received nothing from the estate. These examples demonstrate the wide discrepancy in the roles Jamaican mothers played in securing bequests for their mixed-race children. Jeany Tefler's mother was apparently important enough to her daughter's success that, when she lost a sexual connection with Robert, he cut off ties to Jeany as well. Perhaps her mother had been a strong advocate for Jeany, and she could no longer influence Robert's provisions for her once that relationship ended. Mary Graves appears to have exerted far less direct control over her son's fortune. John Whittaker continued to care for their child, regardless of Mary's connection to him. Nevertheless, such changes in the colonial family, albeit ones of sexual partnership, could dramatically alter the fortunes of mixed-race individuals migrating to Britain or for their relations who stayed behind.[16]

Estate executors could also greatly complicate the finances of mixed-raced migrants firmly established in Britain. With many still dependent on their fathers' fortunes for financial support, individuals of color could be left stranded in the metropole by an untoward administrator. After giving a number of bequests to white family, Samuel Smith divided the remainder of his estate between the mixed-race children he had with housekeeper Elizabeth Ford. In a somewhat unusual arrangement, his only son Samuel was to stay

16. Ritchie v. Tefler, Jan. 6, 1817, Jamaica Court of Ordinary, 1B/11/11/4, fols. 61–69, JA, Whittaker v. Green et al., May 18, 1802, 1B/11/13/1, fols. 179–204. Whittaker had hoped to send one of his sons to Britain since at least 1794, but he struggled to have him manumitted from his owner; see Colleen A. Vasconcellos, *Slavery, Childhood, and Abolition in Jamaica, 1788–1838* (Athens, Ga., 2015), 54. Emmeline Garnett presents an interesting case of a legal dispute over a codicil in Lancaster, England; see Garnett, *John Marsden's Will: The Hornby Estate Case, 1780–1840* (London, 1998), 99–122. Non compos mentis allegations were also quite common. Several such cases turned up in a survey of Jamaica's Court of Ordinary records. See, in particular, Rowe v. Mitchell et al., 1811, Jamaica Court of Ordinary, 1B/11/11/2, JA, Ash v. Ratigan, Sept. 3, 1808, 1B/11/11/3, fols. 8–24, Dispute over the Will of John Sleater, Oct. 3, 1789, 1B/11/13/1, fols. 143–154. See also Addy, *Death, Money, and the Vultures,* 113–118; and Michael MacDonald and Terence R. Murphy, *Sleepless Souls: Suicide in Early Modern England* (New York, 1990), 133–142.

in Jamaica, while his four daughters, Elizabeth, Grace, Lucy, and Mary, went to London. The daughters took up residence off Oxford Road and drew on Smith's trust after his passing. Receiving the expected annuity, however, became a frequent problem. In 1791, nearly twenty years after Smith's death, his daughters sued estate executors for improperly allocating his will. Depending almost entirely on their legacies, they claimed that the amounts given them over the years had been "very inadequate to answer the purpose of their maintenance." Similar troubles beset the Goodman children who had also moved to England from Jamaica. Although legally white—their mother was a free mestee and their father was white, making them four degrees removed from a black ancestor and therefore white under Jamaican law—they likewise suffered at the hands of corrupt executors. Making a standard claim that the original estate had been burdened with debt, the executors never provided full payment to the Goodmans. Denied the entirety of their bequests and therefore unable to afford a British lifestyle, two of the children, Rebecca and Frances, were forced to return to Jamaica. Their case sheds further light on the vulnerability of West Indian children in the metropole. As illegitimate offspring, their rights in estate disputes were always tentative. As the children of enslaved and free women of color, prospects outside their fathers' fortunes were not encouraging.[17]

The legal liabilities stemming from race and illegitimacy could not only lead to disinheritance but also result in reenslavement. Joshua Steele split his Barbadian fortune into thirds to be shared by his sister, Mary Ann, and his two children, Catherine and Edward, whom he had by an enslaved woman named Anna Slatia. When crafting his will in 1796, however, the nonagenarian failed to emancipate his offspring. Steele's executor, Francis Bell took control of the estate after Steele's death that year and sent Catherine and Edward to England for an education: "the boy Edward to Norwich school . . . and the girl Catherine to an established place of female education, at Camberwell."[18]

17. Smith v. Rodon, July 30, 1791, Jamaica Chancery Court Records, 1A/3/93, no. 73, lib. 82, fols. 467–476, JA, Goodman v. Wright, Feb. 25, 1802, 1A/3/194, no. 172, fols. 138–141. Rebecca was still living in Jamaica by 1820 as she applied to serve as executor over her mother's intestate finances; see Writ of Grace Meachem, Caveats of Administration, Sept. 12, 1820, 1B/11/16/2, JA.

18. Will of Joshua Steele, Oct. 25, 1796, Labeled "A," Seaforth Papers, GD 46/17/15, NAS; Francis Bell to Mary Ann Steele, July 18, 1797, as quoted in Philip Gibbes, *A Letter to John Beckles, Esq. Attorney General at Barbados* (London, 1802), 6–9. No records were kept about Slatia's life, except that she was "a Mulatto woman" and "a coloured slave" on the Byde Mill plantation of Admiral Thomas Shirley; see Gibbes, *Letter to John Beckles*, 47,

On learning of the news and inquiring with her lawyers, Mary Ann Steele demanded that Bell immediately cease his activities; she rightly suspected fraud. Bell had not properly manumitted Catherine and Edward, whose mother belonged, not to Joshua Steele, but to Admiral Thomas Shirley.[19] Under the guise of helping the children, Bell had embezzled money from Steele's estate. Mary Ann insisted that Catherine and Edward were still enslaved and that she was thus sole heir to her brother's fortune. Yet, rather than keep them in that state, she emancipated the children and won their guardianship, hoping "to provide handsomely for them." She gave them each almost the full thirds' share of Barbadian riches demanded by their father and included an added bequest in her own will, showing a high degree of familial obligation for relatives of color whom she did not know. Nonetheless, Mary Ann Steele's ability to reapply the shackles of slavery onto Catherine and Edward in Britain demonstrated the precarious place that mixed-race migrants held, even in the metropole. The line separating enslaved from free was often tenuous in the colonies, and it could remain so in Britain.[20]

57; and "Case for the Opinion of Mr. Arthur Pigott," Nov. 20, 1798, Seaforth Papers, GD 46/17/16. It is possible that Gibbes and others misnamed Slatia. Baptismal records from Barbados's Saint Philip Parish in 1781 list a mulatto slave named "Anastatia" belonging to the "estate of Thomas Shirley now in possession of Joshua Steele, Esq."; see Joanne McRee Sanders, ed., *Barbados Records: Baptisms, 1637–1800* (Baltimore, 1984), 499. Catherine might have been born in 1783. A mulatto slave from Byde Mill plantation "in possession of J. Steele" named "Kitty Ann" was baptized on February 19 of that year; see ibid., 500. See also David Lambert, *White Creole Culture, Politics, and Identity during the Age of Abolition* (New York, 2005), 52–65.

19. Improper emancipations were not uncommon. Bernard Moitt finds that whites in the French Caribbean regularly manumitted slaves without proper documentation or state consent; see Moitt, "In the Shadow of the Plantation: Women of Color and the *Libres de fait* of Martinique and Guadeloupe, 1685–1848," in David Barry Gaspar and Darlene Clark Hine, eds., *Beyond Bondage: Free Women of Color in the Americas* (Urbana, Ill., 2004), 37–59. Such manumissions were particularly tricky for those slaves with "liberté de savanne"—living semi-independently on a plantation.

20. Mary Ann Steele to Francis Bell, Sept. 28, 1798, in Gibbes, *Letter to John Beckles,* 14–15; Will of Mary Ann Steele, Feb. 20, 1799, PROB 11/1319, NAE. Details of Catherine and Edward's voyage across the Atlantic are few. In the court case arising from Bell's actions, some speculation emerged that he first sent Catherine and Edward to Tobago before they finally embarked for England. According to the register of Steele's plantation, Kendal, the children were sent to the port of Lancaster. From there, Stephen Walcott took them to London, along with an attending servant named James. Along the way, the group stopped in Liverpool, Birmingham, and Bristol. Bell paid £138 to Walcott for his troubles as well as an additional £21 for James's service. Once in London, Bell laid out money for the children's

Challenges to illegitimate heirs of color at the turn to the nineteenth century, therefore, originated from both white and mixed-race relatives. Like all British residents, mixed-race migrants faced off with one another in the metropole when personal finances came up against perceived legacy imbalances. This development should come as no surprise. Inheritance litigation was routine in eighteenth-century Britain, and virtually nothing—not even potential solidarity around factors of race—could prevent family members from suing one another. But white Britons also continued to use legal challenges in their efforts to wrest away large colonial fortunes from mixed-race kin. These were often not explicitly racial attacks. They were primarily the result of normal probate resolutions. But these suits nevertheless could have the effect of imposing colonial markers of race back onto migrants of color. They compelled English courts, if not a wider English audience, to consider the influence of mixed ancestry on the metropole's law, culture, and methods of property transmission.

Estimating the frequency of these attacks as well as the degree to which they changed over time is an incredibly difficult task. Missing, destroyed, and decayed sources make it virtually impossible to follow, let alone compile data on, these cases. Only an impressionistic sense of these suits can be made out. What is clear, though, is the somewhat routine experience of inheritance contests among white and mixed-race family members. Britons did not learn about the Caribbean's population of color or its mixed-race migrants to the metropole only through travel and political literature. They also learned about it firsthand through family networks, probate settlements, and inheritance suits. The accumulation of these contests created a private knowledge about separate households and rival heirs. The British public's interest in the topic emerged from shared experiences as well as abolitionist pamphlets. What

---

room and board as well as their education. The account register includes several presents made to a Dr. Foster for instructing Edward as well as to Catherine's teacher. Their maintenance in the metropolis was not at a bargain: the children's expenses in 1799 surpassed £250. Bell also gave a healthy provision to the children's mother in Barbados. Anna Slatia received £100 per year, despite the lack of provision for her in Steele's will. Mary Ann Steele and her lawyers contended that these were not accurate outlays of expense and that Bell had pocketed much of the money; see Account book for Kendal Plantation, Seaforth Papers, GD 46/17/18, fols. 8–19, NAS; and Gibbes, *Letter to John Beckles*, 45. Bell's fraud was further evident through his own accounting, in which he valued Steele's entire estate at an amount far less than the roughly £20,000 estimate that he originally made when discussing the amounts he would pay to Catherine and Edward; see Account book for Kendal Plantation, Seaforth Papers, GD 46/17/18, fol. 19. For more on the frequency of reenslavement, see Rebecca J. Scott, *Degrees of Freedom: Louisiana and Cuba after Slavery* (Cambridge, Mass., 2005).

piqued Britons' curiosity was, not that these were aberrant and exotic stories, but that they were relatively normal ones.[21]

The Mixed-Race Migrant in Fiction

British novelists reflected and contributed to growing criticism over the presence of mixed-race migrants and their inheritances. This came about, in part, as a result of the political stagnation of abolitionism. Parliament's failure to pass an abolition bill by 1793 sapped much of the polemical fervor driving reform for the rest of the decade. Prophesies of British racial amalgamation in the political press diminished in turn. Yet, this did not mean that mixed-race migrants left the spotlight. Sentimental novels took up the debate by meditating on family composition as it pertained to relatives of color. Mixed-race characters regularly appeared in literature, acting as foils for white protagonists. Metropolitan society's growing worry over family inheritances and composition made the trope of the mixed-race migrant a useful one. As wealthy, illegitimate children with problematic marriage prospects, these characters symbolized the British public's fears of fraught inheritances and racial mixture. Fictional portrayals also extended and expanded on the types of concerns British authors had expressed over mixed-race migration in the years leading up to the Haitian Revolution. Moreover, these characters served as reminders of the types of multiple and complicated households that could be easily spotted throughout the Isles.

Mixed-race migrants did not emerge suddenly in British novels. They had made an initial, though unimpressive, entrance in the early eighteenth century. The first major character of color debuted in the 1720 tale *The Jamaica Lady*. Although centered principally on Bavia, an Irish woman traveling to Britain from Jamaica, the story deals extensively with the character of Holmesia, a quadroon woman from Kingston. The narrator describes Holmesia as "a *Creole*, and consequently of a pale yellow Complexion" whose language was "part[l]y *English*, and part[l]y *Negroish*." This colonial dialect creates severe problems in communication once Holmesia arrives in England; a peddler mis-

---

21. Agnes M. Butterfield's frank description of the early neglect shown to Jamaica's Chancery and Supreme Court records speaks to the challenges of using these sources. Lack of resources combined with infestation and climate issues make many of the hundreds of volumes of the Supreme and Chancery Court ledgers too fragile for inspection. This renders a systematic survey of those records nearly impossible, and most individual cases cannot feasibly be followed in their entirety; see Butterfield, "Notes on the Records of the Supreme Court, the Chancery, and the Vice-Admiralty Courts of Jamaica," *Bulletin of the Institute of Historical Research*, XVI (1938), 88–89.

takes her for a gypsy as do two passersby and a constable. Another woman of color makes a similarly benign appearance in *The Fortunate Transport* (circa 1750). The story follows Polly Haycock, the product of a young woman raped in a haystack in Hampstead, who travels to Virginia and Jamaica. She eventually marries the deputy general of Jamaica and gives birth to several children whom she brings back with her to England. In the second part of the tale, the narrator reveals herself to be Polly's former slave in Jamaica who came to England with her master. She also describes herself as a "Creolian," which might have indicated the author's intention for her to be understood as of mixed ancestry. Yet, the racial component of these migrants operates far in the texts' backgrounds. This was consistent with the relatively fluid conception of race in Britain at midcentury. The first apparent mixed-race migrant protagonist from the period, Unca Eliza Winkfield, featured in *The Female American* (1767), did not bear African ancestry but Amerindian blood instead.[22]

Portrayals of mixed-race Britons at the end of the eighteenth century evolved significantly, inspired by the fashionable genre of sentimental romance. Made famous by Samuel Richardson's wildly popular tales *Pamela* (1740) and *Clarissa* (1748), sentimentality pervaded Georgian literature, philosophy, and correspondence. The genre's overriding interest in emotion—particularly extravagant emotion—captivated the reading public. Novels drove this fascination, while the transatlantic Great Awakening, with its evan-

22. *The Jamaica Lady: or, The Life of Bavia* (London, 1720), 8–9, 85; *The Second Part of the Fortunate Transport; Being a Continuation of the Lady's Adventures, from the Time of Her Arrival in England, to Her Death . . .* (London, [1750]), 18; Unca Eliza Winkfield, *The Female American; or, The Adventures of Unca Eliza Winkfield*, 2 vols. (London, 1767). In *The Jamaica Lady,* most of the commentary about Holmesia fixates on her colonial life, instead of her time spent in Britain. Perpetually crossing the Atlantic, she is conceived on board a transport ship, bound for Jamaica from London, by an English shoplifter and a mulatto shipman. Holmesia emulates her mother and becomes a prostitute to Kingston pirates before eventually being impregnated by her physician's friend. She then travels to London with the goal of marriage. On the voyage, she becomes a mistress to a fellow passenger. Yet, Bavia's actions on board are no different: she also has an affair with a member of the ship's crew, drawing parallels between the two female travelers. Carol Barash notes that both characters undergo similar sexual transgressions on the journey to England, indicating their juxtaposition as a measure of similarities rather than differences; see Barash, "The Character of Difference: The Creole Woman as Cultural Mediator in Narratives about Jamaica," *Eighteenth-Century Studies*, XXIII (1990), 416–422. The author's account of Holmesia's corporeal misbehaviors is therefore tied to her colonial origins, rather than her biological ones. In *The Fortunate Transport,* Barash interprets Polly's description as "Creolian" to mean that she is mixed race, but the term could have simply denoted her birth in the colonies (423–424).

gelical insistence on personal experience with emotion, helped to disseminate these ideas further. Members of the Scottish Enlightenment also spread the belief that individual feelings not only transferred to others but that emotional control could benefit society as a whole. Scholars have credited the rise of consumer and leisure markets to the emergence of sentimentality, which expressed "nostalgia for a social order in the process of being undermined and destroyed by nascent capitalism." In most cases, this was nostalgia for more traditional and stable family relations. Sentimental novels were primarily concerned with issues of legitimacy and legacy. Richardson's works focused on the struggles of female protagonists to marry and secure an inheritance. Many authors, attempting to duplicate Richardson's success, exploited the dramatic potential of a lost inheritance, often through the figure of an illegitimate or orphaned child. Much of the drama of these stories comes from the main character's frustrated passion for much wealthier and more socially advanced partners. Thus, the same forces causing concern within British households — legitimate kin, secure lines of inheritance, and rising capitalist pressures — were simultaneously altering literary customs.[23]

Two conventions that would be central to depictions of mixed-race travelers stand out in these tales. First is the near ubiquity of parental absence. If the protagonists are not either illegitimate or abandoned, then they often have little immediate parental contact. Pamela's interactions with her father and mother in Richardson's novel, for instance, are entirely through correspondence. Female protagonists typically have fractured relationships with fathers, and aunts often replace unseen mothers in the text. Orphanage, then, need not be literal to be perceived. Second, these works show an intense preoccupation with family relations through marriage, particularly in the case of female main characters. Bonds of matrimony replace those of blood in these stories, reflecting the general disinheritance many British women underwent during the period. Equally, bastards and foundlings appear to reflect a general concern about the weakened abilities of women to bargain in the social

23. Fredric Jameson, "Magical Narratives: Romance as Genre," *New Literary History*, VII (1975), 158. The stoic, Hobbesian, Calvinist approach of seventeenth-century philosophers gave way to the eighteenth century's more dynamic interest in passion and self-improvement through a reflection on one's feelings; see Adela Pinch, "Sensibility," in Nicholas Roe, ed., *Romanticism: An Oxford Guide* (New York, 2005), 50–51; and Pinch, *Strange Fits of Passion: Epistemologies of Emotion, Hume to Austen* (Stanford, Calif., 1996), 17–50. Literary obsessions over illegitimacy had long traditions; see Michael Neill, *Putting History to the Question: Power, Politics, and Society in English Renaissance Drama* (New York, 2000), 127–147.

marketplace. For middling Britons unable to pay off illegitimate claimants to a fortune, this interest in bastardy was essentially a preoccupation with how to divide family resources in a changing economic landscape. The figure of the illegitimate daughter represented the starkest version of that vulnerability.[24]

When authors inserted mixed-race figures into their stories, they drew on conventions surrounding inheritance and troubled parentage. Elite travelers of color were hyperbolic manifestations of those concerns. Virtually all mixed-race migrants were born out of wedlock to enslaved or recently freed mothers, and most arrived with large fortunes that appeared to compromise those of legitimate relatives in the metropole. Their legal status, along with large colonial subsidization, naturally made them vehicles for discussing complications in family inheritance. Additionally, migrants' backgrounds fit well within sentimental tropes. When analyzing migrants of color in Georgian literature, issues of race must not be privileged over themes of legitimacy and legacy. Although considerations of race were important, they were nevertheless closely tied to larger literary customs.

A diminished political fervor for abolitionism in the 1790s might have driven authors to include characters of color in their works in order to continue the public debate around race and empire, but an actual increase of these migrants might have also inspired such use. That colonial travelers visited the metropole with greater regularity after the Seven Years' War did not go unnoticed. Novelist Tobias Smollett, who lived briefly in the Caribbean and had been part of Britain's disastrous 1741 siege of Cartagena, put a mulatto rape victim on London's Old Bailey court docket in his 1769 work *The History and Adventures of an Atom*. Two years later, he depicted an English ball "opened by a Scotch lord, with a mulatto heiress from St. Christopher's." The number of Jamaicans who included provisions for mixed-race children in Britain also increased from the 1770s to the 1790s. Twenty-seven testators—nearly one-quarter of white men on the island who gave at least some money to an individual of color—noted between 1793 and 1795 that the mixed-race beneficiary had either spent time in Britain or would soon leave for it. So many individuals of color had traveled to the metropole that by 1796 a white Jamaican woman confidently wrote to her daughter that it would be no problem to

24. Ruth Perry, *Novel Relations: The Transformation of Kinship in English Literature and Culture, 1748–1818* (Cambridge, 2004), 77–106, 336–371, 372–373; Alastair Owens, "Property, Gender, and the Life Course: Inheritance and Family Welfare Provision in Early Nineteenth-Century England," *Social History*, XXVI (2001), 309–313; Lisa Zunshine, *Bastards and Foundlings: Illegitimacy in Eighteenth-Century England* (Columbus, Ohio, 2005), 13–14, 167.

find in Britain a "Brown or a Black person of a Fair character, who has been
already in the Island, and is inclined to return again." This relative swell of
West Indian migrants to Britain as the eighteenth century progressed might
have popularized such characters in British novels. The anxieties provoked by
mixed-race migrants within the confines of sentimental tales reflected insecurities about their real-world presence as well as the general concerns Atlantic
observers had over the domestic realm.[25]

One of the first substantial portrayals of a rich Caribbean migrant of color
dealt heavily with issues of inheritance and marriage in the metropole. The
1791 saga *Memoirs of a Scots Heiress* features Miranda, the daughter of a Dutch
settler and a black Surinamese woman, who lives next door to the titular Scottish heroine Anabel Macgilroy in London. Unlike novelists from earlier in
the century, the author readily discusses Miranda's appearance and ancestry:
"She was almost a negro. The hue of her skin perhaps wanted some shades
of the deep African dye; but it passed the degree of copper colour." Miranda
and Anabel share a number of qualities; both are from the colonies, both
are orphaned, both have claims to substantial legacies from rich uncles, and
both hold affection toward the same man. Yet, whereas Anabel's bequest is
contested, Miranda's inheritance is intact and immense. As would occur in
later novels, the mixed-race migrant puts the white protagonist's struggles further into relief. Miranda is the shadow sentimental heroine. Her fortune and
adherence to sentimental convention makes her understandable to readers,
while her lineage allows them to consider larger matters on race in Britain.[26]

25. [Tobias Smollett], *The History and Adventures of an Atom*, II (London, 1769), 21;
Smollett, *The Expedition of Humphry Clinker*, I (London, 1771), 55, 74; Ann Brodbelt to
Jane Brodbelt, Feb. 1, 1796, in Geraldine Mozley, ed., *Letters to Jane from Jamaica, 1788–
1796* (London, 1938), 129. For a review of Jamaica wills, see Appendix 1, below. For colonial visitors to London in the 1760s and 1770s, see Julie Flavell, *When London Was Capital
of America* (New Haven, Conn., 2010), 4–23; and Trevor Burnard, "Passengers Only: The
Extent and Significance of Absenteeism in Eighteenth Century Jamaica," *Atlantic Studies*,
I (2004), 182. Mulatto attendants crossing the ocean were also present in fiction from the
period. Charlotte Smith's 1794 tale *The Wanderings of Warwick* includes an account of a
mixed-race servant reading a newspaper to a Jamaican woman on the voyage to Britain; see
Smith, *The Wanderings of Warwick* (London, 1992), 97. The 1790s saw an acute literary turn
toward questions of household management and romantic love, as authors such as Mary
Wollstonecraft, William Godwin, and Gilbert Imlay questioned the fundamental structures
of patriarchal families; see Andrew Cayton, *Love in the Time of Revolution: Transatlantic
Literary Radicalism and Historical Change, 1793–1818* (Chapel Hill, N.C., 2013), 28–42,
182–194.

26. [Mrs. Charles Mathews], *Memoirs of a Scots Heiress*, 3 vols. (London, 1791), II,

Adhering closely to sentimental formula, Miranda's romantic interests figure into her juxtaposition to the main character. When Anabel—initially unwilling to embrace any romantic emotions—learns of Miranda's infatuation with her employer's son, Mr. Cyril, she records Miranda's unrestrained passions: "I witnessed the ecstasy of her joy. Wild as her native woods, and free as the gale that agitated them, she was ignorant of the cold reserves fashion enjoins." This depiction trades on simple stereotypes. Anabel's disposition is one of European restraint and moderation; Miranda's is one of Caribbean lasciviousness and uncontrollability. But such love is unrequited. Despite assuring Cyril, after a round of kisses, "Never mind: colour won't come off," Miranda cannot capture his heart. Cyril's attention, instead, is focused on Anabel. Miranda and Anabel's shared sweetheart reflects the novel's continued comparison between the two. The text's world is upended by the presence of a mixed-race grandee with intemperate emotions. It cannot be made stable until the rightful heiress takes her place.[27]

The issue of Miranda's infatuation underscores the novel's discomfort with women of color in the metropole. Her failed courtship with Cyril allows the author to comment directly on the problem of interracial relationships and Britain's future. Sufficiently spurned, Miranda goes into a deep illness, compelling the other characters to face the prospect of a forced union to bring about her recovery. Anabel, trapped between her own emerging desires and the quest to save Miranda, confronts Cyril. She accuses him of holding "narrow prejudices," to which he poses the question, "Can you call it *narrow* prejudice to dislike Miranda's colour?" The realities of marriage to a woman of color make the option unthinkable. "What say you to a brood of tawney children?" Cyril baldly asks. Such genealogical considerations sway Anabel, who

---

183–184; Sara Salih, "The Silence of Miss Lambe: *Sanditon* and Fictions of 'Race' in the Abolition Era," *Eighteenth-Century Fiction,* XVIII (2006), 340–341. Colonial matters saturate the text of *Memoirs of a Scots Heiress.* At the beginning of the novel, Anabel marries in Edinburgh, but, on the wedding day, a poor Irish woman with an indecipherable brogue informs Anabel, through a translator, that her inheritance belongs to the illegitimate Irish daughter of Anabel's benefactor. Anabel's husband immediately initiates the process of annulment, and she flees Scotland. After a fraught journey to London, Anabel is taken in by a family who are soon to travel to America (where the patriarch is staving off rebels in Quebec). Eventually returning to Britain, her ship is taken by American privateers and deposited on an uninhabited island before natives help her back to England. Colonial perfidy pervades this section on Anabel's time in America, indicating the author's sense of disorganization and debauchery on the imperial fringes. After all these adventures, Anabel returns to London, where she meets Miranda.

27. [Mathews], *Memoirs of a Scots Heiress,* II, 193–194.

quickly concedes that "the aversion he manifested comes into the world with us, and reason would in vain subdue [it]." Miranda's uncle also confesses, "Certainly a white man can never love a black woman," and even Miranda herself feels the potential match doomed. "Every body will cry out *black wife*. Mr. Cyril *black wife*," she laments, "Oh they will so laugh! and I shall die." Caught between these prejudices and the expectation of returned love, Cyril fights his instincts and proposes. Miranda is a suitable prospect for a young man seeking out a large dowry, but her African ancestry unsettles the proceedings.[28]

Cyril and Miranda's upcoming marriage pushes the tension over interracial pairings, but, in the lead-up, it underscores the perceived incompatibility of such a match in Britain. Miranda never accepts the authenticity of Cyril's proposal, fully aware of its social transgression. "Why was I not born in happy England," she wonders, "Why am I not of his complexion?" Nevertheless, preparations are made and the ceremony commences. In true sentimental fashion, however, Miranda is struck down as she recites her vows. In despair, she cries out, "Miranda's heart fail—black woman die; but black woman never make laugh at dear Cyril." She expires in Cyril's arms, to the shock of spectators. Her death helps to avoid a major obstacle in the plot: interracial unions in the capital and the prospect of additional Britons of color. Although Miranda is a sympathetic character in the narrative, when she attempts to assimilate fully into British society—in this case by marrying a white man—she violates public perceptions about a sacred boundary between European and African, metropolitan and colonist. Only in death can Miranda's transgression be absolved and avoided. Miranda's threat to Anabel's romantic happiness was a convention of sentimental literature as well as a comment on the social vulnerabilities many Britons felt at the time. Yet, she is also a product of decades of debate surrounding racial demography in both colony and metropole. Readers could thus ponder the meaning of her presence as a woman of color within the established context of the British romantic tale as well as in light of recent political developments.[29]

28. Ibid., II, 207–221, 230.

29. Ibid., II, 230, 238. Anabel describes Miranda's elegance in her wedding dress: "She always wore white of the finest kind, unmixed with any colour, and now she was drest in flowing muslin. . . . [W]ho that had seen Miranda that evening would have wished her a shade fairer than she was?" With fine clothes and luxurious accessories, Anabel emphasizes Miranda's racial difference. Her attire reinforces Miranda's complexion, and the contrast between her white dress and dark skin is portrayed as a futile attempt to downplay heritage (II, 230–236). Miranda's place in the romantic context of the novel is also crucially important. Almost immediately after Miranda's death, Cyril proposes to Anabel. For the remainder of

The sexual connotations of interracial relationships come forward with even greater vigor in a short volume published one year later. Although it reached a much smaller audience, a pornographic compilation entitled *The Cherub* hit on the same themes as *Memoirs of a Scots Heiress*. The collection of short stories opens with a warning about the seduction of young women in typical fashion for sentimental novels fixated on proper love matches. Each of the scenarios within *The Cherub* incorporates seduction into its plot: a young woman is drugged and raped; a West Indian heiress—presumably white—is lured into a sexual attack at a cottage in Wales. In perhaps the lewdest tale, "Boarding Schools," the publication incorporates a mixed-race migrant into its salacious themes. The comically named Mac Stamina, "a gentleman by birth, but . . . a younger son," who gains his wealth through industry rather than heredity, falls in love with "a young lady of great beauty, and immense fortune, from the West Indies" at school in London. The young Jamaican's radiance and exoticism go hand in hand. "She might have been perhaps six or seven degrees removed, by maternal lineage, from a beautiful Ethiope," the narrator observes, "but her features were divinely regular." When the young woman's headmistress secrets her away, after learning that Mac violated and impregnated her, the rake is most distressed that "the fortune, which was his first object, was now likely to slip through his fingers." Eventually, Mac pays off the headmistress and carries the Jamaican north to Gretna Green in Scotland for a quick elopement to secure his new bride's eighty-thousand-pound legacy. The victim's African heritage enlivens the pornographic component of the short story, while her colonial bequest grounds it in formulaic understandings of fictional seduction. Her Jamaican background fits perfectly in the text because it connects so easily to these traditional themes of hypersexuality and complicated inheritance. These were the same ideas expounded in political abolitionism. They now shared a home in literary publications—even those squirreled away in private drawers.[30]

---

the novel, the two struggle through a battery of obstacles to realize their love. One of these barriers is Anabel's reluctance to indulge her passion for Cyril. Miranda's example helps the narrator to overcome her reservations and embrace an emotional connection to her employer's son. She is aided by the fact that her still-husband Linfield finally dies, as does the heir to her uncle's fortune, shuffling the massive inheritance back to the protagonist. Now single and rich, Anabel can claim Cyril for herself and fulfill the twin goals of every sentimental heroine.

30. *The Cherub; or, Guardian of Female Innocence* (London, 1792), iii–9, 15–24; A. D. Harvey, *Sex in Georgian England: Attitudes and Prejudices from the 1720s to the 1820s* (New York, 1994), 61–78. Novels and short stories depicting interracial sexual assaults also found

Male migrants of color were not excluded in these tales and posed the same potential reproductive danger in sentimental works. John Moore's 1794 novel *Edward* includes a man of color, whose sexuality threatened metropolitan purity. Within two short passages of the story, Moore depicted a "young mulatto, whose father had left him a considerable fortune." The young man, accompanied by a local woman, purchases an unfashionable country house that no other buyer in England wants. In particular, the couple fawn over two sphinx sculptures at the house's entrance that locals mercilessly mock. Portrayed as an unsophisticated upstart, the young man's massive fortune is directed toward the gaudy, rather than the elegant. His black servant is also impressed with this sculpture, declaring, "She is very like massa's mother, and if she were made of *black* stone in stead of *white,* her face would be quite almost the same." Moore draws a direct line between the hybridity of the sphinx and the mulatto man as well as their apparent gracelessness. This metaphor extends further in a discussion between the house's former owner and a friend. Appalled that the home's original sculptures of a lion and a unicorn—the two figures in Britain's Royal Coat of Arms—have been reshaped into sphinxes, the friend complains bitterly about the alteration. "This attempt to convert these two royal animals into a couple of base Egyptians" was as disgraceful, he proclaims, "as permitting them to be placed over the shop-doors of perfumers, milliners, cork-cutters, shoe-makers, breeches-makers, and other tradesmen." Such changes are problematic for those "who wish to keep up the proper distinction between the king and the cobler." Once again, Moore connects the West Indian and the sculptures. Not only are both mixtures, of a sort, but they are each seen to degrade the British standard. The sphinx bastardizes the representation of royalty, while the mixed-race migrant supposedly compromises the racial state of Britain's upper classes.[31]

Reinforcing this theme of perceived aristocratic infiltration, the now-landed mulatto man sets about populating his home. Such domestication is presented in the text as an attack on English virtue and purity of blood. Once

---

an audience in the United States in this period; see Daniel A. Cohen, "Social Injustice, Sexual Violence, Spiritual Transcendence: Constructions of Interracial Rape in Early American Crime Literature, 1767–1817," *WMQ*, 3d Ser., LVI (1999), 481–526.

31. John Moore, *Edward; Various Views of Human Nature, Taken from Life and Manners, Chiefly in England,* I (London, 1794), 73, 75, 116–117, 119–120. Amanda Vickery argues that nonorthodox architecture was often used to attack a homeowner for being ill-bred; see Vickery, *Behind Closed Doors: At Home in Georgian England* (New Haven, Conn., 2009), 132.

more, the house serves as an allegory for the grandee. Its garishness only increases, owing to "the taste of three Ladies, who had successively been mistresses of it and of the Mulatto." Each of these women degrades the property's decor in tandem with themselves. One mistress implements a Chinese theme while beginning an affair with the mulatto man's black servant. She gives birth to a child, whom the West Indian provides for, "though of a complexion a shade darker than he expected." The next woman redirects the furnishings towards a Gothic aesthetic, but her lover soon tires of her. His last sweetheart nearly bankrupts the estate. Scared of the prospects of her benefactor's death, she mourns "the criminal state in which they both lived . . . [and] brought him to propose that they should expiate the guilt of their past commerce, and consecrate their future union by marriage." Married and settled, the West Indian is now at his most dangerous. His relationships with several English women pose a threat to the nation's moral fabric, but they also compromise its racial stock. As a landed husband, the West Indian can father legitimate children who might blend even more easily into England's elite circles. As with the sculptures, distinctions can be erased — this time between black and white as well as between rich and poor.[32]

The young mulatto man returns only briefly in the text as a subject of debate between two servants. His attendant argues with the servant of another household over their masters' statuses. The West Indian is attacked by the rival servant as a philanderer, a "mule," and "half a Christian." This latter comment infuriates the mulatto's footman. Asserting his master's religious bona fides, he shouts, "Why I am sure I once saw him in church . . . and he regularly eats cross-buns every Good-Friday, and minced pies at Christmas." The debate is as much about the West Indian's assimilation into English society as it is his colonial ancestry. Although he might perform Englishness, the young man of color is depicted as far from the archetype. "He is no full Christian, being between a Christian and a Blackamoor," the fellow attendant concludes; "his face would condemn him before any court in Christendom." Moore's inclusion of the West Indian migrant is a specific denunciation of the supposed degradation of English national integrity. Although Moore's other works often appealed to the humanity of slaves, his compassion did not extend to those of color in the metropole. *Edward*'s mulatto figure is one to be scorned, not only for his financial freedom in contrast to that of the novel's other characters but for his sexual independence as well. Far less success-

32. Moore, *Edward,* II, 15–16, 18, 21–27.

ful than Moore's previous work *Zeluco, Edward* nonetheless received critical praise on its publication. Undoubtedly its readers responded to the novel's trepidation over landed mixed-race wealth in Britain.[33]

Although containing comedic elements, Richard Cumberland's 1795 novel *Henry* plays with similar tropes of racial mixture, inheritance, and illegitimacy with a male migrant of color. The titular hero, an orphan as one might expect, is dogged for most of the first volume by Robert Blachford, a justice of the peace in a small English village. Blachford is declared to be "as base in heart as he is black in person." This castigation hints at his racial background. Blachford's genealogy is obscure, except that "he had made a fortune in the island of Jamaica from a very abject station in society." His mark as a West Indian influences assessments of his appearance. In one passage, he is described as being "of a stout athletic make, with a swarthy atrabilious complexion, strongly leaning toward the cast of the mulatto, with all his passions hot and fiery as indulgence could make them." Intemperate and dark in color, Blachford fits the stereotypical qualities of a mixed-race man before any evidence is proffered on his origins. Rumors of black ancestry were typical for West Indian characters. The illegitimate and orphaned Caribbean heroine of *The Solemn Injunction* (1798), for instance, endures the insults of a classmate at her English school who "insinuated she was a girl of colour" after becoming jealous of her beauty. For Blachford, these physical and emotional descriptions reflect his villainous personality, as he conspires to assault Henry's sweetheart, Susan, and to take Henry's life. Blachford succeeds in the first goal but fails in the second.[34]

The shadow of Blachford's heritage follows him throughout the text, until his death brings the issue starkly to light. On his deathbed, Blachford crafts a will giving nearly all of his riches to a single beneficiary. Henry receives the fortune and learns that Blachford was "the son of a certain planter in Jamaica, long since dead, by a Mulatto wench, who was his property." More news of Blachford's private life dampens Henry's excitement over his foe's conversion. Blachford had not only assaulted Susan but also impregnated her. Susan's young son, Henry declares, must be made the full beneficiary of the

---

33. Ibid., II, 21, 28–33. *Zeluco*, in particular, decried the inhuman punishment of slaves; see E. M. McClelland, "Sidelights on Universal Benevolence, 1789–1820," *Comparative Studies in Society and History*, IX (1967), 359–360. On the reception of Moore's more popular work, *Zeluco*, see, for instance, *Critical Review; or, Annals of Literature . . .*, XIX (London, 1797), 15–21.

34. [Richard Cumberland], *Henry*, 2d ed., 4 vols. (London, 1795), I, 47, 48, 153; Agnes Musgrave, *The Solemn Injunction*, 4 vols. (London, 1798), I, 182–184.

will, and he refuses Blachford's bequest. The dying Jamaican obliges Henry's appeal, leaving his illegitimate son an annuity of two thousand pounds. Blachford clearly begins the novel as a villain, and he is never fully exonerated, despite his attempt at absolution. His colonial and ancestral roots are meant to make him overly emotional and aggressive, inciting his lust to spread the sin of interracial relationships and illegitimacy further into the metropole. Blachford is a character comparable to Henry, but racial status clearly distinguishes the two. As with *Memoirs of a Scots Heiress,* the mixed-race character serves to put the experiences and problems of the white protagonist in relief. Blachford's rape of Henry's sweetheart emphasizes the tragedy of lost love in an extreme fashion, as does the child born from the attack. Cumberland uses the issue of paternal mixed ancestry to gild the lily. As with the other novels of the period, the birth of a mixed-race child in Britain provided the starkest example of the types of sentimental themes popular at the time. Moreover, it connected to the wider debates of the period around ethnicity and blood purity in the metropole.[35]

The regularity of tales with mixed-race migrants helped to propel sales of John Gabriel Stedman's 1796 autobiography of time spent in the Caribbean. Stedman had traveled to Suriname with the Scots Brigade in 1773 to put down an enslaved rebellion. His adventures there inspired him to write a memoir a decade and a half later. Although Stedman's original manuscript underwent significant revision by its publisher, the first edition of his *Narrative of a Five Years Expedition against the Revolted Negroes of Suriname* won wide acclaim. With a sympathetic attitude toward the enslaved — though altered by its publisher — the account appealed greatly to abolitionists, who used engravings and passages from the text to support their ongoing movement. Readers also responded to the personal details of Stedman's life, particularly his relationship to Joanna, an enslaved mulatto woman whom he married in a local custom. Though flesh and blood, Joanna served like many fictional characters of the time as the intermediary between the white colonizer and nonwhite subalterns. Her life appeared to follow a sentimental script. Joanna gave birth to the couple's son, Johnny, who traveled to England for school while his mother stayed in the tropics. Stedman accepted his mixed-race son into his new, legitimate home in England, and his European bride "tenderly loved" young Johnny. Adhering so closely to sentimental formula, Stedman's memoir took an easy place in an established genre. It energized interest in those

35. [Cumberland], *Henry,* II, 292, 327, III, 185; Wylie Sypher, "The West-Indian as a 'Character' in the Eighteenth Century," *Studies in Philology,* XXXVI (1939), 514.

tropes even more, especially as Stedman's humane portrayal of the enslaved connected strongly with abolitionism. His *Narrative* undoubtedly inspired literary authors to continue including mixed-race migrants in their sentimental works.[36]

As sentimentalism and abolitionism converged, popular publications often depicted mixed-race migrants in ways generally disconnected from real experience. Vicar-turned-novelist Edmund Marshall used a wrongly cast character of color in his 1797 tale *Edmund and Eleonora*. Passing through an English village, the novel's orphaned protagonist Edmund finds "a tall, elegant Mulatto girl" at the side of the road. Born in western Jamaica, Alicia Seldon is the daughter of a wealthy white planter and a formerly enslaved African. In a rather unrealistic fashion, Alicia's parents are married, a status that was not only exceptionally rare in Jamaica but had virtually no precedent in fiction. Marshall drew inspiration from the abolition movement and even employed his Jamaican character to address slave reform and imperial demography. Alicia's parents visit, and her father announces that he has freed his slaves. "They are no longer licentious like other negroes—polygamy is not permitted as heretofore, they marry, and are so prolific, that I now purchase no more slaves." This language borrows wholesale from abolitionist rhetoric around the fecundity of well-treated laborers. Such reproductive interest extends to Alicia as well. On her voyage between Jamaica and England, she is attacked by the ship's captain, who "made no scruple to make love to her." Once she arrives in England, Alicia becomes a model of female domesticity. She marries a music and dance teacher, Mr. Adderley, and gives birth to a daughter, blending seamlessly into the English pastoral. "Alicia is celebrated for her hams and her guinea-fowls," the narrator proclaims. Another character states that her home "was now become one of the most elegant cottages perhaps in the whole kingdom." Unlike previous authors, Marshall marks Alicia's inclusion into this society, not as destructive of metropolitan domesticity, but as an enhancement of it. She is an appropriation of a standard narrative trope, yet her portrayal diverges significantly from other accounts.[37]

36. For more on the publication history of Stedman's *Narrative,* see Richard Price and Sally Price, "Introduction," in John Gabriel Stedman, *Stedman's Surinam: Life in an Eighteenth-Century Slave Society; An Abridged, Modernized Edition of Narrative of a Five Years Expedition against the Revolted Negroes of Surinam,* ed. Price and Price (Baltimore, 1992). On the trope of the mixed-race intermediary, see Mary Louise Pratt, *Imperial Eyes: Travel Writing and Transculturation* (New York, 1992), 97–105. For the response of Stedman's bride to Johnny, see Stedman, *Stedman's Surinam,* ed. Price and Price, 318.

37. Edmund Marshall, *Edmund and Eleonora; or, Memoirs of the Houses of Summerfield*

Although promoted, rather than condemned, Alicia and Adderley's relationship nevertheless takes on a qualified endorsement. Marshall does not include any significant protests to the couple's interracial status. When Alicia's
African uncle arrives in England and proposes to a white woman, the town
celebrates. Only Eleonora offers a complaint to Alicia, declaring, "I could
wish, my dear Brunette, that your uncle could resolve to take a lady of his
own complexion, I mean one of his own countrywomen." But this objection
is stated primarily because he plans to marry Eleonora's governess, whom she
does not want to leave. Interracial unions are thus not a pointed threat in Marshall's novel, either for the mixed-race woman or the African man. Yet, Alicia's
nuptials come only under certain conditions. She is not entitled to marry the
novel's protagonist but rather one of its more peripheral characters. Moreover,
Adderley is, in many ways, the male version of Alicia. He privileges music
and dance, retains little distinguishing features, and comes undeservedly into
a large fortune—in his case by winning the lottery. Although certainly not
villains, Adderley and Alicia are not highly sympathetic characters. The for-
midable circumstances required to advance them into a state of contentment
speak to fundamental flaws in their natures. Alicia is not to be oppressed because of her African heritage, but neither is she to be privileged. In a story in
which "every body is *so good,* and every circumstance turns out *so happily,*"
according to the *Critical Review,* any such marks against Alicia's character are
likely larger concerns about a mixed-race presence in England than the author
was willing to betray.[38]

Such relatively positive portrayals, grounded in abolitionist sentiment,
were nevertheless the exception to more regular depictions based on racial
and familial insecurities. Latent fears over mixed-race migrants' inheritances
and sexuality came out more forcefully in stories without a firm abolitionist
message. Helena Wells's 1800 novel *Constantia Neville* played on the relationship between white and mixed-race colonists in Britain in order to criticize
this migration. Much the same as Anabel Macgilroy in *Memoirs of a Scots
Heiress,* the white heroine Constantia Neville is orphaned and dispossessed
of her fortune by the time she arrives in London. Born on Barbados, Constan-

and Gretton, 2 vols. (London, 1797), I, 95, 96, 126, 102, II, 214, 265; Seymour Drescher, *The
Mighty Experiment: Free Labor versus Slavery in British Emancipation* (New York, 2002),
42–53. Alicia's mother is an African princess, a literary throwback to the seventeenth-century
tale *Oroonoko,* which demonstrates Marshall's wholesale adoption of established ideas over
personal experience.

38. Marshall, *Edmund and Eleonora,* I, 193; *The Critical Review; or, Annals of Literature . . . ,* XX (London, 1797), 117.

tia's whiteness is closely guarded and cultivated in the colonies. "The pains taken to keep Constantia from the negroes . . . gave her at twelve years old a fluency of speech, and a correctness of language, which many of her seniors would have been proud to possess," the narrator informs the reader. Although a creole, she is not to be confused with those possessing African ancestors. The difference becomes important when she learns of two mixed-race siblings from Nevis who have recently settled in Dorset. Older brother Ned is set to inherit nearly half a million pounds and younger sister Felicia is entitled to ten thousand. Constantia is shocked to learn that they are the children of two separate enslaved women by the same English father. Her disgust at such colonial impropriety is exacerbated by her belief that metropolitan decorum has been violated. Mixed-race children should never be advanced and certainly not with such large fortunes. Like Anabel, Constantia's poverty is considered all the more shameful in light of the legacies of two descendants of slaves. Once again, mixed-race success in England, despite bloodlines, reinforces the sentimental notion of the protagonist's persecution in an unfair world.[39]

Although Ned and Felicia only hover in the background for a short period, the narrator takes extensive pains to disparage them. Nothing presents a greater problem than their inheritance. In direct mimicry of actual colonial anxieties regarding the disruption of family finances by illegitimate offspring of color, the mixed-race siblings' legacy comes at the expense of their extended white family in Dorset. After leaving Ned and Felicia the greater part of his estate, their father bequeaths only "the paltry sum of five thousand pounds to a brother, a clergyman . . . who had two sons and four daughters but slenderly provided for, and who had been buoyed up with the hope of succeeding to great part of their uncle's possessions." As inheritance challenges indicate, mixed-race legacies often infuriated white relatives awaiting a colonial fortune. Wells reinforces the ridiculousness of the bequests by casting Ned as an indolent grandee. Not only is he "idle," she apprises the reader, but he "knows that money will command all that he now considers necessary to happiness." Colonial notions of mixed-race laziness and degeneracy in-

39. Helena Wells, *Constantia Neville; or, The West Indian*, 2d ed., 3 vols. (London, 1800), I, 73–74, 77, II, 263–268. Still a young woman, Constantia discovers that her older brother has squandered the family's West Indian fortune. The financial trauma drives Constantia's father to an early grave and forces her mother back to Barbados to sort out the family's affairs, but she, too, dies there. Ned and Felicia's fortune is part of a larger set of comparisons drawn between the siblings and the protagonist. As Sara Salih notes, the two arrive in the novel at Constantia's most despondent point, and they are a foil to Constantia; see Salih, "The Silence of Miss Lambe," *Eighteenth-Century Fiction*, XVIII (2006), 344.

form the portrait of Ned. Both illegitimate and sluggish, he conforms to the worst prejudices against West Indians of color, making him unfit to receive his father's substantial estate.[40]

Constantia's fears about Ned and Felicia are ultimately realized, emphasizing the text's disgust with their status as elite mixed-race persons in Britain. Asked by Ned to move into their home in order to become young Felicia's governess, Constantia recoils, parroting her father's opinion that mulattos possess "the predominate [sic] bad qualities of both Europeans and Africans." Constantia then declines the offer, averting any threat of rape posed by an independent man of color with whom she would have lived. The author casts Ned as a West Indian lothario with poor judgment and no self-control, just like his white father had been. Given his African roots, he is the apparent symbol of Caribbean degeneracy and dissipation. His arrival in Britain therefore undermines the social boundaries of the metropole. But his colonial status is not the primary offense; Constantia herself is a West Indian in London. Instead, the siblings' racial heritage is the root problem. Their behavior, status, and class are all compromised by origins in slavery and interracial cohabitation. When Constantia learns that Ned has unsuccessfully attempted to court a "beautiful, highly-accomplished, and amiable young woman," she is excited to discover that the young woman rebuffed Ned on the grounds "that those who sent the issue of such connections [as Ned's] to Europe, were not aware of the evil consequences that might result to society from so doing." Wary of the prospect of Ned fathering children with the English elite, Constantia congratulates the woman as "she would be amply rewarded for not having been led to sacrifice her hopes of connubial happiness at the shrine of wealth."[41]

Race, therefore, is a central component to Wells's views on individuals of color in England. In many ways, she draws the most explicit and stark representation of racial purity of those authors who deployed a mixed-race British character in their writings. Ned and Felicia's inheritance is intensely problematic, primarily because of racial difference. More importantly, Ned's failure to woo an English bride toward the end of the novel speaks to the necessity of restricting his sexuality. Although the siblings appear only briefly in the

40. Inheritances were divided between families on either side of the Atlantic. The English wife of Jamaica's governor lamented of an army captain's death in 1805: "He died without seeing his children, and it is said has left all he is worth to his black mistress and her child. This is, I am afraid, but too common a case in Jamaica"; see [Lady Maria Nugent], *Lady Nugent's Journal of Her Residence in Jamaica from 1801 to 1805*, ed. Philip Wright (Kingston, Jamaica, 1966), May 17, 1805, 234; Wells, *Constantia Neville*, II, 265–272, 319, 322.

41. Wells, *Constantia Neville*, II, 273–282, III, 9–10, 67–69, 70–71.

text, their presence frames the debate on metropolitan sexuality: ethnic purity stands at the pinnacle of colonists' potential romance in the home country. According to Wells, interracial pairings were already far too common in the colonies; the prospect of continuing such a practice in Britain was too forbidding for the novel to have entertained seriously.[42]

Sentimentality in literature could evoke empathy for mixed-race migrants, but it could also solicit fear. *Constantia Neville, Henry,* and *Edward* each damn their figures of color as scourges preying on white Englishwomen. Interracial pairings in Britain are thus rebuked outright and not put into a wider romantic context. Equally, the characters' inheritance facilitates their sexual dalliances, while also upending Britain's emerging class system. Although some authors could reflect on mixed-race migration within an abolitionist context of racial tolerance, others represented the matter as unmistakably horrific. Abolitionism, therefore, influenced sentimental literature of all stripes, although the message could deviate substantially.

Ultimately, sentimental tales featuring mixed-race characters in the last decade of the eighteenth century reinforced the same themes touted by abolitionists and polemicists in previous years. Mixed-race sexuality in Britain loomed as a major problem in these texts, just as authors debating abolition worried over the potential impact of elites of color on British bloodlines. Illegitimacy and inheritance also saturated these novels, in keeping with society's general interest in such topics. Legitimacy and legacy had long dominated questions of family organization, including those with mixed-race members. Fictional accounts of migrants of color, then, effectively continued a long-standing discourse around the real-world arrival of mixed-race West Indians. Authors adopted that language to energize the emotional aspect of their sentimental stories, but they also included these characters to comment directly on mixed-race migration. That so many writers used such characters demonstrates how interested the British public was in the continued occurrence of this social phenomenon. It also reveals the anxiety many Britons held toward multiple and contested families.

42. Wells introduces yet another colonist in England to reinforce the importance of metropolitan racial purity. In the novel's third volume, the character of Luke appears as Constantia's love interest. A young European kidnapped and raised by native Americans in New York, Luke is recovered and sent to Britain for an education. After Constantia learns that Luke's parents were friends of her family, she falls deeply in love, and the two soon marry. Raised in a native culture, Luke embodies the trappings of a mixed-race man, yet he is not biologically hybrid. Although Luke might be partly Indian in behavior, he is entirely European in blood and thus adequate for marriage; see Wells, *Constantia Neville,* III, 12–20, 49.

Competing Households

Visitors to John Tailyour's grand Scottish home, newly purchased after his return from Jamaica in 1792, must have been impressed. After passing by dozens of sheep and cattle grazing on the estate's fourteen hundred acres on the outskirts of Montrose, they saw Kirktonhill rise up from its surroundings. The building was spacious. Tailyour entertained his guests in a large drawing room filled with more than twenty chairs and two sofas. Occasionally, Tailyour would tempt callers into a circular gaming room to play cards. A stable of fifteen horses offered more active diversions for those who enjoyed foxhunting. Quieter recreation could be found in the home's well-stocked library. In the evening, servants plated meals on fine china with silver utensils in an airy dining room. During such banquets, visitors could drink liberally from a selection of more than four thousand bottles of wine kept in the cellar: Tailyour himself preferred Madeira and claret. Nine bedrooms and a nursery housed the growing family within Kirktonhill, attended to by servants boarded in three separate chambers. At the heart of the estate was the business room, where Tailyour dispatched regular letters to associates, oversaw the management of his finances, and kept up contact with friends across the Atlantic. Tailyour did not cut himself off wholly from the West Indies after he left Jamaica, but Kirktonhill allowed him to rebuild an identity as a Scottish laird, rather than as a West Indian grandee.[43]

The splendor of Kirktonhill blessed the offspring of Tailyour's new, legitimate family, not those whom he fathered in Jamaica. Among a host of reasons, Tailyour left the Caribbean to get married and raise children who did not hold genealogical ties to slavery. This decision came, in part, from the pressure put on him by British relatives who hoped that he might distance himself from his colonial household. But he also did so as the result of his desire to establish a legitimate line of succession through which to pass on his property. Within a year of arriving back in Scotland, he wed Mary McCall, the daughter of his former employer, and the two soon welcomed children into their home.

43. Details of Kirktonhill and its contents can be found in the inventory of John Tailyour's will, Feb. 18, 1816, Commissary Court Records, CC 20/7/8, fols. 666–680, NAS. See also George Robertson, *A General View of Kincardineshire; or, The Mearns* . . . (London, 1810), 135, 171–172. Many other imperial adventurers in the seventeenth and eighteenth centuries used the colonies as a stepping-stone toward the landed classes back in Britain; see Nuala Zahedieh, "An Open Elite? Colonial Commerce, the Country House, and the Case of Sir Gilbert Heathcote and Normanton Hall," in Madge Dresser and Andrew Hann, eds., *Slavery and the British Country House* (Swindon, U.K., 2013), 69–77.

Scotland was supposed to offer Tailyour a relatively clean break from the life he led in the tropics. Yet, his Jamaican family did not simply disappear from view. Tailyour continued to pay for his offspring of color to come to Britain and supported them while there, but none of them stayed at Kirktonhill. Many other West Indian sojourners traveled this same path.

The principal casualties of these new, legitimate households in Britain were the colonial women of color who had served and cared for their white companions dutifully. Interracial partnerships in Jamaica could resemble British marriages, but white men almost never formalized them, making the women virtually powerless if abandoned. Jamaica held no laws barring marriage between whites and individuals with non-European ancestry, but legality did not induce compulsion, even though white colonists regularly referred to black and mixed-race lovers as wives. Monitoring James Stothert's plantation in Martha Brae, for instance, John Fowler updated the absentee in Scotland about the estate's white overseer and "Mulatto wife." These households were, not poor simulacra of British marriages, but roughly functional copies of sacralized relationships. White men frequently freed and financed colonial partners, especially when they shared children. Stothert later received a letter about his own mixed-race daughter, Rebecca, whom he had left behind in Jamaica. In this case, the correspondent asked if Stothert could free Rebecca, as she was now the author's mistress. Declarations of affection also brought these relationships closer to a companionate model. John Tailyour wrote of the high esteem he held for his mistress Polly when manumitting her. Likewise, James Wood expressed intense grief at the funeral of his mixed-race partner Ann Parsons when he drunkenly berated the minister conducting her service. Regardless of these factors, matrimony between whites and those with African heritage was essentially unheard of. The prejudices surrounding race in Jamaica hindered white interest in marrying lovers of color, but commentators swore that men in the islands were uninterested in nuptials of any kind. Thomas Atwood noted in 1791 of Dominica: white men "flatter themselves they shall soon return wealthy to their own countries. Buoyed up with these notions, they look upon matrimony as a bar to their expectations." This repulsion to West Indian marriages, Atwood claimed, spurred British men to cohabit instead with women of color. But the desire to marry ultimately did push many to leave.[44]

44. John Fowler to James Stothert, Apr. 15, 1787, James Stothert Letters, WCL, Isaac Grant to Stothert, June 10, 1799; John Tailyour to Simon Taylor, Jan. 3, 1790, Simon Taylor Papers, ICS 120 XIV/A/50, ICS; John Barton to Beilby Porteus, May 21, 1796, Fulham

Pressures to wed and have legitimate children often originated from British kin upset with their relatives' colonial arrangements. John Tailyour's mother Jean wasted no opportunities to comment disapprovingly on his actions in Jamaica. His move to the island never sat well with her, and Jean insisted that he not spend too much time there. She worried that Tailyour would "Stay long and have many Children." Jean kept up this refrain in her letters to the Caribbean. After learning second-hand that Tailyour's mistress Polly was pregnant with another child, Jean scolded her son, "I would wish you to have no more till you have a Wife." Not surprisingly, she penned a glowing letter after learning that Tailyour intended to return to Scotland to pursue such nuptials. She made no comment on his leaving Polly. For as much as Tailyour opened up about his mixed-race offspring and depended on his family to watch over them in Britain, he said virtually nothing about his children's mother. Equally, his relatives in Scotland did not care to discuss her either. If families across the Atlantic were willing to care for the children of interracial partnerships, they nonetheless did not wish to reflect too closely on the origins of those offspring.[45]

Biases against mixed-race children, along with perceived scandals around interracial relationships in Britain, almost universally kept Jamaican mistresses in the Caribbean. Although they were the mothers of these men's mixed-race offspring now crossing the Atlantic, they could not be recognized in the same way as their children. Understandings of patriarchal obligation validated the care of mixed-race kin, both in Jamaica and Britain, but European notions of sexuality and gender roles rarely countenanced any legitimization of conjugal relations across the color line. Such lack of metropolitan recognition was also the product of general British attitudes against women—especially poor women—with illegitimate children. Both their racial and gendered status made them unable to accompany their children to Britain. This travel prohibition not only strained relationships with their offspring but also potentially risked severing the connection to their children's fathers as well. Without the ongoing backing of a white companion, these Jamaican women retained far less financial and social support. They were, in effect, abandoned.[46]

Palace Papers, XVIII, fols. 78–79, LPL; Bryan Edwards, *The History, Civil and Commercial, of the British Colonies in the West Indies*, 2 vols. (Dublin, 1793), II, 21–22; J. B. Moreton, *Manners and Customs in the West India Islands . . .* (London, 1790), 106; Thomas Atwood, *The History of the Island of Dominica . . .* (London, 1791), 210.

45. Jean Tailyour to John Tailyour, Mar. 29, 1785, Tailyour Papers, WCL, Apr. 21, 1788, Feb. 21, 1789, Nov. 20, 1789.

46. Patricia Crawford, *Parents of Poor Children in England, 1580–1800* (New York,

John Tailyour left Jamaica soon after his eldest son James had departed for Britain. Multiple reasons motivated his decision. Many migrants to Jamaica never intended on staying permanently, especially Scots who saw few trappings of home on the island. Three years before Tailyour left, Scottish residents in Kingston—perhaps including Tailyour himself—had petitioned the assembly for help in erecting the colony's first Presbyterian kirk, to no avail. Ultimately, continued illness and a desire to marry compelled Tailyour to quit the island. Throughout his residence in Jamaica, Tailyour complained regularly of bad health. After a fall from a horse left his body severely bruised in 1791, he wrote to cousin Simon, "I sincerely think a change of Climate absolutely necessary if not for the preservation of any Life to prevent my constitution being broke and ruined beyond all hopes of recovery." In August of the next year, he sailed for London. After several weeks in the capital, Tailyour decided to visit Scotland, partly in the hope of finding a bride there. On his way up through England to Montrose, he marveled at how Britain had changed since he left it more than a decade earlier. "Anarchy and madness seem to gain ground" in Europe, he proclaimed. The French Revolution disturbed him, but equally Tailyour worried over the "democratic and levelling Principles" popularly expressed by Britons. Fortunately, he reassured Simon Taylor in December 1792, such political upheaval had distracted the public from abolitionism, which Tailyour believed to have effectively died out. Perhaps more comforting still to Tailyour, his health improved dramatically in Scotland. He declared to have felt better than he had the previous three years.[47]

With improved spirits, John Tailyour set about courting a wife. In his letters, Tailyour did not reveal his criteria for a future bride. If he was anything like fellow Jamaican resident James Johnston, Tailyour might have simply felt excited to observe so many white women after years in the Caribbean. Writing two years after Tailyour started looking for a wife, Johnston asked his brother to find him a potential mate in England but warned, "They must have no Negroe blood or else I am off." Johnston's comment demonstrates the unease some West Indian men had in domesticating with women of color generally. But it also reveals his understanding that a portion of elite English women

2010), 38–48. There were some exceptions to this ban on mothers of color coming to Britain, including a man known to John Tailyour, Robert Cooper Lee, who married his mixed-race mistress Priscilla Lee in London; see Anne M. Powers, *A Parcel of Ribbons: The Letters of an 18th Century Family in London and Jamaica* (n.p., 2012), 151–155.

47. *JAJ*, Oct. 22, 1788, VIII, 413; John Tailyour to Simon Taylor, Feb. 12, 1792, Simon Taylor Papers, ICS 120 XIV/A/86, ICS, Dec. 1, 1792, ICS 120 XIV/A/90; John Tailyour to William Miles, July 31, 1792, Tailyour Papers, Letter Book 3, WCL.

were either mixed-race Jamaicans themselves or their offspring. This made them — at least in his eyes — inappropriate wives. Tailyour made no such pronouncements. Ever pragmatic, he mostly hoped to find an affluent partner. He did not have to look far. Within months of arriving in Glasgow, he asked his former employer George McCall for the hand of his daughter Mary. George ran a successful merchant house specializing in the Virginia tobacco trade and had given Tailyour his first start in the mercantile profession. The business fell on hard times after the American Revolution, but both McCall and Tailyour anticipated an eventual return to prosperity. Mary would cement that trade connection as her groom hoped to expand and oversee his affairs from Scotland. Tailyour likely saw in Mary a path toward even deeper merchant networks solidified through matrimony, rather than simply professional association. George likely felt the same way, as he voiced approval of the match. Although Mary's personal thoughts about the union are unknown, her father flattered Tailyour that he had "long lain near [Mary's] heart." Fifteen years his junior, she also impressed Tailyour with her "good disposition, [and] affectionate Temper . . . with notions of Gaiety and extravagance." On June 25, 1793, just months after proposing, John Tailyour wed Mary McCall in Glasgow. Together they would start their own family, opening a new chapter in the merchant's life.[48]

For ascendant Scots, purchasing a landed estate completed the picture of social success, and Tailyour could not avoid this pressure. Many houses struck his fancy, but he had long held designs on one particular property. Kirktonhill had originally belonged to Tailyour's father, but the family had sold it shortly before the patriarch's death in 1780 to pay off debts. Losing the home, along with a subsequent property named Balmanno, had diminished the family's standing, and John Tailyour wished to rehabilitate its reputation. Although he had made a fortune in Jamaica, Tailyour knew that purchasing the old manors would strain his finances, especially as he had just begun the

48. James Johnston to Robert Johnston, Aug. 26, 1795, Powel Family Papers, box 44, folder 1, Historical Society of Pennsylvania Library, Philadelphia; George McCall to John Tailyour, Mar. 30, 1793, Tailyour Papers, WCL; John Tailyour to Simon Taylor, Apr. 3, 1793, Simon Taylor Papers, ICS 120 XIV/A/95, ICS; Marriage of John Taylor and Mary McCall, June 25, 1793, Marriages, Parish of Glasgow, OPR, ref. no. 644/1, GROS. John was born in Montrose on June 18, 1755; Mary was born in Glasgow on June 27, 1770; see Baptisms, Parish of Glasgow, June 27, 1770, OPR, ref. no. 318/00, ref. no. 644/1, GROS. Arranged marriages without the consent of the bride were by no means unknown for the gentry and aristocracy in this period; see Judith Schneid Lewis, *In the Family Way: Childbearing in the British Aristocracy, 1760–1860* (New Brunswick, N.J., 1986), 20–25.

process of divesting himself from colonial slave markets. He begged cousin Simon for a loan in 1795—a request Simon immediately refused. Still more requests followed, but, by 1797, Tailyour had collected enough money to buy Kirktonhill himself. At the end of that year, he purchased the estate back for the hefty sum of £16,500 sterling, paying an almost equal amount for an adjacent parcel of land. Without any hesitation, he began making plans to refurbish the home and update its appearance. Over the next three years, workers expanded Kirktonhill to reflect Tailyour's grand taste. In the meantime, he and Mary expanded their family in turn. Before moving into Kirktonhill permanently in 1800, Mary gave birth to three children: Robert, Simon, and Mary. Named after Tailyour's brother and cousin, with the daughter christened after her mother, each child reflected the importance that kinship continued to play in the household. Seven more children would eventually arrive, ready to fill up Kirktonhill's spacious interior.[49]

Despite all these efforts to root himself firmly in Scotland, Tailyour remained intimately connected to his Jamaican family. Over the next few years, at least two more of Tailyour's Jamaican children would arrive in Britain, and he kept himself involved in their lives through correspondence. Yet, he tried his best to ignore their mother Polly. Owing to strained relations, a direct command from Tailyour, or the later destruction of letters, Tailyour's correspondence contains no notes from Polly updating him on her condition. Perhaps she simply could not write letters herself. Instead, friends still on the island kept Tailyour abreast of his erstwhile mistress and her children. His business partner James Fairlie gave reports on Polly in the final stages of her pregnancy with Catherine, the couple's last child together. He also noted when Simon and John, the two middle children, had come down with colds. When Polly finally gave birth to Catherine, Tailyour received multiple notices from Jamaican contacts eager to inform the absent father. One of his closest friends, James Renny, congratulated Tailyour on "an addition to your family a fine Girl." These letters did not spare on information. Fairlie wrote once more several months later to reassure Tailyour that Catherine "will be fairer than John." Intent on sending all of his children to Britain, Tailyour likely breathed a sigh of relief that Catherine's light skin might make it easy to assimilate in

49. John Tailyour to Simon Taylor, Aug. 29, 1795, Simon Taylor Papers, ICS 120 XIV/A/113, ICS, Jan. 6, 1795, ICS 120 XIV/A/118, July 31, 1795, ICS 120 XIV/A/123; Andrew Jervise, *Epitaphs and Inscriptions from Burial Grounds and Old Buildings in the North-East of Scotland* (Edinburgh, 1875), 134; John Tailyour to Simon Taylor, Feb. 2, 1798, Simon Taylor Papers, ICS 120 XIV/A/141, May 4, 1798, ICS 120 XIV/A/142.

the metropole. Other Jamaican friends agreed. Proving just how connected John Tailyour was to his wife's relatives — and just how difficult it was to keep his Jamaican and British families separate — John McCall, Tailyour's new brother-in-law, had also moved to Jamaica at a young age and knew Polly and her children well. McCall checked in on Catherine after her birth and echoed Fairlie's assessment of the newborn's fair skin and resemblance to her older brother. He also raved over Catherine's substantial red hair.[50]

Updates from John McCall continued to arrive, and they reveal Polly's ability to lobby successfully for herself and her children, even though she stayed behind in Jamaica. Polly appears to have trusted McCall most, and he wrote comfortably about their regular interactions. Because of his frequent correspondence with Tailyour, McCall soon acted the diplomat between Polly and her former companion. The loss of Tailyour's influence and presence once he departed Jamaica undoubtedly worried Polly, who now had to depend chiefly on the kindness of his old friends. Moreover, Tailyour did not provide generously for his former mistress, handing out, instead, a basic subsistence to cover her expenses as well as those of their offspring who had not yet left for Britain. Furthermore, within a year of leaving, Tailyour put his Kingston home, in which she and the children were still living, up for sale. This development made Polly "a little anxious," particularly because Tailyour did not inform her of where they would go next. The uncertainty of her living situation was especially stressful because Polly had just given birth to Catherine, while caring for five-year-old Simon and three-year-old John. The matter was still unsettled when George Atkinson purchased the home for fourteen hundred pounds. Polly convinced either Atkinson or McCall to delay the property transfer until she had found a new residence. Atkinson agreed, but, after a month passed without Polly moving out, he demanded that she leave. Once again, Polly had to solicit the help of John Tailyour's colonial friends. His business partners found her and the children a temporary home — which McCall noted cost the extravagant sum of fifty pounds per year — but much of the furniture she shared with Tailyour was now sold. Tailyour also got rid of his domestic slaves, who had been attending the Jamaican family. Now living in a small home, poorly furnished, without the help of enslaved servants or the presence of a white companion, Polly's life had changed abruptly. Likewise,

50. James Fairlie to John Tailyour, Sept. 16, 1792, Tailyour Papers, WCL, James Renny to John Tailyour, Oct. 5, 1792. See also Peter Ballantine to John Tailyour, Oct. 14, 1792, ibid., James Fairlie to John Tailyour, Dec. 25, 1792, and John McCall to John Tailyour, Oct. 14, 1792, May 12, 1793.

her children were now growing up in much altered circumstances, ones she likely thought unbecoming of their newly freed standing.[51]

In correspondence with Tailyour, John McCall gave strong impressions of the consternation and heartache felt by Polly throughout these proceedings. Tailyour had originally settled into a refined home in Kingston, where his young family grew up hearing his intentions of sending them to school in Britain. The dismantling of that home and those possessions after Tailyour left must have torn at Polly's soul. Having only recently been manumitted herself, she no doubt worried about her future in a slave society like Jamaica. She therefore desperately wished to appease Tailyour by reassuring him that she could make do with a modest allowance. Regularly called on by Tailyour's old friends, Polly also worked diligently to show them that she was both "frugal and industrious" and therefore deserving of continued support. These efforts convinced McCall, who backed Polly's request that part of her allowance go toward the purchase of an enslaved servant to help in the house. Ultimately, one wonders how she felt about Tailyour's abandonment. Perhaps she had originally seen their relationship simply as a way out of slavery. Maybe she had grown attached to him—as he admitted being to her—as both a companion and the father of her children. Regardless, their relationship transformed fundamentally when Tailyour left. Reports on the birth of his new son in Scotland did not take long to reach Polly, especially because her closest associate to Tailyour was the child's uncle, John McCall. With utmost grace, she gave "best wishes to Mrs. Taylor and [the] little Boy."[52]

Tailyour's frugal turn toward his Jamaican family persuaded Polly to take greater action for their daughter Catherine. From John McCall's letters, it appears that Tailyour had always planned on sending each of the three boys—James, Simon, and John—to the metropole. Removing boys from their mothers' influence was a long-established tradition among British men when arranging children's education. This practice might have been doubly important for those hoping to distance offspring from any African influence in Jamaica. Catherine's fate hung in the balance. Like many of her colonial peers, Catherine's gender marked her as an unlikely migrant to Britain. Mixed-race girls crossed the Atlantic with much less frequency than their brothers. Among Jamaican wills with bequests for mixed-race children traveling to Britain from 1773 to 1815, 65 percent of the migrants were male. More specifically, 56.1 per-

51. John McCall to John Tailyour, July 14, 1793, ibid., Aug. 11, 1793, Sept. 8, 1793, Oct. 20, 1793, Jan. 19, 1794.
52. Ibid., Mar. 2, 1794, Aug. 10, 1794, Dec. 21, 1794.

cent of these wills made provisions only for boys to be sent abroad. Another 26 percent made stipulations only for girls, and a final 17.5 percent included both in plans for Europe. More revealingly, 14 percent of all wills asked that a son of color be sent abroad, while a daughter of color stayed behind. Only 5 percent made the reverse stipulation. These trends against girls grew worse over time. Whereas roughly equal numbers were asked to go to Britain in wills from 1773 to 1775 (fifteen boys versus thirteen girls), nearly double the number of young men as young women were sent abroad in wills from 1793 to 1795 (thirty-one boys versus seventeen girls). Whites with children of color, then, often paved the way for their sons to receive an education in Britain, while their daughters remained in the colonies.[53]

Popular accounts confirm these gender biases. Physician George Pinckard reported in 1796 that a white father in the Caribbean either apprenticed mixed-race sons to artisans or "sen[t] them to Europe to be educated." Yet, the same man had no qualms about "giving out the daughters, in keeping, to his friends . . . [as] the best provision the parent can make for his daughter [is] to place her with a respectable man as his *bonnie amie.*" A British commissioner to the West Indies later agreed that "the cruelty to sons [of color] is much less when they are sent to Europe for education" but that mixed-race girls received little support from fathers. "How few men have any higher views for their coloured daughters than that they shall be concubines, and shall run all the risks of being thrown from that state into prostitution!" he exclaimed. This was not entirely correct. As shown earlier, a number of fathers sent daughters to British schools, and even many of those kept behind would eventually own businesses, cattle pens, or in rare cases plantations. But the preferential treatment given to mixed-race sons stemmed from general attitudes on both sides of the Atlantic that privileged male over female inheritance. At the same time, colonial employment, albeit in sexual labor, could be better for mixed-race

53. Anthony Fletcher, *Growing up in England: The Experience of Childhood, 1600–1914* (New Haven, Conn., 2008), 149. Educating children at a distance from their mother was also true for Spanish colonists in Peru, who hoped to take their mestizo children away from an indigenous influence by sending their offspring to Spain; see Jane E. Mangan, "Moving Mestizos in Sixteenth-Century Peru: Spanish Fathers, Indigenous Mothers, and the Children in Between," *WMQ*, 3d Ser., LXX (2013), 273–278. For statistics on Jamaican children sent to Britain for an education, see Wills, 1773–1815, LOS 41–42, 49–51, 57–58, 60–61, 70–75, 87–91, IRO. There might be some inaccuracy in these statistics, primarily because fathers did not provide equally for all children. Some wills might have sent a daughter of color to Britain while a mixed-race son was not listed, owing to the father's negligence. However, the trend favoring young men over women in the data seems clear.

women than men. As mistresses and domestic partners, women of color could draw on white patronage beyond immediate family in a way that mixed-race men could not. Such racial divisions in sexual coupling also made free men of color less ideal partners for mixed-race women who hoped to draw on white influence. As Simon Taylor wrote to George Hibbert, Jamaica's mixed-race women "never will have any commerce with their own Colour but only with White People." As a woman of color herself, Polly likely reflected on her own experiences when anticipating her daughter's future in Jamaica. This realization, along with John Tailyour's recent stinginess, pushed her to act.[54]

Speaking through John McCall, Polly asked Tailyour to pay for Catherine's passage to Britain. This request appears to have gone against a previous agreement between the couple. Before leaving Jamaica, Tailyour had made an accord with Polly about the children. Whereas Tailyour wished to send the boys to British schools, Polly asked that any girls that they might have be kept on the island. Did she feel comfortable with her daughter fitting into the stereotypical expectations for colonial women of color? Did she simply want at least some children around her before Tailyour's inevitable flight? Her original motives are unclear, but, once Tailyour was gone, Polly changed her mind. She claimed that her new reasons for wanting Catherine to leave stemmed from her concern that "Girls these times are under no controal of their mother." Yet, the turmoil surrounding the Kingston home and the selling of Tailyour's colonial possessions had clearly inspired this decision. Polly worried about her daughter, admitting that she was "not capable of bringing her up as she would wish," and asked Tailyour that, when Catherine was "old enough, to order her home." Simon and John were both soon to leave for Britain, and John McCall suggested that Polly put Catherine on the same ship. Polly reflected carefully about sending a toddler abroad, but soon her daughter would arrive in Britain as well. She watched each member of her family in Jamaica

54. George Pinckard, *Notes on the West Indies . . .* , 2d ed., 2 vols. (London, 1816), II, 136–137; James Walker, *Letters on the West Indies* (London, 1818), 170; Simon Taylor to George Hibbert, Jan. 14, 1804, Simon Taylor Papers, ICS 120 F/42, ICS. Pinckard's publication was a compendium of letters written beginning in the 1790s. The letter cited here was penned on December 20, 1796. Hector McNeill claimed that "the brown lady considers it as a step *derrogêr a noblesse,* to descend to any thing darker than her own complexion"; see McNeill, *Observations on the Treatment of Negroes, in the Island of Jamaica* (London, [1800]), 42. On the professional options available to elite women of color in Jamaica, see Verene A. Shepherd, ed., *Women in Caribbean History: The British-Colonised Territories* (Kingston, Jamaica, 1999), 73–76; and Shepherd, *Livestock, Sugar, and Slavery: Contested Terrain in Colonial Jamaica* (Kingston, Jamaica, 2009), 85.

sail off. Left alone on the island, Polly eagerly awaited any scraps of correspondence that might let her know how they fared in the world. Meanwhile,
she won some small victories for herself. Lobbying through John Tailyour's
former clerk, David Dick, Polly gained enough money to purchase several
additional household slaves. She would not have her children, but she would
have the higher status of slaveholder, which might "enable her to live comfortably hereafter."[55]

By 1796, all of Tailyour's Jamaican sons, and possibly his daughter, were
in Britain. John went to the same boarding school in Yorkshire as his brother
James. Catherine's early years are unclear, but she eventually lived for a time
with her aunt and namesake in Montrose. Simon's whereabouts are even mur-
kier. Almost nothing is written of him during these years, and it is possible
that he died sometime shortly before, or after, the other children's voyages to
Britain. Each of them visited British family after they arrived, and Tailyour's
brother Robert continued to monitor the boys' progress in school. But they
were considered a different family from the one whom John and Mary Tailyour
were raising at Kirktonhill. Tailyour's correspondents often distinguished his
legitimate household by labeling it the "Kirktonhill family." Nontraditional
families were not unusual in Britain, and certainly not in Scotland. Illegitimacy was a regular feature of early modern life, as were half-siblings. However, in light of the political changes of the period—revolutionary struggles,
abolitionism, imperial reform—these domestic situations took on new meaning. Every one of Tailyour's associates understood that caring for mixed-race
offspring went against much of the recent obsessions over race and family that
these changes brought about. Their willingness to aid and abide such politically charged members of the clan show how powerful the bonds of family
could be.[56]

55. John McCall to John Tailyour, May 12, 1793, Tailyour Papers, June 9, 1793, Oct. 20,
1793, David Dick to John Tailyour, Oct. 23, 1797, Apr. 1, 1798. It is unclear when Catherine
actually left Jamaica. Most likely she sailed with her brothers in 1796, as John McCall wrote
to Tailyour of "your Childrens voyage to Britain"; see McCall to Tailyour, May 8, 1796, ibid.
She was at least there by 1809, as Tailyour noted then that Catherine lived with his sister in
Scotland; see John Tailyour to John Orr, Oct. 28, 1809, Letter Book (1804–10), ibid.

56. John McCall to John Tailyour, May 8, 1796, Tailyour Papers, WCL; John Tailyour to
John Orr, Oct. 28, 1809, Letter Book (1804–1810), Tailyour Papers, WCL; Archibald McCall
to John Tailyour, May 20, 1804, Tailyour Papers, WCL; Roy Porter, "Mixed Feelings: The
Enlightenment and Sexuality in Eighteenth-Century Britain," in Paul-Gabriel Boucé, ed.,
Sexuality in Eighteenth-Century Britain (Totowa, N.J., 1982), 4–11; Naomi Tadmor, *Family
and Friends in Eighteenth-Century England: Household, Kinship, and Patronage* (New York,

Such assistance might have come, not from the sense that Tailyour's circumstances were unique, but that they were completely ordinary. Just a few
miles down the road from Kirktonhill, Hercules Ross had set up a similar
legitimate household in Montrose after his return from Jamaica in 1782. Ross
had also brought his children of color to Britain with him, and, like Tailyour's, they were not part of his new, metropolitan household. Two of his
mixed-race sons had joined the East India Company army with Ross's help,
and his daughters attended school in the southeast of England. In 1785, Ross
married Henrietta Parish in Edinburgh. He had purchased the Rossie Estate
just outside Montrose and built a large manor on it for his new family. Playing
the part of a landed gentleman suited Ross well, and he kept up contact with
Britain's leading lights. William Wilberforce, still grateful for Ross's testimony
to Parliament against the slave trade, cultivated a friendship. Ross even traveled to see Wilberforce, styling him in 1796 a "most esteemed friend." Famed
naval officer Horatio Nelson grew even closer to Ross. The two corresponded
regularly, and when Ross asked Nelson to serve as godfather to his unborn
child, Nelson proudly agreed. Horatio Ross, Hercules's only legitimate son
and heir, was born three months later. In a similar fashion to Tailyour, therefore, Hercules Ross separated his Jamaican and British families. But his
continued provision for his Jamaican children demonstrated that they were
nevertheless still part of an extended kinship. Living within ten miles of one
another, Tailyour and Ross's proximity normalized, to a degree, such familial
organizations for those around them.[57]

At the same time, the physical separation of these families made clear that
colonial children were not suitable members within the immediate ranks of

2001); Stana Nenadic, *Lairds and Luxury: The Highland Gentry in Eighteenth-Century Scotland* (Edinburgh, 2007), 32–38, 108–149. Lisa Forman Cody chronicles how somewhat tolerant British attitudes toward illegitimacy in the eighteenth century constricted to become
much harsher by the early nineteenth century; see Cody, "The Politics of Illegitimacy in an
Age of Reform: Women, Reproduction, and Political Economy in England's New Poor Law
of 1834," *Journal of Women's History*, XI, no. 4 (Winter 2000), 133–134.

57. Agnes M. Butterfield, "Hercules Ross of Kingston, Jamaica, and Rossie, Forfar, 1745–
1816" (unpublished manuscript, 1982), 94–118 (many thanks to Mr. J. H. St J. McIlwaine for
allowing me to read a copy of his aunt's manuscript); "Marriages," *Scots Magazine*, XLVII
(1785), 206; Alexander M. Ross, *History of the Clan Ross with Genealogies of the Various
Families* (Morgantown, W.Va., 1983), 106; Hercules Ross to William Wilberforce, Apr. 9,
1796, in Robert Isaac Wilberforce and Samuel Wilberforce, eds., *The Correspondence of
William Wilberforce*, 2 vols. (London, 1840), I, 123–124; Horatio Nelson to Hercules Ross,
June 9, 1801, in Sir Nicholas Harris Nicolas, [ed.], *The Dispatches and Letters of Vice Admiral Lord Viscount Nelson . . .* , 7 vols. (London, 1845–1846), IV, 404.

their fathers' legitimate British households. Hercules Ross turned away his mixed-race son Daniel when he attempted to visit the family's Scottish home after the birth of Horatio. There is no evidence that Tailyour's mixed-race children ever visited Kirktonhill or that they were even invited. They were, instead, kept at arm's length, away from the household Tailyour and his wife were cultivating. Although Tailyour had brought his Jamaican children to Britain for their education, he indulged them far less than his legitimate offspring. He spent significantly less on the Jamaican children's schooling than those born in Scotland. Moreover, while Polly's children went to institutions in England, at a significant remove from Tailyour's home in Montrose, at least two of his children with Mary attended schools in nearby Edinburgh. These competing households, then, did not operate on level playing fields. Legitimacy and whiteness made metropolitan children far more socially acceptable in Britain than colonial children of color born out of wedlock. Their fathers might have felt a sense of self-satisfaction for continuing to support both branches of the family, but, as the novels and inheritance suits from the period have shown, the wider British public was far less impressed. Undoubtedly, these fathers understood how controversial their complicated families were.[58]

Such distaste for these dual households could have arisen from their increasing regularity at the end of the eighteenth century. John Tailyour and Hercules Ross both returned to Scotland to marry and start legally recognized families. But this was not necessarily a well-worn path. It is challenging to trace the marriage patterns of white fathers in any systematic way, but some general impressions are discernable. Jamaican wills, which offer the most substantial evidence on which mixed-race children left the Caribbean, were lodged primarily by men who stayed on the island with no desire to wed in Britain, so they yield little information on this question. But the principal families examined thus far do reveal, somewhat anecdotally, a change over time. Gibson Dalzell and John Morse both returned to England alongside their mixed-race offspring in the middle of the eighteenth century without ever marrying. Malcolm Laing and Thomas Hibbert, whose children went to England in the 1770s, both stayed bachelors in Jamaica. These white fathers might have seen little reason to marry at all, considering they had made their

58. Butterfield, "Hercules Ross," 102. Advertisements for the Jamaican children's school at Byers Green recorded the annual cost at twelve to thirteen pounds; see *Daily Advertiser* (London), Mar. 20, 1783; and *Diary; or, Woodfall's Register* (London), Aug. 4, 1792. The cost for Tailyour's two Scottish sons a decade and a half later was roughly twelve pounds each month; see George Walker to John Tailyour, Mar. 26, 1808, Tailyour Papers, WCL.

fortunes during Jamaica's Silver Age of sugar production from 1763 to 1776 and therefore had virtually no need for a wife's dowry or financial support. Tailyour and Ross, who left the Caribbean in the last two decades of the eighteenth century, had been less successful and, in Tailyour's case, arrived late to the commercial bonanza. They were not the first men to seek out wives back in Britain, but they might have been part of a growing group of people to do so in order to use matrimonial links to solidify colonial fortunes.[59]

The end of the eighteenth century was not a particularly easy time for men like Tailyour and Ross to join the landed elite. Land had long been expensive, and gaining entry into the landowning class had been difficult for centuries. But land prices reached a peak in Britain during the Napoleonic Wars of the 1790s and 1800s. John Tailyour noticed this when he returned, declaring that landed property—especially in England—was "the most secure in Europe." Moreover, economic historians have tended to see an increasing concentration of wealth among the richest of Britain's landowners in this period. Merchants like Tailyour and Ross continued to chase the dream of owning large estates, but it was harder than ever to do so. Marriage offered an easy path by which the commercial class, especially those coming from the colonies, could either join aristocratic households, buy land from impoverished gentry, or stabilize their finances through broadened family contacts. This produced more of the dual households chastised in the popular press. West Indians of color who came to Britain were no longer simply members of an unconventional colonial family tree. They were competing relatives to newly established legitimate households, already under stress to maintain their social privilege.[60]

59. Wives are not mentioned in Dalzell's and John Morse's wills, nor are there any other pieces of evidence to believe them to have married; see Will of Gibson Dalzell, July 2, 1756, PROB 11/823, NAE, and Will of John Morse, Apr. 18, 1781, PROB 11/1077. On Laing's permanent residence in Jamaica, see David Dobson, *Scots in the West Indies, 1707–1857*, I (Baltimore, 2006), 79; Frank Cundall, *Historic Jamaica* (London, 1915), 179–180, 265; and Richard Pares, *Merchants and Planters,* Economic History Review Supplement, IV (New York, 1960), 46.

60. John Tailyour to Simon Taylor, Dec. 28, 1793, Simon Taylor Papers, ICS 120 XIV/A/106, ICS; W. D. Rubinstein, "New Men of Wealth and the Purchase of Land in Nineteenth-Century Britain," *Past and Present,* no. 92 (August 1981), 139–141; John Habakkuk, "The Rise and Fall of English Landed Families, 1600–1800," Royal Historical Society, *Transactions,* 5th Ser., XXIX (1979), 187–207; Habakkuk, *Marriage, Debt, and the Estates System: English Landownership, 1650–1950* (New York, 1994), 420–425, 453–459; G. E. Mingay, *English Landed Society in the Eighteenth Century* (Toronto, 1963), 36–78; F. M. L. Thompson, *English Landed Society in the Nineteenth Century* (London, 1963), 21–23; J. V. Beckett, "The Pattern of Landownership in England and Wales, 1660–1880," *Economic His-*

Family organization across Britain changed and adapted under these economic stresses. In particular, bequests shifted dramatically in response to the turbulent economic fluctuations brought about by merchant capitalism, political upheaval, and regular warfare abroad.[61] As the economy changed, individual households changed along with it in order to create more successful lines of inheritance and property transfer. British wills in the early modern period had traditionally tended to concentrate wealth among the nuclear family; rarely were extended relatives included in wills to any substantial degree. But rising merchant capitalism reorganized British financing and helped reshape structures of kinship and inheritance, primarily for the middling and upper ranks. Immediate kinship ties no longer guaranteed the accumulation of wealth for modest landowners and the gentry, nor did they offer much assistance for the commercial class to become landlords. Mercantile demands for credit and ready money, instead, called for more creative formulations of

---

tory Review, 2d Ser., XXXVII (1984), 11–18. Habakkuk and Mingay's thesis about wealth concentration in this period has rightly been criticized for not factoring in regional variation, so it might have been easier for Scots like Tailyour and Ross, compared to those in the Home Counties; see James Raven, *Judging New Wealth: Popular Publishing and Responses to Commerce in England, 1750–1800* (Oxford, 1992), 214–215. On the role of marriage in stabilizing elite Britons' finances, see H. J. Habakkuk, "Marriage Settlements in the Eighteenth Century," Royal Historical Society, *Transactions,* 4th Ser., XXXII (1950), 15–30; Habakkuk, *Marriage, Debt, and the Estates System,* 227–231; Christopher Clay, "Marriage, Inheritance, and the Rise of Large Estates in England, 1660–1815," *Economic History Review,* New Ser., XXI (1968), 515; Nicholas Rogers, "Money, Land, and Lineage: The Big Bourgeoisie of Hanoverian London," *Social History,* IV (1979), 444–445; and Lloyd Bonfield, "Marriage Settlements and the 'Rise of the Great Estates': The Demographic Aspect," *Economic History Review,* New Ser., XXXII (1979), 486.

61. Key notions of marriage were undergoing tremendous transformation throughout the Atlantic world; see Nancy F. Cott, *The Bonds of Womanhood: "Woman's Sphere" in New England, 1780–1835,* 2d ed. (New Haven, Conn., 1997); Mary Beth Norton, *Liberty's Daughters: The Revolutionary Experience of American Women, 1750–1800* (Ithaca, N.Y., 1980); Gordon S. Wood, *The Radicalism of the American Revolution* (New York, 1991), 177–189; Linda K. Kerber, *Women of the Republic: Intellect and Ideology in Revolutionary America* (Chapel Hill, N.C., 1997), 157–184; Anya Jabour, *Marriage in the Early Republic: Elizabeth and William Wirt and the Companionate Ideal* (Baltimore, 1998); Suzanne Desan, *The Family on Trial in Revolutionary France* (Berkeley, Calif., 2006), esp. 93–118; Catherine O'Donnell Kaplan, *Men of Letters in the Early Republic: Cultivating Forms of Citizenship* (Chapel Hill, N.C., 2008), 140–183; Carroll Smith-Rosenberg, *This Violent Empire: The Birth of an American National Identity* (Chapel Hill, N.C., 2010), 136–158; Loren Schweninger, *Families in Crisis in the Old South: Divorce, Slavery, and the Law* (Chapel Hill, N.C., 2012), 4–6; and Cayton, *Love in the Time of Revolution.*

family beyond simple calculations of direct consanguinity. Access to capital was becoming as vital to one's standing in the family as genetic proximity was. This had been understood and practiced by Jamaican households for years, as they were wholly dependent on strong merchant networks for the buying and selling of Africans as well as the export of sugar and other colonial crops. But it was a relatively new phenomenon for many elite British families still obsessed primarily with land. Indeed, it was the very fortunes made and lost by families such as the Dalzells, Morses, and Tailyours that helped to over-turn the traditional and rigid systems of inheritance that had long organized metropolitan households. This made the arrival of mixed-race Jamaicans even more problematic for wealthy Britons reluctant to accept these major eco-nomic changes.[62]

Perhaps just as important to the shifting view of migrants of color, though, were general redefinitions of family owing to these economic transformations. Immediate biological relationships might have lost their traditional bonding power in Britain after 1750, but kinship connections of some kind became more vital than they had ever been. Families, especially those connected to the commercial interests of Jamaica, had to reorganize themselves in creative ways in order to gain entry to trade and credit opportunities within booming capitalist markets. Merchants and businessmen therefore relied increasingly

62. For British family inheritance strategies in the early modern period, see Owens, "Property, Gender, and the Life Course," *Social History*, XXVI (2001), 307. Keith Wright-son and David Levine find that kinship networks were relatively small and compact in the early modern village of Terling. Their analysis of wills, correspondence, and other records reinforces the notion that the nuclear family was much more important than the extended one during this period; see Wrightson and Levine, *Poverty and Piety in an English Village: Terling, 1525–1700* (New York, 1979). The aristocracy tended to favor primogeniture to keep large estates intact within their immediate family, and Jamaican planters operated in much the same fashion; see Michael Craton, "Property and Propriety: Land Tenure and Slave Property in the Creation of a British West Indian Plantocracy, 1612–1740," in John Brewer and Susan Staves, eds., *Early Modern Conceptions of Property* (New York, 1995), 513. As Patricia Crawford notes, poor fathers who lacked substantial property did not place a great deal of emphasis on their sons' inheritance; see Crawford, *Parents of Poor Children in En-gland*, 244. This is not to say that Britain had an "open elite," as the difficulties in buying land show. Rather, mercantile wealth did significantly promote members of the rising gentry as well as those in the landed classes; see S[imon] D. Smith, *Slavery, Family, and Gentry Capi-talism in the British Atlantic: The World of the Lascelles, 1648–1834* (New York, 2006), 8–9. For a pessimistic interpretation of how difficult it was for merchants to join the landed elite, see Lawrence Stone and Jeanne C. Pawtier Stone, *An Open Elite? England, 1540–1880* (New York, 1984); and John Cannon, *Aristocratic Century: The Peerage of Eighteenth-Century En-gland* (Cambridge, 1984).

on extended relations in their dealings. Yet, this was not necessarily a widening of the family circle. Structural connections between relatives grew longer and more diffuse, but the concept of belonging to a kin group was still exclusionary. The risks associated with mercantile ventures pushed middling and upper-rank households to consolidate their fortunes into a narrower band of family membership determined primarily by one's ability to expand trading opportunities. This meant that merchant families started intermarrying to solidify business networks. It also meant that the flow of inheritance, and thus relational ties, had moved as well. Principally, wealth still stayed within immediate households, but, increasingly by the end of the eighteenth century, daughters and sisters were pushed out of hereditary lines. Now, women facilitated growing family fortunes through conjugal, rather than consanguineous, relations. Their roles as wives and mothers helped the process of capital hoarding, but they themselves rarely benefited from these transactions. The secure and reliable transference of wealth to beneficial individuals, therefore, dictated the form of family connections among Britain's middling and upper sorts at the end of the eighteenth century. Shared biology, in and of itself, was no longer sufficient to ensure strong relational bonds.[63]

This heightened kinship preference for those with potential wealth was clearly a problem for illegitimate children of color who not only held tenuous claims to hereditary bequests but who also had significantly reduced opportunities to expand their families' networks beyond paternal association. White Britons had long used such rationale to sue relatives of color with confidence. Moreover, attitudes toward illegitimacy in Britain did not soften over the course of the eighteenth century. Those who decided to care for mixed-race kin increasingly operated with the understanding that they were helping marginal relatives at best. John Tailyour's segregation of his two households demonstrates this perfectly: Kirktonhill was not a place for Jamaican sons

63. For merchant families, marriage, and business networks, see, in particular, Steven Ruggles, *Prolonged Connections: The Rise of the Extended Family in Nineteenth-Century England and America* (Madison, Wis., 1987), xvii–xviii, 5–11; Smith, *Slavery, Family, and Gentry Capitalism*, 118–119; and David Warren Sabean and Simon Teuscher, "Kinship in Europe: A New Approach to Long Term Development," in Sabean, Teuscher, and Jon Mathieu, eds., *Kinship in Europe: Approaches to Long-Term Developments (1300–1900)* (New York, 2010), 3–23. On the disadvantages faced by women in these reformations of family networks, see Eileen Spring, *Law, Land, and Family: Aristocratic Inheritance in England, 1300 to 1800* (Chapel Hill, N.C., 1993), 183–186; and Perry, *Novel Relations*, 51–73. The disfavor faced by wives and daughters was true in North America in this period as well; see Toby L. Ditz, *Property and Kinship: Inheritance in Early Connecticut, 1750–1820* (Princeton, 1986), 56–65.

and daughters. Moreover, whites who returned to Britain to start legitimate families generally gave smaller bequests to mixed-race offspring in Britain. Tailyour, for instance, did not mention any Jamaican children in his will. Relations of property and inheritance, which had always been central to British kinship, were now perhaps its most important features. Such conceptions refocused public attitudes toward migrants of color in the last decade of the eighteenth century.[64]

Conclusion

On February 20, 1795, England's House of Commons passed a law that stiffened the penalty for those convicted of bigamy. The bill made the offense equal to a charge of larceny, which could result in forced transportation if found guilty. Concern over improper marriages weighed on everyone's minds that year. Prince George, heir to the British throne, was set to wed Caroline of Brunswick when the bill passed. Few could forget that a decade earlier he had married illegally by failing to secure his father's approval and that his brother had done the same just two years before. Multiple households headed by one patriarch thus presented a fundamental problem of family organization at all social levels, and Westminster needed little compulsion to act. That the law came up for a vote at all signaled the increasing importance British society placed on preserving a perceived tradition of how family units should be structured. Shadow families and competing households created illegitimacy, complicated inheritances, and appeared to violate basic social principles.[65]

West Indian whites who returned to Britain to start legitimate families embodied the central problems of bigamous and nontraditional households.

64. Will of John Tailyour, July 17, 1816, PROB 11/1582, NAE. Matthew Gerber offers a good comparison to explain Britain's continued distaste for illegitimacy. France's National Convention granted full inheritance rights to natural children recognized by their fathers in 1793. This was not just a product of the French Revolution but of a century's worth of growing confidence among the upper class, which felt less need to attack natural children in order to shore up its own power. British aristocrats, in comparison, had been less successful in solidifying their political control by the eighteenth century. Illegitimacy in Britain thus retained its disgrace and destructive capacity for affluent households; see Matthew Gerber, *Bastards: Politics, Family, and Law in Early Modern France* (New York, 2012), 153–185.

65. Laws and Statutes of Great Britain, 35 Geo. III. c. 67 (1795); "A Bill for Inflicting a Greater Punishment on Persons Who Shall Be Convicted of the Crime of Bigamy," Feb. 20, 1795, no. 4500, in *HCSP*, XCV, 119–120. Shadow families and multiple households were highly stigmatized in Britain's middle classes as well; see Alannah Tomkins, "Fragility and Resilience in a Middle-Class Family; Jeremiah Ginders (1777–1845) and His Kin," *Staffordshire Studies*, XIII (2001), 79–108.

They could distance themselves physically from Caribbean lovers and children, but such connections were difficult to sever completely. Mistresses of color frequently kept up some type of contact with their former companions in Britain, and mixed-race children could either demand support in the colonies or travel to the metropole as an ever-present reminder of filial relation. British wives knew intimately of these individuals, and they no doubt had strong opinions on how involved their husbands should remain with West Indian charges. Men like John Tailyour and Hercules Ross kept their children of color at a distance but recognized them nonetheless even as they built new families in the metropole. Meanwhile, those mixed-race migrants, like the Morses and the Dalzells, who were able to extricate themselves from challenges by white relatives, organized new, legitimate, metropolitan households that hoped to sidestep African ancestry altogether.

Such decisions and considerations did not take place only in private parlors and correspondence but in the public arena as well. Political abolitionism lost much of its passion by 1793 after Parliament defeated repeated attempts to end England's slave trade. The ideals of that movement were not lost, however. They found new life in fictional accounts that took up those same issues of race, slavery, and demography that had dominated parliamentary debate. The brief popularity of mixed-race migrants in sentimental tales of the 1790s spoke to the public's continued interest in British residents of color, even if political rhetoric had dissipated. Moreover, sentimental writers used mixed-race characters to reflect on the stress of new familial organizations during that turbulent decade. These fictional concerns overlapped perfectly with those encountered in lived experience. Such characters did not appear all that far removed from an actual British landscape populated by many Tailyours, Rosses, Morses, and Dalzells.

Anxieties around race continued to undergird perceptions of migrants of color at the end of the eighteenth century, but central questions around family organization and hereditary economics were perhaps still of equal concern. Families throughout Britain and the Atlantic world reorganized themselves in light of the great transformations of capitalism and revolutionary politics. Membership within an extended family or even a nucleated household was now up for some deliberation. One's access to credit could increasingly strengthen a kinship bond more easily than proximity on a genealogical tree. Changing attitudes toward family composition, especially among the mercantile class to which Jamaica's multiracial households belonged, meant that individuals thought to have less potential for future wealth were no longer treated as equal kin. Such changes were potentially devastating for Jamaicans of color

who had long depended almost exclusively on blood ties to advance themselves in the metropole. Suddenly, they faced the twin challenges of minimiz-
ing their African ancestry while proving the usefulness of their kinship. This
also meant that they were now taking relational backseats to their legitimate,
white half siblings.

CHAPTER 6

IMPERIAL PRESSURES,
1800–1812

On a spring night in 1805, James Taylor struggled to calm his nerves. The young Jamaican's future appeared to hang in the balance, resting on the results of what was to transpire the next day. He had an interview with the East India Company as a candidate for its officer corps, and the meeting would dictate the path of his professional career. On top of everything else, James was not feeling well. On the journey from his Yorkshire boarding school to London, he had caught a bad cold, which he blamed on a fellow passenger having left the carriage window open all night. Arriving in the capital, James found solace at his uncle Robert Taylor's house. It was the first time the two had met, even though Robert had long helped orchestrate his nephew's education and training. Despite Robert's previous discomfort with the young man's illegitimacy and African ancestry, their meeting proved a happy introduction. Robert fawned over James, and his children quickly grew enamored with their cousin. Writing to his brother, Robert remarked that James "is a favorite with us all." Such familial affections, though, could not reduce James's apprehensions before his interview. Everyone in the house noticed his nervousness. Robert recorded that James "suffered a great deal from Anxiety" that night, enough so that he felt certain that his nephew's complexion had actually grown "a Shade Darker" than before. In focusing on James's skin color before his interview, Robert projected his own concerns onto his nephew's appearance.[1]

The source of James and Robert's joint anxiety was the young man's ancestry, about which they knew they would have to lie in order to get him through the interview. The East India Company had instituted a ban on West

1. Robert Taylor to John Tailyour, Mar. 18, Apr. 5, 6, 1805, Tailyour Papers, WCL. For more on Robert Taylor's supervision of his nephew's education, see Chapter 4, above. Bonds between uncles, aunts, nephews, and nieces were important parts of family relationships throughout the eighteenth and nineteenth centuries, even if capitalist pressures were altering their relative strengths; see Leonore Davidoff, *Thicker Than Water: Siblings and Their Relations, 1780–1920* (New York, 2012), 179–185. It appears that Robert respected his obligation as uncle to James, though he did voice concerns about his nephew's African ancestry.

Indians of color from joining its officer ranks only five years earlier. Members
of the Tailyour clan in Scotland were intimately aware of this prohibition. It
had come as a response to the application of their neighbor Hercules Ross's
mixed-race son, and namesake, to the company's navy. Hercules the younger
had interviewed in 1800 for a spot as third mate on a company ship, but,
"from the appearance of Mr. Ross, the Committee apprehend[ed] that both
his Parents were not Europeans" and declined his application. The company
had begun the process of banning nonwhites from serving as officers starting
in 1791, when it rejected the application of John Turing, a Eurasian man living
in Britain with deep connections to the East India Company. Perhaps nervous
after the recent coup of French-educated *gens de couleur* (people of color) in
Saint Domingue the previous fall, the company instituted a full prohibition
on anyone with East-Indian blood from becoming an officer. Hercules Ross's
application nine years later inspired the company's Committee of Shipping
to extend the ban to "Persons born in the West India Islands, whose Complexion evidently shews that their Parents are not severally Natives of Great
Britain or Ireland." Formal, institutionalized pressures were now mounting
against Jamaicans of color in Britain owing to decades of voiced concern over
mixed ancestry, inheritance lawsuits, competing family lineages, and abolitionist attacks.[2]

The company's ruling against young Hercules, and mixed-race West Indians generally, did not deter John Tailyour from putting forth his son as a
candidate. Tailyour lived just up the road from Hercules's father, and he undoubtedly knew all the details of the failed application. Nonetheless, he still
believed that James could use the company — as so many other mixed-race
Jamaicans had — to cover up a colonial past, should he be successful. After
all, Hercules Ross's two other mixed-race sons, David and Daniel, had passed
their interviews. "Could I get [James] to India as a Cadet," Tailyour insisted
to his friend Sir John Stuart, "I think his Chance of Success would be better

2. East India Company Directors Court Minutes, Apr. 19, 1791, IOR/B/113, fol. 17, APAC,
BL, Feb. 19, 1800, IOR/B/130, fol. 997–998. For more on the decision regarding Hercules
Ross and the general prohibition on West Indians of color, see Agnes M. Butterfield, "Her-
cules Ross of Kingston, Jamaica, and Rossie, Forfar, 1745–1816" (unpublished manuscript,
1982), 95 (many thanks to Mr. J. H. St. J. McIlwaine for allowing me to read a copy of his
aunt's manuscript); C[hristopher] J[ohn] Hawes, *Poor Relations: The Making of a Eurasian
Community in British India, 1773–1833* (Richmond, U.K., 1996), 55–63; Michael H. Fisher,
Counterflows to Colonialism: Indian Travellers and Settlers in Britain, 1600–1857 (Delhi,
India, 2004), 201–207; and Linda Colley, *The Ordeal of Elizabeth Marsh: A Woman in World
History* (New York, 2007), 302.

than in any other area of life I know." India was an immediate and obvious choice for a young man with limited opportunities in Britain and perhaps fewer in the Caribbean. Scots, especially those like Tailyour living near Dundee, had also long found success with the East India Company: the city was a crucial port in the coastal trade to London that eventually went to India.[3]

Tailyour solicited support from his many influential business and personal contacts. His brother Robert was once again vital to helping young James. Robert had spent much of his youth on the subcontinent and knew many important Indian officials. He called on longtime friend Lady Amelia Campbell, cousin of Dido Elizabeth Belle and wife of the late governor of Madras Sir Archibald Campbell, for advice. Robert and John's cousin, Sir David Carnegie, a member of Parliament for the Aberdeen Burghs, also pledged his assistance to obtain "a Cadetship for your young Man" once he traveled to London. Carnegie's influence ultimately proved decisive in securing an interview, owing to his friendship with the recently deposed prime minister Henry Addington, Lord Sidmouth. Soon, Tailyour's relatives and associates began congratulating him on his success in obtaining an interview for his son. Thomas Renny, an old family friend from Montrose, celebrated the news in a letter to Tailyour, confident that James would pass his interview as he was "a Clever Lad." Clearly tapped into the vital channels of imperial business, Tailyour's connections allowed his son James the chance to become as much a citizen of the world as his father.[4]

3. John Tailyour to John Stuart, Jan. 18, 1805, Letter Book (1804–1810), Tailyour Papers, WCL; David Armitage, "The Scottish Diaspora," in Jenny Wormald, ed., *Scotland a History* (New York, 2005), 280, 297; Andrew Mackillop, "Dundee, London, and the Empire in Asia," in Charles McKean, Bob Harris, and Christopher W. Whatley, eds., *Dundee: Renaissance to Enlightenment* (Dundee, U.K., 2009), 160–185.

4. Robert Taylor to John Tailyour, Oct. 2, 1804, Tailyour Papers, WCL, David Carnegie to John Tailyour, Mar. 1, 3, 1805, Thomas Renny to John Tailyour, Mar. 15, 1805; Charles Elphinstone Adam, *View of the Political State of Scotland in the Last Century* (Edinburgh, 1887), 184; East India Company Record of Incoming Cadets, Apr. 9, 1805, L/MIL/9/258/96–97, APAC, BL. Robert Taylor believed that the interview's success was owed to Lady Amelia Campbell, wife of General Archibald Campbell with whom he served in Madras. Lady Campbell also had a close connection to Catherine Foulerton, Robert and John's younger sister who had lodged James in his early days in Britain. In addition, Lady Campbell was the cousin of Dido Elizabeth Belle, through her mother Margaret Lindsay (sister to Dido's father John). See *Oxford Dictionary of National Biography,* online ed., s.v. "Campbell, Sir Archibald (1739–1791)," by J. L. Campbell, http://www.oxforddnb.com/view/article/4479, s.v. "Ramsay, Allan, of Kinkell (1713–1784)," by John Ingamells, http://www.oxforddnb.com /view/article/23073, s.v. "Lindsay, Sir John (1737–1788)," by J. K. Laughton, rev. Clive Wil-

Winning the interview forced Tailyour's family to reconstruct James's racial past quickly. Robert supplied his brother with a copy of the written oath required by the company to confirm James's complete European heritage. Tailyour drafted a response, admitting that James had been born and baptized in Kingston but claiming that he held no copy of the baptismal certificate. Although the latter declaration might have been true, he also knew that James's mother Polly was noted as a "mulatto" on the baptismal register. Deception took a more explicit turn in James's oath to the company. He acknowledged his West Indian birth but stated, "My Father [is] a European and my Mother [was] born in the West Indies, but of European parents." Perhaps for the first time in his life, James's racial ancestry was disguised rather than recognized, and he attempted to pass formally as white. Before his dealings with the East India Company, Tailyour's son had operated in a space of relative tolerance allowing family, friends, and teachers to acknowledge, if not accept, his heritage. As James's extended networks became less personal, or as he encountered official systems of oppression, he camouflaged that heritage. No wonder he was stricken with anxiety the night before his interview.[5]

Robert likewise grew nervous about hiding James's African heritage, but he saw no way around subterfuge. Before meeting James, he outwardly held grand ambitions that he could get the young man recommended "very strongly to Men High in Rank" within the company. However, he confessed privately: "I Hope James's Colour will not be Objected to. . . . [I]f he has much if any of the dark Cast in his appearance — I will do all I can to remove Objections if there are any." He worried about the feasibility of presenting James as white, for he was told that the directors were "rather particular in that respect," most likely because of the growing prejudices in Britain against individuals of color. Having relied so heavily on personal contacts to gain the interview, Robert and his brother risked public scorn, both for themselves

kinson, http://www.oxforddnb.com/view/article/16710. In all likelihood, David Carnegie's influence proved most important in winning James's interview. See Robert Taylor to John Tailyour, May 8, 1805, Tailyour Papers, WCL. Securing an interview had gone so quickly that Tailyour received requests from friends seeking East Indian patronage themselves. His former business partner in Jamaica and namesake of one of his legitimate sons, Peter Ballantine, asked to use Tailyour as a reference for his brother-in-law already stationed on the subcontinent; see Peter Ballantine to John Tailyour, Mar. 19, 1805, ibid.

5. Robert Taylor to John Tailyour, Mar. 8, 1805, Tailyour Papers, WCL; East India Company Military Department, Cadet Papers, Mar. 12, 1805, Apr. 1805, L/MIL/9/114/211–212, APAC, BL; Baptism of James Taylor, Aug. 28, 1786, Kingston Baptisms, copy register, I, fol. 371, IRO.

and their associates, if caught in dishonesty. Finally seeing James, however, brought Robert a measure of relief: he appeared, in Robert's estimation, to be no darker than members of the Scottish family. Nevertheless, Robert still perceived some African characteristics that bothered him enough that he "could not Sleep the first night after [James] Came," especially, as he repeated to his brother, since the company was "particularly strict in not allowing any[one] . . . who can be supposed to have any Black blood in them." Searching for a solution, Robert constructed a disguise. If he could not alter James's heritage, he could at least soften his visage. Desperately, he applied white makeup to James's skin. "I try'd him in Powder and various Colour'd Dresses," Robert informed Tailyour, but "Powder made him much worse." Ultimately, they found a useful combination in short hair and blue cloth, which diminished James's African features, at least to Robert's eyes.[6]

In the days leading to James's interview, Robert introduced him to the extended family and associates responsible for this opportunity. The young man dined with several of Robert's friends, who offered James additional letters of recommendation to Indian officials. He also came into closer contact with his father's legitimate family: he attended a play with his step-grandfather, George McCall, who, James noted, showed him "great kindness." Finally, James met with the man most responsible for his interview, Sir Carnegie, who was "much pleas'd with his appearance." The young Jamaican's familial networks, then, were, not simply abstract associations but ones that bound him materially to white, metropolitan kin.[7]

With such reassurance and with his own particular poise, James passed the interview. After an intensive examination, he convinced the East India Company's Committee of Shipping that his West Indian birth had no connection to an African heritage. But it was not a perfectly executed fraud. Robert qualified James's victory in writing to John, saying, "Some of my friends at the India House told me that no One ever Pass'd under so many Objections." The next day he reiterated this aside, insisting that he had told no one but John about the director's grumbles. Even a month later, Robert indicated that several committee members still complained about the decision. "Some of the Directors have said since, they are not at all satisfied with their own Conduct in passing [James]—as they still think he must have some black blood—and there is nothing they are so particular about." Reinforcing just how lucky

6. Robert Taylor to John Tailyour, Mar. 8, 1805, Tailyour Papers, Mar. 18, Apr. 5, 1805.
7. Ibid., Apr. 6, 1805, James Taylor to John Tailyour, Apr. 9, 1805.

James was, Robert related the story of another candidate recently rejected for suspicion of African heritage even though his father had previously served as the governor of Bengal. The whole affair greatly troubled Robert, and he advised both John and James to speak no more of the interview, fearing further company inquiry.[8]

Public pressures against West Indians of color in Britain had now begun to interfere in private arrangements for their advancement. Concerns sowed in the last two decades of the eighteenth century within the abolition movement and sentimental literature reaped lasting consequences for those mixed-race migrants continuing to arrive in the metropole at the beginning of the next century. Increasingly constrictive notions of kinship exacerbated these problems, as the British families who welcomed Jamaicans of color felt less compelled to accept them fully within their most immediate circles. James's experiences were something of an exception, but they did not wholly diverge from this pattern. His relatives did help to find him a prestigious position, exposing themselves to certain reputational risk. Yet, the position in question was also another opportunity to distance him physically from British family. Just as his father and uncle had not wanted him to grow up alongside his legitimate half-siblings and cousins, his Indian appointment would put him on the other side of the world. Nevertheless, the whole process still provided James with new economic opportunities. That he only narrowly passed his East India Company interview in 1805 indicated that such global movement might not long be tolerated. Two years after James's departure for the subcontinent, the United Kingdom would abolish its slave trade, forcing entirely new ideas to be considered about the future of the Caribbean, its inhabitants, and the Empire as a whole.

The perceived threat of mixed-race migrants was perhaps never as high as when the political wheels of colonial reform and abolition finally began to turn. General warnings and discomfort with the migration of mixed-race West Indians in the metropole turned into formalized institutional pressures, direct rhetorical attacks, and private reluctance to accommodate relatives of color. In many ways, the basic terms of debate stayed the same. Racial demography and unease with interracial sex continued to dominate discussion of the topic. But the supposed nightmare scenarios that proslavery supporters, along with many slave reformers, had long used to exaggerate polemical tirades actually came to fruition: a formerly enslaved people gained their independence (Haiti in 1804), and England abolished its slave trade (1807). Successful slave rebel-

8. Robert Taylor to John Tailyour, Apr. 5, 6, 1805, ibid., May 8, 1805.

lions, black fecundity, and racial mixture were now far less abstract or distant notions. Political observers and family correspondents alike struggled to come to terms with these new realities, particularly after a legal cause célèbre thrust these issues to the top of popular conversation.

Effortless and Challenging Assimilations

West Indians of color continued to travel to Britain at the beginning of the nineteenth century. The principal factors that drove them there — the colonies' lack of jobs, few schools, and entrenched prejudice — remained largely unchanged from before. Moreover, the improved status that came with living in Europe still tempted many parents to send children abroad. Relatives and friends in Britain were nevertheless influenced by escalating concerns over mixed-race migration. Many worried that by caring for such family members they were condoning the types of relationships now publicly thought improper for British households. West Indians of color who journeyed to Britain during this period found a different world than their peers had a generation earlier.

Estimating the numbers of individuals who left the Caribbean for Britain at the beginning of the nineteenth century is more challenging than for previous periods. Jamaica's privilege bills do not offer much data for that century's first decade. From 1801 to 1802, fourteen quadroon individuals petitioned for and won privilege rights. However, in 1802 the assembly stopped approving these appeals. The reasons for this are not entirely clear. Mixed-race Jamaicans did not cease petitioning, and many were still highly connected. That year, the governor's wife, Lady Maria Nugent, noted that her "mulatto friends" were "all daughters of Members of the Assembly." Indeed, between 1803 and 1813, only three Jamaicans of color asked for privileges, though the assembly only read through their petitions once. Many more undoubtedly wished to present appeals, but the assembly would not take them. Most likely the man responsible for this political blockade was George Crawford Ricketts, a member of Jamaica's upper legislative body, the council. A report sent to the Colonial Office in London later claimed that Ricketts and a fellow council member had strong-armed the assembly into refusing to accept privilege appeals altogether so that Ricketts could prevent a rival heir from sharing a Jamaican estate. Without privilege dispensations, mixed-race Jamaicans could no longer use personal connections to skirt official regulations. This struck a major blow to the community, which had petitioned with gusto after the Haitian Revolution. Nearly one-fifth of all individuals who received privilege rights in the eighteenth century did so in its last decade. Owing to this new prohibition on privilege bills, those individuals who left the island for an education in the early nineteenth century no longer had the option to record their travels with the assembly.[9]

Despite diminishing numbers of privilege petitions, Jamaican wills continued to show an engagement with European education. Testators routinely lobbied for mixed-race children to undertake a voyage to Britain, revealing that the practice carried on in the face of legislative and cultural changes. Seven percent of white men's wills proven in Jamaica from 1803 to 1805 contained a bequest for a mixed-race child to travel to the metropole, down less than half a percentage point from the previous decade. When adjusted to look only at white men who gave bequests to children of color, more than 15 percent of testators noted that the child had gone, or would go, to Britain. Effectively, then, there was no shift in hereditary practices, despite increasing calls against this migration. This is not altogether surprising as virtually nothing had changed for interracial households in Jamaica. Schools accepting mixed-race children were still few and far between and those that remained were growing even more limited in number. A small institution in the parish of Saint Thomas in the East had stopped admitting children of color in 1794, and Kingston's preeminent school, Wolmer's, officially barred mixed-race students four years after that. A lack of learning opportunities on the island made a British trip even more necessary for children of color seeking an education. With similar stagnations in professional avenues and legal standing, all of the same factors that had pushed mixed-race children to go to Britain in the eighteenth century continued to exert pressure in the nineteenth.[10]

9. [Lady Maria Nugent], *Lady Nugent's Journal of Her Residence in Jamaica from 1801 to 1805,* ed. Philip Wright (Kingston, Jamaica, 1966), 78. The three petitioners between 1803 and 1813 were William Mackintosh, George Napier, and Samuel Shreyer. For their petitions respectively, see *JAJ,* Oct. 28, 1803, XI, 89, Nov. 22, 1804, 210, 242, 266–267, and Nov. 28, 1810, XII, 300–301, 319–322. Although Ricketts noted Jamaican property in his will, he did not indicate any legal threats to it; see Will of George Crawford Ricketts, May 6, 1811, PROB 11/1522, NAE. For the commissioners' speculations on the reasons behind the ban on privilege petitions, see "Commissioners of Legal Inquiry in the West Indies Report," 1822–1828, CO 318/76, fol. 106, NAE. See also A. Wood Renton, "The Work of the West Indian Commissioners," *Juridical Review,* II (1890), 155–164; Daniel Livesay, "The Decline of Jamaica's Interracial Households and the Fall of the Planter Class, 1733–1823," *Atlantic Studies,* IX (2012), 115.

10. For the percentages of mixed-race children sent to Britain through testamentary bequests, see Appendix 1, below. For the report regarding the small institution in Saint Thomas in the East, see Thomas Barritt to Nathaniel Phillips, Dec. 10, 1794, Slebech Collection, MS 8439, National Library of Wales, Aberystwyth.

White fathers with the desire and means to fund trips to Britain maintained their support, but they were not the only ones. Freemen of color continued to undertake the practice for their own relatives as well. John Reid, a planter of color in the parish of Saint Catherine, bequeathed his entire estate to John Sanders, a fellow mixed-race man living in Britain. Their relationship is unclear, though Sanders might have been an extended relative. As mixed-race fortunes accrued, more and more testators of color provided for kin across the Atlantic. Not only were Protestants shipping their children abroad, but so, too, were the island's Jewish residents. Jamaican law effectively put Jews into the same legal category as free people of color. They could not vote, hold office, or save deficiency, although they were not subject to the 1761 inheritance cap. That many Jamaican Jews themselves had African roots complicated the situation further. Such factors propelled mixed-race Jews to Britain along the same stream as their colonial peers. Hyam Cohen, for instance, sent his two mestee daughters, Catherine and Caroline, to London to live with his associate Lyan Levy. If they came to find husbands, the girls were not altogether successful. Catherine moved to Kensington, where she died unmarried. The allure of a metropolitan upbringing attracted all able parents to spirit their children away, even as British attitudes toward their arrival worsened.[11]

Such enthusiasm and devotion for a British education could lead to complicated familial obligations. Jamaican carpenter William Thomson constructed an elaborate path for his mestee son and namesake in an 1803 will. Young William was to land in Liverpool to stay with his uncle David Clark. Eventually, he was to go to school in southwest Scotland. In addition to providing for his son, William also gave twenty pounds to a mixed-race nephew already living in Scotland. William's brother Robert had fathered the boy and brought him to Britain but had since died. Most likely the young man depended on his uncle's small but welcome bequest. Thomson's will demonstrates the multiple responsibilities that some transatlantic families had to relatives of color. Wealthy Jamaicans had to depend on British kin and friends to ensure that their children succeeded in the metropole. One Jamaican resi-

11. Will of John Reid, Nov. 4, 1804, Wills, LOS 73, fols. 189-190, IRO, Will of Hyam Cohen, July 27, 1803, Wills, LOS 71, fols. 135-138; Will of Caroline Cohen, Apr. 26, 1815, PROB 11/1567, NAE. The shared struggle for rights saw many Caribbean Jews, especially those of mixed race, and gentiles of color observing each other's appeals with interest; see John D. Garrigus, "New Christians / 'New Whites': Sephardic Jews, Free People of Color, and Citizenship in French Saint-Domingue, 1760-1789," in Paolo Bernadini and Norman Fiering, eds., *The Jews and the Expansion of Europe to the West, 1450 to 1800* (New York, 2001), 314-327.

dent, for instance, asked a brother in Gloucestershire to take care of his qua-droon son as he wrote out his last will and testament. Likewise, a prominent white colonist from the island's eastern parish gave added provisions for his sister in Scotland as she oversaw the education of her mixed-race nephew John Fowlis. For some Britons, these deathbed requests to care for relatives of color might have come as a surprise. For others, they simply reinforced and confirmed well-known relationships.[12]

Beyond establishing basic plans, few Jamaicans elaborated on the expec-tations for their offspring once in Britain. Occasionally, fathers expressed deep desires that their children never return to the Caribbean. The merchant William McPherson implored his daughter Anne to stay in Scotland for the rest of her life. Similarly, William Anderson included a provision invalidat-ing his mixed-race son Robert's bequest if he ever came back to Jamaica. Fears of colonial prejudice likely motivated these testamentary requests. In some cases, fathers constructed more complicated demands for their chil-dren. John Ferrier, a wealthy shopkeeper, gave perhaps the most specific in-structions for a child of color in Britain out of a sample of more than twenty-two hundred wills. In 1805, he sketched out his children's marriage prospects in the hope that subsequent generations would become more phenotypically white. Ferrier sent his offspring, whom he had by an enslaved black woman named Venus, to friends in Britain. In his will, Ferrier specifically demanded that these guardians help choose his children's spouses. He worried that they might "marry without Consent or go astray to strange men or women after such marriage or cohabit with worthless persons *as their Mother has done*." Clearly, racialized anxieties about his children's sexual behavior wracked Fer-rier's nerves, perhaps because he felt that Venus had not stayed loyal to him. He might have enjoyed his relationship with a black woman in the colonies, but, fearful that his children would take the same steps as their mother — a worry fostered by cultural claims about African hypersexuality — Ferrier regulated his children's marriage prospects in the metropole intensely. Fer-rier's request was not typical for Jamaican testators. Nevertheless, his expec-tations for their assimilation into British society were undoubtedly shared by many fathers.[13]

12. Will of William Thomson, July 2, 1803, Wills LOS 72, fols. 5–6, IRO, Will of William Simmons, Sept. 10, 1803, Wills, LOS 71, fol. 201, Will of Charles Fowlis, Feb. 15, 1805, Wills, LOS 74, fol. 38.

13. Will of William McPherson, Nov. 6, 1804, Wills, LOS 72, fol. 60, IRO, Will of Wil-liam Anderson, Aug. 1, 1804, Wills, LOS 73, fol. 17, Will of John Ferrier, June 8, 1805, Wills, LOS 75, fols. 104–105 (emphasis mine).

In some cases, West Indian fathers' most fanciful desires for their children to assimilate still came true in the nineteenth century. Nathaniel Wells's experiences perhaps best exemplify this. Born to an enslaved woman named Juggy and a white merchant named William Wells on the island of Saint Kitts, he inherited the majority of his father's estate, valued at two hundred thousand pounds sterling. The younger Wells married and in 1803 purchased the estate of Piercefield in Wales for ninety thousand pounds. There he lived as a landed aristocrat with a large family. Wells acted as sheriff, justice of the peace, and deputy lieutenant for the area. Few could have envisioned a smoother transition into British society. Yet, his West Indian past never left him. Throughout his life, Wells allowed the public to tour the magnificent grounds at Piercefield, and guests were known to comment on his heritage. The famous painter Joseph Farington recorded several mentions of Wells in his voluminous diary, each time noting specific features of Wells's complexion. In 1803, Farington visited Piercefield, describing Wells as "a West Indian of large fortune, a man of very gentlemanly manners, but so much a man *of Colour* as to be but little removed from a Negro." On a second visit five months later, he jotted in his diary that "Mr. Wells is a Creole of a very deep colour, but Miss Wells is fair." Wells's appearance proved endlessly fascinating to Farington and his friends. In 1807, Wells came up in a conversation between Farington and a Mrs. Lee. With curiosity, she scrutinized Wells's two sons and daughter, noting that "the daughter is as *fair* as Her Mother, but the eldest Son *brown,* and the 2d. son dark like His father." Thus, even as the public accepted Wells as a prominent figure, it nevertheless speculated on the character and influence of his ancestry in British society.[14]

Dido Elizabeth Belle, who had grown up in the London mansion of William Murray, Lord Mansfield, did not achieve the same amount of success as Wells but nevertheless found some stability. Although she appears not to have had a strong relationship with her cousin and Robert Taylor's close friend, Lady Campbell, both Dido's great-uncle and great-aunt left bequests to ensure at least a modest financial foothold. Moreover, Lord Mansfield demonstrated a strong degree of tenderness in his will, requesting that his portrait be placed "in her room to put her in mind of one she knew from her Infancy

14. *Oxford Dictionary of National Biography,* online ed., s.v. "Wells, Nathaniel (1779–1852)," by J. A. H. Evans, http://www.oxforddnb.com/view/article/74450; Vere Langford Oliver, ed., *Caribbeana; Being Miscellaneous Papers relating to the History, Genealogy, Topography, and Antiquities of the British West Indies,* 4 vols. (London, 1914–1918), III, 168; *The Diary of Joseph Farington,* ed. Kathryn Cave, 16 vols. (New Haven, Conn., 1979–1984), Apr. 24, 1803, VI, 2017, Sept. 17, 1803, 2132, April 4, 1807, VIII, 3003.

and always honoured with uninterrupted Confidence and friendship." Yet, the end of Mansfield's life also terminated Dido's standing in elite society. She married John Davinier in 1793, but her husband was far from a man of leisure. The two lived in humble, though strongly domestic, circumstances for the remainder of their lives. Dido gave birth to twins John and Charles in 1795, the latter of whom would eventually apply to the East India Company as many of his mixed-race peers had. Sadly, almost nothing is known of Dido in her adult years. She died in 1804, just past her fortieth birthday and significantly distanced from the refined comforts of her upbringing. Still, her marriage and motherhood were signs of victorious assimilation in the ways her benefactors had originally envisioned.[15]

Such qualified success could also occur for the less well-heeled. Despite having a modest inheritance, Bryan Mackey appears to have had no problem adjusting to a new life after leaving Jamaica around 1780. He had received a privilege dispensation that year — Simon Taylor investigated the appeal for the assembly — in which his father William noted that Bryan was already in Britain. As a young man, Bryan either stumbled in the attempt to increase his fortune, or he had no interest in pursuing it. Once in England, Bryan began training as a clergyman, and, by 1799, he had become the rector of Coates in Gloucestershire. He served in that position for the next forty-eight years, got married, and fathered several children. The community seems to have accepted Bryan, although he was not without critics. In 1805, William Holland paid a visit to Bryan's ailing father, now also living in England. The two Williams had become familiar: Holland once commented in his diary that he worried about the profligacy of the elder Mackey's new wife Mary. Bryan Mackey happened to be attending his father on this visit, and Holland remarked on meeting the "young man [who] is his son by a Negro Woman and has had from the father an excellent education." Holland nevertheless

15. Will of William Murray, Mar. 28, 1793, PROB 11/1230, NAE, Will of Margaret Murray, May 9, 1799, PROB 11/1324. Dido's marriage announcement comes from an online database on black and Asian individuals in the Guildhall Library's collection; see London's Marriage Allegations, Nov. 3, 1793, MS 10091/169, GL. For a digitized transcription of the marriage allegations, see http://www.history.ac.uk/gh/baentries.htm. A summary of the bond held by the GL declaring John Davinier's status can be found through the same site, reference MS 10091E/106. Margaret Murray noted in her will that Lindsay was "now married to Mr. Davinier"; see Will of Margaret Murray, May 9, 1799, PROB 11/1324, NAE; and Sarah Minney, "The Search for Dido: Sarah Minney, a Genealogist-Researcher, Solves the Mystery of the Later Life of a Famous Black Beauty of the Late 18th Century," History Today, LV, no. 10 (October 2005), online ed., http://www.historytoday.com/sarah-minney/search-dido.

attributed to Bryan the same squandering ways as Mary, though he admitted, "I am not very partial to West Indians, especially young Negro Half Blood people." Undoubtedly, Holland believed that West Indian extravagance was inherent in mixed-race migrants and saw Bryan Mackey in that light. Likely many others in Britain, including Mackey's parishioners, made the same associations, though his long career in Gloucestershire reveals how trivial those concerns might have been to most of his neighbors.[16]

The precariousness of assimilation was more dramatic for other Jamaicans who crossed the Atlantic. Unlike Bryan Mackey, James Fyffe never solidified his place in British society. Born to planter William Fyffe and a black woman in Jamaica, he came to Scotland as a young man at the end of the eighteenth century. He took up as a wright's apprentice in Kirriemuir, only forty miles from John Tailyour's and Hercules Ross's households in nearby Montrose. Perhaps a failed entrant to Scotland's rising mercantile class, James Fyffe commenced a career in carpentry instead, which he hoped would settle him securely in Britain. A relative, David Fyffe, closely managed his progress in an act of true kinship. David provided small loans fully cognizant that they might not be repaid. "It's likely I shall lose what money I have advanced," he admitted to a correspondent, "but [with] William Fyffe's good intentions towards my family, I cannot regret what I have done for his Son." Nevertheless, James struggled to establish his own practice. Eventually, he took up with a master carpenter after David helped him purchase a new set of tools and vouched for his good standing. Continued hardship, though, ultimately compelled James to leave Scotland. It is unclear if he had always planned on returning to the West Indies, but he held some title to his father's Jerusalem Estate in Jamaica, which might have tempted him back. Keen to hasten his return, James decided to borrow yet again from David for passage to the Caribbean in 1804. Describing him as "that poor Mulatto," David spoke well of his relation. "If the lad James after getting to Jamaica will be industrious and behave decently which from what I know, and have heard of him . . . he may very well earn his own bread." Fyffe's example shows even more clearly

16. *Star* (London), Aug. 20, 1799; *Gentleman's Magazine: And Historical Chronicle*, LXIX, pt. II (1799), 1169; *Gentleman's Magazine*, New Ser., XXIX (1848), 213; William Holland, *Paupers and Pig Killers: The Diary of William Holland a Somerset Parson, 1799–1818*, ed. Jack Ayers (Gloucester, U.K., 1984), Jan. 25, 1805, 106, Oct. 1, 1810, 216. See also Kathleen Chater, *Untold Histories: Black People in England and Wales during the Period of the British Slave Trade, c. 1660–1807* (New York, 2009), 171; and Will of William Mackey, Mar. 6, 1805, PROB 11/1422, NAE.

the importance of British networks to a migrant of color. Even after a failed attempt at integration, metropolitan contacts were still crucial to one's continued livelihood, albeit back in the colonies.[17]

Perhaps the unevenness of these attempts at assimilation drove John Tailyour's plans for his son in India. James Fyffe lived so close to Tailyour that he undoubtedly became aware of his travails, especially because Fyffe's father was a prominent white Jamaican. The younger Hercules Ross's failure to join the East India Company in 1800 would have also been known to Tailyour, owing to their previous family connections and proximity to the same Scottish seaport. As these examples show, success in Britain was by no means a foregone conclusion for migrants of color. Although there had never been such a guarantee, the early years of the nineteenth century witnessed greater explicit references to the racial ancestry of mixed-race family members than in previous periods. This was not simply heightened awareness of physical differences. It was an active concern that these relatives were of a separate kinship line as well as a greater public reluctance to accept their assimilation. For those still wanting to assist relatives of color, though, balancing between these pressures was difficult. John Tailyour might have wished to push James away from his new, legitimate family, but he also grew anxious about the young man's prospects in Britain generally. In the lead up to abolition, public rhetoric grew more vitriolic against mixed-race migrants, and the personal challenges of individuals with whom Tailyour was familiar persuaded him to seek alternatives for his children.[18]

17. David Fyffe to James Fyffe [of Glasgow], May 30, 1804, Fyffe Collection, MS 1165, no. 33, NLJ, Sept. 7, 1804, no. 34, Sept. 14, 1804, no. 36. The exact nature of the relationship between James and David Fyffe is unclear, but most likely David was James's cousin. According to David, James left Kirriemuir for Glasgow to save money for passage to Jamaica. After sailing for Jamaica, James's relationship to David turned formal. William Fyffe's plantation in Jamaica could produce a hefty profit, were it run efficiently, and David believed that James, by returning to the island, was bound for large riches. Therefore, he called back all of his loans, which totaled some £130. However, David accommodated James nicely. He assured James "that neither I nor my attorneys will ever distress him for payment." James quickly paid back the loan; see "State of the Debt Due by James Fyffe to David Fyffe," May 12, 1803, no. 61, ibid.

18. For more on the hardening of racial attitudes at the turn of the nineteenth century, see Roxann Wheeler, *The Complexion of Race: Categories of Difference in Eighteenth-Century British Culture* (Philadelphia, 2000); Felicity A. Nussbaum, *The Limits of the Human: Fictions of Anomaly, Race, and Gender in the Long Eighteenth Century* (New York, 2003); Dror Wahrman, *The Making of the Modern Self: Identity and Culture in Eighteenth-Century*

Regardless of John Tailyour's feelings about the assimilation of his children of color, James's own perceptions shed tremendous light on the personal experiences of mixed-race migrants. The few surviving letters between John Tailyour and his sons — James and John — are some of the only firsthand accounts written by Jamaicans of color traveling to Britain during this period. James's correspondence begins only when he arrives in London to prepare for his interview with the East India Company. They reveal an industrious young man building a personal network in the same way as his father. James visited every family member he could while in the capital. This included his aunt Catherine's in-laws, who were well connected to officials on the subcontinent, as well as his stepfamily. It might have been a strange encounter when James, a formerly enslaved illegitimate child, met George McCall, the grandfather of John Tailyour's legitimate offspring. If there was a degree of awkwardness to the meeting, it went away quickly. James proved himself an admirable companion, and, after attending a play with him in London, McCall decided to take him personally to Gravesend where his passage to India would start. James had successfully familiarized himself with his wider British clan. He was particularly sweet with his grandmother in Montrose, Jean, who had always written with interest about him. The two corresponded directly, and James wrote to her regularly on his trip to India. Throughout it all, James depended on his father and ensured that their relationship stayed strong. John served as James's chief counselor when James set out once more across the ocean. In his last letter before sailing off in April 1805, James admitted his anxiety about being so distant. "You may be assured that your advice both now and ever after shall be my principal study to follow," he informed his father, "and I sincerely hope that I may be so fortunate as to find in India a friend, whose advice I may benefit by, when I shall be too far away from you." Family ties were the crucial, if not some of the only, keys to James's future success, even half a world away.[19]

Despite his eagerness, the long voyage from London to India proved stressful to nineteen-year-old James. He lost his trunk in Portsmouth before even completing the voyage across the English Channel. The numerous months

England (New Haven, Conn., 2004), esp. 83–119; and Kathleen Wilson, *The Island Race: Englishness, Empire, and Gender in the Eighteenth Century* (New York, 2003).

19. James Taylor to John Tailyour, Apr. 9, 1805, Tailyour Papers, WCL. For a note on James's correspondence with his grandmother, see James Taylor to John Tailyour, Apr. 24, 1805, ibid.

spent on open water were unquestionably worse. Fighting seasickness, rough weather, wretched food, and boredom were bad enough by themselves. But Britain's escalating wars with Napoleon terrified James about being attacked. France's navy was a looming threat to the convoy of vessels with which James sailed; at one point, they briefly exchanged fire with a French ship. As the fleet neared the Azores, he proudly shared news of Horatio Nelson's blockade of the French at Cadiz with his father, just months before the more decisive victory at Trafalgar. This stirred the young man's heart as he held some distant personal connections to the war hero; Nelson was familiar with James's father, and he was also a close friend of Hercules Ross. However, James's glee was tempered when his ship, the *Devonshire*, began to suffer problems. The foremast and mainmast of the ship broke. Separated from the rest of the convoy, the crew was lucky when a frigate finally heard the *Devonshire*'s distress signal and helped to repair it. Now far behind the convoy, James and his crewmates faced the rest of the months-long voyage to India without any support.[20]

The entire passage proved an ordeal for James, who grew to resent the miserable conditions and his equally miserable treatment. He barely had enough space for a hammock on board, but, more importantly, he resented the ship's captain, James Murray. James Taylor's uncle Robert had successfully lobbied to get the young man a prized spot at the captain's table, but the honor proved meaningless as Murray ignored the young cadets with whom he dined. "He never I believe spoke 2 words to any one of us during the voyage," James complained to his father. This was not simply a social annoyance but a slap in the face to James's status as an up-and-coming officer. James took great pride not only in his professional rank but also in his education and family status. Murray's shunning of the cadets was, in James's mind, an affront to basic decorum and respect. "Had he even paid us the common civilities due from one Gentleman to another it would not have been required to have done more." Seeing himself a gentleman, James reacted to the events around him in a fashion like his fellow officers. When the ship docked on the African coast after traversing the equator, he was taken aback on witnessing the usual "crossing the line" ceremony that included a number of African performers. "Their bodies bare and painted in different places with white spots," he recounted, "upon the whole in my opinion . . . had a most grotesque appearance." Likewise, he felt put off by "Some thousand Blacks" who surrounded their ship at the Cape of Good Hope, "serving to cheat the unwary stranger."

20. Ibid., May 3, 1805.

Identifying as a member of elite British society, James's encounter with the colonial "other" mimicked those of many whites in the Empire. His fixation on the African bodies before him was part of a greater sense of metropolitan identity, disconnected from his own African past.[21]

James clung to this metropolitan status even more closely when he arrived in Madras. Nothing about India satisfied him. The pay was insufficient, the climate too extreme, and the environment too unhealthy. He felt the trip to have been a mistake. In frustration, he attacked the people around him as symbols of these accumulated aggravations. In each of his letters home from India, James disparaged the local inhabitants. He described the Tamil people as "a set of ignorant and careless fools," "a set of cursed rascals," and "expert thieves." Like many British visitors abroad before him, James decried how hard the women worked for the benefit of the men's supposed idleness. Flexing his own imperial muscle, James proudly declared, "The natives are a most effeminate set of wretches one stout Englishman would be more than a match for ½ a dozen of them." In relating these observations of India back to his father, James displayed the typical characteristics of metropolitan identity and British superiority. James articulated his distinction from the Indian people along racial, class, and gender lines. He was both white and British, elite and masculine. James employed the same markers of difference that white Britons used to distinguish themselves from colonial others when casting aside the natives with whom he interacted. If he did retain a tenuous social existence in Britain, then his Asian adventures removed most of those limiting factors. In Madras, James was not a transported colonial; he was a normalized colonizer who could further refine his fashioned British identity.[22]

James's fiscal expectations in India also reflected a metropolitan upbringing. Having received a learned education in England and been treated in a genteel manner for most of his childhood, James struggled to make compromises to daily comforts. Even before he landed in India, James complained to his father about the exorbitant prices of luxury goods abroad. When stopping on the island of Saint Helena, the costs for European articles shocked him, especially as he believed he could not live happily without them. Once

21. Ibid., June 27, 1805, Robert Taylor to John Tailyour, Mar. 9, 1806.

22. James Taylor to John Tailyour, Nov. 29, 1805, ibid., Jan. 7, 1806. Scottish thinking and identity—if James connected to it—were important parts of British governance in India; see Martha McLaren, *British India and British Scotland, 1780–1830: Career Building, Empire Building, and a Scottish School of Thought on Indian Governance* (Akron, Ohio, 2001).

in Madras, he scoffed at his low salary, which seemed not to match his qualifications. After Warren Hasting's trial in the 1780s, Indian reforms had reined
in the large fortunes previously acquired by soldiers like himself. "All these
nabobs who return home have made their money by having some other situation," James lamented. Almost immediately, James wrote to his father wishing
to return to Britain. He anticipated much greater success outside the military
if he could join a mercantile firm.[23]

James's expectations, however, ran counter to his family's. He complained
to both his father and uncle about India, but Robert, having spent time there
as a young man himself, opposed each grievance. His nephew's clamor for
more money greatly upset Robert, who grumbled to Tailyour that James "has
a disposition to be more extravagant than his situation entitles him to" and
that "he certainly has higher Notions than either you or I had at his age."
Robert's aggravation grew much worse when James began drawing bills of
exchange against his father and uncle without their permission. Nonetheless,
Robert assured his brother that James would eventually discover the advantages given him in India and implored Tailyour not to allow his immediate return. "It would be impossible to get him any thing half so good"; "if he were
to return to England — there is no Situation you could place him in where he
could have anything more than above subsistence." A colonial career was, in
Robert's mind, the best, if not only, option for a mixed-race man straddling
the border of passable whiteness. James's genteel assurance conflicted with
Robert's pessimism. Some of this disagreement undoubtedly stemmed from
the ordinary conflicts between generations, but Robert did not simply see
this as a case of youthful entitlement. With firm memories of James's birth in
slavery, Robert had always believed that his nephew operated at the margins
of British respectability and saw his protests as evidence of social confusion.
"The sudden Change he found in his Situation, commencing the Gentleman
all at once, was too much for him," he surmised. For Robert, then, illegitimate children of color never had full access to elite metropolitan society, nor
should they expect it. Although he undertook the requisite steps to place his

23. James Taylor to John Tailyour, June 27, 1805, Tailyour Papers, WCL, Jan. 7, 1806.
James later wrote to his father to disabuse him of the notion that all migrants to India made
money, especially those in the military; see ibid., Oct. 6, 1807. After a crackdown on private, illicit trade in 1784, Indian merchants' wages increased, but that of soldiers' did not
keep pace; see P. J. Marshall, *East Indian Fortunes: The British in Bengal in the Eighteenth
Century* (New York, 1976). Although Marshall focuses on Bengal, and not Madras, the company's policies extended toward various other areas of the subcontinent.

nephews and niece in relatively privileged positions, he never believed them entirely worthy of such places.[24]

It is highly likely that Robert's diminished expectations for James came partly out of an ongoing public critique of mixed-race migrants. James's voyage to India in 1805 coincided with the uproarious clamor for abolition in Parliament that would come to fruition two years later. These political debates about slavery and race, along with continued diatribes published against individuals of color in Britain and the lasting surprise of Haitian independence in 1804, changed the available paths to success for Jamaicans like James. The East India Company's ban on mixed-race West Indians in 1800 had already started to put official pressure against him and his fellow migrants. Family attitudes — at least among the Tailyours — appear to have shifted in turn. Robert did not necessarily stifle his compassion and familial obligation to James, but he certainly tempered his outlook for the young man's future. He was not alone in this view. Writing to his son in 1801, John Matson warned about transferring children of color from the Caribbean to Britain. "Education, Habits and other Causes, render Persons of this Disposition convenient only in the warm Climate of their Birth," he observed; "it becomes a Misfortune to themselves to be removed to any other Country." This argument followed an intellectual path that joined together climate and race, which also explicitly dictated that geographic separation for ethnic groups was imperative in the Empire. Britain was less appropriate than it used to be for migrants of color. Political observers justified this position in terms of slavery and social stability. Racial theorists defended it in terms of climate. And families enforced it in terms of degrees of accepted kinship.[25]

These moderated attitudes toward mixed-race kin are seen even more clearly with Tailyour's other son, John. After attending the same school outside Durham as James, John left for London in 1809 with some money from his father. John then appears to have disappeared temporarily from the family or ceased contact with them in the years immediately before his majority. His uncle Robert hinted at such a lapse, reassuring Tailyour in 1809 that he would "certainly endeavour to hear of something of your little Boy." By the next summer, John had recommenced communications. Robert placed him

24. Robert Taylor to John Tailyour, Feb. 17, 1806, Tailyour Papers, WCL, Sept. 18, 1806, Oct. 5, 1809.

25. John Matson, Sr., to John Matson, Jr., Dec. 17, 1801, in *Caribbeana,* I (London, 1910), 221.

with a family in London, the Lows, possibly relatives of John Low, Tailyour's Scottish lawyer. Like his brother James, John connected with extended family in London. Another uncle, John Foulerton, began writing to him suggesting that he get in touch with his step-grandfather, George McCall, with whom the younger John was unfamiliar. Perhaps Foulerton hoped that John could follow in his older brother's footsteps by tapping into broader family associations.[26]

Enmeshed once more into his father's network, John took a stable place in the capital. The arrangement, ultimately, was not a happy one. He complained regularly about the Lows; the family appeared to him outrageously fastidious. At breakfast one morning, John's generous use of butter pushed the family to ask him if he knew its cost. Like his brother, eighteen-year-old John had grown used to certain indulgences. These luxuries would require moderation, and he needed a career that could allow greater independence. Once again, John's uncle Robert stepped in to guide his Jamaican relative. He hired John as a clerk at his counting house in order to give him spending money as well as to keep watch over him. Moreover, John moved out of the Lows' home and into his own lodgings. Tailyour wrote back to Jamaica soon after to inform Polly of their son's new position. Young John might have been one of Polly's favored children: this was one of the only messages Tailyour passed to her after leaving the island. Tailyour had virtually ignored Polly after returning to Scotland. He even closed this letter with the note, "I wish her well, but really cannot offer to do more [for her]." Try as he might to keep Polly far away, Tailyour's children kept him tethered to her for the rest of his life.[27]

Despite John's new employment, the pleasures of the capital diverted his mind. Robert had long worried about London's numerous enticements for young men like James and John, and those fears appear to have come true for the latter. John admitted as much to his father, confessing, "What money I received from you . . . I have thrown away foolishly." Nevertheless, in offering such penance, he reassured his father that none of it was "spent in the presence of bad Company." Youth and indiscretion, John chided himself, were the culprits. "There are so many ways of spending money in London that [one] . . . spends it all in a few weeks, not thinking where he shall get more." Moderation might have proved difficult for the young man in an expensive

26. John Taylor to John Tailyour, Oct. 29, 1809, Tailyour Papers, WCL, Robert Taylor to John Tailyour, Sept. 1, 1808.

27. John Taylor to John Tailyour, July 22, 1809, ibid; John Tailyour to John Orr, Oct. 28, 1809, Letter Book (1804–1810), Tailyour Papers, WCL.

city, but his apologies primarily served as a preface to request an increase in allowance. This frustrated both father and uncle. Echoing his previous claims about James's elevated sense of entitlement, Robert declared, "There is nothing I am so apprehensive of, in young men like [John], as getting an expensive turn." Again, Robert anticipated far less success for the boys than Tailyour and bristled when their expectations seemed to exceed his own. He might have thought even less of John, owing to either a darker complexion or weaker sociability.[28]

Just as John lamented his pittance, he begrudged the tedium and long hours of his clerkship. Extended days of work tired the young man and dampened his enthusiasm for a renewed correspondence with his father. "I am very sorry to think that you are displeased with my letters," he explained. "[I] must indeed confess that I have in general very little time when I write." When Tailyour pressed his brother about John's abilities, Robert reported that the young man's penmanship was lacking and not swift enough for the large amount of copying needed by the house. Robert also worried about John's comportment. "He seems to be a Meek quiet Boy"; "quite a Boy — being very little — and awkward in Manner." Having done far less than his brother to impress Robert, John never fit in well with family in the capital. But, over time, John's speed and skill at work improved, and Robert congratulated him on exceedingly high morals. Grooming himself for a career in trade, John began studying French and Spanish outside work. Possessing less social charm than his brother, young John took more time to prove his occupational competency.[29]

Acutely aware of his restricted progress, or perhaps sensing a general prejudice toward him, John quickly grew displeased with metropolitan life and looked for ways out. Work dissatisfied him the most, and he asked his father to help procure a position as a captain's clerk on an outward-bound ship. Taking a cue from his brother's career, he hoped he could sail as a clerk on an East Indiaman. Charged once more to find John such a position, Robert demurred, certain that he would not be able to obtain one for the young man, perhaps owing to his appearance and the company's racial bar. Discouraged, John next considered returning to Jamaica. He said nothing of his motivation to move back, but remigration from Britain to the colonies was certainly com-

28. John Taylor to John Tailyour, Oct. 29, 1809, Tailyour Papers, WCL, Robert Taylor to John Tailyour, June 27, 1810.

29. John Taylor to John Tailyour, Sept. 9, 1809, ibid., Oct. 29, 1809, Sept. 27, 1810, Robert Taylor to John Tailyour, Mar. 14, 1810, Sept. 25, 1811.

mon for West Indians of color. After all, of the seventy-four mixed-race Jamaicans who had gone to Britain and eventually petitioned for privilege dispensations in the eighteenth century, only seven explicitly noted that they were not to come back to the island. Eventually, John relinquished that idea as well. Still eager to leave Britain, he inquired about the possibility of traveling to Île de France (Mauritius), either as a merchant or a clerk. His brother James had just sailed to the island himself with the East India Company, and John most likely wished to join him there, although he had not personally communicated with his brother in more than three years. At this point, in 1811, John's letters to his father stopped, and nothing is said of the young man in Tailyour's other correspondence. James's letters stop at this same point as well. Perhaps something happened to them in their oceanic adventures; perhaps Tailyour cut off ties, feeling their behavior to be capricious. More likely, Tailyour's failing health curtailed his parental interest.[30]

Regardless of why the relationships changed, Tailyour's Jamaican children were slowly being separated from the broader family. Kirktonhill served as Tailyour's fresh start in Scotland. He constructed a new household there that maintained only private ties to illegitimate offspring from the colonies. Pulling away from those natural children by 1811 signified that Tailyour's Scottish household would thereafter be his only acknowledged family. Yet, Tailyour's communication with everyone slowed at this point. His health had been deteriorating, and his correspondence became far less frequent. For years, he complained regularly of headaches, until at the end of July 1812 he suffered a severe stroke. The event paralyzed Tailyour on one side, and he never recovered to any significant degree. Within four years, he was dead. His death had obvious repercussions for the whole family, but perhaps his Jamaican children felt the sting most acutely. They had lost their principal advocate in Britain. Yet, Tailyour's passing only made that split official. The break had been long in coming. When the family read his will, drafted years before his death, they found no mention of his mixed-race children. If Tailyour had been growing reluctant to acknowledge his colonial offspring fully, then death provided the final opportunity to excise them completely from the larger family.[31]

<hr>

30. Robert Taylor to John Tailyour, Sept. 25, 1811, ibid., John Taylor to John Tailyour, Sept. 27, 1810, Mar. 20, 1811, July 16, 1811, Aug. 17, 1811. Given that the Tailyour Papers are organized around the correspondence of John Tailyour, no letters between James and John Taylor and other family members appear in the collection.

31. Robert Taylor to Simon Taylor, Aug. 6, 1812, Simon Taylor Papers, ICS 120/XIII/A/312, ICS; Will of John Taylor (Tailyour), July 17, 1816, PROB 11/1582, NAE.

In several significant ways, James and John Taylor embodied many of the diverse experiences of mixed-race migrants in Britain at the beginning of the nineteenth century. Educated under refined English tutelage, they received the advanced instruction necessary for beginning successful, British careers. James's accomplishments and ability to cast himself as a legitimate participant in distinguished society show the potential that mixed-race individuals had in Britain. His Indian adventures also highlight the ongoing use of imperial travel to advance West Indians of color. Nonetheless, James's precarious advancement and his brother John's faltered progress reveal the burdens and lowered expectations under which mixed-race migrants were beginning to suffer. Failing to construct a privileged identity could cast West Indians of color into a social purgatory between family advantage and racial constraint. Taken together, these children both succeeded and stagnated, realizing the high goals set out by their father while also succumbing to the limitations of the metropole.[32]

Abolition and Demography

If Britain was becoming a far less welcoming place for Jamaicans of color, the transition had long been brewing. Throughout the eighteenth and early nineteenth centuries, questions of race in Britain were considered alongside questions of race in the colonies. As a ban on the African slave trade loomed, it was even clearer that the imperial center and periphery could not be considered separately. Colonial policies always had an impact at home. Proslavery rhetoric in the last quarter of the eighteenth century built its case on that very notion. Commentators such as Edward Long insisted that legal differences between Britain and its colonies on the topic of slavery would draw thousands

32. Almost nothing is known about Tailyour's two other mixed-race children, Simon and Catherine. Simon might have arrived in Britain with his siblings and attended the same school as his brothers; but no letters survive from him, and almost nothing is mentioned about the young boy in his father's papers. Catherine appears only briefly in several letters. When reporting to Polly about their children's lives in Britain, Tailyour wrote that Catherine lived with his sister in Scotland; see John Tailyour to John Orr, Oct. 28, 1809, Letter Book (1804–1810), Tailyour Papers, WCL. This was the same sister who cared for James and John when they were young. John and Catherine, as the two youngest children, retained a tight bond. After moving to London, John wrote regularly to Catherine and frequently asked his father to give her his regards; see John Taylor to John Tailyour, Mar. 15, 1810, Tailyour Papers, WCL. The younger John included a number of letters to his sister in this message to his father (and noted as much in the missive). Unfortunately, copies of these letters to Catherine have not survived.

of black runaways to the more freedom-minded Britain. Likewise, antislavery crusaders insisted that, unless Britain adopted a standard ban on slavery across its Empire, it could not rule effectively. As England inched toward abolishing its slave trade, politicians and political observers took those lessons to heart and engaged once more in debates over demography, ethnicity, and political stability in the Empire. This brought questions of race back to the forefront of public discussion and accelerated concern over the presence of nonwhite people in Britain.

Even though abolitionist fervor had decreased in the 1790s, Parliament continued to investigate human trafficking throughout the decade. Hoping to understand the ramifications of abolition, the House of Commons solicited information on the reproductive capabilities of enslaved laborers should it impose a ban. In 1796, officials in Westminster examined the numbers of bound Africans imported into Jamaica, in part to study the island's tariffs but also to assess the possibility of a self-reproducing enslaved workforce. By the next year, the House of Commons wrote to every Caribbean governor demanding that they adopt measures "to obviate the causes, which have hitherto impeded the natural increase of the negroes already in the islands." Various assemblies were quick to act, but without any kind of meaningful legislation. Saint Kitts's representatives passed an act in 1798 "to promote and encourage" increased slave reproduction, though the law did little to specify how that might happen. Dominica's assembly undertook a survey of its enslaved population in 1799, including birth and death rates, but no resulting legislation followed. That same year the Jamaican assembly publicly read through the House of Commons request, but it also failed to produce a legislative plan. English lawmakers hoped that West Indians could solve this demographic crisis by themselves. However, the entrenched and profitable practices of brutal sugar regimes were at odds with such solutions. This failure of ruling West Indians to act meant that demography would continue to dominate discussions of abolition until the slave trade's prohibition.[33]

33. "Copies of an Act Passed by the Assembly of *Jamaica,* in the Month of February 1774, Imposing Duties on the Importation of Negroes from the Coast of Africa," no. 4609, in *HCSP,* C, 161–181; William Cavendish-Bentinck, duke of Portland, to the Jamaican assembly, Apr. 6, 1797, as quoted in *JAJ,* Aug. 3, 1797, IX, 651; "Further Correspondence between the Secretary of State for the Home Department and the Governors, or Other Civil Authorities, in the West Indies . . . ," Feb. 22, 1799, no. 4905, in *HCSP,* CXII, 99–119; Robert Thomson to William Shipley, May 9–Dec. 16, 1798, in Clare Taylor, ed., *West Indian Attitudes to the American and French Revolutions: As Seen in the MSS. in the National Library of Wales* (Aberystwyth, U.K., 1977); An Act for Ascertaining the Number of Slaves in This Island,

In the absence of an official response, observers hoped that enslaved re-production could be achieved instead through nonstatutory measures. Commentators across the Atlantic believed that the simplest answer would be to compel slaves to marry one another. Europeans often claimed Africans to be heavily licentious, citing polygynous and indiscriminate sexual interactions as an impediment to pregnancy and the impetus for frequent abortions. One abolitionist joked that African marriage was so rare that planters had no need to worry if their enslaved mistresses had husbands. Others blamed slave-owners for the apparent absence of matrimonial connections between en-slaved persons. Lady Maria Nugent, wife of Jamaica's governor, recorded in 1801 that one of the island's planters tried to increase his workforce by giving enslaved women two dollars for every child they bore. The intention seemed admirable, but she felt the policy missed the point, exclaiming that "no mar-riages were thought of!!" To improve this situation, a combined effort had to be made to instruct slaves in proper conjugal relationships as well as to com-pel masters to support matrimony. This fit into a general attempt in the nine-teenth century to impose British notions of sexuality and family organization on colonial populations. Religiously minded reformers hoped to improve the moral state of enslaved workers in preparation for their eventual freedom, and compelling them to wed was simply a first step on that path. One Jamaican visitor felt that slaveowners should do their part as well. He suggested that some kind of reward could be given to those slaves "who have lived faithfully and happily in the marriage-state, and have been the parents of a certain num-ber of children." This would not only improve colonial morality but would also keep West Indian plantations running smoothly after abolition. Cultural change, then, could potentially address the demographic problem of slavery that legislation seemed unable to tackle.[34]

Oct. 11, 1799, Laws of Dominica, PRO 73/11, fol. 14, NAE. The Jamaican assembly did pass an act in 1797 to ban the importation of Africans older than twenty-five, though that was the only significant piece of legislation to address the topic of slave reproduction; see *JAJ*, Dec. 23, 1797, X, 104, Nov. 5, 1799, 320.

34. *The State of Slavery, in the British West Indies, Delineated and Considered* (n.p., circa 1803), 186–191, ICS; [Nugent], *Lady Nugent's Journal*, ed. Wright, 26; Dennis Reid, *An Ad-dress to Every Class of British Subjects, and Particularly to the Legislators and Colonists of the British Empire; in Which Some Observations Are Offered on the Nature and Effects of the Slave Trade* (London, 1802), 29; Robert Renny, *A History of Jamaica . . .* (London, 1807), 186; Catherine Hall, *Civilising Subjects: Metropole and Colony in the English Imagination, 1830–1867* (Chicago, 2002), 112–125; Henrice Altink, "Forbidden Fruit: Pro-Slavery Atti-tudes towards Enslaved Women's Sexuality and Interracial Sex," *Journal of Caribbean His-tory*, XXXIX (2005), 201–235. The link between emancipation and the compulsion to in-

Such idealized notions of enslaved reproduction ignored the many white men who had families with enslaved women. Mixed-race populations always presented a demographic pitfall in the minds of imperial observers. The children of interracial relationships were sometimes freed, which did not contribute to the enslaved population, and those not manumitted were thought to be less able workers. Commentators on the issue of slave marriage frequently reflected on the problems these unions posed. The Scottish poet and traveler Hector McNeill, for instance, did not blame African practices for the lack of slave marriage, but rather he pointed his finger at the behavior of slaveowners. After arriving in Jamaica, he wondered how an enslaved man was supposed to value marriage when "he perceives his superior, and almost every description of white men, totally inattentive to what so materially tends to propagation, namely, an attachment to one woman." Furthermore, he asserted that black women were most fecund with white men, thereby undercutting the plantation economy. "Instead of a Negro child, [she] produces a Mulatto; which, again, instead of turning out a valuable slave, is generally emancipated by the father, and becomes often a vagabond, if a male, and always a lady of concubinage, if a female." James Stewart, who claimed to have lived in Jamaica for a quarter century, agreed. The supposed dearth of civility and Christianity on the island fostered a culture of sexual promiscuity, he insisted, producing a blanket disregard for marriage across all social strata. Perhaps worst of all, Stewart stated, white fathers looked after their illegitimate families in the colony. "His spurious issue he doats [sic] on with as parental a fondness as if they were the offspring of a more virtuous and tender union," Stewart scoffed: "He sends them to Europe, where they are liberally educated, and, if the laws of the colony would permit him, he would, at his decease, bequeath the bulk of his fortune to them." If reformers truly wished to foster enslaved reproduction, they would have to address the issue of interracial unions and the children born from them.[35]

Mixed-race offspring appeared to be such a large problem to West Indian commentators because of their supposed inability to work as productively as

struct free people to wed to stimulate reproduction was especially pronounced in Haiti after its independence; see Elizabeth Colwill, " 'Fêtes de l'hyman, fêtes de la liberté': Marriage, Manhood, and Emancipation in Revolutionary Saint-Domingue," in David Patrick Geggus and Norman Fiering, eds., *The World of the Haitian Revolution* (Bloomington, Ind., 2009), 125–145.

35. Hector McNeill, *Observations on the Treatment of the Negroes, in the Island of Jamaica* (London, [1800]), 41–42; [James Stewart], *An Account of Jamaica and Its Inhabitants* (London, 1808), 200–208.

those with full African heritage. Abolitionists and slaveowners alike had long derided mulattos as inferior laborers, owing to their partial European heritage that they saw as less suited to tropical labor. One political agitator insisted that white West Indians slept with slaves to increase their stock, but in reality this was almost never a policy promoted on the plantation. Instead, planters warned of the ill effects of having mixed-race slaves on their estate. Many echoed McNeill's statement that children of color who were freed turned out either to be vagabonds or concubines rather than productive workers. One Jamaican overseer made this sentiment clear to his estate's absentee owner in an 1807 letter. After a man offered two new slaves to the plantation in return for the manumission of his lover and their child, the overseer implored his boss to take the deal: "The Girl is nearly white and can only be made to do something about the Overseers house. The Child . . . if he should grow up he will be so near white that he will not be of use to the property—These kind of people are far from being desirable on a Sugar Estate." The Caribbean slave regime depended on good workers. Because Europeans had long since concluded that their blood did not respond well to toil in excessive heat, only African labor would suffice. The diminution of that African blood supposedly harmed the productivity of plantations. Mixed-race children also undercut what, by the nineteenth century, had become the central pillar of West Indian society: slaves were to be black, and freemen were to be white. Any softening of that boundary would fundamentally transform the colonies.[36]

All of this demographic discussion circled back to the same topic that had obsessed Caribbean observers from the start: the size and stability of the islands' white populations. Facing the prospect that their supply of captive Africans might soon be cut off, West Indian planters and officials exclaimed that abolition would destroy white settlements in the Caribbean. In particular, they asserted that Britons would no longer venture to the islands if they could not purchase new workers with which to start plantations. When Haiti won its independence in 1804, London's West India Committee lobbied Westminster to view the new black republic as a tragic result of slave reforms. The committee insisted that, should abolition occur, population decline in the

36. Pierre F. McCallum, *Travels in Trinidad* (Liverpool, U.K., 1805), 77–78; Francis Graham to Thomas Milles, Dec. 10, 1807, Georgia Estate Letter Books, MS 132, I, NLJ. For attempts at social engineering on French colonial plantations in this period, see William Max Nelson, "Making Men: Enlightenment Ideas of Racial Engineering," *American Historical Review*, CXV (2010), 1364–1394. For a thorough discussion of the topic and its scholarly debate in the North American context, see Gregory D. Smithers, *Slave Breeding: Sex, Violence, and Memory in African American History* (Gainesville, Fla., 2012).

Caribbean would be inevitable. It sang this refrain repeatedly. Just a month before Parliament finally signed the bill to end the trade, the committee declared that the "immediate consequence of the abolition will be the loss of the white population of the colonies." The Jamaican assembly lobbied Parliament as well, begging it in 1804 to table abolition as white settlement depended on a reliable supply of imported Africans. Those supporting abolition disagreed, claiming that slavery and incivility stood in the way of white reproduction. Granted, some Britons would no longer wish to establish businesses in the Caribbean, but others might be enticed by more moderate policies on slavery. Stewart maintained that increasing white numbers was a simple fix. If more money was given to colonial schools, white children would stay on the islands, marry one another, and bring up large families in turn. Regardless of the position, both sides of the abolition debate still focused on the future of the islands' white populations. Colonial security depended, in their minds, on the strength of white settlement. Abolition would undeniably affect the future of all people living in the West Indies. The question was whether it would provide a secure place for white individuals.[37]

In their personal correspondence, John Tailyour's associates echoed these strident pronouncements on the imminent demise of Jamaica's white population. His cousin Simon Taylor answered repeated letters questioning the island's future should abolition occur. Now in advanced age, especially for a Jamaican, he relished his status as elder statesman, dispensing knowledge to a worried public. At first, Simon offered his own suggestions for increasing white numbers. He petitioned the assembly to hold out inducements for visiting soldiers to settle on the island, which Jamaica's governor considered seriously. Privately, Simon insisted that Jamaica was fighting a losing battle. "Our White Population is dayly nay hourly decreasing," he wrote to George Hibbert, cousin to the mixed-race migrant Jane Harry Thresher. Abolition would only make matters worse by dissuading whites to come over, and he worried that Jamaica might instead "fall into the hands of Negroes or Mulattoes." Such reasoning convinced Hibbert. The year before Parliament banned the slave trade, he wrote in a panic to Simon about the folly of immediate abolition. Not only would the measure hurt Jamaica's small farmers—rarely a group of interest for the island's plantocracy—but he believed that it would

37. West India Committee Minutes, June 12, 1807, West India Committee Records, reel 1, ICS, Feb. 17, 1807, reel 3; *JAJ*, Nov. 23, 1804, XI, 217; *The Horrors of the Negro Slavery Existing in Our West Indian Islands . . .*, 2d ed. (London, 1805), 34–35; [Stewart], *Account of Jamaica*, 167–169.

convince young men, especially Scots, not to cross the Atlantic. These were, not ginned up invectives, but legitimate concerns by a faction struggling to maintain its machinery of human exploitation. As the ax of abolition descended on the shipping lines between Africa and the Caribbean, slaveowners scurried to anticipate their future.[38]

When abolition started to appear inevitable, and especially after its passage, West Indians began rethinking how they might manage colonial settlement without saltwater slaves. For many elite Jamaicans, the diminution of the island's white population seemed a foregone conclusion. For Simon Taylor, there was only one possible way to deal with its effects. Although he did not articulate it in this way, Simon effectively suggested returning to a project forwarded by the policies set in place by the Jamaican assembly in the 1730s but largely abandoned by the 1760s—that is, the creation of a white population from a mixed-race one. Writing again to Hibbert in 1804, he waxed nostalgic about his long life on the island. Reflecting back on his youth, he recalled that, on returning to Kingston in 1760, after completing his studies at Eton, the city had only three quadroon women. Though clearly a gross exaggeration, he was right that the city's mixed-race population was indeed much smaller. By 1804, Simon suggested, there were one hundred times as many women of color. Perhaps more important, though, he intimated that most of these women had no interest in mixed-race men, only whites. European ancestry still maintained its social capital, and Simon believed that women of color cared only to blanch family lines. Spurned by their peers of color, mixed-race men would couple with women of a darker complexion, eventually returning their family lineages back to an effective African stock. Of the quadroon women, however, Simon proclaimed, "Their progeny is growing whiter and whiter every remoove, Their Daughters doing the same [and] from thence a White Generation will come in time." Here, once again, was the basic policy articulated by the Jamaican assembly seventy years earlier: individuals of color could become white. In fact, they had to become white if, indeed, white settlement was a central need of the island. According to Taylor, it was not simply a possibility but the island's only choice. "I have a hundred and a hundred times reflected on the Means of Establishing a white Population here but the Experience of forty three years shews me it is impossible to be

38. *JAJ,* June 21, 1802, X, 671–672; George Nugent to George Grenville, May 25, 1802, Stowe-Grenville Papers, box 44 (3), HL; Simon Taylor to George Hibbert, Oct. 31, 1798, Simon Taylor Papers, ICS 120 B/30, ICS, George Hibbert to Simon Taylor, July 2, 1806, ICS 120 XVII/A/66.

done but in this manner." Perhaps, in his estimation, the Jamaican assembly had wrongly shifted course away from this very plan after Tacky's Revolt in 1761. That notion of socially engineering a white population never wholly disappeared from Jamaican political discourse, but it found renewed favor as the Caribbean faced abolition head-on.[39]

Few West Indians were as bold as Simon Taylor in suggesting increased interracial unions, but the growing disproportion between white and mixed-race colonists demanded attention to the latter's plight. After hearing that a Jamaican preacher was baptizing fifteen children of color for every white child, James Stewart called for some kind of policy to be put in place to address this rise in the population of color. Although far from sympathetic to the group, he nevertheless insisted that "the boundary between them and the whites must at one period give way, or be broken down; either the free browns will be admitted to an equal participation of the rights and privileges of the whites, or they will, at some future day, enforce that admission." Stewart hoped that white marriage would solve the problem, but he understood that a more likely scenario would be to use people of color to support the ruling class. Stephen Gaisford, who had lived in the Windward Islands and spent some time in Jamaica, also felt that the writing was on the wall. In 1811, he commented on the decline of white numbers in the Caribbean and argued that it was time for the islands' assemblies to grant people of color the right to vote. Gaisford stopped short of recommending a blanket allowance for mixed-race people to serve in colonial government, but he did make a startling suggestion. He advised Parliament to conduct an experiment on one or two West Indian colonies that were not seen as potentially rebellious. Once selected, those islands should "devolv[e] to the coloured race in a natural course, [which] may be the necessary means for the regeneration of such islands to a state of prosperity unsurpassed by their former history." Jamaica was not the model island Gaisford envisioned, but the ideas put forward by its assembly in the early eighteenth century had resembled his plan. If establishing a permanent and self-regenerating white population in the Caribbean was an impossible dream, then allowing an elite cohort of color to supplement, if not replace, that population might be the only viable alternative.[40]

39. Simon Taylor to George Hibbert, Jan. 14, 1804, Simon Taylor Papers, ICS 120 F/42, ICS.

40. [Stewart], *Account of Jamaica*, 134–135, 299–300; Stephen Gaisford, *An Essay on the Good Effects Which May Be Derived in the British West Indies in Consequence of the Abolition of the African Slave Trade* . . . (London, 1811), 51–52, 210.

Such interest in allowing mixed-race individuals to take greater control in the colonies came not only out of the abolition movement but out of the Haitian Revolution as well. Vincent Ogé's coup in October 1790, still perceived by many to be the catalyst of the revolution, convinced West Indian observers to try to appease their islands' populations of color in order to prevent another uprising. Colonial officials were terrified that Haitian revolutionaries had spread throughout the Caribbean to organize and radicalize nonwhites. Barbados's governor Francis Mackenzie, Lord Seaforth, labeled freemen of color "unappropriated people" who might find more solidarity with Haiti than the British Empire. Abolitionist-in-chief William Wilberforce agreed. He believed that mixed-race West Indians had built group solidarity around their shared persecution and that the lesson of Haiti was to address the growing disproportion between whites and individuals of color. Colonel Frederick Maitland's military tour through the West Indies at the end of the eighteenth century convinced him of the same. "The Conduct which Government should adopt towards this Class of People, is of the utmost Importance to the Colonies," he wrote in 1800. "They form a Link between the Whites and the Slaves—If this Tye is broken, or not preserved by the former; the Colour'd People must necessarily join their Interest with the Slaves—And the Whites become the common Enemy of each." Maitland bemoaned interracial relationships for raising the imbalance between whites and people of color, which might potentially escalate tensions between the two. However, he felt that the islands had passed a demographic point of no return. West Indians of color were far too numerous not to increase on their own, and the issue under question was now how to manage them effectively. Unlike Gaisford, Maitland did not endorse handing the reins of power to mixed-race subjects. Yet, he advised granting them some guarantee of personal rights. The choice, to him, was clear: "We must receive them, and attach them—or We must destroy them."[41]

Once again, this fixation on colonial demography and West Indians of color bled into parallel discussions about the group in Britain. In some cases, this interest came in the form of public safety, such as when London received news

41. Francis Mackenzie, Lord Seaforth, to Robert Hobart, June 6, 1802, Seaforth Papers, GD 46/7/7, fol. 10, NAS, Lord Seaforth to the attorney general of Barbados, Oct. 17, 1802, fol. 45; W[illiam] Wilberforce, *A Letter on the Abolition of the Slave Trade; Addressed to the Freeholders and Other Inhabitants of Yorkshire* (London, 1807), 171–172, 321–323; Frederick Maitland, "Thoughts on the Situation of the Free Colour'd People in the West Indies and of Those Who Have Pretensions to Freedom," Dec. 28, 1800, Secretary of State Correspondence for Martinique, CO 166/1, no. 3, fols. 10–13, NAE.

in 1801 that a ship of "Mulattoes and Negroes" who served as officers in Saint Domingue had landed in Brest, just across the English Channel. Britain's war office did not feel as much of a threat as its colleagues did in the Caribbean. As a legal ban on slave trading neared, though, commentators began to wonder if Britain itself might provide an answer to the question of mixed-race colonists' future in the Empire. An anonymous pamphleteer sketched out just such a scenario. Advocating generally for better clergymen in the Caribbean, the author proposed that an English college should be erected to train ministers. When deliberating on who might best fill the seats of this seminary, the author considered "the expediency of educating any Negroes or Mulattos in such a College." The appeal of nonwhite clergymen was simple. If an abolition of the slave trade was near, then so, too, might be an eventual emancipation of all bound subjects. Soon-to-be-freed slaves would perhaps listen more intently and respond more effectively to Christianity if taught by someone of like complexion. Mixed-race ministers could stabilize the population in the face of emancipation's dramatic potential. Yet, the author simultaneously worried that these students of color might also present problems. "The consequence which they would derive from having had a learned education in Europe, would enable them to do incalculable mischief, if they should turn out ill." Clearly, the author worried that Jamaicans of color in London might inspire the same type of Caribbean revolt that Dominguans of color, educated in Paris, had seventeen years earlier.[42]

Others contended that, if the potential danger of British-educated West Indians of color arose once they returned to the Caribbean, perhaps they should simply stay in Britain. Many observers sympathetic to abolition did not find the practice of mixed-race education in Britain to be a problem by itself. Gaisford, for instance, did not see Britain as a seedbed for extremism. But he did believe that complications emerged when those students of color arrived back in the colonies where their high status immediately came into conflict with the law. "Rebellion and mischief," he contended, were the natural outgrowths of such disenfranchisement. Stewart echoed these sentiments. He noted that, although a white and mixed-race Jamaican might be friends and schoolmates in Britain, they "discontinue that intimacy on their growing

42. D'Auvergne Bouillon to Robert Hobart, Dec. 25, 1801, Secretary of State for War Correspondence, WO 1/923, fols. 597–598, NAE; *Observations on the Necessity of Introducing a Sufficient Number of Respectable Clergymen into Our Colonies in the West Indies . . .* (London, 1807), 12n. Such a school had been proposed before, but for African children; see C. B. Wadstrom, *An Essay on Colonization, Particularly Applied to the Western Coast of Africa, with Some Free Thoughts on Cultivation and Commerce . . .* (London, 1794), pt. 1, 93.

up and returning to the West Indies; though both may be equally amiable and accomplished." Social prejudices back in the Caribbean were the major root of these distinctions, but the loss of political rights was also key. Free West Indians of color held the same legal status as whites in Britain. When they returned home, though, they fell subject to colonial statutes that kept them from, among other things, voting, holding certain employments, and testifying in court. Such a shift would undoubtedly cause many returning migrants to rethink their place in Caribbean society.[43]

A number of writers offered anecdotal evidence in support of these assertions. Robert Renny claimed personal knowledge of a "young gentleman of fortune, a Mulatto, who had been sent to Europe for his education." Stopping in Barbados on the way home to Jamaica, the young man was refused service at a tavern, causing him to burst into tears. Another author wrote of a free mulatto "of good education" who was fired from an appointed job at Montserrat's customhouse for no other reason than his heritage. Social rejection from white peers might spur West Indians of color trained in Britain to political agitation. British schools could thus radicalize colonial migrants, not because of fanatical instruction, but because of the marked changes in social status when those migrants returned to the colonies. In other words, elites of color might threaten West Indian society simply for not having their privileged metropolitan upbringing recognized.[44]

Public discourse around individuals of color was therefore fraught with anxiety at the start of the nineteenth century. Most of the same demographic arguments put forward in the previous two decades returned once Parliament came back to the question of abolition. Yet, there was not necessarily a uniformity of opinion on the matter. Mixed-race colonists continued to pose problems for imperial reformers hoping to end the slave trade as well as those seeking to keep it in place. Certain commentators such as Simon Taylor nevertheless hoped to ennoble a small branch of the West Indies' population of color in order to stabilize the colonies by any means necessary. In addition, these

43. Gaisford, *Essay on the Good Effects,* 40–41, 151–152; [Stewart], *Account of Jamaica,* 301–303.

44. Renny, *History of Jamaica,* 190n; *State of Slavery,* 232n. East Indian observers certainly felt this to be the case for the subcontinent. George Annesley insisted in 1809 that mixed-race children in India undercut the racial divisions absolutely necessary to maintain rule. The only solution, he felt, was to "oblig[e] every father of half-cast children, to send them to Europe, prohibiting their return in any capacity whatsoever." See [Annesley], *Voyages and Travels to India, Ceylon, the Red Sea, Abyssinia, and Egypt, in the Years 1802, 1803, 1804, 1805, and 1806,* 3 vols. (London, 1809), I, 241–242.

colonial debates inevitably led—as they always had before—to a consideration of the metropole. Abolitionists and proslavery supporters alike continued to wonder what effect mixed-race migrants would have on Britain and especially on the Caribbean should they return. Most writers had grown less sympathetic to their plight as abolition neared. For the relatives taking them in, this made full familial acceptance more challenging. It would become even more difficult after a public scandal emerged involving a woman of color in Britain.

Louisa Calderon's Torture and Thomas Picton's Trial

In the fall of 1803, Louisa Calderon stepped off the ship that had taken her from the Caribbean island of Trinidad to Glasgow. She came to testify against the colony's former governor, Thomas Picton, who stood accused of a number of infractions. The most sensational, and ultimately most important of these, was Calderon's torture during a routine criminal investigation on the island, only recently acquired from Spain by Britain. Lieutenant Colonel Picton had begun serving as the de facto head of Trinidad in 1797, after British forces seized the island, and officially took the position of governor when Spain formally ceded the colony five years later. Immediately, complaints emerged about his strict method of governing. Officials in London, eager to avoid an uprising, sent politician William Fullarton and naval captain Samuel Hood to act as joint governors of the island, alongside Picton. Within seven months of landing in the Caribbean, Fullarton pressed charges against Picton for governmental abuse and returned to Britain with Calderon in tow to testify against him. Calderon, a mixed-race Trinidadian, would provide key evidence for the prosecution. Fullarton, and his wife Marianne, would get her settled and prepared for the trial after they arrived in Scotland.[45]

Commencing the year before England abolished its slave trade, Picton's case enthralled the public. Britons in the midst of considering how best to reform their Empire and potentially cure it of the scourge of slavery were stunned to learn that a colonial governor would stoop to torture a young woman of color. Yet, proslavery forces rising to Picton's defense lashed out at Calderon and insinuated that she carried on an improper relationship with William Fullarton. For a fascinated British audience, Calderon's presence in

45. This chapter, which addresses increasing anxieties surrounding elite mixed-race migrants, does not delve substantively into the details of Picton's trial—a topic other scholars such as James Epstein have cogently addressed; see Epstein, *Scandal of Colonial Rule: Power and Subversion in the British Atlantic during the Age of Revolution* (New York, 2012); Kit Candlin, *The Last Caribbean Frontier, 1795–1815* (New York, 2012), 118–137; and V. S. Naipaul, *The Loss of El Dorado* (New York, 1970), 129–327.

Scotland played out, in miniature, all of the complex issues surrounding anti-slavery, migrants of color, and interracial relationships in Britain. Interest in Calderon's arrival was grounded in the Picton case, which was itself connected to a constellation of debates concerning abolitionism, which had long aroused fears over interracial pairings in Britain.

When Calderon landed in Glasgow, her birthplace was at the epicenter of a rejuvenated discussion of the slave trade. Although abolitionists had gained little ground in the 1790s, Britain's acquisition of fresh Caribbean territory provided the opportunity to reengage with a potential ban on human trafficking. Trinidad's economy had not developed substantially under the Spanish and was thus a potential blank slate for a new slave society. Spain's 1783 Cédula de Población had attempted to spur plantation growth in the colony by encouraging immigration, relaxing laws on land acquisition, and temporarily eliminating slave importation duties. However, those efforts had not yet borne fruit when Britain seized Trinidad in 1797. To speed the development of the island's plantation economy, Britain considered extending the Cédula's enticements. Yet, planters in more-established Anglophone islands resented Trinidad's entry into the sugar economy, and abolitionists railed against the prospect of yet another hothouse of African enslavement. This combined disapproval helped abolition supporters to gain an important victory: in 1799 Parliament banned the interisland slave trade, which all but ended slave imports into Trinidad. This modest success in limiting the slave trade to Trinidad reinvigorated an anemic abolition movement and would open the door to the possibility of full-scale prohibition.[46]

As politicians debated Trinidad's future, Picton came to trial. Proceedings began in 1806, adjudicated by Edward Law, Lord Ellenborough, one of the key attorneys who had defended Warren Hastings, the former governor

46. Carl C. Campbell, *Cedulants and Capitulants: The Politics of the Coloured Opposition in the Slave Society of Trinidad, 1783–1838* (Port of Spain, Trinidad, 1992), 52–53, 90–92. Both Eric Williams and Gelien Matthews point to this period as an important one, not only for Trinidadian history, but for Britain's larger trade in human cargo; see Williams, *History of the People of Trinidad and Tobago* (New York, 1964), 65–66; and Matthews, "Trinidad: A Model Colony for British Slave Trade Abolition," in Stephen Farrell, Melanie Unwin, and James Walvin, eds., *The British Slave Trade: Abolition, Parliament, and People* (Edinburgh, 2007), 84–96. See also Seymour Drescher, "Public Opinion and Parliament in the Abolition of the British Slave Trade," ibid., 61–65; Epstein, *Scandal of Colonial Rule*, 96–101, 184–221; and Candlin, *Last Caribbean Frontier*, 93–95. Banning the interisland slave trade allowed abolitionists to win another victory in 1806: the Foreign Slave Trade bill, which cut off British slave trading to foreign countries. That law effectively paved the way for full prohibition one year later.

of Bengal, in his corruption trial a decade earlier. Picton's attorney Robert Dallas had served on Hastings's legal team as well. In yet another associational twist, Picton had also rented out a room in the London house next door to the mixed-race Jamaican Robert Morse. At the trial, the king's counsel brought forth a litany of charges against the former governor. Of these, the most publicly discussed was his supposed torture of Calderon. The incident dated back to 1801 when Calderon was arrested in conjunction with a burglary. At the time, she lived as the mistress of Pedro Ruiz, whose house had been robbed. Authorities suspected a young man named Carlos Gonzalez of the crime and learned that he and Calderon were rumored to have had a secret relationship of their own. Gonzalez and Calderon were both arrested and later interrogated. When Picton learned of the arrest, he ordered—or at least conceded to—the torture of Calderon to extract evidence. In particular, he had her hung by the arm above a sharp point onto which her feet were occasionally lowered to induce pain (see Plate 10). At question in Picton's trial was whether such torture violated the law.[47]

Multiple legal issues were at stake, but the case almost immediately devolved into competing character attacks, particularly targeting the sexual histories of both Calderon and Picton. Such discourse had started even before the trial. Launching a preemptive salvo against Picton, William Fullarton had exposed the former governor's mistress of color in Trinidad, Rosetta Smith, with whom he had four children. Calderon suffered much worse once the trial began. Her body was subject to intense scrutiny in court, ostensibly to determine her age when tortured. Calderon's treatment could only be considered illegal if she was found to have been a minor when punished. This meant that lawyers spent much of the trial considering the size of her breasts and the imminence of menarche at the time of the event. Depictions of Calderon's ordeal displayed in court also showed a remarkable similarity to abolitionist

47. P[atrick] Boyle's London directory notes that Robert Morse lived at 147 New Bond Street in London, while Picton rented a lodging at 146 New Bond Street from 1797 to 1800; see Boyle, *With Near Five Thousand Alterations; Boyle's New Fashionable Court and Country Guide; and Town Visiting Directory, for 1798* (London, [1798]), 121; [Boyle], *With Near 4000 Additions and Alterations, Carefully Corrected up to January 30, 1800; Boyle's Fashionable Court and Country Guide, and Visiting Directory* . . . (London, [1800]), 22. A nineteenth-century biographical listing of Picton notes the same address; see the *Journal of the Society of Arts, and of the Institutions in Union* (London, 1867), XV, 756. Proving Picton had violated the law was made more complicated given that Spain had not yet ceded Trinidad when the torture occurred. The court in London, therefore, had to determine if Picton's action violated Spanish, not English, statutes.

PLATE 10. Caldron's Torture. Frontispiece. From [Pierre McCallum], *The Trial of Governor T. Picton, for Inflicting the Torture on Louisa Calderon, a Free Mulatto, and One of His Britannic Majesty's Subjects, in the Island of Trinidad . . .* (London, [1806]). Image courtesy of the Senate House Library, University of London

imagery that promoted a "pornography of pain" associated with women of color (see Plate 9). Additionally, the defense attacked her credibility by insisting that Calderon had carried on multiple sexual relationships in Trinidad. That inspired rounds of criticism from Picton supporters who labeled her, among other things, "Louisa Calderon, the mulatto girl, a *perjured prostitute and thief.*" She simultaneously represented, therefore, two different colonial archetypes: the innocent child of color and the sexually ravenous mixed-race paramour. She was both child and mother, which put her body and sexuality on display and open to direct assault. Nevertheless, the jury returned a guilty verdict against Picton for improper torture.[48]

48. [William] Fullarton, *A Statement, Letters, and Documents, respecting the Affairs of Trinidad: Including a Reply to Colonel Picton's Address to the Council of That Island* (London,

Although it would be overturned after a subsequent appeal, the decision prompted immediate attacks against Calderon by Picton's supporters.
Edward Draper, a military officer who had served in the West Indies, cursed
Calderon as a "hypocritical mulata prostitute, a[nd] self-convicted robber"
who had been "brought from another world" and was "introduced into Westminster Hall." He also claimed that William Fullarton and his wife hosted and
looked after Calderon in Scotland but lied about her age "in order that the
tender epithets of *enfant* and *pucelle* might be added to that of the *interesting
Mademoiselle Calderon*." Draper ridiculed the scene of Calderon "paraded
by the Honourable Mrs. Fullarton," who, he alleged, "took her about in her
carriage, and introduced her to her female acquaintances." Once again, then,
Calderon's opponents mocked her for being simultaneously a deceitful prostitute as well as a socially incongruous child of color. Her colonial relationships transformed Calderon's British presence into one of the ultimate taboos:
the mistress of color brought across the Atlantic. But the Fullartons' supervision of her once there—along with the attempts to prove her adolescence in
court—also caused her to resemble the increasingly disparaged figure of the
young, mixed-race migrant.[49]

1804), 192–193; Will of Thomas Picton, July 5, 1815, PROB 11/1571, NAE; Thomas Picton,
Evidence Taken at Port of Spain, Island of Trinidad, in the Case of Luisa Calderon (London,
1806), 61; William Garrow, as quoted in Donald Thomas, ed., *State Trials*, II, *The Public
Conscience* (Boston, 1972), 170; *Anti-Jacobin Review and Magazine; or, Monthly Political
and Literary Censor*, XLV, no. 24 (May 1806), 56; Epstein, *Scandal of Colonial Rule*, 34–38;
Karen Halttunen, "Humanitarianism and the Pornography of Pain in Anglo-American Cul-
ture," *American Historical Review*, C (1995), 303–334. See also Marcus Wood, "John Gabriel
Stedman, William Blake, Francesco Bartolozzi, and Empathetic Pornography in the *Narra-
tive of a Five Years Expedition against the Revolted Negroes of Surinam*," in Geoff Quilley and
Kay Dian Kriz, eds., *An Economy of Colour: Visual Culture and the Atlantic World, 1660–1830*
(New York, 2003), 129–149; and Kirsten Fischer, *Suspect Relations: Sex, Race, and Resistance
in Colonial North Carolina* (Ithaca, N.Y., 2002), 167–169.

    49. Edward Alured Draper, *An Address to the British Public, on the Case of Brigadier-
General Picton* . . . (London, 1806), 58, 150–151, 183. For more on Draper, see James Epstein,
"Politics of Colonial Sensation: The Trial of Thomas Picton and the Cause of Louisa Calderon," Forum: "What is the History of Sensibilities?" *American Historical Review*, CXII
(2007), 727; *Oxford Dictionary of National Biography*, online ed., s.v. "Draper, Edward
Alured (1776–1841)," by H. M. Chichester, rev. Roger T. Stearn, http://oxforddnb.com/view
/article/8036. The evidence of these interactions between Calderon and Scotland's elite,
however, was practically hearsay. Draper cited a letter from John Downie who was himself
not a direct witness. Downie, who had introduced Picton to the Venezuelan revolutionary
Francisco de Miranda in London, claimed to have heard about Calderon's Scottish exploits

Other publications took up the story of Calderon and the Fullartons to lament the supposed racial infiltration of Scotland's genteel society. One reactionary periodical, the *Anti-Jacobin Review*, bemoaned Fullarton's actions. "This introduction of a little abandoned thief and prostitute, in a country where decency and sobriety of manners, respect for virtue, and abhorrence from vice, prevail, in a greater degree, than in almost any other part of Europe, was such a gross and intolerable insult, as will, no doubt, be properly resented by the respectable persons to whom it was offered." Why such added vitriol? The *Review* explained its concern by publishing still more gossip on Calderon. Without citing a source, it noted, "We have heard, from good authority, that this *interesting young lady* has been delivered of a child, since she has had the happiness and the honour of being under the protection of Mr. Fullarton." To reinforce its accusations through faux denials, it stressed, "Let it not be supposed, however, for a moment, that we mean to insinuate, that the Laird of Fullarton is the father of this *bairne* (child)." The same suppositions made by Edward Long about interracial unions in Britain's working classes a generation earlier were now being made about its wealthier orders. Moreover, if William Fullarton had impregnated the young woman, his behavior would have not only transgressed British norms about domestic interracial relationships but also violated his duty as Calderon's guardian and pseudo father. Indeed, Archibald Gloster repeated the rumor a year after the *Review* had first printed it with almost identical language: "This virtuous young lady has insured a continuance of her fair race, by producing an heir . . . whilst under [Fullarton's] philanthropic protection." In this telling, both Calderon and Fullarton were responsible for an illegitimate and improper British household.[50]

William Fullarton's wife, Marianne, retaliated by issuing a number of libel suits but continued to suffer from speculation. After William died in 1808, she

---

when dining with the mayor of Ayr; see Downie, Sept. 8, 1805, as quoted in Draper, *Address to the British Public*, 183. See also Naipaul, *Loss of El Dorado, 333.*

50. *Anti-Jacobin Review; or, Monthly Political and Literary Censor*, XXIV, no. 45 (May 1806), 57n, 64n; Archibald Gloster, *A Letter to the Right Honourable Earl of Buckinghamshire . . .* (London, 1807), 24n. The rumor of Calderon's pregnancy by Fullarton was later repeated; see H. B. Robinson, *Memoirs of Lieutenant-General Sir Thomas Picton . . . ,* 2 vols. (London, 1835), I, 178. James Epstein suggests that the allegations of Calderon's pregnancy might have been true. He has found an 1810 baptism in Trinidad for an illegitimate child born to a "Luisa Canderón"; see Epstein, "Politics of Colonial Sensation," Forum, *American Historical Review*, CXII (2007), 741.

sued Draper for alleging that her husband had impregnated Calderon. Going further, Marianne claimed that she had never entertained Calderon among Scottish friends or that William had even taken care of the young woman. Daniel Baird, the Fullartons' servant, testified that he was "very certain that the said Luisa Calderon did not travel with Mrs. Fullarton." Similarly, her physician, George Charles, claimed that he "never heard, nor doth he believe that Mrs. Fullarton introduced the said Luisa Calderon to any of her female acquaintances." Fullarton and her associates thus pushed Calderon away from their domestic domain in an attempt to make a private family history conform to public expectations. Her suit was ultimately successful, but it did not tamp down the rumors. The *Anti-Jacobin Review* continued to attack the Fullartons, repeating the same allegations. One of its authors challenged Marianne directly for her permissiveness toward Calderon, alleging that "this prostitute lived in your house for some time, and whilst in your family had been got with child by some person; that the reputed father of the child was known to you, and that it was reported you had declared you would protect the offspring of the virtuous Colonel's protegèe." This transgression was not simply a lack of uxorial control but the acceptance of a West Indian familial arrangement in the metropole. Observers frequently castigated white women in the Caribbean for tolerating their husbands' dalliances as well as for taking in their natural children of color. Marianne Fullarton, according to the attacks leveled against her, had done both in watching after Calderon.[51]

With these claims and denunciations, Picton's supporters joined together a number of debates from the previous three decades. They imported the

51. Marianne's claim that she and her husband did little for Calderon during her residence in Scotland was likely true. In one of the few instances in which Calderon's own voice comes through, she had to appeal to the English government for assistance as early as the spring of 1804, claiming that she had no means of support while in Britain; see Louisa Calderon to William Fawkener, May 16, 1804, "Trinidad: Charges Brought against Col Picton, as Governor," PC 1/3557, NAE. For Baird's and Charles's testimony, see Thomas Bayly Howell, ed., *A Complete Collection of State Trials and Proceedings for High Treason and Other Crimes and Misdemeanors*, 34 vols. (London, 1811–1828), XXX, 1365–1367. David Dobson records a John Bowie who worked as a merchant in Ayr in the 1790s and whom the *Anti-Jacobin Review* claimed corroborated John Downie's story; see Dobson, *Scots in the West Indies, 1707–1857*, 2 vols. (Baltimore, 2006), II, 8; *Anti-Jacobin Review and Magazine; or, Monthly Political and Literary Censor*, XXX, no. 69 (May 1808), 99–100. For attacks on the wives of men engaging in interracial relationships, see, in particular, J. B. Moreton, *Manners and Customs in the West India Islands . . .* (London, 1790), 107; and William Jones, "The Diary of the Revd. William Jones," as quoted in Jeannette Marks, *The Family of the Barrett: A Colonial Romance* (New York, 1938), 193–196.

trope of the colonial mixed-race seductress to Britain in order to excoriate Calderon's presence in the metropole. Just as women of color in the Caribbean supposedly tempted and ensnared white immigrants, so, too, had Calderon allegedly nabbed a white suitor once she landed in Scotland. Allegations that Fullarton impregnated her also connected with an Atlantic discourse on Caribbean libertinage. If true, Fullarton's behavior bordered on incestuous, which was a common accusation against white male predation on women of color in the West Indies. Likewise, by stating that she had become pregnant in the metropole, Picton's defenders revived concerns over British racial stock supposedly under threat by immigration. Whereas this anxiety had previously focused on poor white women and freed slaves, Calderon's case catapulted such worry over African ancestry onto the gentry, which had up to that point not been the focus of public diatribes.[52]

Growing prejudice toward elite families and their mixed race-kin was an important turning point in the debate over West Indians of color in Britain, and Calderon's case helped contribute to the shift. Class distinctions, which had traditionally differentiated between poor and rich individuals of African descent, were beginning to collapse. Charles White, for instance, noted in 1799 with some reserve: "There is at this time a gentleman well known in the first circles in London, who was born in Jamaica, and descended from a white and mestize; but he is not to be distinguished from an European by any particular. I have seen several of this description myself." His statement warned that Jamaicans of color were passing as white at the highest echelons of English society. Hester Piozzi recoiled at the number of mixed-race and black individuals in London's finer spaces three years later. "I am really haunted by *black shadows*," she observed; "Men of colour in the rank of gentlemen; a black Lady cover'd with finery, in the Pit at the Opera, and tawny children playing in the Squares." She gave credit for this new reality to abolitionists "Hannah More and Mr. Wilberforce's success towards breaking down the *wall of separation* . . . preparing us for the moment when we shall be made *one fold under one Shepherd*." Abolitionism, in her estimation, was responsible for

52. Marlene L. Daut, *Tropics of Haiti: Race and the Literary History of the Haitian Revolution in the Atlantic World, 1789–1865* (Liverpool, U.K., 2015), 197–204. This trope of "quadroon" sexuality emerged aggressively in the United States after the arrival of some nine thousand Dominguans of color into New Orleans in 1809; see Emily Clark, *The Strange History of the American Quadroon: Free Women of Color in the Revolutionary Atlantic World* (Chapel Hill, N.C., 2013), 49–59. On concerns about incest in the Caribbean, see Doris Garraway, *The Libertine Colony: Creolization in the Early French Caribbean* (Durham, N.C., 2005), 277.

the growing infiltration of mixed-race individuals into polite London society. Whereas elite mixed-race individuals had not been a major point of controversy in previous decades, by 1800 their presence was a primary topic to consider when discussing Britain's racial future. This was especially true in light of the emerging Malthusian view that Britain was now overcrowded and thus needed to monitor its reproductive choices in a more discriminatory fashion. The charges laid against William Fullarton demonstrated that high class standing no longer protected West Indians of color like Calderon from public scorn. Such privilege came to symbolize the very threat perceived by wealthy Britons to their families and finances.[53]

It is difficult to say how much Calderon's case influenced British households helping to raise relations of color. The trial was popularly covered, but families like the Tailyours did not comment on it in their correspondence. Nevertheless, the terms of debate surrounding Calderon's arrival in Britain, along with the general discourse emerging out of abolitionist rhetoric at the time, make it clear that public attitudes were shifting. The end of the slave trade made interracial relationships in the colonies more problematic than ever before because they did not contribute to the growth of what was seen as the most vital population group: enslaved black workers. Likewise, the arrival in Britain of those with African heritage held its own pitfalls, as mixed-

53. Charles White, *An Account of the Regular Gradation in Man . . .* (London, 1799), 117n; Hester Piozzi to Penelope Pennington, June 19, 1802, in Oswald G. Knapp, ed., *The Intimate Letters of Hester Piozzi and Penelope Pennington, 1788–1821* (New York, 1914), 243–244; [Thomas Malthus], *An Essay on the Principle of Population* (London, 1798), 113–117. White listed several cases of mixed-race children in Britain. One he met at an unknown English lying-in hospital, another in York, and three separate cases he studied in London. Most of these he noted for their peculiarity—though some of the stories, if not apocryphal, were exaggerated: a Yorkshire mulatto born as black as the father; a London mulatto born as white as the mother; mixed-race twins, one white, one black; and a Southwark man whose left side was black and his right completely white; see ibid., 116–123. For other examples of interest in unique cases of coloration during this period, see John Barbot, "A Description of the Coasts of North and South-Guinea . . . ," in Awnsham Churchill and John Churchill, eds., *A Collection of Voyages and Travels,* 6 vols. (London, 1732), V, 13; James Parsons, *An Account of the White Negro Shewn Before the Royal Society . . . , Philosophical Transactions of the Royal Society,* LV (London, 1765), 47–49; Printed Books, circa 1725, Broadsides 11.66, GL; John Gottlieb Ernestus Heckewelder to Benjamin Smith Barton, Aug. 29, 1796, Benjamin Smith Barton Papers, Ser. I, American Philosophical Society Library, Philadelphia; Benjamin Moseley, *A Treatise on Tropical Diseases; and on the Climate of the West-Indies* (London, 1787), 63–64; John Lindsay, "A Few Conjectural Considerations upon the Creation of the Human Race; Occasioned by the Present British Quixottical Rage of Setting the Slaves from Africa at Liberty," [Spanish Town, Jamaica, 1788], Add. MS 12439, fol. 141, BL.

race migrants might bring European radicalism or social entitlement back with them to the Caribbean. This general fixation on West Indians of color in Britain during the final years of the abolition debate made Louisa Calderon a particularly fascinating subject. That she did not conform perfectly to the typical migrant was all the more revealing of a general turn against the group, who could now depend even less on their elevated class and social positions.

Conclusion

The year after England abolished its slave trade, the only sentimental novel from the period with a mixed-race migrant as its protagonist was published in London. Although the author's identity is unknown, *The Woman of Colour* was a solidly abolitionist tale, intent on showing the humanity of individuals with African ancestry. Olivia Fairfield, the novel's heroine, is the daughter of a rich Jamaican planter and one of his enslaved workers, who has since died. Fairfield leaves the island at the command of her ailing father to marry her cousin Augustus in England. She explains the necessity of departing for Europe: in Jamaica "the illegitimate offspring of [her father's] *slave* could never be considered in the light of equality by the English planters." As an illegitimate orphan, she embodies the essence of the sentimental heroine. As a mixed-race child of an enslaved woman, she is meant to elicit strong abolitionist sympathies. Olivia was thus the perfect character to explore the new world of a British Empire without a slave trade.[54]

In her engagement to her cousin Augustus, Olivia provides the avenue for the greatest exploration of English racial attitudes in the book. She finds herself to be a marvel in England. "I am an object of general curiosity," she notes, "and many a gentleman follows to repass me, and to be mortified at his folly when he has caught a view of my mulatto countenance." This interest takes on a more sinister tone when she meets with family. Augustus's mother, Mrs. Merton, dislikes her niece from the start. She refuses to shake her hand, causing Olivia to grumble, "*She* considers *me* as but *one* remove from the brute

54. *The Woman of Colour, A Tale,* I (London, 1808), 3. Written in 1808, *The Woman of Colour* built on themes from the author's previous work. In 1803, the novelist penned *Light and Shade,* a story about an orphaned girl who falls in love with a Jamaican boy at school in England. He eventually returns to the islands and marries "a creole" whose "complexion was of a clear brown," painting an ambiguous portrait of her ancestry. Soon the couple moves to England, where the young wife, his "poor little *exotic,*" struggles to acculturate to high society. She dies after learning that her West Indian estate has been given over to a cousin, who also comes to England and is described in racially ambiguous ways; see *Light and Shade: A Novel,* 2 vols. (Bath, U.K., 1803), I, 57–60, II, 18–26.

creation." In a more revealing passage, Mrs. Merton's grandson George is frightened when first encountering the Jamaican. Comparing his hands to Olivia's, George comments that, while his are clean, hers are "dirty." This sets off a lesson on the childlike qualities of racial prejudice. Olivia reveals that George's ignorance comes from parental misinformation. "God chose it should be so, and we cannot make *our* skins white, any more than you can make yours black," she tells the young man. Miraculously cured of discrimination, George lauds, "I could wish . . . that God had made you white, ma'am, because you are so *very* good-natured." Olivia's unassailable argument stuns the Merton household, convincing all but the matriarch of its soundness. Augustus admits, on hearing it, "Prejudices imbibed in the nursery are frequently attached to the being of ripened years . . .[,] and to eradicate them as they appear, is a labour well worthy the endeavour." Bigotry is held up for scorn in the text, but familial discomfort with a relative of color in Britain is nevertheless assumed to be a natural state.[55]

Such ambiguities surrounding race rise to the surface as Olivia prepares to marry Augustus. Much like the character of Miranda in the 1791 tale *Memoirs of a Scots Heiress,* Olivia worries that her groom will prove unable to "get over his own prejudices as to my colour" and denigrates her own potential as a wife, fearing that he "would have to encounter all the sarcastic inuendoes and jeering remarks of his companions." Although Augustus admits to a friend that he initially viewed Olivia with disgust, "for I beheld a skin approaching to the hue of a negro's, in the woman whom my father introduced to me as my intended wife," he later praises her for her "noble and dignified soul." Yet, after the two marry and settle in Devonshire, Olivia learns that Augustus had secretly wed a former lover beforehand. His clandestine vows invalidate those he took with Olivia, and she learns that her dowry has been swindled away by Augustus's brother. Bereft of fortune, Olivia packs her belongings and returns to Jamaica.[56]

Although *The Woman of Colour* proclaims the virtue of human equality, it nevertheless hints at the problem of mixed-race kin and interracial unions in turn-of-the-nineteenth-century Britain. According to the text, individuals of color are improper fits in metropolitan society, not because they lack humanity, but rather because they carry the potential to compromise legitimate family relations and dilute the purity of British blood. Olivia's flight

55. *Woman of Colour,* I, 90–112.

56. Ibid., I, 132–133, 174–175. For analysis of *Memoirs of a Scots Heiress,* see Chapter 5, above.

back to Jamaica confirms the notion that relatives of color had to disappear for white families to be made whole and unadulterated. To a large degree, her story complemented the handfuls of older sentimental tales from the 1790s that portrayed migrants of color. Yet, it also speaks to a specific moment in time. As the walls of slavery came crashing down, mixed-race migrants—even the most affluent and educated among them—increasingly came to be seen as a danger to legitimate British households as well as to Caribbean social stability. Those perceiving such a threat were, not simply polemicists penning blanket diatribes, but family and friends in Britain still being called on to care for mixed-race charges.[57]

Institutional, cultural, and familial pressures against migrants of color emerged as class distinctions among the group began to lose their importance. Outrage over Louisa Calderon's supposed socialization with elites in Scotland reveal heightened anxieties about the soundness of the family structure in Britain's upper ranks. Calderon's humble status meant that the British gentry now faced the same corrupting influence of African blood that Edward Long had warned for Britain's lower orders in 1772. This imagined peril to the nation's first families joined a general abolitionist critique that hinted at the larger imperial problem of mixed-race migrants. If abolition was to come into effect, as it did in 1807, then solid and established white populations on both sides of the Atlantic would be needed for imperial security and stability. Freemen of color, no matter how wealthy, appeared to compromise both. For Britons supporting and taking care of mixed-race relatives, this perspective gave them pause to think through what their familial devotion meant for society at large.

Still at question was how the Caribbean could survive with such a fractured and wavering population. Abolitionists continued to claim that a self-sustaining enslaved workforce could be achieved through natural reproduction. Proslavery supporters disagreed. But both sides conceded that the future did not bode well for West Indian whites. If white numbers continued to decrease, then who would enforce order and keep up the plantations? Seasoned Caribbean observers like Simon Taylor insisted that the "Blackamoor" could be washed white through ongoing sexual interactions with white men. Such advice harkened back to previous ideas of settlement put forth by the Jamaican assembly. However, mixed-race migrants continued to complicate

57. Jennifer DeVere Brody, *Impossible Purities: Blackness, Femininity, and Victorian Culture* (Durham, N.C., 1998), 25. See also Lyndon J. Dominique, "Introduction," in Dominique, ed., *The Woman of Colour* (Buffalo, N.Y., 2007).

that plan. When individuals of color departed for Britain, the colonies lost their most elite mixed-race members who were the best candidates to beget still lighter-skinned offspring. Yet, a British education could also confer the proper cultural refinements to West Indians of color who would eventually return to the Caribbean to bring forth this new white population. These issues would obsess colonial and metropolitan observers alike over the next two decades, while British families struggled to understand their role in these complicated imperial plans.[58]

58. Simon Taylor to George Hibbert, Jan. 14, 1804, Simon Taylor Papers, ICS 120 F/42, ICS.

CHAPTER 7

✿❦✿

NEW STRUGGLES AND OLD IDEAS,
1813–1833

Ann Morse Middleton's final years were ones of desperate struggle. She had led a globe-trotting life. Born to the elite free woman of color Elizabeth Augier and the white merchant John Morse in Jamaica, she had been educated in London, married to the East India Company official Nathaniel Middleton in Calcutta, and finally settled as a mother to a large family in Hampshire. These experiences advanced her socially and financially, but they could not stave off a pronounced battle with mental illness. The turmoil might have begun in 1807 when her fifty-eight-year-old husband died suddenly, but she exhibited no visible symptoms of distress until almost a decade later. By 1816, she was living in London with her sister Sarah Morse Cator and Sarah's daughter Ann, now married to Major General Edward Baynes. Middleton's temper in the house was somber, and her behavior was at times strange. She would often sit awkwardly across a chair, picking at her skin and biting furiously at her nails. Friends and family recognized the changes and sought help. Physicians bled and blistered her in an effort to stabilize her mood, but to no avail. She took frequent trips outdoors, sometimes in a carriage and sometimes in a wheelchair, but continued in a withdrawn state. Her son, Hastings, assumed her affairs as he noticed the decline. He gained power of attorney over her estate but agonized over what to do next. Hastings was convinced that an asylum would never work for his mother and that she would rebel on the least suspicion of surveillance. Further plans to move Ann were scrapped as she descended deeper into solitude. By the spring of 1817, Hastings admitted that his mother's mental state was "impair'd beyond all hope of restoration." Before the year was up, Ann left her sister's home and moved into the house of a stranger in London. Her behavior turned even more erratic, and, in January 1818, she came before the Chancery Court on charges of lunacy.[1]

1. Will of Nathaniel Middleton, Nov. 25, 1807, PROB 11/1470, NAE; *The Diary of Joseph Farington,* ed. Kathryn Cave, 16 vols. (New Haven, Conn., 1979–1984), XIV, Oct. 18, 1817, 5089–5090; Akihito Suzuki, *Madness at Home: The Psychiatrist, the Patient, and the Family in England, 1820–1860* (Berkeley, Calif., 2006), 95–96; Hastings Nathaniel Middleton to Miss Gale, Sept. 29, 1816, Hastings Nathaniel Letter Book, 796/1, fol. 55, City of Westmin-

Ann's psychic break traumatized her family and sent them searching for answers. What caused this agitation? Why was she so troubled? Dissecting mental illness for evidence of rationality is an extraordinarily treacherous exercise — especially from any kind of historical distance — but Ann's obsessions are nevertheless telling. Hastings reported that his mother fixated on two things: finances and family. According to him, Ann would rant regularly about her impoverishment, insisting that she had not a penny to her name. Her mood would then suddenly shift, and she would stroll the streets purchasing all kinds of goods while giving out shillings to beggars, buskers, and beguilers. At the same time, her social disengagements would lead her to grumble about "harassing family occurrences . . . [and] infelicitous marriages." In particular, she worried over her daughter Louisa's match to an Irishman she did not like. For a woman of color raised in an elite Jamaican household, married into a large East Indian fortune, and sued by an English cousin for her birthright, such agonizing over finances and family organization was perhaps understandable. Ann had spent a lifetime cultivating a metropolitan family divorced, to some degree, from its Jamaican origins. Yet, her economic health depended on that very colonial connection. Families were, and are, highly precarious things, routinely constructed and reconstructed. They provide avenues for advancement while simultaneously presenting impediments to improvement. Considering that Ann had to maintain constant vigilance over her family structure, the madness that afflicted her was not entirely delusional.[2]

Social pressures against West Indians of color were increasing in Britain as Ann fought to calm her nerves. Part of this originated from a general heightened prejudice against those with African ancestry in the metropole. Many Britons began identifying themselves along racially exclusionary lines that privileged whiteness above all else. Mixed-race migrants had encountered such bigotry before, but they were now far less protected by the shelter of familial acceptance. By the 1820s, restrictive definitions of family increasingly limited kinship to those who could potentially expand family fortunes. Britons had started to view mixed-race relatives as financial dead ends, draining their fathers' wealth while being simultaneously prevented from building their own

ster Archives, Westminster, U.K., Hastings Nathaniel Middleton to Catherine Green, Sept. 29, 1816, fols. 60–63, Hastings Nathaniel Middleton to Sarah Cator, Oct. 29, 1816, fols. 113–114, and Hastings Nathaniel Middleton to Jasper Atkinson, Feb. 14, 1817, fol. 158; Commissions and Inquisitions of Lunacy, Dec. 19, 1818, C 211/16/M107, NAE.

2. Hastings Nathaniel Middleton as quoted in Suzuki, *Madness at Home*, 97.

assets owing to the legal impediments of the Caribbean. West Indians of color continued to travel to Britain in this period, but they arrived in homes far less willing to assimilate them as full family members, given their attenuated financial prospects as well as the rising bigotry voiced in the British press. Some migrants responded through political protest; others simply hastened their return to the colonies. Regardless, far fewer of them found the same social success as their compatriots of color had only a generation before.[3]

Although many Britons had grown disenchanted with the idea of mixed-race migrants, officials and observers in the Caribbean started to rethink the possibilities for an elite, well-educated cohort of color in the islands. Transatlantic calls for a British end to slavery emerged in earnest in 1823, and they pushed West Indians to prepare for the possibility that their colonies would soon be without enslaved workers. Certain that emancipation would destroy the Caribbean economy, which had already begun losing profitability, Jamaican officials resigned themselves to the idea that whites would no longer come to the tropics. Ever mindful of demography, they anticipated that the islands' inhabitants would inevitably turn a shade darker. For commentators on both sides of the Atlantic, the solution was obvious: free people of color would soon have to be granted legal equality with whites, and the best educated of them would eventually have to be given some control over the colonial government. With that goal in mind, Jamaica's assembly once more promoted British-educated colonists of color. After a twenty-one-year hiatus, the legislature reinstated the practice of accepting privilege petitions in 1823 in the hopes of further advancing an already elite group of mixed-race residents. This time, though, the petitioners' ties to white fathers meant less, if any-

3. Roxann Wheeler, *The Complexion of Race: Categories of Difference in Eighteenth-Century British Culture* (Philadelphia, 2000); Felicity A. Nussbaum, *The Limits of the Human: Fictions of Anomaly, Race, and Gender in the Long Eighteenth Century* (Cambridge, 2003); Dror Wahrman, *The Making of the Modern Self: Identity and Culture in Eighteenth-Century England* (New Haven, Conn., 2004), esp. 83–119; Kathleen Wilson, *The Island Race: Englishness, Empire, and Gender in the Eighteenth Century* (New York, 2003); Catherine Molineux, *Faces of Perfect Ebony: Encountering Atlantic Slavery in Imperial Britain* (Cambridge, Mass., 2012), esp. 110–145; Steven Ruggles, *Prolonged Connections: The Rise of the Extended Family in Nineteenth-Century England and America* (Madison, Wis., 1987), xvii–xviii, 5–11; Ruth Perry, *Novel Relations: The Transformation of Kinship in English Literature and Culture, 1748–1818* (New York, 2004), 51–73; David Warren Sabean and Simon Teuscher, "Kinship in Europe: A New Approach to Long Term Development," in Sabean, Teuscher, and Jon Mathieu, eds., *Kinship in Europe: Approaches to Long-Term Development (1300–1900)* (New York, 2010), 3–23.

thing, compared to their education in Britain. Definitions of family had thus undergone a transformation in the West Indies as well as Britain. Whereas the Jamaican assembly had started hearing privilege appeals in 1733 to advance mixed-race individuals through membership within prominent white house-holds, by 1823, it no longer accorded the same respect to family connections as the sole path to social inclusion.

These twin developments—increasing racial prejudice in Britain and efforts to elevate a privileged class of mixed-race persons in Britain and the West Indies—meant that a metropolitan education continued to have tremen-dous value to individuals of color but that a long-term residence in Britain did not. In the two decades leading up to the emancipation of the Empire's slaves in 1833, free people of color protested strongly and effectively for their rights. At the same time, white officials on both sides of the Atlantic imagined that the group might be the only viable barrier against colonial chaos in the wake of total emancipation. As they had in the previous century, mixed-race elites traveling to Britain were seen as potential leaders for the Caribbean. Yet, few observers anticipated that they would become the seedbed for a new, white population. Rather, they would help rule the West Indies as people of color. Family ties could no longer make them white in the Caribbean, and they cer-tainly could not continue to make them white in Britain.

Changes in Britain

In January 1814, after a two-year engagement, William Farington wed Frances Ann Green, a second-generation member of the British mixed-race Morse family. Frances was the daughter of Catherine Morse Green and niece of Ann Morse Middleton, two of John Morse and Elizabeth Augier's children who had left Jamaica. The London wedding brought together the wider Morse clan with William's uncle Joseph Farington, one of the most prolific diarists in nineteenth-century Britain. Over the next half decade, Joseph would write regularly about his interactions with the family. They dined, took tea, and at-tended balls together, and they even vacationed as a group to the Isle of Wight. Farington grieved in his diary over the death of Robert Morse in 1816 and shared in the sorrow of Frances's stillborn child. In effect, they embraced a newfound kinship. Despite Farington's interest in other West Indians of color in Britain—he penned several observations on Nathaniel Wells's appearance after a trip to Wales—the diarist made no comment on his extended relatives' ancestry. The reasons for this are clear. Morse's descendants had no cause to advertise their heritage, and, for his grandchildren, ties to an enslaved ances-tor were so distant that they might have appeared unimportant to them. In short, John Morse's dream to cut his progeny's ties to an African ancestry — a dream crafted more than a half century earlier — had finally come true.[4]

Yet, even though Morse's descendants lived comfortably as white Britons, their connections to Jamaica did not sever entirely. Farington noted that Frank Green, Morse's grandson and Frances's brother, lived for a long period on the island overseeing the family's property and that he regularly made comments on the state of slavery. Echoing many proslavery supporters of the time, Green once remarked to the diarist, "The condition of the *Blacks* in Jamaica is better than that of the Peasantry in England." Green's livelihood continued to be bound up in the profitability of slavery in Jamaica, as were the fortunes of his cousins. He might not have known about his remote family connections to slavery, or he chose to ignore them. Or, like many thinkers of the time, he believed that the world was composed of orders and that some were made to be free and some to be enslaved. Nevertheless, Farington's diary reveals that family recognitions of a mixed heritage possibly endured for the Morse clan. In May 1818, he recorded that Frank Green sent his relatives in Britain a small print of a "Creole Lady from Jamaica . . . an excellent likeness of a Young Lady, *deceased*." Could the portrait have been Green's grandmother, John Morse's mixed-race companion Elizabeth Augier? Did he recognize in that print the ancestral connection to an enslaved past? Farington commented no further, but Frank Green and his relatives likely lived with the dual understanding of their African heritage and the privileges of their advanced position in British society. They had successfully integrated as white Britons and fulfilled the expectations of many colonists who wished the same fate for their children. At the same time, they might have been the last cohort of mixed-race individuals to do so.[5]

Assimilation into white British society grew increasingly difficult as the general public turned more aggressively against migrants of color. Not all observations were negative. A Cornish newspaper in 1819, for instance, enthusiastically reported the story of a "Mulatto girl" at a local boarding school who helped teach her classmates about human equality. But far more accounts saw the arrival of black and brown migrants as threatening. Stephen Lushington, a member of Parliament for Canterbury, ostensibly lauded British racial tolerance by announcing to Parliament that in England "a gentleman of colour

4. *Diary of Joseph Farington*, ed. Cave, XIII, Feb. 5, 1814, 4454, Feb. 12, 1816, XIV, 4783, Sept. 23, 1817, 5084, July–August, 1818, XV, 5243–5256. For more on Wells, see Chapter 6, above. For the Morse family genealogy, see Appendix 2.

5. *Diary of Joseph Farington*, ed. Cave, Oct. 12, 1815, XIII, 4717, May 26, 1818, XV, 5211 (emphasis in original).

has held a high civil office; and another has enjoyed military rank, and become connected, by marriage, with the family of a member of the [House of Lords]." Yet, this celebration also insinuated that Britain's upper orders were infiltrated by an African presence. Fear spread through all classes. A migrant to Gloucestershire lost his bid for a teaching position in 1815. "Unfortunately he is a Mulatto, a native of the West Indies," one referee commented on the application. "Where so dark a complexion is not objected to, he would make a very valuable Schoolmaster." Britons also continued to protest about the presence of nonwhite sailors and servants among the working poor. Complaints came into the Home Office, bemoaning crowds of color "swarm[ing] about the streets." These were both East Indian "lascars" as well as mixed-race servants who were sent, like the Jamaican Jane Arnold in 1818, to attend white colonists in Britain. Of course, much of the perceived risk posed by mixed-race persons was seen as sexual. At a meeting of the African and Asiatic Society, English parliamentarian Joseph Marryat recoiled at the sight of "a black man [who] led in a white woman, with a party-coloured child, the fruit of their mutual loves" and "a proof of the happy result of that union of colours and races, which all true philanthropists are so anxious to promote." Once more, the prospect of interracial families in Britain gravely concerned onlookers, and many critics blamed abolitionists for speeding that process.[6]

Novelists continued to perpetuate discomfort with mixed-race kin in their characterizations of West Indian migrants. The 1812 work *Montgomery* depicts a white attorney in Jamaica with a mulatto mistress who "had borne him a numerous family of quadroon children, most of whom were in Great Britain for their education."[7] His white peers scold him for this familial arrangement that

6. *Royal Cornwall Gazette, Falmouth Packet, and Plymouth Journal* (Truro, England), May 8, 1819; Stephen Lushington's Speech, June 16, 1825, as quoted in T. C. Hansard, ed., *The Parliamentary Debates,* 2d Ser. (London, 1826), XIII, 1177; Letter of Richard Raikes, July 5, 1815, Gloucestershire County Record Office, as quoted in James Walvin, *Black and White: The Negro in English Society, 1555–1945* (London, 1973), 60–61; George Porter Gale to the Governor's House, Gosport, Oct. 9, 1814, HO 42/141, NAE; James Knask to Henry Addington, Lord Sidmouth, Mar. 11, 1815, HO 42/143, and G. A. Prinsep to Lord Sidmouth, Aug. 7, 1817, HO 42/169; George F. Coward, Jan. 31, 1818, folder 2, box 62, Powel Family Papers, Historical Society of Pennsylvania Library, Philadelphia; Joseph Marryat, *More Thoughts, Occasioned by Two Publications Which the Authors Call 'An Exposure of Some of the Numerous Misstatements and Misrepresentations Contained in a Pamphlet, Commonly Known by the Name of Mr. Marryat's Pamphlet, Entitled Thoughts, etc.' and 'A Defence of the Bill for the Registration of Slaves'* (London, 1816), 103–105.

7. *Montgomery; or, The West-Indian Adventurer,* 3 vols. (Kingston, Jamaica, 1812–1813), II, 49–50, 75–76.

evaded marriage and legitimate offspring as well as opened up his children to inheritance challenges. Jane Austen also included a mixed-race grandee in her final work *Sanditon*. Written, though unfinished, in 1817, the novel features the character of Miss Lambe, a "half mulatto" from the Caribbean. News of Lambe's visit to a seaside resort excites the proprietors of the Sanditon house, primarily because of her wealth. Yet, the home's caretaker recognizes the possible economic drawbacks: "They who scatter their money so freely . . . rais[e] the price of things—and I have heard that's very much the case with your West-injines." As many literary theorists suggest, Austen uses Lambe to convey her uncertainty about emergent capitalism and English enthusiasm over the accumulation of wealth. Considerations of race in *Sanditon* are accordingly surpassed by those of money. The narrator describes Miss Lambe as a "very young lady, sickly and rich." Lambe is therefore a symptom of both the financial and sexual excesses of the West Indies. Though less explicit comment is made on her racial characteristics, her hefty fortune embodies many of the same features of colonial degeneracy. Austen might have felt comfortable using Lambe to make such comments in light of the frequency of such depictions in the period's literature. Nevertheless, by crafting a degraded migrant of color, Austen reaffirmed a popular turning away from mixed-race migrants in Britain.[8]

The deterioration of goodwill toward mixed-race migrants notwithstanding, many people of color still viewed opportunities in Britain, however restricted, as preferable to remaining permanently in colonial society. The rate of mixed-raced migration from Jamaica to Britain stayed at roughly the same level in the second decade of the nineteenth century as it had been over the previous twenty years. Almost one-fifth of white male Jamaican testators who included

8. Jane Austen, *Sanditon*, in *Jane Austen: Lady Susan, The Watsons, and Sanditon*, ed. Margaret Drabble (New York, 2003), 180, 195, 206–207; Sarah Salih, "The Silence of Miss Lambe: *Sanditon* and Fictions of 'Race' in the Abolition Era," *Eighteenth-Century Fiction*, XVIII (2006), 329–335; Elaine Jordan, "Jane Austen Goes to the Seaside: *Sanditon*, English Identity, and the 'West Indian' Schoolgirl," in You-me Park and Rajeswari Sunder Rajan, eds., *The Postcolonial Jane Austen* (New York, 2000), 32, 44; Drabble, "Introduction," in Austen, *Jane Austen*, ed. Drabble, 7–23; and Edward Said, *Culture and Imperialism* (New York, 1993), 80–96. The West Indies famously hover in the background of Austen's novel from three years before; see *Mansfield Park*. In that story, Sir Thomas Bertram's lavish English estate is fueled by the profits of an Antiguan plantation that he visits with his son. The younger Thomas's impropriety and profligacy reflect the novel's disagreeable view of the colonies and the islands' ability to upset social decorum; see Jane Austen, *Mansfield Park: A Novel*, 3 vols. (London, 1814).

provisions for mixed-race children in their wills from 1813 to 1815 also noted that a child of color was traveling to, or had been in, Britain. That number was consistent with the percentages from the 1790s (see Appendix 1). Those who arrived scattered to each corner of the Isles, spreading across England and Scotland in particular. In 1815, Thomas Patterson directed his mulatto sons John and William to their ancestral home in North Britain shortly before he died. Despite greater pressures against migrants of color, Patterson neverthe- less expressed the desire that his children stay put after crossing the Atlantic. Several of his fellow white colonists agreed. Jamaican merchant George Wat- son insisted that his three mestee sons—George, John, and James—should travel to Britain "and never return." Saint Mary planter Thomas Pain sent his son George Godfry to live with an aunt in England and also asked that he re- main there permanently. The hope of establishing one's child of color success- fully in the metropole endured well into the nineteenth century.[9]

The dream of a better life for one's children away from colonial limitations was not held exclusively by white men in the 1810s. Mixed-race women in- cluded provisions for their children to go to Britain in this period as well and in higher numbers than ever before. Indeed, five free women of color lodged wills from 1813 to 1815 with bequests to such migrants. Tereisa Shaw from Trelawney parish noted in her 1814 will that she had sent seven children to Britain in her lifetime. Her sons David and Samuel eventually returned to Jamaica, where David was quick to follow his mother in death. Samuel spent the next two years settling his brother's estate, which included manumitting David's enslaved mistress Frances Graham. Their siblings, however, stayed in Britain. Female testators of color likely provided such directions to make up for broken promises by white paramours to send their children abroad, espe- cially given that many of these women and their children were undoubtedly abandoned by white companions after Parliament abolished the slave trade in 1807. A comparative lack of romantic connections with whites might explain why not a single mixed-race man made similar provisions from this sample of wills. The assembly's revocation of the 1761 inheritance cap in 1813, which legalized large bequests to illegitimate mixed-race offspring, might have also left women of color feeling more confident about their children's financial futures. Cecilia Ann Morris, a free woman of color from Kingston, possibly sent her son to Scotland for these financial and familial reasons sometime

9. Will of Thomas Patterson, June 15, 1815, Wills, LOS 90, fols. 148–149, IRO, Will of George Watson, Sept. 21, 1813, Wills, LOS 88, fol. 121, Will of Thomas Pain, Nov. 2, 1815, Wills, LOS 90, fol. 256. For a survey of wills, see Appendix 1, below.

around 1820. She was also entrenched in the larger Atlantic networks that privileged mixed-race education in Britain. Her child's father was John Orr, a close business associate of John Tailyour. Morris was too young to have known Tailyour personally, but she might have learned of him from Orr and used his example to provide a pathway for her son to escape the Caribbean.[10]

Despite the continued enthusiasm of West Indians to send their children abroad, relatives receiving them in Britain did not necessarily match their excitement. William Macpherson, a Scottish overseer in Berbice, received a strict warning from his parents in 1813 about sending back the two daughters and one son that he had with an enslaved Guyanese woman. Colonel Allan Macpherson cautioned his son that "from the pure delicacy" of his mother Eliza's heart "it would grieve her to see you introduce them with yourself at our home." Allan implored William instead to "leave them a little at Glasgow until you arrive at home, when after you may be able to resolve upon a plan suited for their future care." Clearly, direct family contact was a less palatable option for the Macpherson clan than many of their fellow Scots, such as the Tailyours, in previous years. William complied, temporarily, with his parents' requests as he sought out a more suitable companion than his colonial mistress. Within a year of his arrival, just as John Tailyour had, William Macpherson married. His new bride's attitude toward her husband's illegitimate children of color, however, was anything but positive. William's mother Eliza gossiped that her new daughter-in-law "could not take trouble with [the children]." Eliza ultimately assumed their care, though not until offered a generous allowance to do so.[11]

The children's status as free people of color complicated Eliza's feelings of familial responsibility. She openly condemned her son's experiences in the

10. Will of Tereisa Shaw, Apr. 13, 1814, Wills, LOS 88, fol. 86, IRO; Dispute over David Lyon's Will, Aug. 8, 1817, Jamaica Court of Ordinary Proceedings, 1B/11/11/4, fols. 45–46, JA, Jamaica Court of Ordinary Minutes, Aug. 8, 1817, 1B/11/12/5; Pye v. Linwood, Supreme Court of Judicature, J 90/588, NAE.

11. Allan Macpherson to William Macpherson, Mar. 21, 1813, bundle 202, MBP, Eliza Macpherson to William Macpherson, Dec. 25, 1817, bundle 112, Jan. 1, 1818, Nov. 16, 1816. My deepest thanks to Laird Macpherson for allowing me to read through his family's collection. The family's finances were in dire straits, both from Colonel Allan's losses in India as well as William's economic failure in Guyana. Eliza's dependence on her son's stipend might have been a strong factor in her willingness to care for her grandchildren. For more on the family and its finances, see Stephen Foster, *A Private Empire* (London, 2010), 87–95. On the details of Macpherson's marriage, see W. Cheyne-Macpherson, *The Chiefs of Clan Macpherson* (Edinburgh, 1947), 127.

Caribbean, quoting the abolitionist Henry Brougham that "a Residence in the West Indies tends (speaking generally) to debase the European character." Yet, concerns over her grandchildren's ancestry were tempered eventually by a greater desire to protect them. Eliza declared that her "little moonlight shades" were "more worthy [of her] peculiar care than Handsome fair ones from an unprincipled woman." She often used the phrase "moonlight shades" to call attention to their racial origins and difference from the British side of the family. These comments were part of a new social vocabulary. None of the other British families in this study made such explicit and frequent reference to their relatives' coloration before the 1810s. But Eliza's emerging racial grammar did not mean that she could not form attachments. Instead, she reaffirmed her faith, saying, "You have made them Christians and God's Children—and if they live and aim the Christian's part, our Heavenly father makes no distinction of Persons." "Altho' they were in the line of Egyptian Bondage," she further encouraged her son, "they could become through Gods Grace Heir to an immortal Crown." "God had made a distinction in this world," she acknowledged, "but he had made no distinction for Jew or Gentile." The religious fervor surrounding the abolitionist movement might have influenced Eliza's feelings toward the enslaved as well as those descended from slavery. Her sentiments toward relations of color were similar to many popular attitudes at the time. She could profess religious piety toward them while simultaneously publicizing their difference.[12]

Having agreed to care for the children, Eliza Macpherson struggled to plan the best course for their development. She decided to place the two girls, Eliza and Matilda, in a dame school in Stevenage, on the outskirts of London. The children—who took the surname "Williams" after their father's forename—traveled back and forth between London and Scotland as school went in and out of session. On some occasions, the Macphersons made the trip with them. Eliza hoped that, under this arrangement in the capital, her granddaughters "might become not unworthy Members in a Country Society," a desire indicating that she hoped to have them settle in Britain. The more modest goal was to have them become governesses in affluent homes. The more ambitious one

12. Eliza Macpherson to William Macpherson, Dec. 25, 1816, bundle 112, MBP, Nov. 27, 1816, Oct. 13, 1818. Devoutly religious, she preached to her son of the humanity of Africans, saying, "Nothing can be more opposite to gospel doctrine than the slave trade"; see ibid., Dec. 25, 1816. For Christopher Brown's discussion of the various motivations that brought together a diverse group of people under the common banner of abolition, regardless of general views toward individuals of African descent, see Brown, *Moral Capital: Foundations of British Abolitionism* (Chapel Hill, N.C., 2006).

was to get them married into a well-heeled household. Either way, Britain appeared the better place for social advancement than their birthplace. After all, an English education did less good in the Caribbean for women of color than for men. Single women of color could, and did, become important economic actors in the colonies, but the reluctance of wealthy men to marry them in the West Indies essentially capped their progress there. Eliza's other grandchild, Allan, remained closer to her, attending a school outside Perth. A number of Scottish institutions near the Macphersons instructed children of color. Dollar Academy, not far from Perth, taught a mixed-race boy from Jamaica, John McIntyre, in the 1820s; McIntyre's German teacher was dismissed after calling him an ape. Allan's proximity to his grandparents facilitated supervision and intervention should problems emerge. Moreover, his fate as a young man, unlike his sisters', was back in the colonies, not in Britain. He therefore did not need extensive or expensive schooling in the capital.[13]

As with John Tailyour's children, organizing this path of education was not a private affair. Many of Eliza's friends and contacts were apprised of the plans for her grandchildren. Unlike Tailyour's network, or those of many other British families in earlier periods, Eliza's friends appeared far less encouraging. Instead, they were deeply pessimistic. "All people here who come to me seem very jealous that my ideas for your little girls are too elevated for you and them," she confessed to her son. In particular, these associates complained that she "d[id] wrong not to place them to business" immediately, opting instead to have them educated. The prospect of refined and scholarly children of color clearly bothered these contacts, worried for their potential graduation to elite society. They might have also held the era's common prejudice against overeducating disadvantaged children. But this concern was in stark contrast to families discussed in previous chapters—such as the Tailyours, Rosses, Fyffes, and Laings—who insisted on both schooling and business opportunities for relatives of color in Britain. Nevertheless, Eliza Macpherson promised that her grandchildren of color would receive a better education than what "this Class of People find from the folly of those who have to do with them." Enough children of color had come to live in Scot-

---

13. Eliza Macpherson to William Macpherson, Jan. 1, 1818, bundle 112, MBP. At times, the Williamses would stay with their extended family during their journeys between London and Scotland. In a letter from Eliza Macpherson to William Macpherson, Nov. 20, 1816, bundle 112, MBP, she notes that the children were going to stay with "Major and Mrs. Macpherson." On Dollar Academy, see June Evans, "African / Caribbeans in Scotland; A Socio-Geographical Study" (Ph.D. diss., University of Edinburgh, 1995), 75; and Bruce Baillie, *History of Dollar* (Dollar, U.K., 1998).

land that Eliza provided examples in her correspondence of neighbors who had failed a mixed-race charge by not having them sufficiently educated. If her granddaughters were to fare well in Britain, then they needed to be taught how to present themselves properly.[14]

Despite brushing off criticism, Eliza Macpherson nevertheless diminished her expectations for the children. Race lurked behind most of her considerations, even if it was not stated outright. Her daughter, in fact, mentioned to William that she dared not bring up the sensitive topic of the children's appearance with their mother. Not wishing to focus too intensely on her grandchildren's heritage, Eliza Macpherson preferred instead to address the issue through a consideration of social place. She worried that the Williamses might "think more of themselves than they should" if given too much instruction. Macpherson sought to impose not only limits but also a sense of inferiority, perhaps because she believed that they could never pass as white. "They do, or will soon know, and feel, they are not Honorable Children," she wrote to her son. Rather than see this as an impediment, Macpherson sought to cultivate it. "This feeling I wish them to possess—since this virtue in themselves with modesty would or will draw attention from friends inclined to bestow it—where an opposite Conduct of assurances would deny it them." More than anything, Eliza Macpherson wanted her grandchildren to know their apparent place. Fearful that they might be rejected outright for projecting a haughty manner, she wanted to ensure that their complexion, West Indian origin, and illegitimate birth were permanently fused onto their identities.[15]

The entire British family held such concerns regarding the Williamses' place in society. Harriot Macintyre, William Macpherson's sister, frequently socialized with her nieces in London, where she and her husband lived. Despite reassuring her brother that Eliza Williams "seems a fine disposition and a great tempered girl," Macintyre grew apprehensive that she would find little success in Britain. Although Eliza Macpherson had hoped to instill a sense of inferiority in her grandchildren, Macintyre believed she had instead raised young Eliza's "ideas too high and making her feel worse if she should be obliged to get her own bread." Such doubts about the girls' prospects either to provide for themselves or to marry into a nice household sprang primarily from their appearance. Macintyre admitted, "I am apprehensive

14. Eliza Macpherson to William Macpherson, Dec. 25, 1817, bundle 112, MBP; Alysa Levene, *The Childhood of the Poor: Welfare in Eighteenth-Century London* (New York, 2012), 87.

15. Harriot Macintyre to William Macpherson, Nov. 26, 1819, bundle 60, MBP, and Eliza Macpherson to William Macpherson, Jan. 1, Oct. 13, 1818, bundle 112.

[young Eliza's] colour will always be against her being taken as a Governess."
Eliza Macpherson's lowered expectations for the children, therefore, stood
still too high in her daughter's estimation. Neither class nor legitimacy raised
Macintyre's alarm; only complexion aroused her concern. Writing in 1819,
perhaps her understanding of difference, like much of the British populace,
had been boiled down to simpler notions of color distinction.[16]

As with many of these families, personal relationships could and did
evolve, and Eliza Macpherson softened her approach to her grandchildren as
they grew. Despite Eliza's concerns about too much education, both the Williams girls learned French, Latin, spelling, and mathematics, along with the
requisite instructions of sewing, dance, and music for young women. After
her grandmother paid for additional lessons with a music master, young Eliza
lovingly responded, "I shall take great pains and hope I shall improve according to your wishes both in playing, and singing." She boasted of her
ability to play the "Hallelujah Chorus," "Hear my Prayer," and the "Easter
Hymn." If she was to find employment in a wealthy household, or—more
optimistically—marry into a prosperous family, young Eliza would need to
cultivate musical talent. She would also need to maintain extended kinship
networks. Putting their sewing instruction to practical use, the children often
made handcrafted gifts for their father and his wife back in Scotland. Eliza
confided to her grandmother, "I am desirous of working [a] cap for Papa's
Lady" in preparation for Christmas. Attaining intellectual prowess, as well
as domestic skills, set the Williamses on a path toward gentility and possibly
marriage. It also drew them more closely into British society and away from
their origins in the West Indies. Even with their family's low expectations, the
Williams sisters began cultivating genteel identities.[17]

Sensing their determined aspirations, Eliza Macpherson soon spoke more
encouragingly of her granddaughters' futures. Matilda had long impressed
Macpherson with her sharp wit and quick learning. However, young Eliza's
instruction and training took longer, and she became something of a pet
project for her grandmother. Macpherson regularly scolded her for lack of
assertiveness and her propensity to mumble. Outside the issue of clarity, Macpherson grew anxious that Eliza's speech would frustrate future employment.
"I tell her nobody will take her for a Governess or Teacher, or any thing," she
lamented. Should Eliza not improve her diction, she would have little chance
outside the immediate household. Although she and her grandmother fought

16. Harriot Macintyre to William Macpherson, Nov. 26, 1819, bundle 60, MBP.
17. Eliza Williams to Eliza Macpherson, Oct. 15, 1818, bundle 112, MBP, July 24, 1821.

regularly on the topic, Macpherson reassured her son, "It is all for her own good and to make her get her bread gentily, and like a gentlewoman she promises to mind me and do better." Continued interaction between the two improved their connection, and, ultimately, Macpherson lobbied aggressively for her granddaughter. She appealed to Eliza's teachers to give her extra attention and implored them to help prepare her for a position as a governess. This dutiful upbringing intimately connected the two Elizas; Eliza Williams took care of her grandmother in her final days and stayed closely allied with the rest of the British family.[18]

The story of the Macpherson clan offers an important counterpoint to the relative success of previous generations of mixed-race migrants. Although the Macpherson / Williams family history mirrored those of many other families, the level of racial prejudice openly discussed was something quite novel. John Tailyour's family acknowledged that his children were of mixed heritage, and they made references to complexion, but this was only in contexts in which that information held a specific purpose — such as when James Taylor attempted to pass as white in his interview with the East India Company. The Macphersons' forthright and frequent admissions that the Williamses' complexion would hurt them in life as well as Eliza's regular use of "moonlight shades" to refer to her charges reveal an openness, if not compulsion, to draw attention to color differences. Moreover, the general pessimism expressed about their relatives' futures was more brazen than earlier familial expectations. A more polarized racial discourse in Britain facilitated this newer, franker dialogue. It came out of decades of abolitionist critiques on interracial sex and political handwringing over the role of European-educated people of color in the Haitian Revolution as well as the continued arrival of individuals such as the Williamses. However, a more open acknowledgement of their mixed-raced kin's interracial background did not mean that the family made no effort to incorporate them in much the same way as Britons had in prior years. Not only did the Macphersons send the children to notable tutors and schools, they also pushed for some degree of professional attainment. Yet, such approaches did not fare as well as they had for their predecessors. Either from more pronounced racism in Britain or from the uncertainties of chance, the Williams children seem to have fought harder to achieve a distinguished status in the metropole. Little is known of Matilda, but Eliza struggled in adulthood. She moved from London to Perth, where she died at age thirty.

18. Eliza Macpherson to William Macpherson, Aug. 9, 1819, ibid., and Eliza Macpherson to Miss Brooks, Sept. 21, 1821; Foster, *Private Empire*, 168–193.

Although she had most likely married, Eliza had found little financial security by the time of her death: she had to bill the Macphersons just to purchase working clothes. Allan left Scotland for Australia at a young age, using Britain as a stepping-stone for further colonial advancement, as many of his predecessors had, but he, too, was not altogether successful. Although he was of light complexion—Eliza Macpherson described him as "Allan the fair"—his mixed-raced heritage precluded him from holding office in Australia. Their stories serve as examples of the increasing unpredictability of social assimilation in Britain, and even back in the colonies, for immigrants of color.[19]

Even those tasked to look after mixed-race migrants from a distance were also growing concerned with their presence. In the 1820s, two of the four "natural sons" of Patrick McGregor traveled to Scotland from Jamaica. Each entitled to five hundred pounds under their father's will, they fell under the watch of his contacts in Edinburgh and Glasgow. Correspondence between McGregor and his networks does not reveal the interpersonal dynamics that took place once the children arrived. Regardless, not long after their landing, the boys expressed an immediate wish to return to the West Indies. Perhaps it was owing to regular taunts along the Scottish streets, bad treatment by guardians, or simple disaffection with their new location. For his part, McGregor's friend John Anderson hoped to keep the boys in Edinburgh, according to their father's desires, rather than send them back to an uncertain and possibly oppressive existence. After continual delay by Anderson, the two young men decided to make their voices heard and began sabotaging their metropolitan prospects. John, the eldest, stole regularly from the grocer with whom he was employed, forcing Anderson to apprentice him instead with an upholsterer. Younger brother Robert followed suit, pilfering from the jeweler under whom he was working. Asked if they might prefer to live in the country, to avoid such urban temptations, John and Robert instead demanded to return home. Within a month, they set sail. Neither Anderson nor McGregor commented extensively on the proceedings, but certainly an underlying tension between the boys and their caretakers comes through in these events.[20]

19. A receipt sent to the Macpherson estate labeled her "Miss Williams Inness"; see Receipt, Mar. 21, 1837, bundle 202, MBP. An undated scrap of paper within the same bundle also notes that Eliza died in Perth in January 1837. See also Eliza Macpherson to William Macpherson, May 18, 1821, bundle 112, MBP; and Foster, *Private Empire*, 203–204.

20. John Anderson to William William, Oct. 7, 1826, John Anderson's Letter Book, CS 96/1823, fol. 21, NAS, John Anderson to Nethern Tory, Mar. 16, 1825, fol. 47, John Anderson to Robert McGregor, Mar. 18, 1825, fol. 47, John Anderson to Adam Howatson, Mar. 22, 1825, fols. 48–50, John Anderson to Craig Gibson, Apr. 4, 1825, fol. 60, John Anderson

Social exclusion and bickering were not the only results of these changing family dynamics for migrants of color. Some West Indians who had been denied their relatives' support in Britain turned instead toward radical politics. Familial rejection played a clear part in William Davidson's activism. Davidson arrived in Britain in 1800 with the same intentions as most other children of color. Born in Kingston to a black mother and Jamaica's attorney general, Davidson traveled to Edinburgh to study law and take an elevated social place in Britain like many of his mixed-race peers. He soon moved on to a lawyer's apprenticeship in Liverpool, but, for reasons that are unclear, he ran away not long afterward. The carefully constructed plan for his future crumbled, and Davidson's life took a chaotic turn. Twice, the navy impressed him as he moved from place to place. After his second discharge, he studied mathematics in Aberdeen. An unsuccessful marriage proposal sent him on the road once more. He landed in Birmingham, where he purchased a house and set up shop as a cabinetmaker—a business for which he had no aptitude. Before long, he fled again, this time to London to evade creditors. There, he married a poor widow with four children, Sarah Lane, who gave birth to two of Davidson's offspring. Times were tough, particularly as Davidson's cabinetry business failed to take hold.[21]

Without the support of his father's British family, and now married into an impoverished white household, Davidson struggled to establish himself. He finally found his place in the church and in London's emerging revolutionary politics movement. In particular, he joined the Union Reading Society, formed in the aftermath of the 1819 Peterloo Massacre that killed a number of parliamentary reformers. With the society, he discussed radical publications and heard fiery orations urging social action on various subjects. Swept up by the teachings of Arthur Thistlewood, Davidson organized a new family

to Adam Howatson, Apr. 15, 23, 1825, fols. 64-67, John Anderson to Thomas Thomson, Feb. 25, 1826, fol. 117.

21. George Theodore Wilkinson, *An Authentic History of the Cato-Street Conspiracy; with the Trials at Large of the Conspirators, for High Treason and Murder* ... (London, 1820), 406-411; Peter Fryer, *Staying Power: The History of Black People in Britain since 1504* (Atlantic Highlands, N.J., 1984), 215-220; *Oxford Dictionary of National Biography,* online ed., s.v. "Davidson, William (1786-1820)," by Marika Sherwood, http://www.oxforddnb.com/view /article/57029; Joseph A. Baylen and Norbert J. Gossman, eds., *Biographical Dictionary of Modern British Radicals,* I, *1770-1830* (Atlantic Highlands, N.J., 1979), s.v. "William Davidson," by Howard Mackey; Asher Hoyles and Martin Hoyles, *Remember Me: Achievements of Mixed Race People Past and Present* (London, 1999), 70-72.

PLATE 11. *William Davidson.* By R. Cooper. Circa 1820. British Library Board, Shelfmark: General Reference Collection 6495.aaa.42. Image courtesy of the British Library Board

composed of fanatic protestors in 1819. He joined a small group of dissidents who plotted to blow up the British cabinet in the political turmoil following the death of George III in 1820. But the Cato Street Conspiracy, as it came to be called, was doomed from the start; it had been infiltrated by a government spy who arrested the group before it could execute the plan.

When Davidson came to trial for his involvement, he pointed directly to the challenging issues facing individuals of color in Britain. Initially, he declared mistaken identity in his arrest. Davidson drew on previous personal examples of improper identification to demonstrate the regularity of racial confusion in daily life. He recalled a troubling incident that took place several years before in which a young woman from his church had accused him of molestation. Accounts vary on the incident, but Davidson claimed that another man of color in the largely white church had done the deed for which he fell victim to blame and that whites, making few distinctions, saw all men of color as interchangeable. Davidson held the previous incident up as proof "how one man may be mistaken for another," before concluding his case. "Although I am a man of colour," he argued, "that is no reason that I should be guilty of such a crime." Davidson maintained that such racial profiling had plagued him throughout life. Considering the reigning beliefs about vicious black male sexuality, it is hardly surprising that fingers pointed to Davidson. Any man of color, even a well-educated one, was subject to accusation.[22]

Davidson further asserted that Britain could be a miserable place for a mixed-race person without any strong personal networks. His financial failures in Britain clearly tortured him, and he continued to believe that he was originally destined for the type of luxurious life his father had set out for him. He insisted that he "never associated with men of colour, although one myself, because I always found them very ignorant." His defense was meant to present himself as a member of the educated elite, disconnected from London's rabble of color. Yet, he proclaimed to hold no bonds with whites either; indeed, he claimed to have "no friends in England" at all, nor "a relative who will stretch out his hand to my helpless family." This was all the more frustrating owing to his ambitions and self-identity. At trial, Davidson cast himself as English, if not essentially white, despite these familial rejections. "I am a stranger to England by birth; but . . . educated and brought up in England," he proclaimed; "my father was an Englishman, my grandfather was a Scotch-

22. William Davidson, as quoted in Wilkinson, *Authentic History*, 321–322. The exact wording of Davidson's speech might be an exaggeration or florid retelling on Wilkinson's part, but the substance of the speech is consistent with other summaries of it. For more on Davidson's discussion about mistaken identity, see Howard Mackey, "'The Complexion of the Accused': William Davidson, The Black Revolutionary in the Cato Street Conspiracy of 1820," *Negro Educational Review*, XXIII, no. 4 (October 1972), 138. For the Old Bailey account of Davidson's defense—which essentially contains the same statement, see *The Proceedings of the Old Bailey Online: London's Central Criminal Court, 1674 to 1913*, "Arthur Thistlewood, William Davidson, . . . , Royal offenses, Treason," Apr. 16, 1820, 61–62, reference number: t18200416-1, www.oldbaileyonline.org. On British concerns over black male sexuality, see James Walvin, *The Black Presence: A Documentary History of the Negro in England, 1555–1860* (London, 1971), 15; David Dabydeen, *Hogarth's Blacks: Images of Blacks in Eighteenth Century English Art* (Athens, Ga., 1987), 39; Carol Barash, "The Character of Difference: The Creole Woman as Cultural Mediator in Narratives about Jamaica," *Eighteenth-Century Studies*, XXIII (1990), 410; Jennifer DeVere Brody, *Impossible Purities: Blackness, Femininity, and Victorian Culture* (Durham, N.C., 1998), 8.

man; I may too claim the prerogative of an Englishman." But Davidson's promotion of British blood fell out of step with the growing importance of cultivated family connections, rather than simple calculations of direct blood relation. It mattered less that he had a British relative than that he had no active association with British family. Sensing the diminished power of inert consanguinity, Davidson cried out, "My colour may be against me, but I have as good and as fair a heart as if I were a white." Sensitive to the growing oppression of blacks in Britain—particularly the black poor—Davidson's defense begged for the consideration of a hybrid racial position.[23]

Both the court's and the public's reaction to Davidson reflected an understanding of this mixed ancestry as well as his privileged upbringing. The judge presiding over the trial was none other than William Garrow, who had prosecuted Thomas Picton in 1806 for torturing the mixed-race Trinidadian Louisa Calderon. Davidson presented himself in a nuanced light by citing his education and background, and witnesses corroborated these claims. An associate in Aberdeen described him as possessing "a gigantic mind." Later accounts noted that Davidson conducted himself "with great composure and propriety." Of Davidson's appeal, the *Times* recorded that he was "not of that ignorant and illiterate class of being which he was supposed to be" but that "he was indeed a man of colour . . . neither devoid of a human understanding or human feelings." By juxtaposing Davidson with the "ignorant" class of color in Britain, these testimonials reinforced how stigmatized the group was by the time of the trial. Moreover, the *Times*'s fixation with Davidson's heritage demonstrated its centrality to his social status. Sensing the growing importance of these characteristics to the proceedings, the judge attempted to forestall their influence, solemnly urging, "God forbid that the complexion of the accused should enter, for a single moment, into the considerations of the jury." Indeed, the trial turned frequently around issues of race, but not without reflecting, in part, on Davidson's other attributes. Nevertheless, Davidson was found guilty and hanged in May 1820.[24]

23. Davidson, as quoted in Wilkinson, *Authentic History,* 320–324. During the trial, several witnesses testified that Davidson sang, "Scots wha hae wi' Wallace bled" during the conspiracy; see *Proceedings of the Old Bailey Online,* "Arthur Thistlewood, William Davidson, . . . ," Apr. 16, 1820, 15, reference number: t18200416-1.

24. "Examination of William Davidson by Mendacity Society," Feb. 29, 1820, HO 44/4, fol. 323–324, NAE; Wilkinson, *Authentic History,* 312–313, 317; *Times* (London), Apr. 28, 1820, 3; Baron Garrow, as quoted in Mackey, " 'The Complexion of the Accused,' " *Negro Educational Review,* XXIII, no. 4 (October 1972), 114.

Tried at the end of the Regency period, Davidson encountered stricter notions of racial difference than in previous years, even though allowances for racial hybridity had not dissipated fully. The ability of mixed-race individuals in eighteenth-century Britain to construct identities beyond the boundaries of race was not entirely cut off from Davidson in 1820. He could still claim the rights of Englishmen, grounded in British ancestry, while also calling attention to a privileged upbringing. Without strong connections to those British relations, however, Davidson could not effectively ward off the accusations against him. Britain's government also began to suspect extremism in its community of color as the radicalism and agitation of the nineteenth century wore on. Much of this unrest was dreamed up by Britons nervous about a national solidarity organized around racial uniformity as well as fears of a Haitian Revolution precipitated in their isles by migrants of color. But Davidson's activities demonstrate that mixed-race Jamaicans in Britain were not simply passive subjects in this changing public concern. Instead, the challenges he faced in Britain, owing at least partly to his race, led him toward the nightmare scenario imagined by white observers. In many ways, this process was self-fulfilling. The more Britons turned against migrants of color out of fear of political extremism, the more disenfranchised and radicalized some of those migrants became.[25]

At the same time that Davidson found himself in court, fellow Jamaican of color Robert Wedderburn also fell under government scrutiny. Like Davidson, Wedderburn came from Kingston. He was the child of an enslaved black woman named Rosanna and Scottish planter James Wedderburn. When Rosanna was pregnant with Robert, James sold her with the stipulation that their child be freed at birth, which occurred in 1762. Young Robert matured under the guidance of his black grandmother, "Talkee Amy," while receiving only "paltry assistance" from his father. With little support, in 1778 young Wedderburn left the island aboard a warship. In London, he became a tailor, running a shop near Saint Martin-in-the-Fields. It is unclear whether he had any contact with white relatives in these early years, but in later writings Wedderburn insisted that his Scottish family rejected him. Such scorn pushed Wedderburn, as it had Davidson, toward dissenting religion. He became a Unitarian minister, espousing nontraditional notions of Christianity that questioned Jesus's teachings and denied the Trinity. This extremism aligned with political radicalism when Wedderburn read the philosophy of Thomas Spence, a protocommunist agitator who called for the eradication of

25. Wilson, *Island Race*, 11–16.

PLATE 12. *Robert Wedderburn*. 1824. British Library Board, Shelfmark: General Reference Collection 8156.c.71.(4.). Image courtesy of the British Library Board

private property. Davidson, too, had been a "Spencean," and it is likely the two met at some point in London. The combination of unconventional Christian theology and socialist political philosophy made Wedderburn a subject of suspicion to an increasingly nervous state.[26]

26. Robert Wedderburn, *The Horrors of Slavery* (London, 1824), 49. Robert would later claim that his father had two more children of color in Jamaica, before sending each to

As a political dissenter, Wedderburn called direct attention to his mixed ancestry. Living on Great Windmill Street in London's rough-and-tumble district of Soho, he often held sermons just outside his apartment. His preaching drew significant interest, both from the public and the authorities, and, in 1817, Wedderburn published his views in a pamphlet titled *The Axe Laid to the Root*. In it, he railed against the oppression of disadvantaged people in Britain and the West Indies. Eager for the last vestiges of feudalism to crumble, he openly advocated for the dissolution of the monarchy and the elimination of noble titles and the country's land tax. Fully "Spencean," Wedderburn extended such radical ideas to the Caribbean. He called on enslaved Jamaicans to rise up in rebellion. Antislavery dominated his writing, and he used his own Caribbean experiences to bolster the appeal. "Repent ye christians, for flogging my aged grandmother before my face," he railed from the pulpit. Having witnessed abuse visited on slaves firsthand, Wedderburn affirmed his authority. Casting himself even closer to the heart of the matter, he traced his origins through the islands' sexual violence. He condemned planters, "taking your Negro wenches to your adultrous bed," including his own father. "What do you deserve at my hands?" he cried, "Your crimes will be visited upon your legitimate offspring." Racial mixture, albeit damned, was crucial to Wedderburn's self-portrayal, connecting him to the Empire's worst abuses and validating his authenticity as a provocateur.[27]

By autumn 1819, Wedderburn's rhetoric took a turn toward the revolutionary. The Home Office issued a warrant for his arrest on August 12, 1819, after he gave a sermon calling for the death of the prince regent and the murder of white masters by slaves. Days later, after the Peterloo Massacre, Wedderburn gave vocal support to those hurt and killed. He provoked his audiences to spread the protest to London, declaring that "the revolution had already

Scotland. For more on Wedderburn's biography, see Fryer, *Staying Power*, 220–227; *Oxford Dictionary of National Biography*, online ed., s.v. "Wedderburn, Robert (1762–1835/6?)," by Malcolm Chase, http://www.oxforddnb.com/view/article/47120; Ian McCalman, "Anti-Slavery and Ultra-Radicalism in Early Nineteenth-Century England: The Case of Robert Wedderburn," *Slavery and Abolition*, VII (1986), 99–117; McCalman, *Radical Underworld: Prophets, Revolutionaries, and Pornographers in London, 1795–1840* (New York, 1993), 54; and Hoyles and Hoyles, *Remember Me*, 63–64. Paul Edwards has appropriately called for a differentiation between Wedderburn and other figures of African descent in Britain at this time (namely Olaudah Equiano) based on his radicalism; see Edwards, "Unreconciled Strivings and Ironic Strategies: Three Afro-British Authors of the Late Georgian Period (Sancho, Equiano, Wedderburn)," *Immigrants and Minorities*, XII, no. 3 (November 1993), 28–48.

27. Robert Wedderburn, *The Axe Laid to the Root*, II, no. 1 (London, 1817), 11–13. He later changed the name to *The Forlorn Hope*, selling it from his tailoring stall.

began in blood there, and that it must now also end in blood here." He tied slavery and England closer together, proclaiming that Parliament was responsible for the deaths of enslaved Americans as it had approved slave-produced cotton to flow into English textile mills. Two particularly vituperative sermons given by Wedderburn on October 11 and 13, 1819, convinced London's magistrates of his danger, and they finally arrested him on charges of seditious language. Brought before the King's Bench in May 1820, Wedderburn was sentenced to two years at Dorchester prison.[28]

Incarceration allowed Wedderburn time for reflection. Brought to trial the week after William Davidson's execution, he was lucky to have escaped with his life. In prison, the abolitionist and member of Parliament William Wilberforce came to see him. As one of the capital's more outspoken critics of slavery, Wilberforce might have asked for accounts of his experiences while in Jamaica. The visit appears to have revived Wedderburn's energies and inspired him to take up Wilberforce's cause more directly. Discouraged about the lack of progress on labor reform, Wedderburn refocused his attention on the emerging effort to emancipate the Empire's slaves. In 1824, two years after leaving prison, he published *The Horrors of Slavery,* an autobiographical account that further pressed the case for liberation. He dedicated the tract to Wilberforce.

In his new publication, Wedderburn once again highlighted his past in Jamaica and the fractured relationships that destroyed his life. Describing himself as an "oppressed, insulted, and degraded African," he chronicled the depredations he observed as a young man. From the outset, he claimed harboring strong feelings against his father. "From him I have received no benefit in the world," he bitterly acknowledged. "By him my mother was made the object of his brutal lust, then insulted, abused, and abandoned." Most of Wedderburn's critique revolved around the treatment of his mother; indeed, he met his father only once. "My father's house was full of female slaves," he scoffed, "all objects of his lusts; amongst whom he strutted like Solomon in his grand seraglio, or like a bantam cock upon his own dunghill." Wedderburn's father did little to care for his son, which made their interactions much more representative of interracial relationships in Jamaica than those between most migrants of color and their white kin. This lack of parental affection and support was a key reason Wedderburn not only struggled in Britain but turned against British society as a whole. At their first and only meeting when

28. Deposition of Richard Dalton, circa 1819, TS 11/45, no. 167, NAE, H. Hobhouse to George Maule, Aug. 12, 1819.

Wedderburn was a child, his father berated him with "abusive language," which his grandmother rebuffed, insisting that she would bring up the child "without his paltry assistance." Tying such execrable behavior to Wilberforce's damning reports on the scale of the practice, Wedderburn inserted himself squarely into the story of white depravity in the tropics as well as the terrible mistreatment of slaves.[29]

Adding to this theme of family neglect, Wedderburn challenged a half-brother in Scotland to recognize their relationship. After noting his parentage, Wedderburn revealed that his father's colonial plantations were now "in the possession of a younger brother of mine, by name, A. Colville," living in the City of London. Colville had claimed, before the publication of *Horrors,* that Robert Wedderburn was not his brother. Robert's mother, he argued, "was delivered of a mulatto child, and as *she could not tell who was the father,* her master, in a foolish joke, named the child Wedderburn." Robert supposedly had hassled both him and his father, demanding money. Colville displayed great indignation at the claim of black blood in the family, chiding Wedderburn for "foul slander upon the character of the respected dead." Colville's rebuke demonstrated that the acknowledgment of mixed-race paternity was much less acceptable than before. Whereas previous generations had simply provided a small allowance for an illegitimate child from the colonies, many whites in the 1820s wanted no possible claims on legitimate British family fortunes.[30]

Regardless of his family's rebuttal, Wedderburn insisted on the relation and pointed to the strains of prejudice flowing through his kin's blood. Repeatedly calling Colville his "dear brother," Wedderburn claimed that the two had in fact met in their father's Scottish house and that other mixed-race relatives had also come to Britain. Mocking Colville's memory, Wedderburn predicted he would "remember seeing me at his father's house," at which time his father "threaten[ed] to send me to gaol if I troubled him" and called him a "lazy fellow." Not only had Colville met him, Wedderburn averred, but he also met several other Jamaican half-siblings. "Perhaps, *my dear brother* knows nothing of one Esther Trotter, a free tawny, who bore my father two children, a boy and a girl, and which children my inhuman father *transported to Scotland,*" Wedderburn speculated. Those children had to be known to Colville, as he was "brought up in the same house with them at Inveresk." Additionally, Wedderburn pointed to Colville's older brother who visited the mixed-race

29. Wedderburn, *Horrors of Slavery,* 44–49.
30. Ibid., 45–53.

family in Jamaica and openly acknowledged them during the trip. Racism had kept Wedderburn from receiving any benefit from their relation. Such was "their hatred of any one having black blood in his veins" that it surprised Wedderburn that they had not attempted to hang him for claiming kinship. Clearly, some Britons would no longer have anything to do with relatives of color.[31]

Despite his half brother's disavowal, Wedderburn continued to claim British relations. Augmenting his revolutionary bona fides, he revealed that his "grandfather was a staunch Jacobite, and exerted himself strenuously in the cause of the Pretender, in the rebellion of the year 1745." His lineal ties to Scottish resistance not only bolstered his claims to reform but also connected him more securely to British roots. His black Jamaican grandmother and white Scottish grandfather stood as twin figures in Wedderburn's revolutionary genealogy, reinforcing his identity as a mixed-race figure sprung from two separate but similar traditions. By highlighting his British grandfather, Wedderburn sought to establish the legitimacy of his calls for parliamentary reform. Without this white ancestry, the public might consider him only a disaffected colonial migrant, thereby compromising his attempt to link white, working-class radicalism with enslaved revolt. As a mixed-race man, Wedderburn used his hybridity to advocate simultaneously for a global uprising. In so doing, he took a fairly distinctive position among nineteenth-century reformers. However, the public never embraced him or his message. Wedderburn continued to run afoul of the law, returning to prison after an 1831 incident at a London brothel. He died four years later, leaving behind two children by his white wife: Jabez (1798–1880) and Jacob (1806–1841), both of whom became scale makers. Between them, Wedderburn had fifteen English grandchildren.[32]

As Wedderburn and Davidson's examples show, the increasing challenges faced by migrants of color were as much about contested family ties in Britain as they were outright concerns over race. The racism and social exclusion that both men experienced occurred during a period of intense debate about family organization. Eighteenth-century attempts to impose stricter boundaries around marriage and family membership had done little to resolve anxieties by the nineteenth century. Household finances had changed, demanding looser structures of family that could evolve with the upheavals of merchant

31. Ibid., 58–61.
32. Ibid., 45; Alexander Wedderburn, *The Wedderburn Book; A History of the Wedderburns in the Counties of Berwick and Forfar*, 2 vols. (n.p., 1898), I, 505–506.

capitalism. Moreover, the appearance of easier divorce laws in France and the United States influenced English observers to rethink core issues of marriage. The debate over marriage and family was accelerated by the chaos surrounding George IV's tumultuous union with Queen Caroline. The marriage had been in shambles from the start in 1795, as George had previously wed another woman clandestinely. By 1820, George accused Caroline of having an affair with her servant and brought divorce proceedings against her. At her trial, James Maitland, the earl of Lauderdale, insisted that inferences were just as good as evidence to prove infidelity and thus to invalidate the marriage. Although the House of Commons refused to grant the divorce, the proceedings nevertheless sent a clear message. The king's attempt to alter his household through divorce was emblematic of a heightened confidence in the active reorganization of family lines.[33]

Parliament's potential invalidation of royal nuptials was a far cry from the strictures put forward in Hardwicke's 1753 Marriage Act, three generations earlier. By the time of the queen's trial, English jurists and philosophers began to see that act as severely antiquated. Joseph Phillimore, a professor of law at Oxford, insisted that Hardwicke's Act was one of "undue severity and rigour." More particularly, he worried that its attempt to secure property through inheritance had backfired: the law's strict definition of marriage as solemnized only through specific ecclesiastical procedure made it quite easy to annul a union years later by dredging up a technicality. He also argued that the law's obsession with banns—the required reading of a marriage announcement to the community for three successive weeks before the ceremony—was an outdated practice that could work only in an agrarian society of small villages. It accomplished nothing in the modern cities populating England, where pub-

---

33. Anya Jabour, *Marriage in the Early Republic: Elizabeth and William Wirt and the Companionate Ideal* (Baltimore, 1998); Catherine O'Donnell Kaplan, *Men of Letters in the Early Republic: Cultivating Forms of Citizenship* (Chapel Hill, N.C., 2008), 140–183; Carroll Smith-Rosenberg, *This Violent Empire: The Birth of an American National Identity* (Chapel Hill, N.C., 2010), 136–158; Suzanne Desan, *The Family on Trial in Revolutionary France* (Berkeley, Calif., 2006), 93–118; Loren Schweninger, *Families in Crisis in the Old South: Divorce, Slavery, and the Law* (Chapel Hill, N.C., 2012), 4–6; Andrew Cayton, *Love in the Time of Revolution: Transatlantic Literary Radicalism and Historical Change, 1793–1818* (Chapel Hill, N.C., 2013). On George IV's divorce, see James Maitland, *Substance of the Earl of Lauderdale's Speech in the House of Lords, on Thursday, the 2d of November, 1820, on the Second Reading of the Bill, Entitled an Act to Deprive Her Majesty, Caroline Amelia Elizabeth, of the Titles, Prerogatives, Rights, Privileges, and Exemptions of Queen Consort of This Realm, and to Dissolve the Marriage between His Majesty and the Said Caroline Amelia Elizabeth* (Edinburgh, 1820), 5.

lic familiarity was all but extinct. Phillimore appealed to Parliament to amend the Marriage Act in order to remove some of these nuptial impediments. In 1823, Parliament listened. An amendment passed that year lifting the requirement of attending parental consent when minors obtained marriage licenses. Clandestine marriage was effectively reinstated, so long as the couples did not explicitly attempt to hide their weddings. This amendment reflected an obvious legal shift giving more autonomy to spouses, but it also revealed a cultural change. Britons were experimenting with new ways to run their households, and traditional models were no longer perfect blueprints. Indeed, in an 1815 work entitled *Conversations on Matrimony,* John Ovington vowed that far too much thought was put into the financial appeal of a potential spouse when emotional compatibility was just as important. This was an old refrain, but it serviced a new tune. Creative matches were more vital than ever within the social turbulence of the nineteenth century.[34]

Shifting notions of marriage and divorce did not improve the plight of mixed-race migrants. Changes in family structure were not evidence of a marriage free-for-all, driven by emotion and unchecked by practical considerations. Rather, the growth of merchant capitalism in the eighteenth and nineteenth centuries required new strategies of affiliation. The concentration of property and wealth among a small band of landowners at the turn of the nineteenth century made it increasingly difficult for those in the commercial sector to join the landed elite. Affluent brides could sometimes help merchants buy their way in, but more often they allowed them to create stronger commercial networks to keep business going. Simultaneously, wealthy landowning families directed daughters' marriages into more complicated alliances in order to retain their consolidated holdings. Marriage matches therefore became ones of greater similarity between partners. Class standing was growing increasingly homogenous among spouses in the early nineteenth century, and large numbers of family married kin of near relation to solidify social status. For Britain's middle class and rising gentry, such as those tied to the estates of Jamaica, that simply meant that dowries mattered less than future business associations. This spelled doom for migrants of color. Even those lucky enough to receive a bequest tied to fixed land in the Caribbean would

34. Joseph Phillimore, *Substance of the Speech of Joseph Phillimore, Lld. in the House of Commons, on Wednesday, March 27, 1822, on Moving for Leave to Bring in a Bill to Amend the Marriage Act* (London, 1822), 9–69; *Copy of an Act of Parliament for Preventing Clandestine Marriages . . .* (Leeds, 1822), 3–4; Rebecca Probert, *Marriage Law and Practice in the Long Eighteenth Century: A Reassessment* (New York, 2009), 309–311; John Ovington, *Conversations on Matrimony . . .* (London, [1815]), 30–34.

no longer hold the same appeal for suitors interested in expanding trade networks. It hardly needs to be stated what the prospects were for migrants, such as Davidson and Wedderburn, who did not even stand to receive a meager inheritance. The simultaneous and connected acceleration of prejudices against African descent all but sealed their fates. As G. W. Jordan, Barbados's colonial agent in London, asked about migrants of color in 1816, "What shall we say of submitting the daughters of Great Britain . . . to the embraces of persons, towards whom there is in fact, and confessedly an instinctive feeling . . . [that] would abate even the joy of a mother, that a man child is born into the world[?]" The links between changing notions of race and family made Britain a far less attractive place for West Indians of color to settle permanently.[35]

Yet, growing racial prejudice did not end the practice of sending young men and women abroad. Jamaican testators from 1813 to 1815 gave bequests for children in Britain at roughly the same rates as previous decades. Britain continued to hold the promise of a good education, and—if lucky—the possibility for marriage. The "Atlantic family" was still capacious enough to allow mixed-race relatives to live in the metropole and even receive care from their kin. But the treatment they experienced, and their statuses within those households, had deteriorated. The pressures that the commercial and rising gentry families perceived with regard to their financial futures kept them from tendering too much in the way of filial piety. Moreover, the abolition of the slave trade in 1807, and the impending emancipation of slaves, unsettled the fortunes of Britons with Jamaican property. In their minds, they simply could not offer the same seats at the family table as they had in previous years.

35. G. W. Jordan, *An Examination of the Principles of the Slave Registry Bill, and of the Means of Emancipation, Proposed by the Authors of the Bill* (London, 1816), 115; John Habakkuk, "The Rise and Fall of English Landed Families, 1600–1800," Royal Historical Society, *Transactions,* 5th Ser., XXIX (1979), 187–207; F. M. L. Thompson, *English Landed Society in the Nineteenth Century* (London, 1963), 22–23; J. V. Beckett, "The Pattern of Land Ownership in England and Wales, 1660–1880," *Economic History Review,* 2d Ser., XXXI (1984), 11–18; John Habakkuk, "Marriage Settlements in the Eighteenth Century," Royal Historical Society, *Transactions,* 4th Ser., XXXII (1950), 15–30; Nicholas Rogers, "Money, Land, and Lineage: The Big Bourgeoisie of Hanoverian London," *Social History,* IV (1979), 444–445; Eileen Spring, *Law, Land, and Family: Aristocratic Inheritance in England, 1300 to 1800* (Chapel Hill, N.C., 1993), 183–186; Sabean and Teuscher, "Kinship in Europe," in Sabean, Teuscher, and Mathieu, eds., *Kinship in Europe,* 3. Fears of overpopulation in Britain by 1815 also reduced enthusiasm for colonists to settle in the metropole; see C. A. Bayly, *Imperial Meridian: The British Empire and the World, 1780–1830* (London, 1997), 157–158; and James Belich, *Replenishing the Earth: The Settler Revolution and the Rise of the Anglo-World, 1783–1939* (New York, 2009), 145–147.

Although racial prejudice had infected kinship relations for decades, it was never so pronounced as in the early years of the nineteenth century. Public attitudes against these migrants, popular declamations against those of African descent generally, and growing anxieties about household management amplified and caused these feelings to further degenerate. As Britons began to pull away from their Caribbean colonies, they also began to pull away from their Caribbean relatives.[36]

Changes in Jamaica

Issues of marriage, family, and race were also of paramount importance to Jamaica in this period, as the colony appeared on the verge of massive social transformation. Emancipation was by no means a foregone conclusion after England abolished its slave trade in 1807. But the following quarter century saw an air of excited anticipation among antislavery forces, as well as embittered resignation in proslavery circles, over the seeming inevitability of forced labor's eventual demise. Reformers went to work preparing enslaved Jamaicans for a future life of freedom, while the island's white plantocracy drafted plans on how best to concede as little power as possible to a mixed-race elite. Although it would be many decades before black and brown freemen would take the reins of Jamaican governance, the pre-emancipation period saw an attempt to align rich Jamaicans of color with the social and economic interests of ruling whites in the hope of tamping down their political ambitions. This came after a pronounced time of protest by mixed-race colonists in the 1810s and 1820s, led by individuals who had spent time in Britain. Once more, education and life experience in the metropole would become standards by which mixed-race Jamaicans would be allowed partial entry into the island's ascendant class.

Pressures mounted against colonists of color as demographic planning continued to dominate Jamaican rulers' thinking about how to keep their sugar regime running. Effectively nothing had changed from the previous century in calls for reform: the island needed stronger white and black reproduction to stabilize its populations, and interracial sex worked against that mission. If anything, these appeals grew louder as emancipation appeared on the horizon. An 1816 account argued that incentives toward marriage would stabilize West Indian society, weaning it off a commercial dependence on the United States. The author held that increasing the Caribbean's white population should be the top goal of British imperial policy. If Europeans could be

36. See Appendix 1, below.

compelled to settle and marry in the tropics, and if colonists would end their unofficial policy of "refusing to employ on their plantations married men," then the West Indies would thrive. This observer might have thrust responsibility on the British government because island legislatures had done so little themselves. Besides passing an 1816 law giving greater welfare allotments to the wives of white soldiers, the Jamaican assembly had done virtually nothing to encourage higher marriage rates among either the enslaved or white populations. According to James Walker, a British naval officer who had toured the Caribbean, this failure to act created myriad problems. Walker supported the belief that married white men struggled to find work in the West Indies and alleged that such discrimination encouraged immoral behavior. He went further, though, claiming that this general disdain toward matrimony set a "bad example to the slaves." If demographic stability was to be achieved for all segments of the Caribbean population, then white settlers had to model upstanding metropolitan comportment.[37]

Just as in the previous century, enslaved marriage was promoted by reformers and members of the slave interest alike. Not only would matrimony help improve manners, these writers proclaimed, but women's fecundity supposedly increased when married. Therefore, if marriage was encouraged in enslaved communities, the islands could remain vigorously populated with black laborers. Many rumored, however, that slaves carried over an African prejudice against marriage. A proslavery supporter and former resident of Jamaica believed it would not be easy to "persuade an African . . . to submit to such restraints" of matrimony, while a reform-minded British clergyman who visited Jamaica similarly worried that the "holy institution will never, and can never, be established amongst the slaves." Others pointed out that many slaves were already married, though bound only by loose contracts similar to those allowed in Scotland. Still more insisted that planters had no desire to encourage workers to marry anyhow. Regardless, the steady stream of missionaries flowing into the Caribbean in the first three decades of the nineteenth century went undeterred by these claims. Driven to transform slaves' morals in preparation for eventual freedom, these campaigners felt confident that they could end the practice of slaves "herd[ing] together like the cattle,

37. *The Colonial Policy of Great Britain, Considered with Relation to Her North American Provinces and West India Possessions* . . . (London, 1816), 170–171, 183–184; *JAJ*, Nov. 5, 1816, XIII, 12; James Walker, *Letters on the West Indies* (London, 1818), 166–167; Henrice Altink, "Forbidden Fruit: Pro-Slavery Attitudes towards Enslaved Women's Sexuality and Interracial Sex," *Journal of Caribbean History*, XXXIX (2005), 201–235.

to change mates as often as they are prompted by appetite." As they preached in newly built churches, missionaries railed against the practice of polygamy and infidelity and implored black congregants to settle down and wed. They soon proclaimed victory. Although one Jamaican insisted that few slaves had adopted matrimony, by 1827, a Kingston curate declared that a "considerable number of marriages" had occurred throughout the island. This social change would produce large and dynamic enslaved families, so long as planters ensured that spouses and children were not broken up and sold off.[38]

Once again, this mantra on the importance of marriage to Caribbean demography cast the children of racially mixed unions out of social acceptance. First, interracial sex supposedly destroyed the morals of white men. Multiple observers repeated this claim: "keeping coloured girls . . . the white man [is] ruined"; "father and brothers . . . openly keep their mulatto mistresses; so that it is not accounted in the slightest degree infamous"; "the obstacles to matrimony, too often lead to vicious and immoral connexion with native females." Second, these relationships destroyed the fragile structure of emerging white families in the Caribbean. A West Indian surgeon sneered at white women who tolerated these dalliances, while former Jamaican resident James Stewart

---

38. Alexander Barclay, *A Practical View of the Present State of Slavery in the West Indies; or, An Examination of Mr. Stephen's "Slavery of the British West India Colonies"* . . . (London, 1826), 101; Thomas Cooper, *Facts Illustrative of the Condition of the Negro Slaves in Jamaica* . . . (London, 1824), 41. See also George Wilson Bridges, *A Voice from Jamaica; in Reply to William Wilberforce, Esq. M.P.* (London, 1823), 12–13; William Sells, *Remarks on the Condition of the Slaves in the Island of Jamaica* (London, 1823), 28–32; James Stephen, *The Slavery of the British West India Colonies Delineated* . . . , 2 vols. (London, 1824), I, 23; Richard Watson, *A Defence of the Wesleyan Methodist Missions in the West Indies* . . . (London, 1817), 25; John Riland, *Memoirs of a West-India Planter* . . . (London, 1827), 117–120; R[ichard] Bickell, *The West Indies as They Are; or, A Real Picture of Slavery: But More Particularly as It Exists in the Island of Jamaica* (London, 1825), 91. A strong debate occurred over whether planters broke up families in their slave sales, but both sides in the argument agreed that it was not a good practice. See *Speech of the Right Hon. George Canning, Secretary of State for Foreign Affairs, etc. etc. etc. on Laying before the House of Commons the Papers in Explanation of the Measures Adopted by His Majesty's Government with a View of Ameliorating the Condition of the Negro Slaves in the West Indies, on Wednesday, the 17th of March, 1824* . . . (London, 1824), 18–19; and James McQueen, *The West India Colonies; the Calumnies and Misrepresentations Circulated against Them by the Edinburgh Review, Mr. Clarkson, Mr. Cropper, etc. etc.* (London, 1824), 271–272. Ideas of marriage and sexuality were certainly different between Europe and many West African societies, and enslaved workers in the Americas often did maintain African traditions of polygyny and polyamory; see James H. Sweet, *Recreating Africa: Culture, Kinship, and Religion in the African-Portuguese World, 1441–1770* (Chapel Hill, N.C., 2003), 34–49.

registered shock that white women were so callous to such relationships that they openly socialized with relatives' mixed-race offspring. Letters between the King sisters of Saint George, Jamaica, however, reveal that such apparent nonchalance was chimerical. Both women wrote to an American sister-in-law in 1817, complaining about their brother Richard's actions. One sister denounced the "parcel of Mulattoes" to which Richard had given more than a thousand pounds. The other protested that Richard's charity came at the expense of his family's well-being. As executor of their parents' will, Richard controlled the family estate, and his sisters could do nothing but watch him spend the family fortune on mistresses. "I fear we are from the Frying Pan into the Fire in respect of our Legacies," one sister agonized. "Were We Mulattoes," she continued, "there would be no need of consanguinity to induce him to the tenderest acts of solicitude, and to spend thousands on us." As James Walker insisted in an account written the next year, "White families may be troublesome, but mulatto families are dangerous." The financial stability of white households thus depended on a retreat from interracial coupling.[39]

Perhaps the greater worry over interracial unions in the early nineteenth century was the sense that a mixed-race population would overtake and dominate white settlement in the Caribbean. Despite Edward Long's contention in 1774 that individuals of color were effectively sterile, observers charted with amazement the explosion of their numbers in the last quarter of the eighteenth century. Novelist and absentee planter Monk Lewis explicitly rejected Long's claim when he visited Jamaica in 1816, and a traveler to Grenada joked the next year that women of color "encrease and multiply like rabbits." Jamaica's free population of color far outpaced white inhabitants in this period. Perhaps twice as many mixed-race freemen than whites lived on the island by the time of emancipation (see Table 1). For many contemplating the future of the colonies, such a large middling class between blacks and whites portended doom. In his reflections on emancipation, Joseph Marryat argued that "the progressive increase of the free coloured people, is adverse to the public peace and

39. *Colonial Policy of Great Britain*, 182; John Augustine Waller, "A Voyage in the West Indies," 1820, in *New Voyages and Travels*, III (London, n.d.), 20–21, Rare Books, 44772 ANAL, HL; James Johnson, *The Influence of Tropical Climates on European Constitutions to Which Is Added Tropical Hygiene; or, The Preservation of Health in All Hot Climates*, 2d ed., 2 vols. (Philadelphia, 1818), II, 288; J[ames] Stewart, *A View of the Past and Present State of the Island of Jamaica; with Remarks on the Moral and Physical Condition of the Slaves, and on the Abolition of Slavery in the Colonies* (Edinburgh, 1823), 173–175; E. B. Forbes to Isabella King, Apr. 26, 1817, King Papers, MS 93, NLJ, Louisa King to Isabella King, Mar. 3, 1817; Walker, *Letters on the West Indies*, 168.

security." He believed, like Stewart, that the small amounts of property and civil rights concessions that the group received had frustrated, rather than pacified, them. Should the islands' assemblies not improve the conditions of mixed-race people, some suggested further, the British West Indies would soon erupt into rebellion. Certainly the specter of revolt was on the minds of colonial legislators, especially considering the Caribbean's recent history. Jamaica's assembly regularly debated the steps it could take in the early 1820s to prevent the island from becoming another Haiti, and fears over mixed-race disaffection weighed in those considerations.[40]

In Jamaica's case, the debate about the place of mixed-race individuals in the political future of the island did influence lawmakers. Abolitionism and the Haitian Revolution had persuaded members of the assembly to offer a few token concessions in 1796, when freemen of color were given the right to testify for themselves in court. This was done in the hope of preventing a mixed-race uprising similar to Vincent Ogé's half a decade earlier. Nonetheless, this indulgence was not evidence of a rising tide of racial tolerance. Six years later, a member of the Jamaican council ended the practice of privilege petitioning, severely hampering the social progress of elite Jamaicans of color. After 1802, then, mixed-race Jamaicans were no longer able to ask for added employment rights, nor could they lobby to avoid certain harsh punishments if they were caught committing a crime. The colonial government's revanchism prompted the island's free population of color to appeal en masse to the assembly. In 1813, a group of free black and mixed-race colonists submitted a petition asking for three legal changes: they wished to testify against whites in court, to save deficiency on their properties, and to be able to inherit any amount of money. Clearly, this entreaty came from the island's wealthiest inhabitants of color. The desire to testify against whites primarily originated from businessmen who had little recourse to sue for untoward practices. Saving deficiency was important mostly to planters and shopkeepers who could not escape the

40. [Edward Long], *The History of Jamaica; or, General Survey of the Antient and Modern State of That Island . . .* , 3 vols. (London, 1774), II, 335; M. G. Lewis, *Journal of a West India Proprietor, 1815–17*, ed. Mona Wilson (London, 1929), 94; "Thought on the Political Tendency of the Restrictions at Present Applied to People of Color," Aug. 19, 1817, MS 1834, NLJ; Joseph Marryat, *Thoughts on the Abolition of the Slave Trade, and Civilization of Africa . . .* (London, 1816), 134; Stewart, *A View of the Past and Present State of the Island of Jamaica*, 333–334; *JAJ*, Nov. 27, 1822, XIV, 71, Dec. 12, 1823, 229–230; Gad J. Heuman, *Between Black and White: Race, Politics, and the Free Coloreds in Jamaica, 1792–1865* (Westport, Conn., 1981), 7. See, in particular, Stephen, *Slavery of the British West India Colonies*, I, 429–430; and Bickell, *West Indies as They Are*, 116.

fines associated with having too few white employees. Likewise, the destruction of the inheritance cap only affected those who stood to receive more than two thousand pounds. Despite the petitioners' upper-class origins, their requests represented the revival of political organization among the island's mixed-race residents at large. Coming together as a bloc, they validated those observations that anticipated an end to the political passivity of the island's populations of color.[41]

Jamaica's assembly had little choice but to grant the petition. However, there was not an immediate consensus on how to proceed. Many white Jamaicans protested vociferously against appeasement. Tensions had already been high: a group of Sephardic Jews had complained the year before that they had no more rights than people of color. After the 1813 petition was submitted, a number of Kingston voters lobbied the assembly themselves, proclaiming that "it hath ever been an essential part of the constitution of Jamaica . . . to preserve a marked distinction between the white inhabitants and the free persons of colour and free blacks." They pleaded that nonwhites be kept from testifying in court, and, although they conceded that the inheritance cap might be raised, they nevertheless insisted that its repeal "would lead to very injurious consequences." A committee considering the petition agreed in spirit by stating that "free people of colour in this island have no right or claim whatever to political power." Yet, it persuaded the rest of the assembly to approve the petitioners' essential demands. Few could reasonably defend these laws against a group steadily outnumbering the white population. In fact, members of Parliament in Westminster would later scoff that Jamaica had ever passed the laws in the first place. In quick order, the Jamaican assembly granted the petition's basic requests. On December 4, 1813, free people of color gained the right to testify against anyone in court, save deficiency on their properties, and inherit any amount of money.[42]

The successes of 1813 demonstrated a new political energy among Jamaicans of color, but they showed a connection to the long-standing hierarchies among them as well. As with the aborted petition mixed-race Jamaicans had

41. *JAJ*, Nov. 5, 1813, XII, 506; An Act to Repeal Several Acts and the Clause of An Act of This Island respecting Persons of Free Condition and for Granting to Such Persons Certain Privileges, Jul. 16, 1814, CO 139/60, fol. 110–114, NAE.

42. *JAJ*, Nov. 24, 1812, XII, 467–469, Nov. 16–25, 1813, 519–531; *Report of the Debate in the House of Commons, June the 16th, 1825; on Dr. Lushington's Motion respecting the Deportation of Messrs. L. C. Lecesne and J. Escoffery, Two Persons of Colour, from Jamaica* (London, 1825), 3.

drafted twenty-one years earlier for broad improvements in civil rights, the 1813 appeal was also directed by individuals recently arrived from Britain. In a memorial of their victory written soon afterward, the group recounted, "The return to the Colony of many of the mixed class from their Education in Europe served to give an accession of intelligence to the efforts made in the year 1813." The English education received by those migrants allowed them to draw on common-law precedent and to use the legal language necessary to validate their requests. Their prominent role in the petition also reveals that British-educated Jamaicans still stood at the pinnacle of the island's mixed-race political leadership. If Jamaicans of color were to gain civil equality, they would have to do so either through force or through exacting political and legal maneuvers. For elites of color, desperate to preserve the economic health of the island, the latter option was the only reasonable one. Migration to Britain, therefore, continued to serve a vital function in colonial society.[43]

Spirits remained high among Jamaicans of color in the following decade. The group continued to petition the assembly, calling for greater civil rights. By 1823, these efforts produced two major political moves: the hiring of a lobbyist in Westminster to advocate for their enfranchisement and the drafting of yet another formal appeal to Jamaica's assembly. The latter occurred on a clear night in May of that year. A group of mixed-race men gathered on the back piazza at the Kingston home of Alexander Sympson to craft a petition with four demands: first, that the deficiency laws be struck down so that people of color could be elected to office; second, that they be given the rights to vote and sit on juries; third, that they no longer be asked for proof of their freedom and baptism when testifying in court; and, finally, that funds be raised to create schools for poor children of color. Effectively, they desired roughly equal rights with free white men. It was perhaps a tall order for a government still unwilling to debate the prospect of emancipation, but it showed the resolve held by the colony's leaders of color. Moreover, while crafting the appeal, the men began planning an island-wide campaign to organize individuals of color. They already had requests from nearby parishes hoping that they might "repeal such laws as prevent the free exercise of the faculties, and enslave the mind." When the petition finally came before the Jamaican assembly in November 1823, the legislature considered it and eventually passed a provision making it easier for all free people to provide evidence in trials.

43. "Commissioners of Legal Enquiry in the West Indies," 1822–1828, CO 318/76, fol. 72, NAE. For the 1790s petition, see Chapter Four, above.

Yet, overall, freemen of color would have to wait seven more years before they gained political parity with whites.[44]

The assembly made cautious moves to appease individuals of color in 1823, staying suspicious of their motivations and political ideologies. Twenty-one men had signed the original Kingston petition that year, and officials set out to learn more about each of them. Although little is known of most of the signatories, two names stood out. Louis Lecesne and Edward Escoffery were both Haitians that had fled as young children to Jamaica at the time of the Haitian Revolution. They had established themselves as tradesmen on the island in the intervening years, but their foreign birth now marked them for interrogation. Jamaica's governor, William Montagu, duke of Manchester, had the men arrested on the grounds of conspiring to overthrow the colony. They were eventually deported back to Haiti. The men next sailed to England to clear their names. Their arrival thrust the issue of mixed-race rights back into the British political debate around the future of West Indian governance. It also demonstrated that the white ruling class in Jamaica still worried about the lingering appeal of the Haitian Revolution to free people of color. Rebellion, in their minds, continued to be a viable threat, and they hoped that pacification might ease the tensions between the island's ethnic groups.[45]

Jamaicans of color recognized this quandary and sought to capitalize on it. Two days before the group submitted its 1823 petition, Thomas Drummond lodged a privilege appeal with the assembly to test whether its reluctance to hear these bills still held. It had been twenty-one years since a privilege petition for a Jamaican of color had passed, but clearly the political environment

44. William Burge, *A Letter to the Right Honorable Sir George Murray, G.C.B. His Majesty's Principal Secretary of State for the Colonies, Relative to the Deportation of Lecesne and Escoffery from Jamaica* (London, 1829), 392–393, 511–512; "Commissioners of Legal Enquiry in the West Indies," 1822–1828, CO 318/76, fols. 109–114, NAE; *JAJ*, Nov. 14, 1823, XIV, 179; Heuman, *Between Black and White*, 34.

45. [Richard] Barret, *A Reply to the Speech of Dr. Lushington in the House of Commons, on the 12th June, 1827, on the Condition of the Free-Coloured People of Jamaica* (London, 1828), 15–16; Burge, *A Letter to the Right Honorable George Murray*, 41. The two men signed their names "Lewis Lecesne" and "John Escoffery"; see "Commissioners of Legal Enquiry in the West Indies," 1822–1828, CO 318/76, fols. 114, NAE. See also Mavis Christine Campbell, *The Dynamics of Change in a Slave Society: A Sociopolitical History of the Free Coloreds of Jamaica, 1800–1865* (Rutherford, N.J., 1976), 91. For the trial more generally, see Heuman, *Between Black and White*, 36–41; and T. C. Hansard, ed., *Hansard's Parliamentary Debates*, 2d Ser., 25 vols. (London, 1820–1830), XIII, 1173–1205. For a discussion of the trial's links to abolitionism, see Edward Bartlett Rugemer, *The Problem of Emancipation: The Caribbean Roots of the American Civil War* (Baton Rouge, La., 2008), 101–102.

had changed. The assembly read through Drummond's bill after analyzing the general petition put forward by the island's residents of color. On November 26, it agreed to give Drummond effectively the same legal status as white subjects. Witnessing this success, mixed-race elites began submitting a flurry of similar appeals. The 1820s saw the return of privilege petitioning, with a new crop of residents hoping to distinguish themselves from their fellow colonists of color. The government tolerated it, in part, to curry favor with the growing mixed-race population. William Burge, a member of Jamaica's council, later declared that the assembly began hearing privilege appeals again to tamp down the disaffection felt after Lecesne's and Escoffery's arrest. However, Jamaica's ruling class also allowed privilege petitioning to recommence because it needed to pull elites of color back into its orbit and influence. If all freemen of color would soon achieve legal parity with whites, which many imperial observers believed would have to occur, then whites needed first to guarantee the loyalty of wealthy individuals of color who supported the plantation system. Privilege petitions, the eighteenth-century relic of a similar effort at politicking mixed-race elites, was once more back in fashion.[46]

Elites of Color and Jamaica's Future

Despite being a political throwback, the privilege appeals of the 1820s did not perfectly mimic their predecessors. Between 1823 and 1826, Jamaicans of color submitted thirty-nine petitions, outpacing the eighteenth-century rate of appeals. This enthusiasm sprang up as a result of the assembly's twenty-year moratorium on hearing privilege bills as well as the government's agreement to waive the hefty charge to submit them. According to a member of the assembly, the latter development came about because "there are many free persons of colour, of good education and behaviour, who cannot afford the large fees now payable on private bills." This reopening and expansion of petitioning reveals the assembly's strategy of using privilege appeals to bestow individual empowerment to avoid granting blanket civil rights. The resolution to dissolve petition fees came just weeks after a group in the parish of Saint James — many perhaps individuals of color themselves — demanded equal rights for all free people. There were limits, however, to how widely the assembly would consider expanding these privileges. After abolishing the privilege bill fee, the assembly debated extending the deadline to submit appeals, owing to the large numbers of applications it received. It decided not to grant

46. *JAJ*, Nov. 12–Nov. 26, 1823, XIV, 176–199; Burge, *Letter to the Right Honorable George Murray*, 22.

the extension. Yet, members of the assembly recognized that the eighteenth-century practice of petitioning would not suit the new realities of Jamaican society. At the end of the 1826 session, a proposal came forward asking that all future privilege petitions go through local vestries, rather than the island legislature. This would accommodate many more petitioners of color but would take power out of the hands of the assembly to regulate which Jamaicans could be elevated. Only seven assemblymen voted for the proposition, and it ended in failure. The island's rulers did not want to give up their centralized ability to monitor the social advancement of mixed-race Jamaicans.[47]

Privilege bills in this period also looked different from their eighteenth-century counterparts. In the previous iteration of petitioning, Jamaicans of color frequently recorded the names of white fathers and companions as part of the biographical justification for their appeals. Kinship to a white patriarch, generally a well-connected person on the island, was key to documenting a preeminent status. Yet, by the 1820s, such connections were not only becoming less regular, they were also losing their social power. Of the thirty-nine petitioners in the 1820s, only six highlighted a white relative. William Alcock, for instance, noted that his father Samuel had helped teach him the profession of coffee planting. Thomas Witter Jackson's petition mentioned that his father was the island's former chief justice, while Hugh Smith and John McLean both remarked that their fathers had been members of the assembly. Abingdon Bayly likely did not need to state that he was the nephew of Zachary Bayly, one of the island's most prominent men and an influential power broker of the Jamaican assembly. The large majority of petitioners, however, did not record such relations. With a decreasing white populace and the prospect of eventual rule by mixed-race individuals, kinship to white men was losing its political power on the island.[48]

Petitioners of color might also have failed to note a white relation because they did not have an immediate one. As the mixed-race population increased at the turn of the nineteenth century, the rate of white with nonwhite coupling dipped. This might have been owing to the social realities of fewer white residents, or to the choices of women of color to avoid relationships with white men. Regardless, by the early nineteenth century, cross-racial unions contributed less heavily to the growth of Jamaica's population of color than the unions

47. *JAJ*, Oct. 13–18, 1826, XIV, 601–606, Nov. 23, 1826, 665, Dec. 22, 1826, 760; Heuman, *Between Black and White*, 47.

48. *JAJ*, Nov. 4, 1824, XIV, 252, Nov. 25, 1824, 313, Nov. 10, 1826, 649, Nov. 22, 1826, 661–662, Nov. 28, 1826, 670.

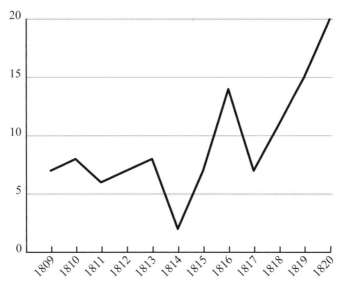

FIGURE 3. Percentage of Free Mixed-Race Children Listed as Legitimate in Baptismal Records, Kingston, Jamaica, 1809–1820. Drawn by Kelly Crawford. Kingston Baptism Records, 1B/11/8/9/3–4, JA

of two mixed-race parents. Figure 3 shows the legitimacy rates of free mixed-race children rising in the island's urban mecca of Kingston between 1809 and 1820. Because virtually no white men married women of color, those who were legitimate almost universally had two mixed-race parents. Many more had two parents of color who had not married, but rising legitimacy rates indicate a lower percentage of children born from interracial relationships. At the same time, decreasing percentages of mixed-race women appear to have cohabited with white men in this period. Although the data is fragmentary and incomplete, Figure 4 plots the proportion of free, mixed-race children in Kingston who had a white father and a mother of color according to the city's baptismal records. Although still a majority, the percentage of children with white fathers steadily decreased as the nineteenth century progressed. By 1820, the numbers of mixed-race people in Kingston with both a father and mother of color approached those who had a white parent. In the early decades of the nineteenth century, then, Jamaica's free population of color started to evolve away from the white community. These new residents of color had weaker connections to whites and thus fewer reasons to mention them in their petitions.[49]

49. A decrease in formalized interracial relationships appears to have occurred in Saint Domingue / Haiti at the turn of the nineteenth century as well; see John D. Garrigus, "'To

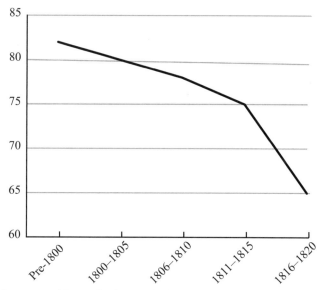

FIGURE 4. Percentage of Free, Mixed-Race Children Listed as Having a White Father in Baptismal Records, Kingston, Jamaica, 1750–1820. Drawn by Kelly Crawford. Kingston Baptism Records, 1B/11/8/9/3–4, JA

The differences in parentage among various individuals of color reflect an important point about group cohesion. West Indians of mixed-race did not form a unified mass in the eighteenth and nineteenth centuries. Slavery versus freedom, poverty versus wealth, social anonymity versus political connection: all were crucial to mixed-race standing. Populations of color retained strong, internal divisions along class and phenotypic lines throughout Jamaica's colonial history. Yet, another prominent distinction emerged between people of color in the nineteenth century — one based on parentage. The lack of a white parent pushed mixed-race West Indians further away from the islands' white residents. Such a development allowed for greater social cohesion among most mixed-race people, rather than less. Without white patrons, individuals of color came to depend on one another for financial and social well-being, if not for self-identification. This eliminated many of the original divisions prominent in the eighteenth century and allowed mixed-race West Indians to form a group dependent less on associations with whites and more on self-organization. Certainly, myriad factors contributed to a growing political energy among the Caribbean's populations of color. But the weakening of kin-

Establish a Community of Property': Marriage and Race before and during the Haitian Revolution," *History of the Family*, XII (2007), 142–152.

ship and personal connections to whites, both in the Caribbean and in Great Britain, forced elites of color to depend more on themselves.[50]

Changing gender expectations also contributed to this shift away from white patrons and indicated a new purpose of privilege petitioning. Unlike in the eighteenth century, when women had constituted a significant portion of appellants who tied their fortunes to a white companion, all of the individuals who received privileges in this period were men. Only one woman of color submitted a petition, and it was on behalf of her son. The gendered shift in petitioners meant that sexual connections to whites were not part of the justifications for obtaining privileges: virtually no elite men of color carried on public relationships with white women. But the absence of female appellants is also emblematic of a much larger transformation in privilege petitioning. Women of color still had every reason to want privileges. Many had large sums of money and suffered under the island's race-based laws. Yet, the assembly's records from 1823 to 1826 show only male petitioners. It is unclear whether women still sent in appeals that were never brought up for debate. What appears more likely is that the function of the revived privilege petitions was altogether different and that women understood that their requests would no longer be met. Going forward, privilege bills were an avenue toward eventual political participation, from which women would continue to be excluded, rather than simply a step up the social ladder. They were meant to bring very

50. David W. Cohen and Jack P. Greene, "Introduction," in Cohen and Greene, eds., *Neither Slave Nor Free: The Freedmen of African Descent in the Slave Societies of the New World* (Baltimore, 1972), 1–18. See, especially, the case of Barbados, Jerome S. Handler, *The Unappropriated People: Freedmen in the Slave Society of Barbados* (Baltimore, 1974), 209; and Melanie J. Newton, *The Children of Africa in the Colonies: Free People of Color in Barbados in the Age of Emancipation* (Baton Rouge, La., 2008). Arnold A. Sio argues that free colored identity in the Caribbean was much more unified than scholars have traditionally believed owing to extended networks across the islands as well as a common African culture; see Sio, "Marginality and Free Coloured Identity in Caribbean Slave Society," *Slavery and Abolition,* VIII (1987), 169–172. Gad Heuman sees its genesis in the spirit of reform following both the American and Haitian Revolutions, particularly after enduring years of protracted civil rights; see Heuman, *Between Black and White,* 23–29. O. Nigel Bolland believes that the end of slave imports in 1807 diminished African influence among people of color, leading them to articulate a more Eurocentric form of political demands; see Bolland, "Creolisation and Creole Societies: A Cultural Nationalist View of Caribbean Social History," in Verene A. Shepherd and Glen L. Richards, eds., *Questioning Creole: Creolisation Discourses in Caribbean Culture* (Kingston, Jamaica, 2002), 23. Mavis Campbell argues that this politicization came from ideological inspiration and the decline of white society; see Campbell, *Dynamics of Change,* 27.

small numbers of elite men into the political fold, not to create more divided social hierarchies between individuals of color.[51]

What had not changed was the importance of highlighting past experiences in the metropole when submitting an appeal. More than half the privilege petitions lodged in the 1820s noted time spent abroad as evidence of distinction. This was a much higher rate of migration than that seen among the appeals submitted in the previous century. Nineteen petitioners mentioned their own education and travel to the United Kingdom, while merchants John Napier Dawes and John Kelly bragged that they had sent children to Britain. Both Dawes and Kelly noted that they were also married, an important detail in a society ever concerned about matrimony and reproduction. Nearly all of those who left for Europe had gone to school in the United Kingdom. Alexander Tulloh was the single exception; his petition noted that he had a "liberal education" and had since "travelled in several parts of England and Scotland" on his adventures as a merchant. The remaining eighteen all described having gone abroad for school. James and Charles Williamson recorded their "good education in England," while John Cuff left "at an early age to Ireland." James Campbell Stewart had not only gone to school in Britain but served twelve years in the Royal Navy before marrying a woman in England. In these new rounds of petitions, therefore, Jamaicans of color sought to advertise themselves as potential leaders, either of the island's mixed-race freemen or eventually of its entire population. As the English politician Robert Wilmot Horton argued in 1826, although a liberal education was not, by itself, sufficient to make an individual of color equal to a white man, it would be improper "to admit to all the privileges of the whites free persons of colour who have not those qualifications." Marriage and a British education were once again prerequisites to admission in this imperial project.[52]

As in the eighteenth century, privilege bills during this period gave legal sanction to an already elevated social position. James Swaby was well known and respected before submitting his petition. Educated at Charterhouse in England before joining the British army, Swaby eventually returned to Jamaica where he became a substantial planter, building his fortune on the backs of 217 enslaved workers. When members of the assembly were sent to

51. Petition of Elizabeth Martha Coakley for Thomas Witter Jackson, Nov. 26, 1824, *JAJ*, XIII, 313.

52. *JAJ*, Nov. 10, 1824, XIV, 261, Nov. 17, 1824, 289, Nov. 24, 1826, 668, Nov. 23, 1824, 304, Nov. 2, 1826, 640, Nov. 6, 1826, 643; Robert Wilmot Horton, *The West India Question Practically Considered* (London, 1826), 99–100.

investigate his petition, they reported back enthusiastically, saying that "[he] is a very humane master; that he has been remarkably well educated, and possesses a very cultivated mind; that he is highly esteemed by the different white inhabitants of Manchester, and is admitted to their society, and treated in every respect as a white person." Clearly, there could be no better recommendation to the legislature than that the petitioner was already, in effect, living as a white individual. When Swaby came up in a parliamentary debate about the struggles of Jamaica's mixed-race population, the Jamaican politician Richard Barret scoffed at the contention in Westminster that Swaby endured any hardship. "He and his fortune are not to be computed," Barret retorted; "Mr. Swaby will marry a woman of manners and education, therefore not a woman of colour, and he will leave his fortune to his legitimate descendants." Once again, such a report showed Swaby's sterling reputation as the model for Jamaicans of color. Not only was he wealthy, educated, and well regarded, but he was bound to fulfill the ultimate function of white settlement: to marry and have legitimate children. Swaby's advancement, therefore, was something of a throwback to the 1730s initiative of creating a permanent settler society through further interracial coupling.[53]

If Swaby did symbolize a return to previous notions of Jamaican demography, it was not without significant debate. The decades preceding emancipation saw a variety of arguments about the future of white West Indians and those of color. Many observers and officials took a zero tolerance policy toward mixed-race enfranchisement. Some contended that conciliation erased the crucial boundary between black and white, while others continued to beat the drum that reform would herald a black uprising. Still others insisted that appeasement had already destroyed the colonies. G. W. Jordan believed that danger lurked behind efforts to promote individuals of color. He decried the attempt to unite mixed-race colonists to white interests, proclaiming, "The experiment has been made and has failed." Individuals of color could be freed,

53. *JAJ*, Nov. 26, 1823, XIV, 200; Barret, *Reply to the Speech*, 8–10. Swaby would inherit two estates from his father John in 1826 and began developing them. In 1828, Swaby's Hope Plantation covered 753 acres, though only 155 of those were cultivated. He would help turn those fortunes around so that four years later the estate produced sixty-five thousand pounds of coffee; see *JAJ*, Nov. 21, 1823, XIV, 194; Heuman, *Between Black and White*, 13; Kamau Brathwaite, *The Development of Creole Society in Jamaica, 1770–1820* (Kingston, Jamaica, 2005), 172; B. W. Higman, *Jamaica Surveyed: Plantation Maps and Plans of the Eighteenth and Nineteenth Centuries* (Kingston, Jamaica, 2001), 181–182; and Vincent Brown, *The Reaper's Garden: Death and Power in the World of Atlantic Slavery* (Cambridge, Mass., 2008), 113.

he went on, but they could never be made white. James Walker agreed. He disputed the idea that elites of color could supplement or replace the West Indies' white ascendancy. Instead, he implored white colonists to enlarge their families. "In each white child that you rear," he stated, "you rear a defender of that ascendancy." Moreover, he passionately attacked the migration of mixed-race individuals to Britain, emphatically importuning parents to "send none of them to Europe who are ever to return." From this perspective, petitioners like James Swaby were, not beacons for the future, but examples of wayward Caribbean policies.[54]

Some commentators took a slightly different approach to their skepticism by claiming that there were not enough men like Swaby. James McQueen's 1824 attempt to correct what he believed were abolitionists' misperceptions of the West Indies highlighted the Spanish colonies' large populations of color that dwarfed those in the Anglo-Caribbean. As a former plantation manager in Grenada, he attributed this difference, in part, to the fact that "a very great number of free coloured children come annually to this country (England), and never return to the Colonies again." A firm supporter of mixed-race education, McQueen worried that the lack of colonial resources for West Indians of color kept them from taking the political mantle from whites. Richard Barret followed a somewhat similar line of logic. Far less supportive of mixed-race individuals than McQueen, the Jamaican assemblyman shuddered to think of them taking over colonial governance. Barret implored Westminster not to interfere in Jamaican politics, mostly because it would cause whites to abandon the colony. The result would be the turning over of the island to "the possession of a class of persons who know not England, and have no ties of consanguinity to bind them to Great Britain." This was not an endorsement of sending mixed-race children abroad but was instead a warning about Jamaica's larger population of color taking over. Barret's polemic nevertheless revealed what so many found appealing about mixed-race education in Britain. Those who had gone to Britain were not only more familiar with Jamaica's position within the larger Empire, but they were also tied more closely—in Barret's words, in a consanguineous way—to the metropole. They would be more united, in this vision, to the interest of whites than to those of their fel-

54. *Brief Remarks on the Slave Registry Bill; and upon a Special Report of the African Institution, Recommending That Measure* (London, 1816), 18–19; *JAJ,* Nov. 27, 1822, XIV, 71, Oct. 30, 1823, 161; "Journal of a Voyage to Jamaica," Feb. 12, 1824, MS 17956, fols. 30–31, NLS; Jordan, *Examination of the Principles of the Slave Registry Bill,* 106, 125; Walker, *Letters on the West Indies,* 172–173.

low colonists of color. If the future of Jamaica's place in the Empire was under threat, then surely the education of mixed-race individuals in Britain would help hem that fraying tether.[55]

Elites of color had their share of supporters on both sides of the Atlantic. Few disputed the reality that the Caribbean's population of color would continue to increase. With that realization in mind, many observers lobbied for some kind of political transition that might better incorporate mixed-race people. England's African Institution, founded in 1807 to colonize Sierra Leone with formerly enslaved West Indians, stated firmly that empowering individuals of color was the "only certain way" to ensure Caribbean stability. The Reverend Richard Bickell concurred, claiming that young men of color should be enfranchised so that they could work as bookkeepers, saving the lives of thousands of white men who came to the tropics every year for such positions only to die within months of arriving. Multiple politicians floated this idea as well. A committee of the Jamaican assembly in 1824 accepted with resignation that the island's white population would not increase and suggested instead that schools be founded to improve the "morals and habits of the rising generation of free coloured people." This educational drive was an explicit appeal to begin considering some kind of transition, or supplement, in colonial rule. For whites, these efforts were largely self-serving: members of the assembly wondered if enfranchised elites of color might join their opposition to Parliament's interference on the question of slavery and colonial governance. But similar positions were taken in Westminster as well. A year after the Jamaican committee's report, James Scarlett spoke in Parliament about the need to educate individuals of color so that they might form "a very important security against the most dreadful of all revolutions." In a later session, Stephen Lushington would further implore members of the Commons to act on the behalf of mixed-race petitioners, this time by appealing to their family connections to the group: "By those who had sons, daughters, brothers, friends, among the petitioners, he trusted he should be supported, in endeavouring to rescue from a state little short of slavery, individuals thus attached to them by the dearest ties of blood and intimacy." By invoking family ties in their speeches, Scarlett and Lushington demonstrated that many wealthy households in Britain were still caring for mixed-race relatives, even if they had grown more reluctant to do so.[56]

55. McQueen, *West India Colonies*, 303–304; Barret, *Reply to the Speech*, 58.

56. *Reasons for Establishing a Registry of Slaves in the British Colonies: Being a Report of a Committee of the African Institution* (London, 1815), 88–89; Bickell, *West Indies as They*

Proposals emerged in the early decades of the nineteenth century to strengthen these links. If educating individuals of color in Britain improved the prospect of West Indian security, then support needed to go toward institutions that would provide such instruction. After England abolished its slave trade, missionaries and religious reformers lobbied for the creation of a British seminary that might train individuals of color, who would then preach to the enslaved. The plan stalled but did not immediately disappear. One West Indian physician revived the call for a school that might "bring a considerable proportion of the *people of colour,* between the whites and the negroes, to England to be educated." Reverend Bickell agreed that West Indians educated in Britain were the only ones capable of preaching effectively to the slaves — though he did not specify if they had to be white. A Scottish minister writing in 1830, the year that Jamaica's free population of color received equal rights, continued the refrain about the merit of mixed-race migrants: "Many of them . . . have been educated in the mother country with a liberality which places them, in point of accomplishments, on a footing little short of the best informed inhabitants of the colony." Not only could British-trained Jamaicans of color serve as the island's leading ministers, they might also serve alongside its politicians as well.⁵⁷

As optimistic as these proposals were, many colonial observers noted the harsh realities facing mixed-race migrants when they returned to the Caribbean. Numerous commentators remarked that well-educated individuals of color still did not receive a warm welcome once home. James Walker lamented, "They find upon their return to the West Indies, that the lowest white person disdains to associate with them." James Stewart complained that migrants of color were "excluded [from] the society of the whites," while Thomas Cooper stated that "much jealousy is entertained of them, especially when they have been educated in England." An 1825 account even speculated that racism was

---

Are, 115–116; *JAJ,* Dec. 18, 1824, XIV, 380; James Scarlett's Speech, 1825, as quoted in Hansard, ed., *Hansard's Parliamentary Debates,* XIII, June 16, 1825, 1201, Stephen Lushington's Speech, 1827, as quoted ibid., XVII, June 12, 1827, 1242–1243; Heuman, *Between Black and White,* 79, 100–119; Matthew J. Smith, *Liberty, Fraternity, Exile: Haiti and Jamaica After Emancipation* (Chapel Hill, N.C., 2014), 28–30.

57. *Observations on the Necessity of Introducing a Sufficient Number of Respectable Clergymen into Our Colonies in the West Indies . . .* (London, 1807), 11–13; [George] Pinckard, *Observations on the Emancipation of the Slaves* (circa 1816), Rare Books, 480000: 1090, HL, 7; Bickell, *West Indies as They Are,* 102; Henry Duncan, *Presbyter's Letters on the West India Question; Addressed to the Right Honourable Sir George Murray, G.C.B, M.P. Colonial Secretary &c. &c.* (London, 1830), 93.

so strong that it would be possible for a mixed-race man to be enslaved in the Caribbean though "he has lived twenty years in England." Authors of fiction also wrote of the rude homecomings faced by migrants of color. In the 1828 novel *Marly,* the title character is chastised for having shaken hands with a Jamaican of color who was his classmate at the University of Edinburgh. Even proslavery supporters had to respond to the charge of whites attacking British-educated people of color back in the Caribbean. Alexander Barclay defended planters' manners, insisting, "A decent person of any colour, earning his bread in an honest way, is no more molested in Jamaica than in England." As a former Jamaican resident, he vouched to knowing several mixed-race migrants who left Britain because it was less welcoming than the colonies.[58]

Personal experiences attested to the struggles awaiting well-educated individuals of color in the Caribbean. John Walker condemned the treatment he witnessed firsthand in Barbados. He recounted the story of a mixed-race surgeon trained in Edinburgh, who was shunned at a dinner in Bridgetown when his fellow guests left the table on his arrival. The Reverend Bickell recorded a similar experience in Jamaica's capital in 1825. At a ball in Spanish Town, he encountered "two coloured sons of one of the most respectable men . . . in the island, who had both been educated in Great Britain." When a white relative spotted them, he ordered them out of the party, and they were soon forced to leave. In an appeal to England's secretary of state for war and the colonies, John Campbell bemoaned that he and many others "have received their education in Great Britain, and consequently on their return to their native country, the more poignantly feel the miseries to which they are exposed." John Baptista Philip, a mixed-race doctor trained at the University of Edinburgh, confirmed these experiences. When returning to the Caribbean, he observed, "Coloured men, aware that whatever advance they make in the sphere of learning, will engage neither encouragement nor favour, become disheartened." He personally attested to having "known a woful catalogue of young coloured men, who have fallen off very shortly after their arrival from Europe." Education could empower young men of color, but, if West Indian society did not validate that training, then their prospects of helping to lead the colonies were severely diminished.[59]

58. Walker, *Letters on the West Indies,* 170; Stewart, *View of the Past and Present State of the Island of Jamaica,* 328; Cooper, *Facts Illustrative,* 24; *West India Slavery; A Review of "The Slavery of the West India Company . . ."* (Aberdeen, 1825), 9; *Marly; or, a Planter's Life in Jamaica* (Glasgow, 1828), 182–184; Barclay, *Practical View of the Present State of Slavery in the West Indies,* 232, 272–273.

59. Waller, "A Voyage," 1820, in *New Voyages and Travels,* III, 95; Bickell, *West Indies as*

Continued discrimination ultimately pushed back the ascension of mixed-race individuals in colonial society. Free men of color in Jamaica, in particular, struggled to build political power in the assembly, even after gaining full political rights in 1830. Suffrage did not immediately translate into political control. Only two mixed-race men were elected to the assembly in 1831, and just five more were added in the first four years after emancipation. The massive enslaved uprising of the Baptist War of 1831, which ended with the loss of hundreds of lives and massive property damage, cooled white Jamaicans' enthusiasm toward reform. Conversely, the conflict persuaded many British parliamentarians to abolish slavery altogether, which they did in 1833, and to take a stronger hand in shaping colonial policy directly. Constantine Phipps, Lord Mulgrave, and Howe Browne, Lord Sligo, two of Jamaica's English-appointed governors during this transition to freedom, both foresaw the importance of mixed-race involvement in island politics and worked to appoint men of color to important positions when they could. They were also swayed by the professed loyalty that individuals of color expressed to the crown. Although it was slow in coming, by the end of the 1840s white colonists lost their majority in the assembly. For some, these changes suggested a dramatic shift in imperial organization. Horace Twiss, a member of Parliament for Newport, railed in the Commons that granting full civil rights to men of color "has rendered the Jamaicans . . . independent of British connexion." That might have been an implicit promotion of mixed-race migration, but Twiss's familial allusion made a more pointed imperial critique. Just as family members in Britain had been cutting ties with mixed-race relatives, so, too, did it seem that the Empire was sloughing off its colonies of color.[60]

Neither the island assemblies nor Parliament in England made mixed-race

They Are, 226; John Campbell to the Henry Bathurst, earl of Bathurst, circa 1816, CO 137/45, fol. 271, NAE; *An Oration, Pronounced on the 29th of July, 1829, after the Funeral Dirge of Doctor John Baptista Philip, Who Died on the 16th of June, 1829, in Trinidad* (London, [circa 1829]), 7–10, 24–25; John Baptista Philip, *An Address to the Right Hon. Earl Bathhurst, His Majesty's Principal Secretary of the State for the Colonies, Relative to the Claims Which the Coloured Population of Trinidad Have the Same Civil and Political Privileges with Their White Fellow-Subjects* (London, 1824), 101–102, 115–116, 191–192.

60. Horace Twiss, as quoted in *Report of the Debate in the House of Commons, on Friday, the 15th of April 1831; on Mr. Fowell Buxton's Motion to Consider and Adopt the Best Means for Effecting the Abolition of Colonial Slavery* (London, 1831), 82; Heuman, *Between Black and White,* 49–58. Heuman notes that the original bill enfranchised only those with a ten-pound freehold, but that restriction was soon taken out. For more on Jamaican politics during the 1830s and 1840s, see Thomas C. Holt, *The Problem of Freedom: Race, Labor, and Politics in Jamaica and Britain, 1832–1938* (Baltimore, 1992), 13, 99–102, 217–219.

migrants part of a specific policy decision for the post-emancipation West Indies, but individuals of color nevertheless carved out that role for themselves. In the case of Jamaica, ruling whites held onto the reins of power for as long as they could. Yet, after emancipation occurred in 1834, and formerly enslaved individuals finished their "apprenticeship" period in 1838, elites of color who had been educated in Britain played an important, though at times only symbolic, role. Several of Jamaica's mixed-race leaders in the second half of the nineteenth century came out of this group. James Mitchell Gibb, for example, had attended an English school and was elected to the Jamaican assembly where he would help deal with the aftermath of the Morant Bay Rebellion in 1865. Thomas Witter Jackson joined his father's profession in the law after finishing school in Britain. He rose to become the stipendiary magistrate of Saint David's parish, where he settled down and had at least one daughter. Eventually, he would become a strong ally to the black cause after emancipation. By the 1860s, Jackson advocated vigorously for firm work regimens to be put in place to train black residents in a trade.[61]

These mixed-race migrants' refined upbringings in the metropole persuaded white rulers to trust them more readily than black subjects, thrusting the group forward in colonial society and politics. This created a great deal of division between individuals of color. Poorer members of the group accused them, especially those who had received privileges, of conforming to white society and betraying their peers. For imperial officials, though, migrants of color seemed the best group to help govern the West Indies not only because of their education but also because of their links back to Britain. When the House of Commons sought information on the future of the West Indies after emancipation, it discovered that this was already a well-discussed topic. A former Jamaican resident testified to a parliamentary committee that "some of the best educated men he has known in Jamaica are people of colour, and they promote education among the young." Likewise, a visitor to Jamaica agreed that mixed-race individuals were "persons of education and understanding," and some were "quite as competent as any white men." For the handful of British islands in the Caribbean Sea, suddenly populated with hundreds of

61. *JAJ*, Nov. 29, 1826, XIV, 673; *Daily News* (London), Apr. 2, 1866; Heuman, *Between Black and White*, 63; *JAJ*, Nov. 25, 1824, XIV, 313; *Morning Chronicle* (London), Dec. 13, 1859; *The Law Times: The Journal and Record of the Law and the Lawyers*, LXXXIX (London, 1890), 228; Catherine Hall, *Civilising Subjects: Colony and Metropole in the English Imagination, 1830–1867* (Chicago, 2002), 206–207. On Jackson in the 1860s, see Monica Schuler, "Coloured Civil Servants in Post-Emancipation Jamaica: Two Case Studies," *Caribbean Quarterly*, XXX (1984), 85–98.

thousands of newly free subjects, that was a strong endorsement of the colonies' future leaders.[62]

Conclusion

At the end of a visit to Jamaica in 1823, the English traveler Cynric Williams contemplated the differences between island life and British society. He claimed to have fallen in love with a mulatto woman named Diana and lamented an affection that could not properly be indulged. Perhaps he could stay on the island and keep her as a mistress; he felt confident that he could not take her to "England, where young women of *colour* are not received in society except under some disadvantages." Such open scorn in Britain's elite ranks was a developing phenomenon, brought on by the debates about demography, slavery, race, and the family over the previous decades. To Williams, it was a curious problem, especially because interracial relationships continued unabated in the West Indies. Moreover, he felt a certain sense of irony that those in the metropole who advocated most passionately for Caribbean reforms were now the ones most wary of racial equality. He challenged William Wilberforce and his fellow abolitionists, asking if they would "consent to their sons and daughters, their nephews and nieces, intermarrying with blacks." It was a loaded jest, poking at the most sensitive spot of familial tension. He pushed further, wondering if British reformers would enjoy seeing "their domestic circles composed chiefly of blacks and Mulattoes." It echoed G. W. Jordan's rhetorical question from seven years earlier about allowing Jamaicans of color into the bedrooms of Britain's daughters. Casting racial concerns into family debates guaranteed public aggravation.[63]

The early decades of the nineteenth century saw tremendous amounts of change for mixed-race migrants and their larger families. Fewer Jamaicans of color in particular had a white relative than those in the eighteenth century,

62. *Analysis of the Report of a Committee of the House of Commons on the Extinction of Slavery* (London, 1833), 41, 169-170; Sio, "Marginality and Free Coloured Identity," *Slavery and Abolition,* VIII (1987), 171-172. Free Jamaicans of color were indeed divided when they gained full political rights in 1830. A letter to the editor of the *Watchman and Jamaica Free Press,* which was published by and for mixed-race individuals, chastised those who had received privilege bills. "The system of private bills or *indulgences* was *a most consummate farce,*" the author railed, whose real intention was to "cause a division in the rising class"; see *Watchman and Jamaica Free Press* (Kingston, Jamaica), Dec. 17, 1831.

63. Cynric R. Williams, *A Tour through the Island of Jamaica, from the Western to the Eastern End, in the Year 1823* (London, 1826), 307-308; Jordan, *Examination of the Principles,* 115.

forcing stronger group dynamics that depended less on white patronage. Ultimately, this was a better position for mixed-race people as a whole, as blanket rights replaced private exemptions and special treatment. Yet, elites of color still managed to lead vastly different lives from their poorer peers. Despite all the changes, mixed-race migrants educated in Britain continued to take exalted spots in colonial society. They were no longer expected to form a new, white settler society, but they were expected to help navigate Jamaica's transition to freedom. Traveling to Britain no longer served a vague, symbolic purpose to advance one's appearance. It was now meant to confer social legitimacy on a group of people suddenly entrusted with the colony's future, and it would continue to do so. It is no coincidence that, when John Bigelow visited Jamaica from the United States in 1850, two of the most prominent men of color that he met were educated in England.[64]

These advances meant little in Britain, however. Intensified anxieties about family composition had pushed relatives of color outside the traditional boundaries of kinship by the 1830s. Mixed-race individuals continued to arrive in Britain throughout the nineteenth century, but they no longer had the same ability to exploit family networks as before. Efforts to construct kin systems that expanded access to capital kept most mixed-race travelers out of the family portrait. For many migrants, this marginalization made little difference; they expected to return to the West Indies anyhow, especially as new leadership possibilities were opening. But, for those individuals who hoped to escape Caribbean prejudices, they arrived in a metropole that looked increasingly similar to the colonial society they had left behind.[65]

64. Robert Harrison, visiting Jamaica from the United States in 1834, worried that the island's newly emancipated black subjects would overrun both the white and mixed-race populations, provoking chaos; see Edward B. Rugemer, "The Harrisons Go to Jamaica: Race and Sexual Violence in the Age of Abolition," *Journal of Family History*, XXXIII (2008), 17. On Bigelow's visit to Jamaica from the United States, see John Bigelow, *Jamaica in 1850; or, The Effects of Sixteen Years of Freedom on a Slave Colony*, ed. Robert J. Scholnick (Chicago, 2006), 23–24.

65. Deborah Cohen, *Family Secrets: Shame and Privacy in Modern Britain* (New York, 2013), 44–46.

CONCLUSION

Not long after putting the finishing touches on an amendment to his will, Edward James Mascall set off on a hunting trip in Southampton, England. It was the early days of 1832, just months away from Parliament's decision to abolish slavery in the British Empire, and the expedition ravaged the septuagenarian's health. Gangrene attacked Mascall's foot, and he died within six weeks. In typical English fashion, a brief dispute rose up over his will, but the estate was not excessively bounteous. The largest bequest, three thousand pounds, went to the only surviving direct descendant, his granddaughter Juliana Dalzell Hamilton. This was a generous gift, but anyone who knew the family's genealogy might have been surprised at the amount. After all, Hamilton was the great-granddaughter of Robert Dalzell, the mixed-race Jamaican whose enormous fortune was cited by the Jamaican assembly to justify its 1761 inheritance cap against individuals of color. Robert Dalzell had lived opulently in England, but he had not secured enough of his father's Jamaican estate to establish an enduring line of landed family wealth. His great-granddaughter Juliana would live quite comfortably, but she could not slide easily into Britain's aristocracy, as members of the Jamaican assembly had claimed to worry about the descendants of slaves doing so many years before.[1]

In the century between 1733 and 1833, a tremendous amount had changed for mixed-race migrants, both in the Caribbean and in Britain. At the start of this period, elites of color who traveled abroad were thought to be the vanguard of a new type of colonial settlement in Jamaica. A permanent and growing cohort of white residents had failed to establish itself, and refined individuals of color were expected to become the progenitors of a new society that was effectively white enough to mimic a European model. Family connections thus became crucial determiners of whiteness and racial standing in the colony. The course of history altered those expectations as enslaved revolts, humanitarian appeals, and family dynamics pushed many to reject the idea that African roots could ever be fully pruned from a family tree. Yet, the repeated failure of an idealized, so-called pure white society to take hold forced

1. Will of Edward James Mascall, July 19, 1832, PROB 11/1803, NAE, Hamilton and Brand v. Hamilton, PROB 18/126/12; *Oxford Dictionary of National Biography*, online ed., s.v. "Mascall, Edward James (1757/8–1832)," by W. A. S. Hewins, rev. M. C. Curthoys, http://www.oxforddnb.com/view/article/18255.

observers to reconsider migrants of color in their imperial schemes. As emancipation neared, the question took on greater urgency. By 1833, elites of color educated in Britain were no longer seen as the seeds of a settler core that was white enough but instead as a mixed-race ascendancy believed to be the best bulwark against colonial anarchy. In certain ways, the initiatives of 1733 were resoundingly similar to those of 1833. Both dates saw slavery under threat, island security under attack, and demographic stability under debate. But subtle policy differences demonstrated just how much had changed in the intervening century.

Britain saw its own transitions in this period as well. Jamaicans of color arrived in the metropole at the start of the eighteenth century to join white families and reap the spoils of a British upbringing. In most cases, they succeeded: few families commented significantly on their relatives' heritage and incorporated them into the fold with little protest. Public discourse began to shift, however, when antislavery protests took off. Most famously, Edward Long worried in 1772 about the possible darkening of England's complexion by the arrival of African-descended people. Yet, individual households weathered these early swells of racial polemic. Kinship connections buffeted the changing ideological tides, but they depended on the social power of consanguinity. When blood relation began to lose its supremacy in family formation, mixed-race migrants were suddenly swept up in these waves of bigotry. Class could no longer outrank race, and Britons began lumping elites of color into the totalizing category of "black." Just as in the Caribbean, though, as much as things changed, they also stayed the same. In an almost perfect retelling of Edward Long's 1772 race-baiting diatribe, an 1830 pamphleteer warned that, if Parliament abolished slavery, "thousands of the freed negroes [would] come to England." Such an eventuality would completely alter "the *countenances and complexions* of the British population." To a degree, this forecast was less sensational in 1830 than it had been in 1772. After all, British families had already started erecting social barriers in an attempt to prevent that very outcome.[2]

Such shifting dynamics demonstrate just how much Atlantic ideas of race fluctuated in the long eighteenth century. Taken as a whole, racial prejudice worsened over the period, or it at least lost some of its early tolerance for ambiguity. Yet, this was not strictly the result of political and cultural debates around blackness and slavery. It was also a product of simultaneous questions about family belonging. When reformers began drafting plans to dismantle

2. *A Letter to the Most Honourable the Marquis of Chandos* (London, 1830), 22–23.

enslavement, they thought about it in familial ways: how to construct stable black families and virtuous white households. Likewise, when officials contemplated the future of colonial administration, they wondered if by holding white kinship ties individuals with some African ancestry might be trusted to govern. Working at the foundation of each of these debates were the people of color themselves, connected by family relationships to some of the most powerful figures on either side of the Atlantic. Those personal associations ensured that any deliberation around race was also a reflection on kinship. After all, Britain's empire was not composed of disconnected parts with isolated intellectual theories. It was composed of families, linked together across thousands of miles, and negotiated in continual and intimate ways. Racial attitudes were hardening, but not into a broad form of racism. Instead, family relations were the prisms through which many Britons and colonists viewed and understood very complex notions of race.

Large social and political forces transformed the status of mixed-race migrants, but West Indians of color were instrumental in shaping those changes as well. Throughout the long eighteenth century, they utilized family connections to better themselves in a brutal colonial regime. The Morses' mother Elizabeth Augier, for instance, appealed to the Jamaican assembly for added civil rights, enticing a white planter's interest and setting the stage for her children's eventual lives in Britain and India. Jamaicans of color like Polly Graham, who pushed John Tailyour to send their offspring to Britain, were often the ones appealing for a mixed-race child's good education. Migrants like the Rosses were the ones who traveled to the metropole and negotiated relations with British kin, even when their fathers kept them at a distance from legitimate relatives. Mixed-race Jamaicans such as the Dalzells were the ones who married into affluent families and established associations with some of the Empire's most influential power brokers. And, many of them, including James Mitchell Gibb and Thomas Witter Jackson, were the ones who returned to the Caribbean to help lead that society into freedom.

When Atlantic ideas of race and family shifted at the turn of the nineteenth century, they did so in part because migrants of color presented challenges to simplistic ideas about belonging. Interracial households emerged at the very beginnings of colonization and later attempts to organize society through basic racial and familial categories were attempts to address their presence. When white administrators in the Caribbean worked to adjust to their nonwhite populations, they did so in part because migrants of color presented a competing notion of race and capability. When British families narrowed the definitions of who could be members, they did so partly as a reaction to mixed-race relatives presenting complications to inheritance and kin networks. Jamaicans of color occupied a narrow band in the social spectrum, but those who crisscrossed the ocean revealed the astonishing determination of individuals born into even the most inhuman of conditions.

Their stories should not redeem the white fathers who systematically oppressed and murdered enslaved workers, but they should serve as a reminder of the complexities around colonial life. Men like John Morse and John Tailyour made their fortunes extracting profit from the bodies of enslaved creole and African individuals. Regardless of what benefits they gave to their children, the society they helped to build was one of horrific racism and civic underdevelopment with which Jamaicans still struggle today. But those stark realities should reinforce just how important it is to differentiate the ways that racial ideas were considered and applied in the long eighteenth century. What else but family connection can best explain the large financial gifts and demonstration of support that Morse and Tailyour offered to children with direct connections to the very slaves they exploited? Moreover, in a free society as small as Jamaica, studying mixed-race individuals as unconnected to colonial white rule is a strange and misrepresentative endeavor. Even in a place as baldly oppressive as colonial Jamaica, there was no singular notion of race, nor was there a total abandonment of familial responsibility.

Likewise, mixed-race migrants' biographies should reinforce Britain's historical diversity. Previous scholars have already proven that the British Isles were far from a racially homogenous society, even in the eighteenth century. But it was not simply the case that whites coexisted and lived alongside nonwhites for centuries. Instead, white Britons across all socioeconomic levels shared lives, homes, and ancestry with those of African descent. Poor whites cohabited with and married black immigrants, and rich whites worked with and wed elite West Indians of color. When family trees merged, most Britons either suppressed or forgot the African branch. The Morses married wealthy Englishmen, and their descendants lived as well-to-do white subjects. Others, like the Tailyours and Rosses, left for imperial adventures where their stories dry up, waiting to be recovered by future historians. Regardless, each of them joined—in their own particular way—a British household. These were not extreme examples of radically tolerant and forgiving relatives. Rather, they were instances of the regular and mundane incorporation of extended kin operating on both sides of the Atlantic Ocean.

APPENDIX 1

𝕬𝕾𝕮𝕬

Percentage of White Men's Wills, Proven in Jamaica,
with Acknowledged Mixed-Race Children That Include
Bequests for Such Offspring in Britain, Either Presently
Resident, or Soon to Be Sent There, 1773–1815

	1773–1775	1783–1785	1793–1795	1803–1805	1813–1815
Explicit References	9.7	4.5	12.2	9.6	9.1
Explicit and Implicit References Combined	17.2	13.6	22.0	15.5	18.9

Sources: Wills, LOS 41–42, 49–51, 57–58, 60–61, 70–75, 87–91, IRO. The specific wills are: Samuel Say, Feb. 11, 1773, LOS 41, fol. 44; John Buck, Mar. 4, 1773, LOS 41, fol. 55; James Goldson, ibid.; John McDonnell, May 6, 1773, LOS 41, fol. 96; George Hall, Oct. 21, 1773, LOS 41, fol. 169–170; Archibald Stewart, Dec. 2, 1773, LOS 41, fol. 193; James Macgrudan, Dec. 23, 1773, LOS 41, fol. 209; John Nixon, July 28, 1774, LOS 41, fols. 387–390; Thomas Blair, Aug. 11, 1774, LOS 42, fol. 2; John Gillespie, Sept. 6, 1774, LOS 42, fol. 14; Donald Campbell, Sept. 15, 1774, LOS 42, fol. 20; Duncan Cuming, Sept. 15, 1774, LOS 42, fol. 21; James Hill, Jan. 26, 1775, LOS 42, fol. 77; John Renny, May 20, 1775, LOS 42, fol. 115; Nathaniel Milward, June 15, 1775, LOS 42, fol. 132–133; Samuel Smith, July 18, 1775, LOS 42, fols. 156–157; Samuel Barrett, Jan. 20, 1783, LOS 49, fol. 133; Alexander McKinnal, May 3, 1783, LOS 50, fol. 16; John Taylor, June 5, 1783, LOS 50, fol. 24; John Dawes, Feb. 7, 1784, LOS 50, fol. 54; John McCulloch, July 21, 1784, LOS 50, fol. 124; James Wilson, Nov. 8, 1784, LOS 50, fol. 178; John Bell, Dec. 9, 1784, LOS 50, fol. 191; Thomas Holt, Apr. 25, 1784, LOS 50, fol. 214; Edward Hoy, July 7, 1785, LOS 51, fol. 64; Alexander Grame, July 28, 1785, LOS 51, fol. 75; Richard Lancelott, Sept. 15, 1785, LOS 51, fol. 83; John Fletcher, Dec. 5, 1785, LOS 51, fol. 114; Matthew Sterling, Jan. 19, 1793, LOS 57, fol. 116; Archibald Thomas, Feb. 1, 1793, LOS 57, fol. 133; Benoni Smith, Feb. 18, 1793, LOS 37, fol. 137; John Eccles, Feb. 21, 1793, LOS 57, fol. 141; Samuel King, May 2, 1793, LOS 57, fol. 189; Archibald MacNeill, June 20, 1793, LOS 57, fol. 195; John Andrews, Oct. 10, 1793, LOS 58, fol. 34; John Ruiz, Oct. 17, 1793, LOS 58, fol. 33; Thomas Gairdner, Nov. 22, 1793, LOS 58, fols. 87–88; Ambrose Carter, Feb. 10, 1794, LOS 58, fol. 150; Donald Smith, Feb. 13, 1794, LOS 58, fol. 119–120; Thomas McNachlane, Feb. 13, 1794, LOS 58, fol. 131; George Leslie, Mar. 18, 1794, LOS 58, fol. 173–174; Joseph Jobling, Apr. 26, 1794, LOS 58, fol. 204; Robert Thomson, May 24, 1794, LOS 60, fol. 5; Samuel Curtin, Aug. 19, 1794, LOS 60, fol. 33; Kenneth McKenzie, Nov. 13, 1794, LOS 60, fols. 74–75; John Smith, Jan. 29, 1795, LOS 60, fol. 92; Charles Stirling, Feb. 12, 1795, LOS 61, fols. 81–82; John Room, Mar. 7, 1795, LOS 61, fol. 93; Hugh Millar, Apr. 11, 1795, LOS 61, fol. 123; John Durney, May 26, 1795, LOS 60, fol. 112; Joseph Stoney, June 11, 1795, LOS 61, fol. 153; Eugene Calnan, June 22, 1795, LOS 61, fols. 171–172; William Low, July 15, 1795, LOS 60, fols. 118–119; Edmund Harbaron, July 28, 1795,

LOS 60, fol. 124; Thomas McKinlay, Dec. 9, 1795, LOS 61, fol. 187–188; John Walford, Apr. 16, 1803, LOS 71, fol. 15; William Thomson, July 2, 1803, LOS 72, fols. 5–6; Hyam Cohen, July 27, 1803, LOS 71, fols. 135–138; Matthew Shea, Aug. 16, 1803, LOS 72, fol. 81; Thomas Banitt, Aug. 18, 1803, LOS 72, fol. 10; William Simmons, Sept. 10, 1803, LOS 71, fol. 201; Alexander Ochterlony, Sept. 23, 1803, LOS 72, fol. 126; Samuel McKie, Nov. 4, 1803, LOS 72, fol. 45; John McIndoe, Dec. 12, 1803, LOS 72, fol. 58; Bartholomew Walden, Jan. 25, 1804, LOS 72, fol. 73–75; John Drummond, Apr. 21, 1804, LOS 72, fols. 189–190; George Morrison, May 8, 1804, LOS 72, fols. 191–192; William McPherson, Nov. 6, 1804, LOS 72, fol. 60; John Frances Hare, Jan. 1, 1804, LOS 73, fol. 15; John Shaw, June 28, 1804, LOS 73, fols. 50–51; William Anderson, Aug. 1, 1804, LOS 73, fol. 17; Edward Davey, Oct. 3, 1804, LOS 73, fols. 121–122; Somerville Forrester, Oct. 25, 1804, LOS 73, fol. 192; John Kelly, Nov. 16, 1804, LOS 73, fols. 131–132; William Grant, Nov. 17, 1804, LOS 74, fols. 4–5; William Galbraith, Dec. 8, 1804, LOS 73, fol. 203; John Finlay, Dec. 15, 1804, LOS 73, fols. 212–213; George Eaton, Jan. 25, 1805, LOS 74, fol. 31; William Coakley, Feb. 2, 1805, LOS 74, fols. 26–27; Charles Fowlis, Feb. 15, 1805, LOS 74, fol. 38; George McKay, Feb. 26, 1805, LOS 74, fol. 53; William Hunter, Feb. 26, 1805, LOS 75, fol. 49; George Dunn, Mar. 30, 1805, LOS 74, fol. 107; James Furguson, Apr. 29, 1805, LOS 74, fol. 87; John Wark, May 2, 1805, LOS 74, fol. 84; Richard Francis, May 11, 1805, LOS 74, fol. 120; John Ferrier, June 8, 1805, LOS 75, fols. 104–105; John Starat, Aug. 13, 1805, LOS 75, fol. 119; Christopher McLean, Dec. 24, 1805, LOS 75, fols. 135–136; George Malcolm, June 16, 1813, LOS 87, fol. 152; James Brodie Rose, June 21, 1813, LOS 88, fol. 13; George Moffitt, June 22, 1813, LOS 87, fols. 46–47; Charles Crooke, June 23, 1813, LOS 87, fols. 178–179; Alexander Stewart, Aug. 7, 1813, LOS 87, fol. 144; George McCulloch, Aug. 24, 1813, LOS 87, fol. 215; George Watson, Sept. 21, 1813, LOS 88, fol. 121; John Buddle, Oct. 2, 1813, LOS 87, fol. 224; Zacharias Daly, Nov. 20, 1813, LOS 88, fols. 93–94; John Kelly, Mar. 2, 1814, LOS 87, fol. 197; Peter Moffatt, Mar. 29, 1814, LOS 88, fol. 156; Matthew Parkinson, Nov. 1, 1814, LOS 89, fol. 214–215; Arthur Savage, Feb. 2, 1815, LOS 90, fol. 77; John Christie, Feb. 27, 1815, LOS 90, fols. 93–94; John O'Meally, Mar. 21, 1815, LOS 89, fols. 220–221; Patterson Thomas, June 15, 1815, LOS 90, fol. 148–149; Henry Palmer, June 20, 1815, LOS 90, fols. 248–250; John Taylor, July 27, 1815, LOS 90, fols. 166–168; John Monteath, Nov. 9, 1815, LOS 91, fol. 210; Archibald Turnbull, Sept. 29, 1815, LOS 90, fol. 220; Richard Dormer, Sept. 30, 1815, LOS 90, fols. 221–222; Edward Dalling Fitzgerald, Oct. 2, 1815, LOS 90, fol. 185; Thomas Pain, Nov. 2, 1815, LOS 90, fol. 256; William Oldham, Nov. 25, 1815, LOS 90, fols. 271–272; John Hamer, Dec. 25, 1815, LOS 91, fol. 201.

Note: An explicit reference is one in which the child is listed with a racial category (such as "mulatto," "quadroon," "mestee," etc.). An implicit reference is one in which the child is noted as illegitimate ("natural" or "reputed"). In nearly all of the latter categories, the testator also noted having a mistress of color who was likely the child's mother.

APPENDIX 2

Genealogical Charts

Morse Family Tree

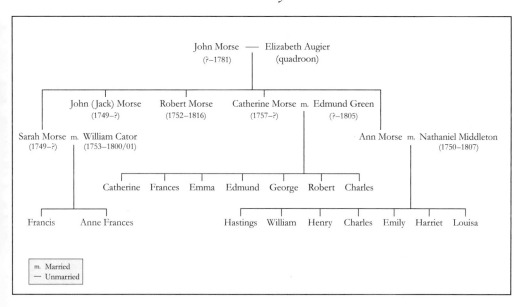

Tailyour Family Tree

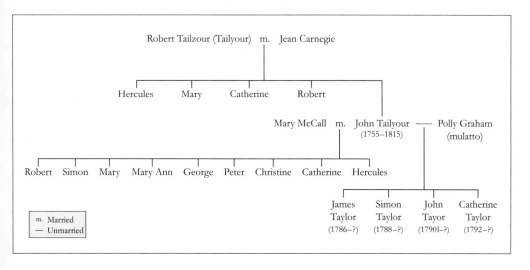

Ross Family Tree

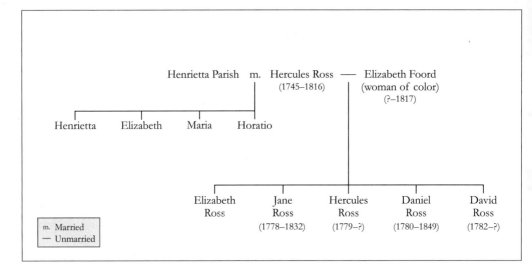

INDEX

Abolitionism. *See* Movement to abolish the slave trade

American Revolution, 133, 142, 144–151, 175–177, 183, 189–192, 200, 208, 285, 387n

Augier, Elizabeth, 49, 77, 109, 162–174, 233, 256, 347–351, 400. *See also* Morse family

Augier, Susanna, 45–49, 75–77, 256

Austen, Jane. *See* Fictional portrayals of mixed-race migrants

Baretti, Giuseppe, 153–157

Bastards. *See* Illegitimacy

Bayly, Nathaniel, 214–218

Bayly, Zachary, 85, 217, 384

Beckford, William, 59, 79, 116, 146

Belle, Dido Elizabeth, 8, 112–114, 140, 151, 156, 303, 311–312

Bennett, Sarah, 100

Board of Trade (London), 29–31, 73–88, 210–212. *See also* Jamaica assembly

Bowman, John, 228–231

Burke, Edmund, 144, 148, 151–160

Calderon, Louisa, 334–345, 365

Campbell, Katharine, 84, 161

Carnegie, David, 303–305

Cator, William, 111, 144, 254. *See also* Morse family

Clarke, Dugald, 21, 95

Clarkson, Thomas, 144, 199, 214, 237–238, 247. *See also* Movement to abolish the slave trade

Clive, Robert, 150–151

Colville, A., 370–371

Court of Chancery. *See* Inheritance bequests; Morse family

Cuming, William, 92

Cunningham, William (younger), 46–47, 65, 94n

Dalzell family, 296–299, 398–400; Frances Duff (née Dalzell), 77, 255–256; Gibson, 77, 255–256, 293; Robert, 77, 255–256, 398

Davidson, William, 362–374

Deficiency legislation, 26–35, 64, 93, 200, 239, 309, 379–381

Demography in Britain, 4, 116–130, 207–212, 269–270, 341–345, 396–401

Demography in Jamaica, 4, 16, 80, 117–121, 142, 195, 200–207, 246–247, 306, 324–331, 396; and mixed-race individuals as settlers, 4–10, 30–41, 51, 131–139, 205–206, 241–243, 329–349, 375, 387–401; and racial imbalance, 10, 24–26, 38–39, 53–54, 70, 80, 90–91, 118, 126, 132–134, 167, 330, 345, 375–378; and plans for European settlement, 11, 22–35, 59, 83, 135–136, 198, 345–349, 375–378, 390–392; and gender imbalance among white population, 12–18, 23. *See also* Enslaved Jamaicans; Whites in Jamaica: as legal category; Movement to abolish the slave trade

Dickson (Jamaican petitioner), 240–244

Draper, Edward, 338–340

East India Company, 111, 150–157, 191, 292, 301–321, 347, 360

Education in Britain, 97–106, 213–215, 228–231, 356–360, 374, 392

Education in Jamaica, 95–100, 137, 207, 213–215, 308, 328; and establishment of free schools, 28, 95n–96n, 381, 391

Edwards, Bryan, 107, 198n, 201–204, 217–219, 235–242

Eliza (ship), 196–197

Emancipation. *See* Movement to emancipate enslaved people

Enslaved Jamaicans: and population size,

24–28, 117–118, 324, 342–345, 376–377; and manumission, 25, 36, 60, 181–188, 282–288, 326. *See also* Mixed-race individuals

Enslaved revolts, 10, 30, 86–91, 129–132, 238, 275, 306–307, 368–371, 390–398; Tacky's Revolt, 4, 20, 49, 66–69, 86–88, 109, 130, 330; Baptist War, 394. *See also* Haitian Revolution; Maroons

Equiano, Olaudah, 7–8, 368n

Family, 19, 52–66, 120, 239–240, 283, 306, 362, 383–384; and race, 4–14, 176, 224–226, 261–263, 291, 304, 318–323, 334, 345, 364–371, 394–401; and encouragement of white families in Jamaica, 29–34, 64, 80, 93, 135–136; and economic effect on membership, 55–58, 231, 250, 266–268, 293–300, 342–350, 375–378, 397–401. *See also* Illegitimacy; Inheritance bequests; Marriage

Farington, Joseph, 157n, 311, 350–351

Fictional portrayals of mixed-race migrants, 16, 122, 264–280, 293, 299, 343–345, 352–353, 393; *The Jamaica Lady,* 264–265; *The Female American,* 265; *The Fortunate Transport,* 265; *The History and Adventures of an Atom* [Smollett], 267; *The Expedition of Humphry Clinker* (Smollett), 267–268; *Memoirs of a Scotts Heiress* (Mathews), 268–277, 344; *The Cherub,* 271; *Edward* (Moore), 272–274, 280; *The Solemn Injunction* (Musgrave), 274; *Henry* (Cumberland), 274, 280; *Edmund and Eleonora* (Marshall), 276–277; *Constantia Neville* (Wells), 277–280; *The Woman of Colour,* 343–345; *Montgomery,* 352–353; *Sanditon* (Austen), 353; *Marly,* 393

Fox, Charles James, 151–152, 160, 191–192

Free people of color. *See* Mixed-race individuals

French policies toward people of color, 208–209

French Revolution, 232–237, 298n

Fullarton, Marianne, 334–340
Fullarton, William, 334–343
Fuller, Stephen, 213, 240–243
Fyffe, James, 313–314, 357

George III (king of England), 73, 122, 152, 191, 232, 363
George IV (king of England), 298, 368, 372
Gibb, James Mitchell, 395, 400
Golding, John, 35–45
Graham, Mary (Polly), 186–189, 282–304, 320–323, 400. *See also* Tailyour / Taylor family
Green family: Edmund, 109, 163–174, 252–254; Charles, 255; Edmund Francis, 255, 351; Frances Ann, 350–351. *See also* Morse family

Haitian Revolution, 4, 196, 232–264, 307, 327–332, 360–366, 379–387. *See also* Ogé, Vincent
Hall, Jasper, 228
Hardwicke's Marriage Act. *See* Marriage
Harry, Charity, 106–107, 178–182, 257. *See also* Thresher, Jane (Jenny) Harry
Hastings, Warren, 143–160, 172, 191, 232, 248, 318, 335–336
Hay family, 1–3
Hibbert, George, 241, 248, 290, 328–329
Hibbert, Thomas (elder), 90–92, 106–107, 134, 177–178, 245–247, 257, 293
Hibbert, Thomas (younger), 109, 178–179
Home, Henry, Lord Kames, 141
Hume, David, 117–118

Illegitimacy, 13, 52, 54–84, 125–128, 204, 223–226, 251, 266, 291–297; and mixed-race people, 13, 52, 60–83, 136–140, 161–176, 204–205, 221–226, 250, 261–264, 274–281, 293–301, 318–326, 343–345, 355–359, 370, 385
India, 109–111, 143–160, 172–174, 191, 254, 347, 400
Inheritance bequests: and lawsuits, 11–17, 84–92, 145, 161, 204, 221–222, 249–264,

302, 353; in Jamaica, 14–15, 74–84, 101–104, 137, 178–185, 212–221, 267–268, 288–293, 326, 353–355, 374–378; and transatlantic settlements, 264–298, 308–310, 400–401. *See also* Morse family

Inheritance cap in Jamaica, 11, 21, 68–89, 92, 128–144, 165–178, 236–242, 257, 309, 354, 379–380

Interracial relationships in Britain: condemnations of, 16, 92, 103–129, 147–149, 175, 208–210, 264–284, 306, 334–374, 396; and general observations, 141–146, 276, 362

Interracial relationships in Jamaica, 2–46, 62–64, 104, 185–192, 282–290, 329, 384–400; and condemnations of, 11–31, 67–71, 80–93, 118–119, 135–139, 203–205, 283, 326, 342, 368–378

Jackson, Thomas Witter, 395, 400

Jamaica assembly, 15, 18, 20–21, 29; and relationship with English government, 29–36, 73–87, 132–134, 324, 380; and relationship with Jamaica council, 30–49, 65–76, 197–198, 307, 379–383

Jamaica council. *See* Jamaica assembly

Jews in Jamaica, 309, 380

Johnson, Samuel, 108, 141n, 156, 177

Kein, Bridget McDermott, 216–219

Ker, Peggy, 175–182, 192

Kirktonhill estate, 229, 250, 281–298, 322. *See also* Tailyour / Taylor family

Knight, Joseph, 141–142

Laing family: Malcolm, 71, 106, 293; Robert, 106, 176–182

Lawsuits. *See* Inheritance bequests

Lee, Robert Cooper, 170, 195, 284n

Long, Edward, 67–68, 123–152, 175, 207–214, 241–242, 323, 339, 345, 378, 399

McCall, George, 285, 305, 315, 320

McCall, John, 287–288, 290

Mackey, Bryan, 190, 312–313

Macpherson family: Allan, 355; William, 355–356, 359–360; Allan Williams, 355–357, 361; Matilda Williams, 355–360; Eliza, 355–361; Eliza Williams, 355–361; Harriot Macintyre, 358–359

Maroons, 28, 50; and warfare with Jamaican settlers, 32–48, 66, 243

Marriage, 52–64, 103–122, 137–142, 180–181, 204, 250, 294–298, 357–359, 371–372, 396; clandestine, 52–58, 80, 121–128, 372–373; and Hardwicke's Marriage Act, 58–64, 79n, 128, 372–373; in Jamaica, 61–64, 104, 136–139, 201–204, 257, 282, 325–326, 353, 375–388

Marryat, Joseph, 239n, 352, 378

Marsh family: John, 219–226, 232, 247; Edward Thomas, 220–226, 231–232

Mascall, Edward James, 256, 238, 398. *See also* Dalzell family

Mathews, John, 210–212

Middleton family: Nathaniel, 111, 153–157, 174, 252–255, 347; Hastings Nathaniel, 157–158, 347–348. *See also* Morse family

Milward, Nathaniel, 102–105

Mixed-race individuals: and education in Britain, 4–15, 22–25, 35, 45–47, 59–85, 100–106, 130–150, 209–229, 237–247, 289, 301–334, 345–365, 381–401; and population in Jamaica, 24–25, 167–172, 242, 331; and poverty, 25–35, 41, 137, 162, 352, 380–381, 395–397; in slavery, 25, 36, 104, 326–327; and legal status in Jamaica, 27–41, 66–69, 87–93, 168–172, 241–243, 308, 330, 349, 392–394; and militia service, 31–35, 66–67; and presence in Britain, 84–120, 142–148, 158–168, 182, 219, 238, 299, 307–324, 337–343, 375, 382–388; and education in Jamaica, 95–100, 137, 213, 307–308, 391; and political protests, 239–244, 332–334, 347–350, 375–386, 397. *See also* Demography in Jamaica; Illegitimacy; Privilege petitions

Morgann, Maurice, 129–132, 148

Morse family, 18–20, 49, 109–112, 152, 175,

256, 296–299, 400–401, 405; Robert, 1–3, 109–111, 158–159, 252–254, 336, 350; and inheritance lawsuit in Court of Chancery, 15, 144–145, 160–174, 191–192, 204, 249–255, 348; John (elder), 20–21, 48–49, 66, 77, 109, 144, 162–173, 195, 233, 249–256, 293, 347–351, 401; Ann Morse Middleton, 109–111, 153–159, 173–174, 252–255, 347–350; Catherine Morse Green, 109, 164, 169, 253–254, 350; John (Jack) (younger), 109, 169, 249–255; Sarah Morse Cator, 109–111, 144–159, 254, 347; Edward, 144–145, 160–174, 191, 248–259. *See also* Augier, Elizabeth

Movement to abolish the slave trade, 4, 89–92, 144, 172–197, 210, 227, 237–250, 263–264, 275–319, 334–360, 399; and colonial demography, 11–16, 91, 132–135, 198–207, 248, 276, 323–334

Movement to emancipate enslaved people, 4, 132, 146, 349–352, 368–370, 374–399

Mulattoes. *See* Enslaved Jamaicans; Mixed-race individuals

Murray, William, first earl of Mansfield, 8, 112–116, 123–129, 137–156, 311–312

Nelson, Horatio, 1, 194, 292, 316

North, Frederick, 191–192

Ogé, Vincent, 232–248, 302, 331, 379

Peterloo Massacre, 362, 368–369

Petty, William, earl of Shelburne, 79, 130

Picton, Thomas, 334–340, 365

Poor whites in Jamaica, 24, 31–37, 48–51, 64, 71, 328–329

Privilege petitions, 15–18, 40–101, 137, 189–190, 212–217, 242, 307–308, 322, 349–350, 379–384, 396–397; and individually named petitions, 21, 44–49, 64–95, 165–171, 190, 215–216, 308–312, 382–389, 400

Quaque, Philip, 105n–106n, 148

Racial attitudes, 16; in Britain, 8–11, 30, 81–88, 125–182, 279–280, 302–317, 343–375, 393–399; in Jamaica, 10, 26, 31–88, 136, 172–177, 282, 310, 393–401

Raimond, Julien, 233

Ramsay, James, 147, 202, 206, 214, 247

Richardson, Samuel, 265–266

Ricketts, George Crawford, 307, 379

Robertson family, 221–222

Ross family, 18, 87, 357, 400–401, 406; Hercules (elder), 87–92, 134, 189–195, 227–248, 292–302, 313–316; Daniel, 293, 302; David, 302; Hercules (younger), 302

Schools. *See* Education in Britain; Education in Jamaica

Scotland: and mixed-race migrants, 1–2, 77, 84, 90–93, 104, 146, 175–176, 189–194, 224–231, 271, 293, 309–314, 323n, 334–345, 354–371, 388, 393; and marriage customs, 54–62, 226, 291, 376; and Scottish migration to Caribbean, 61, 244, 284, 328–329; and education, 98–105, 226–228, 357; and slavery, 117–121, 141–142; Montrose, 193–196, 227–230, 247–250, 281–293, 313–315

Sentimental literature, 264–306, 343–345

Seven Years' War, 66, 73, 81, 82n, 119, 127, 129, 145n, 148, 150, 151n, 267

Sharp, Granville, 120

Sierra Leone, 146, 191–192, 391

Slavery in Britain, 59, 91–92, 113, 123, 141, 146

Slaves. *See* Enslaved Jamaicans

Somerset decision, 112–116, 120–129, 136, 140–141, 146–150, 207–208. *See also* Murray, William, first earl of Mansfield

Spanish Empire: and influence on British West Indies, 18, 38, 132; and warfare with British Empire, 22, 33, 334–335; and comparisons to British Empire, 43, 80–81, 125, 136, 141–142, 166n, 208–209, 336n, 390

Spence, Thomas, 366–368

Stanhope, Lovell, 80–85, 130

Stedman, John Gabriel, 245, 275–276

Steele family: Joshua, 209–210, 261–262; Catherine, 261–262; Edward, 261–262; Mary Ann, 261–262

Stewart, James, 326, 330, 377–379, 392

Swaby, James, 388–390

Tacky's Revolt. *See* Enslaved revolts

Tailyour / Taylor family, 17–18, 296, 342, 357–360, 400–401, 405; John (elder), 182–198, 225–250, 281–328, 355–357, 400–401; John (younger), 187–188, 286–291, 315–323; Catherine, 187–188, 286–291, 323n; Simon (John Tailyour's Jamaican son), 187–188, 286–291, 323n; James, 187–196, 224–232, 244, 247, 284, 288, 290–291, 301–306, 315–323, 360; Jean, 193, 225–226, 229, 283, 315; Robert, 225–238, 291, 301–321; Mary (née McCall), 250, 281, 285, 291–293

Taylor, Simon, 92, 183–188, 195, 228, 284–290, 312, 328–330, 345

Taylor family. *See* Tailyour / Taylor family

Thistlewood, Thomas, 62–64, 100, 245

Thresher, Jane (Jenny) Harry, 106–112, 177–182, 192, 198n, 241, 248, 257

Thresher, Joseph, 179–182, 257n

Tobin, James, 147, 206, 214

Townshend, Thomas, Lord Sydney, 160, 172

Trelawny, Edward, 51, 118, 132

Trinidad, 334–335

Vanheelin, John, 251–255. *See also* Morse family

Vaughan, Benjamin, 188, 205, 242–243

Wedderburn, James, 366–370

Wedderburn, Robert, 17, 142, 366–374

Wells, Nathaniel, 311, 350

Whites in Jamaica: and definition of "mulatto," 18, 37–41, 165–170, 236, 261; as legal category, 38–39, 51, 65, 76, 84–85, 329, 345–346, 398; and privilege bills, 40–41, 137, 171

Wilberforce, William, 194–195, 219, 226, 237–248, 292, 331, 341, 369, 396

Wills. *See* Inheritance bequests

Wolmer's School. *See* Education in Jamaica

Woodart, Anna Petronella, 68, 76, 88n

Yorke, Henry Redhead, 240

Yorke, Philip, earl of Hardwicke. *See* Marriage

Yorke-Talbot decision, 59, 116–117

Zong (ship), 197